Generational Accounting around the World

A National Bureau
of Economic Research
Project Report

Generational Accounting around the World

Edited by   Alan J. Auerbach,
Laurence J. Kotlikoff,
and Willi Leibfritz

The University of Chicago Press

Chicago and London

ALAN J. AUERBACH is the Robert D. Burch Professor of Economics and Law at the University of California, Berkeley, and a research associate of the National Bureau of Economic Research. LAURENCE J. KOTLIKOFF is professor of economics at Boston University and a research associate of the National Bureau of Economic Research. WILLI LEIBFRITZ is head of the Department for Macroeconomic and Fiscal Studies at ifo Institute for Economic Research.

The University of Chicago Press, Chicago 60637
The University of Chicago Press, Ltd., London
© 1999 by the National Bureau of Economic Research
All rights reserved. Published 1999

08 07 06 05 04 03 02 01 00 99   1 2 3 4 5
ISBN: 0-226-03213-2 (cloth)

Library of Congress Cataloging-in-Publication Data

Auerbach, Alan J.
    Generational accounting around the world / edited by Alan J. Auer-
bach, Laurence J. Kotlikoff, and Willi Leibfritz.
        p.   cm.—(National Bureau of Economic Research project
report)
    Includes bibliographical references and index.
    ISBN 0-226-03213-2 (cloth : alk. paper)
    1. Generational accounting.   I. Kotlikoff, Laurence J.   II. Leib-
fritz, Willi.   III. Title.   IV. Series.
    HJ9755.A93   1999
    339.5—ddc21   98-45329
                                                                        CIP

Relation of the Directors to the
Work and Publications of the
National Bureau of Economic Research

1. The object of the National Bureau of Economic Research is to ascertain and to present to the public important economic facts and their interpretation in a scientific and impartial manner. The Board of Directors is charged with the responsibility of ensuring that the work of the National Bureau is carried on in strict conformity with this object.

2. The President of the National Bureau shall submit to the Board of Directors, or to its Executive Committee, for their formal adoption all specific proposals for research to be instituted.

3. No research report shall be published by the National Bureau until the President has sent each member of the Board a notice that a manuscript is recommended for publication and that in the President's opinion it is suitable for publication in accordance with the principles of the National Bureau. Such notification will include an abstract or summary of the manuscript's content and a response form for use by those Directors who desire a copy of the manuscript for review. Each manuscript shall contain a summary drawing attention to the nature and treatment of the problem studied, the character of the data and their utilization in the report, and the main conclusions reached.

4. For each manuscript so submitted, a special committee of the Directors (including Directors Emeriti) shall be appointed by majority agreement of the President and Vice Presidents (or by the Executive Committee in case of inability to decide on the part of the President and Vice Presidents), consisting of three Directors selected as nearly as may be one from each general division of the Board. The names of the special manuscript committee shall be stated to each Director when notice of the proposed publication is submitted to him. It shall be the duty of each member of the special manuscript committee to read the manuscript. If each member of the manuscript committee signifies his approval within thirty days of the transmittal of the manuscript, the report may be published. If at the end of that period any member of the manuscript committee withholds his approval, the President shall then notify each member of the Board, requesting approval or disapproval of publication, and thirty days additional shall be granted for this purpose. The manuscript shall then not be published unless at least a majority of the entire Board who shall have voted on the proposal within the time fixed for the receipt of votes shall have approved.

5. No manuscript may be published, though approved by each member of the special manuscript committee, until forty-five days have elapsed from the transmittal of the report in manuscript form. The interval is allowed for the receipt of any memorandum of dissent or reservation, together with a brief statement of his reasons, that any member may wish to express; and such memorandum of dissent or reservation shall be published with the manuscript if he so desires. Publication does not, however, imply that each member of the Board has read the manuscript, or that either members of the Board in general or the special committee have passed on its validity in every detail.

6. Publications of the National Bureau issued for informational purposes concerning the work of the Bureau and its staff, or issued to inform the public of activities of Bureau staff, and volumes issued as a result of various conferences involving the National Bureau shall contain a specific disclaimer noting that such publication has not passed through the normal review procedures required in this resolution. The Executive Committee of the Board is charged with review of all such publications from time to time to ensure that they do not take on the character of formal research reports of the National Bureau, requiring formal Board approval.

7. Unless otherwise determined by the Board or exempted by the terms of paragraph 6, a copy of this resolution shall be printed in each National Bureau publication.

(Resolution adopted October 25, 1926, as revised through September 30, 1974)

To the next generation

Contents

Introduction   1
Alan J. Auerbach, Laurence J. Kotlikoff, and
Willi Leibfritz

1.   **From Deficit Delusion to the Fiscal Balance Rule:
      Looking for an Economically Meaningful Way to
      Assess Fiscal Policy**   9
      Laurence J. Kotlikoff

2.   **The Methodology of Generational Accounting**   31
      Alan J. Auerbach and Laurence J. Kotlikoff

3.   **Generational Accounting in
      General Equilibrium**   43
      Hans Fehr and Laurence J. Kotlikoff

4.   **An International Comparison of
      Generational Accounts**   73
      Laurence J. Kotlikoff and Willi Leibfritz

5.   **Argentina's Generational Accounts: Is the
      Convertibility Plan's Fiscal Policy Sustainable?**   103
      Marcelo F. Altamiranda

6.   **Generational Accounting in Australia**   141
      John Ablett

7.   **Generational Accounts for Belgium**   161
      Jean-Philippe Stijns

8.   **Generational Accounting in Brazil**   177
      Regina Villela Malvar

9.   **Canada: On the Road to Fiscal Balance**   199
      Philip Oreopoulos

10.   **Public Debt, Welfare Reforms, and**
      Intergenerational Distribution of Tax
      Burdens in Denmark   219
      Svend E. Hougaard Jensen and Bernd Raffelhüschen

11.   **Generational Accounting for France**   239
      Joaquim Levy and Ousmane Doré

12.   **Unification and Aging in Germany: Who Pays**
      and When?   277
      Bernd Raffelhüschen and Jan Walliser

13.   **Generational Accounts for Italy**   299
      Nicola Sartor

14.   **Generational Accounts for the Netherlands** 325
      A. Lans Bovenberg and Harry ter Rele

15.   **Generational Accounting in New Zealand**   347
      Bruce Baker

16.   **Generational Accounting and Depletable Natural**
      Resources: The Case of Norway   369
      Erling Steigum, Jr., and Carl Gjersem

17.   **Generational Accounts in Sweden**   397
      Robert P. Hagemann and Christoph John

18.   **Thailand's Generational Accounts**   413
      Nanak Kakwani and Medhi Krongkaew

19.   **Generational Accounting in Japan**   447
      Noriyuki Takayama, Yukinobu Kitamura, and
      Hiroshi Yoshida

20.   **Generational Accounting in Portugal**   471
      Alan J. Auerbach, Jorge Braga de Macedo, José Braz,
      Laurence J. Kotlikoff, and Jan Walliser

21.   **Generational Accounts for the United States:**
      An Update   489
      Jagadeesh Gokhale, Benjamin R. Page, and
      John R. Sturrock

      Contributors   519

      Author Index   523

      Subject Index   527

Introduction

Alan J. Auerbach, Laurence J. Kotlikoff,
and Willi Leibfritz

Generational accounting is a method of long-term fiscal analysis and planning (see Auerbach, Gokhale, and Kotlikoff 1991; Kotlikoff 1992). Its goals are to assess the sustainability of fiscal policy and to measure the fiscal burdens facing current and future generations. Although generational accounting is only eight years old, there are now 22 countries around the world doing generational accounting: Argentina, Austria, Australia, Belgium, Brazil, Canada, Denmark, Finland, France, Germany, Ireland, Italy, Japan, the Netherlands, New Zealand, Norway, Portugal, Spain, Sweden, Thailand, the United Kingdom, and the United States. Chile, Israel, and Mexico may soon be added to this list.

Much of this generational accounting has been done by or in conjunction with governmental bodies including the Argentine Ministry of Planning; the Bank of England, the Bank of Japan; the Board of Governors of the Federal Reserve System, the Congressional Budget Office, and the Office of Management and Budget of the U.S. Government; the New Zealand Treasury; and the Norwegian Ministry of Finance. The International Monetary Fund (IMF) has constructed generational accounts for France and Sweden. The World Bank has constructed generational accounts for Thailand and is about to begin constructing generational accounts for Slovenia. In addition, the Congressional Budget Office, the European Commission, and the Organization for Economic Cooperation and Development (OECD) have each produced detailed studies of generational accounting (see Sturrock 1995; Leibfritz et al. 1995; Raffelhüschen 1997).

Alan J. Auerbach is the Robert D. Burch Professor of Economics and Law at the University of California, Berkeley, and a research associate of the National Bureau of Economic Research. Laurence J. Kotlikoff is professor of economics at Boston University and a research associate of the National Bureau of Economic Research. Willi Leibfritz is head of the Department for Macroeconomic and Fiscal Studies at ifo Institute for Economic Research.

Generational accounting has also received its fair share of academic scrutiny (see Haveman 1994; Auerbach, Gokhale, and Kotlikoff 1994; Buiter 1997; Cutler 1993; Diamond 1996; Kotlikoff 1997). Its methodology has been debated in leading economics journals, including the *Journal of Economic Perspectives,* the *National Tax Journal,* and the *Economic Journal.* This debate has stimulated ongoing research, some of which is discussed here, on general equilibrium effects, immigration, and the proper way to discount government receipts and payments in light of their uncertainty. Finally, generational accounting has received a fair amount of public attention. Its findings have been discussed in leading newspapers, magazines, and television news shows in many of the countries for which the accounts have been prepared.

The growing interest in generational accounting is stimulated by the rapid population aging taking place in virtually all the developed world and in much of the developing world. This demographic transition portends enormous fiscal bills in the first half of the next century as those generations born since World War II retire and begin collecting social security pension and old-age health care benefits. The tremendous size of this fiscal liability, its dire implications for our children, and its independence from the traditional deficit is leading economists, government officials, and the press to search for a meaningful measure of our fiscal future.

How It Works and What It Does

Generational accounting is based on the government's intertemporal budget constraint, which requires that either current or future generations pay the government's bills—the present value of the government's projected future purchases of goods and services plus its official net financial liabilities. Subtracting from these bills the present value of projected future net tax payments of current generations gives the present value net tax burden facing future generations implied by current policy. Net tax payments are taxes paid less social security, welfare, and other transfer payments received.[1]

By comparing the growth-adjusted lifetime net tax burden facing members of future generations with that facing current newborns (who are assumed to pay, over their lifetimes, only the net taxes implied by current policy), one can assess the sustainability of current fiscal policies. For example, if the growth-adjusted lifetime net tax burden facing future generations is higher than that facing newborns, maintaining current policy through time, which means taxing members of successive new generations at the same rate as members of current generations, is not sustainable because it will not suffice to pay the government's bills.

---

1. The fact that the government's bills left unpaid by current generations must be paid by future generations does not mean that future generations must pay off (retire) official government debt at some finite future date. They do, however, have to service the debt.

Besides comparing the lifetime tax burdens facing members of future generations with that of newborns, generational accounting calculates the present value changes in net taxes of generations, both living and future, resulting from changes in fiscal policies. Take an expansion of pay-as-you-go-financed social security retirement benefits. Generational accounting shows that this policy helps the current elderly and harms current younger and future generations. Specifically, it records the reduction in the present value net tax payments of older generations arising under the policy as well as the increase in the per capita present value net tax payments of young and future generations (whose increased payroll taxes have a larger present value than do their increased social security retirement benefits).[2]

Finally, generational accounting can identify the set of sustainable policies available to the government. For example, generational accounting can calculate the immediate and permanent annual percentage increase in income tax revenues (relative to the baseline projected time path of these revenues) needed to achieve intertemporal budget balance. This calculation takes the government's projected expenditures and other tax receipts as given and asks: By what percentage would one need immediately and permanently to raise income taxes so as to be able (in conjunction with other tax receipts) to pay for the government's projected future expenditures and its current net financial liabilities and never have to raise taxes again?

In forming its calculations, generational accounting considers not only the course of future policy but also the future demographic structure of the economy. Projected population totals of currently living generations are a key element in determining the contribution of current generations in paying the government's bills. Projected population totals of future generations are a key element in determining how large will be the burden per future person of covering the bills left unpaid by those now alive.

This Book's Agenda

This book brings together the latest generational accounting results for 17 of the 22 countries listed above: Argentina, Australia, Belgium, Brazil, Canada, Denmark, France, Germany, Italy, the Netherlands, New Zealand, Norway, Sweden, Thailand, Japan, Portugal, and the United States.[3] The results are presented in separate chapters, one for each country, but they are also summarized and compared in chapter 4. Chapters 1, 2, and 3 set the stage for these analyses. Chapter 1 discusses the severe limitations of traditional fiscal analysis, namely, deficit accounting. Chapter 2 describes the method of generational accounting, and chapter 3 uses a simulation model to consider how well generational

2. This statement assumes that the return to capital exceeds the growth rate of the economy.
3. Unfortunately, accounts for the other countries were not completed in time for inclusion in this book.

accounting approximates policy-induced changes in generations' true fiscal burdens.

Chapter 1 provides the main motivation for generational accounting[4]—the deficit, at its core, is an arbitrary measure. Rather than measure a county's fiscal position, the deficit, in fact, need bear no fundamental relationship to fiscal policy but, instead, simply reflects the government's choice of how to label its receipts and payments. Chapter 1 drives home this point using a series of models that incorporate intergenerational redistribution by the government, uncertainty, economic distortions, and liquidity constraints. These models are stylized. But the point they make would hold in any neoclassical economic model with rational economic agents and institutions: *Regardless of their true fiscal policies, governments can label their policies so as to report any time path of deficits or surpluses they want.*

The fundamental problem with deficit accounting is that the deficit does not represent the answer to a well-posed economic question. Generational accounting, in contrast, attempts to answer two well-defined economic questions. First, what is the magnitude of the fiscal burden being left to future generations by current policy, and second, how does a change in fiscal policy alter the intergenerational distribution of welfare? In short, generational accounting attempts to understand the generational *incidence* (distribution of burdens) of fiscal policy changes. In so doing, it incorporates a set of incidence assumptions that will not, in general, capture the full range of either microeconomic or macroeconomic responses to policy changes. Consequently, generational accounting should be viewed as a method of approximating the policy-induced welfare changes experienced by different generations.

How well do changes in generational accounts succeed in approximating true generation-specific fiscal burdens? Hans Fehr and Laurence Kotlikoff address this question in chapter 3 with the help of the Auerbach-Kotlikoff dynamic life cycle model. Their approach is to simulate various fiscal policies that produce substantial intergenerational welfare changes. They then use the simulated data to form changes in generational accounts according to the methodology detailed in chapter 2. Finally, they compare these generational account changes with the exact welfare changes arising in the model. They conclude that generational accounting does a pretty good job in approximating actual welfare changes particularly in the case of policies that do not involve substantial changes in the structure of economic incentives.

Country Studies

The country studies, which appear in chapters 5 through 21, have a common structure. They each begin with a description of recent domestic fiscal policy,

4. Chapter 1 was originally published in 1993 in the *Journal of Economics* (suppl. 7, 17–41) under the same title and is reprinted here with the permission of the publisher.

present (in 1995 dollars) generational accounts for 1995, discuss the generational impact of recent or pending policies, and then consider alternative ways to restore generational balance. The 30 economists who produced these studies hail from all corners of the globe. They are almost equally divided between academic economists and economists working for central banks, treasuries, ministries of finance, or international economic institutions. A number of the country studies represent collaborations between the two types of economists, but all of the studies owe a significant debt to their respective governments for providing critically important data.

The studies reveal very substantial and very troubling generational imbalances in the majority of the 17 countries. The countries with extreme imbalances are Japan, Italy, Germany, the Netherlands, and Brazil. In these five countries, future generations face fiscal burdens that are at least 75 percent higher than those of current generations when these burdens are measured as a percentage of lifetime labor earnings.[5] In Japan and Italy, future generations face burdens that are more than twice those facing current generations. Another five countries have severe imbalance—the United States, Norway, Portugal, Argentina, and Belgium. In these countries, the growth-adjusted fiscal burdens facing future generations are 50 to 75 percent larger than those of current newborns. Three countries—Australia, Denmark, and France—have substantial imbalances that leave their descendents facing 30 to 50 percent higher lifetime net tax rates. Canada appears to be essentially in generational balance. The remaining three countries—New Zealand, Thailand, and Sweden—have negative imbalances; that is, their policies, if maintained, would leave future generations facing lower lifetime net tax rates than current newborns.

In measuring the fiscal burdens facing future generations or, more precisely, the net taxes (taxes paid less transfer payments received) facing future generations, the baseline generational accounts assume no change in either the net taxes to be paid by current generations over the rest of their lives or in the future course of government purchases of goods and services. Alternative assumptions can be and are entertained in this volume. Specifically, we consider the immediate and permanent tax hikes, transfer cuts, or spending cuts needed to achieve generational balance—a situation in which future generations face no higher rate of lifetime net taxation than do those who have recently been born. These alternative characterizations of generational imbalances deliver a complementary message, namely, that in countries with large generational imbalances, very major policy changes are needed to achieve balance.

Take, as an example, a policy of immediately and permanently cutting government spending (purchases of goods and services) to achieve generational balance. In Japan, this policy would entail a 26 percent reduction in govern-

---

5. The cross-country comparisons of generational accounts in this chapter are based on the results arising from treating educational expenditures as a government purchase rather than a transfer payment. As indicated in chapter 5, treating educational expenditures as transfer payments generates even larger imbalances than those mentioned here.

ment purchases this year and every year into the future. In the United States, roughly a 19 percent reduction is needed, whereas Italy would have to cut its purchases by roughly 53 percent! Proposing such tremendous fiscal adjustments would, presumably, frighten even the most courageous and generationally altruistic politicians. But those politicians who hesitate to act are condemning their nations to more severe fiscal stringency in the future. This is one of the hard lessons of generational accounting: the longer one waits, the larger the adjustment needed to achieve generational balance.

Is official government debt primarily responsible for the generational imbalances reported here? The answer, in general, is no. The real culprit in most of the countries with imbalances is the interaction of their population aging with their large and growing transfer payments to the elderly in the form of pension payments and health care expenditures. The United States is a case in point. Its baseline generational accounts, which treat government education as a form of spending, show future Americans facing lifetime net tax rates that are 51 percent higher than those facing current American newborns. If the U.S. federal debt were miraculously and instantaneously paid off by, say, a philanthropic Martian, future Americans would still face 30 percent higher net tax rates. On the other hand, were the United States able to stop aging, the rate of net taxation of future Americans would actually be 3 percent smaller!

Whither Generational Accounting?

Generational accounting is clearly catching on and appears to be influencing a growing number of policy debates. But will it ultimately replace deficit accounting as our central gauge of a nation's fiscal behavior? It is hard to say. The decision to use generational accounting is not just an intellectual one. It also involves political considerations, some of which militate against generational accounting. But the decision also involves ethical considerations, which have a power of their own. Generational accounting makes us look ahead. It makes us refine our long-term fiscal projections. It makes us consider the rising cost of policy procrastination. It makes us ask tough questions about who will pay the government's bills. It makes us address economic issues, rather than play accounting games. And it makes us acknowledge the extent to which we are expropriating our children's resources by accumulating fiscal liabilities, be they implicit or explicit.

Whether or not generational accounting replaces deficit accounting, the papers collected here make one thing clear: serious discussion of a country's generational policy necessitates producing a set of generational accounts and using these accounts to consider the generational impact of alternative policies. Moreover, keeping track of changes over time in a country's generational policy requires doing generational accounting on an ongoing basis. This is where involvement by governments and international economic institutions, such as the European Union, the OECD, the IMF, the World Bank, the Inter-American

Development Bank, and the Asian Development Bank, is crucial. These entities have the manpower and other resources needed to ensure that accurate and up-to-date generational accounting is done and done routinely. In addition to the means, governments and quasi-governmental entities bear a responsibility to do generational accounting for one simple but very good reason: they represent the collective guardians of our children's economic futures.

References

Auerbach, Alan J., Jagadeesh Gokhale, and Laurence J. Kotlikoff. 1991. Generational accounts: A meaningful alternative to deficit accounting. In *Tax policy and the economy,* vol. 5, ed. D. Bradford, 55–110. Cambridge, Mass.: MIT Press.
———. 1994. Generational accounting: A meaningful way to evaluate fiscal policy. *Journal of Economic Perspectives* 8, no. 1 (winter): 73–94.
Buiter, Willem H. 1997. Generational accounts, aggregate saving and intergenerational distribution. *Economica* 64:605–26.
Cutler, David. 1993. Review of generational accounting: Knowing who pays, and when, for what we spend. *National Tax Journal* 46, no. 1 (March): 61–67.
Diamond, Peter. 1996. Generational accounts and generational balance: An assessment. *National Tax Journal* 49, no. 4 (December): 597–607.
Haveman, Robert. 1994. Should generational accounts replace public budgets and deficits? *Journal of Economic Perspectives* 8, no. 1 (winter): 95–112.
Kotlikoff, Laurence J. 1992. *Generational accounting.* New York: Free Press.
———. 1997. Reply to Diamond and Cutler's reviews of generational accounting. *National Tax Journal* 50, no. 2 (June): 303–14.
Leibfritz, Willi, Deborah Roseveare, Douglas Fore, and Eckhard Wurzel. 1995. Aging populations, pension systems, and government budgets: How do they affect saving? OECD Economics Department Working Paper no. 156. Paris: Organization for Economic Cooperation and Development.
Raffelhüschen, Bernd. 1997. Generational accounting in Europe. Luxembourg: European Commission, October.
Sturrock, John. 1995. Who pays and when? An assessment of generational accounting. Washington, D.C.: Government Printing Office.

1

From Deficit Delusion to the Fiscal Balance Rule: Looking for an Economically Meaningful Way to Assess Fiscal Policy

Laurence J. Kotlikoff

Notwithstanding its widespread use as a measure of fiscal policy, the government deficit is not a well-defined concept from the perspective of neoclassical macro economics. From the neoclassical perspective the deficit is an arbitrary accounting construct whose value depends on how the government chooses to label its receipts and payments. This paper demonstrates the arbitrary nature of government deficits. The argument that the deficit is not well defined is first framed in a simple certainty model with nondistortionary policies, and then in settings with uncertain policy, distortionary policy, and liquidity constraints. As an alternative to economically arbitrary deficits, the paper indicates that the "fiscal balance rule" is one norm for measuring whether current policy will place a larger or smaller burden on future generations than it does on current generations. The fiscal balance rule is based on the economy's intertemporal budget constraint and appears to underlie actual attempts to run tight fiscal policy. It says take in net present value from each new young generation an amount equal to the flow of government consumption less interest on the difference between (a) the value of the economy's capital stock and (b) the present value difference between the future consumption and future labor earnings of existing older generations. While the rule is a mouthful, one can use existing

Laurence J. Kotlikoff is professor of economics at Boston University and a research associate of the National Bureau of Economic Research.

Reprinted from *Journal of Economics,* suppl. 7 (1993): 17–41, by permission of Springer-Verlag.

The author thanks Alan Auerbach, Doug Bernheim, Christophe Chamley, Michael Darby, Jacob Frenkel, Jagadeesh Gokhale, Fumio Hayashi, Elhanan Helpman, Michael Manove, Robert Rosenthal, Assaf Razin, Bernd Spahn, and Andrew Weiss for very helpful comments. Section 1.2 draws on the author's August 1987 article in *Science.* This paper was written, in part, while the author was a visiting scholar at the International Monetary Fund. He is very grateful to the International Monetary Fund for research support. This paper is part of NBER's research program in taxation. The view expressed here are solely the author's; they are not necessarily the views of the International Monetary Fund, Boston University, or the National Bureau of Economic Research.

data to check whether it is being obeyed and, therefore, whether future generations are likely to be treated better or worse than current generations.

1.1 Introduction

Recent years have witnessed a growing unease about using government deficits to measure fiscal policy. Martin Feldstein (1974) pointed out that vast amounts of unfunded Social Security retirement liabilities are not picked up in official debt figures. The 1982 *Economic Report of the President* and Leonard (1986) stressed the same is true of unfunded civil service and military pensions and a range of other programs such as FSLIC commitments, etc. Eisner and Pieper (1984, 1985), Boskin (1987), and Boskin, Robinson, and Huber (1987) faulted the official U.S. deficit for ignoring government assets. These and a host of related complaints about conventional deficit accounting coincided with demonstrations by Kotlikoff (1979), Summers (1981), Chamley (1981), Auerbach and Kotlikoff (1983), and others that (1) major intergenerationally redistributive fiscal policies can be conducted under the guise of a "balanced budget" and (2) identical fiscal policies can be conducted concomitant with dramatically different time paths of reported deficits.

While some economists including Eisner and Pieper (1984, 1985) and Leonard (1986) suggest that the deficit can be fixed, the arbitrary nature of such corrections raises the question of whether the deficit is a well-defined economic concept. Unfortunately, it is not. In a series of articles (Kotlikoff 1984, 1986, 1988) I have pointed out that from a neoclassical perspective the deficit is an arbitrary accounting construct with no necessary relationship to the fundamental stance of fiscal policy. The equations of neoclassical models do not uniquely define the size or sign of government deficits, and "the deficit" in such models is purely a reflection of how the government chooses to label its receipts and payments.

Since rational households and firms see through accounting labels, the predictions of neoclassical models are free of fiscal illusion. Not only does the choice of accounting labels have no implications for actual fiscal policy in neoclassical models, but the reverse is also true: in neoclassical macro models the government can conduct any sustainable fiscal policy while simultaneously choosing its accounting so as to report any size surplus or deficit it desires. In neoclassical macro models fiscal policies have real effects, not because of their labels, but because they either (1) alter economic incentives, (2) redistribute from different generations to the government, (3) redistribute within generations, or (4) redistribute across generations. It is this fourth policy, intergenerational redistribution and its implications for saving and investment, that appears to underlie recent concern about loose U.S. fiscal policy. Intergenerational redistribution occurs whenever a government policy expands the consumption opportunities of one generation at the expense of another.

This paper describes a new rule for assessing whether the government's intergenerational policy is in balance in the sense that future generations are not being made worse off as compared to current generations. The rule is denoted the "fiscal balance rule." In contrast to the "balanced budget rule," the fiscal balance rule is economically well defined. The fiscal balance rule is based on the economy's intertemporal budget constraint and appears to underlie actual attempts to run tight fiscal policy. It says take in net present value from each new young generation an amount equal to the flow of government consumption less interest on the difference between (a) the value of the economy's capital stock and (b) the present value difference between the future consumption and labor earnings of existing older generations. While the rule is a mouthful, one can use existing data to check whether it is being obeyed and, therefore, whether future generations are likely to be treated better or worse than current generations. This paper proceeds in section 1.2 by demonstrating the arbitrary nature of "deficit" accounting with a simple two period life cycle model with no uncertainty. Section 1.3 shows that the economically arbitrary nature of "deficit" accounting arises equally in models in which government policy is uncertain and distortionary and in which agents face liquidity constraints. Section 1.4 describes the fiscal balance rule and its use as a norm for considering whether fiscal policy is intergenerationally loose or tight. Section 1.5 discusses how this rule might be implemented empirically. Section 1.6 summarizes and concludes the paper.

1.2   A Two Period Life Cycle Model

A simple two period, one good life cycle model with zero population or productivity growth is convenient to show both the concern with loose fiscal policy that redistributes toward earlier generations and the fact that the government's reported deficit bears no necessary relation to the stance of fiscal policy. At the beginning of each period a new generation of constant size is born, and members of each generation live for two periods, their youth and old age. When individuals are young they work full time, and when they are old they are retired. Each individual born at time t chooses how much to consume when young at time t, C_{yt}, and how much to consume when old at time $t + 1$, C_{ot+1}, subject to the budget constraint given in equation (1):

(1) $$C_{yt} + C_{ot+1}/(1 + r_{t+1}) = W_t.$$

In equation (1) r_{t+1}, is the interest rate at time $t + 1$. The equation states that the present value of consumption expenditure (the price of consumption is numéraired to 1) over the life cycle equals the present value of lifetime resources which, in this model, is simply earnings when young, W_t. The maximization of utility given in (2) subject to (1) gives the demands for consumption when young and old written in equation (3):

(2) $$U_t = \beta \log C_{yt} + (1 - \beta) \log C_{ot+1}$$

$$C_{yt} = \beta W_t$$
(3)
$$C_{ot+1} = (1 - \beta)W_t(1 + r_{t+1}).$$

At the beginning of any time period the young have no assets. Hence, the capital stock in the economy at time $t + 1$ corresponds to the asset holdings of the elderly at time $t + 1$. The assets of the elderly at time $t + 1$ equal the savings they accumulated when they were young at time t. This savings per elderly equals $W_t - C_{yt}$, which is simply saving out of first period labor earnings. This fact and (3) permit one to write capital per young worker at time $t + 1$, K_{t+1}, as

(4)
$$K_{t+1} = (1 - \beta)W_t.$$

To close the model assume that the economy's single good is produced according to the production function in (5) that relates output per worker at time t, Y_t, to capital per worker, K_t:

(5)
$$Y_t = K_t^{\alpha}.$$

Given the production function, profit maximization by representative firms implies the following expressions relating factor demands to factor returns:

$$W_t = (1 - \alpha)K_t^{\alpha}$$
(6)
$$r_t = \alpha K_t^{\alpha-1}.$$

Substitution of the first equation in (6) into (4) yields a nonlinear difference equation determining the time path of the economy's capital stock:

(7)
$$K_{t+1} = (1 - \beta)(1 - \alpha)K_t^{\alpha}.$$

If α and β are less than one, this model has a locally stable, nonzero stationary state capital stock denoted by K, where

(8)
$$K = [(1 - \beta)(1 - \alpha)]^{1/(1-\alpha)}.$$

1.2.1 Adding Loose Fiscal Policy to the Model

Consider now an ongoing government policy commencing at time t that takes an amount H from each young person and gives an amount H to each contemporary old person. For young individuals born at time t their lifetime budget constraint is now

(9)
$$C_{yt} + C_{ot+1}/(1 + r_{t+1}) = W_t - H + H/(1 + r_{t+1}).$$

Holding the time path of the wage rate, W_t, and the interest rate, r_t, constant, this fiscal policy leaves generation t as well as all subsequent generations worse off; each generation from t onward gives up H when young and must wait until old age to receive H back. Hence, each generation from t onward loses, in present value, interest on the amount H. The first generation of elderly alive at time t, in contrast, benefits from this policy since they receive H but don't have to pay it back. Their second period budget constraint is now

$$(10) \qquad C_{ot} = (1 - \beta)W_{t-1}(1 + r_t) + H.$$

With (9), rather than (1), holding, $C_{yt} = \beta[W_t - Hr_{t+1}/(1 + r_{t+1})]$, and the capital stock at time $t + 1$ is given by (11) since the saving of the young at time t now equals $W_t - H - C_{yt}$.

$$(11) \qquad K_{t+1} = (1 - \beta)W_t - H[1 - \beta r_{t+1}/(1 + r_{t+1})].$$

The new capital stock transition equation is

$$(12) \qquad K_{t+1} = (1 - \beta)(1 - \alpha)K_t^\alpha - H[1 - \beta\alpha K_{t+1}^{\alpha-1}/(1 + \alpha K_{t+1}^{\alpha-1})].$$

The new stationary state capital stock, K', is found by setting $K_t = K_{t-1} = K'$ in (12). Denoting by r the initial stationary state value of the interest rate, the derivative of the stationary state capital stock with respect to H evaluated at $H = 0$ is given by

$$(13) \qquad \delta K'/\delta H = -[1 - \beta r/(1 + r)]/(1 - \alpha) < 0.$$

Equation (13) indicates that this intergenerational transfer policy crowds out the economy's long-run capital stock. Of course, the crowding out process takes some time, and (12) determines the transition path from K to K' associated with an increase in H.

The intuitive explanation for this crowding out of capital formation is that the redistribution to the initial elderly generation of H at time t leads to an increase in their consumption by the amount H (see eq. [10]), while the young at time t reduce their consumption by an amount $\beta Hr_{t+1}/(1 + r_{t+1})$, which is less than H. Hence, aggregate consumption is larger at time t, and since output at time t is given, aggregate saving and investment at time t declines. This explains why the capital stock is smaller at time $t + 1$ as a consequence of the policy, but why does the economy end up in a stationary state with a permanently reduced capital stock? The answer is that although each successive generation will consume less because of this policy, their reduced consumption will, at any point in time, not yet have fully offset the initial increase in consumption of the time t elderly; i.e., at any point in time there will always be generations yet to come whose consumption has yet to be reduced by the policy. In addition, the reduction in capital at time $t + 1$ means a lower level of wages at time $t + 1$ (see eq. [6]), which feeds back into lower savings by the young at time $t + 1$, and an even lower capital stock at time $t + 2$, with the process converging to the permanently lower capital stock of the new stationary state.

1.2.2 Deficit Delusion and the Arbitrary Nature of Fiscal Labels

In presenting this simple example of loose fiscal policy care was taken not to use any fiscal language to label the payment of H by each young generation to the government and the receipt of H from the government by each old generation. It now remains to show that this policy can be conducted with the government reporting a balanced budget, a debt, or a surplus. In each case the real effects of the policy are identical, and the reported size of the debt has no relationship whatsoever to the stance of fiscal policy.

First, take the case that the government labels the receipt of H from the young each period as "taxes" and the payment to the old each period as "spending on transfer payments." In this case the government would report a balanced budget each period, since "taxes" equals "spending" each period, despite the fact that the government is running a loose fiscal policy. Furthermore, the budget would remain in balance the looser the fiscal policy, i.e., the larger is the value of H.

Next let the government (1) label its payment of H to the elderly at time t as "spending on transfer payments," (2) label its receipt of H from each young generation as "borrowing," and (3) label its net payment of H to each elderly generation at time s for all $s > t$ as "repayment of principal plus interest in the amount of $H(1 + r_s)$" less a "tax in the amount of Hr_s." While each generation of elderly starting at time t still receives H, and each generation of young starting at t still pays H, with this new labeling the government's deficit at time t is H, and its stock of debt remains at H forever. To see this note that at time t the government's "spending" is H, and its reported "taxes" are zero. Hence, the time t deficit ("spending" less "taxes") is H. At time s, for $s > t$, the government's "spending on transfer payments" is zero, but its "spending on interest payments" is Hr_s. Since its "taxes" are also Hr_s, its deficit (change in the debt) after time t is zero, and its debt remains permanently equal to H.

As a third case, let the government (1) label its payment of H to the elderly at time t as "spending on transfer payments," (2) label its net receipt of H from each young person at time t and thereafter as "receipt of taxes in the amount of $2H$" less a "loan in the amount of H," and (3) label its net payment of H to each elderly person at time s for $s > t$ as "spending on transfers payments in the amount of $2H + Hr_s$" less "receipt of principal plus interest in the amount of $H(1 + r_s)$." At time t the government will now report a negative deficit ("taxes" less "spending") of $-H$. And at time $s > t$ the government will report a balanced budget, since "taxes" of $2H$ plus "interest received" of Hr_s will equal "spending on transfer payments of $2H + Hr_s$." Hence, the government will report a positive stock of assets, a surplus of H at time t, and, since its budget will be balance in each period after t, the government's surplus (negative debt) will remain at H.

These three labeling cases show that a fundamentally loose fiscal policy can be conducted with the government reporting zero debt, positive debt, or negative debt. Furthermore, there is nothing to preclude the government from changing its labeling through time with the consequence that the same real policy could first be reported as generating a deficit, then be reported as generating a surplus, and finally be reported as being conducted on a balanced budget basis. Finally, there is no requirement that the labeling produce either a zero debt, a debt of H, or a surplus of H. To see this, consider again the labeling leading to the reporting of a surplus. If the government labels its net receipt of H from the young as "taxes in the amount of $5H$" less "a loan of $4H$" and labels the net payment of H to the elderly at $s > t$ as "spending on transfer payments of $5H + 4Hr_s$" less "receipt of principal plus interest in the amount of $4H(1 + r_s)$," the reported surplus will be $4H$ rather than simply H. Hence, the government can report any size surplus or debt while engaging in exactly the same economic policy. And individuals, since they care only about their budget constraints, not the government's choice of labels, will behave exactly the same regardless of the announced, as opposed to actual, stance of fiscal policy.

1.3   Demonstrating the Arbitrary Nature of Fiscal Labels When Fiscal Policy Is Uncertain, When Fiscal Policy Is Distortionary, and When There Are Liquidity Constraints

1.3.1   Uncertain Fiscal Policy

One possible objection to the above demonstration that fiscal labels are economically arbitrary is that it assumes that government policy is certain. Surely, the objection goes, "future 'transfer payments' and 'taxes' are less certain than the future payment of interest on government bonds, which, in the absence of inflation, is very safe. Hence, this demonstration that rests on the equivalence of receipts and payments in a world of certainty does not go through in a world of uncertainty." Fortunately or unfortunately, this objection is not valid, and the risk properties of government payments and receipts do not provide a basis for fiscal labeling; i.e., the definition of "the deficit" is just as arbitrary in models with uncertainty as it is in certainty models. The reason is that any uncertain payment (receipt) $\tilde{X}$ (where ~ refers to a variable that is uncertain) made by (received by) individuals to (from) the government in the future can be relabeled as the combination of a certain payment (receipt) $\overline{X}$ plus an uncertain payment (receipt) $\tilde{X} - \overline{X}$. Since current payments (receipts) are certain and future payments (receipts) can be described as a combination of certain and uncertain payments (receipts), the labeling of the current and future certain payments and receipts remains economically arbitrary.

To see more precisely why the "deficit" is no less arbitrary in uncertainty models consider again the two period life cycle model in which the government transfers from the young and to the old. But now denote by $\tilde{H}_t$ the amount taken by the government from the young and given to the old at time t. The young at time t know the value of $\tilde{H}_t$ (hence the ~ is dropped below for this variable) but are uncertain about the value of $\tilde{H}_{t+1}$. To add to the realism of this example let us assume that output in the future is also uncertain due to a random productivity shock. The young now maximize expected utility given by

$$(14) \qquad E_t U_t = \beta \log C_{yt} + (1 - \beta) E_t \log \tilde{C}_{ot+1}$$

subject to

$$(15) \qquad \tilde{C}_{ot+1} = (W_t - H_t - C_{yt})[1 + \bar{r}_{t+1} + \theta_t(\tilde{r}_{t+1} - \bar{r}_{t+1})] + \tilde{H}_{t+1}.$$

In (15) $\tilde{r}_{t+1}$ and $\bar{r}_{t+1}$ are respectively the risky and safe rates of return at time $t + 1$. At time t, $\tilde{r}_{t+1}$ is uncertain. The term θ_t is the proportion of the saving of the young at time t that is invested in the risky asset.

Equations (16) and (17) are the respective first order conditions for the optimal choices of C_{yt} and θ_t:

$$(16) \qquad \frac{\beta}{C_{yt}} = (1 - \beta) E_t \frac{[1 + \bar{r}_{t+1} + \theta_t(\tilde{r}_{t+1} - \bar{r}_{t+1})]}{\tilde{C}_{ot+1}}$$

$$(17) \qquad E_t \frac{(\tilde{r}_{t+1} - \bar{r}_{t+1})}{\tilde{C}_{ot+1}} = 0.$$

Insertion of (15) into (16) and (17) yields two equations in the period t choice variables C_{yt} and θ_t.

To close the model assume that the production function at time t is given by

$$(18) \qquad Y_t = \tilde{A}_t K_t^\alpha$$

where $\tilde{A}_t$ is uncertain at time t. The wage at time t and the risky rate of return at time $t + 1$ are determined according to (19):

$$(19) \qquad \begin{aligned} W_t &= A_t(1 - \alpha) K_t^\alpha \\ \tilde{r}_{t+1} &= \tilde{A}_{t+1} \alpha K_{t+1}^{\alpha-1}. \end{aligned}$$

Since the net supply of safe assets to the economy is zero, θ_t will equal 1 in equilibrium, and (16) and (17) can be solved, given (19), for C_{yt} and $\bar{r}_t$.

The economy's capital stock evolves according to equation (20):

$$(20) \qquad K_{t+1} = A_t(1 - \beta)(1 - \alpha)K_t^\alpha - H_t - \hat{C}_{yt}(K_t),$$

where C_{yt} is chosen to satisfy (16). Note that the optimal choice of C_{yt}, $\hat{C}_{yt}$, can be written as a function of K_t; the function $\hat{C}_{yt}$ incorporates information about the distributions of $\tilde{A}_{t+1}$ and $\tilde{H}_{t+1}$ since these variables are integrated out in equation (16).

1.3.2   The Arbitrary Nature of Fiscal Labels, Once Again

As in the case of the certainty model, I have described the uncertainty model without labeling either H_t or $\tilde{H}_{t+1}$. Suppose now that the amount H_t received by the government from the young at time t is labeled "taxes" and the payment of H_t to the elderly at time t is called "spending." In this case the government will report a "balanced budget." If it proceeds in this fashion the government will announce a "balanced budget" and a "zero stock of debt" forever.

Next let the government (a) label its payment of H_t to the elderly at time t as "spending," (b) label its receipt of H_t from the young as "borrowing," and (c) label its payment of $\tilde{H}_{t+1}$ as "a certain repayment of principal plus interest in the amount of $H_t(1 + \bar{r}_t)$" less an uncertain "tax" on the elderly at time $t + 1$ equal to $H_t(1 + \bar{r}_t) - \tilde{H}_{t+1}$. In words, the random second period payment is described as a combination of a certain payment equal to "principal plus interest on H_t" plus an uncertain "tax" equal to the difference between the certain amount $H_t(1 + \bar{r}_t)$ and the random amount $\tilde{H}_{t+1}$. In this case the government will report a "deficit" of H_t at time t. At time $t + 1$ the "deficit" (the change in the debt) will equal zero assuming the government labels the $\tilde{H}_{t+1}$ that it gets from the young at time $t + 1$ as "borrowing" in the amount of H_t plus "transfers" to the young at time equal to $H_t - \tilde{H}_{t+1}$. The sum of time $t + 1$ "transfers" to the young, $H_t - \tilde{H}_{t+1}$, plus the government's time $t + 1$ "interest payments," $H_t\bar{r}_t$, equals the time $t + 1$ "taxes" on the old, $H_t(1 + \bar{r}_t) - \tilde{H}_{t+1}$, and the time $t + 1$ deficit is zero. If the government proceeds in this manner through time it will report a stock of debt equal to H_t forever.

If the government prefers to announce a debt of say $20H_t$ forever rather than a debt of only H_t it need only label its period t receipt from the young of H_t as "borrowing of $20H_t$," less a "transfer payment" to the young at time t of $19H_t$. If the government continues to label the payment of H_t to the old at time t as a "transfer payment" its deficit at time t and debt at the beginning of time $t + 1$ will equal $20H_t$. At time $t + 1$ the government now labels its payment of $\tilde{H}_{t+1}$ to the old at time t as a certain "repayment of principal plus interest" of $20H_t$ $(1 + \bar{r}_t)$ plus a "tax" equal to $20H_t(1 + \bar{r}_t) - \tilde{H}_{t+1}$. If the government labels the $\tilde{H}_{t+1}$ it takes from the young at time $t + 1$ as "borrowing" of $20H_t$ less a "transfer" of $20H_t - \tilde{H}_{t+1}$, its reported deficit at time $t + 1$ will equal zero; time $t + 1$ "transfers" of $20H_t - \tilde{H}_{t+1}$ plus "interest payments" of $20H_t\bar{r}_t$ will equal time $t + 1$ "taxes" of $20H_t(1 + \bar{r}_t) - \tilde{H}_{t+1}$. If the government proceeds in this fashion through time it will report a stock of debt equal to $20H_t$ forever.

I leave it to the reader to convince himself that despite the uncertainty of government policy, the government can equally well label its receipts and payments so as to report forever any size surplus it desires.

1.3.3   Distortionary Fiscal Policy

So far the discussion has ignored distortionary fiscal policies. The presence of distortionary policies does not alter the conclusion that the "deficit" is not well defined. I demonstrate this point again using the simple life cycle model. In the context of the simple life cycle model with no uncertainty distortionary policy can be exhibited through the introduction of a wedge between the marginal rate of substitution between consumption when young at time t, C_{yt}, and consumption when old at time $t + 1$, C_{ot+1}, and the marginal rate of transformation between consumption at time t and consumption at time $t + 1$. Suppose this distortion is effected through a proportional "capital income tax." In this case the lifetime budget constraint of generation t is given by

$$(21) \qquad C_{yt} + C_{ot+1}/[1 + r_{t+1}(1 - \tau_k)] = W_t.$$

In (21) τ_k stands for the rate of "capital income taxation" and represents a distortionary policy since the marginal rate of substitution now equals $1/[1 + r_{t+1}(1 - \tau_k)]$ while the marginal rate of transformation equals $1/(1 + r_{t+1})$, where r_{t+1} equals the marginal product of capital at time $t + 1$ (see eq. [6]).

If the receipts from "capital income taxation" are used each period to pay for government consumption and there are no other sources of government receipts and no other government payments, the government will be reporting a "balanced budget." Now suppose the government wishes to run the same real policy but report a "surplus." One method it can use is to levy a nondistortionary "tax" on the young at time $s \geq t$ of say H_s, lend this to the young at time s, and at time $s + 1$ use the return of "principal plus interest" on this "loan" to finance a transfer payment to the old. This policy will leave each generation facing exactly the same lifetime budget constraint, including the same distortion with respect to current and future consumption, but permit the government to report a surplus of H_s at $s \geq t$. The new policy also leaves unchanged the net flow of payments from each generation to the government in each period; the only thing that has changed is the words used to describe the policy.

The reader may prefer an example in which the government maintains its identical policy but uses distortionary "taxes" in "running its surplus." Here's one such example. Let the government announce at time t that it is eliminating the "capital income tax" from time $t + 1$ onward but is imposing a "tax" at rate m_s on the purchase of assets at time $s \geq t$. To illustrate this policy let us write the lifetime budget constraint of individuals born at time $s \geq t$ in two parts:

$$(22) \qquad \begin{aligned} C_{ys} + (1 + m_s)A_{s+1} &= W_s \\ C_{os+1} &= A_{s+1}(1 + r_{s+1}). \end{aligned}$$

In (22) A_{s+1} stands for the assets the young at time t accumulate and bring into period $s + 1$. If m_s is set equal to $r_{s+1}\tau_k/[1 + r_{s+1}(1 - \tau_k)]$ for $s \geq t$ the lifetime budget constraints of each generation born at time t and thereafter will be unaffected by the "new" policy and the distortion between consumption when young and consumption when old will remain unchanged. The only thing that will change is the government's reported "debt." Rather than report a "debt" of zero, the government will now report a "surplus" of mA_{t+1} at time t since "taxes" will exceed "spending" by this amount. At time $t + 1$ the government's "spending" will be covered precisely by this time t "surplus" including interest earned by the government on this surplus; i.e., the value at time $t + 1$ of the time t surplus is $m_t A_{t+1}(1 + r_{t+1})$ which, given the definition of m_t, equals $r_{t+1} \tau_k(W_t - C_{yt})$, the "tax revenue" under the "capital income tax." However, since the government will collect another m_{t+1} in "taxes" at time $t + 1$, its reported "surplus" (stock of government assets) at time $t + 1$ will equal $m_{t+1} A_{t+2}$. At time $s \geq t$ the government's reported "surplus" will equal $m_s A_{s+1}$.

Note that in this example if the government lends its surplus each period to that period's young, the net payments from each generation to the government will again remain unchanged. Hence, to a Martian observer the only thing that will make this policy different from the previous policy is the government's choice of words.

If the government prefers to report a "debt" from time t onward it can do so with no change in policy by "borrowing" say D_s for $s \geq t$ and making transfer payments to the young at time $s \geq t$ equal to D_s. At time $s \geq t + 1$ it "taxes" the old an amount equal to D_s plus interest and uses these receipts to finance its payment of "principal plus interest" on its borrowing of D_s at time s. This policy will leave the government reporting a "debt" of D_s for $s \geq t$.

Another way the government can do nothing real while reporting a "debt" is to announce a subsidy on the acquisition of assets for $s \geq t$. In terms of equation (22) m_s is set equal to a negative number. If the government also announces an increase in the rate of capital income taxation for $s \geq t + 1$ equal to τ'_{ks} such that $(1 + m_s)/[1 + r_{s+1}(1 - \tau'_{ks+1})] = 1/[1 + r_{s+1}(1 - \tau_k)]$, the intertemporal distortion will remain unchanged, but the government will announce a "debt" of $m_s A_{s+1}$ for $s \geq t$. While hardly exhaustive, these examples illustrate that the distortionary nature of the government's policy does not restrict its ability to announce any size deficit or surplus while running the same underlying fiscal policy.

1.3.4   Liquidity Constraints

Another response to the above demonstration that "deficit" policies are not well defined is that the demonstrations ignore the possibility that at least some agents are liquidity constrained. If some young agents can't borrow against future income will they be indifferent between policy a, in which the government takes H from each young person and returns H to them when old, and policy b, in which the government "borrows" H per young person from those young who volunteer to make loans, repays these "loans" with interest when the leaders are old, and "taxes" each old person Hr_s at time s?

An affirmative answer is given in a very insightful article by Hayashi (1987) (see Yotsuzuka [1986] for an expanded treatment of Hayashi's argument). Hayashi points out that the riskiness of future government payments is different from the riskiness of an individual's earnings. Hence, even though an individual may not be able to borrow more than a specific sum against future earnings, he may still be able to borrow against future government payments. As an illustration of this point I present one of Hayashi's examples although with different notation. The example relies again on the two period life cycle model, but incorporates the assumption that there are two types of young agents each period, denoted type A and type B. Both the A and B agents earn W_s when young (assuming they are born at time s). The A type agents earn $\lambda_A W_{s+1}$ when old, while the B types earn $\lambda_B W_{s+1}$ when old, where $\lambda_B > \lambda_A$. The problem for banks in lending money to the A and B types is that the banks don't know who is who. If they lend more than $\lambda_A W_{s+1}/(1 + r_{s+1})$, where r_s is the safe rate, to the A types, the A types will default on a part of the loan since their second period earnings are only $\lambda_A W_{s+1}$.

While Hayashi's argument also goes through in the case of a pooling equilibrium, I focus here on the separating equilibrium. I first examine the equilibrium with no government policy and then introduce the government policy. If one assumes a configuration of preferences such that a separating rather than a pooling equilibrium arises, the banks will separate the two types by offering a maximum loan, M (which exceeds $\lambda_A W_{s+1}/(1 + r_{s+1})$), such that (a) the A types are indifferent between borrowing this maximum and defaulting and borrowing and repaying a smaller amount, and (b) the B types borrow the maximum amount and repay. The indifference relationship for the A types is given by

$$
(23) \quad \begin{aligned}
\beta \log[\beta R_{As}] &+ (1 - \beta) \log[(1 - \beta)R_{As}(1 + r_s)] \\
&= \beta \log(W_s + M) + (1 - \beta) \log C.
\end{aligned}
$$

In (23) the left hand side gives the indirect utility of the A types if they borrow less than M and repay their loans. The term R_{As} equals $W_s + \lambda_A W_{s+1}/(1 + r_{s+1})$, the present value of the lifetime resources of the A types valued at the safe interest rate. The right hand side gives the utility of the A types if they borrow the maximum M and then default when old. The term C stands for the subsistence level of consumption provided by society to people who have defaulted. Equation (23) is used to solve for M. Given M the consumption of the B types when young will equal $W_s + M$, i.e., their first period wages plus the maximum they can borrow. Their second period consumption will equal $\lambda_B W_{s+1} - M(1 + r_{s+1})$. The B types are, therefore, liquidity constrained in this separating equilibrium; they would like to borrow more than M but cannot.

The question posed above amounts to asking whether type A or type B agents will change their consumption when young if the government takes away H from each of them when young and returns $H(1 + r_{s+1})$ to each of them when old. This policy leaves the left hand side of (23) unchanged since the present value of resources valued at the riskless rate r_{s+1} is unchanged. The right hand side of (23) will also remain unchanged if the maximum loan amount increases to $M + H$. In this case the consumption when young of those borrowing from the bank equals $W_s - H$ plus the maximum loan $M + H$; i.e., it equals $W_s + M$, the same amount that is consumed prior to this present value neutral government policy. The banks are willing to increase their loan amount to the type B agents because they understand that the A types will, on net, be no better off if they select into the group borrowing the now larger maximum because they will need the larger maximum just to remain indifferent between borrowing the maximum and borrowing less than the maximum. Hence, at the margin the type B agents are not liquidity constrained with respect to government-determined changes in the timing of their income flows, and the "liquidity constrained" B type agents will consume the same when young despite the government's taking H from them when young.

Perhaps the easiest way to understand the argument is to note that in each of the above examples of relabeling the same policy, the cash flows between the young and old households and the government at each point in time are the same. Since these cash flows determine the degree of liquidity constraint, fiscal policy can be arbitrarily relabeled with no impact on liquidity constraints. For the United States there is conflicting evidence on whether even a minority of households are liquidity constrained (e.g., Hayashi [1987] and Altonji and Siow [1987]). But even if the great majority of households were so constrained, the argument would be valid.

1.4   Can We Discuss Fiscal Policy without Using the Words "Taxes," "Spending," and "Deficits"?

After some reflection on the labeling illustrations of the previous sections, one might offer the following defense of the use of the terms "taxes," "spending," and "deficits": "Well, I agree that the quantities we measure as 'taxes,' 'spending,' and 'deficits' are not meaningful measures of fiscal policy in and of themselves, but the important thing is not what the government labels its receipts and payments, rather the important thing is thinking comprehensively about the government's receipts and payments. As long as I keep track of all of the government's lump sum and distortionary receipts and payments extracted from and made to particular individuals, I can use any words I want to describe particular receipts and payments." True! But thinking comprehensively about the distortionary and nondistortionary net payments extracted from particular individuals is equivalent to specifying their lifetime budget constraints. Once one realizes this point, there is no reason to use potentially misleading language when one can describe precisely how government policy affects individuals' lifetime budget constraints. Indeed, the policy description in section 1.2 is an example of how one can discuss fiscal policy without ever using the words "taxes," "spending," and "deficits" and without classifying assets as "private" assets or "government" assets.

This section offers some new terminology, centered around lifetime budget constraints, to describe fiscal policies. The section first discusses nondistortionary policies and then considers distortionary policies. The new fiscal vocabulary succinctly summarizes the government's fundamental policy instruments. One can think about policy in terms of changes in these instruments. In addition to describing these instruments, this section discusses the choice of these instruments through time. In this regard this section examines a rule to which the government must ultimately adhere (if the economy reaches a steady state) in setting policy through time so as to obey the economy's intertemporal budget constraint. This rule, which I denote the fiscal balance rule, has no relationship to conventional "budget balance"; i.e., the government can obey "budget balance" while violating the fiscal balance rule.

1.4.1 Describing Nondistortionary Policy

If policy is not distortionary and there is no uncertainty, the government's treatment of each individual over his lifetime can be fully summarized by the present value of the individual's lifetime net payment (LNP) to the government. The LNP (the generational account) is a sufficient statistic for the government's treatment of individuals; any intertemporal equilibrium will be unaffected by changes in the timing of lifetime net payments to the government that leave individual LNPs unchanged. Equation (24) shows how the LNP (denoted N_t) enters the lifetime budget constraint of individuals born at time t in the simple two period OLG model.[1]

$$(24) \qquad C_{yt} + C_{ot+1}/(1 + r_{t+1}) = W_t - N_t.$$

Let us now consider a stationary state of a two period Cobb-Douglas economy in which government consumption equals G and $N_t = N$. In the stationary state income equals consumption; hence, the capital stock is defined by

$$(25) \qquad k^\alpha = [\beta + (1 - \beta)(1 + r)](W - N) + G$$

where $r = \alpha k^{\alpha-1}$ and $W = (1 - \alpha)k^\alpha$. In (25) $\beta(W - N)$ is the consumption of the young and $(1 - \beta)(1 + r)(W - N)$ is the consumption of the old. There is no need for N to equal G. Different combinations of N and G are consistent with different stationary states. In the stationary state N may be negative, and G may be zero or positive. Larger values of G and smaller values of N will be associated with larger values of stationary state capital. This may seem surprising. How can larger values of government consumption and a smaller LPN be consistent with more long-run capital accumulation? The answer is that equation (25) only tells us about the stationary state; it says nothing about the transition leading up to the stationary state. To see how the transition matters, start in a stationary state with a given N and G and consider a policy in which the government permanently raises G. According to (25) there is a new stationary

---

1. Note that in the policy of section 1.2 $N_t = -H + H/(1 + r_{t+1})$.

state with the original N, but larger values of G and k that is feasible. But will the economy ever get there? The economy can get there, but only if the government raises the LNPs on some generations during the transition. In other words, a new stationary state with a higher G, a higher k, and the same N is only feasible if the government makes generations alive in the transition to the new stationary state pay the bill.

Starting at time t from an initial stationary state what is the transition equation determining the evolution of the economy's capital stock? Equations (26) and (27) answer this question.

$$(26) \qquad k_{t+1} = k_t + k_t^\alpha - \beta(W_t - N_t) - C_{ot} - G_t$$

$$(27) \qquad \begin{aligned} k_{s+1} &= k_s + k_s^\alpha - \beta(W_s - N_s) \\ &\quad - (1 - \beta)(1 + r_s)(W_{s-1} - N_{s-1}) - G_s \quad s \geq t. \end{aligned}$$

Equation (26) states that capital at time $t + 1$ equals income at time t less total private plus government consumption at time t. The consumption of the young at time t, $\beta(W_t - N_t)$ incorporates the new (if $N_t \neq N$) choice of an LNP for the generation born at time t. The term C_{ot} is the consumption of the old at time t. If the policy does not involve any change in consumption of the initial elderly, C_{ot} will equal $(1 - \beta)(1 + r)(W - N)$, otherwise it will equal this amount less an additional net payment extracted from the elderly. Equation (26) holds for periods after time t. At time $s \geq t$ consumption of the elderly can be written as $(1 - \beta)(1 + r_s)(W_{s-1} - N_{s-1})$.

To summarize, the government's choice of policy can be fully described as (a) a decision whether to extract an additional net payment from the initial elderly, (b) the choice of a time path of LNPs (the time path of N_s for $s \geq t$), and (c) the choice of a time path of government consumption (G_s for $s \geq t$). The government need only announce these elements of its policy and need never use the ill-defined words "taxes," "spending," and "deficits."

1.4.2 The Fiscal Balance Rule

The next question that this new vocabulary raises is, If the government abandons the rule of "balancing the budget," what rule should it use to guide it in choosing the time paths of the N_s and the G_s; i.e., what rule can the government use to make sure it is obeying the economy's intertemporal budget constraint? To consider this question let us first look at the economy's intertemporal budget. Equation (25) turns out to be simply the flow version of the stationary economy's intertemporal budget constraint. Since $k^\alpha = rk + W$, equation (25) can be rewritten in the standard form for the intertemporal budget constraint, viz.:

$$(25') \qquad \begin{aligned} &k(1 + r) + \frac{W(1 + r)}{r} \\ &= \frac{(W - N)(1 + r)}{r} + (1 - \beta)(1 + r)(W - N) + \frac{G(1 + r)}{r} \end{aligned}$$

or, after subtracting $W(1 + r)/r$ from both sides:

$$(25'')   k(1 + r) - (1 - \beta)(1 + r)(W - N) + \frac{N(1 + r)}{r} = \frac{G(1 + r)}{r}.$$

Equation (25') states that the present value of the economy's resources (the sum of its nonhuman and human wealth) equals the present value of the consumption of young and future generations (the first term on the right hand side of the equation) plus the consumption of the current old plus the present value of government consumption. Equation (25") states that the present value of what the government consumes must be financed by the difference between the economy's nonhuman wealth and the consumption of the current old plus the present value of the LNPs from future generations. Intuitively equation (25") says that the government's resources for financing the present value of its consumption are the economy's capital left over after the elderly have consumed plus the amount that will be taken from young and future generations.

Equation (25") also represents the stationary state rule for setting fiscal policy. Let the stationary state level of government consumption be $\overline{G}$. Then in the stationary state N_s must be set each period to satisfy

$$(25''')   N_s = \overline{G} - \frac{r_s}{(1 + r_s)}[k_s(1 + r_s) - C_{os}].$$

The rule says: set the net lifetime payment of each successive generation equal to the flow of government consumption less the interest on the economy's capital stock left over after the current elderly consume. A more intuitive statement of the fiscal balance rule is: "extract enough from each successive generation such that if you were in the stationary state you would stay there and not impose a larger or smaller burden (NLP) on subsequent generations."

In a more realistic model where each period refers to a single year and in which adulthood begins at say age 20, the fiscal balance rule would be to set the net lifetime payment of each new cohort of 20-year-olds equal to annual government consumption less the product of the interest rate times the sum of the economy's current (in the year the cohort hits age 20) capital stock and human wealth (the present value of labor earnings of existing adults) less the present value of consumption of existing adults. If there is population or productivity growth the rule needs to be adjusted slightly; in the case of the two period model the rule with growth is given by $N_s = \overline{G} - [(r_s - n)/(1 + r_s)][K(1 + r_s) - C_{os}]$, where $1 + n$ stands for the product of one plus the rate of population growth and one plus the rate of productivity growth.

Now consider a policy transition starting at time t from a stationary state that involves keeping G constant at $\overline{G}$ but altering the time path of N_s for $s \geq t$. While the time path of N_s can be chosen arbitrarily for a period of time, if the economy is to converge to a stationary state the government must ultimately choose a rule for setting N_s that leads to stationary state convergence.

Table 1.1   One Time 10 Percent Reduction in N for the Young

t	K	W	r	N	G	C_y	C_o	S
1	0.138	0.3864	1.2	0.1104	0.1104	0.138	0.3036	0.138
2	0.138	0.3864	1.2	0.0994	0.1104	0.1435	0.3036	0.1325
3	0.1325	0.3817	1.2348	0.124	0.1104	0.1288	0.3208	0.1178
4	0.1178	0.3685	1.3406	0.1252	0.1104	0.1216	0.3016	0.1106
5	0.1106	0.3616	1.4011	0.1259	0.1104	0.1179	0.2921	0.1068
6	0.1068	0.3578	1.4357	0.1263	0.1104	0.1158	0.2871	0.1048
7	0.1048	0.3558	1.4555	0.1265	0.1104	0.1146	0.2843	0.1036
8	0.1036	0.3546	1.4668	0.1266	0.1104	0.114	0.2828	0.1029
9	0.1029	0.3539	1.4734	0.1267	0.1104	0.1136	0.2819	0.1026
10	0.1026	0.3535	1.4771	0.1267	0.1104	0.1134	0.2814	0.1024
11	0.1024	0.3533	1.4793	0.1267	0.1104	0.1133	0.2811	0.1022
12	0.1022	0.3532	1.4805	0.1268	0.1104	0.1132	0.281	0.1022
13	0.1022	0.3531	1.4812	0.1268	0.1104	0.1132	0.2809	0.1021
14	0.1021	0.353	1.4816	0.1268	0.1104	0.1131	0.2808	0.1021
15	0.1021	0.353	1.4818	0.1268	0.1104	0.1131	0.2808	0.1021
16	0.1021	0.353	1.482	0.1268	0.1104	0.1131	0.2808	0.1021
17	0.1021	0.353	1.4821	0.1268	0.1104	0.1131	0.2808	0.1021
18	0.1021	0.353	1.4821	0.1268	0.1104	0.1131	0.2808	0.1021
19	0.1021	0.353	1.4821	0.1268	0.1104	0.1131	0.2808	0.1021
20	0.1021	0.353	1.4821	0.1268	0.1104	0.1131	0.2808	0.1021

Note: $\alpha = 0.5$, $\beta = 0.3$, and $\lambda = 0.2$.

Any policy rule can be described as a function $N_s = R(\overline{G}, k_s, C_{os-1})$, since the three arguments of this function fully circumscribe the government's choice of N_s; i.e., the government needs to finance a constant time path of $\overline{G}$, it needs to honor (if it is time consistent) the consumption of the elderly, C_{os-1}, and it needs to think about the resource base of the current and future economy which is fully described by k_s. Since the rule $N_s = N(\overline{G}, k_s, C_{os-1})$, where the function $N(\ ,\ ,\ )$ is given by the right hand side of (25''') , must be satisfied in the stationary state, any policy rule $R(\overline{G}, k_s, C_{os-1})$ which leads the economy to converge to a stationary state must, itself, converge to $N(\overline{G}, k_s, C_{os-1})$. I denote the rule $N_s = N(\overline{G}, k_s, C_{os-1})$ the underlying "fiscal balance rule."

While there is no guarantee that any particular rule $R(\overline{G}, k_s, C_{os-1})$ will lead the economy to converge to a stationary state, the simulations of Auerbach and Kotlikoff (1987) in their 55 period life cycle model used the "fiscal policy rule" itself (i.e., they set $R(\overline{G}, k_s, C_{os-1}) = N(\overline{G}, k_s, C_{os-1})$) and found no problems with convergence to a unique stationary state for a range of reasonable parameter values (see Laitner [1988] for an analysis of uniqueness in the Auerbach-Kotlikoff model).

Table 1.1 gives an example of a loose fiscal policy using the simple two period model and the fiscal balance rule. The economy, whose parameters are given in the table, is initially at a stationary state with values of $k = 0.138$, $G = 0.1104$, and $N = 0.1104$. The new policy involves reducing by 10 percent the NLP of the generation born at time t. At time $s > t$ the value of N_s (the NLP of generation s) is set by the fiscal balance rule. Note that this policy raises the consumption of generation s, but lowers that of subsequent generations. Associated with this intergenerational redistribution is a 30 percent crowding out of capital.

Before turning to the issue of distortionary policy, it is useful to consider the nonrelationship between the fiscal balance rule and conventional "budget balance." An easy illustration of the point that "budget balance" does not necessarily imply fiscal balance is given by the case of a "pay as you go" social security system. Suppose the economy is initially (at time t) in a stationary state with no government policy whatsoever ($N = 0$ and $G = 0$). At time t the government announces that starting at time t it will "tax" each young generation s for $s \geq t$ an amount X_s and "transfer" the proceeds to the contemporaneous old. Since at each point in time "taxes" equals "spending," this policy satisfies "budget balance" forever. For the old at time t the new policy means an increase of X_t in their consumption. For generation s, where $s > t$, the policy involves setting $N_s = -X_s + X_{s+1}/(1 + r_{s+1})$. Suppose the government chooses its initial X_t and then sets $X_{s+1} = (1 + r_{s+1})X_s$ thereafter for $s > t$. In this case $N_s = 0$ for all $s \geq t$, and this "balanced budget" policy never obeys the fiscal balance rule and, since it violates the economy's intertemporal budget constraint, leads the capital stock to implode.

If the fiscal balance rule rather than the "balanced budget" rule were obeyed starting at $t + 1$, the government would set $N_s = -[r_s/(1 + r_s)]X_t$ for $s \geq t$, leading the economy to converge to a stationary state with a lower, but positive capital stock. Depending on the policy's labeling, obeying the fiscal policy rule in this case might be described as "keeping the level of old age benefits (transfers) constant and adjusting taxes to meet the fixed level of benefits plus pay for government consumption" or it might be described as "keeping debt per young worker constant."[2] Again, announcement of "social security trust fund balance" or "federal budget balance" may be associated with policies obeying fiscal balance, but they also may not.

2. If the amount X_t taken from the young at time t is labeled "borrowing," the amount given to the old at time t is labeled a "transfer payment" and subsequent receipts from each new young generation are taken when young and labeled "taxes," then for $s > t$ the quantity $-[K_s(1 + r_s) - C_{os}]$ in the fiscal balance rule will correspond to "debt per young person," and the fiscal balance rule would read "tax each new generation an amount N_s equal to government consumption plus interest on government debt; i.e., keep debt per young person constant." If the amount X_t taken from the young at time t is labeled "taxes," rather then borrowing, the amount given to the old at time t is labeled a "transfer payment," and receipts taken from generation $s > t$ when young are labeled "taxes" and payments made to generation $s > t$ when old are labeled "transfers" and there is no "debt," then the amount $-[K_s(1 + r_s) - C_{os}]$ in the fiscal balance rule will correspond to "transfers to the elderly" and the fiscal balance would be read "set taxes high enough to cover government consumption and keep transfers to the elderly at the current level of $-[K_s(1 + r_s) - C_{os}]$; i.e., keep transfers to the elderly constant through time." In addition to paying "taxes" to cover G at time s, the young at time s pay "taxes" sufficient to cover "transfers" to the elderly at time s, $-[K_s(1 + r_s) - C_{os}]$; but when they are old the generation born at time s will receive

1.4.3   Describing Distortionary Policy

As in the case of nondistortionary policy, fiscal policy can be characterized with reference to individual lifetime budget constraints. Take, as an example, the case of a distortionary capital income tax. In this case the lifetime budget constraint equation (24) still holds, but the lifetime net payment, N_t, now includes the net present value of distortionary payments to the government plus the present value of nondistortionary payments.[3] With this budget constraint the share of net lifetime resources (valued at the pretax interest rate) spent on consumption when young, β, depends on the interest rate and the rate of capital income taxation. Hence, equation (28), defining stationary state capital, expresses β as a function of r and τ_k. In (28) N should be understood to include the net present value of lifetime distortionary payments to the government.

(28) $$k^\alpha = [\beta(r, \tau_k) + (1 - \beta(r, \tau_k))(1 + r)](W - N) + G.$$

The transition equations are

(29) $$k_{t+1} = k_t + k_t^\alpha - \beta(r_{t+1}, \tau_{kt+1})(W_t - N_t) - C_{ot} - G_t$$

(30)
$$k_{s+1} = k_s + k_s^\alpha - \beta(r_{t+1}, \tau_{kt+1})(W_s - N_s)$$
$$- (1 - \beta(r_{t+1}, \tau_{kt+1}))(1 + r_s)(W_{s-1} - N_{s-1}) - G_s.$$

The form of the fiscal balance rule is not changed. However, in determining N_s in (25''') the government needs to consider the net present value of its receipts from each new generation arising from its distortionary as well as nondistortionary policies; i.e., in setting its capital income tax rates the government must consider how this policy will influence its time path of N_s.

1.5   Can We Implement the Fiscal Balance Rule Empirically?

The fiscal balance rule represents a means (but not a unique means) for judging the stance of current policy. The use of this rule does not require describing how policy changes will affect the economy. Hence, the use of this rule does not require a fully articulated model that would determine, for example, how factor prices respond to changes in policy. Use of the fiscal balance rule does, however, require one to specify what one believes current policy to be. This, in turn, requires specifying current future policy, i.e., the time path of

---

"transfers" of $-[K_s(1 + r_s) - C_{os}]$; hence the present value of their lifetime payment, N_s, is $G + [K_s(1 + r_s) - C_{os}] - [K_s(1 + r_s) - C_{os}]/(1 + r_{s+1})$, which is the fiscal balance rule except for the difference between r_s and r_{s+1}.

3. One can always express a budget constraint with distorted prices as a budget constraint with nondistorted prices, but with the present value of lifetime resources now reduced by an amount equal to the present value of distortionary payments to the government. Thus eq. (21) can be written as $C_{yt} + C_{ot+1}/(1 + r_{t+1}) = W - N$, where $N = r_{t+1} \tau_k C_{ot+1}/(1 + r_{t+1})$.

policy in the future currently expected to prevail. For example, in forming the value for N_s in $(25''')$ based on an economy with a social security system one would need to consider what generation s will pay to the government when young and what it will receive when old. It is this receipt when old that constitutes an aspect of current future policy.

In addition to specifying current future policy, determining whether the government is obeying the fiscal balance rule requires projecting future factor prices. The prevailing term structure of interest rates can be used to value future earnings and consumption streams, but the levels of future earnings will have to be projected. Projecting future earnings of those currently alive requires specifying the growth rates of population and productivity. It remains to be seen how sensitive will be the evaluation of the fiscal balance rule to these assumptions.

Another issue that needs to be examined is how to deal with life span uncertainty in forming the present value of the future earnings and consumption of existing adult generations. Treatment of this kind of uncertainty as well as the uncertainty of future earnings and government policy need to be considered prior to actually implementing the fiscal balance rule. Still, even at this stage the empirical implementation of the fiscal balance rule seems eminently feasible.

An advantage of the fiscal balance rule is that its implementation would take into account nongovernmental intergenerational redistribution. For example, a reduction in the stock market, like the crash of October 1987, will redistribute from older to younger generations. In terms of the fiscal balance rule, the change in stock values spells a lower present value of consumption of older generations and makes it easier to satisfy the fiscal balance rule.

1.6 Conclusion

Deficit delusion is far from a hypothetical possibility. As Feldstein (1974) has shown, under the guise of "balanced budgets" the U.S. engaged in an enormous program of intergenerational redistribution through Social Security in the 1960s and 1970s. In 1983 the government dramatically reduced the future generosity of Social Security without the new legislation having any impact on the 1983 "deficit." Other programs such as the 1981 Accelerated Cost Recovery System and the 1986 Tax Reform Act have had important generational implications that, again, were not reflected in the "deficit." By ignoring or placing little emphasis on these and other intergenerational policies and focusing on the "deficit," we have generally come to believe that fiscal policy was tight in the 1960s and 1970s and loose in the 1980s. In contrast, it appears that an analysis based on the fiscal balance rule would lead to the exact opposite conclusion.

The concern with deficit delusion is heightened by the "social security surpluses" projected for the 1990s and beyond. These impending "surpluses" are already leading many commentators to suggest that fiscal policy will be tight in the 1990s. In contrast, the fiscal balance rule perspective suggests there will be no particular tightening of policy in the 1990s. In focusing on the "surpluses" of the 1990s we could well end up with a much looser fiscal policy than will likely be justified by the fiscal balance rule.

The use of the fiscal balance rule or closely related rules will not be easy. Given the kinds of projections and assumptions required for its implementation we may well end up with a quite rough measure of fiscal policy. Still, even a rough measure of actual fiscal policy would appear to be more accurate than the precise measure of accounting whims that constitutes current description of fiscal policy.

References

Altonji, J. G., and Siow, A. (1987): "Testing the Response of Consumption to Income Changes with (Noisy) Panel Data." *Quarterly Journal of Economics* 102(2):293–328.

Ando, A., and Modigliani, F. (1963): "The Life Cycle Hypothesis of Saving: Aggregate Implications and Tests." *American Economic Review* 53(1):55–84.

Auerbach, A. J., and Kotlikoff, L. J. (1983): "National Savings, Economic Welfare, and the Structure of Taxation." In: *Behavioral Simulation Methods in Tax Policy Analysis,* edited by M. Feldstein. Chicago: University of Chicago Press.

Auerbach, A. J., and Kotlikoff, L. J. (1987): *Dynamic Fiscal Policy.* Cambridge: Cambridge University Press.

Boskin, M. J. (1987): *The Real Federal Budget.* Harvard University Press, forthcoming, manuscript 1987.

Boskin, M. J., Robinson, M. S., and Huber, A. M. (1987): "Government Saving, Capital Formation and Wealth in the United States, 1947–1985." NBER working paper no. 2352, August 1987.

Chamley, C. (1981): "The Welfare Costs of Capital Income Taxation in a Growing Economy." *Journal of Political Economy* 89(3):468–96.

Eisner, R., and Pieper, P. J. (1984): "A New View of the Federal Debt and Budget Deficits." *American Economic Review* 74:11–29.

Eisner, R., and Pieper, P. J. (1985): "How to Make Sense of the Deficit." *The Public Interest* 78:101–18.

Feldstein, M. S. (1974): "Social Security, Induced Retirement, and Aggregate Capital Accumulation." *Journal of Political Economy* 82:905–26.

Hayashi, F. (1987): "Tests for Liquidity Constraints: A Critical Survey and Some New Observations." In: *Advances in Econometrics. Fifth World Congress. Vol. 2,* edited by F. Truman. Bewley: Cambridge University Press.

Kotlikoff, L. J. (1979): "Social Security and Equilibrium Capital Intensity." *Quarterly Journal of Economics* 93:233–53.

Kotlikoff, L. J. (1984): "Taxation and Savings: A Neoclassical Perspective." *Journal of Economic Literature* 22:576–629.

Kotlikoff, L. J. (1986): "Deficit Delusion." *The Public Interest* 84:53–65.

Kotlikoff, L. J. (1988): "The Deficit is Not a Well-Defined Measure of Fiscal Policy." *Science* 241:791–95.

Laitner, J. (1988): "Tax Changes and Phase Diagrams for an Overlapping Generations Model." *Mimeo.*

Leonard, H. B. (1986): *Checks Unbalanced.* New York: Basic Books.

Modigliani, F., and Brumberg, R. (1954): "Utility Analysis and the Consumption Function: An Interpretation of Cross-Section Data." In: *Post-Keynesian Economics,* edited by K. K. Kurihara. New Brunswick, N.J.: Rutgers University Press.

Sargent, T., and Wallace, N. (1981): "Some Unpleasant Monetarist Arithmetic." *Federal Reserve Bank of Minneapolis Quarterly Review* 5:1–17.

Summers, Lawrence H. (1981): "Capital Taxation and Capital Accumulation in a Life Cycle Growth Model." *American Economic Review* 71:533–44.

Yotsuzuka, T. (1986): "Ricardian Equivalence in the Presence of Capital Market Imperfections." *MIT mimeo.*

2 The Methodology of Generational Accounting

Alan J. Auerbach and Laurence J. Kotlikoff

This chapter describes the standard method of generational accounting that is used, with minor modifications, in all the country studies. This methodology was first developed in Auerbach, Gokhale, and Kotlikoff (1991), on which this chapter closely draws.

Generational accounting is based on the government's intertemporal budget constraint. This constraint, written in equation (1), requires that the future net tax payments of current and future generations be sufficient, in present value, to cover the present value of future government consumption as well as service the government's initial net indebtedness.[1]

$$(1) \qquad \sum_{k=t-D}^{t} N_{t,k} + (1 + r)^{-(k-t)} \sum_{k=t+1}^{\infty} N_{t,k} = \sum_{s=t}^{\infty} G_s(1 + r)^{-(s-t)} - W_t^g.$$

The first summation on the left-hand side of equation (1) adds together the *generational accounts*—the present value of the remaining lifetime net payments—of existing generations. The term $N_{t,k}$ stands for the account of the generation born in year k. The index k in this summation runs from $t - D$ (those aged D, the maximum length of life, in year 0) to t (those born in year 0).

The second summation on the left-hand side of equation (1) adds together the present values of the generational accounts of future generations, with k again representing the year of birth. As each of these generational accounts is expressed in dollars of the respective generation's birth year, they must be

Alan J. Auerbach is the Robert D. Burch Professor of Economics and Law at the University of California, Berkeley, and a research associate of the National Bureau of Economic Research. Laurence J. Kotlikoff is professor of economics at Boston University and a research associate of the National Bureau of Economic Research.

1. The constraint does not assume that government debt is ever fully paid off, merely that the debt grows less quickly than the rate of discount—that it does not explode. Thus it is consistent with the long-run existence of government deficits, as long as these deficits are smaller than the amount needed simply to service the level of outstanding debt.

discounted back to year t in the summation, using the government's real before-tax return r.

The first term on the right-hand side of equation (1) expresses the present value of government consumption. In this summation the values of government consumption in year s, given by G_s, are also discounted to year t. The remaining term on the right-hand side, W_t^g, denotes the government's net wealth in year t—its assets minus its explicit debt.

Equation (1) indicates the zero-sum nature of intergenerational fiscal policy. Holding the present value of government consumption fixed, a reduction in the present value of net taxes extracted from current generations (a decline in the first summation on the left-hand side of eq. [1]) necessitates an increase in the present value of net tax payments of future generations.

The generational account $N_{t,k}$ is defined by

$$(2) \qquad N_{t,k} = \sum_{s=\kappa}^{k+D} T_{s,k} P_{s,k} (1 + r)^{-(s-\kappa)},$$

where $\kappa = \max(t,k)$. In expression (2) $T_{s,k}$ stands for the projected average net tax payment to the government made in year s by a member of the generation born in year k. The term $P_{s,k}$ stands for the number of surviving members of the cohort in year s who were born in year k.[2] For generations who are born prior to year t, the summation begins in year t and is discounted to year t. For generations who are born in year $k > t$, the summation begins in year k and is discounted to that year.

A set of generational accounts is simply a set of values of $N_{t,k}$, one for each existing and future generation, with the property that the combined present value adds up to the right-hand side of equation (1). Though we distinguish male and female cohorts in the results presented below, we suppress sex subscripts in equations (1) and (2) to limit notation.

Note that generational accounts reflect only taxes paid less transfers received. With the exception of government expenditures on health care and education, which are treated as transfer payments, the accounts do not impute to particular generations the value of the government's purchases of goods and services because it is difficult to attribute the benefits of such purchases. Therefore, the accounts do not show the full net benefit or burden that any generation receives from government policy as a whole, although they can show a generation's net benefit or burden from a particular policy change that affects only taxes and transfers. Thus generational accounting tells us which generations will pay for government spending not included in the accounts, rather than

---

2. As discussed in chap. 6 in this volume, by Ablett, the population weights $P_{s,k}$ incorporate both mortality and immigration, implicitly treating immigration as if it were a "rebirth" and assigning the taxes paid by immigrants to the representative members of their respective cohorts. This approach does not, therefore, separate the burdens of natives and immigrants. Such an extension is desirable, particularly if one wishes to study the effects on generational accounts of changes in immigration patterns.

telling us which generations will benefit from that spending. This implies nothing about the value of government spending; that is, there is no assumption, explicit or implicit, concerning the value to households of government purchases.

2.1   Assessing the Fiscal Burden Facing Future Generations

Given the right-hand side of equation (1) and the first term on the left-hand side of equation (1), we determine, as a residual, the value of the second term on the left-hand side of equation (1), which is the collective (aggregate) payment, measured as a time t present value, required of future generations. Based on this amount, we determine the average per capita present value lifetime net tax payment facing members of each future generation under the assumption that the average per capita lifetime net tax payment of members of successive generations rises at the economy's rate of productivity growth. This makes the lifetime payment a constant share of lifetime income. Controlling for this growth adjustment, the average per capita lifetime net tax payments of future generations are directly comparable with those of current newborns, since the per capita generational accounts of both newborns and individual members of future generations take into account net tax payments over these agents' entire lifetimes and are discounted back to their respective years of birth.

Our assumption that the generational accounts of all future generations are equal, on a per capita basis, except for a growth adjustment, is just one of many assumptions we could make about the distribution across future generations of their collective net payment to the government. We could, for example, assume a phase-in of the additional fiscal burden (positive or negative) to be imposed on future generations, allocating a greater share of the burden to later future generations and a smaller share to earlier ones. Clearly, such a phase-in would mean that generations born after the phase-in period has elapsed would face, on a per capita basis, larger values of lifetime burdens (the $N_{t,k}$) than we are calculating here.

Another way of measuring the imbalance of fiscal policy, illustrated in the chapters that follow, is to ask what permanent change in some tax or transfer instrument, such as an increase in income taxes or a reduction in old-age social security benefits, would be necessary to equalize the lifetime growth-adjusted per capita fiscal burden facing current newborns and future generations. Because such policies satisfy the government's intertemporal budget constraint, they are also sustainable.

2.2   Assumptions Underlying Generational Account Calculations

To produce generational accounts, we require projections of population, taxes, transfers, and government expenditures; an initial value of government wealth; and a discount rate. We consider the impact of total, not just national, government.

Typically, we assume that government purchases grow at the same rate as GDP, although in some cases we break these purchases down into age-specific components and assume that each component remains constant per member of the relevant population, adjusted for the overall growth of GDP per capita. This causes different components of government purchases to grow more or less rapidly than GDP according to whether the relevant population grows or shrinks as a share of the overall population.

Government infrastructure purchases are treated like other forms of purchases in the calculations. Although such purchases provide an ongoing stream rather than a one-time amount of services, they must still be paid for. Generational accounting clarifies which generation or generations will have to bear the burden of these and other purchases. For government wealth, we measure the government's net financial assets—its financial assets less its gross debt. We do not include the real assets of state enterprises in this measure but instead subtract projected net profits from state enterprises from projected government spending. This procedure effectively capitalizes the value of these enterprises.

Government wealth does not include the value of the government's existing infrastructure, such as parks. Including such assets would have no impact on the estimated fiscal burden facing future generations because including these assets would require adding to the projected flow of government purchases an offsetting flow of imputed rent on the government's existing infrastructure.

Taxes and transfer payments are each broken down into several categories. Our general rule regarding tax incidence is to assume that taxes are borne by those paying the taxes, when the taxes are paid: income taxes on income, consumption taxes on consumers, and property taxes on property owners. There are two exceptions here, both of which involve capital income taxes. First, we distinguish between marginal and inframarginal capital income taxes. As described below, inframarginal capital income taxes are distributed to existing wealth holders, whereas marginal capital income taxes are based on future projected wealth holdings. Second, in the case of small open economies, marginal corporate income taxes are assumed to be borne by (and are therefore allocated to) labor. The need for this later adjustment is discussed in chapter 15, for example.

The typical method used to project the average values of particular taxes and transfer payments by age and sex starts with government forecasts of the aggregate amounts of each type of tax (e.g., payroll) and transfer payment (e.g., welfare benefits) in future years. These aggregate amounts are then distributed by age and sex based on cross-sectional relative age-tax and age-transfer profiles derived from cross-sectional microdata sets. For years beyond those for which government forecasts are available, age- and sex-specific average tax and transfer amounts are assumed to equal those for the latest year for which forecasts are available, with an adjustment for growth.

2.3 Calculating Inframarginal Capital Income Taxes

Capital income taxes require special treatment because, unlike other taxes, they may be capitalized into the values of existing assets. Also, the time pattern of income and tax payments may differ. As a result of these features of capital income taxes, such taxes must be attributed with care to ensure that they are assigned to the proper generation. If all forms of capital income were taxed at the same rate, there would be no such problem: all assets would yield the same rate of return before tax (adjusted for risk), and each individual would face a rate of return reduced by the full extent of the tax. However, if tax rates on the income from some assets, typically older ones, are higher than those facing income from new assets (e.g., because of investment incentives targeted toward new investment), a simple arbitrage argument indicates that the extra tax burden on the old assets should be capitalized into these assets' values.

To illustrate the nature of the necessary correction, consider the case of cash-flow taxation in which assets are written off immediately. A well-known result is that the effective marginal capital income tax rate under cash-flow taxation is zero. However, taxes would be collected each year on existing capital assets, and such assets should therefore be valued at a discount. Assigning these taxes to the assets' initial owners, rather than to members of future generations who may purchase the assets, is consistent with the fact that such future generations of individuals may freely invest in new assets and pay a zero rate of tax on the resulting income. Our correction to actual tax payments should, in this case, result in a zero tax burden on the income from new assets.

For the general case, we use the following methodology. Our calculation begins with expression (3) for the user cost of capital, to which firms set their marginal products:

$$(3) \qquad C = \frac{(r + \delta)(1 - k - \tau z)}{(1 - \tau)},$$

where r is the investor's required after-tax return, δ is the investment's economic rate of depreciation, τ is the investor's marginal tax rate, k is the investment tax credit or grant received on investment, and z is the present value of depreciation allowances. We wish to calculate two measures. The first, which we denote by Q, is the tax-based discount on old capital, which equals the difference between tax savings from depreciation allowances and investment credits per unit of new capital and those available per unit of existing capital:

$$(4) \qquad Q = k + \tau(z - z^\circ),$$

where z° is the present value of depreciation allowances per unit of old capital.

Measured capital income tax payments are not based on the effective rate of tax on new capital m, where

$$(5) \qquad\qquad m = \frac{C - (r + \delta)}{C - \delta}.$$

Instead, they are based on an average tax rate, α, where

$$(6) \qquad\qquad \alpha = \frac{\tau(C - b) - k}{C - \delta}$$

and b is the average current depreciation deduction per unit of total capital. Comparing equations (5) and (6) indicates that we must correct measured taxes per unit of capital by subtracting from $\alpha(C - \delta)$ the term Δ, where

$$(7) \qquad\qquad \Delta = (\alpha - m)(C - \delta).$$

The values of z° and b depend on past patterns of investment and the depreciation schedules permitted existing assets. For the case in which investment grows smoothly at rate n and all capital (new and old) is written off at rate ψ based on historic asset cost, the value of undepreciated basis per unit of existing capital may be shown to equal

$$(8) \qquad\qquad \frac{n + \delta}{n + \pi + \psi},$$

where π is the rate of inflation. Thus the value of b, the average current depreciation deduction per unit of capital, is ψ multiplied by this basis:

$$(9) \qquad\qquad b = \psi \frac{n + \delta}{n + \pi + \psi},$$

and the value of z°, the present value of depreciation deductions per unit of existing capital, equals

$$(10) \qquad\qquad z^\circ = z \frac{n + \delta}{n + \pi + \psi},$$

where z is the present value of depreciation deductions per unit of basis (and per unit of new capital),

$$(11) \qquad\qquad z = \frac{\psi}{r + \pi + \psi}.$$

Substituting equations (5), (6), (9), and (11) into equation (7), we obtain

$$(12) \qquad \Delta = (r + \delta)\tau z \left[1 - \frac{(r + \pi + \psi)(n + \delta)}{(n + \pi + \psi)(r + \delta)} \right].$$

Substituting equation (10) into equation (4), we obtain

$$(13) \qquad\qquad Q = k + \tau z \left(1 - \frac{n + \delta}{n + \pi + \psi} \right).$$

Based on parameter values for the United States in the 1990s, Auerbach et al. (1991) estimated values of $\Delta = .00111$ and $Q = .111$.

There are other possible assumptions we could make about the incidence of capital income taxes. For a small open economy, for example, it may make sense to assume that taxes on mobile corporate capital are borne by local, fixed factors such as labor.[3]

2.4 Discount Rates and Uncertainty

For base-case calculations, generational accounts typically use a real rate of discount in the neighborhood of 5 percent, a rate that exceeds the real government short-term borrowing rate in most developed countries. This rate seems justified given the riskiness of the flows being discounted. However, as we now discuss, the "right" discount rate to use is in sufficient question to merit presenting results based on a range of alternative discount rates—a practice routinely followed by generational accountants.

The appropriate discount rate for calculating the present value of future government revenues and expenditures depends on their uncertainty. If all such flows were certain and riskless, it would clearly be appropriate to discount them using the prevailing term structure of risk-free interest rates. However, even in this simple and unrealistic case, such discounting could be problematic since it would require knowing the values of this term structure. To discern these values, one might examine the real yields paid on short-term, medium-term, and long-term inflation-indexed government bonds. But this presupposes the existence of such bonds. Many countries do not issue indexed bonds, and those that do don't necessarily issue indexed bonds of all maturities. The United States is a case in point. It has just begun to issue indexed bonds but so far has limited its issue of such bonds to those with 10-year maturities. Even if a country issues indexed bonds of multiple maturities, equating their real yields with the risk-free rate requires assuming no default risk, which for many countries is a very strong assumption.

In the realistic case in which countries' tax revenues and expenditures are uncertain, discerning the correct discount rate is even more difficult. In this case, discounting based on the term structure of risk-free rates (even if it is observable) is no longer theoretically justified. Instead, the appropriate discount rates would be those that adjust for the riskiness of the stream in question. Since the riskiness of taxes, spending, and transfer payments presumably differ, the theoretically appropriate risk-adjusted rates at which to discount taxes, spending, and transfer payments would also differ.

Is risk adjusting really important? A priori, one might think that forming the expected present value of future taxes and transfers of current and future generations, with discounting done at risk-free rates, would yield a meaningful

---

3. This approach is taken in Auerbach et al. (1997) for New Zealand.

measure of the fiscal burdens facing different generations on average.[4] But this is not the case as the following line of argument, relying on the invariance of economic outcomes under changes in fiscal labels, makes clear.

Chapter 1 points out that there are an infinite number of ways to label a country's underlying fiscal policy. If economic agents are rational, the choice of labels will have no real impact, including no impact on the intergenerational distribution of well-being—which generational accounting seeks to help illuminate. This proposition that economic outcomes are invariant under changes in the government's vocabulary is true regardless of whether the economy features uncertainty, including uncertain government policy. However, in the context of uncertain government policy, relabeling fiscal policy can easily alter expected future taxes and expected future transfer payments. Such relabeling will also alter the riskiness of reported taxes and transfer payments and, therefore, the proper rates at which to discount expected future tax and transfer streams. If one discounts these altered expected values with the proper risk-adjusted discount rates, one finds what one should find: no change in the expected utilities of any generation. However, if one simply uses the time path of risk-free rates of return to discount the expected value of future taxes and transfers, one gets nonsensical results: the "expected" fiscal burdens facing alternative generations depend on how the fiscal policy is labeled; that is, they depend on the government's choice of vocabulary.

An example may help clarify this point. Take the case of a fully funded defined-benefit social security system. Suppose the government has held risk-free bonds and now chooses instead to invest in risky stock. To acquire the stock, the government sells the public its bonds. Consequently, the public ends up holding stock through the government and bonds in its private portfolio. If the stocks perform well, the government rebates to the public (in the form of a transfer payment) the amount beyond what is needed to cover its social security pension obligations. If the stocks perform poorly, the government taxes the public to cover its social security obligations.

Hence, under the "new" policy, the public receives a sure income on the bonds that it has purchased from the government but a risky stream associated with the transfers or taxes it now faces. On balance, the public ends up with exactly the same income; that is, it gets the same social security pension income, and the combination of its safe bond income and its now risky net taxes is equivalent to its holding directly the stock sold to the government. This "portfolio" change on the part of the government alters the expected net tax payments of the public but has no real effects—it is nothing more than a relabeling of government receipts and payments. The fact that the government and

4. Diamond's (1996) presentation of "projections" seems to come close to endorsing such analysis, although Diamond's main argument is the same as we make here, namely, that properly valuing uncertain tax and transfer flows requires adjusting for risk when one discounts.

the private sector exchange different securities with the public is simply part of the relabeling process, not evidence that policy has fundamentally changed.

Another issue that arises with respect to risk-adjusted discounting is that the proper risk adjustments may be generation specific. To see this, consider a two-period model in which there are two generations and no government purchases—just an initial stock of debt that needs to be serviced and repaid in the second period. Generation 1, currently alive, will pay some tax rate, τ, times its uncertain income, and generation 2, not yet alive, will pay the residual. Since, by construction, the payments of the two generations equal principal plus interest on the debt in every state of nature, the government's intertemporal budget constraint is always satisfied.

In this example, aggregate tax payments are certain, although each generation's own tax payments are not. For generation 1, the uncertainty of its tax payments are actually a plus, since its risky income is being insured. Thus we would be justified in applying a discount rate of $\rho > r$, where r is the risk-free rate, in valuing the expected tax payments from generation 1's perspective. From generation 2's point of view, the situation is more complicated. It depends on how much generation 2's marginal utility of consumption is correlated with that of generation 1. If there were perfect correlation (say, because of a single source of income or complete intergenerational risk sharing), then generation 2's burden would be *greater* than that implied by discounting at the risk-free rate—its burden would be relatively higher in bad (low income) states of nature—so its expected tax payments should be discounted at a rate $\rho < r$.

Hence, by discounting the burdens of each generation at an appropriate discount rate (higher than the risk-free rate for generation 1, lower than the risk-free rate for generation 2), we would still find that the sum of the burdens satisfied the government's intertemporal budget constraint but get a better measure of the impact on individual utility.

To see the implications of this result, let us go back to the general, multi-period and multigeneration model and assume again for the moment that there is a single set of state-contingent future prices that all generations use to evaluate future flows. Then our current approach, to define the burden on future generations as a residual, gives a correct measure of the aggregate burden on future generations. That is, we define this collective burden as

$$(18) \qquad N_{\text{fut}} = \sum_{k=-D}^{0} N_{0,k} - \sum_{t=0}^{\infty} (1 + \rho)^{-t} G_t - B_0,$$

where $N_{0,k}$ is the generational account for the generation born in year k, formed by discounting that generation's flows using the discount rate ρ. As long as ρ is chosen appropriately (as already discussed, this would include, perhaps, using different values of ρ for government purchases than for taxes and transfers), N_{fut} is the value of the burden placed on future generations. Note that this procedure *will not* give us a measure of the expected values of net tax payments by future generations, but rather the value of these payments based on the valuation that would be placed on such payments by existing generations.

But now we must come back to consider how to value the residual flows that must be paid by future generations under incomplete risk sharing across generations. Consider again the simple model with two agents. In this instance, we cannot use a discount rate based on generation 1's valuation of generation 2's burden. If we evaluate generation 2's burden from its own point of view, the burden may be lower. For example, suppose that the income of the two generations is negatively correlated; the negative correlation might arise if, for example, the source of shocks was to the relative productivity of capital and labor and generation 1 (2) supplied capital (labor). Then generation 2's burden, from its own perspective, will be less onerous than a certain burden with the same expected value. This is because generation 2's taxes will be higher in states in which its income is higher (even though generation 1's income is lower). Hence, we should discount generation 2's expected burden at a rate higher than the risk-free rate. Thus both generations will perceive lower burdens than would be implied by discounting their respective expected tax payments at the risk-free rate. Since the total burden in the second period is $(1 + r)B_0$, this means that the sum of the burdens from the individual perspectives will be lower than the present value of the debt repayment—because government policy improves intergenerational risk sharing.

In short, with incomplete risk sharing, we cannot use the valuations of existing generations to discount the flows of future generations. Indeed, we do not even have the valuations of existing generations to rely on for future years that occur after all current generations are deceased.[5]

Our standard approach, then, may overstate the burdens on future generations to the extent that government policy improves intergenerational risk sharing. However, it may be justified with the argument that such benefits of government policy should be considered separately from the first-order redistributions among generations, in the same way that, as discussed in chapter 3, we ignore changes in deadweight loss associated with fiscal policy changes.

In summary, measuring fiscal policy's welfare effects on different generations, as generational accounting seeks to do, requires an evaluation of the risk characteristics of fiscal flows and an appropriate risk adjustment of these flows or, as an approximate substitute, the use of risk-adjusted discount rates. Attempts to sidestep this issue simply by discounting expected flows with a risk-free rate of interest are plagued by the same fundamental problem as deficit accounting—the resulting measures would not be invariant with respect to changes in the superficial labels attached to government transactions. As generational accounting methods to date have not fully identified the appropriate

---

5. Adding the possibility of incomplete *intra*generational risk sharing would simply extend the complexity one additional step. Even within a generation, the total burden might be lighter than would be implied by discounting that generation's overall payments with a market discount rate.

adjustment for risk, it remains standard practice to estimate generational accounts for a range of discount rates.

References

Auerbach, Alan J., Bruce Baker, Laurence J. Kotlikoff, and Jan Walliser. 1997. Generational accounting in New Zealand: Is there generational balance? *International Tax and Public Finance* 4, no. 2 (May): 201–28.

Auerbach, Alan J., Jagadeesh Gokhale, and Laurence J. Kotlikoff. 1991. Generational accounts: A meaningful alternative to deficit accounting. In *Tax policy and the economy,* vol. 5, ed. D. Bradford, 55–110. Cambridge, Mass.: MIT Press.

Diamond, Peter. 1996. Generational accounts and generational balance: An assessment. *National Tax Journal* 49, no. 4 (December): 597–607.

3   Generational Accounting in General Equilibrium

Hans Fehr and Laurence J. Kotlikoff

3.1   Introduction

Generational accounting is a relatively new tool of long-term fiscal analysis.[1] It is based on the government's intertemporal budget constraint, which requires that the government's bills be paid by current or future generations. These bills refer to the present value of the government's projected future spending plus the current value of its official net debt. The payments of current and future generations are also measured in present value and equal the projected value of their future net tax payments (taxes paid less transfer payments received).

Generational accounts measure, in present value, the projected future net tax payments of current and future generations. The difference between the government's bills and the collective generational accounts of current generations determines the present value of the net tax burden facing future generations. Comparisons of the generational accounts of current and future generations indicates the extent to which fiscal policy is, generationally speaking, out of balance. Generational accounting also reveals changes in the generational distribution of fiscal burdens arising from policy reforms. Since generational accounting considers the taxes paid to, and transfers received from, all levels

Hans Fehr is assistant professor at the chair of public economics at the University of Tübingen. Laurence J. Kotlikoff is professor of economics at Boston University and a research associate of the National Bureau of Economic Research.

Reprinted from *Finanzarchiv* 53, no. 1 (1996/97): 1–27, by permission of the publisher.

Parts of this paper were written when Hans Fehr was a visiting scholar at the Department of Economics, Boston University. His fellowship from the German Research Foundation (grant no. Fe 377/1-1) is gratefully acknowledged, as is the research support extended to Laurence Kotlikoff by The World Bank, Mr. Charles Benenson, and Mr. Lawrence Benenson. The authors thank Alan Auerbach and Jagadeesh Gokhale for helpful comments.

1. See Auerbach, Gokhale, and Kotlikoff (1991, 1992, 1994) and Kotlikoff (1992; chap. 1 in this volume).

of government (federal, state, and local), it provides a comprehensive picture of the fiscal treatment of different generations.

Although it is less than five years old, generational accounting has made significant inroads in fiscal analysis, both in the U.S. and abroad. It has been included in the *Budget of the United States Government* and is being used by the governments of Norway, Italy, Japan, and New Zealand. The IMF is preparing generational accounts for Sweden, the World Bank is preparing them for Thailand, and academic economists have prepared or are preparing them for Germany, Canada, and Australia.[2]

Given its growing use, it is important to understand the limitations as well as advantages of generational accounting. One concern about generational accounting is the accuracy of its implicit incidence assumptions. Generational accounting assumes that taxes on labor income are paid (in the economic sense) by workers, that taxes on capital income are paid by suppliers of capital, and that sales, excise, and value added taxes are paid by consumers. It also assumes that recipients (in the economic sense) of transfers, such as social security benefits, are those individuals who receive these payments. Given its incidence assumptions, generational accounting simply adds together the taxes paid by members of particular generations when they work, receive capital income, and purchase commodities and subtracts from the total tax payment the total amount of transfer payments received.

Another way of stating these incidence assumptions is that generational accounting takes pre-tax factor returns as given; i.e., it ignores potential policy-induced changes in factor returns which can alter the ultimate incidence of fiscal policies. In addition, generational accounting may not accurately reflect those changes in generations' utility levels associated with their efforts to avoid fiscal burdens, such as consuming less of taxed goods. Buiter's (1997) generational accounting critique stresses both shortcomings.

In order to set these disadvantages against the advantages of the existing method of generational accounting—namely, its simplicity and clarity—one needs to study, as this paper does, their magnitude. This paper uses the Auerbach-Kotlikoff (1987) dynamic life-cycle model (henceforth, the AK model) to study the degree to which generational accounting captures the changes in generations' utilities resulting from particular policy reforms. It does so by simulating a range of alternative policies and comparing the resulting changes in generations' utilities with the associated changes in generational accounts. Since the AK model can be run as either a closed or a small open economy, the paper also sheds light on how an economy's openness may affect the accuracy of its generational accounting.

In our simulations of closed economies with no capital adjustment costs, generational accounting does quite well in capturing the sign pattern and mag-

---

2. See U.S. Office of Management and Budget (1992, 1993, 1994), Franco et al. (1994), Auerbach et al. (1993), Boll et al. (1994), and Gokhale, Raffelhüschen, and Walliser (1995).

nitudes of generations' utility changes. This is not entirely surprising. In closed economies with no adjustment costs, factor returns are determined by the capital-labor ratio. Since the capital stock is fixed in the short run and since labor supply is fairly inelastic in the AK model, the capital-labor ratio changes gradually in response to policy changes.[3] Consequently, factor returns also change gradually. In addition, the income effects from the initial direct changes in tax burdens play the key role in altering household saving and labor supply, which, in turn, determine the changes in the capital-labor ratio and factor returns. Hence, the changes in factor returns are second-round or feedback effects from the policy change. Since the model is stable, these second-round changes in factor returns are smaller in magnitude than the first-round effects, which are, to a considerable extent, captured by changes in generational accounts. Moreover, although policy-induced changes in behavior are nontrivial, they are nonetheless a relatively small factor in generations' utility changes.

Adding capital adjustment costs weakens the link between the return to capital and the capital-labor ratio. This return is no longer determined simply by capital's marginal product (which depends on the capital-labor ratio), but also by revaluations of the stock market (the market price of capital). When capital adjustment costs are large, policy changes can produce sharp changes in stock market valuations that alter generations' welfare but are not captured in generational accounting. This finding—that generational accounting misses a portion of generations' changes in utilities in the presence of sizable adjustment costs—needs, however, to be considered in light of the limited empirical evidence in support of adjustment costs (Cutler 1988).

Running the AK model as a small open economy is another way to generate significant and immediate changes in factor returns. The reason is that an economy's capital-labor ratio can change instantaneously in response to capital inflows and outflows. Our simulations of corporate tax changes in small open economies suggest the need to modify generational accounting in such economies by allocating changes in corporate capital income taxes to generations in proportion to their labor income. The reason is that an increase in the corporate income tax rate in a small open economy will produce an immediate capital outflow, thereby lowering the marginal product of labor and the wage; i.e., the corporate tax will be immediately shifted to workers.

The paper continues in section 3.2 by first considering the analogy between generational accounting and tax incidence analysis in a supply and demand diagram and then using a simple two-period life-cycle model to illustrate how one can decompose policy-induced changes in generations' utilities into three components: (1) the change in their generational accounts, (2) the change in their factor income, and (3) the change in their economic behavior, which we refer to as their net tax avoidance. Section 3.3 presents our simulation model,

---

3. The utility function of the AK model is calibrated based on empirical studies of U.S. labor supply and consumption.

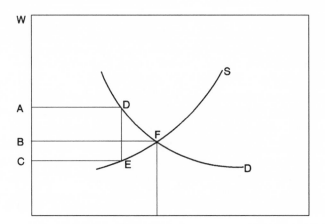

Fig. 3.1   Incidence of a wage tax

and section 3.4 reports our results using the 55-period AK model for closed as well as small open economies. In the case of the small open economy, we consider both corporate and personal taxation of capital income. Section 3.5 summarizes our findings and draws conclusions.

3.2   Fiscal Reforms and Changes in Generations' Utilities

3.2.1   Generational Accounting—The Analogy
to Incidence in a Simple Static Model

Before considering the relationship between changes in generational accounts and changes in utility in a dynamic model, it may be helpful to draw the analogy between generational accounting and tax incidence in a simple static setting. Figure 3.1 considers a tax on labor. The demand for labor is governed by the demand curve D, and the supply of labor is governed by the uncompensated supply curve S. The area BCEF indicates the change in worker's surplus, i.e., the change in utility that workers experience from the tax. Generational accounting, in effect, approximates the change in workers' surplus by the change in tax revenue, ACED. In so doing, it fails to subtract from the change in tax revenues the tax-induced increase in workers' factor income, ABFD, or add to the change in tax revenues the change in tax avoidance, DEF.[4] Making both of these adjustments produces the exact change in workers' utility.

---

4. DEF partly reflects the excess burden from the tax. In particular, if one compensates workers for the changes in their nominal tax payments and their factor incomes, one would, in effect, replace the uncompensated supply curve with the compensated supply curve and end up with a triangular area equaling the excess burden of the tax. The closer in value are the compensated and

Clearly, how well the change in tax revenues approximates the change in workers' surplus depends on the relative values of supply and demand elasticities. If supply is perfectly inelastic, the change in tax revenues exactly equals the change in workers' surplus. This also occurs if the change in workers' pre-tax income exactly equals the change in tax avoidance. At the other extreme, if demand is perfectly inelastic, workers' surplus is unchanged, and the change in tax revenues is a very bad measure of workers' utility change.

3.2.2 Incidence in a Simple Two-Period Model

Next consider fiscal incidence in a simple two-period life-cycle model. Each generation has the same size population, which we normalize to one, and each agent has one unit of time each period to spend working or enjoying leisure. The utility function of a generation born at time s depends on consumption and leisure when young and old; i.e.,

$$(1) \qquad U_s = u(c_{ys}, c_{os+1}, M_{ys}, M_{os+1}),$$

where c indexes consumption, M indexes leisure, y indexes young, and o indexes old.

Now suppose a change in policy occurs at time t. To understand its welfare effects, we need to examine the changes in utility of the old at time t, the young at time t, and all subsequent generations. We start by considering the old at time t, whose consumption is constrained by

$$(2) \qquad c_{ot} = k_t(1 + r_t) + w_t(1 - M_{ot}) - T_{ot},$$

where k_t is the capital owned by the old at time t, T_{ot} is the remaining net tax payment of the old at time t (their generational account), w_t is the wage per unit of labor supply, and r_t is the time t return per unit of capital.[5] The generational account of the old at time t, T_{ot}, as well as those of other generations, includes all net tax payments, whether or not they are distortionary.

The budget constraint facing the generation born at time $s \geq t$ is

$$(3) \qquad c_{ys} + \frac{c_{os+1}}{1 + r_{s+1}} = w_s(1 - M_{ys})$$
$$+ \frac{w_{s+1}(1 - M_{os+1})}{1 + r_{s+1}} - \left(T_{ys} + \frac{T_{os+1}}{1 + r_{s+1}} \right).$$

---

uncompensated labor supply elasticities (i.e., the smaller in absolute value is the income elasticity), the greater the degree to which the change in tax avoidance will reflect the excess burden of the tax.

5. To keep the analysis simple, we assume that the young and old receive the same wage per unit of labor supply at a point in time.

The term in the large brackets on the right-hand side of (3) is the present value of net taxes of the generation born at time s, i.e., its generational account.

Total net payments of the young and old at time $s \geq t$ equal government consumption spending G_s; i.e.,

$$(4) \qquad T_{ys} + T_{os} = G_s.$$

Although (4) appears to ignore government borrowing, it is, in fact, a general formulation. As Kotlikoff (chap. 1 in this volume) shows, any government fiscal policy involving borrowing can be relabeled as one in which government debt is always zero.

We now consider changes in different generations' utilities arising from a policy reform introduced at time t. In so doing, we begin with the utility change of the elderly at time t who were born in $t - 1$:

$$(5) \qquad dU_{t-1} = \frac{\delta U}{\delta c_{ot}} dc_{ot} + \frac{\delta U}{\delta M_{ot}} dM_{ot}.$$

Differentiating (2) and using the first-order condition of the elderly at time t, which involves marginal after-tax prices, we get the normalized utility change

$$(6) \qquad \frac{dU_{t-1}}{\lambda_{t-1}} = (1 + \tau_{ot})dc_{ot} + w_t(1 - \theta_{ot})dM_{ot}$$
$$= -dT_{ot} + [k_t dr_t + (1 - M_{ot})dw_t] + [\tau_{ot}dc_{ot} - w_t\theta_{ot}dM_{ot}],$$

where λ_{t-1} is the marginal utility of income of the elderly at time t (who were born at $t - 1$), τ_{ot} is the marginal consumption tax rate facing the elderly at time t, θ_{ot} is the marginal tax on labor income facing the elderly at time t, and where we have used the fact that at time t, k_t is given, so dk_t equals zero.

In (6), the utility change of the elderly is decomposed into three components: changes in their generational account $(-dT_{ot})$, changes in their factor incomes (the first bracketed term on the equation's right-hand side), and changes in their tax payments due to changes in their economic behavior (the second bracketed term on the right-hand side). The utility change of those born at time $s \geq t$ can be similarly decomposed. Differentiating equation (1) and using relevant first-order conditions leads to

$$(7) \qquad \frac{dU_s}{\lambda_s} = (1 + \tau_{ys})dc_{ys} + w_s(1 - \theta_{ys})dM_{ys}$$
$$+ \frac{(1 + \tau_{os+1})dc_{os+1} + w_{s+1}(1 - \theta_{os+1})dM_{os+1}}{1 + r_{s+1}(1 - \phi_{os+1})},$$

where ϕ_{os+1} is the marginal capital income tax faced by the elderly at time $s + 1$. Combining (7) with the differential of (3) gives

(8)

$$\frac{dU_s}{\lambda_s} = -\left[dT_{ys} + \frac{dT_{os+1}}{1 + r_{s+1}} \right]$$

$$+ \left[(1 - M_{ys})dw_s + \frac{(1 - M_{os+1})dw_{s+1} + k_{s+1}dr_{s+1}}{1 + r_{s+1}} \right]$$

$$+ \left[\tau_{ys}dc_{ys} - w_s\theta_{ys}dM_{ys} + \frac{[\tau_{os+1}(1 + r_{s+1}) + r_{s+1}\phi_{os+1}]}{1 + r_{s+1}(1 - \phi_{os+1})} \frac{dc_{os+1}}{1 + r_{s+1}} \right.$$

$$\left. + \frac{[r_{s+1}\phi_{os+1} - (1 + r_{s+1})\theta_{os+1}]w_{s+1}}{1 + r_{s+1}(1 - \phi_{os+1})} \frac{dM_{os+1}}{1 + r_{s+1}} \right].$$

In (8), the normalized utility change of generation $s \geq t$ consists of the same three components encountered in (6): the change in its generational account (the first right-hand side term in large brackets), the change in factor income (the second right-hand side term in large brackets), and the marginal change in tax revenue associated with a change in economic behavior (the third right-hand side term in large brackets).

To determine the generations' changes in utility arising from a finite, rather than an infinitesimal, change in policy, one needs to integrate (6) and (8) over a dummy variable indicating the degree to which the policy reform is implemented. To be more precise, let z run from 0 to 1, where, for example, a value of z equal to .5 means that the policy has been 50 percent implemented and a value of 1 means it has been fully implemented. The change in utility of generation s, for $s \geq t - 1$, ΔU_s, is given by

(9)
$$\Delta U_s = \int_0^1 \frac{1}{\lambda_s} \frac{\delta U_s}{\delta z} dz.$$

Substituting from (6) and (8) for the integrand in (9) yields an expression for generations' utility change that has three pieces (three areas) corresponding to the integrals of the three terms on the right-hand sides of (6) and (8). These three areas are exactly analogous to the three areas in figure 3.1; i.e., one reflects the change in tax revenues (in this case, changes in generational accounts), one reflects changes in factor incomes, and one reflects changes in tax avoidance.

To summarize this section, the changes in the utilities of all generations alive after a policy reform depend on more than just the changes in their generational accounts. Changes in generational accounts will not, except in special circumstances, provide a full accounting of the intergenerational incidence of fiscal reforms. Hence, the question is not whether generational accounting gets intergenerational incidence exactly right. It doesn't. Rather the question is how accurately it approximates true intergenerational incidence. This is the issue which we now explore with the AK model.

3.3   The Auerbach-Kotlikoff Model

The AK model contains three sectors: households, firms, and government. The household sector consists of 55 overlapping generations, with the total population growing at a constant rate n. Each adult agent lives for 55 years corresponding to ages 21 to 75 and is concerned only with his own welfare; i.e., there is no bequest motive. Since all agents within a cohort are identical, economic opportunities differ only across cohorts. The model incorporates variable labor supply, including endogenous retirement. Preferences over current and future consumption and leisure are governed by the CES utility function

$$(10) \qquad U = \frac{1}{1 - 1/\gamma} \sum_{a=1}^{55} (1 - \delta)^{1-a} (c_a^{1-1/\rho} + \beta M_a^{1-1/\rho})^{\frac{1-1/\gamma}{1-1/\rho}},$$

where δ is the "pure" rate of time preference, ρ is the intratemporal elasticity of substitution between consumption and leisure at each age a, γ is the intertemporal elasticity of substitution between consumption of different years, and β is the leisure preference parameter. Since government spending does not enter into the utility function, changes in generations' utilities reflect only the incidence of the method of financing the spending.

Agents are assumed to have perfect foresight and experience realistic growth in their wages during their working years. This age-wage profile is separate from the general level of wages, the time path of which is determined by the model. The model's production sector is characterized by perfectly competitive firms operating with a CES production function. The capital adjustment cost function depends on the level of investment at time t, I_t, the capital stock at time t, K_t, and a coefficient b. It is given by

$$(11) \qquad \varphi(I_t, K_t) = .5b \frac{I_t^2}{K_t}.$$

The model incorporates income taxes, wage taxes, capital income taxes, and consumption taxes, all of which can be levied at proportional or progressive rates. The government's policy instruments include borrowing and a pay-as-you-go social security system. Government policy is constrained by the government's intertemporal budget constraint. As mentioned, this constraint requires that the present value of net taxes of current and future generations be sufficient to cover the present value of government consumption plus the value of existing government debt. The perfect foresight path of the AK model is calculated using an iterative Gauss-Seidel algorithm. The algorithm assumes that the economy reaches its new steady state after 150 years. Table 3.1 displays our baseline parameter values.

Our simulations all start in year 1 from an initial steady state. They are quite similar to simulations reported in Auerbach and Kotlikoff (1987), and conse-

Table 3.1   **Baseline Parameters**

Parameter	Value
Population growth rate	0.01
Intertemporal elasticity of substitution (γ)	0.25
Intratemporal elasticity of substitution (ρ)	0.80
Pure rate of time preference	0.015
Leisure preference parameter	1.5
Elasticity of substitution between capital and labor	1.0

quently, we provide only a brief description of their impacts on macroeconomic variables. Our initial steady state features a 20 percent income tax which is used to finance public consumption, no government debt, and, except where indicated, no social security system. After solving for the transition path of the economy arising from a change in fiscal policy, we compute the difference between each generation's utility under the new policy and the initial steady-state level of utility, which represents the utility that the generation would have realized in the absence of the policy change.

Generations' changes in utility are divided by the post-policy-reform marginal utilities of income. Changes in generational accounts and factor incomes are calculated using the post-policy-reform pre-tax interest rates to discount changes in net tax payments and factor income.[6] In order to approximate ΔU_s in (9) and the integrals of the three right-hand-side components of (6) and (8), we simulated each policy reform in five steps.[7] Then we (a) added together the resulting ratios of the change in utility divided by the marginal utility of income in that step, (b) added together changes in the net tax payments and factor incomes discounted at the interest rate in that step, and (c) computed the change in tax avoidance as the difference between (a) and (b).

In presenting our calculated changes in each generation's utility, generational account, factor income, and tax avoidance, we scale these numbers (divide them) by the present value of the generation's expenditure on consumption and leisure, valued at the initial steady-state pre-tax prices.

3.4   How Well Does Generational Accounting Track Changes in Generations' Utilities?

This section considers two questions: First, how do changes in generational accounts compare with generations' actual utility changes? Second, are changes in generational accounts less accurate indicators of utility changes for young and future generations than they are for older generations because of the time needed in closed economies (without adjustment costs) for factor prices

---

6. The post-policy-reform pre-tax interest rate in year s is the one that prevails in year s in the transition to the new steady state.

7. Using more than five steps in the numerical integration does not materially affect the results.

Table 3.2   20 Percent, Income-Tax-Financed Increase in Government Spending: Transition Path

Year	Capital	Labor	Output	Wage	Interest Rate	Income Tax Rate	Saving Rate
0	89.9	19.2	25.7	1.000	.071	.200	.035
1	89.9	19.2	25.6	1.001	.071	.241	.020
2	89.5	19.2	25.6	1.000	.071	.241	.021
3	89.1	19.2	25.6	.988	.072	.241	.021
4	88.8	19.2	25.5	.997	.072	.241	.022
5	88.4	19.2	25.5	.996	.072	.241	.023
10	87.1	19.3	25.5	.992	.073	.242	.025
20	85.4	19.3	25.4	.986	.074	.242	.029
60	83.9	19.4	25.4	.981	.076	.242	.033
∞	83.9	19.4	25.4	.980	.076	.242	.033

to change? We consider a variety of different policies, including increases in government spending financed by raising either income or consumption taxes, a partial shift in the tax structure from income to consumption taxation, a deficit-financed short-term tax cut, and an expansion of social security benefits.[8]

3.4.1   Generational Accounting in a Closed Economy

Financing Additional Government Spending

Our first simulation involves a permanent 20 percent rise in government spending financed by an increase in the rate of income taxation. As one would expect, this policy crowds out capital, lowers the real wage, and raises the real interest rate. Table 3.2 reports initial steady-state (year 0) macro variables as well as the values of these variables along the economy's transition path. The capital stock, which initially equals 89.9, declines over time to 83.9. Associated with this decline is a 2 percent long-run decline in the wage and a 5 basis point increase in the interest rate. The income tax rate converges over time to 24.2 percent.

The first three columns of table 3.3 decompose each generation's utility change into changes in its generational account (multiplied by minus 1), factor income, and tax avoidance. The total change in utility is given in the fourth column. Since the tax avoidance column is calculated as the difference between the sum of the first two columns and the fourth column, the tax avoidance figures will pick up the error in our method of approximating the integrals of the components of the change in utility.

---

8. Although we report results for only a fixed set of parameters, we have run our policy experiments for a wide range of alternative parameters and found essentially the same results with respect to the ability of changes in generational accounts to track changes in welfare.

Table 3.3   **20 Percent, Income-Tax-Financed Increase in Government Spending: Decomposing Generations' Utility Changes**

Generation's Year of Birth	Generational Account	Factor Income	Tax Avoidance	Generation's Utility
−54	−0.11	−0.01	0.00	−0.12
−50	−0.23	0.01	−0.11	−0.33
−45	−0.57	0.08	−0.19	−0.68
−40	−0.96	0.15	−0.20	−1.01
−35	−1.31	0.21	−0.23	−1.33
−30	−1.61	0.24	−0.26	−1.63
−25	−1.86	0.24	−0.29	−1.91
−20	−2.04	0.21	−0.33	−2.16
−15	−2.17	0.15	−0.36	−2.38
−10	−2.23	0.08	−0.42	−2.57
−5	−2.25	−0.01	−0.46	−2.72
0	−2.22	−0.10	−0.50	−2.82
5	−2.20	−0.19	−0.51	−2.90
10	−2.17	−0.28	−0.53	−2.98
20	−2.14	−0.39	−0.54	−3.07
50	−2.12	−0.48	−0.54	−3.14
∞	−2.11	−0.49	−0.55	−3.15

Note: Table reports changes, expressed as percentages of remaining lifetime expenditure.

In general, generational accounting does a very good job in this simulation in approximating generations' changes in utility. For the oldest generation, the change in generational account equals 91 percent of the total utility change. For 30-year-olds it equals 98 percent of the total, and for those born in year 0, the year before the policy is enacted, it equals 78 percent of the total. For generations born after the transition begins, however, generational accounting does less well. For example, in the case of those born in the long run, the change in generational accounts equals 67 percent of the total change in utility.

The slow rate at which factor prices change in this simulation is the main reason that changes in generational accounts provide a worse approximation to utility changes of younger generations. The younger the generation, the more of its lifetime will be spent experiencing the lower wage, but higher interest rate, resulting from the policy change. For example, those born in the new steady state earn a 2 percent lower wage for their work effort and a 5 basis point higher interest rate on their savings.

Tables 3.4 and 3.5 report the results of a simulation that is identical to that underlying tables 3.2 and 3.3 with the exception that the increase in government spending is financed using a proportional consumption tax. Unlike the income-tax-financed increase in government spending, there is no crowding out of capital. Indeed, there is some minor crowding in. The reason is that the consumption tax falls more heavily on the initial elderly who have high propensities to consume. Since there is very little change in capital per work,

Table 3.4   **20 Percent, Consumption-Tax-Financed Increase in Government Spending: Transition Path[a]**

Year	Capital	Labor	Output	Wage	Interest Rate	Consumption Tax Rate	Saving Rate
0	89.9	19.2	25.7	1.000	.071	.000	.035
1	89.9	19.4	25.8	.998	.072	.053	.036
2	89.9	19.4	25.8	.998	.072	.053	.036
3	89.9	19.4	25.8	.998	.072	.053	.035
4	89.9	19.4	25.8	.998	.072	.053	.035
5	89.9	19.4	25.8	.998	.072	.053	.035
10	90.0	19.4	25.8	.999	.072	.053	.035
20	90.1	19.4	25.8	.989	.072	.053	.035
60	90.1	19.4	25.8	.989	.072	.053	.035
∞	90.1	19.4	25.8	.999	.072	.053	.035

[a]Simulation includes a 20 percent proportional income tax.

Table 3.5   **20 Percent, Consumption-Tax-Financed Increase in Government Spending: Decomposing Generations' Utility Changes**

Generation's Year of Birth	Generational Account	Factor Income	Tax Avoidance	Generation's Utility
−54	−2.11	0.02	−0.04	−2.13
−50	−2.03	0.04	−0.06	−2.05
−45	−2.00	0.05	−0.10	−2.05
−40	−1.97	0.06	−0.15	−2.06
−35	−1.95	0.05	−0.18	−2.08
−30	−1.93	0.04	−0.22	−2.11
−25	−1.92	0.03	−0.25	−2.14
−20	−1.90	0.01	−0.29	−2.18
−15	−1.90	0.00	−0.32	−2.22
−10	−1.90	−0.02	−0.34	−2.26
−5	−1.90	−0.03	−0.38	−2.31
0	−1.91	−0.04	−0.41	−2.36
5	−1.91	−0.03	−0.42	−2.36
10	−1.91	−0.03	−0.42	−2.36
20	−1.91	−0.03	−0.41	−2.35
50	−1.91	−0.02	−0.42	−2.35
∞	−1.91	−0.02	−0.42	−2.35

Note: Table reports changes, expressed as percentages of remaining lifetime expenditure.

there is little change in either the wage or interest rate. Hence, the factor income changes reported in table 3.5 are quite small. The changes in generational accounts of particular generations are, however, significant. These changes account for most of the changes in generations' utility levels. The fraction of the utility change captured by the change in generational accounts ranges from 98 percent for the oldest cohort to 81 percent for cohorts born in the new steady state.

Table 3.6   **Structural Tax Reform: Transition Path**[a]

Year	Capital	Labor	Output	Wage	Interest Rate	Consumption Tax Rate	Saving Rate
0	89.9	19.2	25.7	1.000	.071	.000	.035
1	89.9	19.5	25.9	.997	.072	.064	.054
2	90.4	19.5	25.9	.998	.072	.064	.053
3	90.8	19.5	25.9	1.000	.071	.064	.052
4	91.3	19.4	26.0	1.001	.071	.064	.051
5	91.7	19.4	26.0	1.003	.071	.063	.050
10	93.4	19.4	26.0	1.008	.070	.062	.047
20	95.5	19.3	26.1	1.015	.068	.061	.042
60	97.2	19.2	26.1	1.021	.067	.061	.037
∞	97.3	19.2	26.1	1.021	.067	.061	.037

[a]Simulation entails an immediate and permanent reduction in a proportional income tax from 20 percent to 15 percent with the reduction in revenues made up through the introduction of a proportional consumption tax.

Table 3.7   **Structural Tax Reform: Decomposing Generations' Utility Changes**

Generation's Year of Birth	Generational Account	Factor Income	Tax Avoidance	Generation's Utility
−54	−2.39	0.03	−0.05	−2.41
−50	−2.13	0.02	0.08	−2.03
−45	−1.64	−0.04	0.08	−1.60
−40	−1.16	−0.12	0.06	−1.22
−35	−0.72	−0.19	0.04	−0.87
−30	−0.36	−0.24	0.05	−0.55
−25	−0.06	−0.25	0.05	−0.26
−20	0.17	−0.24	0.06	−0.01
−15	0.32	−0.19	0.08	0.21
−10	0.40	−0.12	0.09	0.37
−5	0.41	−0.03	0.11	0.49
0	0.37	0.06	0.12	0.55
5	0.36	0.18	0.14	0.68
10	0.35	0.29	0.16	0.80
20	0.34	0.42	0.18	0.94
50	0.33	0.52	0.19	1.04
∞	0.33	0.53	0.19	1.05

Note: Table reports changes, expressed as percentages of remaining lifetime expenditure.

Structural Tax Change

Our next simulation, the macroeconomic and utility effects of which are reported in tables 3.6 and 3.7, holds government spending fixed but switches the tax structure from a 20 percent income tax to a 15 percent income tax plus a consumption tax whose rate is set to maintain the same revenues on an annual basis. In the first year of the transition the consumption tax is 6.4 percent and falls through time to 6.1 percent. In the long run, the capital stock increases (relative to its initial steady-state value) by 8.2 percent, the wage rises by 2.1 percent, and the pre-tax interest rate falls by 4 basis points.

As table 3.7 indicates, changes in generational accounts again do a very good job in capturing the general pattern of generation-specific utility changes. They do less well, for certain generations, in capturing the magnitude of those generations' utility changes. The changes in generational accounts are pretty close to the changes in utility for those initially over age 25. Unlike tables 3.3 and 3.5, however, changes in generational accounts capture only about one third of the utility change for generations born in the long run.

The pattern of factor income changes in table 3.7 deserves comment. In the first two years following the reform the substitution effects of a lower tax on labor income induces an increase in labor supply. This lowers the capital-labor ratio, reducing the real wage and raising the interest rate. The oldest generations benefit from this increase in the interest rate, which explains why the changes in factor incomes for those born 50 and 54 years before the reform are positive. Through time, the capital stock rises in response to the partial shifting of the burden of taxation from the young, with low propensities to consume, onto the elderly, with high propensities to consume.[9] This raises the wage. The income effects of this higher wage reduce labor supply, leaving labor supply in the new steady state at its initial steady-state value (at least to one decimal place). The increase, along the transition path, in the wage benefits initial future generations the most, because they work primarily or exclusively during years when the wage has reached or neared its peak. The counterpart of the rise in the wage is a decline in the interest rate. The loss to initial young and middle-aged generations from the lower interest income they receive on their accumulated assets exceeds the gain to these generations of the rising wage. On net, they experience a decline in their factor incomes, whereas future generations experience, on net, an increase.

In this and the previous two simulations a pattern is emerging that merits comment; namely, generational accounting is providing a lower bound estimate of the absolute change in welfare of those born in the long run. The reason is that policies which, over time, lower (raise) the economy's level of capital intensity are generally policies which redistribute from young and future (older) generations toward older (young and future) generations.[10] Since a lower (higher) long-run degree of capital intensity means a lower (higher) long-run wage, the direct redistribution from those alive in the long run, which is captured by generational accounting, will understate the reduction (improvement) in welfare of those born in the long run.

---

9. Recall that in the life-cycle model, propensities to consume rise with age in light of the shorter remaining life span.

10. Income effects generally play a much more important role than do substitution effects in altering consumption and labor supply decisions, and policies that redistribute toward older generations are policies that redistribute toward generations with higher marginal propensities to consume.

Table 3.8   **Deficit-Financed Three-Year Income Tax Cut: Transition Path**

Year	Capital	Labor	Output	Wage	Interest Rate	Income Tax Rate	Saving Rate
0	89.9	19.2	25.7	1.000	.071	.200	.035
1	89.9	19.8	26.2	.993	.073	.160	.044
2	90.1	19.8	26.2	.994	.073	.160	.043
3	90.4	19.8	26.2	.994	.073	.160	.043
4	90.6	19.1	25.5	1.004	.070	.206	.028
5	90.4	19.1	25.5	1.003	.071	.206	.028
10	89.6	19.1	25.5	1.001	.071	.207	.030
20	88.4	19.1	25.4	.997	.072	.207	.031
60	86.8	19.2	25.4	.992	.073	.207	.034
∞	86.8	19.2	25.4	.992	.073	.208	.034

Debt Policy

Tables 3.8 and 3.9 consider the effects of a deficit-financed temporary tax cut, specifically a three-year reduction from 20 percent to 16 percent in the rate of income taxation. After the three-year period, debt per capita is held fixed and the income tax rate is increased in order to cover government spending and interest on this level of debt. As table 3.8 shows, the policy crowds in capital in the short run, but crowds out capital in the long run. The reason is the short-run increase in labor supply and earnings (some of which is saved) arising from the substitution effects associated with the temporary tax cut; i.e., in the short run, when taxes are temporarily low, workers have an increased incentive to supply more labor. Once tax rates are raised, this incentive effect disappears. In the long run, the wage ends up 0.8 percent lower and the interest rate 2 basis points higher. These are small changes in relative factor returns. Accordingly, generation-specific changes in factor incomes reported in table 3.9 are quite small.

There is, however, a substantial intergenerational redistribution from the policy, most of which is picked up by the changes in generational accounts. The policy is particularly advantageous to the oldest cohorts, because many are deceased after the tax rate is raised. Generational account changes are quite similar to generations' utility changes for all generations already born at the time of the policy change. For example, for those aged 35 at the time of the policy change, the change in generational accounts equals 0.32 percent of remaining lifetime expenditures, whereas the change in utility is equivalent to a 0.35 percent reduction in expenditure. For generations born after the policy's enactment, generational account changes capture from 57 percent to 98 percent of the corresponding utility changes. Again, since this policy ultimately crowds out capital by redistributing to early from later generations, generational accounting provides a lower bound for the decline in the welfare of long-run generations.

Table 3.9   **Deficit-Financed Three-Year Income Tax Cut: Decomposing Generations' Utility Changes**

Generation's Year of Birth	Generational Account	Factor Income	Tax Avoidance	Generation's Utility
−54	0.10	0.06	0.00	0.16
−50	0.19	0.10	0.08	0.37
−45	0.33	0.05	0.04	0.42
−40	0.34	0.02	0.03	0.39
−35	0.32	0.01	0.02	0.35
−30	0.27	0.01	0.02	0.30
−25	0.22	0.02	0.02	0.26
−20	0.16	0.02	0.02	0.20
−15	0.10	0.02	0.02	0.14
−10	0.04	0.02	0.02	0.08
−5	−0.02	0.02	0.01	0.01
0	−0.07	0.01	0.01	−0.05
5	−0.40	0.04	−0.05	−0.41
10	−0.40	−0.01	−0.06	−0.47
20	−0.39	−0.09	−0.07	−0.55
50	−0.38	−0.29	−0.08	−0.66
∞	−0.38	−0.21	−0.08	−0.67

Note: Table reports changes, expressed as percentages of remaining lifetime expenditure.

Increasing Social Security Benefits

In tables 3.10 and 3.11 we simulate a 25 percent increase in social security benefits starting with a "pay-as-you-go" social security system with a 40 percent benefit replacement rate. In the AK model, social security benefits are received at age 46 and continued until death at age 55. The actual benefits a generation receives are calculated from the average earnings over the first 45 years of their life span times the replacement rate, a parameter set by the government. Given the total sum of the benefits for a given year, the social security tax is calculated endogenously to meet social security benefit payments.

Table 3.10 shows that the policy crowds out the capital stock, reducing, in the process, the wage by 1.2 percent. The social security payroll tax, which is initially 6.5 percent, rises to over 8 percent. The income tax rate (not shown) rises from 20.0 percent to 20.4 percent. As in the previous simulations, the changes in capital intensity occur slowly. Consequently, the changes in generational accounts reported in table 3.11 do an excellent job in capturing the utility of generations initially alive. They also capture over 60 percent of the utility changes of those born in the long run.

Adjustment Costs

Up to now we have assumed that the economy exhibits no adjustment costs, i.e., that the installation of new capital is costless. As described by Hayashi (1982), increasing marginal costs of investment generate inframarginal rents to existing capital. The market valuation of the existing capital stock will there-

Table 3.10   **25 Percent Increase in Social Security Benefits: Transition Path**

Year	Capital	Labor	Output	Wage	Interest Rate	Social Security Tax Rate	Saving Rate
0	76.4	18.5	24.6	1.000	.081	.065	.031
1	76.4	18.1	24.3	1.005	.079	.082	.014
2	76.0	18.1	24.2	1.003	.080	.082	.015
3	75.6	18.1	24.2	1.002	.080	.082	.016
4	75.2	18.2	24.2	1.000	.081	.082	.017
5	74.9	18.2	24.2	.999	.081	.082	.018
10	73.6	18.2	24.2	.994	.082	.082	.023
20	72.6	18.3	24.1	.990	.083	.081	.028
60	72.1	18.3	24.1	.988	.084	.081	.030
∞	72.1	18.3	24.1	.988	.084	.081	.030

Table 3.11   **20 Percent Increase in Social Security Benefits: Decomposing Generations' Utility Changes**

Generation's Year of Birth	Generational Account	Factor Income	Tax Avoidance	Generation's Utility
−54	3.56	−0.03	0.07	3.60
−50	3.44	−0.05	0.17	3.56
−45	3.84	−0.01	−0.23	3.60
−40	2.02	0.03	−0.27	1.78
−35	1.07	0.08	−0.23	0.92
−30	0.47	0.11	−0.18	0.40
−25	0.05	0.14	−0.16	0.03
−20	−0.26	0.14	−0.15	−0.27
−15	−0.50	0.12	−0.14	−0.52
−10	−0.69	0.08	−0.13	−0.74
−5	−0.83	0.03	−0.12	−0.92
0	−0.92	−0.04	−0.12	−1.08
5	−0.88	−0.15	−0.13	−1.16
10	−0.84	−0.23	−0.15	−1.22
20	−0.81	−0.30	−0.15	−1.26
50	−0.80	−0.33	−0.16	−1.29
∞	−0.80	−0.33	−0.16	−1.29

Note: Table reports changes, expressed as percentages of remaining lifetime expenditure.

fore differ from its replacement cost. Tax policies that stimulate (depress) capital formation will immediately increase (reduce) the stock market value of existing capital.[11] Since the elderly are the primary owners of existing capital, this capital gain (loss) will raise (lower) their wealth and welfare.

11. This abstracts from investment tax credits and other investment incentives that discriminate between new and old (existing) capital and, therefore, change the price of existing capital relative to new capital. As described in Auerbach et al. (1991), changes in Q that arise directly because of investment incentives are incorporated in the formation of generational accounts.

Table 3.12   **Structural Tax Reform with Capital Adjustment Costs: Transition Path**

Year	Capital	Labor	Output	Wage	Interest Rate	Q	Consumption Tax Rate	Saving Rate
0	81.9	19.2	25.6	1.000	.072	1.100	.000	.032
1	81.9	19.5	25.8	.997	.097	1.100	.046	.040
2	82.2	19.4	25.7	.999	.072	1.127	.063	.041
3	82.4	19.3	25.7	1.000	.069	1.130	.065	.041
4	82.6	19.3	25.7	1.001	.069	1.129	.065	.041
5	82.9	19.3	25.7	1.002	.069	1.128	.065	.041
10	83.9	19.3	25.8	1.005	.069	1.123	.064	.040
20	85.4	19.3	25.9	1.010	.068	1.115	.063	.038
60	88.0	19.2	26.0	1.019	.067	1.103	.061	.035
∞	88.7	19.2	26.1	1.021	.067	1.100	.061	.034

In tables 3.12–3.15 we repeat our structural tax reform and deficit-financed tax cut but assume an adjustment cost parameter b equal to 10. This value for b is reasonably large. It implies that 5 percent of steady-state investment expenditure is spent on adjustment. It also produces a steady-state value of Q—the ratio of the market value of capital to its replacement cost—equal to 1.10.[12]

Consider first the structural tax reform reported in table 3.12. This reform raises the market value of capital in the short run by roughly 3 percent. Over time, Q falls back to its initial steady-state value of 1.10. Since older generations alive at the time of the tax reform can sell their capital at a 3 percent higher price, this capital gain (the value of which is included in the change in factor income column in table 3.13) represents an offset to the reduction in utility of these generations associated with their being forced to absorb a larger tax burden. As table 3.13 shows, the change in generational accounts overstates the reduction in welfare of initial older generations. Indeed, for the very oldest generation alive at the time of the reform, the true reduction in utility is roughly half of that suggested by the change in the generation's generational account. For younger generations and those born shortly after the reform, the change in generational accounts provides a fairly accurate assessment of the generations' ultimate change in utility. For those born in the long run, generational accounting captures about one third of the ultimate increase in utility.

In sum, in this simulation with adjustment costs, the changes in generational accounts overstate the losses to the initial elderly and understate the gains to the future young. But given the fact that the actual size and importance of adjustment costs are uncertain, the changes in generational accounts still represent a useful point of reference for considering the intergenerational welfare effects of this policy. Why? Because they provide, respectively, upper and lower bounds on the welfare losses and gains of those who are hurt and helped

12. Q equals one in the absence of adjustment costs.

Table 3.13   **Structural Tax Reform with Adjustment Costs: Decomposing Generations' Utility Changes**

Generation's Year of Birth	Generational Account	Factor Income	Tax Avoidance	Generation's Utility
−54	−1.89	1.02	−0.02	−0.89
−50	−2.12	0.89	0.03	−1.20
−45	−1.69	0.60	0.05	−1.04
−40	−1.21	0.33	0.04	−0.84
−35	−0.77	0.11	0.03	−0.63
−30	−0.39	−0.07	0.03	−0.43
−25	−0.07	−0.19	0.02	−0.24
−20	0.17	−0.26	0.03	−0.06
−15	0.34	−0.28	0.03	0.09
−10	0.43	−0.26	0.05	0.22
−5	0.45	−0.20	0.06	0.31
0	0.40	−0.11	0.08	0.37
5	0.36	−0.01	0.08	0.43
10	0.36	0.08	0.10	0.54
20	0.35	0.23	0.13	0.71
50	0.34	0.43	0.18	0.95
∞	0.33	0.53	0.20	1.06

Note: Table reports changes, expressed as percentages of remaining lifetime expenditure.

Table 3.14   **Deficit-Financed Three-Year Income Tax Cut with Adjustment Costs: Transition Path**

Year	Capital	Labor	Output	Wage	Interest Rate	Q	Income Tax Rate	Saving Rate
0	81.9	19.2	25.6	1.000	.072	1.100	.200	.032
1	81.9	19.7	26.1	.994	.087	1.100	.160	.036
2	82.1	19.7	26.1	.994	.071	1.115	.160	.036
3	82.2	19.7	26.1	.994	.071	1.114	.160	.035
4	82.3	18.7	25.0	1.008	.033	1.113	.237	.019
5	82.1	19.3	25.7	.999	.096	1.073	.192	.033
10	81.7	19.1	25.5	1.001	.071	1.092	.206	.029
20	81.1	19.1	25.4	.999	.072	1.093	.206	.029
60	79.7	19.2	25.4	.994	.073	1.098	.207	.030
∞	79.2	19.2	25.3	.992	.073	1.100	.207	.031

the most by the policy. Thus, they provide a "worse case" scenario which a prudent policymaker who is unsure of the extent of general equilibrium price adjustments can use in thinking through the costs and benefits of the policy reform.

Turn now to the deficit-financed tax cut policy, the results of which are presented in tables 3.14 and 3.15. Due to the initial crowding in of capital in this policy, the price of existing capital initially rises. Consequently, the initial el-

Table 3.15   **Deficit-Financed Three-Year Income Tax Cut with Adjustment Costs: Decomposing Generations' Utility Changes**

Generation's Year of Birth	Generational Account	Factor Income	Tax Avoidance	Generation's Utility
−54	0.02	0.60	0.00	0.62
−50	0.20	0.16	0.06	0.42
−45	0.36	−0.05	0.02	0.33
−40	0.36	−0.08	0.01	0.29
−35	0.32	−0.07	0.01	0.26
−30	0.27	−0.05	0.01	0.23
−25	0.21	−0.02	0.01	0.20
−20	0.15	0.00	0.01	0.16
−15	0.08	0.02	0.02	0.12
−10	0.02	0.03	0.02	0.07
−5	−0.04	0.04	0.01	0.01
0	−0.09	0.04	0.01	−0.04
5	−0.35	0.07	−0.03	−0.31
10	−0.37	0.04	−0.04	−0.37
20	−0.37	−0.02	−0.05	−0.44
50	−0.36	−0.14	−0.07	−0.57
∞	−0.36	−0.20	−0.07	−0.63

Note: Table reports changes, expressed as percentages of remaining lifetime expenditure.

derly experience a windfall gain, and their utility improvement exceeds the reduction in their generational accounts. Once the tax cut ends, the saving rate falls, as does the price of capital. This capital loss produces a temporary decline in the interest rate. With the exception of those over age 50, the changes in generational accounts accord quite closely with the changes in the utilities of those generations alive at the time the policy is initiated. As in previous simulations that involve long-run crowding out of capital, the change in generational accounts provides a lower bound for the decline in welfare for those alive in the long run.

Tax Progressivity

Tables 3.16 and 3.17 report the effects of switching from a 20 percent proportional income tax to a progressive one, where, as described in Auerbach and Kotlikoff (1987), the marginal tax rate is assumed to be linear in the tax base. Average tax rates in the year of the tax reform range from 19.1 percent for the cohort aged 1, to 21.9 percent for the cohort aged 25, to 15.3 percent for the cohort aged 55. The corresponding marginal tax rates are 23.2 percent for those initially aged 1, 28.8 for those aged 25, and 15.7 percent for those aged 55. This age pattern of average and marginal taxes reflects the life-cycle profile of income in which income is highest in middle age. The changes in generational accounts reflect, of course, not just the immediate changes in a generation's net tax payments, but future changes as well. As table 3.17 shows, the

Table 3.16   **Increasing Tax Progressivity: Transition Path**

Year	Capital	Labor	Output	Wage	Interest Rate	Saving Rate
0	89.9	19.2	25.7	1.000	.071	.035
1	89.9	18.3	24.7	1.013	.069	.014
2	89.3	18.3	24.7	1.011	.069	.014
3	88.8	18.3	24.6	1.010	.069	.015
4	88.3	18.3	24.6	1.008	.070	.016
5	87.8	18.3	24.6	1.006	.070	.016
10	85.7	18.4	24.5	.999	.072	.020
20	82.9	18.5	24.4	.990	.074	.026
60	80.8	18.6	24.4	.982	.075	.033
∞	80.7	18.6	24.4	.982	.075	.033

Table 3.17   **Increasing Tax Progressivity: Decomposing Generations' Utility Changes**

Generation's Year of Birth	Generational Account	Factor Income	Tax Avoidance	Generation's Utility
−54	0.15	−0.11	0.00	0.04
−50	0.28	−0.23	0.08	0.13
−45	0.46	−0.25	−0.02	0.19
−40	0.45	−0.19	−0.16	0.10
−35	0.31	−0.10	−0.31	−0.10
−30	0.11	0.00	−0.47	−0.36
−25	−0.09	0.09	−0.60	−0.60
−20	−0.22	0.16	−0.72	−0.78
−15	−0.28	0.21	−0.78	−0.85
−10	−0.25	0.22	−0.79	−0.82
−5	−0.15	0.20	−0.75	−0.70
0	−0.01	0.16	−0.68	−0.53
5	0.01	0.01	−0.69	−0.67
10	0.04	−0.14	−0.70	−0.80
20	0.08	−0.31	−0.73	−0.96
50	0.10	−0.43	−0.74	−1.07
∞	0.10	−0.45	−0.74	−1.09

Note: Table reports changes, expressed as percentages of remaining lifetime expenditure.

switch to a progressive tax structure lowers the generational accounts of older and middle-aged generations, raises the accounts of initial young generations, and lowers the accounts of generations born in the long run.

The policy change produces a very interesting set of dynamics with respect to capital intensity and factor payments. The increase in marginal tax rates produces an immediate and sustained decline in labor supply. The initial impact of less labor supply is a decline in capital intensity and a concomitant rise in the wage and decline in the interest rate. Over time, the decline in labor earnings plus the increase in consumption associated with the intergenerational redistribution toward the initial elderly crowds out investment, lowers the capital-labor ratio, and lowers the wage.

The nonlinear pattern of factor-price changes over the transition coupled with significant changes in tax avoidance in response to higher marginal tax rates means that changes in generational accounts do poorly in measuring the total changes in different generations' levels of utility. Indeed, in this case the sign of the change in generational accounts of those living in the long run is opposite to that of their utility change.

3.4.2 Generational Accounting in a Small Open Economy

We turn now to generational accounting in a small economy that faces perfectly elastic inflows and outflows of foreign capital. Let r^* stand for the rate of return foreigners can earn abroad (after foreign corporate income taxes, but before personal capital income taxes). Then since foreign investors must receive the same return (before personal capital income taxes) whether they invest at home or abroad, we have

$$(12) \qquad f_s'(k_s)(1 - \phi_s) = r^*,$$

where $f_s'(\ )$ is the time s domestic marginal product of capital, which depends on the capital-labor ratio k_s, and ϕ_s is the time s corporate income tax rate.[13] According to (12), policy reforms that do not involve changes in corporate income taxation will leave pre-tax factor incomes unchanged. The reason is that the marginal products of capital as well as labor, which determine the pre-tax interest rate and wage, depend on the capital-labor ratio, which, according to (12), is pegged by r^*. Increases in the corporate tax rate, ϕ_s, will raise the marginal product of capital and, consequently, lower the capital-labor ratio and, thus, the wage; i.e., a corporate income tax increase will be shifted onto workers. This suggests the need to modify generational accounting in small open economies by allocating corporate income taxes to generations in proportion to their labor income, rather than their assets.

To make this point more precise, suppose that the government of a two-period life-cycle small open economy uses only a corporate income tax to finance its spending. Now consider the changes in generations' utilities associated with an increase, beginning at time t, in the rate of corporate taxation. According to (6) and (8), the changes in utilities of the old at time t and those born in $s \geq t$ are given by

$$(13) \qquad \frac{dU_{t-1}}{\lambda_{t-1}} = (1 - M_{ot})dw_t$$

and

---

13. We assume here that $f'(\ ) > 0$ and $f''(\ ) < 0$.

(14) $$\frac{dU_s}{\lambda_s} = \left((1 - M_{ys})dw_s + \frac{(1 - M_{os+1})dw_{s+1}}{1 + r^*} \right)$$

since all other terms in (6) and (8) are zero. Now competition plus the assumption of constant returns to scale in production implies that $w_s = f(k_s) - f'(k_s)k_s$, where $f(k_s)$ is output per unit of labor input. Differentiating this expression as well as (12) and using the results to rewrite (13) and (14) leads to

(13′) $$\frac{dU_{t-1}}{\lambda_{t-1}} = -(1 - M_{ot})dT_t^c + (1 - M_{ot})r^* \frac{\phi_t}{(1 - \phi_t)}dk_t$$

and

(14′)
$$\frac{dU_s}{\lambda_s} = -\left((1 - M_{ys})dT_s^c + \frac{(1 - M_{os+1})dT_{s+1}^c}{1 + r^*} \right)$$
$$+ (1 - M_{ys})r^* \frac{\phi_s}{(1 - \phi_s)}dk_s$$
$$+ (1 - M_{os+1})r^* \frac{\phi_{s+1}}{(1 - \phi_{s+1})} \frac{dk_{s+1}}{1 + r^*},$$

where T_s^c is corporate tax revenue per unit of labor input. Equations (13′) and (14′) indicate that apportioning changes in the corporate income tax to generations in proportion to their labor supply will leave each generation's change in its generational accounts equaling the change in its utility minus terms reflecting corporate tax avoidance arising from net capital outflows.

Structural Tax Change

Our first fiscal policy simulation in a small open economy involves a switch from income taxation to a combination of income and consumption taxation. Specifically we lower the tax on wage and corporate capital income from 20 percent to 15 percent and make up the loss in revenues by raising the consumption tax.

Table 3.18 documents the transition path for the economy under both personal and corporate taxation of capital income. In the case of personal capital income taxation, we assume that the government of the small open economy taxes the capital income received by its residents at the same rate regardless of whether that capital income is earned at home or abroad. In this case, (12) is replaced by

(12′) $$f_s'(k_s) = r^*,$$

which indicates that the pre-tax return to capital is pegged from abroad. This also means that the domestic capital-labor ratio and wage are pegged from abroad. In calculating changes in generational accounts with personal capital

Table 3.18   Generational Accounting in a Small Open Economy; Structural Tax Change: Transition Path[a]

Year	Personal Capital Income Tax				Corporate Capital Income Tax				
	Capital	Labor	Output	Saving Rate	Capital	Labor	Output	Wage	Saving Rate
0	89.9	19.2	25.7	.035	89.9	19.2	25.7	1.000	.035
1	91.6	19.6	26.2	.064	99.7	19.7	26.8	1.020	.052
2	91.5	19.6	26.1	.059	99.6	19.7	26.8	1.020	.052
3	91.3	19.5	26.1	.058	99.4	19.6	26.7	1.020	.051
4	91.1	19.5	26.0	.057	99.3	19.6	26.7	1.020	.050
5	91.0	19.5	26.0	.057	99.2	19.6	26.7	1.020	.050
10	90.2	19.3	25.8	.053	98.6	19.5	26.5	1.020	.047
20	89.2	19.1	25.5	.048	97.8	19.3	26.3	1.020	.043
60	88.0	18.9	25.1	.039	97.1	19.2	26.1	1.020	.037
∞	88.0	18.9	25.1	.039	97.1	19.2	26.1	1.020	.037

[a]Simulation entails an immediate and permanent reduction in proportional wage income and corporate income taxes from 20 to 15 percent with the reduction in revenues made up through the introduction of a proportional consumption tax.

Table 3.19   **Generational Accounting in a Small Open Economy; Structural Tax Change: Decomposing Generations' Utility Changes**

Generation's Year of Birth	Personal Capital Income Tax		Corporate Capital Income Tax			
				Generational Account Allocated By		
	Generational Account	Utility	Factor Income	Assets	Labor	Utility
−54	−2.35	−2.40	0.00	−2.10	−2.22	−2.27
−50	−2.11	−2.02	0.03	−2.00	−2.31	−2.10
−45	−1.62	−1.54	0.12	−1.61	−2.06	−1.77
−40	−1.14	−1.09	0.23	−1.19	−1.71	−1.41
−35	−0.71	−0.67	0.35	−0.80	−1.32	−1.02
−30	−0.35	−0.30	0.46	−0.46	−0.92	−0.63
−25	−0.05	0.01	0.57	−0.17	−0.54	−0.25
−20	0.17	0.26	0.68	0.06	−0.18	0.09
−15	0.31	0.44	0.77	0.23	0.13	0.40
−10	0.39	0.54	0.85	0.34	0.38	0.64
−5	0.39	0.57	0.90	0.38	0.56	0.81
0	0.34	0.54	0.93	0.36	0.65	0.91
5	0.35	0.56	0.93	0.34	0.64	0.89
10	0.36	0.57	0.93	0.32	0.64	0.88
20	0.37	0.58	0.93	0.30	0.63	0.85
50	0.37	0.59	0.93	0.29	0.62	0.84
∞	0.37	0.59	0.93	0.29	0.62	0.84

Note: Table reports changes, expressed as percentages of remaining lifetime expenditure.

income taxation, policy-induced changes in personal capital income taxes are distributed to domestic residences in proportion to their holdings of assets.

Under corporate income taxation, the foreign country taxes its residents only on their capital income earned at home and does not credit taxes paid to other countries for capital income earned in those countries. Consequently, (12) holds, and an increase in the domestic corporate income tax leads to a reduction in capital intensity and a decline in the wage.

As table 3.18 shows, the transition path of the economy is quite different depending on how capital income is taxed at the personal or corporate level in our small open economy. Under personal capital income taxation, there are no changes in the wage or interest rate. However, there are some minor changes over time in the stock of capital and the supply of labor (although not in their ratio) as labor supply responds to the new tax environment. In contrast, under the corporate capital income tax, there is an immediate rise in the capital-labor ratio (as the decline ϕ_s in [12] implies) and a concomitant 2 percent rise in the wage.

Table 3.19 compares changes in generations' utility with their changes in generational accounts. Consider first the results based on personal capital

Table 3.20   Generational Accounting in a Small Open Economy; Deficit-Financed
                  Three-Year Income Tax Cut: Transition Path

	Personal Capital Income Tax				Corporate Capital Income Tax				
Year	Capital	Labor	Output	Saving Rate	Capital	Labor	Output	Wage	Saving Rate
0	89.9	19.2	25.7	.035	89.9	19.2	25.7	1.000	.035
1	93.0	19.9	26.6	.046	98.3	20.0	27.0	1.013	.056
2	92.9	19.9	26.5	.046	98.3	20.0	27.0	1.013	.057
3	92.8	19.9	26.5	.046	98.3	20.0	27.0	1.013	.059
4	88.8	19.0	25.3	.027	87.8	19.0	25.3	.997	.027
5	88.8	19.0	25.4	.028	87.9	19.0	25.3	.997	.028
10	89.0	19.1	25.4	.028	88.1	19.1	25.3	.998	.028
20	89.4	19.1	25.5	.029	88.6	19.1	25.4	.998	.029
60	90.3	19.3	25.8	.034	89.5	19.3	25.6	.999	.035
∞	90.2	19.3	25.8	.034	89.4	19.3	25.6	.999	.034

income taxation. In this case, pre-tax factor incomes are unchanged by the change in tax structure, and the changes in generational accounts do a very good job for existing generations in approximating actual changes in utility. For generations born in the long run, the change in generational accounts represents about two thirds the change in utility.

Turn next to the results based on corporate income taxation. Again, changes in generational accounts do a very good job in capturing changes in generations' utilities when the change in corporate tax revenues is allocated by labor supply. For the sake of comparison, the table also shows the changes in generational accounts resulting from allocating changes in corporate taxes according to generations' holdings of assets. In this case, changes in generational accounts also provide a good approximation to changes in utilities for initial living generations but provide a much poorer approximation for generations alive in the long run.

Debt Policy

Table 3.20 shows the transition path resulting from running our previously discussed debt policy in a small open economy. As in the closed economy, the temporary reduction in tax rates leads to temporary increases in labor supply, labor earnings, saving, and the capital stock. But here we also have an immediate inflow of capital from abroad. Consequently, the short-run increase in the capital stock is greater in the open than in the closed economy (see table 3.8). In the case of personal capital income taxation, there is, of course, no change in the wage associated with this debt policy. This is not true in the case of corporate income taxation. Indeed, with corporate income taxation, the wage rises in the very short run by more than 1 percent. This rise in the wage may be contrasted with the almost 1 percent short-run decline in the wage that arises

Table 3.21   **Generational Accounting in a Small Open Economy; Deficit-Financed Three-Year Income Tax Cut: Decomposing Generations' Utility Changes**

Generation's Year of Birth	Personal Capital Income Tax		Corporate Capital Income Tax	
	Generational Account	Utility	Generational Account	Utility
−54	0.11	0.11	0.00	0.00
−50	0.19	0.29	−0.10	0.07
−45	0.33	0.37	0.12	0.20
−40	0.34	0.37	0.21	0.24
−35	0.31	0.33	0.24	0.25
−30	0.26	0.28	0.25	0.25
−25	0.21	0.23	0.24	0.23
−20	0.15	0.17	0.21	0.20
−15	0.09	0.10	0.18	0.16
−10	0.03	0.04	0.13	0.11
−5	−0.02	−0.02	0.08	0.06
0	−0.07	−0.08	0.03	0.01
5	−0.37	−0.47	−0.36	−0.40
10	−0.38	−0.48	−0.34	−0.37
20	−0.38	−0.48	−0.30	−0.32
50	−0.38	−0.48	−0.25	−0.26
∞	−0.38	−0.48	−0.26	−0.27

under the closed economy debt policy. Table 3.21 compares generational account and utility changes under both personal and corporate capital income taxation. All in all, there is a very close correspondence in the table between generational account changes and utility changes.

Increasing Social Security Benefits

Our final simulation, the results of which are reported in tables 3.22 and 3.23, involves raising social security benefits by one quarter. The transition paths of the economy are similar under both personal and corporate capital income taxation. But unlike the closed economy case, in which the long-run capital stock was crowded out and the wage fell by 1.2 percent, there is no crowding out in these simulations and no long-run change in the wage. Changes in generational accounts again do very well in approximating changes in generations' utilities.

3.5 Conclusion

This paper shows how changes in generational accounts relate to the generational incidence of fiscal policy. Specifically, it uses the Auerbach-Kotlikoff dynamic life-cycle simulation model to compare policy-induced changes in generational accounts with actual changes in generations' utilities. The paper

Table 3.22   **Generational Accounting in a Small Open Economy; 25 Percent Increase in Social Security Benefits: Transition Path**

	Personal Capital Income Tax				Corporate Capital Income Tax				
Year	Capital	Labor	Output	Saving Rate	Capital	Labor	Output	Wage	Saving Rate
0	76.4	18.5	24.6	.031	76.4	18.5	24.6	1.000	.031
1	74.2	17.9	23.9	.008	72.6	17.8	23.6	.997	.002
2	74.4	18.0	24.0	.009	73.0	17.9	23.7	.997	.004
3	74.6	18.0	24.0	.010	73.4	17.9	23.9	.997	.006
4	74.8	18.1	24.1	.011	73.8	18.0	24.0	.998	.008
5	74.9	18.1	24.1	.012	74.1	18.1	24.0	.998	.010
10	75.5	18.3	24.3	.017	75.3	18.3	24.3	.999	.018
20	76.2	18.4	24.6	.024	76.4	18.5	24.6	1.000	.026
60	76.6	18.5	24.7	.028	76.4	18.5	24.6	1.000	.029
∞	76.6	18.5	24.7	.029	76.4	18.5	24.6	1.000	.029

Table 3.23   **Generational Accounting in a Small Open Economy; 25 Percent Increase in Social Security Benefits: Decomposing Generations' Utility Changes**

Generation's Year of Birth	Personal Capital Income Tax		Corporate Capital Income Tax	
	Generational Account	Utility	Generational Account	Utility
−54	3.56	3.62	3.56	3.63
−50	3.42	3.60	3.45	3.52
−45	3.75	3.50	3.71	3.27
−40	2.04	1.74	2.05	1.60
−35	1.10	0.86	1.13	0.78
−30	0.49	0.29	0.55	0.28
−25	0.07	−0.12	0.14	−0.07
−20	−0.25	−0.43	−0.17	−0.32
−15	−0.49	−0.67	−0.41	−0.51
−10	−0.68	−0.87	−0.58	−0.66
−5	−0.81	−1.01	−0.70	−0.75
0	−0.90	−1.12	−0.78	−0.81
5	−0.88	−1.09	−0.70	−0.71
10	−0.86	−1.07	−0.63	−0.64
20	−0.86	−1.07	−0.60	−0.59
50	−0.88	−1.10	−0.64	−0.64
∞	−0.88	−1.09	−0.64	−0.63

considers changes in government spending, the tax structure, debt policy, social security benefit changes, and tax progressivity. It also considers a subset of these policies in an economy with capital adjustment costs and in a small open economy in which capital income is taxed either at the personal or corporate level.

In general, changes in generational accounts provide fairly good approximations to generations' actual changes in utilities. The approximations are better for living generations. They are worse for policies that involve significant changes in the degree of tax progressivity and for economies with sizable capital adjustment costs.

Finally, generational accounting needs to be adjusted in the case of small open economies to take into account the fact that the incidence of corporate taxation is likely to fall on labor. The method of adjustment is simply to allocate changes in corporate tax revenues to generations in proportion to their labor supply.

References

Auerbach, Alan J., Jagadeesh Gokhale, and Laurence J. Kotlikoff. 1991. "Generational Accounts: A Meaningful Alternative to Deficit Accounting." In D. Bradford, ed., *Tax Policy and the Economy,* vol. 5. Cambridge, Mass.: MIT Press, pp. 55–110.

Auerbach, Alan J., Jagadeesh Gokhale, and Laurence J. Kotlikoff. 1992. "A New Approach to Understanding the Effects of Fiscal Policy on Saving." *Scandinavian Journal of Economics* 94:303–18.

Auerbach, Alan J., Jagadeesh Gokhale, and Laurence J. Kotlikoff. 1994. "Generational Accounting: A Meaningful Way to Evaluate Generational Policy." *Journal of Economic Perspectives* 8:73–94.

Auerbach, Alan J., Jagadeesh Gokhale, Laurence J. Kotlikoff, and Erling Steigum, Jr. 1993. "Generational Accounting in Norway: Is Norway Overconsuming Its Petroleum Wealth?" Ruth Pollak Working Paper Series on Economics, no. 24. Boston: Boston University, Department of Economics, October.

Auerbach, Alan J., and Laurence J. Kotlikoff. 1987. *Dynamic Fiscal Policy.* Cambridge: Cambridge University Press.

Boll, Stefan, Bernd Raffelhüschen, and Jan Walliser. 1994. "Social Security and Intergenerational Redistribution: A Generational Accounting Perspective." *Public Choice* 81 (October): 79–100.

Cutler, David. 1988. "Tax Reform and the Stock Market—An Asset Price Approach." *American Economic Review* 78 (December): 1107–17.

Franco, Daniele, Jagadeesh Gokhale, Luigi Guiso, Laurence J. Kotlikoff, and Nicola Sartor. 1994. "Generational Accounting—The Case of Italy." In Albert Ando, Luigi Guiso, and Ignazio Visco, ed., *Saving and the Accumulation of Wealth.* Cambridge: Cambridge University Press, pp. 128–62.

Gokhale, Jagadeesh, Bernd Raffelhüschen, and Jan Walliser. 1995. "The Burden of German Unification: A Generational Accounting Approach." *Finanzarchiv* 52: 141–65.

Hayashi, Fumio. 1982. "Tobin's Marginal q and Average q: A Neoclassical Interpretation." *Econometrica* 50:213–24.

Kotlikoff, Laurence J. 1992. *Generational Accounting.* New York: Free Press.

U.S. Office of Management and Budget. 1992. *Budget of the United States Government, Fiscal Year 1993.* Washington, D.C.: Government Printing Office.

U.S. Office of Management and Budget. 1993. *Budget of the United States Government, Fiscal Year 1994.* Washington, D.C.: Government Printing Office.

U.S. Office of Management and Budget. 1994. *Budget of the United States Government, Fiscal Year 1995.* Washington, D.C.: Government Printing Office.

4 An International Comparison of Generational Accounts

Laurence J. Kotlikoff and Willi Leibfritz

Generational angst—the fear that we are bequeathing enormous fiscal bills to our children—is global, affecting countries as diverse as Japan and Brazil. The angst is rooted in three facts. First, the affected countries have spent decades accumulating large official liabilities. Second, they have spent the same time accumulating even larger unofficial liabilities. And third, they are aging quite rapidly, leaving relatively few workers to pay the government's bills. Generational accounting, as we have seen, helps countries confront, although not necessarily allay, their generational anxieties. It spells out how much each generation will pay under different policy scenarios, including trying to maintain the status quo.

For most of the 17 countries considered in this book, generational accounting's message is highly unpleasant. The reason is that most of these countries are running fiscal policies that if left unchanged will sentence their children to sky-high rates of net taxation. This chapter documents this contention. It compares the countries' generational accounts, the role of demographics in producing their generational imbalances, and the policies they could adopt to achieve generational balance—a situation in which future generations face the same lifetime net tax rates as current newborns. In drawing these comparisons, this chapter provides an overview of each country's generational policy. But it leaves to each country chapter the task of describing recent fiscal events, discussing the generational impacts of past and pending fiscal actions, and identifying data sources underlying the generational accounts.

Laurence J. Kotlikoff is professor of economics at Boston University and a research associate of the National Bureau of Economic Research. Willi Leibfritz is head of the Department for Macroeconomic and Fiscal Studies at ifo Institute for Economic Research.

4.1   Methodology and Assumptions

As detailed in chapter 3, generational accounts are defined as the present value of taxes paid minus transfer payments received (net taxes) that individuals of different annual cohorts (generations) pay on average over their remaining lifetimes. The accounts consider only future net taxes; that is, they do not include taxes that have been paid or any transfers that have been received before the base year. Thus among living generations only the newborn generation (the generation born in the base year) has a generational account consisting of its entire lifetime net tax payments, measured in present value.

Generational accounts are based on the government's intertemporal budget constraint, which implies that the sum of future government consumption spending has to be equal to the sum of all future net taxes (taxes minus transfers all in present value terms) plus current government net wealth. The imbalance in existing generational policy is calculated by assuming that future generations (those born after the base year) pay, in the form of net taxes, all of the government's bills left unpaid by current generations. This assumption ensures that the difference between generational accounts of the newborn generation and generational accounts of future generations reflects the policy adjustment required to satisfy the government's intertemporal budget constraint.

If future generations face, on a growth-adjusted basis, a higher lifetime net tax burden than do current newborns, current policy is neither sustainable nor generationally balanced. The same is true if future generations face a smaller growth-adjusted lifetime net tax burden than do current newborns. However, in this case, generational balance can be achieved by reducing the fiscal burden facing current generations rather than the other way around. The calculation of the extent of generational imbalance is an informative counterfactual—not a likely policy scenario. Hence, we also entertain alternative means of achieving generational balance that do not involve foisting all the adjustment on future generations.

Generational accounting depends on various assumptions, in particular about future economic developments and demographic trends. In the base-case generational accounts presented here, labor productivity is assumed to grow at 1.5 percent per year and all future flows of real taxes and real transfer payments are discounted at a 5 percent real rate. We also present results for higher and lower productivity growth and discount rates.[1] Demographic projections are generally taken from national sources. The base-case fiscal policy considered is that prevailing at the time of the writing of the respective chapters, 1996 and

1. The calculations are also carried out for 1 percent and 2 percent productivity growth. Labor productivity increased on average in OECD member countries by 1.8 percent during the 1980s and by 1 percent during the first half of the 1990s. There are different views about how aging of populations affects productivity. Some argue that aging slows technical progress as innovation is less profitable in shrinking markets and as the aging society loses "dynamism" (Simon 1981;

the first half of 1997. The authors who wrote these chapters chose the data to be used in their accounts. They also produced their accounts themselves, using, in most cases, the original generational accounting software package developed by Alan Auerbach, Jagadeesh Gokhale, and Laurence Kotlikoff.

In the first incarnations of generational accounting, educational expenditure was treated as a government purchase rather than as a transfer payment to those on whose behalf the expenditure is made. This treatment followed the classification of educational expenditures of the U.S. National Income and Product Accounts. To maintain comparability with previous work, we present generational accounts treating educational expenditure both as a government purchase (case A) and as transfer payments (case B).

4.2 The Demographic Transition

Table 4.1 considers the demographic trends under way in each of our 17 countries. The first four columns show projected population growth rates for this decade and the next three. The next two columns compare the elderly shares of the population in 1990 and 2030, and the last two columns compare 1990 and 2020 elderly dependency ratios—the ratio of those aged 65 or older to those aged 15 to 64.

In this decade, each country's annual population growth rate is positive. But each is projected to decline dramatically over time. Indeed, in the 2020s, 6 of the 17 countries will experience negative population growth. In Brazil, Argentina, and Thailand population growth is projected to decline from 1 to 1.5 percent per year in the 1990s to 0.6 to 0.7 percent per year after 2020. In the United States, Canada, Australia, and New Zealand, population growth will decline from this decade's rates of 0.9 to 1.2 percent per year to 0.3 to 0.4 percent per year after 2020. Starting at the turn of the century, the German, Italian, and Belgian populations will actually begin to shrink. Thailand, whose elderly currently make up only 4 percent of the population, will have a population that is 11 percent old in 2030.

Of the 17 countries, Germany, Italy, Japan, and the Netherlands will be the oldest in 2030, with over one-quarter of their populations in the ranks of the elderly. In these countries as well as Belgium, there will be over 4 oldsters for every 10 workers (working-age persons). In Germany and Italy, there will be almost 5 oldsters per 10 workers. In another 9 countries—the United States,

---

Wattenberg 1987), while others find empirical evidence that innovation increases when labor gets scarce (Habakkuk 1962; Cutler et al. 1990).

Discount rates convert projected annual flows into net present values. A higher discount rate would reduce the net present value of future flows compared with a lower discount rate, and the longer the time period under consideration, the greater the sensitivity of the results to the choice of the discount rate. As explained in chapter 2, there are differing views about how to choose an appropriate discount rate for this analysis. The range of discount rates used in this study (3, 5, and 7 percent) encompasses differing interpretations of the appropriate choice of the discount rate and permits sensitivity analysis of the discount rate assumption.

Table 4.1   Demographic Trends

Country	Population Growth Rates (% per year)				Elderly Share of the Population[a]		Elderly Dependency Ratio[b]	
	1990–2000	2000–2010	2010–20	2020–30	1990	2030	1990	2030
United States	1.0	0.8	0.6	0.4	12.9	21.9	19.1	36.8
Japan	0.3	0.1	−0.2	−0.3	11.9	26.1	17.1	44.5
Germany	0.2	−0.3	−0.3	−0.4	14.0	28.1	21.7	49.2
Italy	0.0	−0.2	−0.3	−0.4	14.8	27.9	21.6	48.3
Canada	1.2	0.8	0.6	0.3	11.3	23.1	16.7	39.1
Thailand	1.4	1.1	0.8	0.7	3.8	11.0	6.0	16.3
Australia	1.2	0.8	0.5	0.3	10.7	20.3	16.0	33.0
Denmark	0.2	0.0	0.0	−0.1	15.4	22.6	22.7	37.7
Netherlands	0.5	0.1	0.0	−0.1	13.2	26.0	19.1	45.1
New Zealand	0.9	0.6	0.5	0.4	11.1	18.9	16.7	30.5
France	0.5	0.3	0.2	0.1	13.8	23.3	20.9	39.1
Norway	0.5	0.2	0.2	0.2	16.3	23.0	25.2	38.7
Portugal	0.0	0.0	0.0	0.0	13.0	20.9	19.5	33.5
Sweden	0.4	0.2	0.2	0.1	17.8	23.1	27.6	39.4
Argentina	1.0	0.8	0.8	0.6	9.1	13.9	15.0	21.3
Belgium	0.2	−0.1	−0.1	−0.1	15.0	24.3	22.4	41.1
Brazil	1.5	1.2	1.0	0.7	4.7	11.9	7.7	17.8

Source: World Bank, *World Bank Projections* (Washington, D.C., 1994).

[a]Population aged 65 or older as a percentage of total population.

[b]Population aged 65 or older as a percentage of population aged 15 to 64.

Canada, Australia, Denmark, New Zealand, France, Norway, Portugal, and Sweden—there will be between 3 and 4 oldsters per 10 workers. And in Thailand, Argentina, and Brazil, there will be roughly 2 oldsters for every 10 workers.

4.3   Generational Accounts of Living Generations

When people are young, they receive transfers (e.g., child benefits or educational allowances) and pay consumption taxes. During their working lives, they continue to pay consumption taxes but also pay taxes on their labor and capital income in the form of personal income taxes and payroll taxes. The present value of a generation's remaining lifetime net tax payments—its generational account—is generally highest for generations at the beginning of their work spans, as it does not include child and educational benefits received in youth. When workers reach older ages, the sum of future net tax payments tends to decline as future transfer receipts (e.g., pensions) gain in importance compared with future tax payments. Between ages 50 and 60, future transfer receipts generally start to exceed future tax payments so that generational accounts become negative (net transfers). The absolute amount of net transfers declines during retirement as the remaining lifetime shortens.

Table 4.2 shows the generational accounts of each of our 17 countries. Each set of accounts exhibits a hump-shaped pattern with respect to age. This is true whether one considers case A (educational expenditures treated as a government purchase) or case B (educational expenditures treated as a transfer payment). All amounts in this and subsequent tables are expressed in 1995 U.S. dollars.

Although the accounts all rise and then fall with age, the absolute levels of the accounts vary considerably across countries. Much of this variation—for example, the difference between U.S. and Thai accounts—reflects the level of development. But there is great variation even among developed countries. Take case A, and compare the accounts of 40-year-old Germans and those of 40-year-old Swedes. The Swedish age 40 account equals $228,500, which is 43 percent larger than the corresponding $160,100 German age 40 account. The difference between the two accounts reflects the much higher net transfers paid to older Germans compared to older Swedes. Or compare the 70-year-old Norwegian account with the corresponding Japanese account. The Norwegian account is $135,000 smaller than the Japanese account.

These big cross-country differences in the accounts should not obscure their similarities. Take Italy and Canada. Both countries have quite similar accounts through roughly age 25. But beyond this age, the Italians have much smaller accounts than do the Canadians. Or compare the German and French accounts, on the one hand, or the Argentine and Brazilian accounts, on the other. They are quite similar across all ages.

There are four features of the accounts that particularly merit comment.

Table 4.2   Generational Accounts, 1995 (thousands of 1995 U.S. dollars)

Generation's Age in 1995	United States		Japan		Germany		Italy		Canada		Thailand	
	A	B	A	B	A	B	A	B	A	B	A	B
0	86.3	28.5	143.4	73.0	165.0	97.1	114.2	68.4	113.8	56.3	8.3	5.9
5	102.0	35.3	169.3	90.9	194.3	123.6	132.9	80.3	130.1	66.4	9.6	6.8
10	121.7	71.4	200.1	135.4	233.8	179.0	154.1	112.4	152.0	99.0	10.9	8.9
15	144.6	115.0	235.9	187.4	287.9	252.2	178.4	158.9	176.9	138.5	12.3	11.3
20	168.7	159.3	278.1	257.4	333.6	313.6	193.5	186.6	199.0	177.0	13.6	13.2
25	175.4	172.7	295.2	295.2	309.7	303.4	184.4	183.7	183.7	193.1	14.2	14.1
30	170.0	168.7	297.8	297.8	271.8	271.8	155.2	155.2	189.1	183.3	14.1	14.1
35	157.5	156.9	287.4	287.4	224.4	224.4	113.5	113.5	165.2	161.1	13.3	13.3
40	135.7	135.6	263.8	263.8	160.1	160.1	63.4	63.4	137.3	134.5	11.8	11.8
45	101.3	101.3	227.7	227.7	94.0	94.0	10.7	10.7	98.9	97.1	10.0	10.0
50	56.4	56.4	173.1	173.1	-4.2	-4.2	-46.8	-46.8	51.8	50.8	8.1	8.1
55	4.0	4.0	99.0	99.0	-98.9	-98.9	-103.1	-103.1	5.8	5.5	6.2	6.2
60	-51.7	-51.7	11.9	11.9	-183.6	-183.6	-142.0	-142.0	-45.3	-44.8	4.8	4.8
65	-96.0	-96.0	-47.7	-47.7	-206.7	-206.7	-138.3	-138.3	-84.7	-83.6	3.7	3.7
70	-104.6	-104.6	-44.8	-44.8	-180.7	-180.7	-117.5	-117.5	-89.1	-87.9	2.8	2.8
75	-101.9	-101.9	-36.0	-36.0	-150.2	-150.2	-94.7	-94.7	-85.6	-84.4	2.1	2.1
80	-89.5	-89.5	-26.7	-26.7	-109.6	-109.6	-72.2	-72.2	-80.9	-79.8	1.5	1.5
85	-74.4	-74.4	-18.2	-18.2	-68.0	-68.0	-52.7	-52.7	-69.4	-68.5	1.0	1.0
90	-56.7	-56.7	-9.7	-9.7	-3.2	-3.2	-7.4	-7.4	-11.0	-10.9	0.5	0.5
Future generations	130.4	73.9	386.2	319.4	316.8	248.8	264.8	209.9	114.0	58.0	1.0	-1.5
Generational imbalance												
Absolute	44.1	45.3	242.8	246.4	151.8	151.7	150.6	145.1	0.2	2.7	-7.3	-7.4
In percent	51.1	159.0	169.3	337.8	92.0	156.1	131.8	223.8	0.0	3.1	-88.0	-125.4

	Australia		Denmark		Netherlands		New Zealand		France	
	A	B	A	B	A	B	A	B	A	B
0	79.6	49.4	84	−18	110.0	49.4	57.3	18.0	151.5	82.2
5	95.3	60.1	134	14	139.8	68.9	68.2	26.4	191.7	125.4
10	112.8	85.4	178	79	171.0	113.8	74.4	39.0	229.4	175.4
15	134.3	115.8	211	143	205.0	164.0	82.8	57.9	264.8	222.2
20	148.4	138.3	243	209	231.7	209.9	91.9	78.7	304.4	284.8
25	147.7	141.9	251	232	237.3	237.3	104.2	95.3	321.9	318.7
30	138.5	134.2	238	225	220.0	222.0	102.9	95.9	293.7	293.7
35	128.2	124.4	214	202	196.7	196.7	94.1	88.7	242.7	242.7
40	111.9	108.5	166	157	161.2	161.2	79.0	75.1	166.8	166.8
45	87.4	84.5	99	91	116.3	116.3	57.9	55.6	77.5	77.5
50	57.4	55.1	14	9	62.2	62.2	31.3	30.3	−12.5	−12.5
55	25.9	24.2	−61	−64	5.5	5.5	2.5	2.4	−134.7	−134.7
60	1.5	1.5	−143	−143	−46.5	−46.5	−26.3	−26.3	−197.0	−197.0
65	−12.7	−12.7	−172	−172	−91.4	−91.4	−50.2	−50.2	−199.9	−199.9
70	−17.6	−17.6	−186	−186	−103.4	−103.4	−55.8	−55.8	−151.5	−151.5
75	−16.1	−16.1	−194	−194	−113.0	−113.0	−53.7	−53.7	−162.1	−162.1
80	−13.8	−13.8	−202	−202	−118.8	−118.0	−47.1	−47.1	−93.9	−93.9
85	−11.3	−11.3	−202	−202	−116.6	−116.6	−44.5	−44.5	−102.9	−102.9
90	−9.4	−9.4	−49	−49	−110.9	−110.9	−36.3	−36.3	−94.4	−94.4
Future generations	105.2	73.4	124	26	193.8	137.0	55.3	16.0	222.8	161.4
Generational imbalance										
Absolute	25.6	24.0	40	44	83.7	87.6	−2.0	−2.0	71.3	79.2
In percent	32.2	48.6	46.9	–	76.0	177.7	−3.4	−10.8	47.1	96.3

(continued)

Table 4.2 (continued)

Generation's Age in 1995	Norway A	Norway B	Portugal A	Portugal B	Sweden A	Sweden B	Argentina A	Argentina B	Belgium A	Belgium B	Brazil A	Brazil B
0	106.3	1.4	61.8	43.5	184.3	121.8	22.7	13.9	93.5	43.3	14.3	10.2
5	112.3	-7.5	67.1	45.5	203.4	140.8	25.3	15.7	132.4	76.2	17.1	12.3
10	123.7	14.7	73.0	50.9	226.4	162.9	28.7	20.3	170.1	116.0	20.9	17.1
15	135.3	58.4	79.6	65.3	253.5	211.3	32.6	26.3	210.5	172.3	25.0	22.6
20	140.8	106.3	86.0	82.7	281.2	265.1	34.0	30.8	242.3	232.9	28.9	27.0
25	143.2	127.1	85.1	84.5	295.2	284.2	33.5	31.6	272.5	270.8	31.2	30.1
30	138.1	129.6	75.0	75.0	283.7	278.9	29.8	28.2	278.6	278.6	31.5	31.3
35	120.9	116.2	60.0	60.0	261.9	258.3	22.8	21.6	259.3	259.3	28.0	28.0
40	93.1	90.3	39.7	39.7	228.5	226.5	13.6	12.6	215.5	215.5	19.7	19.7
45	40.5	38.9	15.9	15.9	177.2	175.8	2.1	1.5	149.3	149.3	6.9	6.9
50	-22.0	-22.3	-10.6	-10.6	105.3	104.6	-11.0	-11.3	65.1	65.1	-6.3	-6.3
55	-73.0	-73.0	-33.9	-33.9	16.5	16.1	-25.2	-25.2	-34.6	-34.6	-18.1	-18.1
60	-135.0	-135.3	-47.1	-47.1	-66.3	-66.4	-39.9	-39.9	-130.6	-130.6	-28.0	-28.0
65	-170.6	-170.6	-49.4	-49.4	-110.8	-110.9	-42.9	-42.9	-165.7	-165.7	-33.3	-33.3
70	-179.8	-179.6	-42.7	-42.7	-97.8	-97.8	-43.0	-43.0	-172.4	-172.4	-32.9	-32.9
75	-170.0	-170.0	-33.3	-33.3	-79.7	-79.7	-41.2	-41.2	-163.7	-163.7	-22.1	-22.1
80	-155.1	-155.1	-24.8	-24.8	-58.1	-58.1	-34.3	-34.3	-153.1	-153.1	-14.1	-14.1
85	-139.4	-139.4	-15.4	-15.4	-33.2	-33.2	-32.5	-32.5	-138.6	-138.6	-9.6	-9.6
90	-122.6	-122.6	-4.1	-4.1	-6.5	-6.5	-7.1	-7.1	-119.0	-119.0	-2.7	-2.7
Future generations	173.5	57.3	98.7	73.2	143.5	83.8	36.1	24.3	147.8	89.5	27.0	22.1
Generational imbalance Absolute	67.2	55.9	36.9	29.7	-40.9	-38.0	13.4	10.4	54.2	46.3	12.7	11.9
In percent	63.2	4,091.8	59.7	68.3	-22.2	-31.2	58.6	74.8	58.0	107.0	88.8	116.7

Note: A: Educational expenditure treated as government consumption. B: Educational expenditure treated as government transfers and distributed by age groups.

Table 4.3   **Absolute and Relative Levels of Per Capita GDP, 1995**

Country	Per Capita GDP (U.S. $)	Per Capita GDP as a Percentage of U.S. GDP
United States	26,980	100.0
Japan	22,110	81.9
Germany	20,070	74.4
Italy	19,870	73.6
Canada	21,130	78.3
Thailand	7,540	27.9
Australia	18,940	70.2
Denmark	21,230	78.7
Netherlands	19,950	73.9
New Zealand	16,360	60.6
France	21,030	77.9
Norway	21,940	81.3
Portugal	12,670	47.0
Sweden	18,540	68.7
Argentina	8,310	30.8
Belgium	21,660	80.3
Brazil	5,400	20.0

Source: World Bank, *World Development Report 1997* (Washington, D.C., 1997).

First, the Japanese, Germans, Swedes, Danes, Dutch, French, and Belgians are confronting their young and middle-aged citizens with strikingly high levels of remaining lifetime net taxes. At age 25, the respective case A accounts of these countries are $295,200, $309,700, $295,200, $251,000, $237,300, $321,900, and $272,500. These values are large not only in absolute terms, but also relative to each of the countries' annual average labor earnings. They are also much higher than the corresponding $175,400 age 25 U.S. account.

Second, with the exception of Thailand, which does not yet have a pay-as-you-go social security system, the accounts of all the countries are negative after age 65. In a number of the countries they are negative at earlier ages. For example, Brazil's accounts turn negative at age 50. Third, certain countries are much more generous to their current elderly than are others. Comparing Australia and Norway makes this point. Both countries have quite similar case A accounts prior to age 40. But for older cohorts, Norway has substantially lower levels of net taxation. Indeed, at age 75 the Norwegian account is $154,000 less than the Australian account. Fourth, as expected, the case B accounts are much lower for all countries at younger ages since educational expenditures are allocated to children and young adults on whose behalf the expenditure is made. For example, in Canada the case B account for 5-year-olds is $66,400—less than half the corresponding case A account.

Table 4.4 repeats table 4.2 except it scales each country's accounts by the ratio of U.S. per capita GDP to the country's per capita GDP. Table 4.3 reports the absolute levels of 1995 per capita GDP for each country as well as the

Table 4.4   Scaled Generational Accounts, 1995 (thousands of 1995 U.S. dollars)

Generation's Age in 1995	United States		Japan		Germany		Italy		Canada		Thailand	
	A	B	A	B	A	B	A	B	A	B	A	B
0	86.3	28.5	175.1	89.1	221.8	130.5	155.2	92.9	145.3	71.9	29.7	21.1
5	102.0	35.3	206.7	111.0	261.2	166.1	180.6	109.1	166.2	84.8	34.4	24.4
10	121.7	71.4	244.3	165.3	314.2	240.6	209.4	152.7	194.1	126.4	39.1	31.9
15	144.6	115.0	288.0	228.8	387.0	339.0	242.4	215.9	225.9	176.9	44.1	40.5
20	168.7	159.3	339.6	314.3	448.4	421.5	262.9	253.5	254.2	226.1	48.7	47.3
25	175.4	172.7	360.4	360.4	416.3	407.8	250.5	249.6	234.6	246.6	50.9	50.5
30	170.0	168.7	363.6	363.6	365.3	365.3	210.9	210.9	241.5	234.1	50.5	50.5
35	157.5	156.9	350.9	350.9	301.6	301.6	154.2	154.2	211.0	205.7	47.7	47.7
40	135.7	135.6	322.1	322.1	215.2	215.2	86.1	86.1	175.4	171.8	42.3	42.3
45	101.3	101.3	278.0	278.0	126.3	126.3	14.5	14.5	126.3	124.0	35.8	35.8
50	56.4	56.4	211.4	211.4	-5.6	-5.6	-63.6	-63.6	66.2	64.9	29.0	29.0
55	4.0	4.0	120.9	120.9	-132.9	-132.9	-140.1	-140.1	7.4	7.0	22.2	22.2
60	-51.7	-51.7	14.5	14.5	-246.8	-246.8	-192.9	-192.9	-57.9	-57.2	17.2	17.2
65	-96.0	-96.0	-58.2	-58.2	-277.8	-277.8	-187.9	-187.9	-108.2	-106.8	13.3	13.3
70	-104.6	-104.6	-54.7	-54.7	-242.9	-242.9	-159.6	-159.6	-113.8	-112.3	10.0	10.0
75	-101.9	-101.9	-44.0	-44.0	-201.9	-201.9	-128.7	-128.7	-109.3	-107.8	7.5	7.5
80	-89.5	-89.5	-32.6	-32.6	-147.3	-147.3	-98.1	-98.1	-103.3	-101.9	5.4	5.4
85	-74.4	-74.4	-22.2	-22.2	-91.4	-91.4	-71.6	-71.6	-88.6	-87.5	3.6	3.6
90	-56.7	-56.7	-11.8	-11.8	-4.3	-4.3	-10.1	-10.1	-14.0	-13.9	1.8	1.8
Future generations	130.4	73.9	471.6	390.0	425.8	334.4	359.8	285.2	145.6	74.1	3.6	-5.4
Generational imbalance												
Absolute	44.1	45.3	296.5	300.9	204.0	203.9	204.6	197.1	0.3	3.4	-26.2	-26.5
In percent	51.1	159.0	169.3	337.8	92.0	156.1	131.8	223.8	0.0	3.1	-88.0	-125.4

	Australia		Denmark		Netherlands		New Zealand		France	
	A	B	A	B	A	B	A	B	A	B
0	113.4	70.4	106.7	−22.9	148.8	66.8	94.6	29.7	194.5	105.5
5	135.8	85.6	170.3	17.8	189.2	93.2	112.5	43.6	246.1	161.0
10	160.7	121.7	226.2	100.4	231.4	154.0	122.8	64.4	294.5	225.2
15	191.3	165.0	268.1	181.7	277.4	221.9	136.6	95.5	339.9	285.2
20	211.4	197.0	308.8	265.6	313.5	284.0	151.7	129.9	390.8	365.6
25	210.4	202.1	318.9	294.8	321.1	321.1	171.9	157.3	413.2	409.1
30	197.3	191.2	302.4	285.9	297.7	300.4	169.8	158.3	377.0	377.0
35	182.6	177.2	271.9	256.7	266.2	266.2	155.3	146.4	311.6	311.6
40	159.4	154.6	210.9	199.5	218.1	218.1	130.4	123.9	214.1	214.1
45	124.5	120.4	125.8	115.6	157.4	157.4	95.5	91.7	99.5	99.5
50	81.8	78.5	17.8	11.4	84.2	84.2	51.7	50.0	−16.0	−16.0
55	36.9	34.5	−77.5	−81.3	7.4	7.4	4.1	4.0	−172.9	−172.9
60	2.1	2.1	−181.7	−181.7	−62.9	−62.9	−43.4	−43.4	−252.9	−252.9
65	−18.1	−18.1	−218.6	−218.6	−123.7	−123.7	−82.8	−82.8	−256.6	−256.6
70	−25.1	−25.1	−236.3	−236.3	−139.9	−139.9	−92.1	−92.1	−194.5	−194.5
75	−22.9	−22.9	−246.5	−246.5	−152.9	−152.9	−88.6	−88.6	−208.1	−208.1
80	−19.7	−19.7	−256.7	−256.7	−160.8	−159.7	−77.7	−77.7	−120.5	−120.5
85	−16.1	−16.1	−256.7	−256.7	−157.8	−157.8	−73.4	−73.4	−132.1	−132.1
90	−13.4	−13.4	−62.3	−62.3	−150.1	−150.1	−59.9	−59.9	−121.2	−121.2
Future generations	149.9	104.6	157.6	33.0	262.2	185.4	91.3	26.4	286.0	207.2
Generational imbalance										
Absolute	36.5	34.2	50.8	55.9	113.3	118.5	−3.3	−3.3	91.5	101.7
In percent	32.2	48.6	46.9	–	76.0	177.7	−3.4	−10.8	47.1	96.3

(continued)

Table 4.4   (*continued*)

Generation's Age in 1995	Norway A	Norway B	Portugal A	Portugal B	Sweden A	Sweden B	Argentina A	Argentina B	Belgium A	Belgium B	Brazil A	Brazil B
0	130.8	1.7	131.5	92.6	268.3	177.3	73.7	45.1	116.4	53.9	71.5	51.0
5	138.1	−9.2	142.8	96.8	296.1	204.2	82.1	51.0	164.9	94.9	85.5	61.5
10	152.2	18.1	155.3	108.3	329.5	237.1	93.2	65.9	211.8	144.5	104.5	85.5
15	166.4	71.8	169.4	138.9	369.0	307.6	105.8	85.4	262.1	214.6	125.0	113.0
20	173.2	130.8	183.0	176.0	409.3	385.9	110.4	100.0	301.7	290.0	144.5	135.0
25	176.1	156.3	181.1	179.8	429.7	413.7	108.8	102.6	339.4	337.2	156.0	150.5
30	169.9	159.4	159.6	159.6	413.0	406.0	98.6	91.6	346.9	346.9	157.5	156.5
35	148.7	142.9	127.7	127.7	381.2	376.0	74.0	70.1	322.9	322.9	140.0	140.0
40	114.5	111.1	84.5	84.5	332.6	329.7	44.2	40.9	268.4	268.4	98.5	98.5
45	49.8	47.8	33.8	33.8	257.9	255.9	6.8	4.9	185.9	185.9	34.5	34.5
50	−27.1	−27.4	−22.6	−22.6	153.3	152.3	−35.7	−36.7	81.1	81.1	−31.5	−31.5
55	−89.8	−89.8	−72.1	−72.1	24.0	23.4	−81.8	−81.8	−43.1	−43.1	−90.5	−90.5
60	−166.1	−166.4	−100.2	−100.2	−96.5	−96.7	−129.5	−129.5	−162.6	−162.6	−140.0	−140.0
65	−209.8	−209.8	−105.1	−105.1	−161.3	−161.4	−139.3	−139.3	−206.4	−206.4	−166.5	−166.5
70	−221.2	−220.9	−90.9	−90.9	−142.4	−142.4	−139.6	−139.6	−214.7	−214.7	−164.5	−164.5
75	−209.1	−209.1	−70.9	−70.9	−116.0	−116.0	−133.8	−133.8	−203.9	−203.9	−110.5	−110.5
80	−190.8	−190.8	−52.8	−52.8	−84.6	−84.6	−111.4	−111.4	−190.7	−190.7	−70.5	−70.5
85	−171.5	−171.5	−32.8	−32.8	−48.3	−48.3	−105.5	−105.5	−172.6	−172.6	−48.0	−48.0
90	−150.8	−150.8	−8.7	−8.7	−9.5	−9.5	−23.1	−23.1	−148.2	−148.2	−13.5	−13.5
Future generations	213.4	70.5	210.0	155.7	208.9	122.0	117.2	78.9	184.1	111.5	135.0	110.5
Generational imbalance												
Absolute	82.7	68.8	78.5	63.2	−59.5	−55.3	43.5	33.8	67.5	57.7	63.5	59.5
In percent	63.2	4,091.8	59.7	68.3	−22.2	−31.2	58.6	74.8	58.0	107.0	88.8	116.7

Note: A: Educational expenditure treated as government consumption. B: Educational expenditure treated as government transfers and distributed by age groups.

ratios of these living standards to 1995 U.S. per capita GDP. Living standards are measured on a purchasing price parity basis. In absolute terms, the countries' living standards range from $5,400 in Brazil to $26,980 in the United States. Brazil's living standard is only a fifth of that of the United States. Japan's living standard, in contrast, is 82 percent of the U.S. standard.

Scaling the accounts is informative. It shows remarkable differences across countries in the extent of net taxation even after one has taken into account differences in levels of income. Take 40-year-olds. The largest case A account for this cohort is found in Japan. It equals $322,100. The smallest—equal to $42,300—is found in Thailand. The age 40 U.S. case A account is $135,700. In addition to Japan, Germany, Canada, Australia, Denmark, the Netherlands, France, Sweden, and Belgium have higher scaled age 40 generational accounts than the United States. Next consider 65-year-olds. The smallest age 65 scaled account is −$277,800 and belongs to Germany, whereas the largest—$13,300—is that of Thailand. The age 65 U.S. account is −$96,000. In addition to Germany, the age 65 accounts of Italy, Canada, Denmark, the Netherlands, France, Norway, Portugal, Sweden, Argentina, Belgium, and Brazil are less than that of the United States. Finally, consider newborns. The U.S. case A account is $86,300. This is less than one-third the corresponding scaled Swedish newborn account of $268,300. It is also smaller, and in most cases a lot smaller, than the scaled newborn accounts of Japan, Germany, Italy, Canada, Australia, Denmark, the Netherlands, New Zealand, France, Norway, Portugal, and Belgium.

4.4   Imbalances in Generational Policy

The comparison of the generational account facing newborns with that facing future generations indicates the degree of imbalance in generational policy. These accounts can be found in the "age 0" and the "future generations" rows of table 4.2. The last two rows of table 4.2 show the imbalance in both absolute and percentage terms. Take the United States: The case A generational account of newborn Americans is $86,300, whereas that facing future Americans is $130,400. The difference between these numbers—$44,100—is the absolute imbalance. This absolute imbalance is 51.1 percent of the account of current newborns; that is, unless currently living Americans are forced to pay more in net taxes or unless government in the United States can curtail its purchases, future Americans will face net tax rates that are more than 50 percent higher than those facing current newborn Americans! The case B absolute imbalance is quite close to the case A imbalance, but since the case B generational account of newborns is only about one-third the size of the corresponding case A account, the case B percentage imbalance is much larger than the case A percentage imbalance—indeed, three times larger!

Whether one considers the case A or case B imbalance, one thing is clear: there is a very large imbalance in U.S. generational policy. But the United

States is certainly not alone in placing the next generation in harm's way. According to table 4.2, Japan, Germany, Italy, the Netherlands, Norway, and Belgium have larger percentage imbalances than the United States under case A, and Japan, Italy, Denmark, the Netherlands, and Norway have larger percentage imbalances under case B!

The country with the largest absolute imbalances is Japan. Its case A and case B imbalances are $242,800 and $246,400, respectively. These amounts are startling. If future Japanese are asked to pay these sums in addition to what current newborn Japanese are now being asked to pay, they will, in effect, be handed a net tax at birth in excess of $300,000. To view this number in a different light, compound it to age 20 at the 5 percent real discount. The resulting amount exceeds $800,000 and represents the effective lifetime net tax bill that would be handed to future Japanese upon entering the workforce.

In percentage terms, the Japanese imbalance is 169 percent in case A and 338 percent in case B. In other words, absent some other, quite dramatic fiscal adjustment, future Japanese face lifetime net tax rates that are 2.7 to 4.4 times the lifetime net tax rates facing current newborn Japanese. These findings, which are detailed in Chapter 19, were developed in a year-long Bank of Japan study by Yukinobu Kitamura and Hiroshi Yoshida of the Bank of Japan working in collaboration with Noriyuki Takayama, one of Japan's leading academic economists. They are remarkable in light of the relatively high level of generational accounts facing young and middle-aged Japanese and the relatively small (in absolute value) negative accounts of Japanese elderly. The explanation for Japan's particularly severe generational imbalance lies in its particularly rapid rate of aging.

Although Japan has the worst generational imbalance, the German, Italian, Dutch, and Brazilian imbalances are also grave. In these countries, the tax burden on future generations will have to rise by more than 75 percent under case A and by more than 100 percent under case B unless those now alive pay more or their governments spend less. Another five countries have severe imbalances: the United States, Norway, Portugal, Argentina, and Belgium. In these countries, the growth-adjusted fiscal burdens facing future generations are 50 to 75 percent larger than those facing current newborns.

Three countries—Australia, Denmark, and France—have substantial imbalances that leave their descendents facing 30 to 50 percent higher lifetime net tax rates. Canada appears to be essentially in generational balance. The remaining three countries—New Zealand, Thailand, and Sweden—have negative imbalances;[2] that is, their policies, if maintained, would leave future generations facing lower lifetime net tax rates than current newborns. The main reason is that in these countries the aging of the population is less rapid and

2. In contrast to the Swedish findings reported here, the latest generational accounting for Sweden by Lundvik, Lüth, and Raffelhüschen (1998) reports a very severe imbalance in Swedish generational policy. As of the time of publication of this volume, the precise explanation for the different findings had yet to be determined, although different assumptions concerning baseline fiscal policy appear to be very important.

Table 4.5   **Official Deficit and Debt as a Share of GDP, 1995**

Country	Deficit	Primary Deficit	Gross Debt	Net Debt
United States	2.0	−0.4	63.4	48.2
Japan	3.7	3.1	80.6	10.3
Germany	3.6	0.4	62.2	45.0
Italy	7.0	−3.1	124.7	110.2
Canada	4.1	−1.7	100.5	69.6
Thailand	−8.1[a]	n.a.	n.a.	n.a.
Australia	2.0	−0.2	43.4	28.2
Denmark	1.9	−1.5	76.9	46.6
Netherlands	4.1	−1.0	79.5	46.1
New Zealand	−3.2	−4.7	n.a.	n.a.
France	5.0	1.7	60.7	36.1
Norway	−3.3	−3.9	42.8	−23.4
Portugal	5.0	−0.8	68.4	n.a.
Sweden	7.7	5.2	80.3	32.9
Argentina	n.a.	n.a.	n.a.	n.a.
Belgium	4.1	−4.4	133.5	126.1
Brazil	13.3	n.a.	n.a.	n.a.

Source: Organization for Economic Cooperation and Development, unless otherwise indicated.

Notes: Deficits and debts are for general government (federal, state, local, and social security sectors) and are derived from national income accounts. Primary deficit is the official deficit minus interest on net debt. Net debt refers to gross liabilities (gross debt) less financial assets. Negative values indicate surpluses.

[a]From World Bank, *World Development Report 1997* (Washington, D.C, 1997), central government current deficit.

the government is currently following a strict course of fiscal consolidation. In these countries, intergenerational equity could be restored by reducing (somewhat) the tax burden on currently living generations.

Australia is another country whose recent policy measures have had a significant impact on its generational accounts. There, a compulsory savings scheme has been established that leads individuals to accumulate savings for retirement, while public pensions are steadily reduced; these measures increased the net taxes of current generations (as pension benefits of newborns were reduced) while net taxes of future generations declined. However, during the transition from the pay-as-you-go pension system to a privately funded system, current young Australians have to finance both the pensions of the currently retired generations and the accumulation of reserves for their own retirement; that is, they have to "pay twice."

4.5   Generational Accounting versus Deficit Accounting

It is interesting to compare generational accounting's assessment of fiscal sustainability with that suggested by official deficits and debts. Table 4.5 records, as a share of GDP, government deficits, primary deficits (taxes minus noninterest expenditures), levels of gross debt (gross government liabilities), and levels of net debt (gross government liabilities minus the government's financial assets) for our 17 countries. Consider Japan and Norway: Although Japan has the largest and Norway one of the largest generational imbalances, the two countries have the lowest ratios of net debt to GDP. Indeed, Norway's net debt is negative; the Norwegian government has positive net wealth. If one considers gross rather than net debt, Japan's and Norway's debt levels are still relatively modest. And if one considers deficits, one finds that the Japanese deficit is lower than that of Canada and that Norway is running a surplus. The correlation of generational imbalance with the primary deficit is no better. Norway's primary deficit is negative, and Japan's is lower than Sweden's, even though the Swedes have a negative generational imbalance.

The complete lack of any consistent relationship between nations' generational imbalances and their deficit or debt positions is not surprising given that from a theoretical perspective, there is no intrinsic connection between the two measures. Nonetheless, this finding should be of interest to those who believe deficit or debt levels represent useful criteria for assessing a country's fiscal responsibility. Two institutions that immediately come to mind in this regard are the International Monetary Fund (IMF) and the European Union. The IMF routinely uses budget deficit targets in determining structural adjustment policies for its client countries. And the European Union has adopted a deficit target as the principal requirement for membership in its proposed single-currency monetary union.

In considering the desirability and sustainability of European monetary union, it is worth bearing the following in mind: imposing higher net taxes on current generations by printing money (and exacting a seigniorage tax) is one of the easiest "solutions" to the major generational imbalances facing the various countries who are now likely to join the union. Because their imbalances are quite different, each country will wish to turn on the printing presses to a different degree. This may place significant stress on the union and lead to its eventual collapse. The other and better solution is, however, that countries address the roots of the problems by implementing major fiscal reforms, particularly in old-age pension systems.

4.6   Sensitivity of the Results

Estimates of generational accounts are based on the assumption that except for demographic influences, no other fundamental changes in the economy occur. But with a given working-age population, labor supply could increase if (female) labor participation increases, and this would raise labor tax revenues and reduce transfers. Furthermore, if private saving increases (which may result from a shift toward privately funded pension systems), receipts from capital income taxes would rise. As illustrated for the Netherlands (chap. 14), the combined effects of increasing the labor participation rate of women and increasing aggregate savings could significantly raise the future tax base and reduce the generational imbalance. Also, if population aging were slower than assumed here (e.g., if fertility rates were higher or if there were more immigration of young workers), the imbalance against future generations would be reduced. This would result from a larger number of taxpayers available to help finance government expenditures. The impact of the various demographic assumptions on generational accounts is illustrated in some country chapters (e.g., the assumption of fertility rates in chap. 13, on Italy, and the assumption of immigration in chap. 6, on Australia).

The results are also sensitive to assumptions about productivity growth and the discount rate. For a given discount rate, higher productivity growth increases the absolute amounts of net tax payments of both existing and future generations. For a given productivity growth rate, a higher discount rate reduces these present value amounts. Table 4.6 shows case A generational imbalances for three discount rate assumptions (3, 5, and 7 percent) and three productivity growth assumptions (1, 1.5, and 2 percent). Table 4.7 does the same for case B.

It is clear from the two tables that the absolute sizes of the accounts of current newborns as well as future generations are fairly sensitive, particularly to the choice of discount rates. On the other hand, the values of both variables move in the same direction in response to changes in the rates of productivity growth and interest. Consequently, the absolute generational imbalance in many countries is rather invariant to the choice of these rates. In Japan, for example, the absolute case A imbalance across the nine combinations of growth and discount rates ranges from $220,900 to $294,500. Or take Thailand, whose absolute case A imbalance ranges from −$6,400 to −$8,400.

Even in countries where the absolute imbalance is fairly sensitive to the choice of growth and discount rates, the basic message of generational accounting may be the same. France is a good example. Its absolute imbalance ranges from $33,600 to $167,800. But the $33,600 imbalance, arising from the assumption of a 7 percent discount rate and a 1 percent growth rate, represents a percentage imbalance of 49 percent, and the $167,800 imbalance represents a percentage imbalance of 71 percent; hence, both sets of parameters indicate that future Frenchmen and Frenchwomen face much higher rates of lifetime net taxation than do current newborns assuming current newborns face, over their lifetimes, the panoply of French taxes and transfers now in existence.

Another message emerging from tables 4.6 and 4.7 is that the sensitivity of the generational accounts to growth and interest rate assumptions depends on the country in question. Norway makes this clear. The Norwegian absolute imbalance switches from a small negative to a large positive value depending on parameter values. For Norway the choice of the discount rate is particularly critical. With the base-case 1.5 percent growth rate and 5 percent discount rate, Norway has a sizable generational imbalance. But with a 7 percent discount rate and a 1.5 labor productivity growth rate, Norway is roughly in generational balance.

Table 4.6   Generational Accounts: Sensitivity to Growth and Discount Rates, Case A (thousands of 1995 U.S. dollars)

Country	g = 1			g = 1.5			g = 2		
	r = 3	r = 5	r = 7	r = 3	r = 5	r = 7	r = 3	r = 5	r = 7
United States									
Newborn generation	149.1	86.7	48.9	147.4	86.3	48.8	145.6	85.9	48.7
Future generations	243.7	146.7	93.9	203.5	130.4	86.2	163.6	114.2	78.5
Absolute imbalance	94.6	60.1	45.0	56.0	44.1	37.4	18.0	28.3	29.8
Japan									
Newborn generation	242.1	120.1	62.4	291.0	143.4	73.8	349.8	171.4	87.4
Future generations	510.6	356.5	283.3	571.5	386.2	297.6	644.3	421.6	314.9
Absolute imbalance	268.5	236.4	220.9	280.5	242.8	223.8	294.5	250.2	227.5
Germany									
Newborn generation	255.7	140.2	72.6	292.3	165.0	86.7	329.1	193.1	103.0
Future generations	431.8	284.3	196.7	472.8	316.8	214.6	504.3	353.3	235.8
Absolute imbalance	176.1	144.1	124.1	180.5	151.8	127.9	175.2	160.2	132.8
Italy									
Newborn generation	157.2	101.1	62.5	171.6	114.2	70.9	183.2	128.4	80.5
Future generations	312.6	249.5	212.8	331.5	264.8	221.0	347.6	282.1	230.9
Absolute imbalance	155.4	148.4	150.3	159.9	150.6	150.1	164.4	153.7	150.4
Canada									
Newborn generation	190.1	93.1	44.8	231.9	113.8	54.8	281.8	138.5	66.9
Future generations	198.3	94.2	44.3	232.8	114.0	49.6	271.9	129.6	57.2
Absolute imbalance	8.2	1.1	-0.5	0.9	0.2	-5.2	-9.9	8.9	-9.7
Thailand									
Newborn generation	14.1	7.0	3.9	17.2	8.3	4.5	21.1	9.9	5.3
Future generations	6.1	-0.1	-2.5	8.9	1.0	-2.0	12.6	2.4	-1.5
Absolute imbalance	-8.0	-7.1	-6.4	-8.3	-7.3	-6.5	-8.4	-7.6	-6.8

Australia									
Newborn generation	138	66	32	167	80	39	203	96	47
Future generations	187	91	58	247	105	63	362	124	70
Absolute imbalance	49	25	26	80	25	24	159	28	23
Denmark									
Newborn generation	156	66	17	183	84	27	211	105	38
Future generations	196	103	49	224	124	61	251	147	75
Absolute imbalance	40	37	32	41	40	34	40	42	37
Netherlands									
Newborn generation	191	92	41	222	110	50	257	131	61
Future generations	299	170	111	344	194	122	396	222	136
Absolute imbalance	108	78	70	122	84	72	139	91	75
New Zealand									
Newborn generation	106.7	57.3	30.2	106.7	57.3	30.2	106.7	57.3	30.2
Future generations	130.2	62.9	32.1	100.4	55.3	29.4	70.3	55.3	26.7
Absolute imbalance	23.5	5.6	1.9	-6.3	-2	-0.8	-36.4	-2	-3.5
France									
Newborn generation	205.1	134.4	71.7	222.1	151.5	82.5	236.8	169.9	94.5
Future generations	350.6	202.4	105.3	377.8	222.8	116.9	404.6	245.5	130.0
Absolute imbalance	145.5	67.9	33.6	155.7	71.3	34.4	167.8	75.6	35.5
Norway									
Newborn generation	138.3	95.2	61.9	145.2	106.3	69.1	145.1	117.8	77.4
Future generations	270.1	128.8	40.4	327.8	173.5	71.7	381.3	220.3	104.9
Absolute imbalance	131.8	33.6	-21.5	182.6	67.2	2.6	236.2	102.5	27.5
Portugal									
Newborn generation	86.9	54.9	35.5	97.2	61.8	39.6	107.9	69.6	44.3
Future generations	123.7	92.2	76.6	134.1	98.7	79.4	44.8	106.3	83.1
Absolute imbalance	36.8	37.4	41.1	36.8	36.9	39.8	36.9	36.7	38.8

(*continued*)

Table 4.6   (continued)

Country	g = 1			g = 1.5			g = 2		
	r = 3	r = 5	r = 7	r = 3	r = 5	r = 7	r = 3	r = 5	r = 7
Sweden									
Newborn generation	292.4	163.2	97.5	333.0	184.3	108.3	378.8	208.8	120.7
Future generations	268.3	119.2	40.8	309.6	143.5	53.2	351.4	171.2	67.5
Absolute imbalance	−24.1	−44.0	−56.7	−23.4	−40.9	−55.1	−27.3	−37.5	−53.2
Argentina									
Newborn generation	28.0	20.6	13.5	28.3	22.7	15.1	26.6	24.9	16.9
Future generations	50.1	32.3	22.7	55.5	36.1	24.6	60.8	40.4	26.8
Absolute imbalance	22.1	11.7	9.3	27.2	13.4	9.5	34.1	15.5	10.0
Belgium									
Newborn generation	243.9	138.9	73.9	272.5	162.4	87.5	295.8	188.6	103.2
Future generations	369.7	229.4	158.6	415.2	258.8	171.4	462.1	292.8	188.0
Absolute imbalance	125.8	90.5	84.7	142.7	96.4	83.9	166.3	104.2	84.7
Brazil									
Newborn generation	21	12	7	23	14	8	24	17	9
Future generations	41	23	14	47	27	16	54	31	18
Absolute imbalance	20	11	7	24	13	8	30	14	9

Note: g is productivity growth (percent); r is discount rate (percent).

Table 4.7   Generational Accounts: Sensitivity to Growth and Discount Rates, Case B (thousands of 1995 U.S. dollars)

Country	g = 1			g = 1.5			g = 2		
	r = 3	r = 5	r = 7	r = 3	r = 5	r = 7	r = 3	r = 5	r = 7
United States									
Newborn generation	75.8	28.9	2.6	74.1	28.5	2.5	72.3	28.1	2.4
Future generations	160.3	82.6	43.1	134.9	73.9	39.8	109.6	65.2	36.4
Absolute imbalance	84.5	53.7	40.5	60.7	45.3	37.2	37.3	37.1	34.0
Japan									
Newborn generation	159.7	53.3	7.4	203.8	73.0	16.0	257.5	97.1	26.7
Future generations	431.3	293.6	232.5	487.2	319.4	243.9	554.7	350.9	258.1
Absolute imbalance	271.6	240.3	225.1	283.4	246.4	227.9	297.2	253.8	231.4
Germany									
Newborn generation	174.1	76.4	21.8	205.1	97.1	32.8	236	120.6	45.9
Future generations	351.5	220.2	144.4	389.6	248.8	159.8	423	281.1	178
Absolute imbalance	177.4	143.8	122.6	184.5	151.7	127.0	187	160.5	132.1
Italy									
Newborn generation	99.2	54.3	24.2	110.3	64.8	30.6	118.3	76.3	38.0
Future generations	249.2	197.5	169.5	264.4	209.9	175.4	276.5	224.1	182.9
Absolute imbalance	150.0	143.2	145.3	154.1	145.1	144.8	158.2	147.8	144.9
Canada									
Newborn generation	118.6	39.7	3.8	154.6	56.3	11.0	107.9	76.8	19.9
Future generations	130.7	47.1	12.2	158.0	58.0	14.1	191.5	72.9	17.9
Absolute imbalance	12.1	7.4	8.4	19.3	1.7	3.1	-6.4	3.9	-2.0
Thailand									
Newborn generation	11.2	4.7	2.0	14.1	5.9	2.5	17.8	7.3	3.2
Future generations	3.2	-2.4	-4.3	5.8	-1.5	-4.0	9.3	-0.3	-3.6
Absolute imbalance	-8.1	-7.1	-6.3	-8.3	-7.4	-6.5	-8.5	-7.6	-6.8

(continued)

Table 4.7 (continued)

Country	g = 1			g = 1.5			g = 2		
	r = 3	r = 5	r = 7	r = 3	r = 5	r = 7	r = 3	r = 5	r = 7
Australia									
Newborn generation	101	38	10	127	50	16	158	64	22
Future generations	143	62	36	193	73	39	289	89	44
Absolute imbalance	42	24	26	66	23	23	131	25	22
Denmark									
Newborn generation	29	−29	−56	46	−18	−51	61	−5	−46
Future generations	74	13	−20	93	26	−13	110	42	−4
Absolute imbalance	45	42	36	47	44	38	49	47	42
Netherlands									
Newborn generation	115	34	4	143	49	3	173	67	12
Future generations	226	117	70	267	137	79	313	161	90
Absolute imbalance	111	83	66	124	88	76	140	94	78
New Zealand									
Newborn generation	54.1	18.0	−0.1	54.1	18.0	−0.1	54.1	18.0	−0.1
Future generations	65.1	18.2	−1.1	50.2	16.0	−1.0	35.2	13.8	−0.9
Absolute imbalance	11.0	0.2	−1.0	−3.9	−2.0	−0.9	−18.9	−4.2	−0.8
France									
Newborn generation	125.3	66.6	15.9	140.3	82.2	25.6	153.1	99.0	36.5
Future generations	264.9	147.5	187.2	285.1	161.5	99.3	304.4	178.5	94.2
Absolute imbalance	139.6	80.9	171.3	144.8	79.2	73.7	151.4	79.5	57.7

Norway									
Newborn generation	9	−3	−14	5	1	−11	−6	5	−9
Future generations	126	22	−41	170	57	−16	212	95	11
Absolute imbalance	117	25	27	165	56	−5	218	90	20
Portugal									
Newborn generation	64.5	37.9	22.4	73.1	43.5	25.6	82.0	50.0	29.4
Future generations	93.9	68.0	56.7	102.7	73.2	58.5	111.8	79.4	61.0
Absolute imbalance	29.4	30.2	34.2	29.7	29.7	32.8	29.8	29.4	31.6
Sweden									
Newborn generation	214.9	103.2	49.7	251.8	121.8	58.8	293.5	143.5	69.4
Future generations	191.2	62.3	−1.0	229.3	83.8	9.4	268.0	108.8	21.7
Absolute imbalance	−23.7	−40.9	−50.7	−22.5	−38.0	−49.3	−25.5	−34.7	−47.6
Argentina									
Newborn generation	17	12	7	17	14	8	14	15	10
Future generations	35	21	14	39	24	16	43	28	17
Absolute imbalance	18	9	7	22	10	8	29	13	7
Belgium									
Newborn generation	170.2	80.9	27.5	193.9	100.8	38.4	212.0	123.1	51.2
Future generations	286.4	162.4	104.7	327.5	187.8	114.4	370.2	217.7	127.6
Absolute imbalance	116.3	81.5	77.2	133.6	87.0	76.0	158.2	94.6	76.4
Brazil									
Newborn generation	16	9	4	17	10	5	18	12	6
Future generations	35	19	11	41	22	12	47	26	14
Absolute imbalance	19	10	7	24	12	7	29	14	8

Note: g is productivity growth (percent); r is discount rate (percent).

Table 4.8   Sources of Generational Imbalance (percentage imbalance)

Country	Base Case		No Demographic Change		Zero Debt	
	A	B	A	B	A	B
United States	51.1	159.0	−2.9	21.6	30.5	96.5
Japan	169.3	337.8	42.2	77.2	154.5	308.6
Germany	92.0	156.1	−4.7	−7.6	47.5	80.6
Italy	131.8	223.8	12.9	18.0	60.2	97.6
Canada	0.0	3.1	−46.7	−57.8	−41.0	−51.6
Thailand	−88.0	−125.4	−143.4	−174.6	−190.4	−228.8
Australia	32.0	48.6	20.0	62.4	18.0	25.1
Denmark	46.9	a	−13.6	−168.4	12.7	b
Netherlands	76.0	177.0	7.0	14.0	42.0	100.0
New Zealand	−3.4	−10.8	−5.0	−5.2	−15.9	−15.9
France	47.1	96.3	4.0	6.0	20.0	39.0
Norway	61.0	4,378.6	−12.1	−91.8	69.3	5,000.2
Portugal	48.7	68.2	17.5	24.9	16.2	22.0
Sweden	−22.2	−31.2	−51.2	−66.9	−31.0	−44.6
Argentina	58.6	74.8	−0.8	1.7	37.9	41.0
Belgium	58.0	106.8	29.3	63.2	−92.0	−217.6
Brazil	88.8	116.7	41.8	64.1	76.2	99.0

Note: A: Educational expenditure treated as government consumption. B: Educational expenditure treated as government transfers and distributed by age groups.

[a]Percentage imbalance is not defined. Newborns' account is −$17,800 and future generations' account is $26,400.

[b]Percentage imbalance is not defined. Newborns' account is −$17,800 and future generations' account is −$2,300.

4.7   Sources of Generational Imbalances

Table 4.8 asks how much of the imbalance in generational policy in the various countries can be traced to the country's demographic transition and how much can be traced to its official net debt. The demographics experiment considers how large the generational imbalance would be were each country to experience no change whatsoever over time in the size or age-sex composition of its population. The zero-debt experiment sets official net debt to zero and recalculates the generational imbalance.

Demographics make a very substantial difference to the imbalance in almost all of the countries. The reason is that the countries are aging and the elderly are net beneficiaries of the governments' tax-transfer systems. For instance, Argentina's imbalance is essentially wiped out if there is no change in demographics. The same is true for Germany, the United States, Denmark, Italy, the Netherlands, France, and Norway. In the case of Japan, zero demographic change would eliminate about three-quarters of the case A imbalance and about four-fifths of the case B imbalance.

Eliminating the government official net debt has a range of impacts on generational imbalances. Eliminating official debt would have a minor impact on the Japanese imbalance. The same goes for the imbalances in Norway and Brazil. For the United States, the absence of net debt would eliminate only about one-third of the outstanding imbalance. About half of the imbalance would be eliminated in Germany, Argentina, France, Australia, and Italy. The majority, then, of the 17 countries would still face very significant generational imbalances even were there no official net debt. This provides yet more evidence that official deficit and debt figures fall far short of being sufficient statistics for generational policy.

4.8   Restoring Generational Balance?

Apart from the moral dimension of restoring generational balance, doing so represents an economic imperative. Countries that take no action to achieve generational balance will find their generational imbalances worsening over time. Why? Because failure to act in the short run means permitting each new generation that is born in the short run to experience the status quo policy and thus pay the same lifetime net taxes as those now alive. In terms of generational accounting, this confronts generations born in the more distant future with an even larger lifetime net tax rate. But there is a limit—100 percent—to the rate of lifetime net taxation; that is, governments cannot extract more from people in net taxes than they earn. Moreover, the marginal tax rates that would be associated with trying to collect anything close to a 100 percent average net tax would eliminate people's interest in working and, in the process, the government's net tax base.

Eliminating generational imbalances can be done in only two ways. The government can either force those now alive to pay higher net taxes by raising their taxes or by cutting their transfer payments or it can reduce the time path of its spending. Table 4.9 explores each of these alternatives. It considers (1) immediately and permanently reducing the time path of government spending by a fixed percentage, (2) immediately and permanently cutting all government transfers by a fixed percentage, (3) immediately and permanently raising all taxes by a fixed percentage, and (4) immediately and permanently raising all income taxes by a fixed percentage. These percentages are determined such that the residual growth-adjusted net tax bill facing future generations is the same as that facing newborns. Thus each of these policy alternatives achieves generational balance on its own. Obviously, combinations of the policy instruments could achieve the same end, and if the instruments were combined, less would be required of any single policy instrument.

In considering the magnitude of these alternative immediate fiscal adjustments, it is important to bear in mind that larger adjustments are needed if the policies under consideration are not enacted immediately. It is also important to note that the different types of adjustments would affect different currently living generations differently. For example, an income tax hike would hurt current workers more than would a cut in transfer payments.

Table 4.9   Alternative Ways to Achieve Generational Balance

Country	Cut in Government Purchases A	B	Cut in Government Transfers A	B	Increase in All Taxes A	B	Increase in Income Tax A	B
United States	18.7	27.0	19.8	20.3	10.5	10.8	23.8	24.4
Japan	26.0	29.5	28.6	25.3	15.5	15.5	53.6	53.6
Germany	21.1	25.9	17.6	14.1	9.5	9.5	29.5	29.5
Italy	52.7	87.9	41.0	40.0	66.7	61.4	198.4	188.8
Canada	0.0	0.1	0.0	0.1	0.0	0.1	0.0	0.2
Thailand	−38.1	−47.7	−185.1	−114.2	−25.0	−25.0	−81.7	−81.8
Australia	8.8	10.2	12.1	9.1	5.1	4.8	8.5	8.1
Denmark	9.9	29.0	4.7	4.5	3.4	4.0	5.8	6.7
Netherlands	21.0	28.7	21.4	22.3	8.5	8.9	14.9	15.6
New Zealand	−1.0	−1.6	−0.8	−0.6	−0.4	−0.4	−0.8	−0.8
France	17.2	22.2	11.5	9.8	7.1	6.9	66.0	64.0
Norway	11.5	9.9	9.4	8.1	7.4	6.3	11.3	9.7
Portugal	7.6	9.8	9.6	7.5	4.2	4.2	13.3	13.3
Sweden	−7.6	−8.7	−7.7	−6.0	−3.4	−3.1	−9.3	−8.6
Argentina	24.6	29.1	16.8	11.0	10.7	8.4	97.1	75.7
Belgium	11.2	12.4	6.0	4.6	3.7	3.1	11.7	10.0
Brazil	23.8	26.2	21.3	17.9	12.4	11.7	78.9	74.0

Note: A: Educational expenditure treated as government consumption. B: Educational expenditure treated as government transfers and distributed by age groups.

Restoring the balance between newborns and future generations would require immediate and permanent cuts in government purchases of more than one-half in Italy, of about one-quarter in Japan, Argentina, and Brazil, and of about one-fifth in the United States, Germany, the Netherlands, and France. These are very sizable adjustments. Their enactment would materially alter the official deficits now being reported by these countries. In the United States, the government sector (federal, state, and local) deficit would fall by roughly $200 billion. The U.S. federal surplus is now small. Thus achieving generational balance in the United States requires immediately running what would be, from a historical perspective, huge official surpluses.

Not all countries would need to cut spending to achieve generational balance. Thailand, Sweden, and New Zealand need to raise government spending—by about 40 percent, 8 percent, and 1 percent, respectively—since their baseline generational imbalances are negative.[3] Another point is that the spend-

3. Lundvik, Lüth, and Raffelhüschen's (1998) figures for Sweden, corresponding to table 4.9 above, are 34.6, 48.8, 21.2, 18.0, 14.8, 14.8, 40.3, and 40.3. These figures tell a dramatically different story than those reported in this study. Sartor's (1998) update of Italy's generational accounts, based on Italy's recent dramatic pension reform, shows a much smaller generational imbalance in Italy. For example, the case B 61.4 percent requisite increase in all taxes is now less than 10 percent.

ing adjustment needed to achieve balance is quite similar across alternatives A and B; that is, how one allocates educational expenditures does not matter much to the adjustments needed to achieve generational balance.

An alternative to cutting government spending is cutting all transfer payments be they government-provided health care, unemployment benefits, social security pensions, or welfare benefits.[4] Achieving generational balance in this way means transfer cuts of roughly two-fifths in Italy, one-quarter in Japan, and one-fifth in the United States, the Netherlands, and Brazil. For other countries, the requisite cut is smaller. Germany's case A required transfer cut is 17.6 percent. The corresponding U.S. cut is 19.8 percent. Germany's cut is smaller because transfer payments relative to GDP are somewhat larger in Germany than they are in the United States. Thailand's current transfers are so small relative to GDP that they would need to be more than doubled to achieve generational balance.

Restoring generational balance in Italy through higher taxes translates into more than a 60 percent across-the-board tax hike. The corresponding general tax hike needed for generational balance in the United States, Japan, Germany, the Netherlands, Brazil, and Argentina ranges from 9 to 16 percent. In France and Norway, a roughly 7 percent hike is needed. Portugal, Australia, Denmark, Canada, and Belgium require about a 2 to 5 percent hike. In Thailand, New Zealand, and Sweden across-the-board tax cuts of about 25 percent, 0.4 percent, and 3 percent, respectively, would produce generational balance.

The corresponding income tax hikes needed to achieve generational balance have a much greater range across countries because the ratio of income taxes to GDP varies more across countries than does the ratio of total taxes to GDP. In Italy, which has a relatively small ratio of income tax to GDP, almost a tripling of the income tax rate would be needed to achieve generational balance. This assumes no erosion in the income tax base. If one were to take such erosion into account, it might well be the case that achieving generational balance in Italy solely through a hike in the income tax is infeasible.

Argentina, Brazil, and France would also need to raise their income taxes dramatically to bring their accounts into balance. The requisite income tax hikes for these countries range from 64 to 97 percent. Japan is not far behind. It would need over a 50 percent income tax hike. The corresponding U.S. and German income tax hikes range from 24 to 30 percent. These tax increases are modest compared to what would be needed in Italy, but they would be viewed as enormously painful by current generations of Americans and Germans. Indeed, the focus of U.S. politicians is now on cutting, not raising, federal income taxes. For other countries—Belgium, Portugal, Norway, Australia, Denmark, and Canada—a more modest income tax hike would do the trick. At the other end of the imbalance spectrum is Thailand, which would have to cut its

---

4. In the case of social security pensions, the cuts might come in the form of raising early and normal retirement ages.

income taxes by 82 percent to achieve balance. Sweden could achieve balance with a 9 percent income tax cut, and New Zealand with a 1 percent cut.

4.9 Summary and Conclusion

Policymakers take official budget deficits and debts as their primary fiscal indicators. For example, European countries are currently aiming at budget deficits below 3 percent of GDP—the target for European monetary union membership—while others are aiming at balancing their budgets over the medium term. Such deficit reductions may succeed in stabilizing debt-to-GDP ratios in the near future, but they do not represent fiscally sustainable policies that will achieve generational balance—a situation in which today's and tomorrow's children pay, in net taxes, the same share of their lifetime labor incomes. In fact, by focusing on budget balance, rather than generational balance, many countries appear to be doing too little to achieve generational balance. This makes their long-term fiscal situations worse. The reason is that the longer a country waits to adjust, the more painful the ultimate adjustment will be. And adjusting too little in the short run is a form of waiting too long to adjust.

The international generational accounts presented here are quite shocking. The world's leading industrial powers—the United States, Japan, and Germany—all have severe imbalances in their generational policies. Unless currently living members of these countries pay more in net taxes or unless these countries dramatically cut their purchases of goods and services, future Americans, Japanese, and Germans will face dramatically higher rates of lifetime net taxation. Leaving current Americans untouched and maintaining the current projected time path of government purchases will leave future Americans collectively facing roughly 50 percent higher net tax rates over their lifetimes than those confronting a newborn American based on current U.S. tax-transfer policy. For future Germans, the imbalance, if not rectified, means they will face lifetime net tax rates that are roughly twice as high as those now in place. And for future Japanese, policy inaction means lifetime net tax rates that are more than 2.5 times as high as current values.

These three countries are not alone in running imbalanced generational policies. Of the 17 countries examined here, five—Japan, Italy, Germany, the Netherlands, and Brazil—have extreme imbalances. Another five—the United States, Norway, Portugal, Argentina, and Belgium—have severe imbalances. Three countries—Australia, Denmark, and France—have substantial imbalances. Canada appears to be essentially in generational balance. The remaining three countries—New Zealand, Thailand, and Sweden have negative imbalances; that is, their policies, if maintained, would leave future generations facing lower lifetime net tax rates than current newborns.[5]

There are a range of policy options that can be used to restore fiscal sus-

---

5. Again, the Swedish findings are strongly contradicted by Lundvik, Lüth, and Raffelhüschen (1998).

tainability and generational equity. But for most of the 17 countries, their medicine, no matter how they take it, will be very unpleasant. Since conditions differ substantially across the various countries, the best combination of fiscal responses will be country specific. Although each country may respond differently, those with sizable generational imbalances all need to act immediately. Generational accounting's fundamental message is that who pays the government's bills is a zero-sum game. The less those now alive pay, the larger the amounts their descendants will pay. Delay not only makes the situation worse, it also leaves everyone in society uncertain about how long-term fiscal problems will ultimately be resolved.

References

Cutler, David M., James M. Poterba, Louise M. Sheiner, and Lawrence H. Summers. 1990. An ageing society: Opportunity or challenge? *Brookings Papers on Economic Activity,* no. 1:1–73.

Habakkuk, H. J. 1962. *American and British technology in the nineteenth century.* Cambridge: Cambridge University Press.

Lundvik, Petter, Erik Lüth, and Bernd Raffelhüschen. 1998. The Swedish welfare state on trial. Freiburg University. Mimeograph.

Sartor, Nicola. 1998. The long-run effects of the Italian pension reforms. Università degli studi di Verona. Mimeograph, August.

Simon, J. L. 1981. *The ultimate resource.* Princeton, N.J.: Princeton University Press.

Wattenberg, B. J. 1987. *The birth dearth.* New York: Pharos.

5   Argentina's Generational Accounts: Is the Convertibility Plan's Fiscal Policy Sustainable?

Marcelo F. Altamiranda

5.1   Introduction

In this chapter a set of generational accounts is constructed for Argentina. Subsequently, the resulting generational accounting framework is used to identify policies to achieve intertemporal government budget balance, the fiscal role played by the country's recent privatization program, and the fiscal impact of Argentina's recent social security reform.[1]

Argentina's generational accounts indicate a huge intertemporal imbalance that is robust to reasonable variation in assumptions and implies that the nation's current fiscal policy put forward under the convertibility plan is unsustainable. Correcting this imbalance will require substantial cuts in government consumption and pension payments—cuts that are far beyond anything currently being debated.

The analysis of the generational accounting effects of the social security reform concludes that, most likely, the crisis in Argentina's long-term fiscal finances will not be solved solely by this reform. This is due to the fact that the social security reform constituted, to a large extent, simply a reclassification of government liabilities in which implicit government IOUs were made explicit; that is, the reform did not fundamentally reduce the government's long-term expenditure commitments.

Further, this chapter's generational accounting shows that the manner in which Argentine privatization receipts were spent dissipated a large amount of

Marcelo F. Altamiranda is Financial Manager for the AMCAM region at Philip Morris International, Inc.

The author thanks Laurence Kotlikoff for his helpful comments and constant support. He also thanks Alan Auerbach and Jan Walliser for their time, comments, and suggestions.

1. A more detailed study can be found in Altamiranda (1997).

government net wealth and has significantly contributed to the country's long-term generational imbalance.

5.2 Argentine Economic Policy

The current administration of President Menem took office on 9 July 1989, after the disastrous finale of the previous government of President Alfonsín. Alfonsín's electoral results, as well as his resignation, were intimately associated with the economic situation.

Argentina's economy suffered in 1989 its first hyperinflation caused by the lack of sustainable fiscal and monetary policies. In fact, we can say that Alfonsín's administration consistently failed to control public finances and trusted, instead, in heterodox policies. These policies produced, with low political costs, short-lived periods of low inflation. However, once economic agents learned from past errors these periods became shorter and finally hyperinflation and chaos hit the economy.

The first attempts of the present government to manage the fiscal situation were also unsuccessful (see table 5.1). As a result, the economy again got out of hand and the country was bashed by a second hyperinflation in 1990 (see table 5.2).

Finally, during 1991 the current—convertibility—stabilization plan, put forward by Domingo Cavallo as economy minister, was able to stabilize inflation. We turn now to a more detailed description of this plan and of its key fiscal policy tools.

5.2.1 The Convertibility Plan

The economic plan implemented in March 1991 was based on a law that established the convertibility of the austral at a rate of 10,000 australes per U.S. dollar and required full international reserve backing of the monetary base.[2] It is important to remark that the implication of this "full backing" requirement is that, once satisfied, the public sector must produce the necessary funds to meet total services and repayment of the internal debt, as well as of the external debt.[3]

The fiscal situation did not improve as fast as needed, but Cavallo was able to comply, on an "accounting basis," with the law by increasing the central

2. The central bank's holdings of U.S. dollar–denominated government bonds (BONEX) were included in the definition of reserves. This loose end, eventually, provided a way to create money to finance the public sector deficit. In September 1991, backing of the monetary base through these securities was limited to 10 percent of it.

3. These funds may come from overall operational balance (surplus), increases in the internal debt stock (which will affect its future servicing and repayment), and the sale of public sector assets. The external debt is net of external flows not associated with money creation like international reserve interest payments and loans from the International Monetary Fund (IMF), World Bank, or other multilateral organizations. Note also that the latter inflows affect future servicing and repayment of the external debt.

Table 5.1 **Consolidated Nonfinancial Public Sector Accounts 1990–94**
(percent of GDP)

	1990	1991	1992	1993	1994[a]
Revenues	16.5	18.8	21.0	21.6	21.3
Federal government and enterprises[b]	13.8	15.8	17.2	17.4	17.3
Provincial governments[c]	2.7	3.0	3.8	4.2	4.0
Expenditures	20.6	22.0	21.4	21.5	22.5
Federal government[d]	16.5	18.3	17.4	16.4	17.8
Provincial governments	4.1	3.7	4.0	5.1	4.7
Wages	6.6	7.4	7.8	8.1	8.1
Pensions	4.0	5.0	5.6	5.1	5.4
Interest[e]	3.3	2.6	1.5	1.1	1.2
Other current	3.9	4.7	4.6	4.9	4.9
Capital	2.8	2.3	1.9	2.3	2.9
Overall balance	−4.1	−3.2	−0.4	0.1	−1.2
Federal government	−2.7	−2.5	−0.2	0.9	−0.5
Provincial governments	−1.4	−0.7	−0.2	−0.8	−0.8
Privatization receipts in cash	0.4	1.2	0.8	1.5	0.3

Source: International Monetary Fund.

Notes: Prior to 1994, only the balance of various social security operations is included on the revenue side of the national nonfinancial public sector. Since 1994, revenue and expenditures of these operations are included separately. Similarly, prior to 1994, the National Employment Fund is excluded from the accounts, but it is included since 1994. From 1994 onward, contributions to private pension funds are excluded.

[a]1994 data for provincial governments are preliminary estimates.

[b]Includes enterprises' operating results; excludes privatization receipts.

[c]Own-revenue only, excludes revenue transfers received from federal government.

[d]Includes federal government transfers to provinces.

[e]Does not include capitalized interest on BOCONs (debt consolidation bonds).

Table 5.2 **Inflation: Consumer Prices, 1989–94 (percent)**

Month	1989	1990	1991	1992	1993	1994
January	8.92	79.20	7.70	3.04	0.83	0.10
February	9.59	61.57	26.99	2.15	0.73	−0.00
March	17.01	95.53	11.04	2.10	0.75	0.14
April	33.37	11.37	5.51	1.29	1.05	0.24
May	78.47	13.61	2.80	0.67	1.29	0.35
June	114.47	13.90	3.12	0.78	0.72	0.39
July	196.63	10.83	2.59	1.73	0.32	0.92
August	37.86	15.34	1.30	1.50	0.02	0.21
September	9.36	15.68	1.77	1.03	0.82	0.68
October	5.60	7.69	1.35	1.27	0.57	0.32
November	6.52	6.18	0.39	0.46	0.06	0.23
December	40.07	4.68	0.65	0.28	−0.01	0.22
Year	4,923.6	1,343.9	84.0	17.5	7.4	3.9

Source: Techint (various issues).

bank's BONEX[4] holdings. However, compared with past experience, the imbalance size was not out of control.[5] Furthermore, soon after the convertibility launching the government made clear its strategy of expanding and accelerating the privatization program to finance its deficit.[6]

The political scenario began to exert a strong influence on economic policy during 1992 because the government started to work toward presidential reelection. The reason was that the reelection implied as a prerequisite a constitutional amendment. Thus it created a climate of negotiation between Congress and the executive that slowed not only the approval of needed economic laws but also the degree of adjustment of public sector finances. However, public sector accounts improved as a result of the enhancement of tax collection, the revenues coming from the privatization of public enterprises, and the extremely low level of capital expenditure (see table 5.1).[7]

During 1992, the distribution of federal taxes between the federal government and the provinces was affected by a series of laws and decrees aimed at providing funds to increase social security payments.[8] The changes had more impact on the provinces that relied heavily on federal funds.[9] The issue was settled with an agreement signed in September that guaranteed for the provinces a minimum level of funds coming from federal taxes, established limits to provincial expenditure increases, and financed with federal government funds the increase in social security payments.

The public sector accounts showed better results in 1993 than in previous years thanks to improvement in the overall balance of the federal government and the increasing pace of the privatization program (see table 5.1). Furthermore, the tax reform continued to have beneficial effects on tax collection levels, as well as on tax composition; for example, the percentage of value-added tax (VAT) and income taxes in the total gross federal fiscal pressure went from 18.5 percent in 1989 to 48.2 percent in 1993.[10]

In 1994, the combination of public expenditure increase and revenue decline worsened public sector accounts (see table 5.1).[11]

---

4. These bonds have a 10-year maturity date with an 18-month grace period and are repayable in quarterly installments with an interest rate equal to the six-month London Interbank Offer Rate.

5. E.g., BONEX holdings amounted on average during the first six months of the plan to 0.5 percent of GDP, which in light of the recent history of the public sector budget deficit was certainly an achievement.

6. A new currency, the convertible peso, began to circulate on 1 January 1992, replacing the austral. The replacement rate was 1 convertible peso per 10,000 australes.

7. External debt service also contributed to this situation as it experienced relief due to real exchange rate appreciation and the downward trend of international interest rates.

8. The provinces reached the point of initiating legal action in the Supreme Court of Justice regarding these decrees. These modifications were regarded as politically motivated.

9. The tax distribution change also benefited the Buenos Aires province.

10. A major step in this direction was the federal fiscal pact signed between the federal government and the provinces, which, among other things, implied the end of the turnover tax, its future substitution by a sales tax, and the reduction of employers' social security contributions.

11. Moreover, the upward trend in international interest rates limited government action regarding external financing.

In July, a new social security system that would replace the previous public pay-as-you-go system became operational. The new Integrated Pension System included an optional private capitalized pension system and a public pay-as-you-go system.

To summarize, we could say that the current government, perhaps motivated by necessity rather than by ideology, thoroughly addressed the fiscal problem. Fiscal policy during this administration attacked several fronts, among others: tax revenues, especially tax simplification and evasion; social security reform; privatization of state-owned enterprises; rationalization of the central government's administration; and provincial finances.

5.2.2 The New Integrated Pension System

The new Integrated Pension System (IPS) was enacted by law 24.241 on 23 September 1993 after a long and clumsy legislative process initiated on 2 June 1992, when the executive sent to the lower house of Congress its proposal to reform the social security system.[12] Throughout this process, representatives introduced several changes into the original version and the executive was obliged to accept various political compromises in order to speed up its approval, weakening the effectiveness of the reform.

The provincial and municipal social security systems were not affected by the sanctioned reform, which was designed for the National Social Security System.[13] However, the provinces and the Municipality of Buenos Aires were invited to join the new system by the federal pact signed in August 1993.

The IPS became operational on 15 July 1994 with the following characteristics:[14]

I. Affiliates: Participation is compulsory for dependent[15] and self-employed workers.

II. Retirement age: This was increased to 65 years for men and 60 years for women.[16]

III. Revenues

A. Contributions:[17] The employee's contribution to social security was raised to 11 percent. The employer's contribution remained at 16 percent (see previous percentages in table 5.3). However, it was reduced

---

12. For a detailed treatment of this legislative process, see Isuani and San Martino (1993, 1995a, 1995b).

13. The National Social Security System provides about 86 percent of Argentina's total pension benefits, see Administración Nacional de la Seguridad Social (ANSeS 1994, 5).

14. We include here the changes introduced to law 24.241 by the Social Security Solidarity Law (24.463), enacted 23 March 1995.

15. Except for the armed and security forces.

16. The previous retirement age requirement (men, 60 years; women, 55 years) is to be increased gradually until the year 2001.

17. The law establishes a minimum and a maximum social security taxable base equivalent to 3 and 60 times the Average Compulsory Pension Contribution (ACPC; Aporte Medio Previsional Obligatorio). For details about the ACPC, see n. 22 below.

Table 5.3   **Contributions to the Social Security System, 1993 (percent)**

	Employee	Employer	Total
Social Security	10.0	16.0	26.0
Pensioners' Health Insurance	3.0	2.0	5.0
Active Workers' Health Insurance	3.0	6.0	9.0
Family Allowances	–	7.5	7.5
National Employment Fund	–	1.5	1.5
Total	16.0	33.0	49.0

Note: The contribution of self-employed workers was 26 percent calculated on an earnings scale for activity categories established by government. Also it was deposited monthly. Notice that this is equivalent to fixed-amount monthly payments.

afterward, following the federal pact, in a differentiated manner for some sectors and/or regions of the country.[18] Employees' contributions went to the systems chosen by them, while employers' contributions went in all cases to the public system.[19]

B. Earmarked taxes: These are entirely destined for the public system and consist of the following.
   1. Personal assets tax
   2. 11 percent of the VAT[20]
   3. 20 percent of the earnings tax net of the amount allocated to the operating expenses of the National Tax Office (Dirección General Impositiva)
   4. 15 percent of coparticipation funds[21]

C. Additional revenues: These are determined annually by Congress in the National Budget Law.

IV. Public pension system
A. Basic Universal Pension (BUP; Prestación Básica Universal): Every worker has a right to the BUP, but subject to a minimum eligibility requirement of 30 years of contributions. The BUP goes from 27.5 percent of the average covered wage for 30 years of contributions to a maximum of 31.6 percent for 45 years of contributions.[22]

18. It is estimated that the average value of the employer's contribution for 1995 was 14.4 percent.

19. The self-employed worker's contribution was raised to 27 percent, of which 16 percentage points went to the public system and the rest to the system chosen by the contributing worker.

20. Net of export drawback (tax rebates).

21. Coparticipation is the scheme for distributing federal taxes between the federal government and the provinces. In this case, to obtain the value to which to apply the 15 percent we need to deduct from the total amount of federal taxes that are shared the following items: VAT for social security, earnings tax for social security, and a further 16 percent of the earnings tax that is destined directly for the provinces.

22. The BUP is calculated as 2.5 times the ACPC. In turn, the ACPC is calculated twice a year (March and September) by dividing total contributions by the number of affiliates, but with a six-

B. Compensatory Pension (CP; Prestación Compensatoria): The CP compensates workers for past contributions to the old system. It is calculated as 1.5 percent of the average indexed covered salary of the past 10 years before retirement for every year of contribution to the old system, with a maximum of 35 years; that is, the highest CP can be 52.5 percent of said average. Originally, the maximum CP was established at one times the ACPC per year computed of contribution to the old system. However, after the promulgation of the Social Security Solidarity Law, the role of the ACPC fundamentally changed, and consequently, the same happened to the maximum and minimum pension limits based on it. This law stated in its third article: "The National Budget law will determine the minimum and maximum amount of the public system pensions." Although there is no practical experience yet with the new pension system, one could anticipate that the limits established by the original law (24.241) will hold inasmuch as they fall in the range defined by the minimum and maximum values that will be set by the National Budget Law.

C. Additional Public Pension (APP; Prestación Adicional por Permanencia):[23] The APP is for workers who choose to remain in, enter (in the case of new active workers), or return to the public system.[24] It is calculated as 0.85 percent per year of contribution to the new system using the same methodology as for the CP. This system also provides disability, survivorship, and advanced age pension benefits.

V. Public/private pension system: Workers who choose to join the private pension funds managed by Pension Fund Administrators (PFAs; Administradoras de Fondos de Jubilaciones y Pensiones) will receive the following.

A. BUP

B. CP (if applicable)

C. Ordinary Pension (OP; Jubilación Ordinaria): The OP functions as a defined-contribution scheme with individual capitalization accounts. It will be paid basically either in the form of a life annuity or as scheduled withdrawals based on the cumulative balance of each individual

---

month lag. Because the employee's contribution is 11 percent, one can say that the ACPC will amount to 11 percent of the average covered wage, and thus we get the mentioned 27.5 percent. Furthermore, since the BUP will increase by 1 percent for every additional year of contributions over 30 years up to a maximum of 45 years, the highest BUP possible is 31.6 percent of the average covered wage. However, note that as we comment below these maximum and minimum levels and their relationship with the ACPC were affected by the Social Security Solidarity Law.

23. A literal translation of this term would be "Additional Pension for Continuance." However, as new workers entering the labor force also have the choice of going to the public system and receiving this pension, we considered it more appropriate to call it the Additional Public Pension.

24. The last case refers to workers who, having chosen the private system, want to return to the public system. This option will be possible only, according to current legislation, until July 1996.

account. This system also provides disability and survivorship pensions in the form of defined-benefit payments, covered by group disability and term life insurance and paid in the same way as the OP.[25]

VI. Indexation: Public system pensions will be adjusted annually according to National Budget Law guidelines.

VII. National guarantee: This guarantee covers the public pension system up to the amount provided for its financing by the National Budget Law.

5.2.3   The Privatization Program

The privatization of the public enterprise sector was not only a major component of current government economic reforms but also a core subject of its fiscal policy. Traditionally, this sector had an important share of the cash-flow public deficit. Moreover, public enterprises had been a key tool for government policy related to subsidies, employment, and prices.[26]

By the end of the 1980s there were about 300 public enterprises, and 90 percent of them belonged to the nonfinancial sector. More than half of these firms were under federal jurisdiction and the rest under provincial and municipal jurisdiction.

The privatization program gained momentum in the 1990s, becoming ample in scope and expeditious in results. This process included sectors such as communications; commercial aviation; petrochemicals; oil production, refining, and distribution; electricity generation and distribution; natural gas transmission and distribution; defense; water and sewage; and others.[27]

Privatization took the form of either transfer of ownership or granting of concessions. Moreover, employees remaining on the payroll of the privatized firms were eligible to participate in the Employee Ownership Program (Programa de Propiedad Participada—PPP) by means of which they could receive a percentage of the shares of those companies.[28] Additionally, a fraction of the privatization revenues was earmarked for the social security system, and provincial governments received shares of the restructured oil company, as well as a portion of the privatization revenues.

25. Disability and survivorship benefits for workers who switch to the private system will be prorated with the public system in proportion to the number of years of contribution to each system.

26. Subsidies were explicit and implicit; i.e., they originated either in government transfers of fiscal funds to cover public enterprises' deficits or in their pricing policies. Employment policies included public enterprises' regular staffing as well as politically nominated managers at several levels and political favors in the form of employment positions. The prices of public enterprises had been a major tool of most stabilization efforts; in this context, they generally were the first to be frozen and the last to be freed.

27. See Instituto Nacional de Estadística y Censos (INDEC 1995b) for a detailed list. The communications, oil, electricity, and natural gas sectors constituted the majority of the privatization transactions.

28. The percentage earmarked for employees was in most cases 10 percent, except for those companies whose size was too large relative to the number of employees, e.g., the natural gas company and hydroelectric power stations.

Several factors motivated the privatization policy, and certainly, none of them alone suffices to explain it. Among these factors we should mention efficiency; revenues;[29] elimination of explicit and implicit subsidies; easing of the public debt restraint; signaling to the domestic and international communities the political will to reform, modernize, and deregulate the economy; social attitudes toward the "perennial" inefficiency of Argentinean public enterprises;[30] and politicians' time preferences, which favored the privatization revenue motive.[31]

In table 5.4 we present an overview of the privatization process. Total cash proceeds for the period 1990 to October 1994 are estimated at $18.7 billion (U.S. dollars). This figure is composed of $9.9 billion cash, $6.2 billion cash-equivalent public debt reduction, and $2.7 billion transferred liabilities. The face value of the public debt retired amounted to $14.9 billion, implying an average discount of 41 percent.[32]

Argentina's privatization program revenues—$18.7 billion—were concentrated mainly in four sectors: oil (32 percent), electricity (23 percent), telephones (19 percent), and natural gas (19 percent)—see table 5.4.

Table 5.5 shows the breakdown of capital ownership calculated on the basis of the net wealth value of the privatized companies. We observe that the federal and provincial governments still have stakes in those firms amounting to $5.1 billion, about 19 percent of the total public net wealth privatized. Notice also that concessions represented approximately 50 percent of said net wealth. Finally, almost a quarter of the total public net wealth privatized was in the form of shares sold in local and foreign markets.

5.3 The Data

5.3.1 Population Projections

We obtained two sets of projections, one from the Argentinean government, prepared by the National Statistics Office (INDEC), and the other from the

---

29. Including the increase in taxes paid under private ownership by the new firms created from the former state companies.

30. The government's inability to control public enterprises; public enterprises' policy of zero investment, even for maintenance—aimed at controlling the fiscal accounts; and widespread problems with public enterprise services were together the straw that broke the camel's back.

31. Politicians are in general deemed to have short-term planning horizons. By the 1990s, after the two hyperinflation episodes, politicians in Argentina might certainly have had shorter time horizons than elsewhere and, accordingly, stronger incentives to maximize immediate fiscal receipts. This might help to explain why, motivated by the short-run fiscal benefits, they favored the privatization program. See Castelar Pinheiro and Ross Schneider (1995) for a detailed presentation of this issue for Argentina, Brazil, Chile, and Mexico.

32. Note that total revenues considering the public debt retired at nominal value were $27.5 billion. In addition, the estimated total net wealth value of the privatized companies was $26.9 billion, calculating the ownership transfer as if it had been 100 percent.

Table 5.4   Privatization Program Results Overview, 1990 to October 1994 (millions of U.S. dollars)

Sector	Transfer Method	Cash	Cash Value Debt Securities	Transferred Liabilities	Total	Nominal Value Debt Securities	Total[a]	Net Wealth Value[b]
Telephones	Sale of shares	2,270.9	1,257.0	–	3,527.9	5,000.0	7,270.9	3,919.9
Airlines	Sale	260.0	483.0	–	743.0	1,610.0	1,870.0	891.6
Railroad	Concession	–	–	–	–	–	–	–
Electricity[c]	Sale/sale of shares	867.0	1,931.3	1,556.4	4,354.7	3,769.0	6,192.4	6,813.9
Ports	Concession/sale	9.8	–	–	9.8	–	9.8	9.8
Maritime transport	Sale	14.6	–	–	14.6	–	14.6	14.6
Roads[d]	Concession	–	–	–	–	–	–	–
Television and radio	Concession	–	–	–	–	–	–	–
Oil	Association/concession	2,060.2	–	–	2,060.2	–	2,060.2	3,220.3
National oil company	Sale of shares	3,040.0	884.0	–	3,924.0	1,271.1	4,311.1	6,710.8
Natural gas[e]	Sale/sale of shares	820.6	1,541.1	1,110.0	3,471.7	3,082.1	5,012.7	4,476.1
Water and sewage[f]	30-Year concession	–	–	–	–	–	–	–
Meat processing	Sale	1.9	–	–	1.9	–	1.9	1.9
Petrochemicals	Sale of shares	55.7	28.4	–	84.1	133.6	189.3	262.9
Shipbuilding	Sale	59.8	–	–	59.8	–	59.8	59.8
Steel	Sale	143.3	22.1	–	165.4	41.8	185.1	166.9
Electrical conductors	Sale	12.4	2.6	–	15.0	3.5	15.9	15.0
Other military plants	Sale	11.3	–	–	11.3	–	11.3	11.3
Financial sector	Sale	86.3	–	–	86.3	–	86.3	135.6
Buildings	Sale	202.5	–	–	202.5	–	202.5	202.5
Other	Sales	3.7	2.4	–	6.1	12.0	15.7	6.1
Total		9,920.0	6,151.8	2,666.4	18,738.2	14,923.1	27,509.5	26,919.0

Source: MEyOySP (1995a).

[a]Sum of cash; transferred liabilities and nominal value of debt securities.

[b]Total financial result calculated as if the transfer had been 100 percent.

[c]Includes sales of shares for $230.6 million.

[d]The concessionaire must undertake investments.

[e]Includes sales of shares for $520.6 million.

[f]Awarded to bidder that offered the larger discount over the existing residential tariff (26.9 percent).

Table 5.5   **Privatization Program: Capital Ownership in Privatized Companies, October 1994**

	Net Wealth Value	
Capital Ownership	U.S. dollars (million)	%
Concession[a]	13,345	49.6
National firms	6,117	22.7
Foreign firms	7,026	26.1
Not classified[b]	203	0.8
Shares	5,848	21.7
Local market	3,192	11.9
Foreign markets	2,656	9.9
Other	7,726	28.7
PPP (Employee Ownership Program)	1,745	6.5
Federal and provincial government	5,097	18.9
BOCON exchange	884	3.3
Total	26,919	100.0

Source: MEyOySP (1995a).
[a]Includes transferred liabilities.
[b]Includes the sale of 999 government buildings.

World Bank.[33] The government's projections extend until the year 2050 and are available by age range (from ages 0–4 to 80+) and sex every five years starting in 1995. The World Bank's projections extend until the year 2150 and are available yearly by single age (from age 0 to 75+) and sex starting in 1995.[34]

INDEC's data are based on more optimistic assumptions about population growth that include higher rates of fertility and life expectancy at birth and a positive net migration rate for part of the projected period. Thus the total population projected by INDEC for the year 2050 is 8.7 percent higher than the World Bank's projection.[35]

We chose to use the World Bank's projection for Argentina's generational accounts because it covers a longer period of time. However, we still had to extend it until the year 2200 and disaggregate single ages from 75 up to 90+. In order to undertake this task we assumed first that fertility and mortality rates as well as the age structure after 2150 equal those projected for that year. We assumed next that the 1991 age structure for single ages from 75 to 90+ will

33. See INDEC (1994, 1995a, 1995c) and Bos et al. (1994). Note that the last population census in Argentina took place in 1991.
34. I wish to thank Eduard Bos from the World Bank for providing special and updated demographic tabulations for Argentina and Alejandro Giusti and Alberto Karmona from INDEC for providing the Argentinean government's projections.
35. The differences for the male and female population projections are 8.6 and 8.9 percent.

Table 5.6   **Demographic Projections for Selected Age Ranges and Years**

Year	Age 0–17	Age 18–64	Age 65+	Total	Elderly	Child	Total
	Population (thousands)				Dependency Ratio (%)		
1991	11,737	17,985	2,893	32,616	16.1	65.3	81.3
1994	11,831	19,174	3,213	34,218	16.8	61.7	78.5
1995	11,959	19,381	3,247	34,589	16.8	61.7	78.5
2000	11,554	21,122	3,541	36,215	16.8	54.7	71.5
2005	11,293	22,726	3,827	37,839	16.8	49.7	66.5
2010	11,130	24,291	4,184	39,603	17.2	45.8	63.0
2015	11,137	25,562	4,658	41,361	18.2	43.6	61.8
2020	11,533	26,248	5,220	43,006	19.9	43.9	63.8
2025	11,587	27,095	5,793	44,478	21.4	42.8	64.1
2030	11,482	27,933	6,376	45,796	22.8	41.1	63.9
2035	11,334	28,718	6,961	47,009	24.2	39.5	63.7
2040	11,301	29,115	7,728	48,148	26.5	38.8	65.4
2045	11,369	28,985	8,851	49,202	30.5	39.2	69.8
2050	11,449	28,880	9,811	50,137	34.0	39.6	73.6
2055	11,462	28,778	10,692	50,934	37.2	39.8	77.0
2060	11,425	28,740	11,410	51,574	39.7	39.8	79.5
2065	11,387	29,009	11,576	51,975	39.9	39.3	79.2
2070	11,384	29,213	11,664	52,261	39.9	39.0	78.9
2075	11,407	29,227	11,846	52,478	40.5	39.0	79.6
2080	11,423	29,156	12,096	52,674	41.5	39.2	80.7
2085	11,422	29,112	12,373	52,915	42.5	39.2	81.7
2090	11,410	29,164	12,577	53,153	43.1	39.1	82.2
2095	11,405	29,251	12,696	53,347	43.4	39.0	82.4
2100	11,404	29,308	12,792	53,506	43.6	38.9	82.6
2110	11,421	29,310	13,100	53,829	44.7	39.0	83.7
2120	11,410	29,337	13,356	54,101	45.5	38.9	84.4
2130	11,404	29,375	13,478	54,265	45.9	38.8	84.7
2140	11,410	29,375	13,597	54,386	46.3	38.8	85.1
2150	11,401	29,391	13,703	54,504	46.6	38.8	85.4
2160	11,427	29,458	13,734	54,628	46.6	38.8	85.4
2170	11,453	29,525	13,766	54,753	46.6	38.8	85.4
2180	11,479	29,593	13,797	54,878	46.6	38.8	85.4
2190	11,505	29,660	13,829	55,003	46.6	38.8	85.4
2200	11,532	29,728	13,860	55,129	46.6	38.8	85.4

be the same throughout the projection period (INDEC 1993). Population data for the base year 1994 were obtained following a similar procedure.

Table 5.6 contains a summary of the population data. The share in the total population of people over age 65 goes from 9.4 percent in 1995 to 25.1 percent in 2200, and the dependency ratio goes from 0.17 in 1995 to 0.47 in 2200. Thus, while in 1995 there are about six active workers per pensioner, the projected figure for 2200 decreases to about two active workers per pensioner.[36]

36. Note also that the share in the total population of people under age 17 decreases from 34.6 percent in 1995 to 20.9 percent in 2200.

We will analyze the impact of this projected aging of Argentina's population when performing the sensitivity analysis.

5.3.2   Government Revenues, Consumption, and Net Wealth[37]

We excluded from our definition of the total public sector the municipalities[38] and social works institutions (*obras sociales*).[39] The main reason for this exclusion is that we could not obtain reliable statistics on their revenues. Table 5.7 presents in detail government revenues and expenditures.[40]

When implementing Argentina's generational accounts, we will impute the federal stamp tax and the permanent component of both other taxes and nontax revenues as negative government consumption. Further, we will not consider the capital revenues originating from the privatization program; thus we will be assuming that they will not be replicated in the future.

Finally, we estimated government net wealth at −$78.3 billion. This estimate deducts from the stock of total public debt at the end of December 1994 ($83.4 billion)[41] the value of the privatized public enterprises in the hands of the federal and provincial governments ($5.1 billion).[42]

5.3.3   Tax and Transfer Profiles

Argentina has a household survey (Encuesta Permanente de Hogares) that is conducted twice a year, May and October, interviewing 4,512 urban households located in the capital city, the suburbs, and 26 upcountry cities.[43] The sur-

---

37. I wish to thank Guillermo Barris from Dirección Nacional de Investigaciones y Análisis Fiscal and Cynthia Moskovits and Nuria Susmel from Fundación de Investigaciones Económicas Latinoamericanas (FIEL) for providing the data used in this section.

38. Except for the Buenos Aires province municipality, whose revenues and expenditures in the official statistics are reported jointly with those of the provinces themselves.

39. Social works institutions are mostly private; however, their revenues come from tax proceeds. Thus the health services to active workers that they provide should be considered part of the government's health transfers.

40. It should be remarked that unlike public revenues, there is more ample information on government expenditures. See Flood, Gasparini, et al. (1994) and Ministerio de Economía y Obras y Servicios Públicos (MEyOySP [1994a], [1994b], [1995b]). We included on the revenue side the seigniorage that the government collects on private holdings of money balances. We measured it as the change in the nominal M1 stock between December 1994 and December 1993. Note that the seigniorage is usually measured by the change in the central bank's noninterest bearing liabilities, i.e., the monetary base. In Argentina, due to the existence of high and remunerated reserve requirements, M1 is generally used instead of the monetary base to calculate seigniorage.

41. See MEyOySP, Secretaría de Hacienda (1994:IV). We assumed for the baseline case that the debt with pensioners originating from the legally challenged underpayment of pension benefits was totally consolidated after the payments made by the government in 1991 and 1993.

42. See MEyOySP (1995a). Note that we are not considering the value of public infrastructure and of public enterprises that are still completely in the government's hands. Thus we are using a sort of net financial wealth measure. As mentioned by Auerbach, Gokhale, and Kotlikoff (1994), this is not a serious omission because we include neither the value of the assets nor the value of their implicit rents, and they offset each other.

43. The sample was selected by a two-stage probabilistic process. Its starting size of 6,328 households reduces to 4,512 once uninhabited households and households that did not want to participate are discounted. For details, see INDEC (1990, n.d.).

The 26 upcountry cities include almost all provincial capital cities. The surveyed areas contain about 60 percent of Argentina's population.

Table 5.7   **Total Public Sector: Revenues and Expenditures, 1994**
                     (billions of pesos)

Revenues		Expenditures	
Current	60.3	Pensions and other benefits[c]	19.8
Tax revenues	54.7	Pensioners: health and other benefits	2.6
Federal taxes	45.1	Health	4.1
Income	5.8	Education	8.9
Assets	0.4	Housing	1.2
VAT	16.2	Government consumption	24.7
Excise	2.4	Other social and human resources	6.3
Foreign trade	2.9	Government administrative	13.0
Federal stamp	0.1	Public enterprises and infrastructure	5.4
Personal assets	0.2	Public debt	4.5
Liquid fuels	2.1		
Electricity consumption	0.2		
Social security contributions	12.7		
Special tobacco fund	0.2		
Other	2.0		
Provincial taxes	9.6		
Nontax revenues	5.6		
Federal	3.9		
Provincial	1.8		
Capital	1.2		
Federal[a]	0.8		
Provincial	0.3		
Other revenues[b]	0.8		
Seigniorage	2.1		
Deficit	1.5		
Total	65.9	Total	65.9

Sources: MEyOySP ([1994b], [1995b]); Dirección Nacional de Investigaciones y Análisis Fiscal (National Direction of Fiscal Research and Analysis); FIEL.

Note: Exchange rate used throughout chapter is 1 peso per U.S. dollar.

[a]Privatization cash revenues.

[b]Includes Pensioners Institute (PAMI).

[c]Other benefits include discounts on utilities and public transportation and waiver of municipal taxes for certain pension-income groups, burial subsidy, etc.

vey covers six topics, gathering demographic, employment, migratory, housing, educational, and income information.

Income data is net of taxes and social security contributions. Income sources, differentiated in the questionnaire but not reported, are wage, self-employment, profits, rents, return on financial assets, dividends, pensions, and other. Income is used in the survey mainly to classify other information in order to assess the population's socioeconomic situation. Several tables using income in this manner are published; however, data by age and sex are not released. Nevertheless, with access to the database, it is possible to cross-match publicly available information on sex and age from the family questionnaires

Table 5.8   **Tax and Transfer Profiles**

Tax or Transfer	Profile
Tax	
Labor income	Argentina's income
Capital income	Argentina's income
Assets	Argentina's income
Personal assets	Argentina's income
Seigniorage	Argentina's income
VAT	West Germany's VAT 14%
Excise	West Germany's excise
Special tobacco fund	West Germany's excise
Foreign trade	Thailand's import duties
Liquid fuels	New Zealand's fuel
Electricity consumption	Argentina's income
Social security contributions	Argentina's income
Provincial	Argentina's income
Transfer	
Pensions and other benefits	Argentina's pension payments
Pensioners: health and other benefits	Argentina's pension payments
Health	New Zealand's health
Education	New Zealand's education
Housing	New Zealand's housing

and income from the individual questionnaires. From this information we were able to construct income profiles.[44]

It is important to remark that the problem associated with income information obtained by any survey in Argentina is under/overstatement by the participants. Moreover, income data are in general questioned on statistical significance grounds, and government officials frequently claim that this is the reason they are not published regularly. We tried to ameliorate these problems by working with a weighted average of series from three consecutive surveys.[45]

Regarding transfers, the only available figures are the average pension payments by age range and sex constructed by the social security secretary of the Ministry of Labor and Social Security. From these figures we constructed the average profiles.

Table 5.8 summarizes the assignment of profiles. In the case of taxes and transfers that did not have profiles available to assign we used those for similar

44. In Argentina individual information from the questionnaires is confidential by law. For this reason, access to the database is restricted and the information provided is limited.

It was not possible to obtain income information disaggregated by source. I wish to thank Silvia Montoya and Andrés Tcach from IEERAL–Fundación Mediterránea for providing the income data by age and sex used to construct these profiles. Note that we are talking about average profiles across all members of the generation alive in the base year.

45. The average is weighted by the number of observations.

concepts available for other countries that have had generational accounts performed to date.[46]

5.3.4   Labor and Capital Income Tax

The net income tax is levied on companies, individuals, and undivided states' earnings. It can be considered, in practice, a tax on labor and capital income. Although only the total revenue figure is reported ($5.82 billion for 1994), 62 percent of it can be classified as tax on capital income—specifically on individual capital income and corporate profits.

As explained, we have neither profiles for capital and labor income taxes nor profiles for capital and labor income separately. However, as we can differentiate between capital and labor income tax revenues, we will consider these taxes separately in the calculation of the baseline generational accounts and use Argentina's total income profile to allocate them.[47] We will also perform a sensitivity experiment using the U.S. capital income tax profile and Argentina's total income profile for capital income tax and labor income tax, respectively.

Additionally, we will analyze within the latter sensitivity experiment the impact of the capital income tax adjustment. This adjustment accounts for the fact that taxes on capital income require the consideration of factors that imply differential tax treatment of new relative to existing capital assets.

Using the formula derived by Auerbach et al.,[48] we estimate that the 1994 flow of capital income taxes overstated the capital income tax burden on new investment by $0.285 billion and that the capitalized value of excess taxes on existing assets amounts to $40.7 billion.[49] These figures are calculated by multiplying the value of the capital stock ($503.3 billion)[50] by our estimates of the correction from average to effective tax rates (0.057 percent) and of the tax-based discount on existing assets (8.1 percent). These calculations are based on the following data: (1) investor's marginal tax rate, 28 percent; (2) investor's required after-tax return, 4 percent; (3) investment economic rate of depreciation, 5 percent; (4) investment growth rate, 3.3 percent; and (5) inflation rate, 4 percent.[51]

46. I wish to thank Jan Walliser for providing these profiles.

47. Note that this experiment is in line with the adjustment suggested by Fehr and Kotlikoff (chap. 3 in this volume) for a small open economy.

48. See Auerbach et al. (1991, 67–69 and appendix) for a detailed exposition of this method.

49. In the sensitivity experiment, we subtract the $0.285 billion figure from current capital income taxes and assign the $40.7 billion amount as a one-time tax to 1994 cohorts according to the corresponding profile.

50. The value of Argentina's total capital stock for 1994 is $909.2 billion. This figure includes capital equipment, residential capital, industrial buildings and structures, and public infrastructure. We deducted the amounts that correspond to public infrastructure (27 percent of the total) and to owner-occupied housing (17.6 percent of the total) in order to estimate the value of capital stock used for the capital income tax adjustment. The first figure is based on FIEL's estimations, and the second assumes, based on data from the population census (see INDEC 1995b), that 84 percent of residential capital is occupied by owners.

51. The investment economic rate of depreciation (3) corresponds to the annual average depreciation rate of the capital stock considered; the investment growth rate (4) corresponds to the annual average capital growth rate.

Table 5.9   **Generational Accounts: Central Assumptions (present values in thousands of U.S. dollars)**

Generation's Age in 1994	Net Payment		
	Total	Males	Females
0	13.9	21.8	5.7
5	15.7	25.1	6.1
10	20.3	31.7	8.5
15	26.3	39.9	12.4
20	30.8	46.2	15.2
25	31.6	49.1	13.7
30	28.2	46.6	9.8
35	21.6	39.8	4.0
40	12.6	28.8	−2.8
45	1.5	15.0	−11.7
50	−11.3	−0.8	−21.5
55	−25.2	−17.9	−32.0
60	−39.9	−37.5	−42.1
65	−42.9	−42.1	−43.5
70	−43.0	−41.6	−44.0
75	−41.2	−40.0	−42.0
80	−34.3	−32.0	−35.8
85	−32.5	−28.8	−34.4
90	−7.1	−6.6	−7.3
Future generations	24.3		
Percentage difference	74.8		

Note: Central assumptions are a growth rate of 1.5 percent and a discount rate of 5 percent.

5.3.5   Discount and Productivity Growth Rates

On top of the central assumptions used in this book, we will analyze a particular baseline case for Argentina that assumes an 8 percent discount rate and a 1 percent growth rate. This real discount rate is between the real internal rate of return on the BONEX 89 and the real prime lending rate in U.S. dollars, both for 1994; and the productivity growth rate is in line with the evolution of average productivity during the past two decades.

5.4   Basic Findings and Sensitivity Analysis

5.4.1   Basic Results

Tables 5.9 through 5.12 present 1994 generational accounts for the central assumptions and the special baseline cases. These tables were constructed, as said above, for real discount rates (r) of 5 and 8 percent and growth rates (g) of 1.5 and 1 percent and under the assumption of no social security reform.[52] The rationale for the latter assumption is that the new IPS became operational

52. All 1994 dollar values were expressed in 1995 dollars using the U.S. CPI.

Table 5.10 Composition of Generational Accounts: Central Assumptions (present value of receipts and payments in thousands of U.S. dollars)

Generation's Age in 1994	Net Payment	Tax Payments								Transfer Receipts			
		Labor Income Taxes	Capital Income and Assets Taxes	Seigniorage	VAT	Excise, Fuel, and Electricity Taxes	Duties	Social Security Contributions	Provincial Taxes	Social Security Benefits	Health	Education	Housing
0	13.9	1.4	2.7	1.3	12.9	3.2	2.2	8.0	6.1	11.0	3.1	8.8	0.8
5	15.7	1.6	3.1	1.5	13.0	3.7	2.4	9.4	7.1	12.5	2.8	9.7	1.0
10	20.3	2.0	3.7	1.9	13.7	4.4	2.6	11.3	8.5	15.0	3.1	8.4	1.2
15	26.3	2.4	4.3	2.2	14.1	5.2	2.7	13.4	10.1	17.0	3.4	6.3	1.4
20	30.8	2.6	4.9	2.5	13.5	5.7	2.6	15.1	11.4	19.2	3.4	3.2	1.5
25	31.6	2.9	5.3	2.7	13.6	5.9	2.6	16.6	12.5	23.3	3.6	2.0	1.5
30	28.2	2.9	5.4	2.7	13.1	5.9	2.5	16.8	12.6	27.0	3.7	1.5	1.4
35	21.6	2.8	5.1	2.6	12.6	5.4	2.3	15.9	12.0	31.1	3.8	1.2	1.2
40	12.6	2.6	4.7	2.4	12.2	4.9	2.1	14.6	11.0	36.0	3.8	0.9	1.0
45	1.5	2.2	4.1	2.1	11.3	4.3	1.9	12.7	9.6	41.3	3.9	0.5	0.9
50	-11.3	1.9	3.4	1.6	10.2	3.6	1.6	10.4	7.8	46.8	4.0	0.2	0.7
55	-25.2	1.4	2.7	1.3	8.9	3.1	1.4	8.3	6.3	53.9	4.1	0.0	0.6
60	-39.9	1.1	2.3	1.1	7.6	2.5	1.2	6.8	5.1	62.8	4.3	0.0	0.5
65	-42.9	0.9	1.7	0.8	6.1	1.9	1.0	5.4	4.1	59.9	4.5	0.0	0.4
70	-43.0	0.7	1.4	0.7	4.5	1.3	0.8	4.3	3.2	55.6	4.0	0.0	0.3
75	-41.2	0.6	1.0	0.5	3.4	1.0	0.7	3.3	2.5	49.9	4.1	0.0	0.2
80	-34.3	0.4	0.7	0.4	2.3	0.6	0.5	2.3	1.7	40.2	3.1	0.0	0.2
85	-32.5	0.3	0.6	0.3	1.9	0.5	0.4	2.0	1.4	36.8	2.9	0.0	0.2
90	-7.1	0.1	0.1	0.1	0.4	0.1	0.1	0.3	0.2	7.8	0.6	0.0	0.0
Future generations	24.3												
Percentage difference	74.8												

Note: Central assumptions are a growth rate of 1.5 percent and a discount rate of 5 percent.

Table 5.11   **Generational Accounts: Special Baseline (present values in thousands of dollars)**

Generation's Age in 1994	Net Payment		
	Total	Males	Females
0	5.1	7.3	3.0
5	6.4	9.5	3.3
10	10.5	14.9	5.9
15	16.5	22.7	10.0
20	23.4	31.7	15.0
25	27.1	37.6	16.5
30	27.1	39.1	15.2
35	24.5	37.1	12.2
40	19.3	31.1	8.1
45	11.6	21.7	1.7
50	1.6	9.5	−6.0
55	−10.5	−5.1	−15.5
60	−25.8	−24.9	−26.6
65	−31.2	−31.9	−30.6
70	−33.9	−33.8	−33.9
75	−34.3	−34.1	−34.4
80	−30.1	−28.4	−31.1
85	−29.8	−26.7	−31.6
90	−7.1	−6.6	−7.3
Future generations	12.7		
Percentage difference	146.1		

Note: Special baseline assumptions are a growth rate of 1 percent and a discount rate of 8 percent.

by law on 15 July 1994. Thus, not only because of the nature of the reform implied by the IPS but also because of the way in which it took place, we can safely assume that the fiscal statistics of 1994 do not reflect any major change due to it.

Afterward, we will simulate a case that assumes the social security reform fully operational. In this way, comparing the two cases, we will be able to study the effects on generational accounts of the social security reform.

The accounts in tables 5.9 and 5.11 indicate the average amount an individual belonging to a specific age cohort will pay in net taxes (net payment) over the rest of his or her life. For example, under the central assumptions the projected present value net payments of 40-year-old individuals are $12,600, $28,800, and −$2,800 for the total, males, and females, respectively. The corresponding values for the special baseline case are $19,300, $31,100, and $8,100.[53]

Moreover, these tables show that net payments present a life cycle pattern,

53. The difference in net payments between males and females arises because the latter earn less and therefore pay less income taxes and social security contributions.

Table 5.12   Composition of Generational Accounts: Special Baseline (present value of receipts and payments in thousands of U.S. dollars)

Generation's Age in 1994	Net Payment	Tax Payments								Transfer Receipts			
		Labor Income Taxes	Capital Income and Assets Taxes	Seigniorage	VAT	Excise, Fuel, and Electricity Taxes	Duties	Social Security Contributions	Provincial Taxes	Social Security Benefits	Health	Education	Housing
0	5.1	0.4	0.7	0.4	6.5	0.9	1.0	2.3	1.7	1.2	1.5	5.8	0.3
5	6.4	0.5	1.0	0.5	6.7	1.3	1.1	3.1	2.4	1.6	1.1	7.1	0.4
10	10.5	0.7	1.4	0.7	7.3	1.9	1.4	4.4	3.4	2.3	1.3	6.7	0.5
15	16.5	1.1	2.1	1.0	7.8	2.7	1.5	6.2	4.7	3.1	1.5	5.1	0.7
20	23.4	1.4	2.7	1.3	7.8	3.2	1.5	8.2	6.3	4.1	1.5	2.6	0.9
25	27.1	1.7	3.2	1.6	8.0	3.6	1.5	9.9	7.5	5.8	1.7	1.5	1.0
30	27.1	1.9	3.5	1.7	7.9	3.8	1.5	10.7	8.0	7.8	1.9	1.2	0.9
35	24.5	1.9	3.5	1.7	7.9	3.6	1.4	10.7	8.0	10.6	2.0	1.0	0.8
40	19.3	1.7	3.3	1.6	8.0	3.4	1.4	10.2	7.6	14.5	2.1	0.8	0.7
45	11.6	1.6	3.0	1.4	7.8	3.1	1.2	9.2	6.9	19.4	2.2	0.5	0.6
50	1.6	1.3	2.5	1.2	7.3	2.7	1.1	7.6	5.8	24.8	2.4	0.2	0.5
55	-10.5	1.0	2.1	1.0	6.6	2.4	1.0	6.2	4.7	32.4	2.6	0.0	0.5
60	-25.8	0.9	1.7	0.8	5.9	2.0	0.9	5.2	3.9	43.8	2.9	0.0	0.4
65	-31.2	0.7	1.4	0.7	4.9	1.5	0.8	4.3	3.3	45.1	3.4	0.0	0.3
70	-33.9	0.6	1.1	0.6	3.7	1.1	0.7	3.6	2.7	44.6	3.2	0.0	0.2
75	-34.3	0.5	0.9	0.4	2.9	0.8	0.6	2.8	2.2	41.8	3.5	0.0	0.2
80	-30.1	0.3	0.6	0.3	2.1	0.6	0.4	2.1	1.5	35.3	2.7	0.0	0.2
85	-29.8	0.3	0.6	0.3	1.6	0.5	0.4	1.9	1.3	33.8	2.7	0.0	0.2
90	-7.1	0.1	0.1	0.1	0.4	0.1	0.1	0.3	0.2	7.8	0.6	0.0	0.0
Future generations	12.7												
Percentage difference	146.1												

Note: Special baseline assumptions are a growth of 1 percent and a discount rate of 8 percent.

characterized by younger generations making positive payments to the government over their remaining lifetimes and older generations being net beneficiaries of government transfers. Note that under the central assumptions, males aged 50 or older and females aged 40 or older have negative generational accounts; that is, in present value they can expect to receive more from future transfers than they pay in taxes.[54] The change of sign in the generational accounts occurs at age 55 for males and age 50 for females in the special baseline case.

Tables 5.10 and 5.12 present in detail the present values of each of the various tax payments and transfer receipts. From them, we can further qualify 40-year-old total net payments. In the central assumption case, the generational account ($12,600) reflects the difference between total projected present value of tax payments ($54,500) and total projected present value of future transfers ($41,700).[55] For the special baseline assumptions these figures are $19,300, $37,300, and $18,100.

In addition, we estimate that under the central assumptions newborn generations in 1994 will pay $13,900 in present value over their entire lifetimes while future generations will pay a (estimated) growth-adjusted amount of $24,300, which is about 75 percent larger. The corresponding amounts for newborn and future generations in the special baseline case are $5,100 and $12,700, with an imbalance of 146 percent. These differences indicate that—in both cases—under our assumptions regarding Argentina's fiscal policy, there is a huge generational imbalance. This imbalance implies that future Argentinean generations will have to pay on average net taxes that are 1.8 to 2.5 times larger, after adjusting for growth, than the ones current generations are estimated to pay if they continue to be subject to the 1994 fiscal policy for the rest of their lives.

5.4.2 Sensitivity Analysis

Discount and Growth Rates

In table 5.13 we present the percentage difference between newborns' and future generations' net payments for different combinations of discount rate and growth rate. As the table indicates, the extent of the generational imbalance is quite sensitive to discount and growth rate assumptions. For discount rates larger than 5 percent we observe that the larger the discount rate the larger the difference between accounts of current and future generations, while the effect of growth rates does not show a clear trend. Thus, according to these results, future generations of Argentineans will pay, in present value, net taxes that range from 1.7 to 7.5 times the amount 1994 newborn Argentineans are expected to pay, given the current policy. Note that all the combinations confirm the imbalance of Argentina's fiscal policy.

---

54. Note that social security benefits are the main factor that explains the change in sign of the generational accounts.

55. Here and in similar comments below, differences are due to rounding off.

Table 5.13 Sensitivity Analysis: Net Tax Payments of Newborn and Future Generations (thousands of U.S. dollars)

	$g = 0.5$					$g = 1$					
	$r = 3$	$r = 5$	$r = 7$	$r = 9$	$r = 11$	$r = 3$	$r = 5$	$r = 7$	$r = 8$	$r = 9$	$r = 11$
Present generation	16.5	10.8	6.0	3.2	1.6	17.0	12.3	7.0	5.1	3.8	2.0
Future generations	30.9	18.9	13.4	11.8	12.3	35.0	21.4	14.3	12.7	11.9	12.1
Generational imbalance (%)	88.3	76.2	123.4	272.3	645.3	105.4	73.7	104.0	146.1	217.0	508.8

	$g = 1.5$					$g = 2$				
	$r = 3$	$r = 5$	$r = 7$	$r = 9$	$r = 11$	$r = 3$	$r = 5$	$r = 7$	$r = 9$	$r = 11$
Present generation	16.5	13.9	8.2	4.4	2.4	13.8	15.3	9.6	5.2	2.8
Future generations	39.0	24.3	15.6	12.2	11.9	42.5	27.7	17.3	12.7	11.8
Generational imbalance (%)	137.3	74.8	90.1	174.6	402.0	207.8	79.7	80.9	142.4	318.6

This table also shows that the *sizes* of generational accounts are sensitive to the values assumed for the discount and growth rates. The sizes of generational accounts are lower in absolute value the higher the discount rate. For growth rates the relationship again is not as clear.

Other Assumptions

Table 5.14 presents sensitivity results for changes in several assumptions. This analysis is performed for the central assumptions and the special baseline case.

The first experiment analyzes the case that uses the U.S. profile for the capital income tax. Although the size of the generational imbalance is sensitive to this change of profile, our conclusion that Argentina's fiscal accounts show a huge generational imbalance is robust to it. Then the inframarginal capital income tax adjustment is performed,[56] resulting in a reduction of the generational imbalance. Nevertheless, the size of this imbalance is still very significant. Finally, this adjustment is examined for the case that uses Argentina's total income tax profile for the capital income tax, with similar results.

The second experiment considers the effects of assuming no future demographic change will occur in Argentina; that is, we assume the population age distribution will be constant after 1994. This experiment helps to explain the impact of the aging process, the main feature of the Argentinean population's future development. The conclusion is that if the population structure were to remain constant, younger generations would be better off and the generational imbalance would be significantly smaller in the central assumption case and smaller, though still huge, in the special baseline case.[57]

Third, we analyze the impact of government debt. If we assume no government debt, the generational imbalance is much smaller in the central assumption case, while in the special baseline case the reduction is so important that the imbalance changes sign and is in absolute value almost the same as for the central assumptions.

The last sensitivity test studies the impact of considering government educational expenditure as part of government consumption instead of a transfer. This increases the burden of the newborn generation relative to future generations and, thus, reduces the imbalance in both cases, though more in the special baseline case.

56. The adjustment calculated here was intended as a maximum. This is due mainly to the assumed level of the investor's required after-tax return, which is low in view of the high risk that international investors still assign to Argentina. Note that a 10 percent after-tax return implies a capitalized value of excess taxes on existing assets of about $10 billion.

57. Note that in the cases where the population structure is not constant, younger generations will bear the fiscal burden of the demographic change.

Table 5.14   Sensitivity Analysis: Other Assumptions (thousands of U.S. dollars)

	Central Assumptions			Special Baseline		
	Present Generation	Future Generations	Generational Imbalance (%)	Present Generation	Future Generations	Generational Imbalance (%)
Base case	13.9	24.3	74.8	5.1	12.7	146.1
Capital income tax						
U.S. profile	13.6	23.3	72.1	4.9	12.3	149.8
U.S. profile and inframarginal adjustment	13.5	21.6	61.2	4.9	8.2	68.7
Argentina total income profile and inframarginal adjustment	13.7	22.5	63.9	5.1	8.6	68.8
Population structure	14.7	15.0	1.7	4.6	10.2	119.8
Zero debt	13.9	19.6	41.0	5.1	3.2	−38.0
Government educational expenditure as government consumption	22.7	36.1	58.6	10.9	20.1	84.4

Table 5.15   **Burden Equalization Experiment: Central Assumptions**

Policy	Required Adjustment (%)
All taxes[a]	8.7
VAT	30.0
Social security contributions	34.6
Provincial taxes	45.9
Labor and capital income taxes	75.7
Capital income tax	122.1
Labor income tax	199.3
All transfers	11.0
Social security benefits[b]	17.7
Government consumption	29.1

[a]The required adjustment for all taxes including the seigniorage is 8.4 percent.
[b]Includes pensions and other benefits; see table 5.7.

5.5   The Generational Impact of Alternative Policies

5.5.1   Impact of Policies Needed to Achieve Generational Balance

In this section we will calculate the magnitude of the immediate and permanent increase in alternative tax revenues, or reduction in alternative transfers or government expenditure, required to achieve generational balance (or intertemporal budget balance).[58] Note that these adjustments are alternative ways to evaluate the size of the generational imbalance.

In tables 5.15 and 5.16 we present a list of alternative policies, relative to our central assumptions and baseline projected time path of revenues and expenditures, required to restore Argentina's generational balance. For example, in the special baseline case of the VAT an increase in revenues of 22.8 percent is required for this purpose.[59] It is important to remark that the adjustment needed is in revenues and that the target can be attained not only by increasing the average taxation rate but also by reducing the degree of tax evasion, or by a mix of both effects.[60]

The list of policies also considers increases in all taxes, in social security contributions, in provincial taxes, and in different combinations of income taxes, as well as reductions in all transfers, social security benefits, and government consumption. The magnitude of the required adjustments is, obviously, associated with the weight of the policy instrument chosen within total reve-

58. Note that this is a partial equilibrium statement. In other words, it ignores the effect that changes in taxes, transfers, or government expenditure might have on the country's economic performance, as well as the feedback impact of any modification of this performance on said variables.
59. Note that this huge increase in VAT revenues, equivalent in 1994 to 1.3 percent of GDP, will just restore generational balance.
60. Tax evasion still plays a crucial role in Argentina's fiscal accounts.

Table 5.16   **Burden Equalization Experiment: Special Baseline**

Policy	Required Adjustment (%)
All taxes[a]	6.7
VAT	22.8
Social security contributions	27.2
Provincial taxes	36.1
Labor and capital income taxes	59.5
Capital income tax	96.0
Labor income tax	156.6
All transfers	9.4
Social security benefits[b]	16.1
Government consumption	22.0

[a]The required adjustment for all taxes including the seigniorage is 6.5 percent.
[b]Includes pensions and other benefits; see table 5.7.

nues or expenditures. Furthermore, while the impact on future generations is fairly similar whichever policy instrument is used, the distribution of the additional net payment burden across current generations is sensitive to the choice of tax or transfer instrument.

One interesting feature to note is that the huge Argentinean generational imbalance is associated with adjustments needed for certain policy instruments that are not reasonable. In this sense, for example, the increases in labor or capital income taxes alone are certainly not feasible. Likewise, the increases required for provincial taxes, social security contributions, and VAT are huge enough to raise doubts about the reasonability of applying them in practice.

Thus we are left with few choices, mainly social security benefits and government consumption.[61] Regarding these instruments, on the one hand, the social security benefits issue was already addressed by current economic authorities with the social security reform, and we will analyze it below. On the other hand, the huge reduction needed in government consumption, about 1.3 percent of GDP in 1994, needs further qualification. First, government expenditure in Argentina proved to be extremely—"politically"—rigid downward even after the numerous "announcements" of reductions and reforms made by the current government. Second, our concept of government consumption includes primarily salaries, and thus its required reduction implies a drastic head count cutback. Third, the social consequences of such adjustment should be taken into consideration, and a comprehensive program would unquestionably be required. Finally, expenditure reductions applied to provincial finances would have to take into account their individual situations and would imply complicated political maneuvers; their net impact is difficult to assess.[62]

61. Note that we are also implicitly discarding either increases of taxes or decreases of transfers across the board.
62. The scope of this problem is well beyond the limits of our work. However, the issue is highlighted here to remark the difficulties of the aggregate policy adjustment required to attain

5.5.2   Generational Account Effects of the Privatization Program

In terms of the government's intertemporal budget constraint we have two effects of the privatization program: first, a change in government net wealth—equation (1); second, a variation in the present value in year t of all future net tax payments—equation (2):

$$(1) \qquad\qquad \Delta W_t^G = \Delta A_t^G - \Delta L_t^G,$$

where ΔW_t^G is change in government net wealth in year t due to the sale of public enterprises. ΔA_t^G is change in government assets in year t; this term will decrease by the value of the public companies sold and increase by any cash withheld by the government. ΔL_t^G is change in government liabilities in year t; this term will decrease by the value of the repaid public debt.

$$(2) \qquad\qquad \Delta N_{t,k} = N_{t,k}^{PO} - N_{t,k}^{GO},$$

where $\Delta N_{t,k}$ is change in total net payments to the government, $N_{t,k}^{PO}$ is net payments to the government under private ownership of public enterprises, and N_{tk}^{GO} is net payments to the government under government ownership of public enterprises.

Equation (2) captures the elimination of explicit and implicit public enterprise subsidies when they are privatized, as well as the difference in future taxes and dividends paid to the government by these companies under the distinct ownership-type assumptions. The latter concept includes not only taxes paid by the privatized firms that were not paid before by these companies (for whatever reason) when they were under government ownership but also the increase in taxes and dividends due to the change in the profitability and scale of the new private enterprises.[63]

Estimation of the total effect of the privatization program as measured by equations (1) and (2) is not possible with the available statistical data, especially in the case of equation (2). For this reason, we will only address the change in government net wealth associated with this program.

First, considering that by 1994 most of this process had already been concluded, we can assume that both the net tax payment and government net wealth impacts were by that time included in the fiscal accounts. In this sense, our calculation of Argentina's generational accounts has taken care of these effects, and they are also included in the generational imbalance found.

---

generational balance. Consider, e.g., that currently there are no reliable statistics on provincial finances.

63. Note that when we set up Argentina's generational accounts we did not address either the efficiency of the government's transfers or of its current expenditure because they were beyond the scope of our work. Similarly, we are not evaluating the effect of the change in the quality of services provided by the privatized firms vis-à-vis the former state enterprises. Furthermore, we will not attempt to measure the impact of other aspects of the privatization program, such as the increase in market competition, technological improvements, the adequacy of the price paid for the companies sold by the government, etc.

Second, we can isolate in the generational accounts the government net wealth impact from the rest by means of the following reasoning. If all the privatization revenues had been used to cancel outstanding public debt, this impact would have been zero; otherwise it would have been negative, implying a reduction in government net wealth.[64] The problem is that changes in the stock of public debt also respond to other causes. We propose to sort out this problem by ascribing all the estimated reduction in the stock of public debt during the period under analysis to the privatization program. Then, comparing the net wealth value of the state firms sold less the current government's share of them with our estimate of the reduction in the stock of public debt, we will obtain the effect on government net wealth. Finally, incorporating this effect into the generational accounts, we will be able to calculate its impact on the size of the generational imbalance.[65]

In table 5.17 we present the stock of public debt at the beginning of the current administration and for our baseline year. The nonconsolidated debt figure for 1989 includes debt with pensioners, suppliers, and other creditors originated and accrued before that year,[66] while the figure for 1994 encompasses the estimated public debt pending consolidation by then.[67] We obtain an estimated total reduction in the stock of public debt for the period 1989–94 of $11.8 billion dollars by comparing total figures (in 1994 dollars) for these years.

The estimated net wealth value of the public enterprises that the government sold net of the current government's share of them amounts to $21.8 billion (see table 5.5). Thus the negative effect on government net wealth is $9.98 billion.

Subsequently, we need to plug this last figure into our accounts to calculate its impact on the generational imbalance. As said before, this effect was already included in our calculations, so for our purposes we will need to simulate an increase instead of a reduction in government net wealth.

The result of this simulation is that future generations will pay to the government (estimated) growth-adjusted amounts[68] of $23,800 (central assumptions) and $11,600 (special baseline) in net taxes, which are about 70.7 and 124 percent larger than the net payments of newborn generations. These figures compare with our base-case outcomes: $24,300 and $12,700; 74.8 and 146.1 per-

---

64. We can safely assume that the government did not withhold any privatization cash revenues.

65. Note that the privatization's net wealth impact is analyzed with reference to a country's generational imbalance that already includes the (most likely positive) net tax payment effect of this program.

66. The public debt figures exclude provinces and public (government owned and managed) banks—except for the central bank. The current government began to consolidate previously originated and accrued public debt as of April 1991.

67. We assume for 1994 the same amount Melconian and Santángelo ([1996]) assumed for 1995. We also adopt their criterion regarding the nonconsolidated debt; i.e., this debt is considered as debt of the period when it was accrued but for the value that it was consolidated.

68. Generational account currency figures are in 1995 dollars.

Table 5.17   **Stock of Public Debt (billions of U.S. dollars; end of December)**

Debt	1989	1994
Registered public debt	63.7	83.4
Nonconsolidated public debt	25.7	5.0
Public enterprises liabilities	3.0	–
Foreign exchange adjustment	4.1	–
Other	–	0.6
Total	96.5	89.0
Total in 1994 U.S. dollars	100.9	89.0
Difference (1994 vs. 1989)	−11.8	

Sources: IMF, *International Financial Statistics,* annual volume (Washington, D.C., 1995); Melconian and Santángelo ([1996]); MEyOySP, Secretaría de Hacienda, *Boletín Fiscal,* annual volume (Buenos Aires, 1995).

Note: To express the 1989 public debt in 1994 U.S. dollars we adjusted the index used by Melconian and Santángelo ([1996]) by the U.S. inflation rate, producer prices, during 1995.

cent. Thus the negative effect on government net wealth of the privatization program net of its contribution to government tax revenues implied increases in Argentina's generational imbalance of 2 and 10 percent, respectively.[69]

5.5.3   Generational Effects of the Social Security Reform

In this section, we will set up a theoretical case in which the social security reform is fully functional as of 1994. In this way, we will be able to analyze whether the reduction in social security expenditures associated with the reform could be enough to restore generational balance or whether additional austere fiscal policies are required. The need for additional policies in this theoretical case will certainly reinforce the need for such policies in the actual case, which will produce its eventual benefits gradually and further in the future.

Our strategy will be first to determine the government's total debt with current pensioners. Then we will aim at finding out what should be the reduction in pension payments needed to restore generational balance and at appraising its empirical feasibility as single fiscal policy tool.[70]

In other words, we are making explicit the government's implicit liabilities with current pensioners. Therefore, the resulting reduction in pension payments required to restore generational balance will have two parts: one required to restore the original imbalance and the other to match the increase in public debt generated by this reclassification of liabilities.

In order to estimate the actuarial debt, which is the main component of the

69. From 70.7 to 74.8 percent and from 124 to 146.1 percent, respectively.

70. Note that first we will add the burden of the total debt with current pensioners to our base-case generational accounts, and then we will analyze the reduction in pension payments needed to restore generational balance.

government's total debt with current pensioners, we make the following assumptions: (1) debt is discounted and adjusted for growth in the same way as our central assumption or special baseline case generational accounts; (2) the base-year relationship between total payments obtained from the data of the social security secretary of the Ministry of Labor and Social Security with both total payments of the National Social Security System and the Total Social Security System is assumed constant throughout;[71] and (3) as we do not have pension payment data by single ages, we will make additional assumptions on the number of future years during which each cohort will receive these payments.[72] Our estimates of the actuarial debt amounts are $160.1 billion for the central assumption case and $125.8 billion for the baseline case.[73]

Another element of the total debt with current pensioners, though a minor component compared with our previous figure, is the amount originating from legal actions taken by them against the government.[74] We will assume that the $5.0 billion of nonconsolidated public debt estimated in the preceding section all corresponds to debt with current pensioners of the kind just described. We consider that this is most likely the case because the majority or perhaps the totality of public debt with suppliers and other creditors accrued before 1989 should have been consolidated by 1994.[75]

Consequently, adding these two components we obtain our estimates of the total debt with current pensioners. These estimates, for the cases under analysis, are $165.1 billion and $130.8 billion.

Next, we plug these debt figures as liabilities into government net wealth and run the policy experiment that entails reducing pension payments while maintaining social security contributions at their baseline level to restore generational balance.[76] The needed reductions are 33.5 and 47.8 percent for the cases under analysis.

71. The Total Social Security System includes the National Social Security System, provincial and municipal social security systems, and other activity-specific social security systems. The base-year relationships mentioned in assumption 2 are 71 and 87 percent, respectively. See Cristini (1995) and FIEL–Consejo Empresario Argentino (1995).

72. Specifically, we will assume that (1) 0–18-year-old pensioners will be paid until they are 18 years old; (2) 18–85-year-old pensioners will be paid until they are 80 years old in the case of males and until they are 85 years old in the case of females; and (3) 80+-year-old males and 85+-year-old females will be paid only for one year.

73. FIEL estimates this debt at $140.9 billion using a 4 percent discount rate and not adjusting for growth. This figure is in line with our estimations provided we take into account the different discount rate and growth rate assumptions. See FIEL–Consejo Empresario Argentino (1995), in 1994 dollars.

74. This is the debt with pensioners pending consolidation originated by the legally challenged underpayment of pension benefits.

75. If we only include this debt in our baseline accounts the results change in the following manner: the generational imbalance increases from 74.8 to 77.1 percent in the central assumption case, and from 146 to 158 percent in the special baseline case.

76. The item of the fiscal accounts database that we are reducing is pensions and other benefits. It encompasses pension payments; benefits such as discounts on utilities and public transportation, waivers of municipal taxes for certain pension-income groups, and burial subsidies; and overhead

These reductions seem likely to suffice as single fiscal policy if we consider that by 1995 a third of all social security affiliates were in the public pension system and the rest were in the mixed (public/private) system. However, a more detailed analysis of the data may lead us to a completely different conclusion.

First, consider, for example, that the percentage reduction required in our baseline case implies annual pension and other benefit payments of $10.3 billion. Then assume that the government pays the BUP to all pensioners, that is, that the new IPS is fully functional. The total annual BUP payment will be about $8.4 billion.[77] The remaining funds, net of overhead expenses,[78] are $1.5 billion and seem scarcely enough for the government to be able to meet the rest of its social security commitments. These commitments are the other benefits classified under social security expenditures and the payments to workers who chose the public system, namely, the APP and the disability, survivorship, and advanced age pension benefits.[79]

Therefore, this conclusion reinforces the need for additional austere fiscal policies to complement the social security reform and restore generational balance. In addition, it highlights the fact that considering government fiscal programs separately may be misleading. In other words, the social security system may attain balance or even a small surplus as a result of the reform; however, this is not enough to guarantee the balance of the overall government intertemporal budget.

Along this same line of thought, it is important to remark that 58.2 percent of the funds deposited with PFAs by the end of 1995 were invested in public bonds (see Superintendencia de Administradoras 1995). Therefore, the reform channeled workers' social security contributions to the private PFA funds, and these institutions, in turn, used more than half of the funds to purchase government bonds. This process provided additional government borrowing that will be used over time to meet public expenditures, among them the pension benefits of retirees who opted for the public system, as well as the BUP of all retirees. In government intertemporal budget terms the present value of net taxes was reduced but the public debt was increased, and thus, as Kotlikoff (1994) points out, it amounts to a "change of words," specifically social secu-

---

expenses associated with all these payments. The details of this item are not published in the official statistics, but we estimate that pension payments are 90 percent or more of it.

Note that maintaining social security contributions at their baseline level is in line with the change introduced in Article 13 of the Social Security Solidarity Law. This article established that social security contributions could be reduced only if their reduction was offset by an increase in the collection of other taxes or by transfers from the Treasury.

77. This assumes a total number of affiliates of 3.8 million; an ACPC of $63 (this was actually the value of the ACPC from April to December 1994); and an average BUP of 2.7 times the ACPC. Consider also that there are 13 pension payments during the year, 12 monthly payments and an extra payment paid half in July and half in December.

78. We estimate annual overhead expenses of $0.4 billion. See FIEL–Consejo Empresario Argentino (1995).

79. Similar reasoning applies to the central assumption accounts.

rity contributions are changed—partially—into loans to the government (see also Kotlikoff, chap. 1 in this volume).[80] Note that this "change of words" is also applicable to our above reclassification of government liabilities.

Another characteristic of the PFA portfolio composition that needs to be highlighted, although it is not the object of our present analysis, is the low percentage participation of investments in foreign markets. Specifically, by the end of 1995, only 0.8 percent of the funds deposited with PFAs were invested in foreign government bonds and 0.6 percent in foreign securities (see Superintendencia de Administradoras 1995). This situation was caused mainly by the influence of government regulations and incentives oriented toward fostering domestic savings and protecting investors, justified by the standard arguments associated with developing countries' capital market characteristics.[81] The cost of this policy is that Argentinean investors do not benefit from the reduced risk associated with international diversification of their portfolios.

The other economic changes associated with the social security reform process, whose analysis requires the utilization of a more comprehensive model, are beyond the scope of this work. However, we will briefly consider some of their likely implications from Argentina's perspective.[82]

In Argentina, before the introduction of the IPS, the perceived linkage between social security benefits and contributions was practically zero; that is, workers regarded contributions entirely as a marginal tax on their labor supply. Furthermore, ever escalating inflation, together with the government's constant manipulation of the indexes used to adjust pension payments and policies that diverted social security funds to other purposes, may have resulted in very low actual linkage.[83] Thus, concerning the benefit-tax linkage, chances should be high that the reform will bring about an efficiency gain. However, given the profound impact that the social security crisis had on workers this effect will probably be gradual.

In addition, Argentina has nonregistered employment in the so-called informal sector of the economy that is estimated at about 20 percent of total employment. For this reason, we can expect that the reform will produce an additional efficiency gain related to the relative reduction of the incentive to work in the informal sector, which does not pay, among others, labor taxes. Nevertheless, this gain will be of a smaller magnitude and come at an even more gradual pace than the previous one.[84]

---

80. See Kotlikoff (1995) for a detailed discussion in these terms of the paradigmatic Chilean social security reform.

81. These percentages are below the legal maximum (10 percent), which gives an idea of the influence of PFAs' financial planning policies.

82. For an analysis of these changes applied to the U.S. economy and using the Auerbach-Kotlikoff model, see Kotlikoff (1995, 1996a, 1996b) and references therein.

83. We could not obtain statistics on this linkage.

84. Note that there are still employers' contributions, and consequently, there is incentive to work in the informal sector on these grounds. Note also that a worker can contribute as self-employed and still work in the informal sector.

A last point to consider with respect to the efficiency gains mentioned here is that they need to be calculated together with the potential distortions that the fiscal mechanisms used to finance the transition might produce in the economy (e.g., they may distort, themselves, the labor supply). Argentina's method is not clear. It changed substantially since the draft law project up to the rulings of the law, and subsequently with the Social Security Solidarity Law. However, we may safely state that it will largely involve deficit financing by increasing the public debt and selling the government's remaining share in public enterprises.

Finally, note that initial generations must stay at least in the same welfare situation following the reform. If this is not the case, long-run gains may be originated basically at their expense. By the same token, certain policies like short-term deficit financing of the transition may help to protect initial generations from the negative impact of the reform. However, if these policies get out of control, the opposite situation will arise; that is, they will make initial generations better off and future generations worse off. In this sense, the calculation and payment of the government's total debt with current pensioners play key roles. These issues are ambiguous in Argentina, with most of the ambiguity originating after the promulgation of the Social Security Solidarity Law.

5.6   Summary and Conclusions

In this chapter we used the generational accounting technique to assess the sustainability of the convertibility plan's fiscal policy and to analyze two fundamental aspects of it, namely, the public enterprise privatization program and the social security reform.

We found, under the central assumptions, a significant generational imbalance of 75 percent, and the imbalance turned out to be as huge as 146 percent for the special baseline case. This implies that future Argentinean generations will have to pay on average net taxes that are 1.8 to 2.5 times larger, after adjusting for growth, than the ones current generations are estimated to pay if they continue to be subject to the 1994 fiscal policy for the rest of their lives.

Therefore, based on this imbalance, we conclude that the convertibility plan's fiscal policy is not sustainable as it implies that future Argentinean generations will have to pay intolerably high net taxes (taxes minus transfers).

This result is robust to reasonable variations in the discount rate and growth rate assumptions. In particular, we detected large imbalances for all combinations of these variables. According to these imbalances, future generations of Argentineans will pay, in present value, net taxes that range from 1.7 to 7.5 times the amount 1994 newborn Argentineans are expected to pay, given the current policy.

We also tested the robustness of the above baseline results to our choice of capital income tax profile and to the inclusion of the inframarginal adjustment of this tax to account for differential treatment of new and old investment. In both cases all our results are confirmed. However, we should remark that in the latter instance, as the adjustment allocates the burden of the capital income tax away from future generations, the generational imbalance is reduced. Moreover, the size of this reduction is fairly large. This point notwithstanding, the imbalances are still significant and in several cases huge.

Then we analyzed the impact of the aging of Argentina's population. We concluded that if the population structure were to remain constant, younger generations would be better off and the generational imbalance would be significantly smaller in the central assumption case and smaller though still huge in the special baseline case.

Another result of the sensitivity analysis highlights the importance of government debt, whose hypothetical cancellation would reduce drastically the generational imbalance. Finally, the alternative treatment of government educational expenditure as government consumption also reduced the size of the generational imbalance as it implied an increase in the tax burden of newborn generations relative to future generations.

A study of the alternative policies needed to achieve generational balance, which included the calculation of the immediate and permanent increase in alternative tax revenues or reduction in alternative transfers or government expenditure, led us to the following conclusions. First, the magnitude of the required adjustment is, obviously, associated with the weight of the policy instrument chosen within total revenues or expenditures. Second, the huge Argentinean generational imbalance implies adjustments for certain policy instruments that are not reasonable. Third, we are left with few choices, mainly social security benefits and government consumption, and fourth, in view of the size of the required adjustments, a mix of policy instruments should be used rather than a single one of them.

We identified two potential generational account effects of the privatization program, namely, a change in government net wealth and a variation in the present value in year t of all future net tax payments. With the statistical information available we were able to address the first of these changes. We concluded that the privatization program had an estimated negative impact on government net wealth of $9.98 billion (about 3.5 percent of 1994 GDP) implying 2 and 10 percent increases in Argentina's generational imbalance under the central and special baseline assumptions, respectively.

Subsequently, we assessed the generational account effects of the social security reform. In particular, we studied the magnitude of the reduction in pension payments required to achieve generational balance and to match the increase in public debt generated by the reclassification of liabilities associated with this reform. We concluded that after this reduction (34 or 48 percent), the remaining funds seem scarcely enough for the government to be able to meet the BUP benefit, the payments to the workers who chose the public pension system (APP, disability, survivorship, and advanced age pension benefits), and the other pensioners' benefits classified under social security expenditures.

Thus this reinforces our previous conclusion that a mix of policies is needed to restore intertemporal budget balance.

Additionally, it is necessary to remark that about 60 percent of the funds that workers deposited with PFAs were in turn invested in public bonds. Therefore, in government intertemporal budget terms the present value of net taxes was reduced but public debt was increased. Specifically, social security contributions were changed—partially—into loans to the government, that is, a "change of words."

Finally, we must highlight that while based on the cash-deficit approach multilateral organizations and international investors considered the convertibility plan within a stabilization paradigm, the results of the generational accounting technique introduced a series of doubts about it and, in particular, allowed us to judge its fiscal policy unsustainable.

References

Altamiranda, Marcelo F. 1997. Argentina's stabilization experience: Orthodoxy and the Primavera plan; sustainability of the convertibility plan's fiscal policy. Ph.D. diss., Boston University, Boston.

ANSeS (Administración Nacional de la Seguridad Social). Ministerio de Trabajo y Seguridad Social. 1994. Breve análisis del sistema nacional de previsión social Argentino en el período 1983–1993 y proyecciones al 2000. Informe Técnico no. 23. Buenos Aires: Subgerencia General Económico Financiera. Mimeograph.

Auerbach, Alan J., Bruce Baker, Laurence J. Kotlikoff, and Jan Walliser. 1995. Generational accounting in New Zealand: Is there generational balance? Boston: Boston University, Department of Economics. Mimeograph.

Auerbach, Alan J., Jagadeesh Gokhale, and Laurence J. Kotlikoff. 1991. Generational accounts: A meaningful alternative to deficit accounting. In *Tax policy and the economy,* vol. 5, ed. David Bradford, 55–110. Cambridge, Mass.: MIT Press.

———. 1992. Generational accounting: A new approach to understanding the effects of fiscal policy on saving. *Scandinavian Journal of Economics* 94:303–18.

———. 1994. Generational accounting: A meaningful way to evaluate fiscal policy. *Journal of Economic Perspectives* 8:73–94.

———. 1995. Restoring generational balance in U.S. fiscal policy: What will it take? *Federal Reserve Bank of Cleveland Economic Review* 31:2–12.

Auerbach, Alan J., Jagadeesh Gokhale, Laurence J. Kotlikoff, and Erling Steigum, Jr. 1993. Generational accounting in Norway: Is Norway overconsuming its petroleum wealth? Ruth Pollak Working Paper Series on Economics, no. 24. Boston: Boston University, Department of Economics.

Auerbach, Alan J., and Laurence J. Kotlikoff. 1987. *Dynamic fiscal policy.* Cambridge: Cambridge University Press.

Bos, Eduard, My T. Vu, Ernest Massiah, and Rodolfo A. Bulatao. 1994. *World population projections: Estimates and projections with related demographic statistics, 1994–95.* Baltimore: Johns Hopkins University Press.

Broda, Miguel Angel M., and associates. Monthly. *Carta Económica.* Buenos Aires.

Castelar Pinheiro, Armando, and Ben Ross Schneider. 1995. The fiscal impact of privatisation in Latin America. *Journal of Development Studies* 31:751–85.

Cristini, Marcela. 1995. Crisis y reforma del sistema previsional Argentino. Buenos Aires: Fundación de Investigaciones Económicas Latinoamericanas. Mimeograph.

Durán, Viviana. 1993. La evasión en el sistema de seguridad social Argentino. Serie Política Fiscal, no. 50. Santiago: Naciones Unidas, Comisión Económica para América Latina y el Caribe.

FIEL–Consejo Empresario Argentino. 1995. El sistema de seguridad social: Una propuesta de reforma. Buenos Aires: Manantial.

Flood, M. Cristina V. de, Leonardo Gasparini, M. Marcela Harriague, and Benigno Vélez. 1994. El gasto público social y su impacto redistributivo. Buenos Aires: Ministerio de Economía y Obras y Servicios Públicos, Subsecretaría de Programación Económica.

Flood, M. Cristina V. de, M. Marcela Harriague, Laura Lerner, and Leticia Montiel. 1994. Educación y salud: Resultados de mediciones sobre acceso y cobertura. Serie Gasto Público, Documento de Trabajo no. GP/04. Buenos Aires: Ministerio de Economía y Obras y Servicios Públicos, Subsecretaría de Programación Económica.

Franco, Daniele, Jagadeesh Gokhale, Laurence J. Kotlikoff, and Nicola Sartor. 1994. Generational accounting: The case of Italy. In Saving and the accumulation of wealth, ed. Albert Ando, Luigi Guiso, and Ignazio Visco, 128–60. Cambridge: Cambridge University Press.

Gokhale, Jagadeesh, and Laurence J. Kotlikoff. 1994. Passing the generational buck. The Public Interest 114:73–81.

Gokhale, Jagadeesh, Bernd Raffelhüschen, and Jan Walliser. 1995. The burden of German unification: A generational accounting approach. Finanzarchiv 52:141–65.

IMF (International Monetary Fund). Various issues. International financial statistics. Washington, D.C.: International Monetary Fund.

INDEC (Instituto Nacional de Estadística y Censos). Ministerio de Economía y Obras y Servicios Públicos. 1988. Encuesta de gastos e ingresos de los hogares. Estudios no. 11. Buenos Aires: Instituto Nacional de Estadística y Censos.

———. 1990. Encuestas de hogares: Errores de muestreo y efectos de diseño. Estudios no. 19. Buenos Aires: Instituto Nacional de Estadística y Censos.

———. 1993. Censo nacional de población y vivienda 1991: Resultados definitivos, series B. Buenos Aires: Instituto Nacional de Estadística y Censos.

———. 1994. Estimaciones y proyecciones de población 1950–2050. Total del país. Estudios no. 23. Buenos Aires: Instituto Nacional de Estadística y Censos.

———. 1995a. Estimaciones y proyecciones de población—Total del país (versión revisada) 1950–2050. Serie Análisis Demográfico, no. 5. Buenos Aires: Instituto Nacional de Estadística y Censos.

———. 1995b. Statistical yearbook: Republic of Argentina, 1995. Buenos Aires: Instituto Nacional de Estadística y Censos.

———. 1995c. Tabla completa de mortalidad de la Argentina por sexo 1990–1992. Serie Análisis Demográfico, no. 3. Buenos Aires: Instituto Nacional de Estadística y Censos.

———. n.d. Encuesta permanente de hogares: Marco teórico y metodológico de la investigación temática. Buenos Aires: Instituto Nacional de Estadística y Censos.

Isuani, Ernesto A., and Jorge A. San Martino. 1993. La reforma previsional Argentina. Opciones y riesgos. Buenos Aires: Miño y Dávila Editores.

———. 1995a. El nuevo sistema previsional Argentino: Punto final a una larga crisis? part 1. Boletín Informativo Techint 281 (January–March): 41–56.

———. 1995b. El nuevo sistema previsional Argentino: Punto final a una larga crisis? part 2. Boletín Informativo Techint 282 (April–June): 43–67.

Kakwani, Nanak, Laurence J. Kotlikoff, Mehdi Krongkaew, Sudhir Shetty, and Jan Walliser. 1995. Generational accounting in Thailand. Boston: Boston University, Department of Economics. Mimeograph.

Kotlikoff, Laurence J. 1992. *Generational accounting: Knowing who pays, and when, for what we spend.* New York: Free Press.

———. 1994. A critical review of the World Bank's social insurance analysis. Boston: Boston University, Department of Economics. Mimeograph.

———. 1995. Privatization of social security: How it works and why it matters. Boston: Boston University, Department of Economics. Mimeograph.

———. 1996a. Privatization of social security at home and abroad. Boston: Boston University, Department of Economics. Mimeograph.

———. 1996b. Privatizing social security in the United States: Why and how? Burch Working Paper no. B96–18. Berkeley: University of California.

Kotlikoff, Laurence J., and Philip Oreopoulos. 1995. Restoring generational balance in Canada. Boston: Boston University, Department of Economics. Mimeograph.

Kotlikoff, Laurence J., and Jan Walliser. 1995. Applying generational accounting to developing countries. Boston: Boston University, Department of Economics. Mimeograph.

Leibfritz, Willi. 1995. Generational accounting: An international comparison. Paris: Organization for Economic Cooperation and Development. Mimeograph.

Melconian, Carlos A., and Rodolfo A. Santángelo. [1996]. El endeudamiento del sector público Argentino en el período 1989–1995. United Nations Development Program Project no. ARG/91/R03.

MEyOySP (Ministerio de Economía y Obras y Servicios Públicos). [1994a]. *Argentina en crecimiento. La reforma económica y sus resultados: 1989–1993. El programa "Argentina en Crecimiento 1994–1996."* Buenos Aires: Ministerio de Economía y Obras y Servicios Públicos.

———. [1994b]. *Argentina en Crecimiento 1995–1999. Proyecciones macroeconómicas.* Buenos Aires: Ministerio de Economía y Obras y Servicios Públicos.

———. 1994c. *Argentina un país para invertir y crecer.* Buenos Aires: Ministerio de Economía y Obras y Servicios Públicos.

———. 1995a. *Argentina un país para invertir y crecer.* Buenos Aires: Ministerio de Economía y Obras y Servicios Públicos.

———. [1995b]. *Financiamiento de la transferencia de los regímenes previsionales provinciales.* Buenos Aires: Ministerio de Economía y Obras y Servicios Públicos. Photocopy.

———. Secretaría de Hacienda. Quarterly. *Boletín Fiscal.* Buenos Aires.

Rofman, Rafael. 1995. Moving social security toward fully funded schemes: Who pays the cost. Paper presented at the Seminar on Intergenerational Economic Relations and Demographic Change sponsored by the IUSSP Committee on Economic Demography and the East-West Center Program on Population, Honolulu, September.

Schulthess, Walter Erwin. 1994. La reforma de la previsión social en la República Argentina. Buenos Aires. Photocopy.

Superintendencia de Administradoras de Fondos de Jubilaciones y Pensiones. 1995. *Boletín estadístico.* Buenos Aires: Superintendencia de Administradoras de Fondos de Jubilaciones y Pensiones, December.

Techint. Monthly. *Boletín Informativo.* Buenos Aires.

Tendencias Económicas—Business Trends. *Yearbook* (in Spanish and English). Buenos Aires.

U.S. Office of Management and Budget. 1994. *Budget of the United States government: Analytical perspectives, fiscal year 1995,* chaps. 3 and 21–31. Washington, D.C.: Government Printing Office.

World Bank. 1994. *Averting the old age crisis: Policies to protect the old and promote growth.* World Bank Policy Research Report. New York: Oxford University Press.

6 Generational Accounting in Australia

John Ablett

6.1 Introduction and Overview of Findings

Intergenerational issues have become increasingly important in fiscal policy debates in Australia in the past few years. The recently elected Liberal-National coalition government has vowed to bring the national government budget into surplus within the next few years and has announced its intention to slash expenditure in almost all areas. The baseline Australian generational accounts for 1994/95 reveal a moderate imbalance in favor of current generations, and thus a reversal of the imbalance evident in the 1990/91 base-year accounts (Ablett 1996). Such a deterioration in generational balance appears to vindicate the need for fiscal restraint. However, as shown in section 6.5, the fiscal constraint implied by recent official government projections should be sufficient to correct the projected generational imbalance. This result should add perspective to discussions of the need for further drastic expenditure cuts.

Specific attention is given in this country study to the effects of migration on generational accounts. The simulations suggest post-base-year migrants belonging to age cohorts alive in the base year are likely to make a significant net positive contribution to the Australian public sector. Furthermore, post-base-year migration will tend to result in a reduction in the generational accounts of future generations in Australia.

John Ablett is lecturer in economics and finance at the University of Western Sydney, Macarthur, Australia. He completed his economics education at Brussels Free University and the University of New South Wales and held a previous academic appointment at the latter university.

6.2 Brief History of Australian Fiscal Policies
and Current Fiscal Debates

Recent fiscal policy debates in Australia have been dominated by the issue of whether fiscal policy should be generally tightened, particularly in terms of restraining expenditures. Politically, those advocating significant fiscal tightening appear to have won the argument, with the new Liberal-National coalition government elected in March 1996 announcing wide-ranging cuts to expenditure as well as some revenue-raising measures. The main arguments put forward for fiscal tightening have been the desirability of reducing the relative size of the public sector in the economy, the need for government to play a role in improving national saving, and more recently, concerns about the fiscal burden to be inherited by young and future Australians. It is important to view these arguments in the context of recent history.

Throughout the 1970s and the first half of the 1980s the Australian national government consistently recorded official budget deficits ranging to over 4 percent of GDP. Shortly after its election in 1983 the Labor Party government promised that over the life of its term of office it would not increase tax revenue or government expenditure as a proportion of GDP and would reduce the budget deficit as a proportion of GDP. These promises were largely fulfilled. The federal government budget moved into surplus in 1987/88 and remained so up to the 1990/91 fiscal year.

The economic recession of the early 1990s was, however, met with a significant loosening of fiscal policy, demonstrating that the then federal Labor government had not completely abandoned traditional Keynesian pump-priming as a means of macroeconomic management. As a result of the economic recession and discretionary spending measures, general government net debt as a percentage of GDP increased from a low of 11 percent in June 1990 to 26 percent in June 1995. Most of this increase was caused by increases in federal government debt as opposed to state and local government debt. General government outlays rose from 31 percent of GDP in 1988/89 to almost 36 percent of GDP in 1992/93, while government revenue fell as a proportion of GDP over the same period. Recent government projections that assume significant fiscal constraint imply the underlying general government deficit will fall to 0.4 percent of GDP by 1998/99 (*National Fiscal Outlook* 1996). However, the current national government has announced that it will take additional measures to tighten fiscal policy even more rapidly.

Since 1993, Australia's economic growth performance has improved, but unemployment has remained at unacceptably high levels. In 1996 the official unemployment rate remained at around 8.5 percent of the workforce.

Against this backdrop there have been calls for an acceleration of the microeconomic and labor market reforms commenced by the Labor government in the mid-1980s. Centerpieces of microeconomic reform have been financial market deregulation, the lowering of domestic industry tariff protection, and the promotion of competition in formally monopolized industries such as telecommunications and power generation. Numerous formerly government-owned enterprises such as the Commonwealth Bank have been fully or partly privatized. Labor market deregulation has focused on replacing centralized wage fixing by individual contracts between workers and their employers.

The growing opposition in Australia to big government implies that fiscal tightening should primarily be achieved through expenditure constraint, rather than general increases in the burden of taxation. Nevertheless, taxation reform is a keenly debated issue in Australia, with numerous economic commentators advocating a change in the tax mix to one with less distortionary effects on economic incentives to work, save, and invest. In this regard, the proposal to introduce a comprehensive consumption (value added) tax in Australia, first suggested in 1985, is now again being discussed seriously, despite being rejected by voters at the 1993 national election; the current government has promised not to introduce such a tax before the next national election.

The Australian social security system is also the subject of expenditure cuts. This is despite the fact that over the past decade most social security benefits have been increasingly means tested and targeted to specific disadvantaged groups. Some argue that there is still scope for reducing so-called middle-class welfare outlays, including family payments (related to the number of dependent children) to middle-income households. There is considerable political resistance to reducing such outlays; however, the current government has recently announced measures that reduce benefits to the middle class in the form of subsidized higher education and nursing home care.

Australia has a national health scheme (Medicare), originally introduced in the 1970s, that provides free public hospital care and free or subsidized consultations with medical practitioners.[1] Individuals may also purchase private insurance to cover the costs of private hospital treatment and a number of other medical expenses not included in the national scheme. Currently, about 15 percent of the cost of Medicare is met by a levy currently set at 1.5 percent of taxable income for most taxpayers. Historically the Medicare system has been reasonably successful in keeping down the cost of public health care in Australia, compared to other developed countries. This has changed somewhat in recent years with large increases in government health outlays, especially for pathology/diagnostic services and subsidized pharmaceuticals. The public hospital system has also been put under pressure by a continuing exodus of individuals from private health insurance. The present national government has announced some measures to limit the growth in public health care outlays and encourage people to take out private health insurance, but it is unlikely these will be sufficient.

---

1. Over time, out-of-pocket medical expenses have tended to increase in line with a widening gap between actual doctors' fees and the amount Medicare reimburses. This is especially so for specialist services, although competition has ensured a zero copayment for most visits to general practitioners.

As in other countries, a major concern with public health care and other social security expenditures in Australia is aging of the population. The fear is that the public cost of supporting the elderly will lead to exaggerated tax burdens on future generations. In response to this perceived problem, compulsory saving for retirement has been introduced, as represented by the Superannuation Guarantee Charge (SGC). One of the main aims of the SGC is to moderate future growth of public retirement pension outlays. Under the SGC provisions, each employee has an individual retirement savings account, to which the employer makes contributions on behalf of the employee; these contributions are to be increased in stages to at least 9 percent of gross earnings by 2002. Additional contributions to the savings accounts by employees themselves amounting to at least 3 percent of earnings are also foreseen. The future retirement incomes of those who have accumulated retirement account savings throughout their working lives will be mainly composed of income derived from these savings, perhaps supplemented by a reduced public pension. In view of the lengthy phase-in time, it is not expected that the SGC will lead to significant moderation of public retirement pension outlays over the next 20 years. However, over the long term, the effects should be large.

An additional key, but contested argument for compulsory saving for retirement in Australia is its supposed positive effect on national saving. Average household saving as a percentage of after-tax income fell from about 11 percent in the late 1970s to 3 percent in 1994/95. Australian public sector dissaving has also generally increased over the past decade. The country's reliance on foreign savings has manifested itself by substantial current account deficits over the past 15 years ranging between 3 and 6 percent of GDP. The 1994/95 ratio of current account deficit to GDP was 5.9 percent, higher than in all OECD countries except Mexico. At the present time, the main component of the Australian current account deficit is the net income deficit, largely representing interest payments on foreign debt accumulated during the past decade.

While Australian governments have historically rejected the extreme view that there is a direct link between government budget deficits and current account deficits, there is widespread support for measures to reduce the public sector's dissaving and demand for loanable funds. Indeed the perceived need to increase national saving is the principal reason advanced by the current national government for fiscal tightening.

6.3   Brief Description of Data Sources

The Australian generational accounts refer to the base year of 1 July 1994 to 30 June 1995, since the Australian financial year starts in July.

Four sets of population projections for years up to 2100 are used in this chapter's calculations, each corresponding to a different migration scenario. All four are based on assumptions described in the published projections of the Australian Bureau of Statistics (1994), which suppose improvements in age/gender-specific mortality rates up to 2041 and a constant total fertility rate per woman of 1.884. For the purposes of the Australian generational accounts it was assumed that no further improvements in mortality would occur after 2041.

The first set of population projections represents a zero post-base-year migration counterfactual. It was calculated by applying the assumed age/gender-specific mortality rates and age-specific fertility rates to the cohorts alive in each year, starting with the resident population surviving to year 1994/95. Thus it assumes zero net migration after the base year. In this case the total Australian population is projected to reach a maximum of about 20.2 million in 2030 and then decrease steadily, reaching a level of 16.7 million by 2100, which is less than the current population.

Two further sets of population projections ("low" and "high") were calculated by extending the Australian Bureau of Statistics low and high population series for 1993–2041 up to 2100. These projections incorporate steady increases in net migration up to 2001, after which annual net migration remains constant at 70,000 and 100,000 for the low and high series, respectively. They assume the relative age and gender composition of migration by category of movement (permanent or long-term arrivals or departures) after 1994/95 will remain constant at the average composition for the years 1990/91 to 1992/93. Total population increases steadily for both the low and high series, reaching 27.8 and 32.2 million, respectively, by 2100.

A third "super high" population scenario assumes net annual migration to Australia of 150,000 for all years after 1994/95. The relative age and gender composition of this net migration is assumed to be the same as that for the other sets of population projections incorporating positive migration. Total population increases to 40.6 million by 2100 under the super high scenario.

Results given in section 6.4 and subsection 6.5.1 are based exclusively on the low series (low migration) scenario. Under this scenario the elderly dependency ratio (the number aged 65 or older as a percentage of the number aged 18 to 64) rises from 19.2 percent in 1995 to about 38.5 percent in 2040, after which it remains stable; the child (ages 0 to 17) dependency ratio is projected to decrease from 41.2 percent in 1995 to 36.0 percent in 2020. The projected changes in elderly and child dependency ratios roughly cancel each other out over the next 20 years, leaving the total dependency ratio fairly stable over this period at about 60 percent. Beyond this time frame, a stable child dependency ratio and continued aging of the population result in the total dependency ratio increasing steadily to its long-run level of about 75 percent by 2040.

In establishing the Australian generational accounts, payments to government were divided into indirect taxes and taxes on labor income, capital income, and property. Benefits from government included age pension, family and child, unemployment, and other social security benefits, and transfer payments related to education and health care. Age/gender profiles of all these payments and benefits in 1994/95 were derived using data from the Australian

Bureau of Statistics 1988 Household Expenditure Survey and 1990 Household Income Survey, benchmarked against national account and government finance aggregates.

Recent educational participation rates and profiles of health care consumption (from survey data) by age and gender were used to adjust the educational and health components of projected government consumption expenditure projections for changing demographic composition. Except for subsidies to industry, all other components of government consumption expenditure were assumed to increase at the general per capita income growth rate, unless otherwise stated.[2] Subsidies to industry were assumed to remain constant at their real 1994/95 level; these have remained fairly constant over the past half-decade, and both the new Australian national government and the major opposition party are committed to reducing industry protection. Net transfers to government from public trading enterprises in the base year were treated as negative government consumption expenditure. The government net wealth estimate used was general government net debt.

6.4 Basic Findings and Sensitivity Analysis

The following baseline Australian generational accounts, referring to the base year 1 July 1994 to 30 June 1995, use the low population (low migration) described in section 6.3. A low migration scenario is considered most realistic given recent experience and moves to limit the growth of annual migration to Australia. In the results of this section, all per capita payments, benefits, and government consumption expenditure (except for subsidies to industry) are assumed to grow at the general rate.

As can be seen in tables 6.1 and 6.2, there is a moderate generational imbalance in favor of current generations for all discount rate and growth rate combinations presented. The deterioration in generational imbalance in Australia since 1990/91 is mainly due to increased government purchases, increased government indebtedness, and cyclical changes in government revenues and transfer payments. Fiscal year 1990/91 was the last in which the federal government officially recorded a surplus; an economic recession was experienced over the next few years.

Table 6.3 provides a decomposition of the baseline accounts of table 6.1 for persons by the various tax and transfer components used. It can be seen that the major component affecting the accounts of elderly generations is age pension receipts.[3]

2. Government consumption aggregates from the Australian national accounts include estimates of consumption of fixed capital.

3. The health component in the accounts does not include in-kind benefits such as free treatment in public hospitals. Expenditure on these services is included in public consumption expenditure in establishing the accounts.

Table 6.1   **Present Value of Net Tax Payments per Capita (thousands of U.S. dollars)**

Generation's Age in 1994/95	All Persons	Males	Females
0	79.6	105.1	52.8
5	95.3	125.0	64.0
10	112.8	147.5	76.7
15	134.3	174.2	92.1
20	148.4	192.2	102.6
25	147.7	196.0	98.5
30	138.5	187.0	90.6
35	128.2	171.3	85.0
40	111.9	149.1	75.0
45	87.4	119.7	54.4
50	57.4	85.1	28.7
55	25.9	46.9	3.6
60	1.5	15.6	−12.6
65	−12.7	−3.9	−21.3
70	−17.6	−9.6	−24.6
75	−16.1	−7.4	−23.0
80	−13.8	−6.3	−18.6
85	−11.3	−5.3	−14.4
90	−9.4	−6.1	−10.7
Future generations	105.2		

Note: Real income growth assumed to be 1.5 percent; discount rate, 5 percent.

In view of the comments about fiscal tightening made previously, there is reason to believe that these base-case results present a somewhat pessimistic assessment of generational imbalance, a point taken up in the next section.

6.5   Generational Impact of Alternative Policies

6.5.1   Effects of Budget Restraint and the Small Country Assumption

Table 6.4 reveals how the Australian accounts change as a result of several immediate and permanent policy changes that would imply generational balance: a 5.1 percent increase in all tax revenues, a 12.1 percent decrease in all transfer payments, and an 8.8 percent decrease in government purchases. Comparing the first two of these scenarios, we see that current generations up to 40 years of age would be marginally better off under a cut in transfer payments, but those older than 40 years would be decidedly worse off under this policy. This result is expected given the importance of transfer receipts to the elderly and taxation payments by the young.

The results of four other simulations are given in table 6.5. The assumptions behind each of these and a discussion of the results are given below.

Table 6.2 Present Value of Net Tax Payments per Capita for All Persons (thousands of U.S. dollars)

	g = 1			g = 1.5			g = 2		
	r = 3	r = 5	r = 7	r = 3	r = 5	r = 7	r = 3	r = 5	r = 7
Present generation	138	66	32	167	80	39	203	96	47
Future generations	187	91	58	247	105	63	362	124	70
Absolute imbalance	49	25	26	80	25	24	159	28	23
Percentage imbalance	36	38	80	47	32	63	78	29	50

Note: g is productivity growth rate (percent); r is discount rate (percent).

Table 6.3   Decomposition of Generational Accounts for All Persons by Tax and Transfer Components (thousands of U.S. dollars)

A. Ages 0 to 45

Generational Account Component	Generation's Age in 1994/95									
	0	5	10	15	20	25	30	35	40	45
Labor income tax	53.3	62.2	72.0	84.1	91.5	89.5	81.4	73.0	61.5	47.9
Capital income tax	21.2	24.7	28.6	33.5	37.4	41.9	45.9	48.0	49.4	50.0
Property tax	9.9	11.5	13.4	15.6	17.7	20.1	21.6	21.9	21.6	20.1
Indirect tax	43.5	50.6	58.8	68.5	72.2	66.5	60.5	55.8	51.3	44.5
Total payments (1)	127.9	149.0	172.8	201.7	218.8	218.0	209.4	198.7	183.8	162.5
Age pension	10.1	11.8	13.7	16.0	18.1	20.8	24.0	27.5	31.9	37.1
Family benefits	6.5	7.5	8.8	10.1	11.3	11.7	10.2	7.1	3.8	1.6
Educational benefits	3.5	4.0	3.6	3.2	2.2	1.3	0.9	0.8	0.7	0.7
Health benefits	11.5	10.9	11.3	11.7	11.5	11.5	11.3	10.9	11.0	11.0
Other social security	16.7	19.5	22.6	26.4	27.3	25.0	24.5	24.2	24.5	24.7
Total benefits (2)	48.3	53.7	60.0	67.4	70.4	70.3	70.9	70.5	71.9	75.1
Generational account (1) − (2)	79.6	95.3	112.8	134.3	148.4	147.7	138.5	128.2	111.9	87.4

(continued)

Table 6.3   (continued)

B. Ages 50 to 90

Generational Account Component	Generation's Age in 1994/95								
	50	55	60	65	70	75	80	85	90
Labor income tax	33.8	20.0	8.8	2.6	1.2	0.7	0.4	0.3	0
Capital income tax	49.1	46.6	43.1	36.6	29.5	23.5	18.4	14.0	10.5
Property tax	18.3	16.1	14.0	11.8	9.4	7.5	6.0	4.6	3.5
Indirect tax	36.1	27.2	20.5	15.4	11.2	8.2	6.8	4.5	3.3
Total payments (1)	137.3	109.9	86.4	66.4	51.3	39.9	31.6	23.4	17.3
Age pension	43.4	50.8	60.1	61.1	54.6	45.5	37.0	28.2	21.7
Family benefits	0.6	0.2	0	0	0	0	0	0	
Educational benefits	0.5	0.4	0.2	0	0	0	0	0	0
Health benefits	10.8	10.5	9.8	9.2	7.7	6.2	4.9	3.7	2.8
Other social security	24.6	22.1	14.8	8.8	6.6	4.3	3.5	2.8	2.2
Total benefits (2)	79.9	84.0	84.9	79.1	68.9	56.0	45.4	34.7	26.7
Generational account (1) − (2)	57.4	25.9	1.5	−12.7	−17.6	−16.1	−13.8	−11.3	−9.4

Note: Real income growth assumed to be 1.5 percent; discount rate, 5 percent.

Table 6.4   **Policy Options: Present Value of Net Tax Payments per Capita for All Persons (thousands of U.S. dollars)**

		Policy Scenario Implying Generational Balance		
Generation's Age in 1994/95	Base Case	5.1% Increase in Tax Revenues	12.1% Decrease in Transfers	8.8% Decrease in Government Purchases
0	79.6	86.1	85.5	79.6
5	95.3	102.9	101.8	95.3
10	112.8	121.6	120.1	112.8
15	134.3	144.6	142.5	134.3
20	148.4	159.5	156.9	148.4
25	147.7	158.7	156.2	147.7
30	138.5	149.1	147.1	138.5
35	128.2	138.3	136.7	128.2
40	111.9	121.2	120.6	111.9
45	87.4	95.6	96.5	87.4
50	57.4	64.4	67.1	57.4
55	25.9	31.4	36.0	25.9
60	1.5	5.9	11.8	1.5
65	−12.7	−9.3	−3.1	−12.7
70	−17.6	−15.0	−9.2	−17.6
75	−16.1	−14.1	−9.4	−16.1
80	−13.8	−12.2	−8.3	−13.8
85	−11.3	−10.1	−7.1	−11.3
90	−9.4	−8.5	−6.1	−9.4
Future generations	105.2	86.1	85.5	79.6

Note: Real income growth assumed to be 1.5 percent; discount rate, 5 percent.

Small Country Assumption

In this simulation the "small country assumption" is used, whereby the incidence of corporate income taxes is supposed to fall on labor income. This assumption is based on the hypothesis that in a small open economy (such as Australia) taxes on mobile capital are borne by the nonmobile factor of production (labor). Its application results in generational imbalance increasing to 49 percent, with quite large decreases in the accounts of middle-aged and elderly current generations, and marginal increases in the accounts of those under age 30 in the base year. Since capital ownership is more concentrated among older generations, this result is not surprising.

Moderate Fiscal Constraint

This scenario applies the public sector total outlay and revenue projections up to fiscal year 1998/99 contained in the *National Fiscal Outlook* (1996). These projections take account of specific announced policy measures as at May 1996 but do not include the A$8 billion (about U.S.$6.2 billion) cut to the official national government deficit over 1996/97–1997/98 foreshadowed

Table 6.5   **Other Assumptions: Present Value of Net Tax Payments per Capita for All Persons (thousands of U.S. dollars)**

Generation's Age in 1994/95	Base Case	Small Country Assumption	Moderate Fiscal Constraint	High Fiscal Constraint	Zero Age Pension Growth
			Scenario		
0	79.6	83.0	84.1	85.1	86.2
5	95.3	99.3	100.4	101.5	102.7
10	112.8	117.4	118.6	119.8	121.0
15	134.3	139.7	140.8	142.2	143.4
20	148.4	153.5	155.2	156.6	158.0
25	147.7	149.1	154.5	155.8	158.0
30	138.5	134.4	145.2	146.6	149.5
35	128.2	119.8	134.8	136.2	139.7
40	111.9	98.7	118.4	119.8	123.8
45	87.4	69.2	93.8	95.3	99.5
50	57.4	35.0	63.7	65.3	69.3
55	25.9	0.5	31.9	33.5	37.1
60	1.5	−25.4	7.0	8.6	11.3
65	−12.7	−37.2	−8.0	−6.5	−4.9
70	−17.6	−37.8	−13.7	−12.5	−11.8
75	−16.1	−32.8	−13.2	−12.3	−12.2
80	−13.8	−26.8	−11.6	−10.9	−11.3
85	−11.3	−21.2	−9.8	−9.3	−9.9
90	−9.4	−16.7	−8.4	−8.1	−8.6
Future generations	105.2	123.7	75.3	66.2	82.6
Percentage imbalance	32.2	49.0	−10.5	−22.1	−4.2

Note: Real income growth assumed to be 1.5 percent; discount rate, 5 percent.

by the recently elected government. They foresee total government outlays falling from 34.9 percent of GDP in 1994/95 to 32.6 percent of GDP in 1998/99, with total government revenue falling marginally as a percentage of GDP up to 1998/99. In calculating the accounts for this scenario, the annual percentage changes in total outlays and revenue implied by the projections were applied uniformly to all generational account benchmarking aggregates; the general per capita growth rate was applied to all years after 1998/99.

The fiscal constraint (compared to 1994/95) implied by the *National Fiscal Outlook* projections leads to substantial changes in the generational accounts, indicating that the baseline 1994/95 Australian accounts represent a somewhat pessimistic view. Generational imbalance is reversed with the generational account of future generations becoming 10.5 percent less than that of base year newborns.

High Fiscal Constraint

This scenario is similar to the moderate fiscal constraint scenario except that it factors in additional A\$4 billion (about U.S.\$3.1 billion) cuts to projected government outlays in both 1996/97 and 1997/98. The implied percentage changes in total outlays are applied uniformly to all benchmarking outlay aggregates.[4] This scenario is designed to give an approximate indication of the possible effects of the current federal government's stated goal of balancing the official federal government budget by the end of the 1997/98 financial year. It leads to a doubling of the percentage imbalance in favor of future generations evident in the results for the moderate fiscal constraint scenario.

Zero Age Pension Growth

This scenario is the same as the baseline scenario except that it assumes zero growth in per capita public age pensions after the base year. Such a scenario is relevant in view of the move toward self-funded retirement incomes in Australia, although under current rules compulsory saving for retirement is unlikely to have a significant moderating effect on public age pension benefits until well into the next century (Ablett 1996). It leads to a marginal imbalance in favor of future generations, representing a significant shift compared to the baseline accounts.

6.5.2 Role of Migration in the Net Fiscal Contributions of Generations

Do immigrants contribute less to the public sector of the host country than they receive in return?[5] Australia has traditionally been among those countries with the highest ratios of migrant to native born; therefore, it is of interest to investigate how immigration affects the generational accounting results for this country.

Two conclusions emerge from the simulation results presented in this section.[6] First, future migrants belonging to generations alive in 1994/95 (the base year of the calculations) are likely to make a substantial net positive direct contribution to the Australian public sector. Second, when the implied per capita fiscal burden to be borne by future generations is considered, future migration per se is also projected to have a net positive effect on public sector resources.

The above conclusions can be understood by way of an example. Consider a historically typical migrant to Australia who arrives after completing her formal education in her country of origin. Arriving at the start of her working life, she will tend to make net positive contributions to the public sector over many

---

4. There will of course be a number of changes on the revenue side of government finances as well, such as the raising of the national health care (Medicare) levy on high-income earners who do not have private health insurance. It is felt, however, that reducing projected outlays in the manner described captures the main generational implications of the announced generalized fiscal constraint.

5. The general issue of economic gains from migration is not considered here. Borjas (1994, 1995) provides comprehensive reviews of the issues involved.

6. Except for varying migration assumptions, this section makes the same assumptions as used in establishment of the base-case accounts of section 6.4 (including a 5 percent discount rate and a 1.5 percent growth rate). The qualitative results reported in this section are the same under all the discount and real income growth rate combinations considered in section 6.4.

years through the taxation and social security system. In present value terms, the burden she will represent for the public sector once retired will be minimal. If the experience of a sufficient number of migrants approaches this stylized example, the first conclusion above is not surprising.

However, the second conclusion need not be so clear-cut. Our "typical" migrant, being younger than the average age of all Australian residents, contributes to a moderation in the aging of the population. Supposing she is indeed a female, she renders the age pyramid of females younger, and hence the overall birthrate higher than it would have been otherwise. This will be the case even if, as assumed here, migrant women display the same age-specific fertility rates as women in Australia generally. The increased birthrate will, however, lead to increased demands on public sector resources associated with the education and welfare of greater numbers of children; there will also be greater infrastructure needs for the larger population. The results presented in this section suggest that these increased demands on the public sector are not sufficiently important to lead to an increase in the generational accounts of future generations.

There have been numerous studies that specifically try to gauge the impact of migration on the public purse, particularly in North America and Australia.[7] In contrast to the long-term generational accounting approach used here, most previous studies in this area have tried to assess the impact of migrants on public sector finances in a given year and have not considered all payments to and all benefits received from all levels of government.

Some could argue that generational accounting is an inadequate vehicle for examining the direct net contribution of migrants to government because it ignores differences in average payment and benefit levels between migrants and nonmigrants belonging to the same age/gender cohort. However, previous Australian studies (e.g., Whiteford 1991) suggest that such differences may not be great and are mainly associated with the settling-in period of recent arrivals. More important, the validity of generational accounting in this context does not depend primarily on whether there are systematic differences between net payments to government by migrants and nonmigrants, but rather on the extent to which the average net payments of post-base-year migrants differ from those of the resident base-year population. Inasmuch as the resident population already contains a relatively high proportion of migrants, as in Australia, the average net payment differences between residents and future migrants of the same age may not be large. If this is the case, it is reasonable to conclude that general population level and age composition considerations hold the key to gauging the likely overall direct long-term contribution of future migration to the public purse. The approach used here is based on this view.

---

7. Notable North American studies include Blau (1984), Jensen (1989), and Simon (1989). Australian studies include Whiteford (1991) and Centre for International Economics (1992).

Migration and the Generational Accounts of Current Generations

To understand how migration affects generational accounts, one should first recall that the per capita generational account for each currently living cohort is usually calculated by dividing the cohort's total account by the number of members of the cohort *alive and resident* in the country in the base year. However, the cohort's total account will be affected by migration. Consider the case of 20-year-olds in the base year. If there is no migration of people belonging to this age cohort after the base year and all the other assumptions of the generational accounting exercise are satisfied, then calculation of this cohort's generational account in the manner described above will indeed give a valid indication of the average remaining lifetime net fiscal burden facing base-year resident members of this cohort. However, if foreigners aged 20 in the base year migrate subsequent to the base year, then, ceteris paribus, the generational account so calculated will not, strictly speaking, represent the net present value of tax contributions of 20-year-olds resident in the country in the base year. This is explained by the fact that post-base-year migration swells the numbers of members of a given cohort alive in future years, leading to a change in the cohort's total calculated net contribution. The same reasoning obviously applies to all cohorts alive in the base year.[8]

A failure to separate out the impact of migration on the generational accounts of generations alive in the base year effectively means that these generations are projected to live longer than they actually do. Thus the future arrival of migrants will increase the survival rate of a generation to a given future year if this is calculated as the ratio of the number of cohort members (including post-base-year migrants) resident in the given future year to the number of cohort members resident in the base year.

Table 6.6 shows generational accounts of those alive in the base year under zero post-base-year migration and the low, high, and super high population scenarios described above that assume successively higher levels of future migration. The last row of the table gives the percentage increase in the aggregate generational accounts of all currently living generations compared to the zero migration scenario.

The message from table 6.6 is quite clear. For generations up to 50 years of age in 1994/95, post-1994/95 migrants belonging to these generations are projected to contribute directly, in aggregate, positive net present value amounts to the Australian public sector, at least before government consumption expenditure is considered. This is implied by the increased generational accounts of these cohorts compared to the zero post-1994/95 migration scenario. It is also evident that higher migration accentuates this positive net con-

8. In view of the argument presented here, it may be desirable in general to calculate the accounts of currently living (resident) generations by excluding the contributions of post-base-year migrants from the aggregate account of each generation.

156   John Ablett

Table 6.6 **Population Scenarios: Present Value of Net Tax Payments per Capita for All Persons (thousands of U.S. dollars)**

Generation's Age in 1994/95	Zero Migration	Post-1994/95 Population Scenario		
		Low	High	Super High
0	66.1	79.6	84.9	94.1
5	81.6	95.3	100.7	110.3
10	98.9	112.8	118.3	128.0
15	120.0	134.4	140.1	150.5
20	138.0	148.4	153.6	163.2
25	139.4	147.7	151.7	160.6
30	132.5	138.5	141.1	147.0
35	125.0	128.2	129.4	132.4
40	110.2	111.9	112.4	113.9
45	86.9	87.4	87.6	88.2
50	57.4	57.4	57.4	57.8
55	26.1	25.8	25.8	26.0
60	1.8	1.5	1.4	1.5
65	−12.3	−12.7	−12.8	−12.6
70	−17.2	−17.6	−17.6	−17.4
75	−15.8	−16.1	−16.2	−15.9
80	−13.5	−13.8	−13.8	−13.5
85	−11.0	−11.3	−11.4	−11.0
90	−9.1	−9.4	−9.6	−9.1
Percentage aggregate increase		6.96	9.90	15.74

Note: Real income growth assumed to be 1.5 percent; discount rate, 5 percent.

tribution. The greatest net positive contributions are associated with young cohorts. This is largely explained by two factors. First, the composition of currently recorded and future projected migrant intakes is such that many migrants receive all or most of their education in their home countries before migrating to Australia between ages 20 and 40 and joining the (taxpaying) adult workforce. Second, there will be significantly more future migrants coming from younger 1994/95 age groups than from older age groups.

The story for those over 50 years of age in 1994/95 is different. As future migrants in these cohorts will arrive either shortly before retirement or after retirement, their generational account contribution will mostly be negative, thus adding to the public burden of supporting the aged population. However, since migrants in these age groups represent a relatively minor proportion of migrant intakes, their negative contributions are not sufficient to make the total net contribution over all cohorts negative.

The total percentage increases over all cohorts given in the last row of table 6.6 are arguably quite significant. For example, under the high population

Table 6.7   **Contribution of Future Migration of Cohorts Alive in 1994/95 (thousands of U.S. dollars per migrant)**

	Population Scenario		
	Low	High	Super High
Per migrant generational account contribution	58.8	59.3	60.2
Government consumption per migrant	44.1	43.1	41.7
Net contribution per migrant	14.7	16.2	18.5

Note: Real income growth assumed to be 1.5 percent; discount rate, 5 percent.

(high migration) scenario, future migration of members of generations alive in 1994/95 is projected to increase directly the aggregate generational account contribution of these cohorts by almost 10 percent.

Whether future migrants belonging to generations alive in the base year will make an overall net positive contribution to the public sector also depends on the increase in public consumption expenditure associated with them. However, it is possible to calculate this amount given the assumptions relating to government consumption expenditure in the base-case generational accounts. For each migration scenario, table 6.7 shows the per migrant generational account contribution, government consumption expenditure and the difference between these two amounts (the "net contribution") for those alive in (but migrating after) the base year.[9] Note that the first of these amounts is not comparable to the generational accounts of base-year residents since it refers to contributions by post-base-year migrants belonging to many different generations and migrating over possibly many future years.

One notes that the overall net contributions in table 6.7 are indeed positive. The simulations also show a significant reduction in the net contribution of migrants when the migration-associated increase in government consumption expenditure is included. Since the assumed age structure of arriving migrants is the same under each scenario, the differences in results across scenarios in table 6.7 are purely due to differences in the timing of net migration increases.

Migration and the Generational Accounts of Future Generations

So far we have considered only the contributions of future migrants alive in the base year. To gauge the net contribution of future migration per se on government resources it is necessary to investigate its effect on the per capita generational accounts of future generations.

By definition, the change in the projected aggregate generational account of all future generations due to post-base-year net migration will equal the change

9. The per migrant averages in table 6.7 were calculated by dividing the appropriate aggregate contributions of all post-1994/95 migrants alive in 1994/95 by the projected total net migration of these cohorts post-1994/95.

in the present value of future government consumption expenditure minus the change in the aggregate generational accounts of currently living generations; migration affects future government consumption not only directly, but also indirectly by increasing the number of future births. Some care is needed, however, in calculating the per capita generational accounts of future generations if the overall effect of migration is to be assessed. To clarify this, we can decompose the total generational accounts of future generations in the following way:

$$(1) \qquad \sum_{s=1}^{\infty} N_{t,t+s} = \sum_{s=1}^{\infty} N_{t,t+s}^{d} + \sum_{s=1}^{\infty} N_{t,t+s}^{m}.$$

In equation (1), $N_{t,t+s}^{d}$ is the aggregate generational account of domestic born members of future generations (born after the base year), while $N_{t,t+s}^{m}$ is the present value of the aggregate net fiscal contribution (in terms of generational account components) of future migrants belonging to future generations. In calculating the results so far presented in this country study, it has been assumed implicitly that the net fiscal burden on a given future generation is borne completely by domestic born members of that generation. In other words it has been assumed that $N_{t,t+s}^{m}$ ($s \geq 1$) is zero. But where migration is significant, it is important to make some alternative assumption about how a future generation's net fiscal burden is to be shared between domestic born and migrant members of the generation; otherwise, any positive effect of migration will be understated. The assumption made here is that future migrants born in the future make the same age-specific generational account contributions as those resident in the base year, except for an adjustment for growth (using the assumed general growth rate). Under this assumption, an individual born overseas in year $t + s$ ($s \geq 1$) and migrating to Australia in year $t + x$ ($x \geq s$) would on average face a generational account burden on arrival of $n_{t,t-(x-s)}(1 + g)^{x}$, where $n_{t,t-(x-s)}$ is the per capita generational account of those aged $x - s$ years in the base year and g is the annual growth rate.[10]

Table 6.8 shows the generational accounts of future generations *born in Australia* under the above assumption about the division of the projected total net fiscal burden on future generations between Australian- and overseas-born members of these generations. It is assumed that the generational accounts (at birth) of Australian-born members of all future generations are the same except for the general per capita growth.[11]

It is evident from table 6.8 that under the assumptions of the generational

10. In obtaining the results in table 6.8 using this assumption, the generational accounts of base-year residents were calculated excluding the contributions of post-base-year migrants from the aggregate account of each generation.

11. A comparison of table 6.8 with table 6.1 shows that the assumption regarding the sharing of a future generation's net fiscal burden between migrants and nonmigrants leads to a reduction in the account of future generations from $105,200 to $92,000.

Table 6.8   **Generational Accounts of Future Generations Born in Australia (thousands of U.S. dollars per migrant)**

	Post-1994/95 Population Scenario			
	Zero Migration	Low	High	Super High
Generational account	95.9	92.0	90.1	86.5
Percentage change due to migration		−4.1	−6.0	−9.8

Note: Real income growth assumed to be 1.5 percent; discount rate, 5 percent.

accounting exercise positive post-base-year migration is projected to have a favorable effect on the generational accounts of future generations, and that this effect is greater the higher the level of migration. For example, the high population (high migration) scenario would reduce the generational accounts of future generations by 6.0 percent compared with the zero migration counterfactual.

6.6   Brief Summary and Conclusion

The Australian baseline accounts for 1994/95 show a generational imbalance of 32.2 percent. This result is based on applying the uniform growth rate of 1.5 percent per annum to all per capita payments and benefits after the base year and assuming a low net migration scenario. If the fiscal constraint inherent in recent government projections is indeed realized, the baseline imbalance result is likely to be reversed, as suggested by the simulations of the previous section. A similar reversal of imbalance is projected to occur if the baseline scenario is altered simply by holding real per capita age pension benefits constant at their base-year levels.

The results reinforce the view that the level of net payments by government to older generations is the most important policy factor in the redistribution of resources between generations in Australia. Discretionary government expenditure is also important; however, it is more easily altered over the short term. The move to privately funded retirement incomes could prove the most significant element in the determination of generational imbalance over the long term.

The simulations relating to migration imply that post-base-year migration should have an overall positive generational effect, as reflected in a reduction in the generational accounts of future generations. This result is mainly driven by the relative dominance of young working-age people in the composition of migrant intakes, compared to the resident Australian population. In the future it would be desirable to see whether this conclusion is supported by similar analyses in other countries with relatively high rates of migration.

References

Ablett, J. 1996. Generational accounting—An Australian perspective. *Review of Income and Wealth* 42 (1): 91–105.

Australian Bureau of Statistics. 1994. Projections of the populations of Australia, states and territories 1993–2041. Catalogue no. 3222.0. Canberra: Australian Bureau of Statistics.

Blau, F. 1984. The use of transfer payments by immigrants. *Industrial and Labour Relations Review* 37:222–39.

Borjas, G. J. 1994. The economics of immigration. *Journal of Economic Literature* 32 (4): 1667–1717.

———. 1995. The economic benefits of immigration. *Journal of Economic Perspectives* 9 (2): 3–22.

Centre for International Economics. 1992. Immigration and the Commonwealth budget. Canberra: Government Publishing Service.

Jensen, L. 1989. *The new immigration: Implications for poverty and public assistance utilization.* Studies in Social Welfare Policies and Programs, vol. 10. New York: Greenwood.

National fiscal outlook—Report to the 1996 premiers' conference. 1996. Canberra: Government Publishing Service.

Simon, J. 1989. The economic consequences of immigration. New York: Blackwell.

Whiteford, P. 1991. Immigrants and the social security system. Bureau of Immigration Research. Canberra: Government Publishing Service.

7   Generational Accounts for Belgium

Jean-Philippe Stijns

7.1   Introduction

In most governmental and academic discussions about budgetary discipline, the budget deficit—or the net financial balance—is often cited as the key variable to control. Belgium is not different in that respect. Hence, in section 7.2, I present a brief review of Belgian fiscal policy from a debt-deficit point of view. This partial vision suggests that Belgian public finances are, overall, under control.

My aim in this paper is to go beyond this and present generational accounts for Belgium. Auerbach, Gokhale, and Kotlikoff (1991) have introduced generational accounting as an alternative or at least a complement to the traditional measure of budget deficit. The data and conventions that are the basis for the generational accounts for Belgium are set up in the last part of section 7.2.

The generational accounts themselves are presented in section 7.3. Next, the estimate of the burden on future generations is computed. This estimate is compared to the "birth bill" that typical members of future generations will have to face given the intertemporal budget constraint of the government. Finally, the conclusions of generational accounting about the burden imposed by old-age pensions will be compared to the results of other kinds of studies.

In section 7.4, I examine the generational accounts for Belgium in terms of potential fiscal policy. Alternative policy measures are simulated and conclusions are drawn about the relative efficacy and political feasibility of the corresponding fiscal instruments. I analyze in section 7.5 the influence of the

When this paper was written, Jean-Philippe Stijns was SSTC researcher at the University of Liège.

The author is indebted to Paul Perdang whose memorandum has served as an important starting point for this paper. He is thankful to Alan Auerbach, Etienne de Callataÿ, Sergio Perelman, Pierre Pestieau, and Laurence Kotlikoff for their useful comments and to SSTC (Belgian Science Foundation) for financial support.

treatment of education on generational accounts. Finally, in section 7.6, I summarize my findings and present some paths for further research.

7.2   The Belgian Setting

With a debt-to-GDP ratio around 128 percent in 1995, the issue of the need for budget discipline is obviously compelling in Belgium. Table 7.1 summarizes the evolution of the Belgian government budget from the mid-1980s up to 1995. Some substantial efforts have in fact already been accomplished. Indeed, during the 1980s, the Belgian government net financial balance fell by more than half as a share of GDP, decreasing from 13 percent in the early 1980s to roughly 5.7 percent in 1990. From 1991 until 1993, however, the net financial balance deteriorated and went back up to 7.5 percent of GDP. Since 1994, the net financial balance has been decreasing again.[1]

The first objective of Belgian budgetary policy is currently to meet the Maastricht Treaty criteria. Accordingly, in 1992, the government set targets for the gradual mitigation of the government deficit to 3 percent of GDP in 1996 (compared to 7 percent in 1992). In fact, this pace of deficit reduction is comparable to that observed in the 1980s. The second objective is to eliminate the risk of a "snowball effect," that is, a self-sustaining increase in the debt-to-GDP ratio as a result of interest payments. The third is to create in the long run a sufficient degree of freedom for public finances to confront the problems of population aging.

In practice, the plan introduces three guidelines: the welfare system is to be in equilibrium, fiscal receipts must have "unit elasticity" (increase in line with GDP), and primary expenditure must not increase in real terms. A supplementary rule consists in keeping the primary surplus above 6 percent of GDP beyond 1996, with a view to bringing up a "countersnowball" effect.

Since 1992, in order to compensate for the negative incidence of unforeseen macroeconomic shocks, the government has implemented a series of structural corrective measures. According to the National Bank of Belgium (1995), these additional measures implied budget reductions of 1 percent in 1992, 2.5 percent in 1993, and 1.75 percent in 1994. Also, approximately 60 percent of these are due to new direct and indirect taxes and to a lesser extent to increased payroll taxes, 30 percent result from cutbacks in expenditures, and 10 percent stem from other sources, including asset auctions. Indeed, the Belgian primary surplus in percent of GDP is clearly high (5 percent vs. −0.7 percent for the European Union). This reflects the high level of taxes: compared to the EU average, direct and payroll taxes are 5.5 percent higher whereas primary expenditures, at 42.7 percent, are only slightly higher.

In 1994, the snowball effect seems to have practically stopped: the debt-to-GDP ratio has slightly decreased below 128 percent. Nevertheless, with a debt-to-GDP ratio twice the EU average, interest payments relative to GDP were

1. See also Organization for Economic Cooperation and Development (OECD 1995).

Table 7.1   General Government Budget (percent of GDP)

	1986	1987	1988	1989	1990	1991	1992	1993	1994	1995
Total receipts	48.7	49.0	47.3	45.8	46.2	46.3	46.2	46.9	48.2	47.6
Direct taxes	19.3	19.0	18.2	16.9	17.1	16.7	16.6	16.6	17.9	18.3
Indirect taxes	11.9	12.4	12.1	12.2	12.3	12.2	12.2	12.5	12.9	12.4
Social security contributions	15.1	15.4	15.0	14.7	14.8	15.3	15.5	15.7	15.3	15.1
Primary expenditure	47.0	46.0	44.2	41.9	41.2	42.5	42.6	43.5	43.2	42.7
Transfers to households	25.4	25.4	24.5	24.0	23.8	24.7	25.0	25.4	25.1	25.1
Pensions[a]	9.2	9.1	8.8	8.5	8.5	8.7	8.8	9.1	9.0	9.1
Health care	4.6	4.9	4.7	4.7	4.8	5.2	5.4	5.4	5.3	5.4
Unemployment benefits[b]	3.4	3.3	3.1	2.8	2.8	3.0	3.0	3.1	3.0	2.9
Other primary expenditure	21.6	20.6	19.7	17.8	17.4	17.8	17.6	18.1	18.1	17.6
Primary surplus	1.7	3.0	3.1	4.0	5.0	3.7	3.7	3.4	5.0	5.0
Interest payments	11.3	10.7	10.2	10.4	10.7	10.3	10.9	10.9	10.1	9.1
Net financial balance	−9.5	−7.7	−7.1	−6.5	−5.7	−6.6	−7.2	−7.5	−5.2	−4.1
Debt-GDP ratio[c]	117.5	121.7	122.1	119.4	119.3	120.2	122.0	128.2	127.6	127.9

Source: National Bank of Belgium; author's computations. I am grateful to Mr. Modart of the Department of General Statistics of the National Bank of Belgium for these data.

[a]Including pensions of public sector employees.

[b]Including early retirement and career interruptions.

[c]The value for 1995 is based on an estimate of the National Bank of Belgium (1996).

Table 7.2   **Transfer and Tax Taxonomy**

Transfers	Taxes
Birth allowances	Direct taxes
Family allowances	Social security contributions
Unemployment benefits	Wealth taxes
Old-age pensions	Indirect taxes
Child care[a]	
Education[b]	
Health care	

[a]"Child care" corresponds to public spending relative to child care institutions.
[b]Educational spending has been attributed to students. This does not exactly reflect the private benefits of education, but it surely is a better assumption than including it in nonspecific government consumption. See Ablett (1996); see also section 7.5.

still twice as high as the EU average (10.1 percent vs. 5.3 percent in 1994). In 1995, lower interest rates induced lower interest payments. This resulted in an improvement of the net financial balance (-4.1 percent of GDP in 1995 vs. -5.2 percent in 1994).

In terms of trend, whereas the primary surplus and the global deficit of the European Union have both been relatively stable for a decade, these two budget indicators have improved in Belgium, and the global deficit has tended to get closer to the European average. This reading of the situation suggests that simple commitment to the current fiscal policy could be enough to return to a reasonable debt-to-GDP ratio. Indeed, according to the National Bank of Belgium (1996), even under a relatively conservative macroeconomic scenario,[2] the budget would be in surplus by the beginning of the next century. By 2020, the debt-to-GDP ratio would fall below 60 percent.

This paper will contrast these conjectures with the results of generational accounting. Table 7.2 provides the taxonomy of transfers and taxes used in this paper. I distinguish between seven kinds of transfers, which I derive from Lambrecht, Fasquelle, and Weemaes (1994). Note that a part of public expenditure is treated as pseudotransfers. Taxes are estimated using aggregate results of the Belgian Households Budget Survey (Institut National de Statistique 1994). Income data comes from the Caisse Générale d'Epargne et des Retraite (1988). Belgian national accounts are used for 1995. For purposes of comparability across countries, all results are expressed in equivalent U.S. 1995 dollars.[3]

7.3   The Generational Accounts

Let me select reasonable, though arbitrary, values for the interest and growth rates. I assume a 6 percent real interest rate and a 0.75 percent real growth rate.

2. A 2 percent real growth rate, a little less than 5 percent in nominal terms, and an effective interest rate of 7.5 percent, i.e., the mean rate over the past decade.
3. I use indicative exchange rates (daily means) of the National Bank of Belgium for this purpose. In 1995 the daily mean exchange rate was 29.51 Belgian francs per U.S. dollar.

Table 7.3   **Generational Accounts (thousands of 1995 U.S. dollars)**

Generation's Age in Base Year	1988			1995		
	Net Payments (1)	Tax Payments (2)	Transfer Receipts (3)	Net Payments (4)	Tax Payments (5)	Transfer Receipts (6)
0	32.02	127.08	95.05	43.26	183.77	140.50
5	55.21	153.19	97.98	76.18	221.32	145.13
10	83.22	183.71	100.49	115.97	265.14	149.17
15	122.75	216.65	93.90	172.32	312.31	139.99
20	165.30	248.42	83.13	232.85	357.59	124.73
25	192.20	273.96	81.76	270.80	393.78	122.98
30	198.26	288.12	89.86	278.56	413.60	135.03
35	185.54	288.19	102.65	259.34	413.22	153.88
40	155.74	274.67	118.93	215.54	393.41	177.87
45	110.21	249.30	139.08	149.26	356.69	207.43
50	51.97	213.11	161.14	65.07	304.62	239.56
55	−17.17	166.27	183.44	−34.58	237.51	272.08
60	−84.03	115.70	199.73	−130.56	165.19	295.75
65	−108.55	89.79	198.35	−165.69	127.71	293.41
70	−113.00	75.35	188.35	−172.37	106.59	278.96
75	−107.01	62.40	169.41	−163.74	87.93	251.67
80	−99.80	50.51	150.31	−153.08	70.97	224.05
85	−89.98	39.73	129.71	−138.64	55.80	194.44
90	−76.79	30.21	106.99	−118.96	42.47	161.43

In table 7.3, the Belgian generational accounts are presented for 1988 and 1995 according to this baseline scenario. This scenario corresponds to a lower bound for intergenerational inequity in 1988. Results under alternative assumptions will also be presented.

Columns (2) and (3) show the current values of taxes and transfers, respectively, that the representative member of each age group faces in 1988.[4] Column (1) subtracts columns (3) from column (2) and thus displays the current value of the net taxes each member of every age group faces over her or his remaining lifetime (negative numbers indicate net transfer receipts).[5] In other words, column (1) shows the generational account of the representative member of each generation in 1988. Columns (4), (5), and (6) provide the same information for 1995.

As expected, most active people in the year of reference are facing the heaviest burden. Indeed, in the year of reference, they face the highest taxes of their lifetimes, whereas they have already received young-age transfers (education, etc.). Young individuals will have to face the same net taxes later. Hence, their present value is less than the discounted value of those paid by the active. On

---

4. In this paper, women and men are not distinguished.
5. Note that I am not considering taxes that have already been paid and transfers that have already been received prior to 1988 and 1995, respectively.

the other hand, people over age 53 (54) in 1988 (1995) can expect more transfers than taxes. Further, an 85-year-old awaits lower net transfers than does a 70-year-old. Indeed, the former will receive less since he or she has already received most of his or her old-age pension transfers.

Imbalance among generational accounts cannot be used as an indicator of intergenerational inequity among existing generations. This does not mean, however, that some degree of intergenerational inequity may not prevail. Indeed, Clokeur and Perelman (1994) find that the transfer-tax ratio has fallen from 99 percent for a citizen born in 1920 to 59 percent for a citizen born in 1980.[6] Hence, an interesting question is whether this imbalance among current living generations has worsened in recent years. Figure 7.1 plots in parallel Belgian generational accounts for 1988 and 1995. Generational accounts for 1988 have been adjusted to take account of GDP growth between the two years of reference.

Once GDP growth has been accounted for, both younger and older living generations appear to have been favored by policy changes between the two years of reference. People under age 53 are facing lower net taxes, and citizens above this age can expect higher net transfers. Despite the fact that the primary surplus has increased over the 1988–95 period, this result should not be surprising. Indeed, transfers to households as a share of GDP have been growing faster than total tax receipts (see table 7.1). From 1988 to 1995, transfers to households grew by 0.6 percent of GDP, whereas tax receipts increased only by 0.3 percent of GDP.

Finally, the higher the discount rate, the lower the absolute value of generational accounts. Younger generations receive most transfers in the short run, whereas the bulk of their taxes is located in the future and thus discounted proportionally to the interest rate. For older generations who will mainly benefit from transfers, the higher the interest rate, the lower the present value of future transfers. The lower the growth rate, the higher the absolute value of generational accounts. The influence of the growth rate is straightforward: transfers and taxes are assumed to grow at this rate.

Let me turn to the level of net public wealth to be considered. This is not a trivial issue. Auerbach et al. (1994) have considered federal net wealth to be roughly equal to minus the sum of the national income account deficits from 1900 through 1991. On the other hand, Ablett (1996) considers two extreme hypotheses regarding Australian net public wealth in order to analyze sensitivity of results to net wealth estimation. First, as a lower bound, net wealth is defined as minus government (net) debt; second, an upper bound is computed as the value of government capital from the Australian national accounts minus government (net) debt. Auerbach et al. (1994) argue that it is not important to measure existing public capital since its value is offset by imputed rents in

---

6. The transfer-tax ratio is defined as the ratio of the life cycle sum of transfers to the life cycle sum of taxes. Both sums are discounted to age 40.

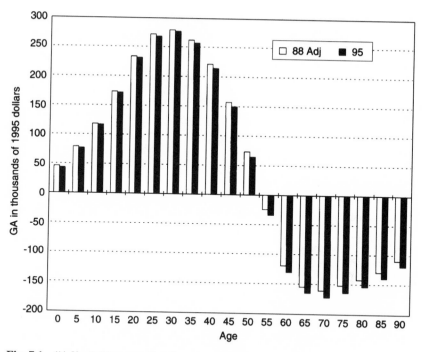

Fig. 7.1   **"Adjusted" generational accounts, 1988 versus 1995**

public consumption. In fact, Belgium is one of the rare countries where a comprehensive inventory of public assets and liabilities has been undertaken (see Commission pour l'Inventaire 1990, 1995). I follow Auerbach et al.'s approach insofar as I take into account public liabilities net of only financial assets yielding returns.

From 1988 to 1995, gross public liabilities have increased from 136 percent of GDP to 141 percent of GDP. Gross financial assets yielding returns went down from 46 percent of GDP to 25 percent of GDP. Hence, net public liabilities increased from 89 percent of GDP in 1988 to 116 percent of GDP in 1995. Net public liabilities are, of course, the mirror image of net public wealth. I tend to use the former term in the rest of this paper, as net public wealth turns out, as usual, to be negative. Non-(age)-specific government consumption is estimated to be approximately equal to 16 percent of GDP in 1988 versus 15 percent of GDP in 1995, based on Belgian current accounts.[7]

Table 7.3 provides per capita figures. The present value of net contributions of living generations is in fact needed. In table 7.4, each transfer and tax per capita has been multiplied by the corresponding generation size over time. The

7. Non-(age)-specific government consumption is government consumption less the amount corresponding to transfers and pseudotransfers (education, etc.) that are taken into account in generational accounts.

168   Jean-Philippe Stijns

Table 7.4   Present Value of Net Taxes of Current Living Generations (billions of 1995 U.S. dollars)

	1988		1995	
Transfer or Tax	Total	Percent of GDP	Total	Percent of GDP
Health care	320.40	170	522.89	195
Birth allowances	0.34	0	0.48	0
Family allowances	37.78	20	54.10	20
Child care	0.20	0	0.28	0
Education	81.74	43	117.40	44
Unemployment benefits	108.98	58	159.17	59
Old-age pensions	694.14	368	1,069.91	399
Sum of transfers	1,243.58	660	1,924.22	717
Indirect taxes	468.82	249	724.59	270
Social security contributions	804.81	427	1,151.84	429
Wealth taxes	53.44	28	75.05	28
Direct taxes	628.53	333	909.40	339
Sum of taxes	1,955.57	1,037	2,860.88	1,066
Sum of net taxes	711.96	378	936.66	349

first rows give estimates of transfers; following rows concern taxes. The last row shows that in present value the sum of net taxes of current living generations has risen; however, as a share of GDP, the present value of net taxes of current living generations has declined by 29 percentage points.

To compute the burden on future generations, net public liabilities, nonspecific government consumption, and the sum of net transfers to current living generations have to be combined. Table 7.5 shows that in 1988, future generations would have to have to have paid back a bill equivalent to 48 percent of GDP in order to meet the intertemporal budget constraint of the government. In 1995, this figure had risen to 74 percent of GDP.

The sum of net transfers is strongly negative and outweighs nonspecific consumption. This indicates that a heavy net fiscal burden has already been placed on current living generations (and particularly on younger ones). On the other hand, the change in the burden on future generations is quite striking. As a share of GDP, it has risen by 26 percent. This is due to the decrease in net taxes and the growth in net public liabilities as a share of GDP. Belgian budgetary efforts are reflected in the decrease of nonspecific government consumption as a share of GDP. This observation illustrates that budget equilibrium may be a necessary condition for budgetary soundness but cannot be considered a sufficient condition.

Finally, I turn to the equivalent of this burden in terms of the "birth bill" to be paid by each member of future generations, assuming that members of future generations pay a constant net tax adjusted for growth. Table 7.6 compares

Table 7.5   **Present Value of the Burden on Future Generations (billions of 1995 U.S. dollars)**

	1988		1995	
	Total	Percent of GDP	Total	Percent of GDP
Sum of net transfers	−711.96	−378	−936.66	−349
Net public liabilities	168.72	89	377.38	116
Nonspecific consumption	633.68	336	823.82	307
Burden on future generations	90.41	48	264.54	74

Table 7.6   **Newborn versus Future Generations (thousands of 1995 U.S. dollars)**

	1988	1995
Total future burden	90,410,000	198,480,000
Equivalent "birth bill"	40.72	89.49
Newborn generational account	32.02	43.26
Percentage difference	27	107

Table 7.7   **Percentage Difference for 1988 under Alternative Assumptions**

Real Interest Rate (%)	Real Growth (%)						
	0.50	0.75	1.00	1.25	1.50	1.75	2.00
3	41	43	45	47	50	127	131
4	35	37	38	40	41	43	45
5	30	31	33	34	36	37	39
6	27	27	28	29	30	32	33
7	34	30	28	27	27	27	28

newborns' generational account with future generations' birth bill in the baseline scenario. The percentage difference is 27 percent in 1988 and reaches 107 percent in 1995.

As table 7.7 shows, the baseline assumptions correspond to a lower bound for the 1988 percentage difference.[8] Results range in fact from 27 to 131 percent. The latter figure is reached with a 3 percent discount rate and a 2.0 percent growth rate.

In table 7.8, I present results for 1995 under alternative assumptions. Results now range from 61 percent (vs. 27 percent in 1988) to 235 percent (vs. 131 percent in 1988). Failure to face the intertemporal government budget constraint between 1988 and 1995 has the consequence that future generations

8. Baseline assumptions are a 6 percent real interest rate and a 0.75 percent real growth rate.

Table 7.8   Percentage Difference for 1995 under Alternative Assumptions

Real Interest Rate (%)	Real Growth (%)						
	0.50	0.75	1.00	1.25	1.50	1.75	2.00
3	61	61	61	62	64	67	71
4	66	64	63	61	61	61	61
5	82	77	72	69	66	64	62
6	121	**107**	96	88	81	76	72
7	235	190	158	135	118	105	94

Table 7.9   Present Value of Gross Burdens (billions of 1995 U.S. dollars)

Transfer	1988		1995	
	Total	Percent of GDP	Total	Percent of GDP
Health care	320.40	170	522.89	195
Birth allowances	0.34	0	0.48	0
Family allowances	37.78	20	54.10	20
Child care	0.20	0	0.28	0
Education	81.74	43	117.40	44
Unemployment benefits	108.98	58	159.17	59
Old-age pensions	694.14	368	1,069.91	399
Sum of transfers	1,243.58	660	1,924.22	717
Gross public liabilities	256.18	136	378.41	141
Nonspecific consumption	633.68	336	823.82	307
Total of gross burdens	2,133.45	1,132	3,126.45	1,165

now face a *minimum* 61 percent increase in their lifetime net taxes as compared to 1995 newborns.[9] A 61 percent change in net tax rates is in fact already an unsustainable figure. As future generations will probably keep receiving some form of transfers, their gross tax rates will have to be raised by much more than 61 percent.

In a nutshell, a considerable effort has to be made as soon as possible. Indeed, under the baseline scenario, an 80 percent increase has been observed in the ratio of the net fiscal burden of future versus present generations over a period of only seven years. At this pace, Belgium will reach the twenty-first century with an unsustainable net fiscal burden to impose to its citizens.

Table 7.9 weighs gross burdens in 1988 and 1995 (i.e., public transfers, gross public liabilities, and nonspecific consumption) against GDP. First, old-age pensions come up quite expectably with the highest relative weight: 368

9. The reader should keep in mind that the consumer/worker is not expected to react in any way to tax increases in this model. If that were the case, the net tax rate would have to be raised further.

percent of GDP in 1988 and 399 percent of GDP in 1995. Health care programs correspond to 170 percent of GDP in 1988 and 195 percent in 1995. Other transfers are more reasonable. It is noteworthy that in the two years, both old-age pensions and health care transfers to existing generations outweigh not only net but also gross public liabilities.

Nonspecific consumption also represents a very important burden, with 336 percent of GDP in 1988 and 307 percent in 1995. It should be noticed that though nonspecific consumption is projected ad infinitum, it is still outbalanced in current value by old-age pension transfers to current living generations.

The OECD (1994) has found gross pension liabilities to amount to 571 percent of GDP in 1990. The difference between my estimates for both years and that of the OECD comes most likely from the fact that I have assumed old-age pensions follow the economic growth rate. However, were the current rules for pension computation to be respected, this transfer would grow faster than the rest of the Belgian economy.[10] My observations and those of the OECD (1994) lead to the common conclusion that pension rights definitely outweigh all other kinds of liabilities the government will have to face.[11]

Second, old-age pensions and health care transfers have grown to higher shares of GDP between 1988 and 1995, whereas the rest of the transfers have been rather stable as shares of GDP. Third, the heavier the weight on future generations a transfer imposes, the faster it grows as a share of GDP.

I conclude that strict discipline over the net financial balance will guarantee neither the sustainability nor the generational equity of the current fiscal system.[12] The only way to reach another conclusion is to arbitrarily impose the condition that social security (taken broadly) be in equilibrium over time.

7.4   Economic Policy Implications

What change in one of the transfer and tax flows would be required to obtain a 1:1 ratio of future to newborn generational accounts? Table 7.10 summarizes my findings for 1988 and 1995. For each of the instrument variables, that is, taxes and transfers, columns (1) and (2) give the rates of change in the tax or

10. This is the case mostly because female workers will increasingly obtain complete career pensions instead of receiving household pensions together with their husbands. Another reason behind this is that the pension system is increasingly coming to maturity: social security receipts are computed with an increasing number of working years accounted for proportionally rather than as a lump sum.

11. Two other different kinds of studies are also worth mentioning. Callataÿ and Turtelboom (1996) have also reviewed the financial implications of aging for the pension system in Belgium. They estimate that if all net liabilities (except those of the self-employed) were financed through debt from 1995 to 2050, the stock of new pension debt would be around 260 percent of GDP in 2050. Bouillot and Perelman (1994) found that under their reference scenario, pension rights accumulated proportionally to a worker's career would grow from 292.5 percent of GDP to 388.8 percent from 1987 to 2040.

12. See Kotlikoff (1988, 1992) for a systematic illustration of this.

Table 7.10   Solving Values for "Generational Equity" (thousands of 1995
                    U.S. dollars)

	Percentage Change		Birth Bill	
	1988	1995	1988	1995
Transfer or Tax	(1)	(2)	(3)	(4)
Old-age pensions	−3	−9	32.26	44.42
Health care	−5	−17	33.07	48.60
Unemployment benefits	−16	−57	33.05	48.63
Education	−12	−45	36.26	65.77
Indirect taxes	+4	+12	33.38	50.31
Social security contributions	+2	+8	33.05	48.60
Wealth taxes	+31	+119	33.21	49.35
Direct taxes	+3	+10	33.02	48.46

transfer value, per member of each age group, with 1988 and 1995 as years of reference. Hence, this policy simulation assumes that members of each age group see the value of this particular tax (transfer) increased (decreased), per capita, by the reported percentage.

Columns (3) and (4) give the new values of the newborn generational account, with 1988 and 1995 as years of reference. This value is by definition equal to the birth bill of future generations. Though all the fiscal instruments are able to solve for generational equity, they do not leave newborn and future generations equally well off. Consequently, one natural way of evaluating the relative advantages of each instrument is to rank them according to the size of the generational account with which they leave the newborn and future generations. This is appropriate since it is known from section 7.3 that young generations are already facing important generational accounts.

Old-age pensions score first according to this criterion. Then follow direct taxes. In 1995, solving for the Auerbach et al. (1991) criterion for generational equity with old-age pensions (direct taxes) would leave newborn and future generations with a $44,420 ($48,460) generational account. In comparison, recall that in case of no change in fiscal policy the generational accounts amount to $43,260 for the newborns and $89,490 for future generations. I conclude that both instruments are able to solve for generational equity; that is, they can keep future generations' situation no worse than the newborns' while putting a limited additional strain on young generations. The case for direct taxes can be questioned since generational accounting does not take into account the potential reaction of economic agents to tax changes.

These two potential policy proposals would seem to be easier than others to implement politically. Indeed, they require a relatively reasonable 9 to 10 percent reduction (increase) in old-age pension transfers (direct taxes). However, to be effective, this change would have to be adopted immediately and completely from 1995 onward. One could of course choose a balanced combination

Table 7.11   **Solving Values for "Generational Equity" with a Ten-Year Burden Rollover until 2005 (thousands of 1995 U.S. dollars)**

Transfer or Tax	Percentage Change	Birth Bill
Old-age pensions	−13	44.86
Health care	−25	50.87
Unemployment benefits	−81	50.92
Education	−75	81.01
Indirect taxes	+17	53.46
Social security contributions	+11	50.87
Wealth taxes	+170	51.99
Direct taxes	+14	50.67

of these two instruments. Health care reductions would also leave young generations with reasonable generational accounts. However, health care cuts would have to be of considerable magnitude, that is, 17 percent. In any case, this instrument could perhaps represent a useful complement to pensions and direct taxes. All other programs leave the newborn and future generations with high generational accounts or would represent very high proportional increases (decreases) in taxes (transfers) per member of each age group.

It is worth noting that the ranking of the instruments on either criterion has hardly changed over time. Yet the increase in magnitude of required fiscal policy changes is considerable. For pension receipt cuts, the required change has increased from 3 to 9 percent. The change is from 3 to 10 percent for income tax changes. Thus "wait and see" policies are not conceivable. The data in table 7.11 help to support this claim.

Table 7.11 assumes that the burden on future generations from table 7.5 is rolled on until 2005. In other words, from 1996 until 2005 (inclusive), the annual budget constraint is met, after which, needed policy changes are implemented in order to face the government intertemporal budget constraint. As for old-age pension receipt cuts, the required change has increased from 9 to 13 percent. The change is from 10 to 14 percent for income tax changes.

The reader should bear in mind that these increases are solely due to a failure to cope with the government intertemporal constraint and not to a failure to present a balanced budget. Put differently, this simulation assumes a zero net financial balance. Furthermore, the above-mentioned policy changes have been derived under the baseline assumptions, which are far from the most pessimistic.

7.5   The Treatment of Education

Finally, I deal with the assumption of educational spending as a transfer to students. Ablett (1996) suggests that this is a better rule than assuming that education is a pure public good. Table 7.12 illustrates the influence of this

Table 7.12   **Generational Accounts in 1995 under Different Treatments of Education (thousands of 1995 U.S. dollars)**

Generation's Age in 1995	Education as a Transfer	Education Included in Nonspecific Consumption
0	43.26	93.52
5	76.18	132.35
10	115.97	170.13
15	172.32	210.45
20	232.85	242.33
25	270.80	272.50
30	278.56	278.56
35	259.34	259.34
40	215.54	215.54
45	149.26	149.26
50	65.07	65.07
55	−34.58	−34.58
60	−130.56	−130.56
65	−165.69	−165.69
70	−172.37	−172.37
75	−163.74	−163.74
80	−153.08	−153.08
85	−138.64	−138.64
90	−118.96	−118.96

choice on Belgian generational accounts in 1995 under the baseline assumptions.

First, young generations end up with lower generational accounts when educational spending is attributed to students as a pseudotransfer. Second, the baseline percentage change between future generations' "birth bills" and newborns' generational account decreases from 107 to 58 percent when failing to attribute education to specific age groups. In my view, the treatment of education as part of non-age-specific government consumption tends to seriously understate intergenerational inequities.

7.6   Conclusions

The analysis in section 7.2 suggests that since 1992 Belgium has been taking steps in the right direction. However, the results of section 7.3 dampen any optimism. Indeed, future generations will have to face a *minimum* 61 percent increase in their *net* taxes as compared to the newborn generation in 1995. This indicator ranges up to 235 percent if growth and interest rate assumptions vary from the baseline. Under the baseline scenario, an 80 percent increase in the ratio of the net fiscal burden of future versus present generations has been observed over only seven years. At this pace, Belgium will reach the twenty-first century with an unsustainable net fiscal burden to impose on its citizens.

Old-age pensions and health care transfers come in first place as determinants. Strict discipline over the net financial balance will guarantee neither the sustainability nor the generational equity of the current fiscal system. In terms of economic policy, reforming old-age pensions and direct taxes would allow equilibrium to be restored between future and newborn generations while leaving them with the lowest generational accounts to cope with. Again, required tax increases and transfer cuts have been increasing substantially from 1988 to 1995. The same conclusion holds if needed policy changes are to be implemented with some delay. Quick fiscal policy change is therefore absolutely necessary.

Finally, three complementary paths for further research could be followed. First, it would be interesting to distinguish between lifetime income categories in order to simultaneously analyze *intra-* versus *inter*generational issues. Second, it would be worthwhile to link Belgian generational accounts with a general equilibrium model for Belgium.[13] This would endogenize some parameters used here and would allow an assessment of generational equity issues in terms of utility. Third, alternative scenarios as regards the evolution of transfer receipts per age group could be contrasted with the assumptions of generational accounting. I conjecture that such a modeling of consumer behavior and of transfer receipts may well call for even larger transfer cuts and tax increases.

References

Ablett, J. 1996. Generational accounting—An Australian perspective. *Review of Income and Wealth* 45 (1): 91–105.
Auerbach, A. J., J. Gokhale, and L. J. Kotlikoff. 1991. Generational accounts: A meaningful alternative to deficit accounting. NBER Working Paper no. 3589. Cambridge, Mass.: National Bureau of Economic Research.
———. 1994. Generational accounting: A meaningful way to evaluate fiscal policy. *Journal of Economic Perspectives* 8 (1): 95–111.
Bouillot, M., and S. Perelman. 1995. Evaluation patrimoniale des droits a la pension. *Revue Belge de Sécurité Sociale* 4 (3): 803–31.
Caisse Générale d'Epargne et des Retraite. 1988. *Statistique du salaire moyen journalier.* Brussels: Service du Compte Individuel de Pension des Travailleurs Salaries.
Callataÿ, E. de, and B. Turtelboom. 1996. Pension reform in Belgium. IMF Working Paper no. 96.74. Washington, D.C.: International Monetary Fund.
Clokeur, R., and S. Perelman. 1994. Transferts et arbitrage entre les générations. In *Héritage et transferts entre générations,* ed. Pierre Pestieau, 111–27. Brussels: De Boek.
Commission pour l'Inventaire du Patrimoine de l'Etat. 1990. *Rapport sur les activités de la commission pour l'inventaire du patrimoine de l'etat au cours des années 1988 et 1989.* Brussels: Ministère des Finances.
———. 1995. *Le bilan consolidé de l'etat à fin 1992.* Brussels: Ministère des Finances.

13. See Fehr and Kotlikoff (chap. 3 in this volume) for such an analysis for the United States.

Institut National de Statistique. Several years. *Annuaire statistique de la Belgique.* Brussels: Ministère des Affaires Economiques.

———. 1994. *Enquête sur les budgets des ménages 1987–1988,* tome 1. Brussels: Ministère des Affaires Economiques.

Kotlikoff, L. J. 1988. The deficit is not a well-defined measure of fiscal policy. *Science* 241:791–95.

———. 1992. *Generational accounting.* New York: Free Press.

Lambrecht, M., N. Fasquelle, and S. Weemaes. 1994. L'évolution démographique de long terme et son incidence isolée sur quelques grandeurs socio-économiques (1992–2050). Planning Paper no. 68. Brussels: Bureau du Plan.

National Bank of Belgium. 1995. *Rapport 1994.* Brussels: Banque Nationale de Belgique.

———. 1996. *Rapport 1995.* Brussels: Banque Nationale de Belgique.

Organization for Economic Cooperation and Development (OECD). 1994. *Etudes économiques: Belgique—1994.* Paris: Organisation de Cooperation et de Developpement Economique.

———. 1995. *Etudes économiques: Belgique—1995.* Paris: Organisation de Cooperation et de Developpement Economique.

8 Generational Accounting in Brazil

Regina Villela Malvar

8.1 Introduction

Brazilian economic experience in most of the recent past has been characterized by unstable growth and high inflation rates. Between 1986 and 1991 the economy was subjected to five stabilization plans, which were unable to control price pressures. Between 1988 and 1992 real per capita income declined by an average rate of 2 percent. In mid-1994 a new stabilization scheme known as the "Real Plan" was implemented, and at least until late 1996 inflation remained at a low and stable rate.[1] The performance of the economy also improved: between 1994 and 1995 real GDP grew at an average rate of 5.1 percent.

The Constitution of 1988 altered virtually all aspects of fiscal policy. Of particular relevance was the reform in social insurance. Mainly because of the new constitutional rules, expenditures on social insurance benefits and welfare jumped from 2.6 percent of GDP in 1988 to 5.0 percent of GDP in 1995, while

Regina Villela Malvar is a legislative advisor at the Board of Legislative Advisors of the Brazilian House of Representatives.

The author thanks Larry Kotlikoff for the opportunity to write this chapter, and Kotlikoff and Jan Walliser for invaluable comments. The author was also fortunate to have had the help of many colleagues from Brazil, especially Flávio Faria, Cláudia Deud, Sandra Almeida, and Osmar Lannes, Jr., from the House of Representatives; Marta Albuquerque from the Senate; Marcia Caldas, Josefa Cardoso de Ávila, Manoel Veras, and Celecino de Carvalho Filho from the Ministry of Social Insurance; Rosângela Villela Pedro and Victor Almeida from the Ministry of Finance; Paulo Machado from the Ministry of Labor; Luciano Oliva Patrício from the Ministry of Education; Kaizô Beltrão, Fernando Fernandes, Gilda Santiago, Ricardo Zarur, Edilson Silva, and Luis Antônio Pinto de Oliveira from IBGE (Brazilian Bureau of Statistics); Carlos Mussi and Juan Chackiel from ECLAC (Economic Commission for Latin America and the Caribbean); and Sérgio Piola from IPEA (Institute for Economic Applied Research of the Ministry of Planning). The opinions expressed in this chapter do not reflect the views of the Board of Legislative Advisors of the Brazilian House of Representatives.

1. The *real* is the new Brazilian currency; it replaced the *cruzeiro*.

social insurance sources of revenue increased only moderately, from 4.6 to 5.3 percent of GDP. As expenditures on benefits increased, the traditional procedure of allocating part of payroll contributions to public health could no longer be accomplished. The crisis in social insurance was then extended to public health financing.

Since 1993 the Brazilian federal government has relied on transitory taxes to finance health expenses, while constitutional amendments (including in the social insurance system) are being debated in Congress. There is little room, however, to address the social insurance crisis in the short run because the level of expenditures with existing retirees is fixed and payroll taxes are already considered to be at prohibitively high levels. Long-run prospects are dim, as an aging population and a decline in total fertility rates signal additional pressures in the future.

Constitutional amendments in the tax system and in the structure of public administration are also being discussed in Congress. Some of the main issues in the tax reform debate include the large number of taxes, overlapping bases of incidence, and high payroll taxes. The proposal for public administration reform aims to contain the level of government consumption expenditure.

The purpose of this paper is to address how current and alternative fiscal policies, like some of those being discussed in Congress, can affect the distribution of resources between current and future generations. In addition, it estimates by how much the social insurance reforms of 1988 helped the current elderly at the expense of their grandchildren. The general conclusion is that the actual path of fiscal policies, coupled with the demographic transition, imposes a heavy burden on future generations of Brazilians.

To bring the issues into perspective, section 8.2 summarizes major facets of economic policy in Brazil since 1988, as well as the course of some recent debates on fiscal reform. Section 8.3 presents a description of data sources used in the calculations. Brazilian baseline generational accounts for 1995 are reported in section 8.4. That section also investigates the impact of changes in social insurance, performs a sensitivity analysis for different choices of parameters, including the evolution of the population, and examines the implications of alternative fiscal policies for intergenerational balance. A summary of the main results and general conclusions is presented in section 8.5.

8.2   Summary of Recent Fiscal Policies and Current Fiscal Debates

In 1986, after 22 years of military regimes, Brazilians were eager to adopt changes that could promote stable growth and a more equitable society. The result of a long participative process, the Constitution of 1988 altered important aspects of political, economic, and social life. In terms of fiscal policy, the major changes were the increase in the process of decentralization of tax revenues and the expansion of the welfare state.

The decentralization of tax revenues resulted mainly from two factors. First, compulsory intergovernmental tax revenue transfers from the central administration to the other two federated units increased. Second, the state and municipal tax base was enlarged, with a corresponding decrease in the tax base at the federal level. The new division benefited local and state governments, whose share of total disposable income increased, at a cost to the federal government.

In an attempt to improve social conditions, the Constitution of 1988 integrated and enlarged previous public programs in health, social insurance, and social assistance under a new order, denominated social security system.

Public health remained a universal program available to all, regardless of age or economic condition. The scope of social assistance was broadened. Social insurance was maintained as a pay-as-you-go system of benefits, due to workers of the private sector. Its main objective continued to be the maintenance of income in numerous circumstances, such as old age, disability, length of service, sickness, death, and maternity, as well as child benefits, among others. Most important, however, the Constitution imposed expensive obligations on the social insurance system, to be effective in 1989 or, at the latest, in 1992, without the accumulation of sufficient previous financing. The main measures in terms of their impact on outlays were recalculation of the value of all existing benefits, in order to recuperate their initial real value; periodic readjustment of benefits to maintain their real value through time; increase in the minimum value of benefits to one minimum wage (most rural workers received half this amount); and decrease in the age of retirement for rural workers (by five years for males and ten years for females).

A new structure of taxation was designed to finance the higher level of expenditures of the health, social assistance, and social insurance programs. The federal budget was fragmented, and social security was granted its own budget (apart from the fiscal one). Since 1992, as a result of the fiscal changes promoted by the Constitution, social security contributions have surpassed federal fiscal revenues.

The Brazilian economic environment was very unstable during the period that lasted from the formation of the National Assembly that gave rise to the Constitution of 1988 through the implementation of its main rules. In the six-year period from 1986 to 1991 the economy was subject to five stabilization plans, which were able to control price hikes for only short periods of time. In fact, as shown in table 8.1, inflation rates skyrocketed from an annual rate of 65 percent in 1986 to 2,700 percent in 1993. From 1988 to 1992, average real GDP decreased by 0.3 percent and average real per capita income by 2 percent.

Starting at the end of 1993 until July 1994, Brazil implemented a stabilization scheme known as the "Real Plan." Policies were structured in three stages. The first stage, designed to improve federal fiscal revenues, was based on a temporary increase in taxes and decrease in constitutional compulsory transfers. The second stage lasted as long as four months. It consisted of a gradual conversion of wages and prices in a new monetary value, which by itself was adjusted daily. The objective was to eliminate distortions in relative prices pro-

Table 8.1   General Indicators, 1988–95

Year	GDP[a] (billion U.S.$ at 1995 prices)	Population[b] (millions)	Inflation Rate[c] (%)
1988	635.3	139.8	1,037.6
1989	655.6	142.3	1,782.9
1990	627.4	144.7	1,476.6
1991	629.3	147.1	480.2
1992	624.3	149.4	1,158.0
1993	650.5	151.6	2,708.6
1994	689.5	153.7	1,093.8
1995	718.5	155.8	14.8

Note: Exchange rate assumed to be 1.0917 U.S. dollars per real (BACEN 1996b, table I.1).
[a]Value for 1995 is from BACEN (1996b, table I.1). Values for other years are calculated retroactively based on GDP real growth rate.
[b]BACEN (1996b, table I.2).
[c]Indice Geral de Preços; Deflator Implicito. Fundação Getúlio Vargas, *Conjuntura Econômica* (Rio de Janeiro, May 1996).

duced by years of high inflation, so that economic agents could again take the price system as a reliable indicator of investment opportunities. The third stage took place in July 1994, when all values were converted into the new currency—the *real*.

Unlike plans implemented during 1986 to 1991, the Real Plan brought price stabilization. In 1995 Brazilians had the lowest annual rate of price increase in 35 years: 15 percent. With inflation under control and an international environment of sustainable growth, GDP grew by a yearly average rate of 4.8 percent from 1993 to 1995. In 1995 real per capita income reached U.S.$4,610, its highest level since 1987.

Overvalued exchange rates and a process of import liberalization (in effect since 1990) were essential in containing price pressures, but they contributed in 1995 to the first trade deficit since 1980 (Banco Central do Brasil [BACEN] 1996c, 121). High domestic interest rates and an international market in search of emerging economies were able to attract a net inflow of capital equivalent to 4.2 percent of GDP in 1995.[2] As a result, in 1995, the balance of payments still registered a surplus equivalent to 1.8 percent of GDP (BACEN 1996b, table IV.1).

Public national debt in 1995 represented 30 percent of GDP (BACEN 1996b, table III.13). In an attempt to make adjustments in public sector financing, the central government is promoting reforms in the tax system, social insurance, and public administration. The difficulty is that any one of these re-

2. In 1994 and 1995 real annual federal securities rates were 25 and 34 percent, respectively. Data are from BACEN (1996a, table II.24).

forms implies changes in the Constitution, which requires the approval, in two rounds of voting, of three-fifths of the members of Congress.

An important issue in fiscal reform is the complexity of the fiscal system. Brazil has approximately 80 taxes (Almeida and Cavalcanti 1995). Of these, 14 are fiscal taxes, 20 are social contributions, and the rest comprise a multitude of specific taxes and economic contributions.

A related problem is the inefficiency caused by overlapping bases of incidence. There are two value-added taxes, one at the federal and another at the state level. In addition, two social security contributions have very similar bases of incidence—gross revenue. What exacerbates the distortions is that each of these two social security contributions is cumulative, since it is not based on the concept of value added and is applied in every stage of production.

The complexity of tax rules and overlapping bases of incidence have contributed to the growth of the informal economy, reducing even more the base of incidence of taxes and social contributions. In 1993 and 1994, when the Constitution was under general revision (and changes could be made by a smaller quorum) several proposals were made to reform the fiscal system. At that time, reactions by enraged taxpayers popularized proposals in favor of a unique tax on monetary transactions or a consumption tax on a small number of products, in place of the actual fiscal system.

Since 1988, the financing of social security and the scope of social insurance have been among the most debated topics of government policy. The level of imposition to finance social security is high. Employers' contributions are levied on three different criteria: wage bill, gross revenue, and "social profits." Employers pay, on average, a monthly tax of 22 percent levied on *total* payroll,[3] a tax of 2 percent on gross revenue,[4] and a tax of 8 percent on social profits.[5] Workers contribute with a tax that varies from 8 to 11 percent of net wages up to a cap, and all levels of government are required to allocate resources to the social security budget.

In 1991 and 1992, when most of the new rules regarding social insurance were implemented, it became apparent how feeble the structure of social security financing really was. In 1988 social insurance benefits and welfare to the poor (old or disabled) consumed 57 percent of payroll contributions, whereas in 1992 this ratio had risen to 87 percent (Ministério da Previdência e Assistência Social [MPAS] 1995). As social insurance and welfare consumed more and more of payroll contributions, less and less of that source could be transferred

3. Employers contribute with an additional 5.8 percent levied on payroll to finance education and programs of a private nature.
4. To finance unemployment benefits and programs of economic development, there is an additional tax of 0.65 percent levied on a basis that is very similar to gross revenue.
5. The rules for financial institutions are different. As of 1996, they do not pay taxes on gross revenue, but the levy on social profits is 18 percent.

to health (decreased from 28 percent in 1988 to 13 percent in 1992). At the same time, proceeds from other sources (gross revenues and social profits) were not enough to finance the gap in health expenditures plus remaining social security costs.

Without conditions to promote radical changes in the structure of social security, in 1993 the central administration started a cycle in which transitory taxes are created as soon as old ones expire. From 1993 to 1996, new legislation (including three amendments to the Constitution) was introduced in an attempt to provide the system with enough financing. As of 1996, public health has had an additional source of revenues: a transitory tax of 0.20 percent on all monetary transactions, to be in effect until 1998. Another set of temporary taxes, aimed at the whole social security system, was in effect until 1997.

Since 1994 revenues from payroll contributions have not been transferred to public health. Even so, social insurance is in a financial crisis. In 1995 and 1996 expenditures with benefits consumed 94 percent from payroll contributions. The ratio between the number of contributors and the number of beneficiaries dropped from 2.5 in 1982 to 1.8 in 1995 (Instituto Brasileiro de Geografia e Estatística [IBGE] 1982, 1995; MPAS 1994, 1995). The system does not count on a trust fund to ensure the payment of benefits when expenditures exceed revenues, or for the payment of future benefits. In 1995, the average value of social insurance checks was 1.7 minimum wages.[6] This situation has imposed a policy dilemma. The system of collection imposes a heavy burden on economic agents and, perhaps as a consequence, is not able to provide enough financing. On the other hand, it is difficult to cut expenses because the majority of beneficiaries already receive low benefits.

During the revision of the Constitution in 1993 and 1994 several propositions tried to change the nature of social insurance. A few recommended its privatization. Others suggested a system composed of two parts: (1) a compulsory pay-as-you-go plan with a lower cap of contributions and benefits and (2) an optional plan based on capitalization. The final proposition addressed another very sensitive issue—social security of federal public workers. In this regime, pensions and survival benefits correspond mainly to full earnings. The proposal suggested the integration of public workers (except the military) into the social insurance system and the adoption of rules limiting the access to benefits within that unified regime. By that time, however, with general elections only a few months away, the political environment did not support the approval of any relevant reforms.

During 1996, most of the negotiations between the Congress and the federal government were channeled toward a constitutional amendment of social insurance. Due to strong political pressures, however, the proposition approved in the House of Representatives did not change the structure of social insur-

---

6. This represented 46 percent of the average remuneration of the economy (IBGE 1995).

ance. The plan preserves the basic characteristics of the social insurance system for private workers and increases the cap of contributions and benefits from eight to ten minimum wages. Public workers continue to have the right to receive full pensions, but access is restricted to those with more than 10 years of service. As of 1997, the proposal is being discussed in the Senate, and it seems that the general lines approved in the House of Representatives will be maintained.

Long-term prospects are dim. In addition to the problems emphasized before, Brazil is experiencing swift changes in its demographic characteristics, particularly a decrease in the fertility rate and an aging population. The total fertility rate decreased from 5.8 in 1970 to 2.4 in the first half of the 1990s. Between 1970 and 1991, the proportion of young generations decreased from 43 to 35 percent; middle-aged cohorts expanded moderately, while the proportion of the elderly in the total population increased from 3 to 5 percent (Instituto de Pesquisa Econômica Aplicada [IPEA] 1996c, chap. 4). The Ministry of Social Insurance is particularly concerned. A smaller rate of growth of middle-aged cohorts and an aging population will add stress to the already debilitated pay-as-you-go system. Health officials expect increasing pressures because diseases typical of older generations are associated with high costs.

To date, regardless of many distortions, social security remains under the same rules that created it. Radical changes will have to come, but no one knows when they will be made or how effective they will be.

8.3 Description of Data Sources

A broad database is required to produce generational accounts. It includes population projections; the age-sex composition of tax payments and transfer receipts; the value of taxes, transfers, and government consumption; an estimate of government net debt; and alternative growth and interest rates.

The Brazilian population was projected up to 2200. From 1995 to 2050 the estimates are from CELADE.[7] In this scenario, the total fertility rate is equal to 2.1 in 2000, remaining at this level thereafter. Moreover, life expectancy improves over time for all age groups. In particular, life expectancy at birth is projected to increase from 67.9 years in 1995–2000 to 78.4 years in 2045–50. From 2050 to 2200, estimates followed a program of the Brazilian Bureau of Statistics.[8] Baseline calculations were conducted under the assumption that the total fertility rate and age-sex mortality rates would remain constant at their

7. CELADE is the Latin American Demographic Center. It is the institution within the United Nations organization ECLAC (Economic Commission for Latin America and the Caribbean) responsible for population studies, including population projections. See Latin American Demographic Center (1996).

8. The program used to project Brazilian population from 2050 to 2200 was designed by Fernando Fernandes from DEPIS/IBGE (see Fernandes 1995).

Table 8.2   Public Sector Tax Revenues and Transfer Payments, 1995 (billions of
                   U.S. dollars)

Revenues	Amount	Expenditures	Amount
Labor income taxes	15.1	Welfare	2.9
Capital income taxes	13.2	Social insurance benefits: private workers	33.7
Seigniorage	4.4	Unemployment benefit[e]	3.6
Value-added taxes[a]	69.4	Other social security benefits	11.2
Social security contributions	62.7	Social security of public workers	16.1
Payroll	31.2	Transfers to state and local workers	17.8
Gross revenue[b]	16.6	Education	21.9
Social profits	6.1	Total expenditures	107.1
Gross revenue: unemployment[c]	6.4		
Federal public workers	2.3		
Other taxes[d]	38.9		
Total revenues	203.6		

Sources: IBGE, "Carga Tributária 1994 e 1995" (Rio de Janeiro 1996); IBGE, "Tabulação Especial: Trans-
ferências de Assistência e Previdência" (Rio de Janeiro, 1996); Ministério da Educação e do Desporto
(1996); BACEN (1996a).
Note: Exchange rate assumed to be 1.0917 U.S. dollars per real.
[a]Includes tax on industrialized products (IPI), state value-added tax on the circulation of products (ICMS),
and tax on credit, exchange rate, and insurance (IOF).
[b]Social contribution incident on gross revenue (COFINS) and allocated to social security.
[c]Social contribution incident on gross revenue (PIS/PASEP) and allocated to finance unemployment benefit and bonus to low-income workers.
[d]Includes state and local administrations taxes, tax to finance trust fund for employees (FGTS) and other
taxes or social contributions.
[e]Includes unemployment benefit plus bonus to low-income workers.

2050 levels until 2200. Because Brazil is considered a closed country in population flows, the projection does not incorporate immigration or emigration
variables.

Table 8.2 shows the composition of overall public sector tax revenues and
transfer payments in 1995. Tax payments to federal, state, and local governments include labor and capital income taxes,[9] seigniorage, indirect taxes, and
social security contributions. Transfer payments include welfare, social insurance benefits to private workers, unemployment benefits (including bonuses to
low-income workers), social security to public workers, transfers paid by state
and local governments to their public employees, expenditures with education,
and other transfers.[10] It is worth noting that the total value of revenues and
expenditures reported in table 8.2 does not coincide exactly with the value
presented in national accounts statistics. There are two reasons for the differ-

9. Capital income taxes were not adjusted to account for investment incentives.
10. In the Brazilian national accounts, part of health expenditures are in government consumption and part in transfer payments. However, up to now, the available data do not permit the separa-
tion of those amounts. Hence, it was not possible to isolate health benefits and distribute their
value across a health profile.

ence. First, the values in table 8.2 are in dollars and not in reals. Second, in table 8.2 revenues include seigniorage, and transfer payments include educational expenditures.

Specific age-sex profiles are used to distribute the total amount of the corresponding tax or transfer among males and females from ages 0 to 90. The distribution of income taxes and payroll contributions are from the Ministry of Finance database for 1994. The composition of indirect taxes is derived from the Brazilian Bureau of Statistics 1987 Household Expenditure Survey. The age-sex profile of social insurance benefits used in the baseline calculations refers to the Ministry of Social Insurance database for 1992. To account for changes in social insurance legislation, the profile for 1987 is used instead. Finally, the unemployment benefit profile corresponds to the Ministry of Labor composition for 1994.

All profiles were benchmarked against national accounts values for 1995 and seigniorage against the change in aggregate monetary base between December 1994 and December 1995, as registered by the central bank.

Public expenditure on preschool, elementary, middle, and superior education corresponds to the Ministry of Education estimates for 1995. These four kinds of expenses were distributed equally among the population of males and females of the appropriate educational category.

The level of consumption of federal, state, and local governments (including consumption expenditures associated with social security programs) was U.S.$105.7 billion in 1995. This value was derived from national accounts statistics and includes wage payments to public workers, government consumption of goods and services, and subsidies; it excludes educational expenditures.

Government net debt for 1995 corresponds to internal and external government net debt held by federal, state, and local governments as well as public enterprises (BACEN 1996b, table III.13). The expected present value of resources to be obtained with privatization, estimated by the Ministry of Planning as 7 percent of GDP,[11] was deducted from that amount. As a result, the value of net public debt for 1995 used in the calculations corresponds to $167.6 billion.

Tax payments, transfer receipts, and government consumption after 1995 are projected by assuming that the corresponding per capita values will grow at the same rate as the economy. Those future values are discounted to the base year of 1995 by using a specified interest rate.

8.4 Brazilian Generational Accounts

How much can living and future generations of Brazilians expect to pay to the government due to current and alternative fiscal policies? How will the demographic transition and the reform of social insurance in 1988 affect the

11. Estimated at 7 percent of GDP (see Giambiagi and Pinheiro 1996).

Table 8.3   **Generational Accounts of Current and Future Generations: Baseline (thousands of U.S. dollars)**

Generation's Age in 1995	Average (1)	Males (2)	Females (3)
0	10.2	17.3	2.8
5	12.3	20.6	3.8
10	17.1	27.0	6.9
15	22.6	34.3	10.6
20	27.0	41.0	13.1
25	30.1	46.5	13.9
30	31.3	48.9	14.0
35	28.0	45.6	10.8
40	19.7	36.0	4.0
45	6.9	19.4	−4.9
50	−6.3	0.9	−13.0
55	−18.1	−16.3	−19.7
60	−28.1	−30.5	−25.9
65	−33.4	−44.3	−23.9
70	−32.9	−47.7	−20.7
75	−22.1	−33.6	−13.1
80	−14.4	−22.3	−8.7
85	−9.6	−13.5	−6.9
90	−2.7	−4.1	−1.8
Future generations	22.1	37.5	6.1
Percentage difference	116.4	116.2	116.2

Note: Growth rate assumed to be 1.5 percent; interest rate, 5 percent.

fiscal burden of those currently alive and of future generations? Those are some of the questions addressed in this section.

8.4.1   Baseline Results

Table 8.3 shows baseline generational accounts as of 1995 for a typical member of a living generation between ages 0 and 90 years, and generational accounts for an average member of future generations (those born after the base year of 1995). The baseline calculation assumes an economic growth rate of 1.5 percent and a rate of interest of 5 percent. It also assumes that current policies will prevail in the future.

Column (1) of table 8.3 reports "net payments" of living and future generations. "Net payment" is the difference between the present value of all taxes a typical member of each generation can expect to pay to the government over his or her remaining years of life and the present value of all transfers he or she can expect to receive from the government from the base year into the future. Generational accounts (net payments) are forward looking. They disregard net payments made in the past (before the base year of the calculations) and estimate remaining lifetime bills.

Given the prospective nature of the calculations, net payments are smaller for young cohorts, reach a maximum for those in middle age, and are negative for older living individuals. This life cycle pattern can be observed in table 8.3. During the remaining years of their lives, newborns can expect to pay U.S.$10,200 to the government. Net payments increase with age and reach a maximum value of $31,300 at age 30. This happens because members of this age group are near the peak of their taxpaying years, while retirement is still some years away. Generational accounts become negative at age 50, as the present value of transfer payments they will receive from the government outweighs the present value of taxes they will pay during their remaining years of life. Net payments decrease for older cohorts and reach a minimum at age 65, when they can expect to receive net transfers from the government of $33,400. Finally, the value of future net payments increases for those aged 70 or older, because they are approaching the end of their lives (90 years) and so have a reduced number of transfers to receive from the government.

As reported in table 8.3, lifetime net payments for an average member of future generations amount to $22,100, which is 116 percent higher than expected net payments of newborns. This means that if the current path of fiscal policies prevails in the future, generations born after 1995 will have to pay much more in taxes and social security contributions throughout their lifetimes, or will receive much less in benefits (or a combination of both), than those born in 1995.

Table 8.3 also shows an assessment of how generational accounts differ according to gender. During working years males pay more taxes than females, and during inactivity they generally receive more than their female counterparts. The contrast arises because women receive lower wages than men and have lower rates of participation in the labor market. Moreover, since in Brazil the value of pensions is a function of workers' wages and years of contribution, women are entitled to receive, on average, lower social insurance checks than men. Those differences are highlighted by what happens at age 35: remaining net payments of a typical male in this age group ($45,600) are four times higher than net payments of his female counterpart ($10,800).

Generational accounting methodology also shows that in Brazil women start collecting pensions earlier than men. As table 8.3 shows, on average, women at age 45 can expect to receive, during their remaining years of life, a net transfer from the government of $4,900, while men in the same age group can expect to pay, over their remaining years, a net amount of $19,400. The contrast can be attributed to different eligibility criteria for granting social insurance benefits. Females from the urban sector can retire at age 60 and males at age 65. For rural workers the age limits are lower: 55 years for women and 60 years for men. Females can start receiving length-of-service pensions after 25 years of work, while for men the minimum required is 30 years.

A detailed description of the distribution of different payments and receipts among age groups is reported in table 8.4. The present value of remaining income tax payments and payroll contributions is concentrated among those

Table 8.4   Composition of Generational Accounts: Present Value of Payments and Receipts (thousands of U.S. dollars)

	Payments						Receipts						
			Social Security				Social Security						
Generation's Age in 1995	Income Taxes	VAT	Payroll Contributions	Net Revenue and Social Profits	UI	Other[a]	Welfare	Social Insurance of Private Workers	Other	UI	Social Security of Federal Public Workers	Education	State and Municipal Transfer Payments
0	3.8	9.5	4.1	3.4	0.9	5.7	0.6	4.9	1.8	0.5	2.4	4.1	2.7
5	4.4	11.0	4.7	3.9	1.0	6.6	0.7	5.7	1.8	0.6	2.7	4.8	3.1
10	5.3	13.1	5.6	4.7	1.2	7.9	0.7	6.8	1.7	0.7	3.2	3.8	3.7
15	6.2	15.3	6.6	5.5	1.4	9.2	0.8	7.9	1.7	0.8	3.8	2.4	4.3
20	7.2	17.3	7.8	6.2	1.6	10.8	0.9	9.2	1.6	0.9	4.4	1.9	5.0
25	8.5	18.1	9.1	6.5	1.7	12.5	1.2	10.8	1.6	0.8	5.1	1.1	5.8
30	9.8	18.1	10.3	6.6	1.6	14.0	1.2	12.7	1.5	0.7	6.1	0.2	6.8
35	10.6	17.3	10.8	6.3	1.6	14.7	1.2	14.9	1.4	0.6	7.1	0.0	8.0
40	10.6	15.7	10.2	5.6	1.4	14.0	1.3	17.2	1.3	0.4	8.3	0.0	9.3
45	10.1	13.5	8.9	4.8	1.2	12.4	1.5	20.1	1.2	0.3	9.8	0.0	10.9
50	8.8	11.6	6.9	4.0	1.0	10.0	1.7	22.4	1.1	0.2	11.0	0.0	12.3
55	7.3	8.2	5.0	2.7	0.7	7.4	1.9	22.7	1.0	0.1	11.2	0.0	12.5
60	6.2	6.0	3.5	1.9	0.5	5.3	2.3	23.5	0.9	0.0	11.7	0.0	13.0
65	4.7	4.2	1.8	1.2	0.3	2.7	2.6	21.7	0.7	0.0	10.9	0.0	12.1
70	3.7	2.5	0.3	0.6	0.2	0.5	3.1	17.9	0.6	0.0	9.1	0.0	10.1
75	2.8	1.6	0.0	0.4	0.1	0.1	3.4	11.2	0.5	0.0	5.7	0.0	6.3
80	2.3	1.1	0.0	0.2	0.1	0.0	3.7	6.8	0.4	0.0	3.5	0.0	3.9
85	1.6	0.8	0.0	0.2	0.0	0.0	3.8	4.0	0.3	0.0	2.0	0.0	2.3
90	0.4	0.1	0.0	0.0	0.0	0.0	0.9	1.1	0.1	0.0	0.5	0.0	0.6

Note: Growth rate assumed to be 1.5 percent; interest rate, 5 percent.

[a]Includes seigniorage, tax to finance the trust fund for employees (FGTS), and remaining taxes.

Table 8.5   **Baseline Results and Sources of Generational Imbalance**

Scenario	Generational Imbalance (%)
Baseline	116.4
Zero debt	99.0
No demographic change	64.1

Note: Growth rate assumed to be 1.5 percent; interest rate, 5 percent.

between ages 30 and 45, whereas the payment of indirect taxes (value-added taxes and gross revenue contributions) is distributed over a wider range of ages (5 to 50). Welfare is targeted toward older cohorts, since most assistance benefits in Brazil go to the old poor. Social insurance payments for private and public workers are highest for those at age 60. Those between ages 25 and 55 also benefit substantially from social insurance, as this program comprises a wide range of benefits regardless of age, such as disability and length-of-service pensions and survival benefits payable to the living spouse. Educational expenditures are targeted to younger cohorts, reflecting the concentration of public funds on elementary education.

The burden imposed on future generations would be lower if the public sector did not hold any debt or if the structure of the population remained constant in the future. Table 8.5 outlines some of the sources of intergenerational imbalance and compares the associated burdens with the baseline calculation. In the absence of public sector debt, net payments of future generations would be 99 percent higher than those of newborns. In a hypothetical scenario where the population of each age cohort is maintained constant from 1995 to 2200, unborn generations would have to pay on average 64 percent more than newborns. Why is the burden imposed on future generations lower in these two cases than in the baseline calculation? A smaller net debt (in the absence of changes in the current path of government consumption expenditures or in net payments it will receive from living generations) means that the government can reduce the net payments it will impose on future generations and still balance its intertemporal budget constraint. With a constant population structure, the proportion of old cohorts in the total population will remain constant over time and, as a consequence, will not constitute an increasing pressure on the level of transfer payments.

What can be done to ensure that future generations will not have to pay more to the government than today's newborns? Table 8.6 reports spending cuts and tax increases required to eliminate generational imbalance. In all cases, considerable changes are necessary. Net payments of future generations will equal those of newborns if the level of government consumption, net of educational expenditures, decreases by 26.2 percent. Equilibrium between current and future newborns can also be attained if total revenue has an immediate and permanent increase of 11.7 percent, or if the value of all transfer payments has an

Table 8.6   **Spending Cuts or Tax Increases Required to Eliminate Generational Imbalance**

Change	Cut or Increase (%)
Cut in government purchases	26.2
Increase in all tax revenues	11.7
Cut in all transfer payments	17.9
Increase in payroll contributions	74.1
Cut in social insurance outlays	47.2

Note: Growth rate assumed to be 1.5 percent; interest rate, 5 percent.

immediate and permanent reduction of 17.9 percent. Alternatively, if only the social insurance program is adjusted, a 74 percent increase in revenues from payroll taxes or a 47.2 percent reduction in all outlays is required to produce balance.

8.4.2   Impact of Changes in Social Insurance

As discussed earlier, the implementation of the Constitution of 1988 substantially increased the level of social insurance outlays. The objective of this section is to investigate how baseline generational accounts would be affected if the Constitution of 1988 had not changed the structure of social insurance benefits. This is a purely hypothetical exercise and was conducted only with the purpose of illustrating how social insurance reform can affect living and future generations in opposite ways.

To explore this hypothetical situation it is necessary to assume that social insurance legislation in 1995 is the same as it was in 1988 (the last year of the old legal regime). For that, some of the baseline values need to be revised. First, the profile of social insurance and welfare outlays for 1987 is used, so as to capture the age-sex composition of benefits prior to the reform. Second, the hypothetical value of benefits in 1995 under the old rules is estimated[12] and used instead of the observed level of outlays, so as to incorporate the lower level of expenditures before the reform. With those corrections it is possible to project net payments of current and future generations under the old social insurance rules. Those results can then be compared with the baseline calculations, which reflect current policy.

Table 8.7 shows net payments of living and future generations of males and females for the scenarios "current policy" and "old social insurance rules," as well as the absolute and relative differences between them. The conclusion is that the reform of 1988 involved a substantial redistribution of resources toward living generations at the expense of those born in the future. As the last

12. This was done by assuming that the average value of benefits in 1995 would be equal to the average value of benefits observed in 1988 times the number of beneficiaries that would have existed in 1995 had the law not changed (and rural workers had to retire at later ages).

Table 8.7   **Impact of Changes in Social Insurance Legislation: Net Payments of Males and Females (thousands of U.S. dollars)**

Generation's Age in 1995	Males				Females			
	Current Policy (baseline) (a)	Old Social Insurance Rules (b)	Absolute Difference (a) − (b)	Relative Difference (%) (a)/(b)	Current Policy (baseline) (a)	Old Social Insurance Rules (b)	Absolute Difference (a) − (b)	Relative Difference (%) (a)/(b)
0	17.3	18.5	−1.1	−6.2	2.8	5.5	−2.7	−48.6
5	20.6	21.9	−1.3	−6.1	3.8	6.8	−3.1	−45.1
10	27.0	28.6	−1.6	−5.5	6.9	10.6	−3.6	−34.4
15	34.3	36.1	−1.8	−5.1	10.6	14.8	−4.2	−28.5
20	41.0	43.1	−2.1	−5.0	13.1	18.0	−4.8	−26.9
25	46.5	49.0	−2.4	−4.9	13.9	19.8	−5.9	−29.9
30	48.9	51.7	−2.8	−5.3	14.0	20.7	−6.7	−32.4
35	45.6	48.9	−3.3	−6.7	10.8	18.4	−7.6	−41.2
40	36.0	39.8	−3.8	−9.6	4.0	12.9	−8.9	−69.1
45	19.4	24.0	−4.6	−19.2	−4.9	5.7	−10.6	−186.6
50	0.9	6.5	−5.7	−86.6	−13.0	−0.7	−12.3	1,692.6
55	−16.3	−11.9	−4.4	36.8	−19.7	−6.0	−13.7	229.6
60	−30.5	−20.1	−10.4	51.5	−25.9	−9.7	−16.2	167.8
65	−44.3	−25.5	−18.8	73.9	−23.9	−8.3	−15.7	189.4
70	−47.7	−23.2	−24.5	105.9	−20.7	−6.5	−14.2	218.7
75	−33.6	−15.7	−17.9	114.4	−13.1	−3.6	−9.6	269.1
80	−22.3	−10.6	−11.7	110.4	−8.7	−2.7	−6.0	223.4
85	−13.5	−7.4	−6.1	82.7	−6.9	−1.6	−5.3	330.6
90	−4.1	−1.5	−2.6	178.1	−1.8	−0.4	−1.4	401.7
Future generations	37.5	20.3	17.2	84.9	6.1	6.1	0.1	1.4
Percentage difference	116.2	9.7			116.2	9.7		

Note: Growth rate assumed to be 1.5 percent; interest rate, 5 percent.

row of table 8.7 shows, if social insurance rules had not changed, unborn generations would pay 9.7 percent more than newborns. Under current policy, the burden facing future generations is much greater, since they can expect to pay 116 percent more than newborns.

Why were future generations left with this sizable burden? The reason is that since all members of living generations can expect to receive, during their remaining years of life, higher transfer payments from the government, the only way to balance the government intertemporal budget constraint (in the absence of a reduction in consumption expenditures or the debt) is to increase net payments to be received from future generations.

An additional result drawn from this analysis is that even though social insurance reform benefited all members of living generations, the gains were not distributed uniformly across all age groups or between males and females. To see this, it is useful to look at the absolute and relative difference columns presented in table 8.7. The first reports the absolute difference between net payments (taxes minus transfers) under current policy and net payments under the old social insurance rules. The absolute difference is negative for all age cohorts of living generations, indicating that as a result of the reform, males and females currently alive can expect to receive higher levels of transfer payments than they would otherwise. The relative difference is negative for younger cohorts, showing that under current policy they will have to make lower net payments than they would under the old social insurance rules. That difference is positive for older cohorts, indicating that with current policy they will receive higher levels of net transfer payments than they would otherwise.

All members of current generations are better off, but males aged 60 to 80 gained more than other males and females aged 45 to 70 benefited more than other females. This can be seen in the absolute difference columns. For example, if the old rules still prevailed, net payments of a typical male aged 65 would be −U.S.$25,500 (indicating that during his remaining years of life, transfer receipts exceed tax payments). Under the new rules, his expected net payment is −$44,300. The difference of $18,800 represents what he can expect to receive in terms of higher social insurance benefits. Why did older cohorts benefit more than younger ones? The new rules increased the value of all existing benefits and hence represented a sizable gain for those already receiving social insurance checks. Younger cohorts also benefited from the reform, but their gain will occur only in the future. Since all the calculations are in present value terms, a payment received today has a higher present value than the same payment received in the future.

Another conclusion is that women benefited more than men. This can be seen by noting that the absolute value of the relative difference columns is always higher for women than for men in the same age cohort. This pattern probably accrues because some aspects of the new legislation favored women more than men: the retirement age for female rural workers was reduced more than for male rural workers, and female workers gained the right to ask for length-of-service retirement earlier than males.

8.4.3   Sensitivity Analysis

The baseline result gives generational accounts for a particular choice of parameters. It is useful, then, to measure how the calculations would change if a different set of values were more appropriate.

Table 8.8 shows net payments of living and future generations for reasonable assumptions regarding productivity growth and interest rates. The choice of these parameters affects the burden to be imposed on future generations, but it does not change the overall conclusion that if current fiscal policies, including social insurance, are maintained in the future, net payments of unborn generations will be much higher than those of newborns.

The calculations are sensitive to the hypothesis regarding the population projection, as well. Those results are reported in table 8.9. If the structure of the population observed in 1995 remained constant in the future, that is, in the absence of an aging population and a declining fertility rate, the burden on future generations would be 64 percent higher than that on newborns. Different assumptions concerning the behavior of the fertility rate also affect the results. If the number of children per woman of reproductive age remains at 2.1 after 2000, future generations will pay 116 percent more than newborns. However, if the total fertility rate falls from 2.1 to 1.8 after 2055, net payments of unborn generations will be 349 percent higher than those of newborns. This happens because with lower fertility rates there will be fewer members of future generations left to pay the bills not paid by current generations.

8.4.4   Effect of Policy Changes

Another important application of generational accounting is to assess how policy changes affect net payments of different generations. Table 8.10 reports generational accounts of males and females under three alternative scenarios. A general conclusion drawn from these experiments is that policy changes are not neutral with respect to gender or age.

In Brazil, given the high level of payroll taxes, one proposition often suggested is a shift in the tax base, from payroll contributions to value-added taxes. As column (2) of table 8.10 shows, this change in tax structure benefits males aged 0 to 60 as their net payment to the government declines. Young females and older cohorts of both sexes lose, since they will have to pay higher taxes than they would otherwise. Why do the elderly lose? They did not pay payroll taxes and hence do not benefit from their elimination, but they are hurt by higher value-added taxes. Young females are worse off because the ratio of young females' to young males' indirect tax payments is higher than the ratio of payroll taxes. As a result, an increase in indirect taxes hurts young females more than young males, and a cut in payroll taxes favors young males more than young females.

The second experiment is a 1 percent increase in social insurance expenditures every year until 2030. All living generations gain from this measure, since they benefit from higher transfers from the government. Females gain more

Table 8.8   Sensitivity with Respect to Productivity Growth and Discount Rate (U.S. dollars)

| | $g = 1$ | | | $g = 1.5$ | | | $g = 2$ | | |
	$r = 3$	$r = 5$	$r = 7$	$r = 3$	$r = 5$	$r = 7$	$r = 3$	$r = 5$	$r = 7$
Net Payments									
Present generation	15,726	8,498	3,579	17,304	10,229	4,611	18,174	12,097	5,811
Future generations	35,203	18,791	10,481	40,840	22,132	12,080	46,791	26,042	14,041
Generational imbalance (% difference)	123.9	121.1	192.8	136.0	116.4	162.0	157.5	115.3	141.6

Note: g is productivity growth (percent); r is interest rate (percent).

Table 8.9   **Sensitivity with Respect to Population Parameters**

Assumption Regarding Population	Generational Imbalance (%)
Constant population structure from 1995 to 2200	64.1
Fertility rate of 2.1 after 2000 (baseline)	116.4
Lower fertility rate of 1.8 after 2055	349.2

Note: Growth rate assumed to be 1.5 percent; interest rate, 5 percent.

Table 8.10   **Generational Accounting under Alternative Policy Changes: Net Payments of Males and Females (thousands of U.S. dollars)**

Generation's Age in 1995	Baseline (1)	Switch from Payroll to Value-Added Taxes (2)	Increase in Social Insurance Benefits by 1% Every Year until 2030 (3)	Reduction in Government Consumption by 2% Every Year until 2200 (4)
		Males		
0	17.3	16.9	14.9	17.3
10	27.0	26.4	23.6	27.0
20	41.0	39.7	36.6	41.0
30	48.9	44.3	43.7	48.9
40	36.0	29.8	30.6	36.0
50	0.9	−2.9	−3.6	0.9
60	−30.5	−32.8	−33.5	−30.5
70	−47.7	−46.8	−49.0	−47.7
80	−22.3	−22.0	−22.7	−22.3
90	−4.1	−4.1	−4.1	−4.1
Future generations	37.5	38.8	52.1	35.9
Percentage difference	116.2	129.4	250.8	107.4
		Females		
0	2.8	3.7	0.9	2.8
10	6.9	8.1	4.4	6.9
20	13.1	14.3	9.8	13.1
30	14.0	13.7	9.9	14.0
40	4.0	2.8	−0.2	4.0
50	−13.0	−13.5	−16.6	−13.0
60	−25.9	−26.0	−28.3	−25.9
70	−20.7	−20.3	−21.8	−20.7
80	−8.7	−8.4	−9.1	−8.7
90	−1.8	−1.8	−1.8	−1.8
Future generations	6.1	8.4	3.3	5.9
Percentage difference	116.2	129.4	250.9	107.3

Note: Growth rate assumed to be 1.5 percent; interest rate, 5 percent.

than males. Women in their 40s and men in their 50s profit more than the other age groups, since they are closer to retirement and will be granted higher pensions during their entire period of inactivity. The gain to living generations, however, hurts future generations, whose burden is 250 percent higher than that of current newborns.

The last experiment is a reduction in government consumption by 2 percent every year until 2200. This policy does not change what living generations pay or receive from the government because it does not entail alterations in tax policy or social security transfers. As a result, the beneficiaries of a thriftier government are future generations who face lower net payments.

8.5 Conclusions

The application of generational accounting to the Brazilian case suggests that if the actual path of fiscal policies, including social insurance, remains unchanged, future generations will face a burden 116 percent higher than current newborns.

What are the sources of intergenerational imbalance in the Brazilian situation? The level of public debt and an aging population associated with lower fertility rates can partially explain why expected net payments of future generations are much higher than those of current generations. Most of the imbalance, however, can be attributed to the changes in social insurance legislation brought by the Constitution of 1988. The reform increased the value of all existing benefits and decreased the age for retirement of rural workers without securing appropriate financing. If this windfall to the initial elderly had not taken place, the burden on future generations would be 9.7 percent higher than that on newborns, which is significantly lower than the burden associated with current social insurance policy.

Several measures can ensure that future generations will not pay more to the government than current newborns. They encompass a cut in government spending by 26.2 percent, an increase in revenues from taxes and social contributions by 11.7 percent, or a reduction in all transfer payments to public and private workers by 17.9 percent. Any of those changes are, without doubt, extremely hard to accomplish. However, if relevant corrections are postponed to a later date, the intergenerational imbalance against future generations gets even worse. For instance, if during the next five years the Brazilian government is unable to promote structural reforms in fiscal policies, generations born five years from now will face a burden 153 percent higher than that on newborns. And if the lag period is ten years, the onus will be almost 200 percent.

Another important lesson from generational accounting is that policy changes are not neutral with respect to gender or age. For example, a shift in the tax base from payroll to indirect taxes helps current males but hurts young females and the elderly. The social insurance reform of 1988 benefited all members of living generations, but in general, women gained more than men and the current elderly gained more than young and middle-aged cohorts. Finally, why should Brazilian policymakers or politicians be concerned about the burden on future generations? The government strives, almost daily, to find resources to pay public employees, keep hospitals open, and pay current retirees. The answer is that the intergenerational distribution of resources can have important consequences for a nation's capacity to save. For instance, if the marginal propensity to consume out of remaining lifetime income rises with age, policies that increase social insurance benefits (like the reform of 1988) may tend to stimulate current consumption and reduce domestic savings.

References

Afonso, J. R. R. 1995. A questão tributária e o financiamento dos diferentes niveis de governo. In *A federação em perspectiva: Ensaios selecionados,* ed. Rui Affonso and Pedro Luiz Silva, 315–28. São Paulo: Fundação do Desenvolvimento Administrativo.
Almeida, S. C., and C. E. G. Cavalcanti. 1995. As contribuições sociais e a reforma tributária. In *Federalismo no Brasil: Reforma tributária e federação,* ed. Rui Affonso and Pedro Luiz Silva, 95–128. São Paulo: Fundação do Desenvolvimento Administrativo.
Auerbach, A. J., J. Gokhale, and L. J. Kotlikoff. 1991. Generational accounts: A meaningful alternative to deficit accounting. In *Tax policy and the economy,* vol. 5, ed. David Bradford, 55–110. Cambridge, Mass.: MIT Press.
———. 1994. Generational accounting: A meaningful way to evaluate fiscal policy. *Journal of Economic Perspectives* 8 (1): 73–94.
Banco Central do Brasil (BACEN). 1996a. *Boletim do Banco Central do Brasil* 32, no. 2 (February).
———. 1996b. *Boletim do Banco Central do Brasil* 32, no. 12 (May).
———. 1996c. *Relatório do Boletim do Banco Central do Brasil: 1995,* vol. 32. Brasilia: Banco Central do Brasil.
Dain, S. 1995. Visões equivocadas de uma reforma prematura. In *Federalismo no Brasil: Reforma tributária e federação,* ed. Rui Affonso and Pedro Luiz Silva, 43–74. São Paulo: Fundação do Desenvolvimento Administrativo.
Fernandes, F. 1995. Sistema previdenciário e desigualdades inter e intrageracionais no Brasil: O papel da dinâmica demografica. Belo Horizonte: Centro de Desenvolvimento e Planejamento Regional.
Fundação Getúlio Vargas. 1996. *Conjuntura econômica.* Rio de Janeiro: Fundação Getúlio Vargas.
Giambiagi, F., and A. C. Pinheiro. 1996. Lucratividade, dividendos e investmentos das empresas estatais: Uma contribuição para o debate sobre a privatização no Brasil. Texto para Discusção no. 34. Brasilia: Banco Nacional de Desenvolvimento Econômico e Social, Departamento Econômico.
Instituto Brasileiro de Geografia e Estatística (IBGE). 1982. Pesquisa nacional por amostra de domicilios. Rio de Janeiro: Instituto Brasileiro de Geografia e Estatística.
———. 1995. Pesquisa nacional por amostra de domicilios. Rio de Janeiro: Instituto Brasileiro de Geografia e Estatística.

198   Regina Villela Malvar

———. 1996. *Contas consolidadas para a Nacão, 1990–1995.* Rio de Janeiro. Instituto de Pesquisa Econômica Aplicada (IPEA). 1996a. *Boletim conjuntural 1996.* Rio de Janeiro: Instituto de Pesquisa Econômica Aplicada.

———. 1996b. *Carta de conjuntura 1996.* Rio de Janeiro: Instituto de Pesquisa Econômica Aplicada.

———. 1996c. *Relatório sobre o desenvolvimento humano no Brasil: 1996.* Brasilia: Instituto de Pesquisa Econômica Aplicada.

Kotlikoff, L. J. 1992. *Generational accounting: Knowing who pays, and when, for what we spend.* New York: Free Press.

Kotlikoff, L. J., and J. Walliser. 1995. Applying generational accounting to developing countries. Boston: Boston University, Department of Economics. Mimeograph.

Latin American Demographic Center (CELADE). 1996. Brazil—Demographic indicators estimated by quinquennia. Santiago: Economic Commission for Latin America and the Caribbean.

Ministério da Educação e do Desporto. 1996. Desenvolvimento da Educação no Brasil. Brasilia: Ministério da Educação e do Desporto.

Ministério da Fazenda. 1996. Boletim de acompanhamento macroeconómico. Brasilia: Secretária de Política Econômica.

Ministério da Previdência e Assistência Social (MPAS). 1994. *Anuário estatístico da previdência social,* vol. 2. Brasília: Ministério da Previdência e Assistência Social.

———. 1995. *Anuário estatístico da previdência social,* vol. 3. Brasilia: Ministério da Previdência e Assistência Social.

Oliveira, F. E. B., K. Beltrão, and M. T. M. Pasinato. 1995. Projeções da situação econômico-financeira da previdência social 1995–2030 e impactos de políticas institucionais alternativas. Brasilia: Ministério da Previdência e Assisténcia Social.

Piola, S. F., S. M. Vianna, and V. C. Pinheiro. 1995. *Gasto social federal e investimento na infância.* Brasilia: UNICEF.

Quadros, W. L. 1995. A tributação indireta no Brasil. In *Federalismo no Brasil: Reforma tributária e federação,* ed. Rui Affonso and Pedro Luiz Silva, 75–96. São Paulo: Fundação do Desenvolvimento Administrativo.

Rezende, F. 1995. O financiamento de políticas públicas: Problemas atuais. In *A federação em perspectiva: Ensaios selecionados,* ed. Rui Affonso and Pedro Luiz Silva, 241–59. São Paulo: Fundação do Desenvolvimento Administrativo.

9   Canada: On the Road to Fiscal Balance

Philip Oreopoulos

9.1   Introduction

On the whole, Canadians have enjoyed exceptional economic and social growth over the past 35 years. Average incomes have been rising steadily, international trade has increased substantially, and a highly skilled labor force has been promoted. In 1961, per capita GDP in Canada was 70 percent of that in the United States; by 1990 it had virtually caught up, to 92 percent, establishing Canada as one of the richest countries in the world.[1] During the same period, a broad and extensive social safety net was entwined, which soon became recognized as one of the defining characteristics of the country.

Yet, despite these past fiscal arrangements, it had become apparent in the early 1990s that the country's method of financing its welfare state through deficit spending could not be sustained. A slowdown of economic growth, underestimation of debt-servicing costs, and lower than expected tax revenue base had led the ratio of total net debt to GDP in Canada to rise steadily, from 11.3 percent in 1975 to 70.1 percent in 1995, the second highest level (next to Italy) among the G-7 countries.[2] Moreover, should the government try to maintain the 1995 level of social programs without further reform, this ascending trend would continue.

Philip Oreopoulos is a graduate student in economics at the University of California, Berkeley. He received his B.A. from the University of Western Ontario, Huron College, and his M.A. from the University of British Columbia.

The author thanks Bill Robson, Irwin Gillespie, and François Valliancourt for helpful comments and discussion and gratefully acknowledges financial assistance from the Social Sciences and Humanities Research Council of Canada. Any errors or omissions are the author's sole responsibility.

1. Cairns et al. (1996) note that although this convergence was not unique, the degree to which it occurred in Canada was greater than for most industrialized countries.

2. For purposes of consistency and international comparison, all references to government debt are based on a national accounts basis.

199

Over the past several years, the federal and 10 provincial governments have instigated a number of initiatives specifically designed to realign fiscal policy on a more sustainable path. Social policy has now been placed at the front of the political agenda, as individual programs are assessed for efficiency and effectiveness in light of current economic pressures. The reforms are intended to reverse the trend of spiraling interest costs—not just for the following year, but for the coming decades as the population ages.

This chapter applies the generational accounting approach to Canada, to examine whether these changes have been enough to actually reach fiscal balance.[3] Despite persistent government deficits in recent years, the main findings suggest that Canada's fiscal policy is at a state of sustainability. The recent federal budget, the prevalent pattern of partial indexing of particular expenditures, and the anticipated payroll tax hikes for the Canada and Quebec Pension Plan (C/QPP) all have significant influence in reducing the estimated net tax burden on future Canadians. After these changes are factored in, future generations are projected to face lifetime net tax burdens 3.1 percent more than that of today's newborns under current policy. It would take, for example, only a 0.1 percent hike in personal income taxes to remove this generational imbalance. That no further reform is required is due largely to these policies, which have not yet had their full impact on currently living Canadians.

There is one chief cautionary note, however. Now that the federal deficit is set to become surplus by around the turn of the century, the government is considering using a portion of the surplus for either tax relief or more spending. This may be myopic policy in that the large revenue requirements that will occur beginning around 2015 when the baby boomers start to retire are not taken into account. Simulating this policy using mainly income tax cuts over the first 20 years, I find the net tax burden on future generations would rise to a level 58 percent higher than that on current newborns. (For a more detailed look at the implications of not using the surpluses primarily for debt reduction, see Oreopoulous and Valliancourt [1998b].)

Section 9.2 will outline in brief detail what has happened to Canadian fiscal policy since the 1960s. Section 9.3 will discuss the data sources used to calculate the generational accounts for Canada. In section 9.4, I present the main findings and provide a sensitivity analysis of the results. The impact from the recent federal budget and the projected changes to the C/QPP will be shown in section 9.5. Finally, section 9.6 summarizes and concludes the chapter.

9.2 Canadian Fiscal Policy since 1960

As in most other industrialized countries, the 1960s were a prosperous time in Canada. The country's population was growing rapidly, with high fertility rates of 3.0 and more. Hence, the labor force was also increasing. Economic

---

3. Generational accounting was first introduced by Auerbach, Gokhale, and Kotlikoff (1991).

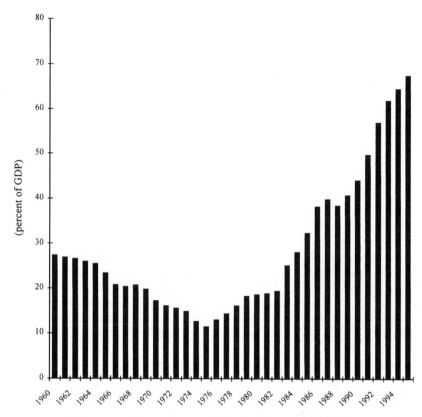

Fig. 9.1   Ratio of net debt to GDP 1960–95 (national accounts basis)
Sources: Statistics Canada, *National Income and Expenditure Accounts,* Catalogue no. 13-201 (Ottawa: Minister of Industry, Science and Technology, various years); Statistics Canada, *National Balance Sheet Accounts,* Catalogue no. 13-214 (Ottawa: Minister of Industry, Science and Technology, various years).

growth and productivity were very robust. Real per capita GDP was rising some 2.0 to 3.0 percent a year, while interest rates were barely higher than inflation levels. The unemployment rate averaged 4.9 percent for this decade, and the debt, relative to the size of the economy, was on a downward track, falling from 27.2 to 17.1 percent of GDP (see fig. 9.1). In short, the 1960s was an affluent period in Canada, which brought promise and optimism. Sustained economic growth was simply taken for granted.

Within this environment emerged a broad expansion of the Canadian welfare state. Policymakers could argue that these newly introduced or expanded programs were affordable by appealing to the economic conditions existing at the time. There were three main developments. First, the Canada Assistance Plan (CAP), enacted in 1966, consolidated and enhanced the existing public assistance programs to meet "basic requirements" of welfare recipients. Second, a comprehensive retirement pension program was also phased in. The pay-as-you-go Canada and Quebec Pension Plans were established in 1966 with the intent of providing social insurance for workers and their families against loss of income due to retirement, disability, or death. Additional income security plans for the elderly were also incorporated: Old Age Security (OAS), the Guaranteed Income Supplement (GIS), and the Spouse's Allowance were introduced in 1952, 1967, and 1975, respectively, to provide revenues for individuals who required additional support. Last, universal public health insurance was adopted by each of the provinces by the beginning of 1972.

In the early 1970s, the federal government continued to expand its level of expenditures while posting only modest deficits and one budget surplus. The rise in spending was financed mostly by an increase in taxation, while government borrowing was kept at minimal levels. Prior to 1975, the primary account was in surplus, large enough that the ratio of debt to GDP maintained a downward trend, falling eventually to 11.3 percent. Demand for debt reduction ceased to be a major issue. But ironically, this apathetic attitude toward debt reduction was the main reason for the beginning of debt creation.[4] As the magnitude of debt decreased, fewer Canadians perceived it as a threat, and greater taxation was deemed unnecessary. The federal government recognized this shift in voters' perception, and primary surpluses were finally allowed to become primary deficits, which led the debt-to-GDP ratio to steadily increase to 18.2 percent by 1979.

The situation quickly worsened after 1980. The rate of growth of national income consistently slowed, while the national unemployment rate doubled. The trend was not one particular to Canada. Almost all industrialized countries experienced smaller productivity growth during this period. What made Canada's situation particularly grave was the added strain from the 1981–82 and 1990–92 recessions, which were the most severe ones felt since the Great Depression, and the worst out of all industrialized countries. In the 1981–82 recession, real GDP fell 5.2 percent, real short-term interest rates rose to 7.5 percent, and unemployment rose from 7.5 to 12.5 percent. And in the 1990–92 recession, real GDP fell by 3.2 percent, real short-term interest rates rose to 10 percent, and unemployment rose from 7.8 percent to 11.0 percent. Higher servicing costs resulting from the higher interest rates, coupled with a substantial rise in expenditures and lower revenues instigated by the 1981–82 recession, produced a doubling of the debt-to-GDP ratio in less than a decade.

The federal government was rather slow to react forcefully to its growing financial problems. It was not until 1987 that it recorded a primary surplus, which amounted to only 1 percent of GDP. Federal taxes were increased throughout the latter part of the decade, from 15.5 percent of GDP in 1979 to

---

4. Gillespie (1996) comments that the influences that led to the rise in relative debt since the mid-1970s are very different from all previous "waves" of debt creation. In the past, substantial increases in federal borrowing occurred during the financing of wars and depressions.

18.0 percent in 1989. It was also during this period that certain welfare payments were de-indexed to economic growth, or at least were no longer periodically adjusted to keep pace with it. This would not have a significant impact right away. Relative federal program expenditures remained virtually the same, representing 15.9 percent of GDP in 1979 and 15.4 percent in 1989. Despite the large increase in tax revenues, the federal government was unable to raise its primary budget above levels that would begin to lower the ratio of debt to GDP. To be sure, the speed of increase for this figure had slowed. However, the arrival of the 1990–92 recession, and the increased servicing costs from the debt, brought further escalation in the ratio. Between 1990 and 1995, the debt-to-GDP ratio climbed from 43.9 to 67.4 percent.

The provinces, whose aggregate total spending is about the same as the federal government, exhibited similar patterns of fiscal policy.[5] Budget imbalances were usually small and fluctuated from deficit to surplus during the 1960s and 1970s. As it had done to the federal government, the recession of the early 1980s impaired the fiscal positions of the provinces. But whereas the federal deficit continued to balloon, the deficits of the provinces started to decline immediately and dramatically after 1983. The return to solid financial ground did not last long, however. The effort by the provinces to forestall further the need for borrowing was not enough to avoid the strain from the 1990–92 recession. In general, budgetary deficits increased substantially.

The 1990s saw concern about the unsustainable path of Canadian fiscal policy snowball into a massive call for deficit reduction. Opinion polls reported that the public debt load was perceived as the most serious threat to economic stability. Several provinces were given strong mandates to take measures to control their spending. As a result, six of the ten provinces have produced, or are expected to produce by next year, a budget surplus, despite reduced transfers from the federal government. The two largest Canadian provinces, Ontario and Quebec, appear to be the slowest in dealing with their budgets, although Ontario has recently reduced its expenditures dramatically. On the federal side, the election in 1993 brought about a phenomenal makeover in Parliament. The Progressive Conservatives, who came to power in 1984 with the second largest majority in Canadian history, were reduced to 2 of the 295 seats in the House of Commons. Dissatisfied with the government's inability to control its budgets, the electorate had made clear they wanted this practice reversed (although this was not the only factor contributing to the Progressive Conservative defeat). The new government under the Liberal Party has instigated a number of reforms to reduce its overall expenditures, most notably in the areas of unemployment insurance and old age security. Large cuts to provincial cash transfers have been announced and will occur over the next three years. The provinces are, of course, upset about this, but their rhetoric suggests that they will accom-

---

5. Kneebone (1996) and Wroberl (1995) provide more detailed accounts of the changing fiscal policies among the provinces.

modate the change without borrowing. Neither the provincial nor federal governments are keen to raise taxes. The past few years have seen ardent opposition to higher taxes, and calls even to lower them. The Canadian governments have generally acknowledged this concern, allowing most of their changes to fiscal policy to come from expenditure cuts only.

In addition to anxiety over current fiscal arrangements, the majority of Canadians perceive that their country will have difficulty in the future supporting its elderly population (Northcott 1994). This concern is not surprising. The fertility rate has fallen dramatically since its peak of 3.8 in 1959. A sharp contraction occurred shortly after this time, with the rate dropping to 1.9 by 1973, and to 1.7 by 1985, where it has remained since. Net migration is large enough to offset the low fertility rate so that the total population in Canada is still growing, although very slowly. The senior dependency ratio—the number of Canadians over age 65, expressed as a percentage of the working-age population— is set to rise from 19.0 percent in 1995 to 36.3 percent by the year 2030 (Statistics Canada 1995).

A number of initiatives have been implemented to address the concerns about an aging Canada. The National Forum on Health was launched in 1994, with the purpose of preserving, or improving, Canada's health care efficiency and effectiveness in the midst of the demographic transition. The most important and recent change made in order to anticipate future revenue requirements has been the readjustment to annual rises in C/QPP contributions. When these schemes were devised in 1966, it was expected that Canadians and their employers would never have to pay more than about 5.7 percent of each individual's earnings to fund this pay-as-you-go scheme. But due to unanticipated demographics, enriched benefits, and slower economic growth, this projection was grossly miscalculated. The Chief Actuary of Canada warned in 1995 that without further reform, contribution rates would have to rise from 5.6 percent of earnings in 1996 to 14.2 percent over the next 30 years to meet benefit commitments (Office of the Superintendent of Financial Institutions 1995). The federal and provincial governments reached an agreement in February 1997 to speed up this process, setting contribution rates to rise from 5.6 to 9.9 percent over the next six years. This change in policy significantly reduces the extra burden of contributions over benefits that younger and future Canadians are expected to pay (Oreopoulos 1996a).

9.3 Data Sources Used to Calculate the Canadian Generational Accounts

Generational accounting methodology provides a means to assess the implications of past borrowing by Canadian governments, in addition to current and expected reforms that would bring fiscal policy to a more sustainable path. Canada in particular is a country in which deficit accounting can give no meaningful information to assess the overall impact of government policy on current and future generations. Projected rises in financial costs from the aging population and forecasted declines in costs from expected future budgets are simply not accounted for when referring to the government's most recent deficit.

To produce generational accounts for Canada, we require (1) a set of population projections; (2) projections of average taxes, transfers, and government purchases by age and sex; (3) an estimate of government net debt for the base year (1995); and (4) a discount rate assumption.

9.3.1 Population Data

Age- and sex-specific population projections were obtained from Statistics Canada (1994) under official medium baseline forecasts up to 2041. Estimates were extended to 2100 using the same component assumptions prevalent at the end of that year. Specifically, the fertility rate remains at 1.70, while life expectancy rises from 74.8 and 81.3 years in 1993 to 78.5 and 84.0 years by 2016 for males and females, respectively. Net migration between 2016 and 2100 is 196,030, contributing to an overall increase in population during this period. A steady state is assumed thereafter.

9.3.2 Fiscal Projections

Projections for aggregated taxes and transfers begin with the 1995 official totals for all levels of government (measured on a national accounts basis). These totals were further consolidated into more general categories, which are displayed in table 9.1. Our baseline results classify educational and health expenditures as implicit transfers, whose remaining present value amounts are allocated to specific generation cohorts and subtracted from overall net tax payments. The Social Policy Simulation Database and Model (SPSD/M), produced by Statistics Canada, was used to distribute expenditures and receipts by age and sex.[6] Data from Health Canada (1996) were also used for allocation purposes. In general, taxes were assumed to be borne by those paying the taxes. The one major exception was that corporate taxes were allocated according to wage and salary income. Elementary, secondary, and postsecondary expenditures were distributed according to profiles discussed in Cameron and Wolfson (1994).

Average tax payments and transfer receipts were projected forward by examining historical, recent, and expected changes to these categories. Productivity growth is assumed to be 1.5 percent per year in the base-case results. All taxes increase in line with productivity, in addition to population served, and inflation. For transfers, several social programs have not remained in step with economic growth in recent years. Under current legislation, the government is only obliged to raise spending on a number of transfers by inflation. Although, historically, these expenditures were increased discretely to keep pace with productivity changes, recent data show them growing at a lesser rate. Oreopoulos

---

6. See Bordt et al. (1990) for a detailed description of the SPSD/M.

Table 9.1   Consolidated Government Expenditures and Receipts, 1995 (percent of GDP)

Receipts	
Personal income taxes	13.95
Capital income taxes	2.64
Commodity taxes	8.78
Property taxes	3.83
Unemployment insurance contributions	2.67
Workers' compensation contributions	0.57
C/QPP contributions	1.73
Public pension contributions	0.51
Other taxes	2.08
Income from government wealth	5.48
Total receipts	42.24
Expenditures	
Government purchases	13.89
Education	5.94
Health care	6.40
Elderly benefits (OAS, GIS, and Spouse's Allowance)	2.93
Social assistance	1.98
Child tax benefits	0.70
Unemployment insurance	2.01
Workers' compensation	0.52
C/QPP	2.65
Public pensions	0.72
GST credits	0.38
Interest	9.17
Total expenditures	47.32
Deficit	5.08

Source: Statistics Canada, *National Income and Expenditure Accounts,* Catalogue no. 13-201 (Ottawa: Minister of Industry, Science and Technology, 1995).

and Valliancourt (1998) discuss the indexing assumptions for projecting social programs. Many of the transfers are assumed to grow only with inflation and population, or only in partial step with productivity. These include elderly benefits, social assistance, child tax benefits, C/QPP, and goods and services tax (GST) credits. Per capita real health care expenditures and general government purchases (excluding education) are projected to grow in line with productivity.[7]

The three-year federal budget projection for 1997 is also included in the base-case results. Successive cuts in cash transfers to the provinces are as-

7. Oreopoulos (1996b) provides the motivation behind assuming health care expenditures grow at the same rate as productivity. Despite the much slower relative growth rates in such expenditures in recent years, a model of real per capital public health spending regressed on lagged per capita real income shows that the slower growth can be explained solely by the recession in the early 1990s. Without further reform, real health expenditure per person is predicted to grow approximately 1:1 with productivity.

sumed to be accommodated by reducing respective government purchases. Unemployment insurance reforms reduce unit costs initially and then grow with productivity. Tuition fees are increased by 10 percent by 2005. Finally, under current legislation, C/QPP contribution rates are increased from 5.6 percent of earnings in 1996 to 9.9 percent by 2002.

9.3.3 Government Net Debt

Consolidated net financial assets, as measured by Statistics Canada's National Balance Sheet Accounts, was used as the estimate for net government debt (or the negative of). Beginning in 1995, this amount was U.S.$374,801 million, or 70.1 percent of GDP.[8]

9.3.4 Discount Rate

The discount rate used to convert amounts to present value was 5 percent. This amount was similar to those used in other studies for calculating particular unfunded liabilities for Canada (e.g., Canadian Institute of Actuaries 1995).

9.4 Main Findings and Sensitivity Analysis

Table 9.2 presents the base-case Canadian generational accounts for males, females, and both combined. The base year is 1995. Educational and health expenditures are classified as implicit transfers. Productivity growth is assumed to be 1.5 percent, and the discount rate used is 5.0 percent.

The accounts exhibit a life cycle pattern, with expected remaining net tax payments to the government peaking at age 25 for both males and females and then falling. The initial rise is due to younger generations' approaching their heaviest taxpaying years. Present values become greater when the time period until actually realizing a payment or receipt gets smaller. The accounts decline for cohorts after age 25, as more taxpaying years fall into the past, and the time in which old-age-related transfers are paid becomes closer. The generational accounts for male cohorts aged 60 or older are negative, indicating that, on average, these generations will receive more in transfers than they will have to pay in taxes for the remaining portion of their lives. Generational accounts for females aged 55 or older are also negative.

Since the accounts measure net tax payments for only the remainder of a cohort's lifetime, we cannot use these values to compare burdens on living generations directly. Older cohorts are projected to pay little, or receive more from government than they will have to pay in taxes. But the taxes that these people paid in the past are not included in the results. The most useful information from this table can be gained from comparing newborn generational accounts with those for future generations, since remaining lifetimes for them are the same.

Recall from chapter 2 that initially the generational accounts assume current

---

8. An exchange rate of 1.389 Canadian dollars per U.S. dollar was used throughout this paper.

Table 9.2   **Generational Accounts: Base Case, Education as Part of Government Transfers (thousands of U.S. dollars)**

	Present Value of Net Tax Payments		
Generation's Age in 1995	Males and Females Combined	Males	Females
0	56.3	88.7	22.1
5	66.4	103.2	27.7
10	99.0	141.8	54.2
15	138.5	187.6	86.7
20	177.0	232.2	119.3
25	193.1	252.9	131.9
30	183.3	242.8	122.2
35	161.1	217.6	103.7
40	134.5	187.5	81.8
45	97.1	142.7	51
50	50.8	85.1	16.1
55	5.5	33	−21.8
60	−44.8	−29.8	−59.4
65	−83.6	−80.9	−86.1
70	−87.9	−85.2	−90.1
75	−84.4	−80.1	−87.6
80	−79.8	−74.3	−83.2
85	−68.5	−62.9	−71.4
90	−10.9	−12.7	−10.3
Future generations	58.0	91.4	22.7
Percentage difference	3.1		

Source: Author's calculations.

policy will remain in place for living generations, while future generations will have to bear any residual net tax burden that would be required to satisfy the government's intertemporal budget constraint (i.e., to make the government's long-term fiscal policy sustainable). The burden is spread equally among the future cohorts, except for a productivity growth rate adjustment. In table 9.2, newborn males and females are projected to pay $56,300 in present value net taxes. This amount includes the expected three-year budget expenditure cuts and anticipated increases in C/QPP contributions in the future. On the other hand, Canadians-to-be are projected to be burdened by net taxes of $58,000, measured in present value, a $1,700 difference, or 3.1 percent more than what newborns face under existing policy. Thus the findings indicate that Canada is approximately at a state of fiscal balance such that no further policy reform would be required to maintain indefinitely the same net tax burden for all future generations (measured in proportion to earnings).

A sensitivity analysis of the base-case productivity and discount rate assumptions is displayed in table 9.3. Smaller productivity growth will mean that future expenditures and receipts will be less than projected before. A greater

Table 9.3   Sensitivity Analysis for Generational Imbalance

	g = 1			g = 1.5			g = 2		
	r = 3	r = 5	r = 7	r = 3	r = 5	r = 7	r = 3	r = 5	r = 7
N	118.6	39.1	3.8	154.6	56.3	11.0	197.9	76.8	19.9
F	130.7	47.1	12.2	158.0	58.0	14.1	191.5	72.9	17.9
Percentage difference	10.2	18.9	218.7	2.2	3.1	28.2	-3.28	-5.1	-9.85
AD	12.1	7.4	8.4	19.3	1.7	3.1	-6.4	-3.9	-2.0
PIT	3.1	2.8	3.3	1.3	0.8	1.3	-2.1	-1.8	-2.3

Source: Author's calculations.

Notes: g is productivity growth (percent); r is discount rate (percent). N: Generational account for newborns (thousands of U.S. dollars). F: Generational account for future generations (adjusted for growth). AD: Absolute difference between F and N (thousands of U.S. dollars). PIT: Percentage increase in personal income taxes required to reach generational balance.

discount rate will also cause expenditures and receipts to be lower, once they are converted to present value. Thus, in general, the larger the gap between the assumed productivity growth and discount rate, the smaller the generational accounts, measured in absolute value. This effect will increase the percentage difference between generational accounts for newborns and future generations. A wide range of alternative productivity growth rates (1.0, 1.5, and 2.0 percent) and discount rates (3.0, 5.0, and 7.0 percent) was used. As shown, the percentage differential between newborn and future generations' net payments ranges widely. When productivity growth (g) is 1.0 percent and the discount factor (r) is 7.0 percent, the generational account for newborns is very small—$3,800. Consequently, the percentage difference of this payment with the $12,200 to be paid by future generations (after growth adjustment) is high—218.7 percent. Conversely, in the three cases where productivity growth is assumed to be 2.0 percent and the discount rate varies among 3.0, 5.0, and 7.0 percent, percentage differences between newborns and future cohorts are actually negative, although not very different from zero.

Examining absolute differences between the two accounts and magnitudes of policy changes shows, in general, that Canada is approximately at a state of fiscal balance, regardless of the assumptions used. When we examine the absolute difference, the amounts range from $6,400, for the case when productivity growth is 2.0 percent and the discount rate is 3.0 percent, to $19,300, when g and r equal 1.5 and 3.0 percent, respectively. The magnitude of policy change required to remove any differential between the accounts is also minimal. For example, personal income taxes would have to adjust by either falling by 2.3 percent for the case where growth is 2.0 percent and the discount rate is 7.0 percent or rising by 3.3 percent when the growth and discount rates are 1.0 and 7.0 percent, respectively. Thus, while the imbalance measured by percentage differences between newborns and future generations varies considerably, the sensitivity for absolute differences and the policies required to remove the gap is relatively small.

9.5   Alternative Policies

The base-case generational accounts for Canada projected net tax payments for living generations under "current fiscal policy" conditions. Current fiscal policy was defined to include a number of reforms that are legislated, or expected to take place in the future, as well as slower relative growth for certain transfer payments. It is useful to examine the extent to which these influences reduce generational imbalance. This section examines such cases, and in addition looks at an alternative policy in which the federal government decides to cut taxes once budget surpluses begin to occur early next decade.

Table 9.4 shows how the generational accounts (with males and females together) would look with alternative projections for future budgets. Column (1) assumes all taxes and transfers are indexed to productivity, inflation, and

Table 9.4   **Effects on Generational Accounts of Expected Future Changes to Fiscal Policy (thousands of U.S. dollars)**

Generation's Age in 1995	Generational Accounts: Males and Females Combined			
	(1)	(2)	(3)	(4)
0	39.9	47.3	49.4	56.3
5	48.5	56.3	58.7	66.4
10	78.9	87.4	90.1	99.0
15	116.5	125.5	128.6	138.5
20	154.2	163.4	166.9	177.0
25	171.4	180.5	183.9	193.1
30	163.6	172.4	175.5	183.3
35	143.2	151.9	154.6	161.1
40	118.1	127.0	129.4	134.5
45	82.4	91.5	93.4	97.1
50	37.7	47.0	48.5	50.8
55	−5.8	3.4	4.5	5.5
60	−54.2	−45.7	−45.1	−44.8
65	−91.0	−84.0	−83.6	−83.6
70	−93.6	−88.1	−87.9	−87.9
75	−88.4	−84.5	−84.4	−84.4
80	−82.3	−79.9	−79.8	−79.8
85	−69.8	−68.5	−68.5	−68.5
90	−10.9	−10.9	−10.9	−10.9
Future generations	111.0	90.4	72.0	58.0
Percentage difference	178.2	91.1	45.6	3.1

Source: Author's calculations.

Notes: Col. (1): All taxes and transfers indexed to population change, inflation, and productivity; no adjustments to budget or C/QPP. Col. (2): Expected slower real growth for old-age security transfers, social assistance, child tax benefits, and GST credits. Col. (3): Slower growth to transfers, and three-year federal budget forecast included. Col. (4): Base-case results: Includes slower transfer growth, 1996 federal budget, and legislated changes to C/QPP contribution rates.

population. The 1997 budget forecasts and the legislated changes to C/QPP contributions are also not included in these results. The difference between newborns' and future generations' net tax payments is much larger than in the base case. Here, newborns are estimated to pay $39,900 in present value net taxes, while future generations would have to pay $110,944 to satisfy the government's intertemporal budget constraint (after adjusting for future changes to productivity). This represents a very significant generational imbalance of 178.2 percent.

This scenario no longer appears likely, however. Several social transfers, legislated to increase with inflation and population, are no longer fully adjusted to also increase with productivity. Column (2) examines the Canadian generational accounts by adding new projections for social transfers that accommodate this recent trend of slower relative growth. The imbalance between newborns and future generations is reduced substantially, from 178.2 to 91.1

percent. The smaller fiscal burden on future generations comes at the expense of those currently living. Net taxes for living generations (except those 90 years of age) are increased—by about the same absolute amount for those younger than 60 years old, and less so for older cohorts who will not be around long enough to experience the relatively smaller benefits. It should be understood that the real value of these transfers to generations has not been reduced— they have only increased at smaller rates than productivity growth or remained constant in per capita terms.

Column (3) uses the same tax and transfer projections but includes the three-year budget forecasts made by the federal government in 1997. The generational imbalance is further reduced as a result of these planned reforms—from 91.1 to 45.6 percent. This decline is mainly due to cuts in cash transfers to the provinces. It is assumed that the provinces correspondingly reduce their own government purchases.[9] Thus net tax payments for living generations are not significantly influenced by these actions.

Column (4) displays the original base-case generational accounts shown in section 9.4. In addition to including the adjusted social transfer index assumptions and the 1997 federal budget, legislative changes to the C/QPP have also been accommodated. Contributions to the C/QPP are raised from 5.6 percent of earnings in 1996 to 9.9 percent by 2002. Net tax payments for newborns are consequently raised from $49,400 to $56,300, while net tax payments for future generations fall from $72,000 to $58,000. This leaves a remaining generational imbalance of 3.1 percent.

Thus, by factoring for these expected future developments to Canadian fiscal policy, we are able to get a much better picture of the government's ability to meet its bills than we would have had we only examined the recent upward trend in the Canadian debt-to-GDP ratio. The policies have substantial impact on reducing the overall net tax burden on future generations but have little or no influence on the recorded yearly deficit. Generational accounting's dynamic approach of examining budgetary effects over time reveals a much smaller generational imbalance compared to other countries, despite a significant aging of the Canadian population. The country is close to fiscal balance because the expected changes to fiscal policy will eventually affect those generations living now, even though they may not feel the effects right away.

It is useful to examine the impact from speeding up the process of raising the contribution rates for the country's pay-as-you-go pension scheme, the C/QPP. Rather than increase contribution rates over a 40-year period, as legislated previously, rates are now set to rise over the next 6 years. Both policies cover the plan's unfunded liabilities, but the impact on different age groups is different. Table 9.5 compares these differences. Column (1) assumes a 30-year

9. As long as the provinces do not resort to greater borrowing to reconcile their budgets with this change, the reduction in the estimated generational imbalance will be about the same, whether taxes are increased, transfers reduced, or government purchases diminished.

Table 9.5   **Change to Base-Case Generational Accounts under Alternative Policy for Canada and Quebec Pension Plan Reform (thousands of U.S. dollars)**

Generation's Age in 1995	Alternative: Raise Contribution Rates to 14.2% by 2025 (1)	Base Case: Raise Contribution Rates to 9.9% by 2002 (2)	Absolute Change from Alternative to Base Case (3)
0	58.6	56.3	−2.3
5	68.2	66.4	−1.8
10	99.8	99.0	−0.8
15	138.1	138.5	0.5
20	175.4	177.0	1.6
25	190.9	193.1	2.2
30	180.8	183.3	2.5
35	158.5	161.1	2.6
40	132.1	134.5	2.5
45	95.1	97.1	2.0
50	49.4	50.8	1.4
55	4.9	5.5	0.7
60	−45.0	−44.8	0.2
65	−83.6	−83.6	0.0
70	−87.9	−87.9	0.0
75	−84.4	−84.4	0.0
80	−79.8	−79.8	0.0
85	−68.5	−68.5	0.0
90	−10.9	−10.9	0.0
Future generations	60.4	58.0	−2.4
Percentage difference	3.0	3.1	

Source: Author's calculations.

transition, with contribution rates raised from 5.6 percent of earnings to 14.2 percent.[10] Column (2) shows the base-case generational accounts, which include the 6-year transition of C/QPP contribution rates.

As shown, the percentage difference between newborn and future generation net tax payments is approximately the same for the 30-year and 6-year transition scenarios—3.1 and 3.0 percent, respectively. However, the absolute net tax burden on future generations is lower for the shorter transition period. The reason is that by increasing contribution rates sooner, the generations who would have retired before any significant contribution rate increases under the 30-year transition are now required to pay more. This results in higher net taxes to be faced by older generations (who are under age 65) and lower net tax

10. The 6-year, 9.9 percent steady state contribution rate is equivalent to the 30-year, 14.2 percent steady state contribution rate in making the self-contained C/QPP program sustainable. In other words, both policies satisfy an intertemporal budget constraint for just the pay-as-you-go system of the C/QPP. Oreopoulos (1996a) discusses in more detail the intergenerational effects from such different paths to a sustainable Canada Pension Plan.

Table 9.6   ֊nange to Base-Case Generational Accounts under Per Capita
Income Tax Freeze until 2010

Generation's Age in 1995	Base Case: No Policy Change	Alternative: Per Capita Tax Freeze	Absolute Change from Base Case to Alternative
0	56.3	46.5	−9.8
5	66.4	55.4	−11.0
10	99.0	86.7	−12.4
15	138.5	124.9	−13.7
20	177.0	162.8	−14.2
25	193.1	179.6	−13.6
30	183.3	171.0	−12.3
35	161.1	150.0	−11.1
40	134.5	124.8	−9.7
45	97.1	89.0	−8.1
50	50.8	44.2	−6.6
55	5.5	0.5	−5.1
60	−44.8	−48.7	−3.9
65	−83.6	−86.8	−3.2
70	−87.9	−90.5	−2.6
75	−84.4	−86.4	−2.0
80	−79.8	−81.4	−1.6
85	−68.5	−69.7	−1.2
90	−10.9	−11.0	−0.2
Future generations	58.0	74.5	16.5
Percentage difference	3.1	60.3	

Source: Author's calculations.

burdens for younger and future generations. Column (3) in table 9.5 shows the differences in generational accounts due to the shorter transition period. The biggest losers from the move to the shorter transition are the 35-year-old cohorts, who have to pay $2,600 more in present value net taxes for the remainder of their lives. The higher net taxes for the generations aged 15 to 60 reduce the required revenues for the younger cohorts. Future generations gain the most with the 6-year transition, having to pay $2,400 less than under the slower transition scenario.

With the rising trend in the debt-to-GDP ratio reversed and surpluses appearing in some government budgets, many Canadians have considered the option of tax relief or spending increases. As was mentioned earlier, however, a balanced budget now does not necessarily correlate with a state of fiscal balance. Much of the strain on the government's finances will not be felt until beginning in 2015, when the baby boomers start to retire. If taxes are lowered or expenditures increased now, policy will have to be reversed later to afford the higher elderly costs.

Table 9.6 shows what would happen if the government froze per capita income taxes at their 1998 levels until 2010, so that they are no longer growing in step with productivity increases during this period. This policy is broadly similar to one designed to maintain balanced budgets during the same period using income tax reductions.[11] In this case, some of the net tax burden on the current age groups is reduced. Newborns are estimated to have to pay $40,800 in net taxes over their lifetimes, compared to the $56,300 under the base case. However, this policy is not sustainable, and at some point later on, the government will have to increase taxes again, or reduce expenditures further. The lifetime net tax payment by a cohort born in the future becomes $74,500 (adjusted for growth), $16,500 higher than before. Thus, to the extent that the government relaxes its policies to reduce or eliminate budget surpluses early in the next century, the net tax burden on future age groups will rise.

9.6 Summary and Conclusion

Canada's fiscal situation worsened in the 1980s and early 1990s mainly because of slower than expected economic growth and two particularly severe recessions. The reaction by the federal and provincial governments was modest, and not sufficient to stop the debt-to-GDP ratio from growing dramatically. The worsening financial situation, coupled with the ominous aging of the population, has caused the public to demand that the governments get their houses in order. Several policies have been implemented to respond to these calls, including large expenditure cuts already imposed or expected in the next few years and a slower pattern of growth for some transfers, in relation to productivity changes.

This chapter has applied the generational accounting approach to Canada to assess the sustainability of the country's current fiscal policy and its potential impact on living and future generations. The findings emphasize the importance of looking not only at borrowing done by governments in the past but also at the financial resources that will be needed in the future. Under the base-case scenario, which includes factoring for contribution rate increases to the C/QPP, the net tax burden on future generations is estimated to be 3.1 percent more than for newborns, who face net taxes under the existing fiscal position. The magnitude of policy change required to remove the remainder of this imbalance is very small, indicating that Canada is just about at state of fiscal balance.

The changes implied in restoring generational balance are permanent ones. Relaxing current policy now would impose a much greater burden on future generations, because of the effects from the demographic transition, which will not begin to have full impact until 2015. Yet, if the Canadian fiscal position remains on its current course, no further tax hikes, transfer cuts, or government purchase reductions will be required to maintain fiscal balance. Canadians

---

11. A more detailed discussion on this alternative policy scenario is given in Oreopoulos and Valliancourt (1998).

have not been a content bunch lately as a result of recent restraint by their governments. But, at least, they can now see light at the end of the tunnel.

References

Auerbach, Alan J., Jagadeesh Gokhale, and Laurence J. Kotlikoff. 1991. Generational accounts: A meaningful alternative to deficit accounting. In *Tax policy and the economy,* vol. 5, ed. D. Bradford, 55–110. Cambridge, Mass.: MIT Press.

Bordt, Michael, Grant J. Cameron, Stephen F. Gribble, Brian B. Murphy, Geoff T. Rowe, and Michael C. Wolfson. 1990. The Social Policy Simulation Database and Model: An integrated tool for tax/transfer analysis. *Canadian Tax Journal* 38 (1): 48–65.

Cairns, Alan, et al. 1996. Group of 22: Making Canada work better. Toronto: C. D. Howe Institute.

Cameron, Grant J., and Michael C. Wolfson. 1994. Missing transfers: Adjusting household incomes for noncash benefits. Paper prepared for the 23d general conference of the International Association for Research in Income and Wealth, St. Andrews, New Brunswick.

Canadian Institute of Actuaries. 1995. *Troubled tomorrows: The report of the Canadian Institute of Actuaries' Task Force on Retirement Savings.* Ottawa: Canadian Institute of Actuaries.

Gillespie, Irwin W. 1996. A brief history of government borrowing in Canada. In *Unnecessary debts,* ed. Lars Osberg and Pierre Fortin, 1–25. Toronto: James Lorimer and Company.

Health Canada. 1996. *National health expenditures in Canada: 1995–1994, Full report.* Ottawa: Policy and Consultation Branch.

Kneebone, Ronald D. 1996. Four decades of deficits and debt. In *Unnecessary Debts,* ed. Lars Osberg and Pierre Fortin, 39–70. Toronto: James Lorimer and Company.

Northcott, Herbert C. 1994. Public perceptions of the population aging "crisis." *Canadian Public Policy* 20 (1): 66–77.

Office of the Superintendent of Financial Institutions (OSFI). 1995. *Canada Pension Plan: Fifteenth actuarial report as at 31 December 1993.* Ottawa.

Oreopoulos, Philip. 1996a. Bad tasting medicine: Removing intergenerational inequity from the CPP. *Choices* (IRPP), vol. 2, no. 7.

———. 1996b. Why worry? Refocusing the debate on the sustainability of public healthcare in Canada. Vancouver: University of British Columbia. Mimeograph.

Oreopoulos, Philip, and François Valliancourt. 1998a. Applying the generational accounting approach to Canada: Findings and fallacies. Paper presented at Statistics Canada's conference Intergenerational Equity in Canada, 20–21 February.

———. 1998b. Taxes, transfers, and generations in Canada: Who gains and who loses from the demographic transition. Commentary no. 107. Toronto: C. D. Howe Institute, June.

Statistics Canada. Population Projections Section. Demography Division. 1994a. *Population projections for Canada, provinces and territories, 1993–2016.* Ottawa: Minister of Industry, Science and Technology.

———. 1994b. *Population projections for Canada, 2017–41.* Ottawa: Minister of Industry, Science and Technology.

―――. 1995. *Population projections for Canada, provinces and territories.* Catalogue no. 91-520. Ottawa: Minister of Industry, Science and Technology.

Wroberl, Marion G. 1995. Fiscal policy in Canada: The changing role of the federal and provincial governments. Research Branch Working Paper no. 91-2E. Ottawa: Library of Parliament.

10   Public Debt, Welfare Reforms, and Intergenerational Distribution of Tax Burdens in Denmark

Svend E. Hougaard Jensen and Bernd Raffelhüschen

10.1   Introduction

Denmark is an archetype of a Scandinavian welfare state. Although the government plays virtually no direct role in the business sector, the public sector is large. An ambition of guaranteeing all residents a respectable living standard has been put into practice by providing collective insurance against temporary or permanent income losses. As a result, the public sector has a near monopoly in the production of children's day care, health care, and education. Old-age provision is also mainly in the hands of the public welfare system. A large number of transfer payments are offered without means testing, and benefits are in many cases unrelated to past contributions. Furthermore, taxes are only to a minor extent earmarked for any specific purpose.

Such large-scale involvement of the public sector has recently come under attack from different angles (Drèze and Malinvaud 1994; Lindbeck et al. 1994). It has been argued that welfare programs may (1) undermine the incentives to work and thereby give rise to rigidities in the functioning of labor markets; (2) increase the size of government and thereby raise the level of distortionary taxation, in turn constituting obstacles to economic efficiency and growth; and (3) lead to cumulative deficits and mounting public debts, thereby passing tax burdens onto future generations that, eventually, may threaten the fiscal sustainability of the welfare state.[1] This paper concentrates on the third issue: for

Svend E. Hougaard Jensen is currently director of research in the Danish Ministry of Business and Industry and a research associate of the Economic Policy Research Unit at the University of Copenhagen. Bernd Raffelhüschen is professor of economics at Albert-Ludwigs-University in Freiburg, Germany, and professor II at the University of Bergen, Norway.

The authors thank Alan Auerbach for comments and Martin Junge for research assistance. Financial support from the Danish National Research Foundation is gratefully acknowledged.

1. Although Atkinson (1995) finds no clear-cut aggregate empirical evidence in support of these charges leveled against the welfare state, these charges may be more serious in the Scandinavian

Denmark, we examine both the generational stance of current fiscal policy and the generational impact of various policy reforms.

As in most other Organization for Economic Cooperation and Development (OECD) countries, the (gross) public debt-to-GDP ratio in Denmark has risen quite dramatically over the past couple of decades, from about 5 percent in the early 1970s to about 72 percent in 1995. In addition, due to rising life expectancy and declining fertility, the Danish population is aging rapidly, as indicated by the projected rise of nearly 30 percent in the ratio of elderly to working-age people from 1995 to 2030. Therefore, future generations of taxpayers may not only be burdened by the costs of providing for an increasing number of elderly, they may also have to service a public debt that meanwhile might have grown large.

In our discussion of these issues we focus on the generational impact of a set of policies that are on the forefront of debate of fiscal policy in Denmark. These fall in three broad categories, namely, (1) a labor market reform with strong fiscal ingredients, aiming at bringing structural unemployment down; (2) a program of public debt reduction, designed in line with official medium- to long-term targets of fiscal policy; and (3) an increase in the (effective) retirement age, aiming at tempering the effects of population aging. As a benchmark for these appraisals we first compute the intergenerational distribution of tax burdens in a baseline scenario in which fiscal policy remains unchanged.

From here we proceed as follows. Section 10.2 offers a brief introduction to the Danish tax and transfer system, and section 10.3 reflects on some topical themes in the debate on fiscal policy in Denmark. Section 10.4 presents our empirical base. The generational stance of current fiscal policy is reported in section 10.5, while section 10.6 evaluates the generational impact of the above-mentioned policy reforms. Finally, section 10.7 provides a brief summary and conclusions of the study.

10.2   The Tax and Transfer System in Denmark

The large involvement of the public sector in the Danish economy has led to a high level of taxation. The ratio of total tax revenue to GDP is around 50 percent, among the highest in the European Union. However, it should be kept in mind that unlike Denmark, most EU countries pay transfers on a net-of-tax basis. Also, in some European countries household subsidies are given in the form of deductions from the tax base rather than through direct transfer payments. For example, these factors have been found to account for almost 5

---

countries where the welfare state has been carried further than in most other countries in Western Europe. See Hagen et al. (1998) for a comparison of the fiscal systems in Scandinavia with those of other Western European countries.

percentage points of the difference in gross tax rates between Denmark and Germany in 1991 (Ministry of Finance 1994a).

The Danish tax structure differs from that in most other European countries. In particular, there are two notable differences. First, the contributions of employers and employees count relatively more in the other European countries, and second, personal income taxes make up a significantly larger part of tax revenue in Denmark than in Europe in general. Indeed, while the revenue from personal income taxes constitutes about half of total tax revenue in Denmark, the corresponding figure for the European Union as a whole is only about a quarter. On the other hand, while social security taxes (paid by employees and employers) only count for about 4 percent of total taxes in Denmark, the EU average is more than a quarter. The revenue collected from indirect taxes has in recent years converged on the European average, with indirect taxes constituting about a third of total tax revenue. The value-added tax is by far the most important indirect tax, accounting for more than 50 percent of total indirect tax revenue.

Denmark was the first Nordic country to move away from the system of *global* income taxation, wherein a single progressive tax schedule is applied to the sum of the taxpayer's income from all sources, toward a system of so-called *dual* income taxation, wherein the taxation of capital income is separated from the taxation of other sources of income (Sørensen 1994). Since much of private sector interest income benefits from special tax concessions, while interest payments are fully deductible from taxable income, the capital income tax in Denmark yields a negative net revenue.

On the expenditure side of public activity, the share of the core expenditures in the welfare state, such as education, health, and social security, account for about three-quarters of all expenditures. It is notable that the share of public expenditures allocated to education and health has gone down over the past decades, while social security expenditures constitute a larger share, reflecting the rise in unemployment and a tendency toward earlier retirement over the period.

The redistributive capacity of the Danish tax and transfer system is quite significant. Although the distribution of incomes between "rich" and "poor" is not particularly even *before* taxes and transfers, the distribution of *disposable* incomes is much more equal (Förster 1994). The redistributive effects of taxes and transfers are enhanced by the provision of public services, such as education and subsidized child care (OECD 1996).

10.3 Current Debates on Fiscal Policy

Tax reform was a key ingredient in a new policy package introduced in January 1993. The reform was designed in the same spirit as most other recent tax reforms in the OECD area. It thus involved cuts in marginal income tax rates, financed by various measures to broaden the tax base and to close existing loopholes. Furthermore, the fall in personal income tax rates was to a large extent financed by increases in energy taxes levied on the household sector and by the introduction of new taxes on refuse, water use, and sewage. From 1996 these initiatives were supported by taxes on the emission of carbon dioxides and sulfur dioxides from the business sector. The reform thus marked an important step toward a so-called green tax reform.

A big theme in the current debate on fiscal policy involves the extent to which wage taxes can be further replaced by green taxes. In particular, would it be possible to reap a "double dividend" in the form of improvements to both the environment and employment? Recent academic research suggests such a switch may lower the efficiency of the tax system as a revenue-raising device. Also, the (intended) substitution of labor for polluting inputs may lower labor productivity. With rigid real wage adjustments, this may lead to higher unemployment. A further concern relates to the fact that so far only a few countries in the world impose green taxes on the business sector. Hence, there is a lively debate in Denmark on what impact these taxes would have on Danish companies exposed to international competition (Koch 1996).

Since the Maastricht Treaty was signed, fiscal policy in Denmark has to a large extent been conducted in accordance with the so-called convergence criteria. At first sight this may appear surprising since Denmark has already announced that it will not participate in the final stage of Economic and Monetary Union in Europe. Nevertheless, the Danish government remains committed to the principles of nominal convergence and fiscal discipline. Indeed, these objectives have been quite successfully accomplished, as witnessed by the fact that Denmark now satisfies all the convergence criteria.

In spite of the recent success of fiscal policy in Denmark, there are some longer term challenges raised by the Danish welfare provisions. The most important challenge relates to the rather sharp increase that has been observed over the past couple of decades in the number of working-age people more or less dependent on public transfer payments. Not only has the number of unemployed increased, but there has also been a rising number of recipients of (1) early retirement pension, available to persons who for health or social reasons are unable to participate in the labor market; (2) early retirement benefits, available to persons aged 60 or older; and (3) cash benefits, available to uninsured unemployed persons from households with income and wealth below a certain threshold.

Altogether, in 1995 around 10 percent of the labor force (2.8 million) were registered as unemployed, and about 18 percent of the total number of working-age people (3.4 million) received some sort of income-compensating public transfer other than unemployment benefits. Hereof, about a third were recipients due to disabilities of various kinds, and a sixth were students. Hence, about 21 percent of the labor force (or 18 percent of all working-age people) were out of work but should in principle have had the ability to work. With the corresponding number in the early 1970s being almost negligible, two tendencies can thus be identified: the work force is retiring earlier, and a larger number of low-skilled workers have been expelled from the labor market. While most analysts would agree that these tendencies are serious, there are different views of their significance.

"Optimists" hold that rather than being associated with a dramatic increase in de facto unemployment, the enormous rise in the number of recipients of public transfers simply reflects a change in political priorities in favor of granting public benefits to people who previously would have been provided for by family or other "local" safety nets, if provided for at all. Thus, although the rise in the number of working-age people receiving transfer payments should not be overlooked, the problem should not be overstressed either. Furthermore, along with expansion of welfare programs, optimists often refer to the fact that it has been possible to keep the employment rate fairly constant at 72 to 75 percent (Callesen 1995).

"Pessimists," on the other hand, tend to claim that not only has the rise in expenditures allocated to public transfers led to higher (marginal) tax rates, but it has also led to cuts in the proportion of expenditures allocated to public consumption and provision of various services. While high marginal tax rates are well known to have distortionary effects, a continuous fall in the share of expenditures to public service production and infrastructure relative to public transfer payments to persons out of employment may in the longer term threaten the legitimacy of the welfare state. For example, middle-class people may perceive their "return" from contributing to large-scale transfer payments as too low; a dissatisfaction that subsequently may translate into increased support for political forces completely opposed to the fundamental structures of the welfare state (Ingerslev and Ploug 1996).

The ongoing process of population aging has also reached the policy agenda (Jensen and Nielsen 1995). Unlike most other OECD countries, Denmark seems to be offered demographic "breathing space": over the next 10 years or so the ratio of elderly (age 65+) to working-age people (ages 20–64) is falling, whereupon it increases rather dramatically. While the generational aspects of this phenomenon are widely recognized, there are different views on what should be done. Optimists argue that the problem will only show up far in the future, and that a successful economic policy in the meantime may reverse the current tendency to early retirement. Pessimists, on the other hand, have emphasized the need for a strong commitment to eliminate the public sector's debt during the breathing space and argue that the population should be more directly confronted with the need for a higher retirement age in the future.

After this brief review of the state of play of fiscal policy in Denmark, we next study the generational impact of alternative policies that may be adopted in the near future. As a benchmark we first present generational accounts in the case where fiscal policy remains unchanged.

Table 10.1   Public Receipts and Expenditures in Denmark, 1995 (millions of dollars)

Receipts		Expenditures	
Labor income taxes	54,286	Social security	18,653
Capital income taxes	−5,896	Health insurance	10,362
Value-added taxes	17,000	Unemployment insurance	5,293
Alcohol and tobacco tax	1,995	Welfare and housing	5,016
Gasoline tax	1,318	Child and youth support	5,402
Vehicle tax	786	Education	10,267
Property and wealth tax	1,994	Long-term care	5,594
Unemployment insurance	2,770	Other transfers	9,580
Other taxes	15,305	Net investments	1,421
Other revenues	5,532	Subsidies	5,072
Public deficit	2,832	Net interest payments	5,335
		Government consumption	15,924
Total	97,920	Total	97,919

Sources: Danmarks Statistik (1996) and data provided by the Danish Ministry of Finance.

10.4   Data

The calculation of generational accounts for current and future generations requires (1) a long-term gender-specific population projection, (2) an aggregate government budget in a base year, (3) microprofiles (age and gender specific) of net taxes to be paid over remaining lifetimes, and (4) an estimate of the government's initial net debt position. Finally, assumptions about exogenous parameters, including the GDP growth rate and the real interest rate, are needed (Auerbach, Gokhale, and Kotlikoff 1991).

The population projections start in 1995. We have retained all assumptions about fertility, mortality, and net immigration made in the official Danish population projections. While the end year of the official projections is 2040, our projections run through year 2200. During the first five years of the projection period, the total fertility rate is assumed to increase from 1.8 to 1.9, and it remains constant at that level from year 2000 onward. Since for females (males) younger than age 50 (65), the mortality rates are assumed to fall during the first 10 years of the projection period, life expectancy at birth rises from 77.9 years (72.7) to 78.1 (73.0) for females (males). Finally, as to the immigration numbers, the official assumptions imply an annual net inflow of 13,500 persons, about 0.25 percent of the base-year population.

The aggregates of taxes and transfers are taken from the official statistics on Danish national income and product accounts (Danmarks Statistik 1996; Ministry of Finance 1996). Table 10.1 summarizes the overall public budget of the base year 1995 in detail. The entire budget includes expenditures and receipts of the federal and local governments as well as public enterprises. All intergovernmental payments have been canceled out.

Public revenues include taxes on labor income, capital income, property, wealth, vehicles, alcohol, tobacco, and gasoline, employees' unemployment contributions, the value-added tax, and other taxes or general revenues.[2] Note that capital income taxes are significantly negative, mainly due to a generous system of tax deductions on owner-occupied housing expenditures. Table 10.1 also lists various transfer payments, including transfers for social security, health care, unemployment insurance, welfare and housing benefits, child and youth support payments, education, and long-term care expenditures as well as other transfers to households and subsidies.

Each aggregate for taxes and transfers is allocated to the representative male and female individuals of each living generation with the help of relative age-gender profiles. Age-specific profiles originate from various Danish microdata surveys. Those taxes and transfers that have not been distributed by age and gender are summarized under other taxes, revenues, or transfers. This is also true for the specific parts of taxes not being entirely distributed due to standard incidence assumptions.[3]

According to official Danish statistics, the government's net financial debt amounts to $61.7 billion.[4] To this number we add a real debt of $33.5 billion, resulting from a present value calculation of deficits from publicly owned enterprises, land, and so forth. Note that this approach excludes public infrastructure, which is provided without user fees. Our estimate of the government's net wealth is thus −$95.2 billion.

Net investment amounts to $1.42 billion. Hence, in the base year, the residual of total government revenues minus expenditures on transfers, subsidies, and net investments—that is, government consumption—amounts to $15.9 billion. However, this number is not used in the calculations. There we constructed a gross figure by including non-age-specific distributed taxes, revenues and transfers, subsidies, net investments, and transfers to the rest of the world. This number is projected to grow in line with GDP, and it is adjusted for the demographic transition in a per capita manner.

10.5 Basic Findings

Table 10.2 reports generational accounts for cohorts ranging in age from 0 to 90 in the base year 1995. The accounts are shown both for the case in which educational expenditures are allocated as a transfer payment on age groups and

2. The aggregate for labor income taxes includes income of the self-employed. The aggregate of unemployment insurance covers both employers' and employees' contributions.

3. In particular, this concerns about a quarter of gasoline and vehicle taxes, which are allocated to the firm sector. Income of the self-employed is not divided into hypothetical shares of labor and capital income. Although this is in contrast to standard incidence, the splitting would be meaningless in the light of the capital income profile, which is dominated by tax deductions for owner-occupied housing. Corporate taxes are distributed uniformly across age and gender. This is due to the lack of true information about the incidence of corporate taxes in Denmark.

4. Although future generations should only be burdened by the service payments, and not be made responsible for the principal, a present value approach focusing exclusively on the debt service flow would lead to similar results given the long time horizon used in the calculations.

Table 10.2   **Generational Accounts of Current and Future Generations: Baseline (thousands of U.S. dollars)**

Generation's Age in 1995	Education as Transfers			Education as Government Consumption		
	Average	Male	Female	Average	Male	Female
0	−18	35	−73	84	135	31
5	14	77	−52	134	194	70
10	79	154	1	178	250	103
15	143	229	52	211	294	124
20	209	304	110	243	337	145
25	232	330	128	251	349	148
30	225	321	123	238	333	136
35	202	297	104	214	308	116
40	157	249	62	166	258	72
45	91	172	9	99	179	16
50	9	78	−63	14	84	−57
55	−64	0	−128	−61	2	−125
60	−143	−93	−190	−143	−93	−190
65	−172	−134	−207	−172	−134	−207
70	−186	−151	−214	−186	−151	−214
75	−194	−155	−224	−194	−155	−224
80	−202	−173	−219	−202	−173	−219
85	−202	−169	−218	−202	−169	−218
90	−49	−44	−51	−49	−44	−51
Future generations	26	−53	110	124	198	45
$GA_{t,t+1}(1+r)/GA_{t,t}(1+g)$	−1.53	−1.56	−1.56	1.52	1.52	1.52

the case in which education is treated as a form of government consumption. Furthermore, the accounts are presented for males and females combined and for males and females separately. The results refer to baseline assumptions, including an annual real GDP growth rate of 1.5 percent and an exogenous real interest rate of 5 percent.

The first remarkable result is that if education is counted as a transfer, the generational account of a current newborn is negative. Since net payments to the government are strictly negative throughout childhood and youth, the accounts steadily increase until a peak is reached at age 25. Over the years of active labor market participation, the generational accounts are positive but falling, before turning negative as individuals approach retirement. Retirees obviously have negative accounts since they pay low income taxes and receive public pensions and other old-age services.

The accounts also reveal big gender-specific differences underlying the average figures. Indeed, while newborn males have a generational account of $35,000, that of a newborn female is negative (−$73,000). To understand this difference between the two sexes—a remarkable one by international standards—we have to look at the more detailed specifications of the net payments.

First, a newborn male in 1995 would over his entire life span contribute about 40 percent more in labor income taxes than his female counterpart. The reason for this is that in spite of their relatively high labor market participation rate, Danish women are mostly recruited to low-wage and part-time jobs. Second, women receive more old-age pensions than men. Since the benefit rate is unrelated to gender, this clearly reflects the fact that women have, on average, longer lifetimes than men. For the same reason the present value of women's transfers in the form of old-age care is higher than the corresponding number for men. Third, as a consequence of the fact that women are more exposed to unemployment than men, they receive relatively more unemployment and cash benefits. Fourth, women's receipts of health insurance and other welfare services by far dominate what men receive.

These patterns are modified considerably if expenditures on education are treated as government consumption. In general, this would increase the generational accounts of current newborns and future generations; indeed, current newborns and future generations would have their accounts increased by the same amount (when adjusted for productivity growth). Since education is concentrated on children and youth, and only differs marginally across gender, this alternative accounting would leave the older generations unaffected. However, massive changes are observed for younger people (ages 0–15). In particular, the generational accounts of current newborns (of both sexes) now become positive.

Following standard practice, the distribution of net tax burdens between current and future generations is assessed in terms of $\pi \equiv (1 + r)GA_{t,t+1}/(1 + g)GA_{t,t}$, where $GA_{t,t}(GA_{t,t+1})$ is the generational account of current newborns (individuals born in the subsequent year), r is the real interest rate, and g is the real GDP growth rate. Generational balance, in the sense that existing and future generations are burdened equally, is achieved when this indicator equals unity. Similarly, if the indicator is greater (smaller) than unity, future generations have to pay higher (lower) net taxes than current generations.[5]

There are two circumstances in which π does not yield meaningful results. First, as $GA_{t,t}$ approaches zero, π would indicate an infinite redistribution to the advantage of current generations. Such an outcome would clearly be difficult to interpret. Second, problems arise if the accounts of current and future generations display changing signs. However, this is due to the fact that π can be substantially biased by gender-specific redistribution (Raffelhüschen 1995). Both of these problems actually occurred in an earlier study on generational accounting in Denmark (Jensen and Raffelhüschen 1997).

The problem of changing signs depends crucially on how we treat educational expenditures. Table 10.3 reports the baseline findings as well as their sensitivity with respect to realistic parameter variations. Only if education is

---

5. $\pi = 1$ is also necessary for maintaining a steady state corresponding to Kotlikoff's (chap. 1 in this volume) fiscal balance rule.

Table 10.3   Sensitivity Analysis

	$g = 1$			$g = 1.5$			$g = 2$		
	$r = 3$	$r = 5$	$r = 7$	$r = 3$	$r = 5$	$r = 7$	$r = 3$	$r = 5$	$r = 7$
Generational accounts, education treated as government consumption									
Newborns in base year	156	66	17	183	84	27	211	105	38
Future generations	196	103	49	224	124	61	251	147	75
$GA_{t,t+1}(1+r)/GA_{t,t}(1+g)$	1.28	1.62	2.98	1.24	1.52	2.40	1.21	1.45	2.06
Generational accounts, education treated as transfers									
Newborns in base year	29	−29	−56	46	−18	−51	61	−5	−46
Future generations	74	13	−20	93	26	−13	110	42	−4
Achieving generational balance, education treated as transfers									
Cut in government purchases	29.2	27.3	24.4	29.9	29.0	26.0	30.6	30.7	27.7
Reducing all transfers	4.4	4.2	3.8	4.4	4.5	4.1	4.4	4.7	4.3
Increasing all taxes	4.0	3.8	3.4	4.0	4.0	3.6	4.0	4.2	3.8
Achieving generational balance, education treated as government consumption									
Cut in government purchases	9.6	9.4	8.4	9.3	9.9	8.9	8.5	10.5	9.5

Note: g is productivity growth (percent); r is discount rate (percent).

included in government consumption does π represent an unbiased indicator of intergenerational imbalance. In this case, and under baseline parameterization, our results suggest that the net tax burdens of future generations will be 52 percent higher than for current generations. A lower discount rate and a higher growth rate both serve to reduce this generational imbalance. The quantitative robustness seems to be fairly low, as witnessed by the fact that for combinations of three real interest rates (3, 5, and 7 percent) with three alternative GDP growth rates (1, 1.5, and 2 percent), the intergenerational imbalance ranges between 20 and 200 percent. However, the qualitative finding of an imbalance in favor of currently living generations is robust. Table 10.3 also shows that if educational costs are counted as transfers, π cannot be given a meaningful interpretation.

In view of the fundamental problems with π, we present the magnitude of intergenerational imbalance with the help of an alternative set of indicators. These indicators show how much fiscal policy should be changed in order to eliminate the "excess burden" on future generations. Specifically, we try to estimate the (immediate and permanent) adjustment of (1) all taxes, (2) all transfer payments, and (3) all government purchases of goods and services that would be needed to ensure equality between the net tax payments of future generations and the (growth-adjusted) net tax payments of newborns ($\pi = 1$). The results are found in table 10.3, both for the baseline and for alternative combinations of interest rate and growth rate. The table shows the necessary fiscal adjustments, reported as percentage differences from what the relevant tax revenue or expenditure level would have been in the absence of these adjustments.

Consider first a policy whereby intergenerational balance is restored through higher overall tax revenue collected from living generations. In this case additional revenue equal to 4.0 percent of the existing tax revenue is required. This is a nonnegligible fiscal adjustment. The net tax payments of current newborns and future generations could also be equalized if all transfer payments were reduced by 4.5 percent, or through an across-the-board cut in government expenditures of 29.0 percent.

It is noteworthy that the required fiscal tightening is fairly robust to parameter variation, ranging within a band of ± 15 percent of the baseline finding. As seen from the last row in table 10.3, the strong sensitivity of measuring imbalance via the indicator π translates into rather robust qualitative findings if we focus on, for example, necessary cuts in government purchases, also for the case of treating education as government consumption. Note that the scale of these cuts differs from those found in the case in which we distributed educational expenditures due to the different denominators referred to in both cases.

An important question is what difference it makes whether generational balance is achieved in one way or another. Indeed, the macroeconomic response to a tax increase may be different from the macroeconomic response to a spending cut. Similarly, if contractionary fiscal actions are implemented through higher income taxes, the wage and employment effects may differ significantly from the case in which fiscal policy is tightened through higher consumption taxes (Jensen 1997). However, generational accounting fails to capture such differences. Nevertheless, it would be of interest to see how sensitive the generational accounts of existing generations are to the specific way of restoring generational balance. Table 10.4 shows the generational accounts by age for current as well as for future generations under each alternative policy change. For comparison we also show the baseline generational accounts.

Let us first see how sensitive the generational accounts of existing generations are to whether the generational balance is restored through higher taxes or lower transfers. Although almost identical total revenue, measured in present value, has to be raised in the two scenarios, and although *all* living generations have to pay higher net taxes, the distribution of burdens across current generations appears to be quite sensitive to the choice of fiscal instrument. In general, higher tax rates place the fiscal burden on current generations of working age, whereas transfer reductions mainly hit the younger and the older generations. If generational balance is restored through an across-the-board cut in government expenditures, there would only be a direct influence on future generations' net tax payments. However, while the generational accounts of currently living generations are left unaffected, there would be an indirect effect in the sense that the utilities derived from use of infrastructure, defense, policing, and so forth, would fall.

In the light of these findings it would be useful to know the sources of the generational imbalance and their quantitative significance. Two main sources can be identified, namely, demographic changes and preexisting public debt. Suppose education is counted as government consumption. In this case we find that if the age structure could be kept constant, future generations' net payments would be 11 percent less than those of current newborns. Hence, changing demographics have a lot to say. Similarly, in the absence of any public debt in the base year, future generations would only have to bear a 13 percent higher burden than current generations. As compared to the baseline results, we can thus conclude that both sources have more or less the same quantitative impact.

10.6   Generational Impact of Policy Reforms

Given the current debt position and given the underlying demographic projections, current fiscal policy *does* pass burdens onto future generations. However, in the case of no demographic change, that is, if the number of persons in each age group could be kept constant, or the case of no public debt in 1995, there would almost be generational balance. Since neither of these alternatives—keeping the age structure constant or getting rid of public debt in a jiffy—can be readily implemented, it might be of interest to consider some less ambitious policy changes that would mitigate the generational imbalance.

Table 10.4   Achieving Generational Balance (thousands of U.S. dollars)

	Education Treated as Transfers				Education Treated as Government Consumption			
	Baseline	All Taxes	All Transfers	Government Consumption	Baseline	All Taxes	All Transfers	Government Consumption
Decrease/increase in expenditure/tax	0.0	4.0	4.5	29.0	0.0	3.4	4.7	9.9
Generation's age in 1995								
0	−18	−7	−5	−18	84	94	93	84
5	14	27	28	14	134	145	142	134
10	79	94	92	79	178	191	187	178
15	143	159	155	143	211	225	220	211
20	209	227	220	209	243	259	253	243
25	232	251	243	232	251	267	261	251
30	225	244	236	225	238	254	249	238
35	202	220	213	202	214	230	225	214
40	157	173	168	157	166	180	177	166
45	91	105	103	91	99	111	111	99
50	9	21	22	9	14	24	27	14
55	−64	−54	−50	−64	−61	−52	−46	−61
60	−143	−136	−128	−143	−143	−137	−128	−143
65	−172	−166	−158	−172	−172	−167	−157	−172
70	−186	−181	−172	−186	−186	−182	−172	−186
75	−194	−191	−182	−194	−194	−191	−181	−194
80	−202	−199	−190	−202	−202	−200	−189	−202
85	−202	−200	−191	−202	−202	−201	−190	−202
90	−49	−49	−47	−49	−49	−49	−47	−49
Future generations	26	−7	−4	−18	124	95	95	86

Three alternative scenarios are considered, each of which is designed with a view to important themes in the current debate on fiscal policy in Denmark.[6]

The first scenario (A) is based on rather optimistic assumptions about the Danish economy. Think of this as a successful outcome of the tax and labor market reforms introduced in recent years. Indeed, these reforms have been motivated by a need for stimulating incentives to work and thereby bringing structural unemployment down. The year 1993 marked the starting point of an expansion in the Danish economy, with rather impressive growth in output and falling rates of unemployment. For example, the registered rate of unemployment has fallen by 3 percentage points since 1994. The question now is whether this is a process likely to continue. It is widely believed that if further underpinned by structural policy adjustments, additional inroads can be made in the number of unemployed.

Following this line of reasoning, the rate of unemployment is assumed to fall by a total of 3.4 percentage points over the years 1996–99. Due to the operation of built-in fiscal stabilizers, an increase in employment not only reduces expenditures on unemployment and cash benefits, it also leads to higher tax revenues. In our calculations we use official estimates (Ministry of Finance 1994b) of the budgetary effects of a fall in the rate of unemployment. Since a better performance of the economy automatically improves the government budget, the question arises whether the extra revenue should solely be used to reduce public debt, or whether it should also translate into a fall in the tax burden on living generations.

We assume that over a period of 15 years, that is, until the year 2010, the extra revenue is used to reduce the government's financial net debt, and there will be no discretionary fiscal adjustment (such as a cut in tax rates). As a result, the public debt, amounting to $61.7 billion in 1995, would be eliminated by the year 2007. By the end of the year 2010 the government will have accumulated a net financial asset position of $14.7 billion. In view of the strength of public finances in the year 2011, two alternative subscenarios are considered. Scenario A-1 assumes that the process of government financial asset accumulation simply continues, while scenario A-2 assumes that a permanent tax cut is implemented so as to ensure that the level of the government's net financial assets can be kept constant in all future years.

The effects of scenario A are reported in table 10.5. In the absence of any discretionary action (A-1), the generational accounts of living generations are seen to increase relative to the baseline findings. People of working age face the highest increases in tax payments, whereas the effects on the elderly's accounts are relatively minor, due to the adjustment of transfer aggregates. The benefits resulting from a better economic performance accrue to future

---

6. As mentioned already, it should be stressed that the implementation of reform measures can involve significant macroeconomic feedbacks that are not taken into account (Buiter 1995; Fehr and Kotlikoff, chap. 3 in this volume; Raffelhüschen and Risa 1997).

Table 10.5   Generational Accounts for Alternative Policies (thousands of U.S. dollars)

Generation's Age in 1995	Baseline	Labor Market Reform		Reducing Government Activity		Higher Retirement Age (C)
		Endogenous Debt after 2010 (A-1)	Reduced Income Tax after 2010 (A-2)	Endogenous Debt after 2010 (B-1)	Reduced Income Tax after 2010 (B-2)	
0	−18	1	−11	1	−11	−10
5	14	37	22	32	17	23
10	79	106	89	96	79	90
15	143	173	157	158	141	154
20	209	241	225	224	208	221
25	232	261	247	246	232	245
30	225	251	239	240	228	238
35	202	226	216	218	209	216
40	157	176	169	174	167	170
45	91	108	102	111	106	104
50	9	22	18	31	27	23
55	−64	−54	−57	−39	−42	−48
60	−143	−137	−138	−117	−119	−141
65	−172	−168	−169	−149	−150	−171
70	−186	−182	−183	−164	−164	−185
75	−194	−192	−192	−175	−175	−194
80	−202	−200	−200	−185	−185	−202
85	−202	−201	−201	−188	−188	−202
90	−49	−49	−49	−49	−49	−49
Future generations	26	−20	1	−20	1	2
Change in government purchases to restore generational balance	−29.0	14.2	7.8	14.2	7.8	8.0

generations, which turn out to be even better off than current newborns. In fact, instead of paying $26,000, as in the baseline scenario, they now receive $20,000. Moreover, to restore generational balance it would be necessary to increase government purchases by 14.2 percent, against a cut of 29 percent as in the baseline. Of course, one would also expect that living generations reap some benefits of successful macroeconomic performance. For example, the higher employment rate would undoubtedly be felt as an improvement in living conditions of those previously unemployed.

More balanced generational results would clearly come out if taxes were lowered in 2011 (A-2). In this case some but not the entire benefits of labor market reforms would accrue to future generations. For current generations, the future income tax relief will thus imply that their accounts range about halfway between the baseline and scenario A-1. The same holds true for future generations. Hence, achieving generational balance in scenario A-2 necessitates a moderate cut in government consumption of 7.8 percent.

Scenario B is based on less optimistic assumptions about the effects of structural reforms and the international conjuncture. In particular, the unemployment rate is assumed to remain at its 1995 level. Yet we assume that policymakers have equally ambitious public debt targets. Indeed, the Danish government has taken the official position that that public debt should be eliminated over the next 10 to 15 years (Lykketoft 1995). We now let scenario A constitute a benchmark for the design of fiscal policy in scenario B. However, rather than getting rid of public debt through automatic stabilization, debt reduction now has to be implemented through discretionary fiscal initiatives. We assume this is achieved through (proportional) contributions from all parts making up the government budget. In view of its breathing space, alluded to above, Denmark seems to have a unique opportunity to bring down public debt relatively fast, although a horizon of 15 years may seem a bit too ambitious.

This scenario will necessarily impose significant burdens on current generations. However, as before the distribution of tax burdens between current and future generations depends on what happens when the public debt target has been reached in 2010. In scenario B-1 we assume that the policy of debt reduction (or asset accumulation) is continued after the year 2010. As compared to scenario A-1, we of course find the same net payments for future generations and current newborns as well as the same increase of government purchase necessary to ensure generational balance. Moreover, young working-age cohorts will gain while old working-age and elderly cohorts lose. As compared to our baseline results, all cohorts will realize lower transfer receipts and therefore higher accounts. Clearly, this strategy would be advantageous solely for future generations. Scenario B-2 is designed with the aim of sharing more equally the changes in net tax payments between current and future generations. Hence, we assume that taxes are cut in 2011, with the magnitude being determined such that the debt ratio arrived at in 2010 can be kept constant permanently thereafter.

The results from scenario B-2 are also shown in table 10.5. Again, as compared to scenario A-2 only the accounts of those at least one year old in the base year are affected, and it will be the young who gain. In comparison to scenario B-1 no generation is worse off, while relative to our baseline, every cohort except those aged 15 to 25 in the base year will be worse off. Note that the gaining cohorts suffer transfer losses only for a few years right after 1995 as well as in the far future, while the income tax effect in year 2010 is high in terms of present value.

The third strategy (C) relates to initiatives to avert the old-age crisis. While the need for debt reduction is well perceived across a broad political spectrum in Denmark (although its specific form of implementation remains controversial), views certainly differ as to whether debt reduction is enough to combat the underlying pressure on public finances due to population aging. Against this background a strategy is considered with the purpose of reversing the strong tendency toward early retirement. This strategy is designed as a reform of the early retirement scheme, currently allowing members of the workforce to retire at age 60. Instead, we examine the generational impact of raising that age stepwise to 63 through the years 2000–2002. Clearly, this announced reform would yield a "double dividend": not only would the workforce be expanded, there would also be a fall in the large number of recipients of public transfer payments.

Table 10.5 reports the generational impacts of scenario C while adjusting solely early retirement benefits and income tax revenues. As compared to the baseline findings, the burden of current generations will rise with age while the current elderly remain basically unaffected. With respect to intergenerational redistribution, we find a significantly reduced burden on future generations. This holds for both absolute net payments amounting to $2,000 instead of $26,000 and for the 8 percent cut in government purchases necessary to ensure generational balance. In fact, reducing the retirement age is a very effective and adequate way of achieving generational balance under the given demographic pressure. One should keep in mind, though, that it will predominantly burden older and therefore—in terms of life cycle planning—not very flexible cohorts. Hence, a fair and longsighted announcement has to be part of that type of reform.

10.7 Conclusion

Using the device of generational accounting, we find that there actually is a generational imbalance associated with current fiscal policy in Denmark. Therefore, current generations would have to face tighter fiscal policies if the generational distribution of net tax burdens were to be more equal. For example, generational balance could be achieved through an increase in income tax revenue of almost 4.0 percent or a cut in transfer payments of around 4.5 percent. Treating educational expenditures as government consumption, our results suggest that the (growth-adjusted) lifetime net tax payments of a representative member of future generations will be around 50 percent higher than those faced by current newborns.

We also assess the generational impact of a number of other policies that are important on the policy agenda in Denmark. In particular, the prospects of future generations would look much lighter if public debt were reduced in line with official declarations of intent, implying that public debt would be eliminated over the next 10 to 15 years. Also, initiatives to expand the workforce, including steps to bring down the large number of recipients of early retirement benefits, could add a significant contribution to restoring generational equity. Furthermore, a fall in structural unemployment, as accomplished through, say, tax and labor market reforms, would not only be good for the unemployed but would also benefit future generations significantly.

Another notable finding of the paper is that not only do men contribute a much larger share of their lifetime incomes to the government than women, womens' net payments are even negative. There are several reasons for this result, unique by international standards. For example, Danish women are mainly recruited to low-paid jobs with higher risks of unemployment; a number of services provided by the Danish welfare system are mainly utilized by women; and Danish women have a greater longevity than men, which implies that they receive public pensions and other old-age benefits for a longer period than men. This bias is aggravated by the flat-rate nature of the Danish pension scheme.

References

Atkinson, A. B. 1995. The welfare state and economic performance. *National Tax Journal* 48:171–98.

Auerbach, A., J. Gokhale, and L. Kotlikoff. 1991. Generational accounts—A meaningful alternative to deficit accounting. In *Tax policy and the economy,* ed. D. Bradford. Cambridge, Mass.: MIT Press.

Buiter, W. 1995. Generational accounts, aggregate saving and intergenerational distribution. NBER Working Paper no. 5087. Cambridge, Mass.: National Bureau of Economic Research.

Callesen, P. 1995. A note on policies to reduce structural unemployment. Copenhagen: Ministry of Finance. Mimeograph.

Danmarks Statistik. 1996. *Statistical yearbook.* Copenhagen: Danmarks Statistik.

Drèze, J., and E. Malinvaud. 1994. Growth and employment: The scope for a European initiative. *European Economy,* no. 1: 77–106.

Förster, M. 1994. Measurement of low incomes and poverty in a perspective of international comparisons. OECD Labor Market and Social Policy Occasional Paper no. 14. Paris: Organization for Economic Cooperation and Development.

Hagen, K., E. Norrman, P. B. Sørensen, and T. Teir. 1998. Financing the Nordic welfare states in an integrating Europe. In *Tax policy in the Nordic countries,* ed. P. B. Sørensen. London: Macmillan.

Ingerslev, O., and N. Ploug. 1996. Velfærdsstatens udvikling. In *Velfærdsstatens fremtid,* ed. E. Dalgaard, O. Ingerslev, N. Ploug, and B. R. Andersen. Copenhagen: Handelshøjskolens.

Jensen, S. H. 1997. Debt reduction, wage formation and intergenerational welfare. In *Pension policies and public debt in dynamic CGE models,* ed. D. P. Broer and J. Lassila. Heidelberg: Physica.

Jensen, S. H., and S. B. Nielsen. 1995. Population ageing, public debt and sustainable fiscal policy. *Fiscal Studies* 16:1–20.

Jensen, S. H., and B. Raffelhüschen. 1997. Generational and gender-specific aspects of the tax and transfer system in Denmark. *Empirical Economics* 22:615–35.

Koch, C. 1996. Green tax reform in a small open economy—From theory to practice. Paper presented at the 52d congress of the International Institute of Public Finance, Tel Aviv, August.

Lindbeck, A., P. Molander, T. Persson, O. Petersson, A. Sandmo, B. Swedenborg, and N. Thygesen. 1994. *Turning Sweden around.* Cambridge, Mass.: MIT Press.

Lykketoft, M. 1995. Den danske pensionsdebat. *Nordisk Forsikringstidsskrift* 76: 28–30.

Ministry of Finance. 1994a. *Budgetredegørelse 94.* Copenhagen: Ministry of Finance.

———. 1994b. *Finansredegørelse 94.* Copenhagen: Ministry of Finance.

———. 1996. *Finansredegørelse 96.* Copenhagen: Ministry of Finance.

Organization for Economic Cooperation and Development (OECD). 1996. *Economic surveys—Denmark.* Paris: Organization for Economic Cooperation and Development.

Raffelhüschen, B. 1995. A note on intertemporal and gender-specific redistribution in generational accounting. Discussion Paper no. 49. Freiburg: University of Freiburg, Institute of Public Finance.

Raffelhüschen, B., and A. Risa. 1997. Generational accounting and intergenerational welfare. *Public Choice* 93:149–63.

Sørensen, P. B. 1994. From the global income tax to the dual income tax: Recent tax reforms in the Nordic countries. *International Tax and Public Finance* 1:57–79.

11   Generational Accounting for France

Joaquim Levy and Ousmane Doré

11.1   Introduction

This paper presents a set of generational accounts to contribute to the assessment of France's long-term fiscal position. Understanding the sustainability of fiscal policy in France from a generational perspective is important in many respects. France has one of the most extensive social security and welfare systems among the large industrialized countries; public expenditure on health as a share of GDP is the highest in Europe; and compared to other Organization for Economic Cooperation and Development (OECD) countries, its pension system is generous (table 11.1). Not only are benefits high, but so is the level of taxation; taxes needed to finance social security funds have risen from less than 15 percent of wage income in 1950 to almost 50 percent in 1996. In recent years, there have been mounting concerns regarding the continuing viability of such an extensive social security system in general, and its unfunded pay-as-you-go pension schemes and its universal health care in particular. Slower rates of economic growth and the prospective aging of the population have led to further concerns that the implied taxation burden on younger (working) generations in the future will be too high, assuming the continuation of the general thrust of current policy settings. Projected trends of changes in the age structure reveal that an increasing number of retirees must be supported by a declin-

Joaquim Levy is an economist in the Research Department of the International Monetary Fund. Between 1993 and 1996 he worked on the French Desk of the European I Department of that institution. Ousmane Doré has been an economist in the European I Department of the International Monetary Fund since 1993. He is currently working as part of the French Desk in the Western Division.

The authors thank without implicating J. Artus for suggesting the computation of the lifetime accounts of baby boomers, and Mr. J. Accardo (Division Revenues et Patrimoine des Ménages, INSEE) for providing the necessary data. Excellent research assistance by B. Casabianca is also acknowledged.

239

Table 11.1   **Comparative Fiscal Indicators, 1994 (percent of GDP)**

	France	United States	Japan	Germany	Italy
General government					
Tax revenue	43.0	30.1	30.6	38.1	37.8
Spending	53.9	33.4	37.4	49.1	52.7
Deficit	5.0	1.8	4.1	2.3	7.8
Gross public debt	59.5	63.0	88.9	62.5	122.1
Public pensions	13.5	7.1	5.7	12.3	14.2
Public health	7.2	6.5	5.1	6.1	6.3
Education	5.0	5.4	2.8	3.1	4.3

Source: OECD (1995).

Table 11.2   **Comparative Demographic Factors, 1990–95**

	France	United States	Japan	Germany	Italy
Population (1994)	57,960	260,651	124,960	81,407	57,190
Fertility rate[a]	1.8	2.1	1.5	1.3	1.3
Life expectancy at birth	77.2	76.6	79.1	75.8	77.4
Net migration rate[b]	1.2	2.5	0.0	5.6	1.0
Participation rate	66.7	76.0	76.1	69.7	58.2

Source: Bos et al. (1994).
[a]Number of children per woman of childbearing age.
[b]Number of net immigrants per 1,000 people.

ing number of workers, with the old-age dependency ratio (for a constant participation rate) likely to rise from 0.35 to 0.60 by 2030 (tables 11.2 and 11.3).

Recent reform efforts have contributed to reducing social security spending below trend, but the long-run sustainability of the system remains in question. A reform of the basic pension system effected in 1993, while formalizing the indexation of pensions to the CPI instead of wages (pensions had been loosely indexed to the CPI since 1987), failed to attack longer term problems, in particular the relatively low minimum retirement age enshrined in legislation passed in 1982. Health expenditure growth has been curbed in recent years, but mainly through the imposition of expenditure ceilings that have created strong pressures for an eventual catch-up process. A far-reaching reform of the health system was announced in late 1995 but has yet to be fully implemented. More generally, a substantial fiscal consolidation has taken place since 1995, reducing the fiscal deficit from around 6 percent of GDP to close to 3 percent of GDP, but it has been achieved largely through the compression of expenditure and an increase in taxes, rather than structural, forward-looking changes in expenditure patterns. Therefore, while current government accounts have improved, and further consolidation is envisaged by the "Stability and Growth Pact" signed by candidates to the European Economic and Monetary Union

Table 11.3   **Demographic Transition**

	1995	2000	2010	2020	2030	2050
Population (thousands)	58,048	59,425	60,993	62,121	62,661	62,120
Elderly dependency ratio[a]	22.1	23.6	24.6	32.3	39.1	43.5
Very elderly dependency ratio[b]	39.2	43.4	49.6	41.9	48.8	56.6
Total dependency ratio[c]	52.2	52.8	51.2	59.6	67.9	73.6

Source: Bos et al. (1994).

[a]Population aged 65 or older as a percentage of the population aged 15 to 64.

[b]Population aged 75 or older as a percentage of the population aged 65 or older.

[c]Population aged 0 to 14 and 65 or older as a percentage of the population aged 15 to 64.

(EMU), sole consideration of the conventional fiscal deficit in assessing France's fiscal policy stance—and particularly its sustainability—would be misleading.

Behind concerns about the sustainability of the welfare system and the current real level of public consumption expenditures looms the fundamental question of how fiscal policy affects the distribution of income between generations. In general, fiscal settings that imply markedly increased burdens on some generations, relative to other generations, constitute a cause for concern. The standard measure of the budget deficit cannot appropriately address this question (Kotlikoff 1992). In contrast, generational accounting provides a tool for the investigation of the intergenerational distributional effects of fiscal policy. The purpose of this paper is thus to use this technique to determine whether current fiscal policies in France can be sustained without requiring future generations to pay higher net taxes over their lifetimes than current generations pay.

Our calculations indicate that France's generational policy is imbalanced against future generations. Despite the ongoing fiscal contraction, the pattern of social benefits (in particular pensions) implies a projected net tax burden adjusted for income growth on future French citizens that is about *twice* as large as that facing current young generations. While the precise size of this generational imbalance depends on a number of assumptions, including the rates of discount and productivity growth, the direction of the imbalance is unmistakable, as it holds under alternative assumptions about these parameters. It is also noteworthy that these projections do not build in feedback effects from policies that may be necessary to ensure the "balancing" in the future of the government's intertemporal budget constraint, such as increases in taxation, which could significantly weaken the underlying growth of income, thereby amplifying the imbalance. The size of generational imbalance existing between selected currently living generations is also computed, taking into account the net tax paid by current adults in the past. On this basis, the calculations show that protecting the "baby boom" generations from any change in fiscal policy (thus leaving to young and future generations the full responsibility to redress any fiscal imbalance) would imply a projected net tax burden on those now under age 25 that is more than *twice* as large as that facing those born around 1950.

Section 11.2 provides an overview of developments in France's public finances. Following a brief presentation of the generational accounting framework, section 11.3 presents estimates of generational accounts for France based on policies in place in 1995. In section 11.4, the lifetime net tax payments of current adults are calculated and compared with those of younger living generations. Sensitivity analysis with respect to key parameters is conducted in section 11.5, and alternative scenarios on policies aimed at redressing the generational imbalance are discussed in sections 11.6 and 11.7. Finally, section 11.8 summarizes these findings and concludes. An appendix provides details on the calculation of the accounts, including the data sources.

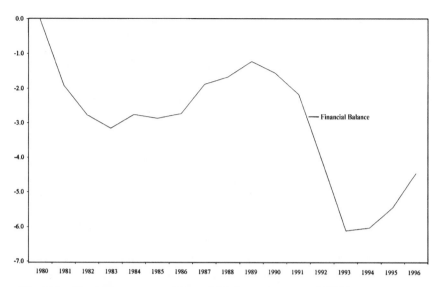

Fig. 11.1   General government financial balance (percent of GDP)
Source: INSEE, quarterly national accounts.

11.2   Public Finances in France

France's overall public finances deteriorated from a surplus in the early 1980s to persistent deficits in the 1990s (fig. 11.1), which have accumulated over the years, leading to a rise in the ratio of public debt to GDP from 20 percent to close to 60 percent. The deterioration of the general government balance that began in the late 1980s reflected in large part a marked increase in overall spending, mainly social expenditures. In the 1990s, it has been aggravated by relatively weak economic growth, which has reduced tax buoyancy and has increased outlays associated with entitlements (e.g., minimum income payments and a number of tax allowances). Public spending as a share of GDP rose from 46.5 percent of GDP in 1980 to about 53.8 percent in 1995, one of the highest levels among large industrial countries.

Meanwhile, a series of tax increases have contributed to a ratio of government revenue to GDP that is both the highest among the seven major industrial economies and heavily dependent on wage-based social security contributions.[1] French public accounts reached a low point in 1993, when, in part due

1. The general government revenue ratio reached 48.9 percent in 1995 after slightly declining in the second half of the 1980s. Contrary to what happened in many other developed countries, France had no major tax reform in the 1980s, but specific changes undertaken almost every year in the tax rules (and in particular a reduction in income tax rates in the late 1980s when the economy was booming) have changed considerably the structure of the tax system: a relatively low share of personal income tax in government, and yet a high burden of taxation. Revenues from income taxes were 7.2 percent of GDP in 1994, compared to an average of 10 percent of GDP for the seven large industrial countries. Social security contributions, on the other hand, are very high,

to the recession that began in 1992, the deficit widened to 6.1 percent of GDP. Thereafter, and under the aegis of the Maastricht Treaty on Economic and Monetary Union, fiscal policy has been oriented toward consolidation in order to meet public deficit and debt criteria established by this treaty.[2] Efforts to strengthen the public finances undertaken since mid-1995 appear on balance to have yielded some results, with the general government deficit declining to close to 3 percent in 1997. This improvement, however, has resulted chiefly from increases in taxes, and to a lesser extent from belt-tightening measures.[3]

Even a cursory analysis of the expenditure dynamics witnessed in the past three decades makes clear that the public sector, which has traditionally played a considerable role in France, has continued to expand, while experiencing some changes in its scope since the early 1970s. As shown in figure 11.2, total outlays of the general government as a share of GDP rose very rapidly between the early 1970s and early 1980s, falling thereafter until the late 1980s as a result of stronger economic growth over this period and some reform efforts aimed at containing spending (e.g., global budgets for hospitals) and shifting the focus of industrial policy (e.g., by cutting subsidies to enterprises). Slower growth since 1991 has in part been responsible for a sharply rising expenditure share in recent years. Current transfers—mainly to households—have been the most rapidly rising item, representing 45 percent of total spending in 1980 and more than half in 1995, whereas the share of public consumption in total gen-

---

at 21 percent of GDP compared to an average of 11 percent for the seven large industrial countries. Some broadening of the income tax base has taken place in recent years, through the introduction of a number of broad-based flat income taxes, notably the Contribution Sociale Généralise (CSG; introduced in 1991 and used to finance social security) and the Remboursement de la Dette Sociale (RDS; introduced in February 1996 and earmarked to finance a sinking fund set up to repay the deficit accumulated by the social security administration in recent years). Reductions in the burden of wage-based social security taxation were initially pursued through the introduction of a system of partial exemptions from payment of employer social security contributions. More recently, a gradual raise of the rate of the CSG was decided upon, to permit the financing of public health care to be shifted away from social security contributions (from 1998, the CSG rate will be raised by 4.1 percentage points to 7.5 percent of capital and wage incomes).

2. These criteria consist of capping the general government deficit at 3 percent of GDP, and the stock of public debt at 60 percent of GDP. While the deficit criterion has been strengthened in 1995 in accordance with the "Stability and Growth Pact," there has been some flexibility in the interpretation of the debt criterion. The latter criterion, while somewhat forward looking, does not take into account the implicit debt of the social security system, which in the case of France was estimated to be at about 100 percent of GDP in 1993 (Kuné, Petit, and Pinxt 1993). Maastricht deficit criteria were set on a national accounts basis, with a view to homogenizing cross-country comparisons and bringing a degree of transparency to fiscal accounts that is absent in most public budgeting accounting. Nevertheless, as 1998 approached, Eurostat endorsed the recording as deficit-reducing current revenues receipts from some operations that could be plausibly classified as exchange of assets (and as such usually classified as financial operations).

3. The contribution of public enterprises to the consolidation effort was mixed, as several of them needed to be recapitalized, in addition to the cases of some public banks that produced large contingent shortfalls. On the other hand, the transfer of France Telecom's future pension liabilities to the state budget, against a lump-sum payment (recorded as a deficit-reducing current revenue), while generating a negative cash flow in coming years (ceteris paribus burdening future generations) contributed to the narrowing of the fiscal deficit in 1997.

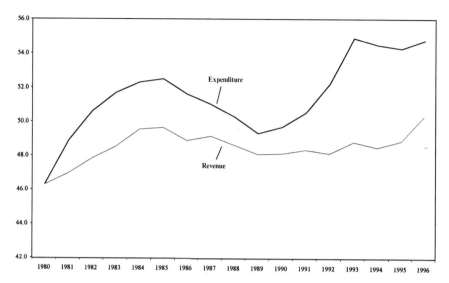

Fig. 11.2   General government revenue and expenditure (percent of GDP)
Source: INSEE, quarterly national accounts.

eral government expenditure has declined, largely as a result of strict public sector wage policy.[4]

A widely observed source of spending growth has been the expansion of the social security system. Previously close to balance, the social security accounts have run deficits of about 1 percent of GDP from 1992 onward.[5] Between 1980 and 1995, social security spending as a share of GDP rose by 5 percentage points. Expenditure on pensions, which represented only about 5 percent of GDP in 1960, rose to 10 percent in 1980 and more than 12 percent in 1995. Health expenditure has increased at an annual rate of 0.7 percentage points greater than that of nominal GDP since 1980; its share in GDP rose from 4 percent in 1960 to over 9 percent in 1995. Demographic factors have accounted for a good share of the rise in social expenditure (according to the OECD, about 50 percent of the increase in health care costs can be attributed to population aging). However, policies and economic conditions have also played a role. For instance, the coming to maturity of the pension system instituted in 1945 lies behind the increase in contribution rates required to balance the pay-

4. The share of compensation of public sector employees in GDP has remained flat despite a continuous increase in total public sector employment, which currently represents 25 percent of total domestic employment as opposed to 20 percent in 1980.

5. By law the social security system has to close the year in balance; in recent years this has required complex financial operations, promptly reversed at the beginning of the new year. This window dressing has not, however, been hidden from the public, as biannual reports of the finances of social security pointing to the sources of imbalances in the accounts of the system have received wide publicity.

as-you-go scheme, and increases in health care expenditure have often been associated with higher income levels. In the case of pensions, while life expectancy had risen substantially, the minimum retirement age was reduced in 1982 from 65 years to 60, and as in other European countries, a number of early retirement schemes were introduced after 1980.

Other social outlays also increased due to changing economic conditions. Most notably, unemployment benefits rose extremely fast in real terms during the 1970s, when the rate of unemployment increased from 2 percent to 8–9 percent. The average annual real growth rate of benefits per capita was, however, curtailed in the 1980s when policy reforms made the system progressively less generous while tightening the eligibility requirements. However, because of the sharp rise in the number of unemployed in recent years, total outlay on unemployment benefits has gone up from less than 1 percent of GDP in 1980 to 1.7 percent in 1995.[6]

The projected impact of population aging has been extensively studied since the late 1980s, particularly regarding pensions (the *Livre Blanc sur les Pensions* summarizing these studies and published in 1992 formed the basis for the reform implemented in 1993). Partly due to a decline in the fertility rate in the 1960s and 1970s and to the continuous lengthening of life expectancy, the old-age dependency ratio (i.e., the ratio of the number of people aged 65 or older to the working-age population) has risen from 12 percent in 1965 to about 15 percent in 1995 and is likely to increase over the coming decades to peak in 2030 at 23 percent. Official demographic projections (taking into account the trend decrease in mortality) show that at the current retirement age of 60 years, there will be 2.6 persons of working age for every person of retirement age in 2000, but only 1.2 persons in 2050. The implication of these demographic developments is that spending on pensions and health care is likely to rise markedly. Recent official French studies (Briet, Zaidman, and Rubenstein 1996) show that under unchanged policies, the average rate of contribution needed for financial balance of the basic pension system would have to increase from 18.9 percent in 1990 to 48 percent in 2040. Other studies indicate that aging by itself would tend to increase the share of health expenditure in GDP by about 3 percentage points by 2050 (e.g., Lenseigne and Ricordeau 1997). A study of the combined impact of these trends on future generations has not, however, been done. The generational accounts computed here are thus the first attempt to bring together these prospective developments in an unified framework.

---

6. For a number of reasons, unemployment benefits as such represent a relatively small part of replacement income. Since the early 1990s, social minima (Revenu Minimum d'Insertion—RMI) have had an increasing importance, while family allowances have increasingly been reoriented from responding to demographic policies toward being a key element of the social safety net (nevertheless, until 1997, the basic family allowance was targeted at encouraging childbearing, not being means tested and being quite generous to families with three or more children).

11.3 Generational Accounting

11.3.1 The Basic Framework

Generational accounting is a new technique developed by Auerbach, Gokhale, and Kotlikoff (1991) and Kotlikoff (1992) that can be used to study the effects on different generations of the government's fiscal policy. In this framework, the explicit analysis of the impact of fiscal policy on the welfare of different generations starts out by computing generational accounts, which simply show the present value of the expected net tax payments of a representative individual of a given generation, where "net taxes" refers to taxes paid less transfers received and a "generation" is defined as a cohort of individuals of the same age and sex.

Generational accounts are based on the premise that all government purchases must be paid for; that is, for a given path of government spending, a reduction in one generation's account can only be achieved through expanding other generations' accounts in a way that respects the government's intertemporal budget constraint. The budget constraint implies that the government's current net wealth plus all future taxes paid to the government minus all transfers paid by the government (future net taxes) must cover all future government spending on goods and services. In order to compare the intergenerational burden, the sum of future net taxes is split into an amount paid by all existing generations from the base year onward to the end of their lives and the remaining amount, which has to be paid by all future generations during their lives. Hence, more formally, the government's intertemporal budget constraint can be written as

$$
(1) \qquad \sum_{s=0}^{D} N_{t,t-s} + \sum_{s=1}^{\infty} N_{t,t+s} + W_t = \sum_{s=t}^{\infty} G_s \prod_{j=t+1}^{s} \frac{1}{1 + r_j}.
$$

The first term on the left-hand side of equation (1) adds together the present value of the net payments of existing generations. The expression $N_{t,k}(k = t, \ldots, t - D)$ stands for the present value of net remaining lifetime payments to the government of the generation born in year k discounted to year t. The index of this summation runs from age 0 to age D, the maximum length of life. Hence, the first element of this summation ($s = 0$) is $N_{t,t}$, which is the present value of net payments of the generation born in year t; the last element ($s = D$) is $N_{t,t-D}$, the present value of remaining net payments of the oldest generation alive in year t, namely, those born in year $t - D$. The second term on the left-hand side of equation (1) adds together the present value of remaining net payments of future generations. The third term on the left-hand side, W_t, denotes the government's net wealth in year t. The right-hand side of equation (1) expresses the present value of government consumption. In the latter expression, G_s stands for government consumption expenditure in year s. All future flows are discounted to year t at the pretax rate of return r_j.

The term $N_{t,k}$ is defined more explicitly as follows:

$$(2) \qquad N_{t,k} = \sum_{s=\max(t,k)}^{k+D} T_{s,k} P_{s,k} \prod_{j=t+1}^{s} \frac{1}{1+r_j}.$$

In expression (2) $T_{s,k}$ stands for the projected average net payment to the government made in year s by a member of the generation born in year k. The term $P_{s,k}$ stands for the number of surviving members of the cohort in year s who were born in year k. For generations who are born in year k, where $k > t$, the summation begins in year k.

Generational accounts are defined simply as a set of values of $N_{t,k}$, one for each existing and future generation, with the property that the combined total value adds up to the right-hand side of equation (1). This formulation makes clear the implications of the government budget constraint; holding the right-hand side of the equation fixed, increased (decreased) government payments to (receipts from) existing generations mean a decrease in the first term on the left-hand side of equation (1) and require an offsetting increase in the second term on the left-hand side of equation (1); that is, they require reduced payments to, or increased payments from, future generations.

This framework can be used easily to make two types of comparison. First, through the use of lifetime net tax rates, it can be used to compare the lifetime net taxes of future generations, of the generation of people just born, and of different generations born in the past; that is, it can be used to determine how much future generations are likely to pay in net taxes as compared to generations alive today. Second, generational accounting can be used to compare the effects of actual or proposed policy changes on the remaining lifetime net tax payments of generations currently alive and on future generations.

11.3.2   The Case of France

Generational Profiles and Benchmarking Aggregates

The construction of generational accounts necessitates first projecting each currently living generation's average taxes less transfers for each future year during which at least some members of the generation will be alive, and then converting these projected net tax payments by individuals into an aggregate present value. This requires projections of population by age and sex, as well as a discount rate to convert flows of net taxes into present values. In the case of France, projections of average future taxes and transfers by age and sex start with the 1995 aggregate taxes and transfers, as well as medium-term projections of transfers and taxes for all levels of government. These aggregate taxes and transfers are distributed across the population by age and sex in each year according to the age and sex pattern observed in 1990 from official survey data. The primary sources for these distributions are the 1990 Enquête sur les Revenus Fiscaux des Ménages, the 1991–92 Enquête sur les Actifs Financiers, and the 1990 Enquête sur les Budgets des Familles. A detailed account of the construction of these profiles can be found in the appendix.

The resulting age and sex profiles of net taxes (i.e., the relative tax weights of different living cohorts) are assumed constant through time, except for adjustments reflecting projected changes in the participation rate of women and pension indexation (the profile for pensions also varies over time, as explained below). The actual value of individuals' taxes and payments in the medium term are found by scaling individuals' payments to achieve aggregate values consistent with taxes in 1995 and the medium-term fiscal projections, which assume inter alia that the economy returns to its "potential" level by year 2002. For years beyond 2002, it is assumed that all taxes and transfers not governed by other explicit factors increase at the same rate as productivity growth.[7] Five categories of taxes are distinguished: income tax, property tax, value-added tax (VAT), social security contributions, and taxes based on individual wealth (including corporate income taxes, the incidence of which was shifted to asset holders). Transfer payments are categorized into pensions, health, education, and unemployment benefits. For each of these items, the aggregate amounts are allocated according to the existing profiles; all other categories of transfers and nondiscriminated government revenues were included in government consumption. Figures 11.3 and 11.4 present the distribution of taxes and benefits in the base year 1995.

The next step in the construction of France's generational accounts involves an estimation of the initial stock of government net wealth and projections of future government consumption. Government consumption is determined by a projection over the medium term (see appendix), then by a rule that assumes that spending grows over time from its 2002 level to keep pace with population and productivity growth. This amounts to assuming that per capita public consumption rises at the productivity growth rate. The estimate of spending includes both government spending on goods and services (excluding health and educational spending) and public investment, netted by those taxes and receipts not included in the five categories described above (it is customary in generational accounts to lump public investment together with public current expenditure and not explicitly record the flow of services from past investment, as this convention has no impact on the present value of the net tax burden to the extent that individual benefits from public investment cannot be identified). For government net wealth, estimates computed by Institut National de la Statistique et des Etudes Economiques (INSEE 1994) are used. In 1995, the consolidated net wealth of the general government was estimated to be FF 800 billion (about 10 percent of GDP), reflecting the 1993 estimate, adjusted for

---

7. E.g., the projected distribution of taxes and transfers by age and sex for, say, 2017 would be equal to the 2002 distribution multiplied by $(1 + n)^{15}$, where n is the rate of productivity growth.

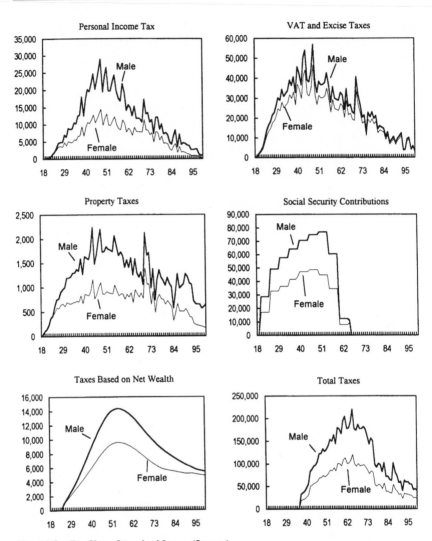

Fig. 11.3   Profiles of tax incidence (francs)
Sources: Data provided by INSEE; authors' calculations.

the growth in government debt and the sale of government assets through privatization in the intervening period. The net financial wealth that is used for the baseline calculation was negative, with net liabilities amounting to FF 2,800 billion, obtained by netting off from the general government debt (estimated at FF 4,059 billion in 1995), the financial assets of the general government.

Using the government intertemporal budget constraint, the average present value lifetime net tax payment of each member of each future generation was then determined as a residual under the assumption that the average lifetime

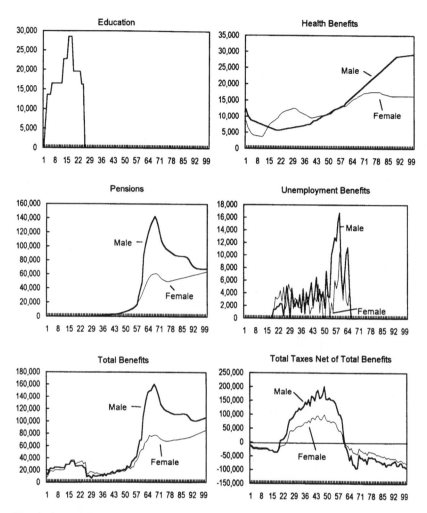

Fig. 11.4   Profiles of government transfers (francs)
Sources: Data provided by INSEE; authors' calculations.

tax payment of successive generations rises at the economy's rate of productivity growth.[8]

The classification of taxes and transfers adopted aimed at minimizing the arbitrariness in the labeling of taxes and transfers. All flows were fully taken into account on a national accounts basis (table 11.4), and the age and gender distribution of the net tax burden was allocated in as large a fraction as possible

---

8. Detailed Excel spreadsheets used in the calculation of the accounts are available from the authors upon request.

Table 11.4   Accounts of the General Government, 1995 (millions of francs)

		Income	Expenditures	Net Taxes		
				Amount	% of GDP	Incidence
Current account						
Operational income	N2	160,512		160,512	2.09	Government consumption
Subsidies	R30		127,910	−127,910	−1.67	Government consumption
VAT	R21	533,338		533,338	6.94	Consumption-based tax
Other taxes on goods and services	R22	563,061		563,061	7.33	Consumption-based tax
Customs taxes	R29	177		177	0.00	Consumption-based tax
Corporate income tax	R611	121,219		121,219	1.58	Net-wealth-based tax
Personal income tax	R612	398,392		398,392	5.19	Income-based tax
Other income, wealth, and property taxes	R613					
Property taxes (*taxe d'habitation*)		40,017		40,017	0.52	Income-based tax
Other income and wealth taxes		168,754	3,314	165,440	2.15	Net-wealth-based tax
Social security contributions	R66	1,479,788		1,479,788	19.27	Wage-based tax
Social security transfers	R641					
Pensions			741,094	−741,094	−9.65	Pensions
Health			406,937	−406,937	−5.30	Health expenditures
Unemployment			98,430	−98,430	−1.28	Unemployment
Others, including family allowances			162,717	−162,717	−2.12	Government consumption
Government pensions and other entitlements	R642		152,453	−152,453	−1.98	Pensions
Other social transfers	R643		220,277	−220,277	−2.87	Government consumption
Government social security contributions (*contribution fictives*)	R63+R65	350,931	205,770	145,161	1.89	Government consumption
Transfers to private agents	R66		15,695	−15,695	−0.20	Government consumption

Item	Code					Category
Other domestic transfers	R69	63,626	102,722	−39,096	−0.51	Government consumption
International official transfers	R67	20,171	78,383	−58,212	−0.76	Government consumption
Interests	R41	38,229	309,487	−271,188	−3.53	Debt service
Income from land	R43	3,763	151	3,612	0.05	Neutral
Dividends	R44	17,078		17,078	0.22	Neutral
Income of "quasi societies"	R45	0		0	0.00	Neutral
Insurance premiums	R51	1,960	2,063	−103	0.00	Neutral
Insurance payments	R52	933	1,060	−127	0.00	Neutral
Total income		3,962,019				
Total nondiscretionary expenditures			2,628,463			
Disposable income	N3	1,333,556				
Final consumption	P30		1,480,894			
Education	F1		380,000	−380,000	−4.95	Education
Culture	F2		47,000	−47,000	−0.61	Government consumption
Health	F3		258,000	−258,000	−3.36	Health expenditures
Social interventions	F4		112,000	−112,000	−1.46	Unemployment
Other			683,894	−683,894	−8.90	Government consumption
Capital account						
Gross savings	N4	−43,589	360,189			
Fixed investment	P41	−147,338	240,321			
Stockbuilding	P42		−1,538			
Purchase of land	P71		5,213			
Purchase of nonmaterial assets	P72		443			
Subsidies to investment	R71	49,343	92,945			
Taxes in capital	R72	47,336	22,805			
Other capital transfers	R79	7,070				

(continued)

Table 11.4   (continued)

| | Income | Expenditures | Net Taxes | | Incidence |
			Amount	% of GDP	
Capital expenditures					
Education		36,019	−36,019	−0.47	Education
Culture		23,412	−23,412	−0.30	Government consumption
Health		25,213	−25,213	−0.33	Health expenditures
Social interventions		18,009	−18,009	−0.23	Unemployment
Other		257,535	−257,535	−3.35	Government consumption
Capital income	103,749		103,749	1.35	Government consumption
Net borrowing requirements	−403,778		−5.26		

Sources: INSEE (1996) and authors' calculations.

to individual cohorts, so as to minimize the problem that the generational accounts do not recognize the intergenerational distributional implications of the government consumption program (see Buiter 1996).

Key Assumptions and Other Technical Aspects

A key ingredient in the calculation of generational accounts is the economic and demographic assumptions needed in order to extend and discount the components of the zero-sum equation. They are the rate of productivity growth, the discount rate, and the rate of population growth. For present purposes, the average annual growth of productivity is assumed to be constant at 1.5 percent per year over the long run (baseline case). A discount rate of 5 percent is assumed in the baseline, but this does not necessarily imply that this rate would be the most plausible actual discount rate. Indeed, alternative values of 3 percent (which could be viewed as close to real long-run risk-free interest rates) and 7 percent are also used to gauge the sensitivity of the results to this particular parameter. The projection of population by age and sex for 1995–2050 provided by INSEE corresponds to the "high growth" case (i.e., a fertility rate of 2.1 percent and no immigration) found in Dinh (1994). This trend is extrapolated through 2200 by assuming that the birthrate stabilizes after 2050.

Other technical assumptions made in this paper concern the rate of participation of the working-age population in the labor force, pension indexation, and the growth rate of medical expenditure. As regards the rate of participation, a number of studies point to past and projected increases in the participation of women in the labor force (see, e.g., Direction de l'Animation de la Recherchée, des Etudes et des Statistiques [DARES] 1997). This trend is captured here by incorporating the observation that the increase in the female participation rate has taken place through two mechanisms. First, women who have entered the labor force when young have in their majority remained active until retirement. Therefore, the future participation rate of cohorts aged 50 to 60 is likely to approach that of cohorts aged 40 to 50 (adjusted for some early retirement). Second, there has been a gradual, albeit small, rise in the participation rate of women in their 20s, which is expected to continue (at a decreasing pace) until about 2020.[9]

The current profile of pension payments reflects several influences, among which are the growth of real wages in the past and the indexation of benefits. This profile, however, is bound to change overtime. Since 1993, and following the proposals in the *Livre Blanc sur les Retraites,* pension benefits (in the *régime général*) have been adjusted in line with the CPI instead of according to wages. Accordingly, baseline projections assume that pensions will continue

---

9. Using the participation rate as a measure of economic activity is akin to assuming that the unemployment rate is constant in the long run; in the baseline, this rate is assumed to correspond to the current NAIRU (nonaccelerating inflation rate of unemployment).

to be indexed to the CPI (although the 1993 pension reform leaves the door open for a change in this rule) and that wages will rise in line with productivity growth. As to health care, it is assumed that aggregate health expenditure as a proportion of GDP will stabilize over the medium term, but beyond the year 2002, individual health care spending is assumed to rise faster than productivity (half a percentage point above the rate of productivity through 2030). This is consistent with the experience of the 1980s and early 1990s, when per capita real public health expenditures after adjustment for demographic changes rose faster than labor productivity, and in contrast with the objectives of the health care reform announced in 1995 (see discussion below on the impact that fully achieving the objectives of such reform would have on the generational accounts).

Main Results

The baseline case compares the generational accounts of males and females born in 1995 with the average of those born after 1995. The projections reflect policies that were in place or had been announced as of late 1995; therefore, they take into account the medium-term fiscal plans contained in the convergence program presented at the time. In the baseline scenario (and except where indicated otherwise), the participation rate of women is projected to rise while that of men is projected to remain constant, and a zero-indexation rule is assumed for pension expenditures, reflecting the fact that accounts are computed in constant prices.

The baseline generational accounts for male and female cohorts for the base year 1995 are presented in table 11.5 under the assumptions of 1.5 percent productivity growth and discount rates of 3, 5, and 7 percent. A negative value means that the generation is projected to receive more in transfers than it will pay in taxes over its remaining lifetime. Not surprisingly, a life cycle pattern emerges, with working-age generations having the higher tax burden and older generations being net recipients (working-age generations face many years of paying taxes before starting to receive pensions, while some of the benefits they receive indirectly, such as free education for their children, are rather assigned to younger generations).

For males in the baseline case (with a 5 percent discount rate), the generational account (i.e., the remaining net tax payments) is about U.S.$82,000 for newborns in 1995, rising to a peak of $320,000 for those who turned age 25 in 1995 (who have thus completed their education and have to wait yet some 35 years before retiring). Thereafter, the account falls, becoming negative for those aged 50 in 1995, individuals approaching retirement and thus a reduced level of income taxes and the receipt of public pension benefits. For females, the lifetime pattern is similar, but the accounts at each age are generally much lower than for males. For example, newborn females in 1995 face a net lifetime fiscal burden of some $37,000, which peaks at $220,000 at age 25. The fact

Table 11.5   **Generational Accounts: Baseline (U.S. dollars)**

Generation's Age in 1995	$r = 3$ Male	$r = 3$ Female	$r = 5$ Male	$r = 5$ Female	$r = 7$ Male	$r = 7$ Female
0	140,348	110,681	82,219	37,221	25,623	−3,714
5	174,584	138,844	125,360	64,988	63,904	17,299
10	211,835	170,319	175,370	99,916	113,065	47,738
15	243,973	195,695	222,248	134,520	164,013	82,022
20	290,671	234,637	284,845	186,730	235,394	138,292
25	306,148	253,627	318,688	223,498	284,190	184,112
30	263,625	227,146	293,748	216,809	278,405	190,447
35	199,287	185,985	242,716	193,579	246,843	180,957
40	115,108	130,656	166,777	153,313	188,989	154,209
45	23,743	67,894	77,456	100,826	112,966	112,738
50	−64,100	7,174	−12,524	44,393	29,276	63,238
55	−184,251	−76,278	−134,743	−39,257	−91,104	−16,650
60	−232,282	−136,466	−197,014	−100,390	−164,612	−76,703
65	−225,530	−134,762	−199,879	−106,926	−175,435	−87,475
70	−168,734	−111,542	−151,497	−91,855	−134,820	−77,305
75	−177,047	−119,018	−162,135	−103,600	−148,190	−91,496
80	−101,447	−76,301	−93,948	−67,958	−86,935	−61,197
85	−109,300	−79,461	−102,905	−73,212	−96,974	−67,889
90	−99,988	−76,940	−94,438	−72,308	−89,642	−68,203
95+	−104,084	−76,387	−99,945	−73,395	−96,111	−70,623
Future generations	285,138	224,865	161,450	73,089	99,330	−14,396
Percentage difference	103	103	96	96	288	288

Source: Authors' calculations.

Note: Productivity growth assumed to be 1.5 percent; r is the discount rate (percent).

that accounts for females are lower than for males reflects, first, the lower female participation rate and lower pay scale, so that their lifetime gross taxes (mainly labor income and social security taxes) are lower, and second, greater longevity, which tends to increase the present value of their pensions receipts.

In the baseline scenario, the average net payment burden of future generations is about *two times* higher than that faced by the youngest generation alive in 1995 (represented by the 0–4-year-old cohort of 1995).[10] If all generations born before 1995 are protected from any change in their lifetime net tax profiles, future generations will have to pay on average about 96 percent more than the youngest "protected" generation, in order to guarantee the ultimate solvency of the government. Assuming that the tax burden of future genera-

---

10. A baseline scenario incorporating recent health care reforms would yield smaller generational imbalance. See, e.g., Levy and Doré (1998).

tions will be shared by men and women proportionally to the net tax burden faced by men and women belonging to the 1995 newborn generation, the lifetime net tax paid by males in future generations would amount to $161,000, while women would pay $73,000 over their lifetimes.

11.4 Sensitivity Analysis

11.4.1 Sensitivity with Respect to the Parameter Values

Generational imbalances are sensitive to assumptions regarding discount and productivity growth rates. Table 11.6 shows the impact of varying these parameters in the range of 3 and 7 percent and 1 and 2 percent, respectively. For a given productivity growth, a higher discount rate tends to increase the generational imbalance as measured by the percentage difference in the present value of taxes paid by future generations and the newly born, since it gives a lower weight to future payments.[11] On the other hand, the effect of rising productivity is ambiguous, lowering the relative burden of future generations for sufficiently high discount rates, and increasing it for low discount rates. (Indeed, when the generational imbalance is expressed as a ratio of the present value of lifetime incomes, the effect of change in productivity can be reversed.) The intuition for this result is that higher productivity increases the present values of both taxes and transfers. However, because of the life cycle pattern of consumption and the discounting factor, when the discount rate is sufficiently high the increase in the present value of taxes (which are paid earlier in life) outweighs the increase in the present value of benefits. For low enough discount rates, the increase in benefits (which come later in life), together with higher government consumption (which also grows at the productivity rate forever), implies a higher burden on future generations (even after adjusting for "effective" labor). For parameters in the range chosen, the imbalance always decreases when productivity growth increases (mainly because pensions are indexed to the CPI and not to wages).

11.4.2 Sensitivity with Respect to Accounting Conventions

Although the technique of generational accounting aims for an analysis of public finances free of labels that can be misleading, some conceptual problems arise when accounts are being calculated. Because generational accounts deal with net flows, differences in the way some taxes or benefits are classified

---

11. In general, the change in the imbalance is not a positive monotonic function of the change in discount rate. Although the net present value of all net taxes decreases monotonically with higher interest rates, the change in the imbalance need not, owing to the uneven distribution of taxes over the lifetimes of current generations (e.g., the impact of a higher discount rate is more marked for women than for men). Moreover, the ratio of net cash flows of newborns and future generations may either rise or fall.

Table 11.6   Sensitivity Analysis with Respect to Productivity and Discount Rates (thousands of U.S. dollars)

	g = 1			g = 1.5			g = 2		
	r = 3	r = 5	r = 7	r = 3	r = 5	r = 7	r = 3	r = 5	r = 7
Newborns									
Male	125.2	66.5	15.8	140.3	82.2	25.6	153.1	99.1	36.4
Female	91.4	25.1	−10.1	110.6	37.2	−3.7	130.8	50.9	3.5
Future generations									
Male	264.9	147.5	187.2	285.1	161.4	99.3	304.4	178.5	94.1
Female	193.2	55.5	−117.9	224.8	73.1	−14.4	260.3	91.8	9.1
Generational balance (% difference)	111	122	1,077	103	96	288	99	80	158

Source: Authors' calculations.

Note: g is productivity growth (percent); r is discount rate (percent).

Table 11.7   Sensitivity with Respect to Accounting Conventions: Education Recorded as Government Consumption (U.S. dollars)

Generation's Age in 1995	r = 3		r = 5		r = 7	
	Male	Female	Male	Female	Male	Female
0	222,079	193,096	151,549	102,057	82,520	48,274
5	249,491	215,546	191,668	128,791	121,403	71,836
10	271,493	230,785	229,356	153,518	161,657	95,668
15	289,738	241,963	264,836	177,480	203,801	122,096
20	311,105	255,172	304,397	206,387	254,158	157,151
25	309,455	256,946	321,884	226,706	287,284	187,219
30	263,625	227,146	293,748	216,809	278,405	190,447
35	199,287	185,985	242,716	193,579	246,843	180,957
40	115,108	130,656	166,777	153,313	188,989	154,209
45	23,743	67,894	77,456	100,826	112,966	112,738
50	−64,100	7,174	−12,524	44,393	29,276	63,238
55	−184,251	−76,278	−134,743	−39,257	−91,104	−16,650
60	−232,282	−136,466	−197,014	−100,390	−164,612	−76,703
65	−225,530	−134,762	−199,879	−106,926	−175,435	−87,475
70	−168,734	−111,542	−151,497	−91,855	−134,820	−77,305
75	−177,047	−119,018	−162,135	−103,600	−148,190	−91,496
80	−101,447	−76,301	−93,948	−67,958	−86,935	−61,197
85	−109,300	−79,461	−102,905	−73,212	−96,974	−67,889
90	−99,988	−76,940	−94,438	−72,308	−89,642	−68,203
95+	−104,084	−76,387	−99,945	−73,395	−96,111	−70,623
Future generations	377,796	328,491	222,801	150,040	116,899	68,386
Percentage difference	70	70	47	47	42	42

Source: Authors' calculations.

Note: Productivity growth assumed to be 1.5 percent; r is the discount rate (percent).

can have an impact. These problems are illustrated by adopting alternative assumptions about the classification of educational expenditure.[12]

In the baseline case presented above, educational expenditures were classified as transfer payments, and thus allocated to specific cohorts of the population. The scenario presented below indicates that if education is treated as government consumption, the generational imbalance would be reduced by 50 percent (table 11.7). While the average lifetime net tax payments of both the

12. The sensitivity of generational accounts with respect to the incidence of particular taxes (capital income tax), and the treatment of selected sources of government income associated with its net wealth, is treated elsewhere. If corporate income taxes are netted off government consumption instead of being lumped with other capital income taxes whose incidence was assumed to be proportional to the net wealth of individuals, the relative additional burden on future generations vis-à-vis the newly born increases. Considering total net wealth of the government instead of its financial net wealth and offsetting it against operational income received by the government would also increase the relative intergenerational imbalance. See Levy and Doré (1998).

newborns and future generations increase, the percentage difference between them actually declines. The intuition for a smaller generational imbalance under this category of classification is as follows: Treating education as government consumption amounts to reducing transfer payments that were to be received when young and having higher government spending to finance. Because future generations would face both the cut in educational transfers and the incipient tax increase in later years, their accounts will fall in relative terms.

11.5   Generational Accounts of Baby Boomers

The standard practice of generational accounting includes only future net tax payments and does not incorporate past net payments of currently living generations. Therefore, the only meaningful comparison of generational accounts is between those of newly born generations in the base year and those of future generations, for whom lifetime net tax payments are available. Although this way of presenting generational accounts yields insightful results regarding intergenerational imbalances, its interpretation may have less policy relevance than measures aimed at comparing the accounts of those presently living. Indeed, by comparing only the tax burden of unborn generations with that of current children, standard generational accounts avoid addressing the real political dilemma, which involves a trade-off among living generations. To address this kind of question, it is rather more interesting to compare the net tax burden of, say, current adults (e.g., some cohorts of baby boomers) with that of young generations (e.g., those under age 25, who have not fully entered the labor force yet) under the assumption that young generations will bear the same tax burden as all future generations. Such estimates involve the retrospective calculations of generational accounts as a first step (such calculations are presented for instance by Auerbach, Gokhale, and Kotlikoff 1994 for the case of the United States). But they also involve the netting out of the present value of past net taxes of those living generations lumped with future generations from the government wealth, and the adjustment of accounts of different generations to past (and varying), as well as projected (and constant), productivity growth.

The advantage of this approach of contrasting living adult and young generations, relative to the standard accounts, which assume that all generations alive in 1995 will be "protected" for their entire lifetimes, is that this assumption is somewhat implausible. Owing to demographic changes evident already in the early decades of the next century, the heavier burden on future generations will start to be apparent at a relatively early date, implying heavy pressure for policy changes that most likely will affect currently living generations.[13] As a

13. Of course, policy changes that formally affect only future generations' accounts can have an impact on the welfare of current generations. For instance, a cut in public expenditure on education for future generations, while not directly affecting the tax profile of current generations

Table 11.8   **Generational Accounts for Baby Boomers: Lifetime Net Tax Payments Converted into 1995 Present Values (thousands of U.S. dollars)**

	$g = 1.5$			Historical Productivity Growth		
	$r = 3$	$r = 5$	$r = 7$	$r = 3$	$r = 5$	$r = 7$
Current generations[a]						
Males	135,233	71,752	27,395	108,607	27,094	−15,094
Females	105,683	53,101	16,666	76,016	15,729	−16,992
Average	120,458	62,427	22,031	92,312	21,412	−16,043
Future generations[b]						
Males	262,600	106,317	30,429	237,188	54,021	−98,530
Females	206,120	58,225	−7,357	186,173	29,585	23,822
Average	234,360	82,271	11,536	211,680	41,803	−37,354
Generational imbalance (% difference)						
Males	94	48	11	118	99	n.a.
Females	95	10	−144	145	88	n.a.
Average	95	32	−48	129	95	n.a.

Source: Authors' calculations.

Note: g is productivity growth (percent); r is discount rate (percent).

[a]The 1950–55 cohort.

[b]Current youngsters (under 25 years of age) and all future generations.

yardstick, the generation born in 1950–55 was chosen to represent adult living generations in the computation of the imbalance between "protected" adult generations and "ultimately unprotected" young and future generations.[14] For this purpose, not only future net transfers were projected (as is done in the standard exercise), but retrospective accounts of past net transfers of adult generations were computed, considering in one case only constant productivity growth of 1.5 percent, and in another case taking into account the historical productivity growth rates observed in 1950–95 (details of the computation of the past net tax burden can be found in the appendix).

The calculations reported in table 11.8 indicate that under the present system of taxes and benefits (and a discount rate of 5 percent), the projected net tax burden on generations currently under age 25 is on average about *two times* as

---

(when public expenditure on education is recorded among transfers), would likely reduce their actual net income to the extent that parents would have to shoulder the cost of educating their children. It should also be kept in mind that differences in the treatment of taxpayers based on specific characteristics that might be implied by the coexistence of "protected" and "unprotected" generations already exist, although they are marginal (e.g., senior citizens often pay lower health contributions than working-age persons, couples and large families tend to benefit from income tax deductions).

14. The generation born in the early 1950s is representative in many ways. It fully experienced what came to be known as the "30 glorious" years of economic growth (which lasted until the 1980s) and is associated with the May 1968 students' movement, as well as subsequent transformations in the university and society in general.

Table 11.9   **Sources of Generational Imbalance (thousands of U.S. dollars)**

	Baseline Case		Constant Demographic		Zero Debt	
	A	B	A	B	A	B
Newborns						
Male	151.5	82.2	176.5	107.5	151.5	82.2
Female	102.1	37.2	109.5	45.1	102.1	37.2
Future generations						
Male	222.8	161.4	184.1	113.7	182.1	114.5
Female	150.1	73.1	114.2	47.6	120.5	51.8
Generational imbalance						
(% difference)	47	96	4	6	20	39

Source: Authors' calculations.

Note: A: educational expenditure treated as government consumption. B: Educational expenditure treated as government transfers.

large as that faced by those born around 1950, when the "historical" rate of productivity growth is used for comparing the burden on current adult generations. If generations are put on an equal footing without considering past fluctuations of the productivity growth rate (i.e., by simply using the 1.5 percent growth rate adjustment), the imbalance is on the order of 35 percent. The imbalance is very sensitive to the discount rate chosen, particularly when the adjustment to productivity is made using the simple constant rate.[15]

11.6   Sources of Generational Imbalance

The generational imbalance reported above reflects three major factors: future demographic changes, the level of public debt, and the underlying fiscal position of the general government (including the extensive social security system). In the absence of demographic changes (i.e., assuming a constant population structure), France's generational imbalance would be much smaller (6 percent). Likewise, the imbalance falls to 40 percent when the debt level is zero (table 11.9). To the extent that generational accounts reflect the current stance of fiscal policy, redressing the generational imbalance can also be achieved by changes in policies that result in strong improvement in fiscal positions. Increasing government revenues from general or specific taxes, cutting government consumption across the board, or addressing the problems in the pension and public health care systems are policies that could help correct the generational imbalance.

15. The use of a high real discount rate yields results that are somewhat curious but not implausible given that real interest rates in the 1970s and early 1980s were actually negative.

Table 11.10   Alternative Ways to Achieve Generational Balance (percentage change from baseline)

Variant	Cut in Government Purchases	Cut in Government Transfers	Increase in All Taxes	Increase in Income Tax
A	17.2	11.5	7.1	66
B	22.2	9.8	6.9	64

Source: Authors' calculations.

Note: A: Educational expenditure treated as government consumption. B: Educational expenditure treated as government transfers.

11.7 Restoring Generational Balance

What changes in taxes and transfers would be required to restore the generational accounts of the newborn and future French to fiscal balance? Table 11.10 suggests the magnitude of the policy adjustments necessary to achieve generational balance in France's fiscal policy. The measures considered there are an across-the-board increase in the overall level of taxes, an increase in the income tax, a cut in transfers, and a cut in government consumption. These measures are assumed to be permanent and to take effect as of 2002. The sizes of the policy adjustments required to restore generational balance are calculated under two variants: educational expenditure treated as government consumption (variant A) and as government transfers (variant B).

The overall level of taxes would have to be raised by 7.1 percent (variant A) and 6.9 percent (variant B) for generational balance to be restored under the baseline assumption of 1.5 percent productivity growth and 5 percent discount rate. If the adjustment is made solely by raising traditional personal income taxes, these will increase by 66 percent (variant A) and 64 percent (variant B), as these taxes represent a small share of government revenues (less than half of French households pay traditional direct income taxes; as mentioned in section 11.2, flat income taxes introduced in the 1990s are much broader based). It appears that a policy of increasing the level of taxation would involve substantial increases in the burden on young and middle-aged generations; for example, newborn and 30-year-old males would be required to pay an additional $40,000 and $30,000 in net terms, respectively. The net payment burden on future generations, on the other hand, falls by about 40 percent. Restoring balance through expenditure reductions would require permanently reducing the size of government purchases by 17.2 percent under variant A and 22.2 percent under variant B. Alternatively, permanent across-the-board reductions in transfers of 11.5 percent (variant A) and 9.8 percent (variant B) would yield a generationally balanced policy.

In view of the already high level of taxation in France, expenditure cuts as a way to achieve intergenerational balance would appear to be preferable to further increases in the tax burden. Moreover, while there may be scope for reductions in government consumption, it is in the area of social transfers that France (together with other European countries) should focus the adjustment. In particular, as noted above, the pending demographic transition, with the projected increase in the dependency ratio, is at the root of a large portion of the intergenerational imbalance implicit in current policies. Therefore, policies need to address the challenges in these areas. In fairness, the recognition by the French of the need for an early adjustment motivated both the health care reforms announced in November 1995 (reflecting discussions among social partners and several studies carried out in past years) and the pension reforms designed in the early 1990s and partially implemented in 1993 (mainly affecting the basic pension scheme, *régime général*) and 1996 (with respect to supplementary mandatory pension schemes)—most notably the indexation of pensions to the CPI instead of to wages.

The baseline scenario discussed in section 11.3 incorporates conservative assumptions about the growth in health care spending. In particular, it builds on trends in the past 20 years, and on the argument that total health care expenditure will increase faster than labor productivity because health care can be viewed as a superior good. This argument carries some weight, and in the case of France where public health care has now been officially recognized as a universal right, it is broadly appropriate. On the other hand, the reforms enacted in 1995 aimed at establishing incentives and mechanisms that would slow down the growth of these expenditures, while guaranteeing the quality of services.[16]

While some aspects of the reform of the health care system have already brought results, it is still too early to judge how fast some of its key provisions will be implemented. The importance of fully implementing the reform can, however, hardly be overestimated. Table 11.11 shows the intergenerational impact of assuming that the reform will take full effect before the year 2000, inter alia limiting the growth in per capita health spending (for a given age) to labor productivity growth after 2000. This alternative future path for outlays on health care would cut the intergenerational imbalance roughly by half, giving a net tax burden on future generations that is one and a half times as large as that facing newborns.

The early pension reform also alleviated the future intergenerational imbalance. The calculations presented in table 11.12 show that, were pensions still indexed to wages, for example, increasing at real rates of 1 to 1.5 percent a year, the intergenerational imbalance would be more than twice as large, rising to more than 140 percent. However, it is clear that if projected increases in

---

16. Expenditure restraints on hospital care, while relatively successful, proved to be increasingly distortionary. A major aspect of the 1995 reform was an attempt to regionalize hospital budgets and consolidate the system, with a view also to correcting the geographic imbalance in the distribution of beds and services entailed by demographic changes that had occurred since the 1970s. For a full discussion of the 1995 health care reform, see International Monetary Fund (IMF 1997, chap. 1).

Table 11.11   Generational Accounts with Slower Health Care Growth (U.S. dollars)

Generation's Age in 1995	$r = 3$		$r = 5$		$r = 7$	
	Male	Female	Male	Female	Male	Female
0	163,911	138,791	91,798	47,767	29,997	1,058
5	197,376	166,135	134,982	75,719	68,356	22,337
10	233,805	196,517	185,072	110,671	117,666	52,941
15	265,136	220,521	232,068	145,103	168,828	87,257
20	310,975	257,625	294,787	196,910	240,460	143,427
25	325,158	274,815	328,539	233,285	289,436	189,176
30	280,868	246,194	303,230	226,044	283,700	195,383
35	214,606	202,881	251,676	202,238	252,103	185,786
40	128,316	145,323	174,998	161,298	194,068	158,880
45	34,954	80,375	84,874	108,062	117,787	117,195
50	−54,870	17,546	−6,049	50,778	33,702	67,372
55	−177,018	−68,199	−129,391	−33,994	−87,273	−13,082
60	−226,786	−130,417	−192,746	−96,225	−161,420	−73,743
65	−221,542	−130,482	−196,657	−103,828	−172,928	−85,178
70	−166,082	−108,793	−149,290	−89,775	−133,045	−75,702
75	−175,118	−117,140	−160,499	−102,119	−146,836	−90,312
80	−100,522	−75,421	−93,155	−67,249	−86,272	−60,621
85	−108,674	−78,918	−102,363	−72,760	−96,511	−67,510
90	−99,533	−76,594	−94,051	−72,009	−89,307	−67,944
95+	−104,084	−76,387	−99,945	−73,395	−96,111	−70,623
Future generations	259,404	219,650	130,203	67,750	50,819	1,793
Percentage difference	58	58	42	42	69	69

Source: Authors' calculations.

Note: Per capita health care grows at the rate of productivity (1.5 percent) beyond the medium term. r is the discount rate (percent).

life expectancy are not accompanied by longer working lives and contribution periods for a full pension, it will be difficult to eliminate the intergenerational problem that is manifest in the baseline projections.

Increasing the participation rate (by tightening eligibility requirements for benefits and increasing the taxation of replacement income, including from early retirement) would thus appear to be a policy that could substantially contribute to improving the generational stance of fiscal policy: a higher participation rate not only widens the tax base by raising labor income and GDP but also reduces pension expenditure as a percentage of GDP. A characteristic of the French labor market since the mid-1980s is the relatively low level of labor participation, particularly for people aged 55–65, while life expectancy continues to increase. As the participation rate of this group of people declined from 31.5 to 16.5 percent despite a significant increase in the participation rate of women, its proportion in the active population fell from 18.7 in the 1960s to 9.4 percent in 1995 (DARES 1997). Between 1968 and 1995, participation

Table 11.12   **Generational Accounts with Pensions Indexed to Wages (U.S. dollars)**

Generation's Age in 1995	r = 3		r = 5		r = 7	
	Male	Female	Male	Female	Male	Female
0	120,266	95,632	77,400	34,150	24,494	−4,375
5	153,501	122,946	119,789	61,416	62,470	16,453
10	189,721	153,537	168,934	95,764	111,244	46,657
15	220,516	177,825	214,740	129,660	161,680	80,633
20	265,813	216,025	276,075	181,148	232,396	136,536
25	280,017	234,012	308,535	217,020	280,375	181,873
30	236,592	206,805	282,164	209,403	273,614	187,630
35	171,357	164,947	229,501	185,122	240,820	177,414
40	86,425	109,011	151,768	143,688	181,442	149,758
45	−6,249	45,385	60,110	89,752	103,347	107,087
50	−95,426	−16,380	−32,550	31,597	17,029	56,039
55	−217,149	−100,465	−158,023	−53,811	−106,825	−25,696
60	−232,282	−136,466	−197,014	−100,390	−164,612	−76,703
65	−225,530	−134,762	−199,879	−106,926	−175,435	−87,475
70	−168,734	−111,542	−151,497	−91,855	−134,820	−77,305
75	−177,047	−119,018	−162,135	−103,600	−148,190	−91,496
80	−101,447	−76,301	−93,948	−67,958	−86,935	−61,197
85	−109,300	−79,461	−102,905	−73,212	−96,974	−67,889
90	−99,988	−76,940	−94,438	−72,308	−89,642	−68,203
95+	−104,084	−76,387	−99,945	−73,395	−96,111	−70,623
Future generations	304,165	241,862	187,446	82,704	134,982	−24,111
Percentage difference	153	153	142	142	451	451

Source: Authors' calculations.

Note: Productivity growth assumed to be 1.5 percent; r is the discount rate (percent).

rates for males aged 60–65 dropped from 68 percent to about 15 percent with virtually no change for those aged 55–59. For females aged 60–65, there was a decline from 35 percent to about 13 percent, whereas those in the 55–59 age group experienced an increase in participation rates from 42 to 55 percent during the same period. Table 11.13 shows that by inducing rises in the male participation rates of those aged 55–59 and 60–65 in 2010 to 75 and 50 percent, respectively (and 73 and 40 percent for women), and keeping the replacement rate of initial pensions unchanged, the imbalance between newborn and future generations is eliminated. Moreover, if the increase starts to take place by the year 2000, so that by 2005 most of the adjustment is completed, the imbalance between baby boom generations and future generations (including current young generations) would be eliminated for the central assumption of a discount rate of 5 percent (table 11.14).

An increase to 50 percent in the participation rate of those aged 60–65 is consistent with both a three-year increase in the retirement age and a five-year

Table 11.13   **Generational Accounts with Changes in Participation Rates (U.S. dollars)**

Generation's Age in 1995	r = 3		r = 5		r = 7	
	Male	Female	Male	Female	Male	Female
0	181,166	139,765	96,847	46,270	30,667	−778
5	217,531	169,622	142,309	75,532	70,329	21,059
10	257,096	202,881	195,039	112,196	121,261	52,548
15	291,917	230,041	245,156	148,747	174,475	88,119
20	342,242	270,757	311,905	203,146	248,913	145,978
25	361,080	291,767	350,320	242,506	301,468	193,831
30	321,878	267,212	330,548	238,703	300,386	202,677
35	261,476	228,326	285,847	218,970	275,050	196,478
40	181,689	176,041	217,529	183,281	225,388	174,340
45	91,219	113,997	133,615	134,064	156,837	137,060
50	−53,935	22,056	−4,363	55,046	35,467	71,003
55	−180,793	−72,449	−132,053	−36,686	−89,124	−14,883
60	−230,286	−134,078	−195,433	−98,753	−163,432	−75,559
65	−224,474	−133,385	−199,026	−105,959	−174,786	−86,785
70	−168,290	−110,899	−151,133	−91,395	−134,540	−76,972
75	−176,883	−118,743	−161,999	−103,400	−148,085	−91,350
80	−101,399	−76,215	−93,908	−67,894	−86,904	−61,149
85	−109,300	−79,461	−102,905	−73,212	−96,974	−67,889
90	−99,988	−76,940	−94,438	−72,308	−89,642	−68,203
95+	−104,084	−76,387	−99,945	−73,395	−96,111	−70,623
Future generations	249,662	192,607	96,817	46,256	−1,752	44
Percentage difference	38	38	0	0	−106	−106

Source: Authors' calculations.

Note: From 2005 onward, the participation rates for males and females increase to 75 and 73 percent for the 55–59 cohorts, 50 and 40 percent for the 60–64 cohorts, and 8 percent for people aged 65 and older. Productivity growth assumed to be 1.5 percent; r is the discount rate (percent).

increase in the retirement age with fewer working hours in later years—thus leaving ample room for a variety of policy alternatives.[17] However, a key measure to achieve this objective would be to consider increasing the number of years required for retiring with a full pension to 45 (adjusting at the same time the formula for computing benefits and the minimum contributive pension). While the 1993 reform included a gradual increase in the number of years from 37 to 40, it fell short of the increase to 42 proposed in the *Livre Blanc*. Its potential effect is thus projected to be quite limited because more than half of workers already retire with 40 years of contributions, while the effective pen-

17. While increasing the proportion of people younger than age 65 who work could lead to a surge in output and taxes (even under the assumption of a constant share of labor in GDP) and reduced pressures on pensions, achieving this goal would require that both labor supply and demand be stimulated. In this regard, calibration of wages and working hours to ensure that the labor market clears for older workers is also likely to be required at an early stage.

Table 11.14   **Generational Accounts for Baby Boomers with Changes in Participation Rates (thousands of U.S. dollars)**

	$g = 1.5$			Historical Productivity Growth		
	$r = 3$	$r = 5$	$r = 7$	$r = 3$	$r = 5$	$r = 7$
Current generations[a]						
Males	169,306	83,277	31,092	139,180	36,903	−11,861
Females	128,755	60,740	19,073	96,718	20,517	−14,888
Average	149,031	72,009	25,083	117,949	28,710	−13,374
Future generations[b]						
Males	244,558	82,779	291	218,910	31,291	−101,547
Females	187,960	47,347	−12	168,248	17,897	4,046
Average	216,259	65,063	140	193,579	24,594	−48,751
Generational imbalance						
Males	44	−1	−99	57	−15	n.a.
Females	46	−22	n.a.	74	−13	n.a.
Average	45	−10	−99	64	−14	n.a.

Source: Authors' calculations.

Note: From 2015 onward, the participation rates for males and females aged 60–65 increase to 50 and 40 percent, respectively. g is productivity growth (percent); r is discount rate (percent).

[a]The 1950–55 cohort.

[b]Current youngsters (under 25 years of age) and all future generations.

sion for those with fewer than 32.5 years of contributions is determined by the relatively high level of the minimum pension (Briet et al. 1996). The increase in the number of years of contributions (if accompanied by an adjustment of the minimum contributive pension) would not require the abolition of the right to retire at age 60, while it would create incentives for longer careers and enhance economic activity.[18] From a fiscal point of view, the increase in the number of years should be accompanied by a change in the formula for computing benefits (i.e., the number of years of contributions used in the denominator of the formula should increase accordingly).

11.8   Conclusions

This paper has presented the first set of generational accounts for France with a view to assessing the implications for future generations, given current

18. In principle, working at increasingly older ages should become less of a burden, as intellectual work tends to be replacing repetitive manual work. It would also be compatible with more flexible working lives (admitting career switches and breaks) that have become increasingly common among skilled workers. In this context, increasing the number of years of contribution, instead of the minimum retirement age, protects those who have entered the labor force at early ages, while being fair to those who entered later. In particular, given that education in France is free, it is equitable to require from those who received more benefits to stay much longer in the labor force. In this connection, if greater wage differentiation is allowed, increasing the number of years of contribution would not need to create disincentives to accumulating human capital.

fiscal rules, of the growth in government spending and debt, taking into account the effects of demographic projections and other factors such as the anticipated change in labor force participation rates. The calculations reported in this study indicate that the present system of benefits and taxes, if continuously maintained for current adults, is out of balance in the long run from a generational perspective. The size of the standard generational imbalance implies that a lack of fiscal policy adjustment will leave future generations of French citizens facing a lifetime net tax burden that is more than one and a half times as large as those confronting current adult generations based on existing policies.

Fortunately, policies can be specified that could help alleviate such an imbalance, in particular those aimed at fostering higher employment and later retirement among cohorts aged 55–65. It is shown that an early but gradual increase to 40 percent in the labor force participation rate of people aged 60–65—combined with longer pension contribution periods—would sharply reduce the generational imbalance between young and future generations, as well as the imbalance between current adult and young generations, with a decrease in the absolute net tax burden on future generations. Moreover, a specific set of policies is presented that could help restore balance; for example, a 10 percent cut in transfer payments, a 17 percent reduction in government spending, a 7 percent increase in taxes, or some combination of these policies could, under plausible economic and demographic assumptions, bring France's generational policy into balance.

Appendix
Source and Data Construction

As explained above, average net tax payments for each generation were calculated by distributing aggregate taxes and transfers across the population of cohorts according to the age/sex profiles of payments and benefits observed. This required first an estimation of a generational profile (i.e., by individual cohorts of age and gender) of different taxes and benefits in some base year. This was done principally using 1990 data from surveys conducted by the tax administration department of the Ministry of Finance and INSEE. In a second step, the aggregate weight of each tax or benefit was computed using information in the annual national accounts published by INSEE.

Computation of Profiles

Figure 11.3 presents the age/sex profiles for the five categories of tax considered (personal income tax, property tax, wealth tax, social security tax, and consumption tax). The profiles corresponding to *personal income taxes, property taxes,* and *consumption taxes* were based primarily on data from a 1990 tax survey conducted by the Ministry of Finance (Enquête sur les Revenus Fiscaux des Ménages). INSEE provided a breakdown of the results of the 1990 survey on these taxes according to the age of the head of household surveyed, but a disaggregation by gender was necessary for the study at hand and was thus inferred from additional sources. This disaggregation is not trivial because the differences in income between men and women vary over the life cycle according to marital status, childbearing, and so forth. Therefore, in order to take these factors into account, a more detailed disaggregation of the 1984 and 1990 tax surveys (Canceill 1989; Campagne, Contenci, and Roineau 1996) and data on the number of individuals at each age living in different types of households (from the 1990 population census) were also used. Canceill (1989) provides several tables showing the average income and personal income tax payments of different types of households (persons living alone; couples without children; couples with one, two, or three children; households headed by single parents; etc.). Crossing this information with census data on the population living in different types of households (*individus selon le sexe, l'age, et le mode de vie;* INSEE 1990), guided us in disaggregating by gender the figures by household in the original survey.[19] The disaggregation of VAT, and other indirect taxes, was computed by assuming similar consumption profiles for men and women (i.e., assuming that for each age cohort, individuals of both genders pay the same amount of consumption-based taxes).

The profiles corresponding to *social security contributions* were based primarily on the distribution of wages and employment. They were estimated using the age profiles of wages computed by INSEE (Colin 1995; Perotin 1989) and the average proportion between the wages received by men and women found in Bayet (1996).[20] The average individual contribution to the social security system was then computed by adjusting the average contribution paid by employed persons to the employment rate of different age and gender cohorts estimated using data in DARES (1997).

The profile corresponding to *corporate income taxes and wealth taxes* was based on the distribution of financial assets across ages (Enquête sur le Patrimoine des Familles). This, along with the profile of other taxes related to wealth and income (*autres impôts sur le revenue et le patrimoine*), was computed using the age distribution of net wealth found in Lollivier and Verger (1996), adjusted for the distribution among genders based on figures in Sturrock (1995) and Franco et al. (1992). Following the generational accounting

19. This approximation is evidently based on a number of assumptions (e.g., in households comprising a couple headed by a man, both adults would have the same age), as well as some judgment about the tax incidence on certain populations (e.g., retired couples, which make up the majority of childless couples on which information could be found in Canceill). The overall impact of imprecisions arising from these assumptions appear to be minor.

20. Age profiles for men and women in different professions shown in Colin (1995) do not provide full coverage of the working population and thus had to be marginally adjusted according to the full-coverage profiles provided in Perotin (1989); for the same reason, the overall average men-to-women wage ratio was taken from Bayet (1996).

study by the U.S. Congressional Budget Office (Sturrock 1995), the incidence of corporate income tax was assumed to be related to the net wealth of individuals.

The profiles of individualized transfers comprising pensions, health benefits, public expenditure on education, and unemployment benefits (in addition to minimum income benefits, typically the RMI) are shown in figure 11.4. The profiles for expenditure on *education* were based on the average cost per student (in 1988) for different school ages (Ministère de l'Education Nationale 1990), attendance rates, and the assumption that these costs were the same for students of both genders. The profiles for expenditure on *health care* were computed using the chart found in Caussat and Glaude (1993) and data in Mizhari and Mizhari (1995). The profiles of expenditure on *pensions* and *unemployment benefits* were based on figures provided by INSEE.[21] The age and gender distribution of pension expenditures found there was smoothed, permitting the elimination of some outliers, especially for old and young ages. Expenditures on *minimum support income and other specific social transfers* were distributed according to the profile of unemployment benefits.[22]

Computation of the Relative Tax Weights

The assignment of the actual weights of individual taxes and benefits was based on national accounts figures (INSEE 1996) and followed closely the taxonomy perfected by French statisticians, which guarantees the internal consistency of fiscal magnitudes. General government *resources* and *emplois* (income and expenditures; see table 11.4) were taken from the national accounts yearbook *Comptes et Indicateurs Economiques* (table 10.17, *administrations publiques,* S60). They were classified as much as possible according to the group of taxes and transfers listed above, with those items that could not be assigned to any group being lumped into general government net consumption (see Hagemann and John 1995 for a rationale behind this choice of aggregation). Government expenditures on services for which beneficiaries could be identified but which are usually included in government consumption in the sense of the national accounts (e.g., payment of hospital personnel and teachers) were lumped with transfers. This breakdown of government consumption (found in the P30 line in the national accounts) and investment was computed based on figures in tables 10.07 and 10.08 of the national accounts yearbook (*ventilation fonctionelle de la consommation et de la formation brute de capi-*

---

21. The profile of unemployment benefits reflects the increase in unemployment in the years before the minimum retirement age (60 years) and before the standard retirement age (65 years). While the first peak is easy to understand, the causes of the concentration of unemployment benefits close to 65 years of age are not obvious.

22. Ideally, these should be allocated according to the distribution of the RMI. However, given the relatively small magnitude of these categories of transfers (about 0.3 percent of GDP in 1995), changing the profile from unemployment benefits to RMI is unlikely to change the results obtained thus far.

tal fixe des administration publiques). Finally, payments of pensions to government employees were lumped with pensions to private sector workers, although the contributions that fund them were left at the charge of the government and not shifted to government employees (in the case of the private sector, both employers' and employees' contributions are shifted to employees).[23]

The taxes and transfers identified in table 11.4 were grouped together in table 11A.1 to show the weight of individual taxes and transfers and of government consumption as percentages of GDP for the period 1995–2002. The aggregate taxes and transfers for 1996–2002 reflect inter alia the changes in taxation that have occurred since 1995 and the government goals for 1997–2002. In particular, it assumes a fiscal rule consistent with the government's convergence targets of a general government deficit below 3 percent after 1997. This fiscal consolidation was assumed to be achieved chiefly through a compression in net government consumption, together with a curbing of health expenditure and unemployment benefits, and a constant tax pressure, except for the gradual reduction in personal income tax included in the 1997 budget (which envisaged a reduction in income taxes totaling 0.8 percent of GDP by the year 2001).

The actual average tax payment and transfer receipts of individuals in each age cohort can then easily be computed by scaling the age and gender profiles of individual taxes and transfers such that the respective figures aggregated by cohorts are made consistent with the aggregate weight of the corresponding tax or transfer for a given year.

Computation of Generational Profiles for the 1950–55 Cohorts

To compute the past net tax burden of the 1950–55 cohort, national accounts flows covering the income and expenditures of the public administration in the 1970–95 period were distributed over individual net payment profiles based on the profiles derived for 1995. The main adjustments to these profiles comprised changes in the age distribution of health expenditure, VAT, and social security taxes (based on Mizhari and Mizhari 1995, and INSEE sources).[24] To compare the net payments of the 1950 and 1995 generations, the present value of net taxes paid by the 1950 generation was computed as of 1950 (i.e., flows in 1995 francs were discounted back to 1950) and then adjusted for productivity growth. The relative burden on each generation was computed by scaling dis-

23. This problem can be dealt with by including government pensions in government consumption, or by distributing the *contributions fictives* made by the government to itself on behalf of its employees according to the age profile of public workers.
24. Changes in the distribution of income taxes were not pursued, because for 1970 only the distribution of taxable income was available. While the distribution of taxable income does not permit an easy estimate of the distribution of taxes, owing mainly to changes in the effective marginal tax rates, it shows a clear concentration of those paying income taxes; as fewer and fewer households were subjected to the income tax over the years, those liable to any tax started to be concentrated in the cohorts of 40 to 55 years of age.

Table 11A.1   France: Medium-Term Fiscal Projection (percent of GDP)

	1995	1996	1997	1998	1999	2000	2001	2002
Personal income tax	5.3	5.3	5.0	4.8	4.7	4.6	4.5	4.5
Property taxes	0.6	0.5	0.5	0.5	0.5	0.5	0.5	0.5
Taxes related to consumption	14.6	14.8	15.0	15.0	15.0	15.0	15.0	15.0
Taxes related to individual net wealth	3.8	3.8	3.8	3.7	3.7	3.7	3.7	3.7
Social security contributions	19.3	19.3	19.3	19.2	19.2	19.2	19.2	19.2
Total taxes	43.6	43.7	43.6	43.2	43.1	43.0	42.9	42.9
Expenditure on pensions	11.6	11.6	11.5	11.5	11.5	11.5	11.5	11.5
Health care expenditure	9.0	8.9	8.8	8.8	8.7	8.6	8.5	8.5
Unemployment benefits								
Narrow sense	1.7	1.7	1.7	1.7	1.6	1.6	1.6	1.6
Large sense	2.7	2.7	2.5	2.4	2.2	2.1	2.1	2.1
Expenditure on education	5.5	5.0	5.0	5.0	5.0	5.0	5.0	5.0
Total transfers	28.8	28.2	27.8	27.7	27.4	27.2	27.1	27.1
Government consumption	16.3	16.1	15.5	15.5	15.1	14.7	14.6	14.5
Interest payments	3.5	3.5	3.3	3.2	3.2	3.2	3.2	3.2
Primary balance	-1.5	-0.6	0.3	0.0	0.6	1.1	1.2	1.3
Overall fiscal balance	-5.0	-4.1	-3.0	-3.2	-2.6	-2.1	-2.0	-1.9
Memorandum item								
Real GDP growth (%)		1.5	2.4	3.0	3.0	3.0	3.0	3.0

Source: Staff projections based on the authorities' convergence plan.

counted net taxes according to a 1.5 percent productivity growth rate and (in the "historical" case) taking into account the fluctuation of past productivity growth.

References

Auerbach, A. J., J. Gokhale, and L. J. Kotlikoff. 1991. Generational accounts: A meaningful alternative to deficit accounting. NBER Working Paper no. 3589. Cambridge, Mass.: National Bureau of Economic Research.

———. 1994. Generational accounts: A meaningful way to evaluate fiscal policy. *Journal of Economic Perspectives* 8 (1): 73–94.

Bayet, Alain. 1996. La hierarchie des salaires à temps complet est restée stable. *Les Dossiers de la DARES,* no. 1 (January).

Bos, E., M. T. Vu, E. Massiah, and R. A. Bulatao. 1994. *World population projections: Estimates and projections with related demographic statistics, 1994–95.* Baltimore: Johns Hopkins University Press.

Briet, Raoul, Catherine Zaidman, and Jean-Christophe Rubinstein. 1996. *Perspectives à long terme des retraites.* Paris: Commissariat Général du Plan.

Buiter, Willem H. 1996. Generational accounts, aggregate savings, and intergenerational distribution. IMF Working Paper no. 96/76. Washington, D.C.: International Monetary Fund.

Campagne, Nathalie, Didier Contenci, and Christelle Roineau. 1996. *Les revenus fiscaux des ménages en 1990.* Paris: Institut National de la Statistique et des Etudes Economiques.

Canceill, G. 1989. *Les revenus fiscaux des ménages en 1984.* Paris: Institut National de la Statistique et des Etudes Economiques.

Caussat, Laurent, and Michel Glaude. 1993–95. Dépenses médicales et couverture sociale. *Economie et Statistique* (INSEE), no. 265 (May).

Colin, Christel. 1995. L'éventail des salaires par profession. *Les Dossiers de la DARES,* no. 336 (March).

Dinh Quang Chi. 1994. La Population de la France à l'horizon 2050. *Economie et Statistique* (INSEE), no. 274 (April).

Direction de l'Animation de la Recherchée, des Etudes et des Statistiques (DARES). 1997. La population active devrait encore augmenter pendant une dizaine d'années, 97.02-no. 07. Paris: Direction de l'Animation de la Recherchée, des Etudes et des Statistiques.

Franco, D., J. Gokhale, L. Guiso, L. J. Kotlikoff, and N. Sartor. 1992. Generational accounting: The case of Italy. Working Paper no. 9208. Cleveland: Federal Reserve Bank of Cleveland, August.

Hagemann, R., and C. John. 1995. The fiscal stance in Sweden: A generational accounting perspective. IMF Working Paper no. 95/105. Washington, D.C.: International Monetary Fund.

Institut National de la Statistique et des Etudes Economiques (INSEE). 1990. Recensement de la population: Ménage-familles. Demographie-Société no. 22-23. Paris: Institut National de la Statistique et des Etudes Economiques.

———. 1994. *25 Ans de comptes de patrimoine.* Paris: Institut National de la Statistique et des Etudes Economiques.

———. 1996. *Comptes et indicateurs économiques: Rapport sur les comptes de la nation.* Paris: Institut National de la Statistique et des Etudes Economiques.

International Monetary Fund (IMF). 1997. France: Selected issues and statistical appendix. IMF Staff Country Report no. 97/19. Washington, D.C.: International Monetary Fund.

Kotlikoff, Laurence, J. 1992. *Generational accounting: Knowing who pays, and when, for what we spend.* New York: Free Press.

Kuné, J., W. Petit, and A. Pinxt. 1993. The hidden liabilities of the basic pensions system in the member states. Louvain-la-Neuve, Belgium: Centre for European Policy Studies.

Lenseigne, F., and P. Ricordeau. 1997. Assurance maladie: Un bilan par génération. *Economie et Statistique* (INSEE), no. 307 (July): 59–76.

Levy, J., and O. Doré. 1998. Generational accounting for France. IMF Working Paper no. 98/14. Washington, D.C.: International Monetary Fund.

Lolliver, S., and D. Verger. 1996. Patrimoine des ménages: Déterminants et disparités. *Economie et Statistique* (INSEE), no. 296-297.

Ministère de l'Education Nationale, Education et Formation. 1990. *Donnees sociales.* Paris: Institute National de la Statistique et des Etudes Economiques.

Mizhari, A., and A. Mizhari. 1995. La consommation médicale selon l'age: Effet de morbidité, effet de génération. Paris: Centre de Recherche en Economie de la Sant.

Organization for Economic Cooperation and Development (OECD). 1995. Aging populations, pension systems and government budgets: How do they affect saving? Economics Department Working Paper no. 156. Paris: Organization for Economic Cooperation and Development.

Perotin, Virginie. 1989. Le clivage des générations. In *Les Francais et leurs revenus.* Paris: Institut National de la Statistique et des Etudes Economiques.

Sturrock, John. 1995. Who pays and when? An assessment of generational accounting. Washington, D.C.: Government Printing Office.

12   Unification and Aging in Germany: Who Pays and When?

Bernd Raffelhüschen and Jan Walliser

12.1 Introduction

Germany has to deal with a double pressure on its fiscal policy that raises concerns about the sustainability of the current path of government spending. The first pressure stems from the unification of East and West Germany in 1990. Because the centrally planned eastern economy was inefficient, output in the East fell sharply after unification and a large number of workers became unemployed during the first years of transition. As a consequence, the federal government continues to transfer resources exceeding 5 percent of West German GDP to the eastern region in order to economically and socially cushion the East German transition. The second pressure stems from the sharp increase in dependency ratios, which is due to a severe aging of the population. If fertility rates continue to be low, by the year 2030 around 25 percent of the population will be age 65 or older, compared to a value of 15 percent in 1995. Consequently, the elderly dependency ratio, measured as the number of individuals aged 65 or older per number of individuals aged 18 to 64, will increase from 23 to 48 percent by the year 2030.

How will the burdens of both a dramatically increasing elderly dependency ratio and the West-East transfers be distributed among current and future generations? Will future generations be stuck with the bill? In order to illustrate the intertemporal impact of present and alternative fiscal policies, we employ the method of generational accounting developed by Auerbach, Gokhale, and Kotlikoff (1991, 1992). We show that both unification and aging will impose

Bernd Raffelhüschen is professor of economics at Albert-Ludwigs-University in Freiburg, Germany, and professor II at the University of Bergen, Norway. Jan Walliser is an economist in the Macroeconomic Analysis Division of the Congressional Budget Office.

The authors thank Daniel Besendorfer, Holger Bonin, and Christoph Borgmann for excellent research assistance. The opinions expressed in this chapter do not necessarily reflect the views of the Congressional Budget Office.

sizable burdens on future German generations if the current paths for spending and revenues are maintained. Recent legislation has increased a number of taxes and reduced social insurance benefits to help finance the costs of aging and economic transition in East Germany. But according to our findings, those measures are far from sufficient to ensure fiscal sustainability.

The paper continues in section 12.2 with a brief description of the macroeconomic performance and fiscal policy in East, West, and unified Germany during the recent past. Section 12.3 documents the data used in the analysis. Section 12.4 contains the basic findings and their sensitivity to alternative assumptions concerning the main parameters, the population projections, and the speed of adjustment of eastern Germany. In section 12.5, we explore the generational impacts of alternative fiscal policies. Finally, section 12.6 summarizes and concludes the paper.

12.2   Fiscal Policy and Macroeconomic Performance

During the 1980s, West Germany went through a period of steady though not miraculous economic expansion. Real GDP growth topped at a rate of 4 percent in 1989.[1] This long-lasting economic upswing prior to the unification of East and West Germany in 1990 allowed the Kohl administration to consolidate government finances substantially. Public expenditures fell from approximately 50 percent of GDP at the beginning of the 1980s to about 45 percent at the end of that decade. During the same period the overall public budget deficit including the deficit of the social insurance system shrank from its initial level of 3.3 percent of GDP until in 1989 the public sector realized a small surplus. As a consequence, the debt-to-GDP ratio rose more slowly after 1980 and eventually started to fall as well. All this was achieved despite a relatively high unemployment rate of 8 percent and above. Overall, West Germany seemed to be well prepared at the eve of unification since inflation was low due to a credible anti-inflationary policy; the overall public budget was balanced, tax burdens had been lowered considerably during the 1980s, and national saving rates continued to be high.

The opposite was true for the then still independent East German state. Despite the economic progress reflected in the socialist government's official statistics, problems of the Soviet-style command economy were aggravated during the 1980s. Timid and reluctantly introduced changes in the early 1980s returned some economic freedom to firms but failed to induce higher efficiency because price controls were still maintained. Similar inefficiencies arose from the fully controlled labor market with an inflexible wage structure and only minor wage differentiation. Additionally, the attempt to catch up with emerging western high-tech industries failed and the concentration of investment in

---

1. If not indicated otherwise, the statistical figures are taken from Council of Economic Advisors (Sachverständigenrat 1995, 1996).

those capital-intensive areas worsened the already severe deterioration of the eastern capital stock in other industries. Most notably, the stock of the consumer durables industry (including housing) as well as the public infrastructure suffered from general capital consumption. Moreover, significant parts of industrial capital became obsolescent because the East German economy was not subject to international competition through trade. In 1989 mounting economic and social pressure ignited political change in Eastern Europe that eventually resulted in the opening of the Berlin Wall and the first free elections in the former GDR. These events were quickly followed by economic and monetary union between the two German states, and official unification in October 1990.[2] Two stylized facts most accurately illustrate the initial economic differences between the two newly unified states. First, labor productivity as well as per capita GDP in the East amounted to only one-third of the western level. Second, the per capita endowment with industrial capital and public infrastructure corresponded to less than 50 percent of that in West Germany. Industrial capital was mostly outdated, and considerable parts of housing and public infrastructure were in bad shape. As a result, the standard of living in East Germany lagged far behind that in West Germany.

Additionally, monetary policy caused a severe adjustment shock for the eastern economy. When both countries agreed on economic, monetary, and social union in July 1990, East Germany adopted the deutsche mark and converted wages and prices at par. As a result the former state-owned firms were overloaded since eastern output prices collapsed and input costs skyrocketed. In fact, many firms did not survive, which caused a transitory drop of full-employment labor productivity to 22 percent of the western level in the beginning of 1991. One year later, both full-employment labor productivity and per capita output caught up with the preunification level. Presently, they reach about 50 percent of those in the West. Despite the economic depression, though, real wages more than doubled from about one-third of the western level in 1990 to around 70 percent of western wages in 1996.

Not surprisingly this wedge between the full-employment marginal product and the actual costs of labor induced massive unemployment. According to the official rates, registered unemployment first increased to a maximum of 15.9 percent of the civilian workforce in 1993 and has decreased slightly since then. However, the eastern numbers do not accurately reflect reality because hidden unemployment exists. If workers participating in retraining and labor creation programs, short-time employees, and early retirees were considered in addition to the officially unemployed, the 1992 unemployment rate would reach 36.7 percent. In 1996, this figure is expected to be around 23 percent. This drop in hidden unemployment can mostly be attributed to the reduced labor force participation rates of women and elderly workers as well as migration and

---

2. A more detailed analysis of the macroeconomic effects of German unification can be found in Siebert (1991), Sinn and Sinn (1992), and Raffelhüschen (1994).

Table 12.1   West-East Transfer, Additional Public Receipts, and Public Debt in
                    Transition (billions of U.S. dollars)

	1991	1992	1993	1994	1995
Net transfers					
Total	73.9	91.6	95.0	91.5	112.6
Percentage of western GDP	3.8	4.5	4.6	4.2	5.0
Total tax revenue					
Total	840.7	921.4	957.5	1,015.2	1,054.7
Percentage of total GDP	42.1	42.8	43.4	43.7	43.6
Public debt					
Total	820.9	940.7	1,055.4	1,162.3	1,394.8
Percentage of total GDP	41.1	43.7	47.8	50.1	57.7

Sources: Council of Economic Advisors (Sachverständigenrat 1995, 1996); Deutsche Bundesbank
(recent issues).

commuting to the West since the growth of East German employment has been
sluggish. During the same period, western unemployment reached a long-term
minimum at a rate of 6.6 percent in 1992, but it has risen dramatically afterward to a level of almost 10 percent.

Given that relatively generous West German social insurance programs were
extended immediately to the East in 1990 it is not surprising that seven years
after unification, unification-related burdens are still at the heart of the fiscal
debate. The assistance provided includes benefits for the unemployed, social security payments for old and early-retiring workers who never contributed to
the West German social security program, income support for employees participating in active labor market programs, welfare for the needy, and other
smaller programs. Furthermore, direct investments in public infrastructure and
private investment subsidies are part of a long-term fiscal strategy aimed at
triggering high growth in the East. Since the latter would reduce the size of
transfers and increase tax revenues, public investment and investment tax credits could be partly self-financing. Currently, however, per capita tax revenues
in the East are less than 40 percent of the western figures. Thus, for the time
being, public expenditures for East Germany must largely be financed by West
German taxpayers and through deficits.

Table 12.1 shows the overall fiscal implications of the German unification
between 1991 and 1995. During these years, net public transfers increased
from $73.9 to $112.6 billion.[3] Net transfers are predicted to stay at a level of
approximately 5 percent of western GDP in the medium-term future. As a rule
of thumb, about two-thirds of these annual transfers represent income support,
one-fourth is spent on public investment, and the remainder provides for substantial investment subsidies (Bröcker and Raffelhüschen 1997). As table 12.1
also indicates, transfers were only partly financed through increases in taxes.
In particular, most additional revenues were collected through (1) the introduc-

3. Throughout the analysis we apply the average 1995 exchange rate of DM 1.43 per dollar.

tion of an income tax surcharge in July 1992, which was suspended between July 1993 and January 1995, (2) higher value-added taxes, (3) a significant increase in receipts from gasoline and insurance taxes, and (4) higher contributions to unemployment insurance and social security. According to the official statistics, total taxes as a percentage of total GDP only rose from 42.1 percent in 1991 to 43.6 percent in 1995. Note that eastern GDP accounts for approximately 12 percent of the western figure. Although it is difficult to attribute the revenue increase to the various sources, table 12.1 indicates that unification-related tax increases account for only a small part of the required transfers. As a consequence of insufficient additional revenues, the deficits of the public sector increased sharply. Furthermore, public debt was pushed up by the debt of the former East German state and the privatization of former state-owned industrial conglomerates. Altogether, the debt-to-GDP ratio rose from 41.1 percent in 1991 to 57.7 percent in 1995.

In addition to unification-related fiscal burdens the German welfare system will suffer from a pronounced aging of the population. For more than 20 years, in both East and West, the fertility rate has been below the replacement value. Presently, the West German gross fertility rate is as low as 1.4. In the East, the number has declined even further to 0.9 after unification. Hence, according to official projections (Sommer 1994), the elderly dependency ratio—measured as the number of individuals aged 65 or older per number of individuals aged 18–64—will rise from 22.9 percent in 1995 to 47.7 percent in 2040. The aging process will have severe implications on three branches of the social security system, that is, the pension system, the health insurance system, and the recently introduced system of long-term care insurance. All of these are financed via pay-as-you-go (paygo) schemes and are fairly generous at the moment. For example, the pension system provides for a net replacement rate that exceeds 70 percent for an average production worker, and the average initial retirement age is approximately 60 years for females and slightly higher for males. If this generosity is to be maintained despite the demographic transition, payroll taxes will rise from 18.6 percent of gross income in 1995 to over 35 percent in 2035 (Boll, Raffelhüschen, and Walliser 1994, 94). Similar increases in contribution rates will be necessary for long-term care insurance and health insurance.

The German government responded to the demographic pressure in 1992 by reducing the incentives for early retirement and lowering the replacement rate for future generations. More recently, the payroll tax rate was increased to 19.2 percent in 1996 and 20.3 percent in 1997. Additionally, expenditure ceilings have been imposed on suppliers of health care. But these reforms are not sufficient to guarantee the financial sustainability of the paygo scheme.

12.3 Data Description

As outlined in chapter 2 of this volume we require (1) a population projection, (2) projections of average net taxes by age and sex, (3) an estimate of government net wealth, (4) a discount rate, and (5) a projection of government

Table 12.2   Public Receipts and Expenditures, 1995 (billions of U.S. dollars)

Receipts		Expenditures	
Labor income taxes	242.4	Social security	243.7
Capital income taxes	68.5	Health insurance	157.8
Seigniorage	4.9	Unemployment insurance	43.0
Value-added tax	164.1	Long-term care insurance	4.7
Excise taxes	23.3	Accident insurance	12.2
Gasoline tax	45.4	Maternity assistance	5.1
Insurance tax	9.9	Welfare benefits	13.0
Vehicle tax	9.7	Housing benefits	4.0
Other taxes	6.4	Youth support	17.4
Social security	185.3	Child allowances	14.4
Health insurance	115.8	Net investment	42.7
Unemployment insurance	61.8	Education (without investment)	77.6
Long-term care insurance	10.5	Subsidies	52.7
Accident insurance	13.7	Interest payments	90.7
Other revenues	64.8	Government consumption	359.2
Total	1,026.4	Total	1,138.2
Deficit	111.8		

Sources: Statistisches Bundesamt (1996a, 1996b); Ministry of Finance (Bundesministerium für Finanzen 1996); Ministry of Labor and Social Affairs (Bundesministerium für Arbeit und Sozialordnung 1996a); Commission of Federal and State Governments (Bund-Länder-Kommission 1996).

purchases. In order to correctly reflect differences in net remaining lifetime payments between the eastern and western parts of Germany we perform generational accounting separately for the two parts of Germany. This requires region-specific projections of the population and of average future tax and transfer payments.

Our demographic projection takes the 1994 population as a starting point. We then closely follow the official baseline projections of the German Bureau of the Census (Sommer 1994) up to the year 2030. In particular, the western gross fertility rate is held constant at its 1994 value of 1.39; the eastern rate linearly increases from an initial value of 0.77 to the western figure until year 2005. Holding this fertility rate constant beyond the year 2030 would result in a continuously shrinking population. Since we consider such an outcome to be unrealistic we assume that fertility rates increase linearly in both regions between 2030 and 2070 and remain stationary at their 2070 levels thereafter. This results in a stationary population of 54 million from 2120 onward. With respect to mortality, we assume in line with the official estimates that life expectancy at birth of males (females) increases from 73.2 (79.6) years in 1994 to 74.7 (81.1) years in 2000 and remains constant thereafter. Net immigration decreases from 420,000 in 1994 to 200,000 in 2010 and all following years; immigration of ethnic Germans from Eastern Europe is phased out until the year 2010.

Table 12.2 quantifies the budget of the overall public sector, that is, federal, state, and local governments, and the social insurance system. Although the numbers of our base year 1995 are drawn from official statistics, some of them are not directly comparable to published statistics due to substantial corrections for intergovernmental or interadministrative payments. Additionally, we generally attribute administrative costs and other non-insurance-related expenditures of the social insurance system to government consumption. Aggregate revenues include taxes on labor income, taxes on capital income, value-added tax, gasoline tax, insurance tax, vehicle tax, and other excise taxes, as well as seigniorage and social insurance payroll taxes.[4] Transfers include payments of the various branches of social insurance,[5] welfare benefits, and housing, child, and maternity support payments. Additionally, we calculate educational transfer spending for public kindergartens, schools, and universities. All revenue and expenditure projections take enacted and planned changes into account. In particular, our numbers reflect a 2 percentage point reduction in the solidarity surcharge tax in 1998, the removal of the wealth tax in 1997, the phasing in of long-term care insurance with concomitant reductions in general welfare spending, the increase of the social security payroll tax in 1997, and increases in retirement age after the year 2000.

Aggregate taxes and transfers are distributed by age and sex in accordance with region-specific relative age-sex profiles. These profiles are retrieved from two microdata surveys, the German Socio-Economic Panel (SOEP) and the Consumer Expenditure Survey. Furthermore, health care spending is distributed according to special health insurance data (Bundesministerium für Arbeit und Sozialordnung 1996b). Finally, education age-sex profiles are estimated from both the SOEP data and the Commission of Federal and State Governments (Bund-Länder-Kommission 1996). Except for the above-mentioned enacted adjustments in revenues and expenditures we assume that 1995 per capita taxes and transfers increase with the rate of productivity growth.

The calculation of government net wealth starts with the official debt of the public sector including all off-budget funds, which are the German Unity Fund, the Unification Debt Fund, the European Recovery Program, and publicly owned railway companies (Deutsche Bundesbank, recent issues). From the entire net financial debt of $1,394.8 billion in 1995, we attribute to East Germany $436.26 billion, which predominantly reflects unification-related special debt funds.[6]

---

4. The aggregate for labor income taxes includes taxes on wages, salary payments, and imputed labor income taxes of the self-employed. For the self-employed, the residual represents capital income taxes. Capital income taxes also include corporate taxes, local business taxes on capital, and various minor taxes on wealth and property. Excise taxes include those indirect taxes not included elsewhere and comprise tobacco taxes and a range of special taxes on commodities.

5. In 1995, the government started to phase in long-term health care insurance. Due to specific arrangements upon introduction, that social insurance realized a surplus (see table 12.2) in our base year. Starting in 1996, we assume that expenditures catch up with growth-adjusted revenues so that the system operates on a pure paygo basis.

6. The division of debt is necessary only for our calculation of hypothetical West German accounts and does therefore not affect the results for unified Germany.

In calculating government consumption we subtracted transfers, other revenues net of subsidies, net investment (without education), educational expenditures, and interest payments from the sum of total expenditures. In 1995 government spending on goods and services amounted to $359.2 billion (see table 12.2). Note that both our residual method and the exclusion of educational services and investment purchases imply that the figure is not directly comparable with the official statistics and should more accurately be labeled "non-age-specific government expenditures." Future government consumption as well as future net investment and other revenues net of subsidies are projected by assuming that per capita spending and receipts grow at a prespecified rate of economic growth after 1995.[7] All future receipts and payments are discounted to the base year 1995 using an interest rate of 5 percent in the baseline calculations, while annual productivity growth is assumed to be 1.5 percent. Those figures approximate the long-run interest rate as well as productivity growth in West Germany during the past two decades.

Capital income taxes receive special treatment since tax-favored investment implies a higher tax burden on old capital relative to new capital. Ultimately, the current owners of assets bear the burden of the tax due to the drop in the market value of old capital. We estimate this tax burden to be equal to 18.5 percent of the value of private western physical capital and impose this amount as a one-time tax on living western generations. Our calculation utilizes empirical findings on German capital taxation by Leibfritz (1993). Moreover, the flow of capital income taxes is also adjusted, since the current flow overstates the burden on future generations due to the difference between the marginal tax rate on new capital and the observable average tax rate over both old and new capital. With the tax burden of existing capital attributed to living generations, future generations are only affected by the marginal tax rate (Auerbach et al. 1991). Owing to high marginal tax rates we estimate a 36 percent downward revision of the flow of western capital income taxes.[8]

12.4   Basic Findings

12.4.1   Baseline Results

For a proper estimate of the intergenerational stance of fiscal policy in Germany we need to address the issues arising from the ongoing convergence process between the eastern and western parts. So far, the immediate adjustment

7. We assume identical per capita government consumption in East and West Germany. However, this is only of importance for our calculation of separate West German accounts.
8. We refrain from similar explicit capital income tax adjustments for the relatively small eastern capital stock. Nevertheless, since we assume that the flow of eastern capital income tax payments will adjust to western levels in the future, they include a correction for the difference between marginal and average tax rates, as for the West. Overall, the adjustments happen to have only minor effects on the results in the German case.

of East German social entitlements to western standards stands in sharp contrast to the slow economic catching-up process. As outlined above, eastern residents' per capita taxes are currently lower than in the West, whereas a number of transfers, specifically unemployment benefits and female social security benefits, exceed western levels on a per capita basis. Upon successful transformation, they may eventually converge toward western levels as eastern per capita income and consumption expenditures approach those of western residents. Whether and when this will occur is uncertain.

As a reference point, we assume full convergence by the year 2010; that is, eastern tax payments and transfer receipts are assumed to increase or decrease uniformly such that equality with western per capita values is achieved within a period of 15 years. This optimistic viewpoint, which is in line with the results by Burda and Funke (1995) and Bröcker and Raffelhüschen (1997), will be subject to further sensitivity analysis. In accordance with recent legislation, the surcharge of 7.5 percent on income tax owed is reduced by 2 percentage points in 1998 and removed after the year 2010 in the baseline simulations because the surcharge was originally intended to be eliminated upon completion of the transition.

Panel A of table 12.3 reports the generational accounts for cohorts between ages 0 and 90 in the base year 1995. Moreover, it shows the future net payments of representative male and female German generations under baseline assumptions. All columns reveal a typical life cycle pattern; that is, young generations face positive net payments to the government over their remaining life cycle while older generations are net recipients. In particular, currently newborn individuals pay $97,100. Due to both negative net payments during childhood and the discounting of future tax payments, the accounts first increase with age. They reach a maximum value of $313,600 at age 20 when the cohort enters the labor force and decrease over the years of active labor market participation. At age 50, accounts turn negative since the present value of gross payments falls short of the present value of benefits received over the remaining life cycle. As individuals approach retirement, the relative weight of future pensions and old-age services increases and the generational accounts further decrease until they reach a minimum at age 65. At this age, the remaining future benefits net of tax payments amount to $206,700. Clearly, with higher ages, the negative values decrease due to a decrease of the remaining life span.

As also shown in table 12.3, the future age-specific net payments of male and female agents display a similar life cycle pattern as those for men and women combined. However, due to both a comparatively low labor force participation rate and substantial gender-specific redistribution via all branches of the social insurance system, female net payments are at most half of the respective male net payments while the accounts during old age range only slightly below those of males.

Future generations are left with a growth-adjusted payment of $248,800, which exceeds the payment of current newborns by 156.1 percent if our (fairly

Table 12.3   **Generational Accounts of Current and Future Generations (thousands of U.S. dollars)**

Generation's Age in 1995	Average	Male	Female
A. Baseline			
0	97.1	155.2	36.0
5	123.6	190.3	53.6
10	179.0	257.8	95.9
15	252.2	345.8	153.3
20	313.6	422.4	199.3
25	303.4	416.4	181.8
30	271.8	382.9	151.1
35	224.4	318.4	124.0
40	160.1	234.4	82.8
45	94.0	147.4	38.5
50	−4.2	26.3	−35.4
55	−98.9	−96.3	−101.5
60	−183.6	−212.4	−155.5
65	−206.7	−245.8	−171.9
70	−180.7	−216.0	−160.3
75	−150.2	−178.4	−136.0
80	−109.6	−133.6	−99.3
85	−68.0	−86.2	−61.6
90	−3.2	−10.8	−0.8
Future generations	248.8	397.9	92.3
Percentage difference	156.1	156.4	156.4
B. Baseline, Education Included in Government Consumption			
0	165.0	224.3	102.5
5	194.3	262.4	122.8
10	233.8	314.2	149.0
15	287.9	383.2	187.4
20	333.6	445.1	216.5
25	309.7	425.1	185.5
30	271.8	383.0	151.2
35	224.4	318.4	124.0
40	160.1	234.4	82.8
45	94.0	147.4	38.5
50	−4.2	26.3	−35.4
55	−98.9	−96.3	−101.5
60	−183.6	−212.4	−155.5
65	−206.7	−245.8	−171.9
70	−180.7	−216.0	−160.3
75	−150.2	−178.4	−136.0
80	−109.6	−133.6	−99.3
85	−68.0	−86.2	−61.6
90	−3.2	−10.8	−0.8
Future generations	316.8	430.9	197.0
Percentage difference	92.0	92.2	92.2

optimistic) baseline representation of German fiscal policy is correct. Despite the increases in revenues related to unification (see table 12.1), there is, in fact, a severe generational imbalance to the disadvantage of future generations. The imbalance can alternatively be expressed as the ratio of present value of net tax payments to present value of lifetime labor income. According to our findings, current newborns' net tax payments will account for 21.3 percent of their lifetime labor income. The respective gender-specific rates are 24.9 and 12.9 percent for males and females. Future generations will face a 156 percent higher burden, which translates into a net lifetime tax rate of 54.5 percent.

Panel B of table 12.3 shows the generational accounts under the assumption that educational expenditures are not distributed to the respective age groups but included in government consumption. Earlier studies built on this approach due to the lack of appropriate data, so we report the corresponding results in order to make our findings comparable to earlier results (see Gokhale, Raffelhüschen, and Walliser 1995). Including education in government consumption increases the present value of net payments of newborn and future generations by the same amount. This is due to the fact that the present value of future government consumption increases by the same amount as the sum of net taxes paid by currently living generations when education is no longer treated as a transfer. The described change in accounting methodology reduces the generational imbalance to 92.0 percent. Note that educational transfers are only geared toward agents below age 30. Thus the generational accounts of older agents are unchanged. Without accounting for educational transfers net tax rates of current newborn and future generations are, of course, significantly higher. In particular, those born in the base year will face a rate of 36.3 percent, while future generations will experience a rate of nearly 70 percent.

Table 12.4 decomposes generational accounts into the specific tax payments and transfer receipts. All components add up to the net payments found in the "average" column in panel A of table 12.3. Note that progressive labor income taxes and the proportional contributions to all social insurance tend to be concentrated on agents, predominantly males, between ages 25 and 65. Other taxes, specifically value-added taxes and excise taxes, are much more equally spread over the life cycle. Social security benefits on the other hand are paid mostly after age 60, and health insurance benefits also are larger for retirees. In contrast, unemployment benefits are targeted toward working-age agents, and general welfare payments support poor families, especially with children, as well as the elderly poor. Youth and maternity assistance are clearly most prominent at childbearing ages and below. The "education" column in table 12.4 reveals the important impact of the assumptions concerning the treatment of educational expenditures. Including education in government consumption would allocate the benefits more or less equally over the cohorts while, in fact, the incidence falls heavily on the young.

Which factors contribute to the intergenerational imbalance? To some extent

Table 12.4   **Composition of Generational Accounts: Present Value of Payments and Receipts (thousands of U.S. dollars)**

	Tax Payments					
Generation's Age in 1995	Labor Income Taxes	Capital Income Taxes	Seigniorage	Value-Added Tax	Excise Taxes and Others	Social Insurance
0	69.6	11.9	1.3	65.8	26.0	115.7
5	79.4	13.6	1.5	65.2	29.6	132.0
10	93.3	15.8	1.8	66.7	34.5	154.8
15	108.5	28.7	2.1	67.9	39.8	180.6
20	125.2	34.6	2.1	69.7	44.6	205.7
25	123.5	29.1	1.9	64.5	41.4	198.1
30	113.9	30.0	1.9	60.2	37.8	183.5
35	102.0	31.3	1.8	57.8	33.9	164.1
40	85.4	30.5	1.7	55.0	29.5	138.8
45	66.9	38.7	1.5	51.6	25.4	109.5
50	42.8	30.0	1.3	46.1	20.9	75.5
55	20.2	25.8	1.1	39.8	16.6	41.0
60	5.9	21.6	0.9	33.6	12.7	12.5
65	0.7	18.5	0.8	27.4	9.4	1.5
70	0	18.5	0.6	21.4	6.7	0.1
75	0	16.2	0.5	15.5	4.6	0
80	0	16.7	0.4	10.9	3.1	0
85	0	14.6	0.2	6.5	1.8	0
90	0	14.9	0.1	1.5	0.4	0

	Transfer Receipts					
Generation's Age in 1995	Social Security and Accident Insurance	Health Insurance	Unemployment Insurance	General Welfare	Youth and Maternity	Education
0	34.5	47.0	8.4	7.6	27.9	67.8
5	39.1	46.1	9.5	6.5	25.8	70.7
10	46.0	49.7	11.3	5.8	20.2	54.8
15	53.9	53.6	13.9	5.2	13.1	35.8
20	63.6	57.5	16.5	5.0	5.8	20.0
25	69.5	56.8	14.6	4.5	3.3	6.3
30	79.2	57.5	13.1	4.1	1.4	0.1
35	92.1	59.2	11.2	3.8	0.5	0
40	106.8	60.8	9.5	3.6	0.1	0
45	124.9	62.8	8.4	3.4	0	0
50	146.2	64.0	7.2	3.5	0	0
55	170.0	64.7	5.0	3.7	0	0
60	199.1	65.7	2.1	3.9	0	0
65	195.6	65.5	0	3.9	0	0
70	161.1	62.9	0	4.1	0	0
75	126.5	57.1	0	3.5	0	0
80	90.0	47.9	0	2.7	0	0
85	55.6	33.9	0	1.8	0	0
90	13.1	6.6	0	0.4	0	0

Note: Productivity growth assumed to be 1.5 percent; discount rate, 5 percent.

Table 12.5   **Four Alternative Ways to Restore Generational Balance (difference from base-year revenues/expenditures)**

Option	Change (%)
Increase in income tax revenues	29.5
Cut in government purchases	25.9
Cut in transfer payments	14.1
Increase in all tax revenues	9.5

the imbalance is due to the base-year financial debt of $1,394.8 billion. Assuming that there were no debt at all in the baseline scenario, the imbalance would decrease. However, future generations would still pay 80.6 percent more than newborns. The major source of generational imbalance in Germany stems from the severe aging process. Without demographic change, that is, if the population structure remained constant at the 1995 proportions, future generations would pay 7.6 percent less than current newborns. The figures for these calculations including education in government consumption are 47.5 for the no-debt scenario and -4.7 percent for the scenario without any demographic change.

As an additional way of indicating the generational imbalance we consider alternative tax or transfer policies that ensure equal burdens on current newborns and future generations. Table 12.5 summarizes specific tax revenue increases or transfer reductions as percentages of base-year revenues or expenditures necessary to restore generational balance. In Germany, an immediate and perpetual increase of 29.5 percent of the income tax or an overall tax increase of 9.5 percent would eliminate the imbalance. This finding implies that income tax revenues must be increased from 12.9 percent of GDP to 16.7 percent of GDP in order to eliminate the burden. Alternatively, increasing total tax revenues from 39.8 percent of GDP to 43.6 percent of GDP would suffice. An equal burden could also be achieved by cutting all transfer payments by 14.1 percent or cutting government purchases by 25.9 percent. Those cuts represent 4.0 and 4.2 percent of GDP, respectively. The policy options for restoring generational balance under the assumption that education is included in government consumption display identical results. Although it is unclear which policy or policy combination is most appropriate, it is important to note that the alternative options differ significantly with respect to the time path of budget deficits and surpluses as well as intragenerational redistribution between currently living males and females.

12.4.2 The Burden of Unification for Western Residents

As outlined above, the German unification imposed not only a burden on future generations but also on presently living western residents through various unification-induced tax increments. To illustrate how the burden of unification is distributed among western residents, we calculate hypothetical generational accounts for the West under a scenario where no unification-related tax or contribution increases are imposed on western residents.[9] Moreover, in this scenario government spending on goods and services excludes spending on the eastern region. The "without taxes" columns in table 12.6 show the net payment burdens for western residents under baseline assumptions but without unification-related tax hikes. The table also exhibits the generational accounts of western residents including these tax payments as well as the differences between the two cases. The age- and gender-specific differences indicate the changes in western net payments due to unification. Western residents of all ages will share in the burden of unification, but the burdens on those aged 55 or younger are especially large. On average, the percentage increase in burden of male and female retirees is only one-tenth of the respective figure for western residents aged 55 or younger. It is clear from table 12.6 that in comparison to males, females contribute generally less in absolute but always significantly more in relative terms.

The reason for this distribution of the additional burden is straightforward. Most of the additional net payment burdens arise from proportional social insurance taxes and indirect taxes for both male and female western generations, while revenues from the progressive solidarity surcharge tax range third. Moreover, the surcharge will be phased out by 2010, which lowers its impact on future direct tax burdens. Indirect tax payments are much more evenly spread over the life cycle and the two sexes. Therefore, the additional tax load of the elderly is almost entirely paid via indirect taxes. To conclude, contributors to social insurance and females contribute more than proportionally to the burden of unification if the preunification tax system serves as a reference.

Our calculations show two effects of unification on the intertemporal redistribution: If we exclude East Germany and all unification-related taxes as defined earlier, the resulting intergenerational redistribution in West Germany would be 229 percent, which is *larger* than the intergenerational redistribution in unified Germany. However, had West Germany raised unification-related taxes without having to finance unification, redistribution would only be 81 percent. This implies that (a) perpetually raising unification-related taxes finances more than the transition of the East, assuming that the transition is completed in year 2010; and (b) taking the tax hikes after unification as given, the additional burden of financing the East German transition is about as large as total current debt; that is, if debt were zero the burden of future generations in unified Germany would be approximately as large as the burden of future western residents without unification. Note, however, that this does *not* imply 50 percent of the current imbalance should be attributed to unification since unification caused both higher spending and higher revenues and these effects cannot be separated.

---

9. The method of decomposing generational accounts with respect to residence was first employed by Gokhale et al. (1995).

Table 12.6   **Burden of Unification on Western Residents**

Generation's Age in 1995	Male Net Payments				Female Net Payments			
	Without Taxes	With Taxes	Male Burden	Percentage Increase[a]	Without Taxes	With Taxes	Female Burden	Percentage Increase[a]
0	133.6	155.5	21.9	14.1	21.9	36.9	15.0	40.7
5	170.3	195.4	25.1	12.9	39.2	56.3	17.1	30.4
10	273.3	267.1	29.8	11.2	80.6	100.8	20.2	20.0
15	331.7	367.4	35.7	9.7	145.2	168.9	23.7	14.0
20	404.9	446.5	41.6	9.3	189.8	216.4	26.6	12.3
25	397.2	438.2	41.0	9.4	169.0	193.5	24.5	12.7
30	370.6	409.8	39.2	9.6	139.4	161.7	22.3	13.8
35	312.4	349.0	36.6	10.5	115.4	136.2	20.8	15.3
40	234.6	267.2	32.6	12.2	78.1	96.8	18.7	19.3
45	150.4	177.8	27.4	15.4	36.9	52.5	15.6	29.7
50	33.3	54.2	20.9	38.6	−35.1	−23.3	11.8	50.6
55	−91.4	−78.0	13.4	17.2	−95.6	−87.4	8.2	9.4
60	−215.5	−208.6	6.9	3.3	−145.0	−139.6	5.4	3.9
65	−247.0	−243.4	3.6	1.5	−160.4	−156.6	3.8	2.4
70	−215.1	−212.7	2.4	1.1	−151.6	−148.9	2.7	1.8
75	−177.4	−175.8	1.6	0.9	−128.3	−126.3	2.0	1.6
80	−132.6	−131.5	1.1	0.8	−91.7	−90.3	1.4	1.6
85	−84.6	−83.8	0.8	1.0	−55.1	−54.3	0.8	1.5
90	−8.3	−8.1	0.2	2.8	3.1	3.3	0.2	6.1

Note: Productivity growth assumed to be 1.5 percent; discount rate, 5 percent.

[a]Refers to increase in burden or decrease in receipts relative to the level without taxes.

12.4.3   Sensitivity Analysis

Table 12.7 summarizes the sensitivity of our results with respect to variations in (1) the key parameters, (2) the underlying population projection, and (3) prolonged adjustment paths for East Germany. The top panel of the table reports percentage differences between newborn and future generations' net payments for alternative interest rate (3, 5, and 7 percent) and growth rate (1, 1.5, and 2 percent) combinations. The imbalance is strictly increasing with lower growth rates and higher interest rates. Differentials span a wide range from 79.3 to 563.4 percent. Apparently, the percentage difference is quite sensitive to parameter variations, while the qualitative result that postunification fiscal policy in Germany is imbalanced is sustained for a realistic range of growth and discount rates. The sensitivity to parameter variations for the results when education is included in government consumption (not shown) is lower but leads to similar conclusions.

Table 12.7 also reports the intergenerational stance of fiscal policy for alternative population projections. As it turns out, the results are not very sensitive to the baseline assumption of increasing fertility rates after the year 2030. If we assume a constant low fertility rate corresponding to the 1994 level of West Germans up to the year 2200, the generational imbalance increases to 161.4 percent at baseline parameter values. However, our results depend on the speed of convergence between East and West Germany. Clearly, the imbalance will increase if the eastern economy does not completely catch up by the year 2010—not surprisingly, given the high transfer level as well as the small tax base in the eastern region. Table 12.7 indicates the quantitative impacts of more pessimistic assumptions concerning the adjustment process. Specifically, if the adjustment process were completed by 2020 instead of 2010 the burden of future generations would increase to 170.2 percent. An adjustment lasting until 2030 causes an imbalance of 181.8 percent. A higher speed of convergence thus significantly reduces the burden of future generations.

12.5   Unification- and Aging-Related Policies

As mentioned above, the Kohl administration has already decided on a partial phase-out of the solidarity surcharge tax, that is, a reduction from 7.5 to 5.5 percent by January 1998. According to initial intentions, the income tax surcharge should last as long as it is "deemed necessary" for facilitating the process of adjustment, and this is exactly what we assumed in the baseline scenario. Nevertheless, a range of possibilities with regard to its adoption and longevity are under discussion. We explore the consequences of the income tax surcharge by examining the results of (a) fully eliminating the surcharge "prematurely" in the year 2000 and (b) maintaining it at a rate of 5.5 percent for all future years. In each case, the transition is assumed to last until 2010.

Table 12.8 shows the changes in net payment burdens from the two

Table 12.7   Sensitivity Analysis: Generational Imbalance between Current and Future Generations (percent)

	g = 1			g = 1.5			g = 2		
	r = 3	r = 5	r = 7	r = 3	r = 5	r = 7	r = 3	r = 5	r = 7
Generational imbalance	101.9	188.3	563.4	89.9	156.1	387.5	79.3	132.6	288.0

		Population Projection			
	Constant Population Structure	Baseline Assumptions	Constant Fertility (1994)	Year East Catches Up	
				2010	2020	2030
Generational imbalance	−7.6	156.1	161.4	156.1	170.2	181.8

Note: g is productivity growth (percent); r is discount rate (percent).

Table 12.8   Generational Accounts for Alternative Surcharge Tax Scenarios and Partial Funding of Social Insurance (thousands of U.S. dollars)

Generation's Age in 1995	Surcharge until 2000	Baseline	Surcharge Maintained	Partial Funding
0	97.1	97.1	101.0	125.2
5	123.5	123.6	127.9	155.7
10	178.3	179.0	183.4	216.7
15	250.7	252.2	256.4	296.5
20	311.6	313.6	317.4	364.5
25	301.3	303.4	306.6	352.7
30	269.5	271.8	274.2	317.5
35	222.0	224.4	226.0	265.4
40	158.0	160.1	161.0	195.0
45	92.3	94.0	94.3	121.6
50	−5.1	−4.2	−4.1	14.9
55	−99.2	−98.9	−98.8	−88.5
60	−183.7	−183.6	−183.5	−180.6
65	−206.8	−206.7	−206.7	−206.7
70	−180.8	−180.7	−180.7	−180.7
75	−150.3	−150.2	−150.2	−150.2
80	−109.6	−109.6	−109.6	−109.6
85	−68.1	−68.0	−68.0	−68.0
90	−3.2	−3.2	−3.2	−3.2
Future generations	253.8	248.8	241.4	130.8
Percentage difference	161.3	156.1	139.0	4.5

experiments relative to the baseline. Fully eliminating the surcharge in the year 2000 reduces net payments of basically all cohorts. This implies a 5.2 percentage point larger burden of future generations compared to the baseline. In contrast, permanently maintaining the surcharge imposes losses on living generations amounting, for example, to $2,400 for 30-year-old agents. However, this policy would reduce the generational imbalance of current German fiscal policy in our baseline scenario from 156.1 to 139.0 percent.

As far as the demographic pressure on the paygo-financed social insurance system is concerned, the recent debate about aging-related problems concentrates on imposing a ceiling for future increases of the contribution rate. However, the discussion is dominated by rather ad hoc fixed upper limits for supposedly sustainable rates. We therefore calculate contribution rates for social security, health insurance, and long-term care insurance that equally distribute the implicit demographic burden of social insurance among living and future generations.[10] Assuming that federal subsidies as well as transfers from unemployment insurance stay fixed, we find that payroll taxes for social security and health and long-term care insurance need to be raised perpetually by 40.2 and 31.8 percent, respectively. This implies a social security payroll tax rate of 26.1

10. For a similar exercise for social security only, see Boll et al. (1994).

instead of 18.6 percent in the base year and all future years, a health insurance payroll tax rate of 17.3 instead of 13.1 percent, and a payroll tax rate of 2.24 percent for the new long-term care insurance.[11] In the first decades, annual surpluses will arise and social insurance schemes will operate as partially funded systems. When the demographic burden becomes aggravated, those funds are sufficient to partially finance the occurring deficits up to the year 2200.

The funding strategy will have significant effects on the net payments of presently living agents. As shown in the last column of table 12.8, net payments of newborns increase by $28,100 in present value. A 25-year-old faces a tax bill of $352,700, an increase of $49,300 over the baseline. Equalizing the implicit intergenerational burden of the social insurance system through partial funding also virtually eliminates the imbalance between living and future generations if total government spending is considered. This result underscores how important the implicit liabilities of the welfare system are for understanding the sources of intergenerational imbalances in German fiscal policy. It also shows that options other than tax increases might have to be considered if raising social security and health insurance payroll tax rates once and for all to 26 and 17 percent, respectively, appears to be politically and economically infeasible.

12.6 Conclusions

This paper applies generational accounting to unified Germany. Our findings indicate that the current fiscal policy is severely imbalanced from an intergenerational point of view. Future generations are projected to pay 156.1 percent more in net lifetime taxes than newborns in 1995, and the imbalance increases substantially if the adjustment process in East Germany lasts longer than expected in the baseline calculations. We also illustrate how fiscal balance can be restored. Intergenerational balance and thereby a sustainable fiscal policy can be achieved by (1) a 29.5 percent increase of income tax revenues, (2) a 9.5 percent increase of all taxes, (3) a reduction of all transfer payments by 14.1 percent, or (4) a reduction of government purchases in the magnitude of roughly one-fourth. However, since each policy has different implications for intragenerational equity the choice of the appropriate combination of measures is up to the politicians.

The generational imbalance is due to the demographic change induced by one of the world's lowest fertility rates. It is only partly due to government debt, of which approximately one-third is related to the East German transition toward a market economy. In addition to purely intergenerational issues, we quantify the distribution of unification-related tax increases among generations

---

11. It should be noted that all these results are very optimistic since they assume that per capita medical expenditures grow with the level of productivity. In the United States, e.g., medical expenditures are projected to grow much faster than productivity.

in West Germany. We find that unification imposes sizable burdens on future generations but also on young western males and females. The paper finally illustrates the intergenerational impacts of some of the most recent unification- and aging-related policies. From an intergenerational point of view, an early elimination of the income tax surcharge alone would lead to a small increase in the burden of future generations. Moreover, we demonstrate the effects of a partial funding strategy for public health insurance and social security. While balancing intergenerational burdens, this policy would require accumulation of capital over the next two to three decades through a once and for all increase in contribution rates of approximately 13 percent of taxable income.

Continuing on the current spending path without adjusting taxes and transfers may cause an exponential increase in the burden of future generations over time. In fact, if another 20 years pass with no changes in policy that address the current imbalance, generations born 20 years from now will already face a 496.6 percent higher lifetime tax burden than newborns.

References

Auerbach, A. J., J. Gokhale, and L. J. Kotlikoff. 1991. Generational accounts: A meaningful alternative to deficit accounting. In *Tax policy and the economy,* vol. 5, ed. D. Bradford, 55–110. Cambridge, Mass.: MIT Press.

———. 1992. Generational accounting: A new approach for understanding the effects of fiscal policy on saving. *Scandinavian Journal of Economics* 94:303–18.

Boll, S., B. Raffelhüschen, and J. Walliser. 1994. Social security and intergenerational redistribution: A generational accounting perspective. *Public Choice* 81:79–100.

Bröcker, J., and B. Raffelhüschen. 1997. Fiscal aspects of German unification: Who is stuck with the bill? *Applied Economics Quarterly* 45:139–62.

Bundesministerium für Arbeit und Sozialordnung. 1996a. *Arbeits- und Sozialstatistik: Hauptergebnisse.* Bonn: Bundesministerium für Arbeit und Sozialordnung.

———. 1996b. *Bundesarbeitsblatt 9/1996.* Bonn: Bundesministerium für Arbeit und Sozialordnung.

Bundesministerium für Finanzen. 1996. *Finanzbericht 1997.* Bonn: Bundesministerium für Finanzen.

Bund-Länder-Kommission für Bildungsplanung und Forschungsförderung. 1996. *Ausgaben der Gebietskörperschaften für Bildung und Wissenschaft in den Jahren 1993 (ist), 1994 und 1995 (soll).* Bonn: Bund-Länder-Kommission für Bildungsplanung und Forschungsförderung.

Burda, M., and M. Funke. 1995. Eastern Germany: Can't we be more optimistic? *IFO-Studien* 41:327–54.

Deutsche Bundesbank. Recent issues. *Monatsbericht der Deutschen Bundesbank.* Frankfurt a.M.

Gokhale, J., B. Raffelhüschen, and J. Walliser. 1995. The burden of German unification: A generational accounting approach. *Finanzarchiv* 52:141–65.

Leibfritz, W. 1993. Germany. In *Tax reform and the cost of capital: An international comparison,* ed. D. W. Jorgenson and R. Landau, 166–90. Washington, D.C.: Brookings Institution.

Raffelhüschen, B. 1994. Migration in Germany after unification. Kiel: University of Kiel. Mimeograph.

Sachverständigenrat zur Begutachtung der gesamtwirtschaftlichen Entwicklung. 1995. *Im Standortwettbewerb, Jahresgutachten 1995/96.* Stuttgart: Poeschel.

———. 1996. *Reformen voranbringen, Jahresgutachten 1996/97.* Stuttgart: Poeschel.

Siebert, H. 1991. German unification: The economics of transition. *Economic Policy* 2:287–340.

Sinn, G., and H.-W. Sinn. 1992. *Jumpstart: The economic unification of Germany.* Cambridge, Mass.: MIT Press.

Sommer, B. 1994. Entwicklung der Bevölkerung bis 2040: Ergebnis der achten koordinierten Bevölkerungsvorausberechnung. *Wirtschaft und Statistik,* no. 7: 497–503.

Statistisches Bundesamt. 1996a. *Statistisches Jahrbuch.* Stuttgart: Poeschel.

———. 1996b. *Volkswirtschaftliche Gesamtrechnungen.* Fachserie 18, Reihe 1.3, *Hauptbericht.* Stuttgart: Poeschel.

13   Generational Accounts for Italy

Nicola Sartor

13.1   Introduction and Summary

Among industrialized countries, Italy represents one of the most interesting cases for applying the generational accounting methodology. The Italian economy is characterized by one of the world's largest public debts, a very generous pension system, and the world's lowest fertility rate. These three features produce effects on public finances that reinforce themselves in the long run.

Since the 1980s, stabilization of the ratio of public debt to GDP has represented the main fiscal policy target. According to official figures, the target was reached in 1995. However, conventional debt and deficit measures, by focusing on the very short run, ignore the pressures that the current demographic transition is placing on the budget. Because the elderly dependency ratio will increase by 50 percent in the next 20 years, public expenditures on health and pensions will increase substantially; at the same time, revenues will decrease insofar as an increasing fraction of the population will be retired. By taking the current demographic transition into account, generational accounting analysis shows that the debt outlook differs substantially from the picture obtained from conventional approaches. It is shown that most of the imbalance in current Italian fiscal policy has nothing to do with officially labeled government debt and that fiscal consolidation in excess of what is needed for achieving short-term debt stabilization is required. When considering the future increase in per capita net taxes required to keep public debt on a stable path, a severe intergenerational imbalance against future generations emerges. However, a substantial fraction of it will be removed by the long-run effects of the pension reform enacted in 1995.

Nicola Sartor is professor of public finance at the University of Verona, Italy.

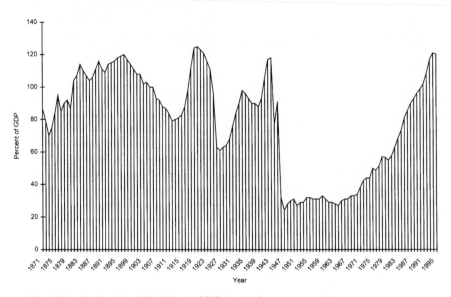

Fig. 13.1   Ratio of public debt to GDP (central government)
Sources: Ministero del Tesoro (1988) and Banca d'Italia, *Relazione Annuale* (various years).

13.2   Public Debt in a Historical Perspective

The existence of a large stock of financial liabilities issued by the public sector is a distinctive feature of Italian economic history. On three occasions (1897, 1920, and 1943) the relative size of debt reached peaks whose orders of magnitude were close to current values (around 120 percent of GDP; see fig. 13.1). Over the years, public debt averaged 90 percent of GDP, with the exception of the 25-year spell of high economic growth and financial stability that followed the Second World War. From a bird's-eye view, the years between 1946 and 1971 appear to be a favorable exception to the historical pattern, as the debt-to-GDP ratio was virtually constant at around 30 percent.

The Italian state, founded in 1861, was burdened from the very beginning by a large debt: its origin goes back to the parliamentary decision to take responsibility for the financial liabilities issued by the previous states,[1] which totaled 45 percent of GDP. The incidence of debt doubled in the following 10 years, as a consequence of the large burst in military spending needed to gain the eastern territories of the nation (Veneto) from Austria. In 1870, when the

1. The decision was shared by the majority and opposition parties. As pointed out by Zamagni (1992), the hypothesis of repudiating the debt issued by the various states previously based on Italian territory was rejected in order to preserve the creditworthiness of the Italian economy in European financial markets. The relevance of Italian standing in the international financial community, in turn, reflected the structural need for foreign savings, aimed at financing economic development. At the same time, oblivion of the previous states was obtained by converting the various debt instruments into a new Italian public debt. Following the experience of the French revolution, the converted debt was accounted for in the "Great Book of Public Debt."

process of creating the new nation ended, the magnitude of public debt was close to the value of the domestic product (96 percent).

While the government's current target of putting financial liabilities on a declining path has not yet been fully achieved, past experience shows that on three occasions the relative size of the Italian debt declined substantially (fig. 13.1). A common feature of all the episodes of debt absorption is the positive role played by economic growth,[2] reinforced by partial debt repudiation in two out of three cases. In the 1898–1912 period, a moderate but steady income growth rate was the major source of stabilization, supplemented by fiscal consolidation in some years. The first (voluntary) repudiation occurred under dictatorship. It took the form of debt consolidation[3] and strengthened the effects of prolonged fiscal discipline during the 1921–27 period. Debt monetization was the form the second (involuntary)[4] repudiation took in the years following the Second World War. In only four years, an average inflation rate above 100 percent per year reduced the 118 percent debt-to-GDP ratio, which had peaked in 1943, to a quarter of its previous level.

From the foundation of the Italian republic (1948) to the end of the sixties, the relative size of public debt fluctuated around 30 percent. A distinctive feature of this period of stability is the favorable macroeconomic conditions summarized in figure 13.2 by a positive real interest rate, which was, however, always lower than the rate of output growth.[5] Under these circumstances, the government could even run "an honest Ponzi game" (Buiter 1985) by financing interest payments through new debt issues. Starting in 1964, the government not only followed the above fiscal rule but even ran a primary deficit (fig. 13.3). Up to the end of the seventies, the rise in public debt was moderate, due to the

2. For a detailed account of past debt policy, see Toniolo and Ganugi (1992) and Zamagni (1992).

3. In 1926, mandatory conversion of public liabilities followed the failure of the voluntary conversion offered two years before. Outstanding debt was converted into consols, yielding a 5 percent coupon. Eight years later, the consols were converted into 25-year bonds, yielding a 3.5 interest rate. The decline of the debt-to-GDP ratio would be larger than it appears in fig. 13.1 if public debt were evaluated at market value. According to Alesina (1991), after the two conversions debt holders suffered an overall loss estimated to be over 50 percent of face value. As a consequence of the loss of reputation, the Treasury faced increasing difficulty in issuing new debt during the next 15 years.

4. According to the interpretation proposed by Toniolo and Ganugi (1992, 137), hyperinflation was initially tolerated by the government, which tightened monetary policy after some delay.

5. The data shown in fig. 13.2 have to be considered with some caution. Due to lack of information, the interest rate refers to the effective ex post rate relative to medium- and long-term bonds (*buoni del tesoro poliennali*) and not to the average interest rate paid on government debt. During some years, the former may not reflect overall financial conditions, as financial markets were not fully developed.

Note that the excess of the growth rate over the interest rate need not imply dynamic inefficiency. As shown by Abel et al. (1989), in a multisector stochastic economy the interest rate on government bonds need not be equal to the marginal product of capital. Under an alternative test, based on the comparison between cash flows generated by capital and the level of investment, the authors dismiss the dynamic inefficiency hypothesis for Italy as well as the remaining G-7 countries in the 1960–84 period.

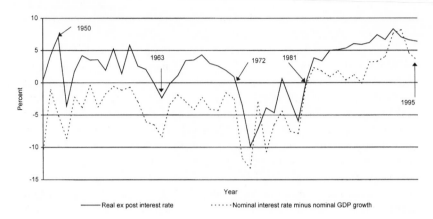

Fig. 13.2   Interest rate on medium-term government bonds
Sources: Ministero del Tesoro (1988) and Banca d'Italia, *Bollettino Statistico* (various years).

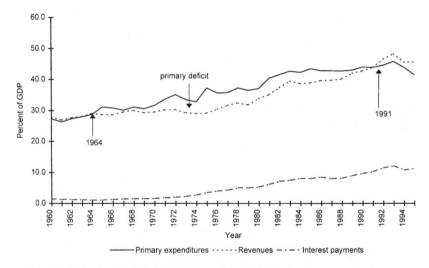

Fig. 13.3   General government revenues and outlays
Sources: Morcaldo (1993) and Banca d'Italia, *Relazione Annuale* (various years).

accommodative stance of monetary policy. Figure 13.2 highlights this situation by showing the persistence of output growth in excess of the interest rate, and also a negative ex post real interest rate over the 1973–80 period.

At the beginning of the eighties monetary policy changed course, following the restrictive stance originating in the United States. The sharp increase in interest rates, which appeared to exceed output growth for the first time in the history of the Italian republic (fig. 13.2), put public debt on a path that would be unsustainable in the long run. The need for a change in budgetary policy was clearly perceived by the prime minister, who in 1985 proposed the first financial plan to reverse debt dynamics.[6] Unfortunately, belief in the need for fiscal tightening was shared neither by all ministers nor by the Parliament.

Two main reasons may be cited to explain the lack of willingness to undergo fiscal discipline. The first is the absence of any macroeconomic sign of financial instability. The frequent calls for fiscal tightening, requested by the central bank and by international organizations such as the International Monetary Fund and the Organization for Economic Cooperation and Development (OECD), appeared to the political body to address a theoretical need not founded on any tangible phenomenon. The second reason, which has been stressed by the recent literature on credibility and politics, lies in the way political institutions shape policymakers' incentives (see, e.g., Persson and Tabellini 1990; Grilli, Masciandaro, and Tabellini 1991). Parliamentary instability and polarization, on one hand, and disagreement among members of coalition governments, on the other, determine the way the future is weighed and make postponement of unpopular policies a rational option. As shown by Grilli et al. (1991), these features seem to explain the existence of large debts and deficits in some industrialized countries. In the Italian case, government durability (estimated in the 1950–90 period at 0.95 years) appears to be the major culprit because, for any individual cabinet, the probability of facing the bad consequences of deficit spending was very low. Under these circumstances, the only phenomenon capable of triggering significant fiscal tightening seems to have been the appearance of a balance-of-payment disequilibrium, which made adjustment unavoidable.[7]

An important opportunity for financial recovery was missed in the second half of the eighties. Average output growth of almost 3 percent per annum would have allowed debt stabilization through the implementation of a small discretionary tightening, as sustained growth (1) reduced the interest-growth rate gap and (2) automatically improved the budget via the effects of built-in stabilizers. This opportunity was clearly understood by the government, which proposed various plans for fiscal consolidation based on keeping (1) current outlays constant in real terms and (2) total revenues a constant share of output,

---

6. In the 1985–86 period, three different financial plans were proposed by the prime minister. In 1986, the Parliament changed the procedure for determining the annual budget, introducing the "Document for Economic and Financial Planning." The document aimed at framing the annual budget within a three-year macroeconomic and financial scenario consistent with debt stabilization. A common feature of those plans was (and still is) represented by the tendency to refer to a too-favorable macroeconomic environment. This, in the end, would underestimate the need for fiscal tightening and for additional restrictions to be adopted during the financial year, thus undermining the government's credibility.

7. This was the case in 1976–77 and in 1991. According to Toniolo and Ganugi (1992), fiscal adjustments in the 1876–1947 period were often triggered by external constraints. This tendency can also be found at the present time. The sole argument for fiscal tightening is represented by the need to fulfill the Maastricht criteria for joining in European Economic and Monetary Union.

thus letting economic growth make the adjustment. In contrast, actual fiscal policy was characterized by simultaneous discretionary increases in revenues and expenditures. Moreover, despite medium-term financial planning, a large part of the restrictive measures deliberately caused one-off effects. In the 1986–90 period, Sartor (1998b) estimates that 46 percent of the effects of deficit-reducing policies had disappeared in the short run. In 1987—a year of general elections—the above proportion peaked at 80 percent. Only in 1991, after a severe exchange rate crisis, was a primary surplus obtained (fig. 13.3). Its size, however, was insufficient to stabilize the relative weight of public debt.

Financial improvement continued in the 1991–95 period, mainly through increases in taxes and social security contributions (the effective overall rate was increased by 1.8 percentage points in the 1990–95 period). Spending cuts were obtained by freezing the wage bill (whose ratio to GDP declined by 1.3 percent in the same period) and investment (its share in GDP decreased by 1.0 percent). If this short-term policy is not backed up by some permanent reduction in the economic role of the public sector, primary spending is likely to reverse its recent downward trend in the coming years. So far, the only structural change to be enacted has been the reform of public pensions. However, because the phase-in period is very long, the reform will not have major effects in the next 10 years (see Sartor 1998a on this point).

The 15-year delay in making fiscal policy consistent with the tight monetary policy followed since the early eighties has caused a dramatic increase in debt, whose relative weight more than doubled, rising from 58 to 120 percent of GDP. The permanent cost of the delay is summarized by the size of the primary surplus needed to stabilize public debt in the short run. Assuming a 3.5 percentage point difference between the interest rate and the rate of output growth— as will be done for the generational accounting simulations—a primary surplus equal to 2 percent of output would have allowed debt stabilization in 1981. Fifteen years later, the debt-stabilizing surplus amounts to over 4 percent.

13.3   The Economic Role of the State

While the relevance of debt and deficits puts Italy among the countries following an unorthodox financial policy, the level and structure of primary public expenditures (e.g., net of interest payments) are similar to those found in the rest of Europe, especially the continental countries. During the first half of the century, public intervention was mainly aimed at closing the gap between the young economy and its more developed European partners. Public policy played a pervasive role in sustaining industrial development and creating basic infrastructures for the unified country, thus closely resembling the German experience. Notwithstanding the relevance of interest payments,[8] total public

---

8. Toniolo and Ganugi (1992) estimate that in 1870 debt servicing absorbed 38 percent of public expenditures.

spending at the beginning of the century was 16.2 percent of GDP (France and Germany reached 14.4 and 11.5 percent, respectively); in 1950, public spending totaled 30.2 percent of GDP, 11.1 points less than France and 3.2 less than Germany (Brosio 1993, table 8.1). The major legacy of the active role played by the state in economic development, however, does not show up in national accounts. A large proportion of companies are owned, directly or indirectly, by the public sector,[9] which until very recently showed no willingness to cease its improper role of entrepreneur. Measuring the relevance of publicly owned corporations by considering the number of employees relative to total employment, the OECD (1993) estimates that in 1988 the market share of public enterprises was 15.8 percent (the equivalent figures for France and Germany are 13.3 and 8.8 percent, respectively).[10]

The most significant increase in public spending occurred in the 1960–90 period:[11] the share of primary expenditures rose from 27.5 to 44 percent of GDP. The increase in public employment was even larger, as labor hoarding was used as a short-run remedy for structural unemployment. The number of public employees more than doubled, rising from 1.6 to 3.6 million. Their share of total employment rose from 7.6 to 15.5 percent.

Expenditure increases were driven by the expansion of the welfare system and public education (fig. 13.4). The main characteristics of the various structural reforms can be summarized as follows: (1) Between 1962 and 1969, compulsory schooling was extended and access to universities eased. (2) In the 1955–65 period, public health care programs increased their coverage from 65 to 90 percent of the population. Starting in 1978, a uniform and universal public health program replaced the heterogeneous regimes. (3) Public pension coverage was gradually extended to workers (both dependent and self-employed) in all economic sectors. Pension financing was gradually switched from fully funded to pay as you go. Moreover, the generosity of the system was increased by linking benefits to income earned in the last few years of work.

Franco (1993) estimates that 59.7 percent of the increase in the ratio of the above spending categories to GDP was determined by the extension of entitlements to larger shares of the population, 48.6 percent was caused by the increase in the amount of real per capita benefits, while demographic factors played only a limited role (13 percent). On the other hand, economic growth

9. As is well known, the United Nations System of National Accounts classifies firms in the market sector and the general government on the basis of the nature of their economic processes, irrespective of the owner of the capital. Thus a company producing goods and services to be sold on the market is reported in the market sector, even if it is fully owned by the state and sells at prices below average costs.

10. The largest stake is held in the energy sector (85.4 percent), followed by transport and telecommunications (81.4 percent) and finance and insurance (50.0 percent). Within the European context, the size of the latter sector appears particularly relevant. The French and German figures are 34.0 and 30.6 percent, respectively.

11. A detailed analysis of the major causes of the increase in public spending can be found in Franco (1993), from which data reported in the text are taken.

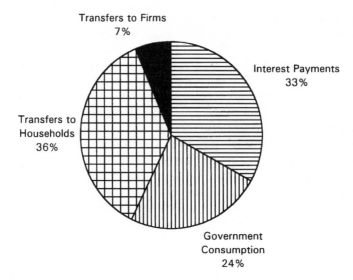

Fig. 13.4   Increase in public expenditures, 1960–90 (breakdown of the change in the ratio to GDP)

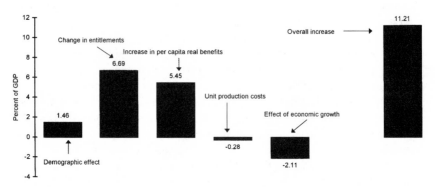

Fig. 13.5   Decomposition of the growth of welfare payments and public education, 1960–90
Source: Franco (1993).

and a moderate decline in production costs dampened the rise in the ratio (fig. 13.5).

At the end of the expansion process, the Italian welfare system closed the gap vis-à-vis the European countries. In the 1970–90 period, its relative weight—proxied by the size of current transfers to households relative to GDP—switched from 0.5 percentage points below the European Community average to 1.6 points above. Its dimension (18.5 percent of GDP) remained smaller than in France and the Scandinavian countries. However, the Italian system has noteworthy peculiarities, some of which are reflected in the composition of benefits. Unemployment allowances are low, while pensions are very high. In 1990, the former absorbed only 2 percent of welfare payments (equivalent to 0.4 of GDP);[12] the latter, 82 percent (or 15.2 percent of GDP—one of the largest figures among OECD member countries). This situation reflects the improper use of public pensions as a tool for social assistance and, in the case of public employees, as a form of deferred income payment. The anomalies in the use of public pensions can be summarized in three stylized facts: (1) Long-term unemployed living in the least developed areas became eligible for invalidity/disability pensions to some extent regardless of their real health conditions.[13] (2) Anticipated old-age pensions are used as a tool for reducing overmanning in declining industrial sectors. (3) Public employees are entitled to a seniority pension provided they have paid contributions for 20 years; per capita benefits equal 2 percent of the last salary per each year of contribution, irrespective of the age of the recipient.[14]

While the growth of the welfare system persisted during the entire 1960–90 period, significant spending increases originated from the active role that the budget played in alleviating the negative effects produced on firm profitability by the supply-side shocks of the early seventies. The first shock was caused by struggles over income distribution between profits and wages. The second was the well-known deterioration of terms of trade due to the increase in the price of oil. Given the downward inflexibility of real wages (due to the indexation

12. Given the severe legal constraints on the possibility of making workers redundant, unemployment is concentrated among young adults facing the labor market for the first time. As these individuals are not eligible for unemployment benefits, their care is the responsibility of their families. On the other hand, temporary redundancies among the employed are dealt with under a compulsory insurance scheme. Firms pay payroll taxes whose revenue is used to finance 80 percent of wages to workers certified to be temporarily redundant.

13. Note that this situation does not depend only on individual misbehavior but also on rather peculiar official rules. As an example, Law 639 passed in 1970 ruled that decisions about the concession of invalidity pensions should take into account the overall social and economic conditions prevailing in the province where the claimant is living. As noted by Onofri (1992, 41), by 1984—when the above law was abrogated—the number of holders of invalidity pensions had almost doubled.

14. As a consequence, the internal rate of return on pension contributions is extremely variable, depending on individual circumstances. Several alternative interpretations can be proposed for explaining this rather awkward situation: (1) Because Italian society as a whole was not ready to accept female participation in the labor market, early pension benefits allowed many women to return to domestic work while children were still living at home. (The minimum working period could be further reduced to 15 years if women were married. When the seniority pension for public employees was introduced, in 1954, the Parliament asked the government to pass "rules that would induce married women to go back to their households"; on this point, see Castellino 1996, 98). (2) By increasing the turnover of public workers, the preferential public pension system broadens the possibility of obtaining political consensus, as many members of the government have the annual opportunity of recruiting new workers. (3) The provision of benefits after 20 years of work represents an effective lock-in that allows public employers to lower wage differentials vis-à-vis the private sector (the system obviously causes negative effects on resource allocation and labor productivity).

mechanism) and the tight legal constraints on the possibility of laying workers off, both shocks severely squeezed profit margins. Under these circumstances, firm profitability was partially restored by the accommodative stance of monetary policy[15] and by public subsidies (fig. 13.4). Firm subsidization took two main forms: (1) workers declared temporarily redundant or employed in firms under restructuring received their wages out of public money (the so-called Cassa Integrazione Guadagni); (2) the effective rate of payroll tax was decreased by 9.6 percentage points in the 1976–80 period. The expansion in transfers to firms did not have any major effect on deficits,[16] because it was partly financed by direct taxes on wages, whose effective rate increased in the same period by 4.6 percentage points. This redistribution was partly reversed in the years after 1986, as profit margins recovered following the sharp decline in the price of oil.

Currently, the overall Italian budget does not appear to be out of range when compared to other EC countries (table 13.1). The primary budget is in surplus, and primary expenditures are below the average of the 12 European countries. On the revenue side, the Italian situation does not appear to be out of range either. The effective rate of taxes and social security contributions is equal to the European average.[17] Direct taxes and social security contributions yield an equal share of total revenues (36 percent each). Among direct taxes, the most revenue is yielded by the progressive tax on personal income, which is applied to all income sources except interest income.[18] Corporate taxes are levied at a high nominal rate (53.2 percent), although generous depreciation allowances, interest deductability, and a plethora of exemptions reduce the effective tax rate, which may even become negative in the case of debt financing (on this point, see OECD 1991). A substantial fraction of revenues are collected through indirect taxation (28 percent), particularly the value-added tax and taxes on petroleum products.

To sum up, the primary burden originates from the excessive deficits run up in the 1980–90 period. Briefly, it consists of large interest payments and an overall deficit, whose ratios to GDP are more than double the EC average.

15. As can be seen from fig. 13.2, the easy money policy produced negative ex post interest rates, redistributing income from households (the net creditors) to firms and the government (the net debtors).

16. In the 1976–80 period, the primary deficit declined by 1.9 percentage points of GDP (1.7 according to OECD estimates of the change in the cyclically adjusted deficit, which can be taken as a proxy for discretionary policy). The changes in effective tax rates mentioned in the text are taken from Giavazzi and Spaventa (1989), who provide a detailed assessment of Italian macroeconomic policy during the supply-side shocks.

17. However, nominal tax rates are often larger than in Europe overall, due to above average tax evasion and avoidance. Evasion is concentrated among small businesses and the self-employed, whose number is very large by European standards (over 20 percent of total taxpayers). Avoidance mainly affects revenues from corporations.

18. Interest income is taxed at a flat rate, currently 12.5 percent for government bonds and 27 percent for bank deposits.

Table 13.1 Structure of General Government Appropriation Account, 1994 (percent of GDP)

	Italy	Germany	France	United Kingdom	EC Average[a]	United States[b]
Government consumption	17.2	19.6	19.4	21.6	19.1	17.1
Gross public investment	2.3	2.7	3.2	1.8	2.7	1.7
Current transfers to						
Households	19.9	19.0	23.3	13.9	19.2	8.7
OASDI[b]	17.2	14.7	14.4	14.2	14.7[c]	n.a.
Firms	2.2	2.1	2.3	1.1	2.1	0.6
Total primary expenditures	43.5	45.9	51.6	40.0	45.3	33.0
Revenues from taxes and social security contributions	41.5	43.8	45.5	34.2	41.8	29.2
Primary deficit[d]	−1.7	−0.9	2.2	3.5	0.6	−0.2
Interest payments	10.7	3.4	3.6	3.3	4.4	4.6
Overall deficit	9.0	2.5	5.8	6.8	5.0	4.4

Source: European Commission.

[a]European countries excluding Italy.

[b]1993.

[c]Including Italy.

[d]Negative numbers are surpluses.

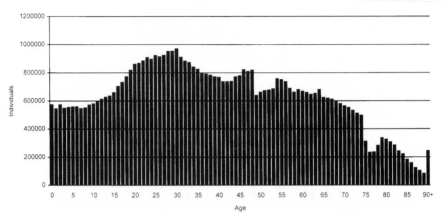

Fig. 13.6   Demographic structure, 1995
Source: ISTAT (1996).

13.4   The Demographic Outlook

The Italian population is expected to experience substantial changes in structure and size. Since 1977 the fertility rate has been below replacement; currently, having reached 1.2, it is the world's lowest. At the same time, life expectancy at birth is on an upward trend, having almost doubled during the first 60 years of the century.

The decline in fertility rates can be appreciated in figure 13.6, where the sizes of cohorts alive in 1995 are reported. The absolute number of births has dramatically decreased since the midsixties and appears to be stable for the past 10 years. This pattern represents three different phenomena pointing in the same direction: the number of women without descendants has steadily increased; the number of households with more than three descendants has declined substantially; and in recent years an increasing number of women are postponing the time for delivering their first child.[19] This overall trend, however, encompasses heterogeneous family structures and behaviors, depending on regional disparities.[20] Simplifying the matter, Italian families can be classi-

19. Forty percent of cohorts born in 1920 had three or more descendants. The proportion was halved in the next 40 years.

Comparing cohorts born between 1945 and 1958, the proportion of women having their first child at ages 30–34 increased by 38 percent. On the other hand, 20 percent fewer women delivered their first baby at ages 20–24. Women aged 25–29 displayed relatively stable behavior (Istituto Centrale di Statistica [ISTAT] 1993, table 9). Note, however, that the process of postponing childbirth has affected women living in northern Italy much more than those living in the south. Average age at the birth of the first child is two years lower in the south.

20. While these trends characterize the demographic outlook of many industrialized countries, Italy stands out in reconciling changes in reproductive behavior with the preservation of historical traditions and convictions; e.g., (1) childless couples have not increased their relevance (less than 15 percent of total marriages); (2) out-of-wedlock births remain a minority (6.2 percent of total births in 1990), notwithstanding the reduced number of marriages; (3) diverse living arrangements

fied into two different groups (ISTAT 1993): (1) The "northern," where the single child model has been prevalent for a long time (total fertility of cohorts born in the second half of the fifties is estimated to be around 1.5), and (2) the "southern," where 75 percent of families have two or more descendants, and a very limited number of women have only one child (less than 10 percent, compared to more than 35 percent in the north). Southern cohorts who have now completed their fertility period still maintain an average number of descendants above the replacement level.

The causes and consequences of the decline in fertility are attracting increasing public attention. Several explanations have been proposed for recent fertility trends, reflecting a multitude of elements (cultural, social, and economic) affecting households' reproductive decisions. On one hand, demographers point out the consequences of the exogenous change in the social role of women, characterized by greater equality vis-à-vis men: (1) the increasing female labor participation rate, particularly for career professions, and the consequent need to reconcile work with household responsibilities,[21] and (2) the substitution for "quantity" (number of children) of "quality" (proxied by per capita expenditures on health, education, and time devoted to child care). On the other hand, economists adhering to the "economics of the family" suggest that the decline in fertility is caused by the development of public pension schemes. According to the theory, generous old-age public transfers, by providing an effective hedge against the decline in earning capacity, substitute for redistribution from middle-aged children to elderly parents.[22] Among the consequences of population aging, policymakers are paying particular attention to projected increases in public expenditures on pensions and health.[23]

For the purposes of generational accounting, three different demographic scenarios have been developed, the first two based on projections recently published by the National Institute for Population Research.[24] All scenarios are

---

are still not common; and (4) the number of legal separations, though on the rise, is still comparatively low. For a recent description of the demographic changes and a suggested interpretation, see Palomba (1995).

21. In the past, the relationship between women's ages and labor participation rates followed an inverted W profile. After an initial increase, the participation rate decreased among cohorts aged 22–35 as many women withdrew from the labor market in order to have babies. When their children had grown up, their labor participation rate increased again, reaching a second local peak at age 43. Since 1986, the age-participation relationship has displayed a single peak, thus following an inverted V profile like that usually observed among men. For empirical evidence on this point, see Ambrosini and Rossi Sciumè (1995, 38, chart 2).

22. Recent empirical evidence for the Italian case is provided by Cigno and Rosati (1996).

23. The Treasury has recently delivered reports on future trends in public expenditures on education, health, and old age (see Ministero del Tesoro 1996a, 1996b, 1996c). An international comparison of national forecasts for public pension expenditures can be found in European Commission (1996).

24. See Istituto di Ricerche sulla Popolazione (1995). For the purposes of generational accounting, projections have been extended from the year 2044 to 2200. The fertility assumptions underlying the scenarios (rates respectively constant at the current level and increasing to 1.8 in the year 2044) resemble very closely the hypotheses adopted by the United Nations (1995) for scenarios C and M, respectively.

based on a three-year increase in life expectancy at birth in the next 20 years and a zero net migration rate.[25] The first projection assumes a gradual increase in the fertility rate, which in the year 2005 reaches 1.8 and remains constant thereafter. This scenario is adopted as a baseline, as the steady state fertility rate equals the completed fertility rate currently estimated for cohorts born in the second half of the fifties. The hypothesis is consistent with the very low total fertility rate currently observed provided the current level is a temporary phenomenon caused by the abovementioned postponement of age at first child-birth. In contrast, the second scenario (fertility constant at 1.3) pessimistically assumes that the current rate is structural and will prevail in the long run. The third scenario, rather implausible,[26] assumes that the fertility rate will rise to 2.1 (the replacement rate) in the next 20 years. It is intended mainly to contrast current generational imbalances with the situation that would prevail under long-term constancy of the population.

Irrespective of the assumptions about the future fertility trend, Italy is bound to experience a sharp increase in the elderly dependency ratio (e.g., the fraction of Italians aged 65 or older), by almost 50 percent in the next 20 years (from 25 percent of total population in 1995 to 38 percent in 2015). Starting from the year 2015, the dependency ratio follows different patterns, depending on the fertility assumption (fig. 13.7). According to the baseline scenario, the dependency ratio continues to grow until the year 2045, when it reaches a peak value of 57 percent. The ratio then declines to the steady state value of 47 percent. Total population steadily decreases from 57 million individuals to 41 million in the year 2100. If the fertility rate currently observed prevails in the long run (the second scenario), the demographic outlook would be substantially bleaker: the Italian population would shrink to 20 million, 66 percent of which would be citizens aged 65 or older.[27]

13.5   Sources and Data Construction

Generational accounting requires the disaggregation of the appropriation account of the general government into a series of individual accounts. The methodology followed for the Italian case is described in detail in Franco et al. (1994). It mainly consists in distributing total revenues and outlays to the different generations alive according to age and gender, on the basis of the information obtained from two sample surveys. The first is the Bank of Italy's Sur-

---

25. The number of third world immigrants living in Italy in 1994 is estimated to be between 0.6 and 1 million. The annual flow is expected to be between 50,000 and 100,000. As many of them are undocumented, the overall effect on public finances is uncertain. This is the main reason for excluding immigration from the generational accounting demographic scenarios.

26. Note, however, that the sharp decline in the Swedish total fertility rate, observed in the decades preceding the eighties, was fully consistent with a stable cohort completed fertility rate around 2. On this point, see Walker (1995).

27. Obviously, such a scenario is inconsistent with a zero net migration rate. The "demographic vacuum" created by the low fertility rate would be filled by relevant immigration flows.

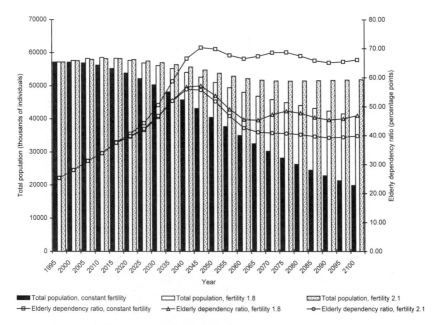

Fig. 13.7   Alternative demographic projections

vey of Household Income and Wealth; the second is the Survey of Consumer Expenditure by the Central Statistical Office (ISTAT). The receipts listed in the appropriation accounts are broken down into taxes on capital, labor, and commodities, social security contributions, and other revenues. The expenditures listed in the appropriation accounts need to be classified according to the different functions pursued. The reclassification greatly benefited from the analysis provided by Franco (1993) and Franco and Sartor (1990), which allowed a distinction between spending on health, education, pensions, household responsibility payments, and other social security transfers (such as unemployment benefits).

For the above spending and revenue items, the relative profiles of each of the 91 cohorts (from age 0 to age 90+) were obtained by benchmarking individual positions against a 40-year-old male.[28] Figure 13.8 summarizes the situation by presenting the levels of net transfers paid or received in 1995 by Italians. Citizens under age 19 receive net transfers, mainly represented by free schooling and health care. As individuals enter the labor market, their fiscal position vis-à-vis the state is reversed. The amount of net taxes paid increases with age, up to 40 years, and then decreases. The inverted V pattern mainly reflects the

28. The relative profile for each spending and revenue item is reported in Franco et al. (1994, fig. 4.1). An exception to the 40-year-old male benchmark is represented by expenditures on education, the profile for which is obtained by benchmarking individual positions against a 15-year-old male.

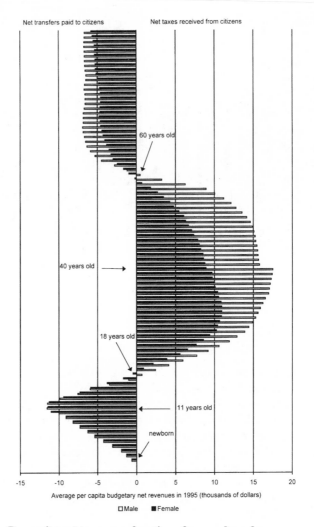

Fig. 13.8   **Per capita net taxes as a function of age and gender**

age structure of labor earnings and thus the amount of direct taxes and social security contributions paid. Above age 59, Italians on average become beneficiaries of net transfers. As they retire, individuals pay less in social security contributions and receive pension benefits. Moreover, the amount of health care benefits increases monotonically with age. Finally, as regards women, it can be noted that the breakeven point occurs at the same age as for men, although the absolute amounts of net taxes or transfers are smaller, due to their lower participation in the labor market.

Table 13.2   **Generational Accounts (thousands of U.S. dollars)**

Generation's Age in 1995	Total Population	Males	Females
0	64.8	89.3	39.0
5	80.3	109.8	49.3
10	112.4	147.4	75.7
15	158.9	200.9	115.0
20	186.6	235.2	136.2
25	183.7	236.5	129.3
30	155.2	209.1	100.3
35	113.5	165.5	61.0
40	63.4	108.7	18.6
45	10.7	45.5	−23.8
50	−46.8	−24.5	−68.6
55	−103.1	−98.3	−107.7
60	−142.0	−153.1	−131.8
65	−138.3	−149.9	−128.3
70	−117.5	−123.4	−112.8
75	−94.7	−96.5	−93.4
80	−72.2	−72.6	−71.9
85	−52.7	−53.0	−52.6
90	−7.4	−8.8	−6.9
Future generations	209.9	289.2	126.2
Generational imbalance	145.1	199.9	87.2
Percentage difference	223.8	223.9	223.6

Note: Economic growth assumed to be 1.5 percent; interest rate, 5 percent.

13.6   Italian Generational Accounts

Table 13.2 presents the baseline generational accounts at every fifth age assuming that the interest rate and the rate of economic growth are 5 and 1.5 percent, respectively. All amounts are in 1995 U.S. dollars. The accounts indicate the amount of net taxes that will be paid on average by an individual in the specified age group over the rest of his or her life. For example, cohorts born in 1995 will expect to pay, on average, $65,000 in net taxes, which will finance public consumption and part of the interest payments on outstanding public debt. The size of generational accounts first rises and then falls with age. This reflects the fact that young citizens are years away from their peak taxpaying periods, while older individuals, being in or near their retirement years, are receiving net transfers from the government. The breakeven age is between 45 and 50 for men and is five years earlier for women. On average, citizens aged 50 in 1995 could expect to receive $47,000 in net transfers from the government during the rest of their lives.

The decomposition of generational accounts into the present value of each of the various tax payments and transfer receipts is presented in table 13.3. In the case of 40-year-old citizens, the generational account of $63,000 represents the difference between $213,000 in the projected present value of future taxes

Table 13.3 Structure of Generational Accounts for Total Population (thousands of U.S. dollars)

	Payments						Receipts				
Generation's Age in 1995	Net Payment	Direct Taxes on Labor	Social Security Contributions	Indirect Taxes	Direct Taxes on Capital	Other Revenues	Pensions	Health	Other Benefits	Household Responsibility	Education
0	64.8	37.6	57.4	47.5	8.2	18.4	26.7	20.3	6.8	1.0	49.4
5	80.3	44.8	68.4	54.1	9.8	18.3	32.0	21.6	7.8	1.2	52.6
10	112.4	53.2	81.1	61.5	11.6	18.0	38.0	22.9	8.9	1.5	41.7
15	158.9	62.2	95.8	69.7	14.4	17.6	45.1	24.4	10.2	1.8	19.4
20	186.6	67.8	106.4	74.7	20.0	17.2	53.2	25.9	11.5	2.1	6.8
25	183.7	69.2	106.4	72.7	23.4	16.7	63.0	27.3	11.7	2.1	0.7
30	155.2	66.8	98.6	66.1	24.1	16.2	74.6	28.6	11.6	2.0	0.0
35	113.5	61.4	84.9	58.8	24.8	15.6	88.7	29.9	11.5	1.8	0.0
40	63.4	54.5	66.8	51.6	25.0	14.9	105.2	31.2	11.5	1.6	0.0
45	10.7	47.3	49.6	44.8	23.7	14.0	123.6	32.3	11.6	1.3	0.0
50	−46.8	38.5	32.0	38.5	22.0	13.0	144.7	33.1	11.9	1.1	0.0
55	−103.1	29.2	15.0	32.5	19.7	11.8	165.9	32.9	11.7	0.9	0.0
60	−142.0	21.3	2.4	27.6	17.7	10.6	179.5	32.0	9.2	0.8	0.0
65	−138.3	15.9	0.0	23.0	15.4	9.2	165.3	30.0	5.9	0.7	0.0
70	−117.5	12.0	0.0	19.5	11.4	7.7	136.6	26.6	4.2	0.6	0.0
75	−94.7	8.7	0.0	16.6	9.0	6.4	108.6	22.9	3.5	0.5	0.0
80	−72.2	5.6	0.0	12.6	6.9	4.9	81.4	17.8	2.6	0.3	0.0
85	−52.7	3.4	0.0	9.2	4.9	3.5	58.5	13.2	1.9	0.2	0.0
90+	−7.4	0.5	0.0	1.7	3.6	0.7	11.2	2.5	0.4	0.0	0.0

Note: Economic growth assumed to be 1.5 percent; interest rate, 5 percent.

and $150,000 in the projected present value of future transfers. The largest payment item is social security contributions ($67,000),[29] while on the receipt side the largest component is public pensions ($105,000).[30]

Under the hypothesis that budgetary policy will in the long run be consistent with financial solvency, table 13.2 also indicates the payment required of generations born from 1996 onward. In order to determine the net taxes of future generations, it is assumed that all unborn citizens will pay the same amount of taxes, adjusted for growth. The comparison between net payments due from future generations and payments expected from newborns under the eligibility rules established by current fiscal policy indicates the degree of intergenerational inequity. If the Italian government's fiscal policy were generationally balanced, the amounts future generations of Italians will pay would be equal to net taxes citizens born in 1995 will pay during their lifetimes. Table 13.2 shows that the current stance of fiscal policy is severely unbalanced against future generations. Net payments required from members of future generations will on average exceed the amount paid by cohorts born in 1995 by $145,000 (more than double the net taxes paid by newborns).

The degree of intergenerational imbalance is negatively correlated with the fertility rate and positively correlated with the difference between the interest rate and the rate of economic growth (the so-called interest-growth gap). Table 13.4 shows that the generational imbalance will be much greater if the long-run fertility rate remains constant at current levels. In this case, net taxes paid by future generations will amount to $275,000, thus increasing the generational imbalance from 224 to 325 percent. On the other hand, under the baseline demographic outlook, the generational imbalance rises from 224 to 473 percent if the interest-growth gap increases from 3.5 percentage points ($r = 5$ percent, $g = 1.5$ percent) to 5.5 percentage points ($r = 7$ percent, $g = 1.5$ percent). For the nine combinations of interest and growth rate assumptions shown in table 13.5, the percentage difference in the treatment of future Italians compared to 1995 newborns ranges from 134 to 601 percent.

13.7 Sources of Generational Imbalance and the Impact of Alternative Policies

In the previous sections it was noted that Italy is characterized by a large public debt, a very low fertility rate, and a generous public pension system. In

29. This is true for men. For women the largest payment is indirect taxes. As some women do not earn their money in the labor market but rather receive transfers from their spouses (or, in the case of widows, from social security under the survivors' pension scheme), the largest payment is linked to consumption rather than to income.

30. The data do not take into account the effects of the pension reform enacted in 1995. An estimation of the change in the present value of pension benefits for cohorts born after 1995 is currently under way (see Sartor 1998a for preliminary results). A critical assessment of the Italian pension system before the reform is proposed by Franco and Frasca (1992). For a description of the reform, see Artoni and Zanardi (1996), Canziani and Demekas (1995), Porta and Saraceno (1996), and Sartor (1998a).

Table 13.4   **Generational Imbalance under Alternative Demographic Projections: Present Value of Net Future Taxes (thousands of U.S. dollars)**

	Fertility Rate		
	Low (1.3)	Baseline (1.8)	High (2.1)
Males			
Newborns	89.3	89.3	89.3
Future generations	379.5	289.2	274.1
Percentage difference	325.0	223.9	206.9
Females			
Newborns	39.0	39.0	39.0
Future generations	165.2	126.2	119.6
Percentage difference	323.6	223.6	206.7
Total			
Newborns	64.8	64.8	64.8
Future generations	275.3	209.9	199.0
Percentage difference	324.6	223.8	206.9

Note: Base year is 1995. Economic growth assumed to be 1.5 percent; interest rate, 5 percent.

order to assess the relative importance of these elements in causing the generational imbalance, we conduct a sensitivity analysis assuming, in turn, that net public debt is zero and that the size and structure of the population remain constant.[31]

Table 13.6 illustrates the results of the counterfactual simulations; all simulations are run under the base-case interest and growth rate assumptions. Contrary to common belief, the most important source of generational imbalance is the pending demographic transition. As the number of future births shrinks, the overall primary surplus needed to keep public debt on a sustainable path must be paid by a decreasing number of citizens, whose per capita net tax payments increase. If the structure of the population remained constant, the generational imbalance would be less than a tenth of the baseline imbalance (18 instead of 224 percent). On the other hand, if it is assumed, counterfactually, that public debt were zero, the generational imbalance would be less than half of the baseline (98 instead of 224 percent). This exercise indicates that most of the imbalance in policy has nothing to do with officially labeled government debt. It illustrates the point that focusing solely on debt can be misleading in assessing a government's generational policy. Combining the two hypotheses (zero debt and constant population) produces a generational imbal-

31. No demographic change means that the number of Italians in each age-gender group in future years equals the corresponding 1995 number of Italians. Clearly, such a hypothesis is made for illustrative purposes only. A more realistic assumption would be a gradual increase in the fertility rate to the replacement level. As can be seen from the last column in table 13.4, such a scenario would still determine a generational imbalance against future generations; its size, however, is smaller than in the baseline case (207 vs. 224 percent).

Table 13.5   **Generational Imbalance under Alternative Macroeconomic Scenarios: Present Value of Net Future Taxes for Total Population (thousands of U.S. dollars)**

	Productivity Growth (%)		
Real Interest Rate (%)	1.00	1.50	2.00
3			
Newborns	99.2	110.3	118.3
Future generations	249.2	264.4	276.5
Percentage difference	151.2	139.7	133.7
5			
Newborns	54.3	64.8	76.3
Future generations	197.5	209.9	224.1
Percentage difference	263.5	223.8	193.7
7			
Newborns	24.2	30.6	38.0
Future generations	169.5	175.4	182.9
Percentage difference	600.8	473.2	381.8

Note: Base year is 1995. Exchange rate assumed to be 0.61 dollars per 1,000 Italian lire.

Table 13.6   **Sources of Generational Imbalance: Present Value of Net Future Taxes (thousands of U.S. dollars)**

	Baseline (A)	Zero Debt (B)	Constant Population (C)	B+C
Males				
Newborns	89.3	89.3	142.4	142.4
Future generations	289.2	176.5	168.0	68.9
Percentage difference	223.9	97.6	18.0	−51.6
Females				
Newborns	39.0	39.0	78.2	78.2
Future generations	126.2	77.0	92.3	37.8
Percentage difference	223.6	97.4	18.0	−51.7
Total				
Newborns	64.8	64.8	111.2	111.2
Future generations	209.9	128.1	131.2	53.8
Percentage difference	223.8	97.6	18.0	−51.6

Note: Base year is 1995. Fertility rate assumed to be 1.8; economic growth, 1.5 percent; interest rate, 5 percent.

ance against the current generation; the percentage difference between net taxes paid by future generations and those paid by cohorts born in 1995 would be −52 percent (table 13.6, last column).

An alternative way to assess the magnitude of the generational imbalance is to consider the sizes of the immediate and permanent increases in alternative tax rates or cuts in alternative spending categories required to restore genera-

Table 13.7   Changes Needed to Restore Generational Balance (percent of baseline)

Policy Option	Change (%)
Cut in government purchases	87.9
Cut in transfer payments (pensions)	40.0
Increase in income tax revenue	188.8
Increase in all tax revenues (including social security contributions)	61.4

Note: Economic growth assumed to be 1.5 percent; interest rate, 5 percent.

tional balance. Table 13.7 reports the results of four alternative experiments: an increase in income taxes or all taxes and social security contributions; or a cut in pensions or government consumption. As the sizes of the above budget items differ by large amounts, the percentage modifications needed to restore generational balance vary considerably. The largest difference is required if only direct taxes are increased (189 percent). The smallest is required if pensions are reduced (40 percent). The latter figure approximates the size of the cuts in future generations' pension benefits enacted by the 1995 reform (Sartor 1998a). Had the reform been applied pro rata to all living generations, the Italian generational accounts would now be very close to balance.

13.8   Conclusions

Since the eighties, stabilization of the ratio of public debt to GDP has been the main target of macroeconomic fiscal policy. According to conventional measures, the target was reached in 1995, as public debt settled at around 125 percent of GDP. Generational accounting acknowledges the great efforts made by the Italian government to put public finances on a sound footing. A measure of the progress in fiscal consolidation can be derived by calculating the generational imbalance under the assumption that the size and structure of population remain constant through time. Under the constant population hypothesis, the first set of generational accounts showed a generational imbalance of 127 percent in 1990.[32] In 1993, the imbalance was reduced to 63 percent by discretionary budgetary policy. If a constant population were a reasonable assumption, the preceding analysis would show that fiscal policy in 1995 had almost reached generational fairness (the imbalance being further reduced to 18 percent).

Conventional debt and deficit measures, however, focus on the very short run and ignore the pressures that the current demographic transition is placing on the budget. When incorporating the demographic change, the preceding analysis has shown that in 1995 the fiscal policy stance was far from balanced

32. See Franco et al. (1992, table 6), where the baseline macroeconomic scenario was the same as for this study (i.e., $g = 1.5$ percent, $r = 5$ percent).

from a generational point of view. If current tax and spending programs remain unchanged, the percentage difference in net lifetime payments between future and newborn generations is 224 percent. The size of the imbalance remains virtually constant (207 instead of 224 percent) even if the fertility rate were to reach the replacement level in the next 20 years. It is substantially smaller, however, if the pension reform enacted in 1995 is taken into account.[33]

The Italian fiscal policy debate is currently focused on European Economic and Monetary Union (EMU). The desire to join the EMU is compelling the Italian government to further restrict its fiscal policy stance in order to fulfill the Maastricht criteria of a deficit-to-GDP ratio below 3 percent and a declining debt-to-GDP ratio. The above targets have been criticized by many observers. Economists criticize the Maastricht fiscal rules for their lack of theoretical foundations.[34] Laymen criticize the criteria for the excessive restriction that would be placed on disposable incomes. While it can be agreed that the Maastricht fiscal rules are not well founded theoretically, the results derived from generational accounting show that the prescription for fiscal consolidation over and above what is needed for achieving short-term debt stabilization can offer a sounder theoretical foundation.

References

Abel, B. A., N. G. Mankiw, L. H. Summers, and R. J. Zeckhauser. 1989. Assessing dynamic efficiency: Theory and evidence. *Review of Economic Studies* 56:1–19.

Alesina, A. 1991. The end of large public debts. In *High public debt: The Italian experience,* ed. F. Giavazzi and L. Spaventa. Cambridge: Cambridge University Press.

Ambrosini, G. C., and G. Rossi Sciumè. 1994. Lavoro extradomestico delle donne, tendenze demografiche e politiche familiari. In *Politiche per la popolazione in Italia,* ed. G. C. Blangiardo, A. Golini, P. De Sandre, R. Palomba, M. Ambrosini, G. Rossi Sciumè, C. Saraceno, and C. Marchese. Turin: Edizioni della Fondazione Giovanni Agnelli.

---

33. According to the estimates of the effects of the pension reform enacted in 1995 reported by Sartor (1998a), the present value of employees' future pension benefits is reduced by 50 percent for newborns, which corresponds to a one-third reduction in overall pension benefits. Applying this percentage reduction to the estimates reported in table 13.3 would reduce the imbalance by $9,000 (and reduce the percentage difference from 223.8 to 184.8 percent).

34. The 3 percent limit on the deficit-to-GDP ratio ignores the differences among initial debt stocks of potential member countries, as well as their past inflation rates. Both factors determine current expenditures on interest payments, which are part of the deficit figure. Moreover, under a future macroeconomic scenario characterized by a common inflation rate and a very similar growth rate for all EMU countries, the 3 percent limit need not be consistent with a stable debt-to-GDP ratio. Consistency requires the debt ratio to be equal to a critical level (e.g., 75 percent if both the inflation and the growth rate are 2 percent). All countries with debt rates higher than the critical value need to to run deflationary fiscal policies in order to fulfill the 3 percent deficit limit (vice versa for countries with debt ratios lower than the critical level). On this point, see, e.g., Buiter, Corsetti, and Roubini (1993).

Artoni, R., and A. Zanardi. 1996. The evolution of the Italian pension system. In *Comparing social welfare systems in Southern Europe.* MIRE Working Paper. Milan: Università Bocconi.

Brosio, G. 1993. *Economia e finanza pubblica,* 2d ed. Rome: La Nuova Italia Scientifica.

Buiter, W. H. 1985. A guide to public sector debt and deficits. *Economic Policy* 1: 13–79.

Buiter, W. H., G. Corsetti, and N. Roubini. 1993. Excessive deficits: Sense and nonsense in the Treaty of Maastricht. *Economic Policy* 16:58–100.

Canziani, P., and D. G. Demekas. 1995. The Italian public pension system: Current prospects and reform options. IMF Working Paper 95/33. Washington, D.C.: International Monetary Fund, March.

Castellino, O. 1996. La redistribuzione tra ed entro generazioni nel sistema previdenziale italiano. In *Pensioni e risanamento della finanza pubblica,* ed. F. Padoa Schioppa Kostoris. Bologna: Il Mulino.

Cigno, A., and F. C. Rosati. 1996. Jointly determined saving and fertility behaviour: Theory, and estimates for Germany, Italy, UK and USA. *European Economic Review* 8:1561–89.

European Commission. 1996. Ageing and pension expenditure prospects in the Western world. *European Economy: Reports and Studies,* no. 3.

Franco, D. 1993. *L'espansione della spesa pubblica in Italia.* Bologna: Il Mulino.

Franco, D., and F. Frasca. 1992. Public pensions in an ageing society: The case of Italy. In *The future of pensions in the European Community,* ed. J. Mortensen. London: Brassey's.

Franco, D., J. Gokhale, L. Guiso, L. J. Kotlikoff, and N. Sartor. 1992. Generational accounting: The case of Italy. Temi di Discussione, no. 171. Rome: Banca d'Italia.

———. 1994. Generational accounting: The case of Italy. In *Saving and the accumulation of wealth,* ed. A. Ando, L. Guiso, and I. Visco. Cambridge: Cambridge University Press.

Franco, D., and N. Sartor. 1990. *Stato e famiglia.* Milan: F. Angeli.

Giavazzi, F., and L. Spaventa. 1989. Italy: The real effects of inflation and disinflation. *Economic Policy* 8 (April): 133–71.

Grilli, V., D. Masciandaro, and G. Tabellini. 1991. Political and monetary institutions and public financial policies in the industrial countries. *Economic Policy* 13 (October): 342–92.

Istituto Centrale di Statistica (ISTAT). 1993. L'evoluzione della fecondità nelle regioni italiane. Notiziario, no. 1. Rome: Istituto Centrale di Statistica.

———. 1996. Popolazione residente per sesso, età e regione. Note e Relazioni, no. 2. Rome: Istituto Centrale di Statistica.

Istituto di Ricerche sulla Popolazione. 1995. *Tre scenari per il possibile sviluppo della popolazione delle regioni italiane al 2004.* Rome: Consiglio Nazionale delle Ricerche.

Ministero del Tesoro. 1988. Il debito pubblico in Italia, 1861–1987. In *Relazione del direttore generale alla commissione parlamentare di vigilanza,* vol. 1, ed. Direzione Generale del Debito Pubblico. Rome: Istituto Poligrafico e Zecca dello Stato.

———. 1996a. Tendenze demografiche e sistema scolastico: Alcuni possibili scenari. Conti Pubblici e Congiuntura Economica, Quaderno Monografico no. 8. Rome: Ragioneria Generale dello Stato.

———. 1996b. Tendenze demografiche e spesa pensionistica: Alcuni possibili scenari. Conti Pubblici e Congiuntura Economica, Quaderno Monografico no. 9. Rome: Ragioneria Generale dello Stato.

———. 1996c. Tendenze demografiche e spesa sanitaria: Alcuni possibili scenari.

Conti Pubblici e Congiuntura Economica, Quaderno Monografico no. 7. Rome: Ragioneria Generale dello Stato.

Morcaldo, G. 1993. *La finanza pubblica in Italia.* Bologna: Il Mulino.

Onofri, R. 1992. La finanza statale negli anni "80." Arel Informazioni. March.

Organization for Economic Cooperation and Development (OECD). 1991. *Taxing profits in a global economy: Domestic and international issues.* Paris: Organization for Economic Cooperation and Development.

———. 1993. *Economic surveys: Italy 1992–93.* Paris: Organization for Economic Cooperation and Development.

Palomba, R. 1995. Italy: The invisible change. In *Population, family and welfare,* vol. 1, ed. H. Moors and R. Palomba. Oxford: Clarendon.

Persson, T., and G. Tabellini. 1990. *Macroeconomic policy, credibility and politics.* Harwood: Academic Press.

Porta, P., and P. Saraceno. 1996. The mandatory pension system in Italy. Contributi di Ricerca IRS. Milan: Istituto per le Ricerche Sociali.

Sartor, N. 1998a. The long-run effects of the Italian pension reforms. Working Paper no. 8. Verona: Università di Verona, Dipartimento di Scienze Economiche.

———. 1998b. *Il risanamento mancato.* Rome: Carocci.

Toniolo, G., and P. Ganugi. 1992. Il debito pubblico italiano in prospettiva secolare (1876–1947). In *Il disavanzo pubblico in Italia: natura strutturale e politiche di rientro,* vol. 2, ed. Ente per gli studi monetari, bancari e finanziari "Luigi Einaudi." Bologna: Il Mulino.

United Nations. 1995. *World population prospects: The 1994 revision.* New York: United Nations Press.

Walker, J. R. 1995. The effect of public policies on recent Swedish fertility behavior. *Journal of Population Economics* 8:223–51.

Zamagni, V. 1992. Debito pubblico e creazione di un nuovo apparato fiscale nell'Italia unificata (1861–76). In *Il disavanzo pubblico in Italia: natura strutturale e politiche di rientro,* vol. 2, ed. Ente per gli studi monetari, bancari e finanziari "Luigi Einaudi." Bologna: Il Mulino.

14 Generational Accounts for the Netherlands

A. Lans Bovenberg and Harry ter Rele

14.1 Introduction

The intertemporal consequences of fiscal policies in the Netherlands are traditionally assessed on the basis of the budget deficit, public debt, and net government wealth. The explicit analysis of the impact of fiscal policy on the welfare of currently living generations and generations that are yet to be born has received only little attention.[1] Generational accounting provides a tool for the investigation of the intergenerational distributional effects of fiscal policy. Moreover, its forward-looking properties allow one to explore how various future developments affect the sustainability of public finances. In particular, in the decades to come, the prospective aging of the population and the depletion of natural gas reserves are expected to put a substantial burden on public finances in the Netherlands. At the same time, increasing participation of the middle-aged in the labor force and increasing taxable income from funded private pension schemes are expected to alleviate this burden by strengthening the tax base. Generational accounting is comprehensive in that it includes all budget items (i.e., both spending and taxes). Hence, it provides a useful framework for exploring how future developments and fiscal policy interact in affecting the sustainability of public finances and the welfare of various generations, thereby offering policymakers an explicit equity choice.

Generational accounting yields two important measures. The first one is the

A. Lans Bovenberg is professor of general economics at the Center for Economic Research at Tilburg University and professor of economic policy at Erasmus University, Rotterdam. He received his Ph.D. at the University of California, Berkeley, held a position as an economist at the International Monetary Fund, and was deputy director of CPB Netherlands Bureau for Economic Policy Analysis. Harry ter Rele is a staff member at CPB Netherlands Bureau for Economic Policy Analysis.

1. Only recently, both the Dutch central bank (see Hebbink 1996) and the Ministry of Finance (see Kempen 1996) started to explicitly explore the intergenerational impacts of fiscal policy.

level of the net tax burden (the gross tax burden minus gross transfers) on future generations. It is found residually from the intertemporal government budget constraint and the net benefits that currently living generations derive from current fiscal policy. Accordingly, future generations are assumed to absorb the entire adjustment required to make the claims of various generations consistent with the intertemporal budget constraint. The level of the net tax burden on future generations is highly sensitive to the level of government purchases because generational accounts do not assign the incidence of public purchases to generations.[2]

The second measure is the *difference* between the tax burden on newborns (these are the youngest members of the current generations), whose net tax burden depends on current fiscal rules unconstrained by the government budget constraint, and the tax burden on future generations, whose net tax burden is determined residually from the government budget constraint rather than on the basis of current rules. The tax burdens on these two generations are comparable because they both apply to an entire lifetime. Measuring the generational imbalance as the difference between these two tax burdens yields two further advantages. First, the difference measure is much less sensitive to the level of government purchases. Second, it provides a measure for the sustainability of public finances. If the net burdens of newborn and future generations coincide, current fiscal policy is consistent with the government budget constraint and is thus sustainable. However, if future generations bear a heavier tax burden than newborns do, current fiscal rules will have to be adjusted in the future to meet the budget constraint. In view of these two advantages, this paper will focus on the second measure, that is, the difference between the tax burdens of newborn and future generations.[3]

The rest of the paper is organized as follows. After providing a historical overview of Dutch fiscal policies (section 14.2) and briefly describing our data sources (section 14.3), we present our results in section 14.4. The standard method of applying generational accounting yields a generational imbalance of $87,600, or 17.1 percent of projected lifetime income. However, if the impact of increasing labor participation and rising pension incomes on the tax base is taken into account, the generational imbalance declines to $24,300, or 4.7 percent of lifetime income. In subsection 14.4.3 we explore the effects of assigning the benefits of government purchases and the public capital stock to generations. Section 14.5 explores various policy reforms aimed at establishing generational balance. Section 14.6 contains the conclusions.

---

2. However, subsection 14.4.3 distributes the benefits from these purchases over generations. This allows us to more readily interpret the net tax burden on future generations as the net "debt" that current generations shift onto future generations.

3. A further advantage of this measure compared to the first measure is that it is less sensitive to the allocation of benefits over the life cycle, which is sometimes rather arbitrary.

14.2   Historical Overview of Fiscal Policy

The Capital Principle. During the first decade after the Second World War, the Netherlands applied the capital principle to the national budget. This principle involves a tax-financed current budget and a debt-financed capital budget. By prohibiting debt financing of current spending, net government wealth is protected. However, fiscal policy in the early fifties was actually tighter than prescribed by the capital principle in order to cut the extremely high level of government debt inherited from the war.

Fine-Tuning. During a short period in the second half of the fifties, the budget was used to pursue activist, countercyclical Keynesian policies. However, experience with countercyclical policies was unfavorable because it was employed in an asymmetric fashion; whereas demand was stimulated in a weak economy, it was barely curbed in a boom. Moreover, identifying the turning points in the business cycle proved to be too difficult for successfully fine-tuning fiscal policy.

Structural Fiscal Policy. A structural budget norm ended activist fiscal policy in the beginning of the sixties. While fine-tuning was abolished, automatic stabilizers were allowed to stabilize the economy. Accordingly, the actual deficit was permitted to differ from its structural level. The structural deficit norm was derived so that government borrowing would match the structural level of net saving in the private sector, adjusted for a desired structural surplus on the current account of the balance of payments to finance development aid. Based on the trend rate of economic growth, the so-called structural budgetary room was established, which defined the resources available for either tax cuts or spending increases. This enhanced overall budget discipline by strengthening the position of the finance minister.

Containing the Tax Burden. In the midseventies, without abandoning the structural deficit norm, a new norm was introduced in order to contain the tax burden. In particular, the rise of the tax burden as a percentage of GDP was limited to 1 percentage point per annum.

Cutting the Actual Deficit. Structural fiscal policy began to show serious weaknesses at the end of the seventies. The projected trend growth rate proved to be too optimistic, resulting in surging fiscal deficits. In the early eighties, during the most serious economic slowdown since the Second World War, Dutch fiscal policy got seriously out of hand. The fiscal deficit rose to almost 10 percent of GDP (see fig. 14.1). Moreover, revenues from natural gas proved to be rather volatile due to changes in oil prices. At that time, taxation and social security contributions accounted for nearly 50 percent of GDP. The structural budget

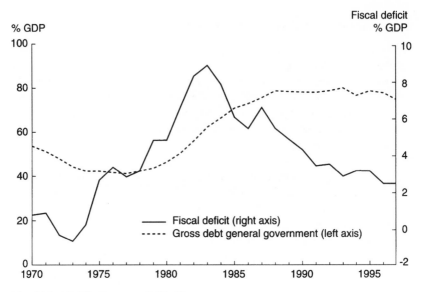

Fig. 14.1   Public finances, 1970–97

norm was replaced by a norm for the actual deficit. Indeed, deficit reduction was to become the leading issue for more than a decade and three successive cabinets. In view of the high tax burden, fiscal adjustment was pursued through expenditure cutbacks.

The Present Situation. By the time the deficit had reached a more sustainable level in the beginning of the nineties, the scope for a more long-term-oriented fiscal policy reemerged. Indeed, two important lessons have been learned from the experience of fiscal policy in the eighties and early nineties. First, the targets for cuts in the actual fiscal deficit made budgetary policy rather sensitive to the cycle. Spending overruns were accommodated in booms. During slumps, in contrast, spending had to be cut substantially to meet the targets for the actual deficits. To avoid unrest in the budgetary process and to better control spending, the present government has set a ceiling on public expenditure for the period 1994–98, which more or less excludes any rise in real terms. So the deficit is allowed to fluctuate with tax receipts up to a certain limit, above which measures have to be taken to cut the actual deficit. The second lesson from fiscal policy in the beginning of the nineties is that a government program based on a favorable economic outlook can seriously disrupt the budgetary process if growth turns out to be slower than anticipated. Accordingly, the present coalition has estimated receipts from taxation and social security contributions on the basis of a cautious economic scenario, which assumes that the economy grows only at a modest rate of 2 percent.

The Economic and Monetary Union Criteria. The Economic and Monetary Union (EMU) convergence criteria set by the Maastricht Treaty are an important yardstick for fiscal policy. Whereas the fiscal deficit in 1997 is projected to satisfy the norm of 3 percent of GDP, the stock of government debt (at about 77 percent of GDP in 1996) still violates the EMU ceiling of 60 percent of GDP. Therefore, the government intends to use the treaty's "escape clause," which states that in case public debt exceeds the 60 percent norm, it should be declining at a reasonable rate. Indeed, general government gross debt fell by more than 5 percent of GDP in 1997 to just below 72 percent of GDP, in part due to a one-off reduction in the government account at the Dutch central bank.

Future Fiscal Policy and Aging. In recent years, several analysts have argued that the prospective aging of the population requires a further reduction of the fiscal deficit, thereby substantially cutting public debt. This would allow lower future interest payments to compensate for the rising cost of old-age benefits and health care. The generational accounting approach pursued in this paper is intended to provide more insights on how aging affects the public finances.

14.3   Data Sources

Statistics Netherlands (CBS), the official Dutch statistical bureau, supplies the data on the present situation. Projections of future economic variables were derived from CPB Netherlands Bureau for Economic Policy Analysis, the independent government bureau producing the official macroeconomic forecasts. CPB constructed the data on the 1995 budget on the basis of national accounts data provided by CBS. The age profiles for taxes were derived from Deelen (1995), which in turn drew its data from a large household survey (Woningbehoefteonderzoek) performed by CBS. This latter bureau also produced the demographic projections. The other future variables are derived from CPB projections. In particular, the long-term scenario analysis of CPB (1992) provided the main guide for future changes expected to take place in the private sector.

14.4   Basic Findings and Sensitivity Analysis

The first part of this section explores the intergenerational effects of current fiscal policies. The second part conducts some sensitivity analyses with respect to future economic developments. The final part explores the sensitivity of the results with respect to an alternative method of generational accounting that assigns the incidence of not only taxes and transfers but also government purchases to generations.

Table 14.1   **Generational Imbalance (present value in thousands of U.S. dollars)**

	Variant 1 (standard)	Variant 2 (including increasing participation)	Variant 3 (including higher private pensions)	Variant 4 (including flattening of wage profile)
Net taxes paid by				
Newborns	49.4	63.0	65.2	65.8
Future generations	137.0	95.8	81.9	90.1
Generational imbalance				
In dollar terms	87.6	32.8	16.7	24.3
As a percentage difference	177.1	52.0	25.6	36.9
As a percentage of				
lifetime income	17.1	6.4	3.3	4.7

Notes: Real income growth assumed to be 1.5 percent; discount rate, 5 percent.

The variants are cumulative. Hence, in addition to the change in parentheses, each variant includes also the changes included in the previous variant.

14.4.1   Current Fiscal Policy

We first apply the standard method for calculating generational accounts to the Netherlands.[4] This standard method, however, ignores several important future changes in the Dutch economic environment affecting the life cycle pattern of taxes. These changes include, first, an increase in labor force participation; second, the maturing of private, funded pension funds; and, third, a flattening of the age-earnings profile. We discuss how sensitive the generational accounts are with respect to these three developments by incorporating them step by step.

Standard Method

The standard practice in generational accounting assumes that the age profiles of the various taxes and transfers change only with legislated or very likely policy reforms. Our first variant (variant 1) employs this traditional approach. The basis for the extrapolation of policies is the projected budget in 1998, when the present government completes its legislative period.[5] This budget incorporates the effects of all policies agreed on by the political parties making up the present government. In addition, for the period beyond 1998, we account for the lagged impact of already legislated measures that restrict the eligibility for disability and survivor benefits. Variant 1 in table 14.1 reveals that current policies appear to be unsustainable, as they benefit current generations at the expense of future generations. In particular, whereas newborns pay

4. In particular, we assume that social security premiums are constant and do not endogenously respond to changes in social security spending in order to maintain balance in the social security accounts.

5. For the period between 1995 and 1998, we adopt the realized and projected budget figures contained in CPB (1996).

Table 14.2   **Present Value of Future Net Tax Payments per Capita (thousands of U.S. dollars; constant prices, adjusted for income growth)**

Generation's Age in 1995	Variant 1	Variant 4
0	49.4	65.8
5	68.9	88.0
10	113.8	135.3
15	164.0	186.9
20	209.9	234.0
25	237.3	261.6
30	222.0	245.4
35	196.7	218.3
40	161.2	180.7
45	116.3	132.3
50	62.2	74.3
55	5.5	14.2
60	−46.5	−40.3
65	−91.4	−87.1
70	−103.4	−100.7
75	−113.0	−111.6
80	−118.0	−117.3
85	−116.6	−116.3
90	−110.9	−110.7
Future generations	137.0	90.1
Generational imbalance		
In dollar terms	87.6	24.3
As a percentage difference	177.1	36.9
As a percentage of lifetime income	17.1	4.7

Note: Real income growth assumed to be 1.5 percent; discount rate, 5 percent.

only $49,400 in net lifetime taxes, future generations bear a lifetime tax burden of $137,000. The difference in the tax burden between newborns and future generations amounts to 17.1 percent of lifetime income.

Table 14.2 (variant 1) shows that the present values of net tax payments over the remaining lifetimes of presently living generations vary substantially with age. The young and middle-aged are net contributors to the budget over their remaining lifetimes. The elderly, in contrast, are net beneficiaries. This lifetime pattern reflects the age profile of both public spending and revenue.

Figure 14.2 contains the age profile of benefits from aggregate public spending (excluding government purchases) and its main components. It indicates that benefits from social security rise with age. This pattern is due mainly to public old-age benefits, which are paid only to citizens over 65 years old, and disability benefits, which increase with age for those younger than 65 years. Benefits from health care also rise strongly with age.

Figure 14.3 reveals that revenues also vary with age. Until about age 50,

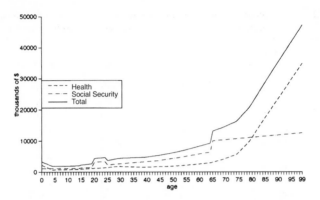

Fig. 14.2   Age profile of expenditures, 1995

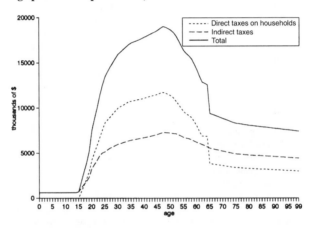

Fig. 14.3   Age profile of taxes, 1995

labor incomes (and hence tax revenues from these incomes) rise with age, explaining the upward slope in the tax profile. Beyond age 50, tax payments fall
because participation in the labor force gradually decreases. The declining labor incomes are not fully offset by various forms of pension income, which
are subject to income tax. Accordingly, both income taxes (which include social security premiums) and indirect taxes (which are linked to net income) fall
with age. Compared to indirect taxes, direct taxes drop more rapidly at age 65
because individuals over 65 years old are exempt from contributing to various
social security schemes, including the public old-age scheme. Overall, compared to the middle-aged, the elderly contribute significantly less to the budget.
Combining the expenditure and revenue sides of the budget, figure 14.4 shows
the age profile of total net contribution to the government budget.

Rising Labor Force Participation

The standard practice in generational accounting implicitly assumes that the
currently observed rate of labor force participation remains constant in the fu-

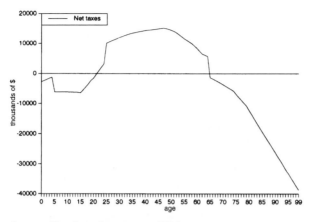

Fig. 14.4   Age profile of total net taxes, 1995

Table 14.3   Participation Rates of Various Age Groups in Full-Time Equivalents, 1995 and 2020

		2020[a]		
Age Group	1995	Low	Base	High
20–34	73.1	76.6	75.8[b]	77.2
35–49	72.0	79.2	84.1	86.2
50–64	37.7	43.7	55.3	60.5
Total	64.1	65.3	70.5	73.9

Source: CBS/CPB (1997).

[a]Adjusted for rise in part-time employment.

[b]This rate is lower than the corresponding rate in the low scenario because the young spend more years in full-time education in the base scenario. The resulting higher stock of human capital allows them to participate at higher rates in later years.

ture. For the Netherlands, this assumption is unrealistic. This country has traditionally featured a low participation rate of women. Over the past decade, however, the participation rate of women has started to rise sharply and is expected to continue to increase substantially in the future. Rising educational levels of women contribute to this development. Indeed, lower fertility not only gives rise to aging but also boosts participation of women. Recent policy measures limiting eligibility for disability benefits are expected to further increase labor force participation, especially of the elderly.

A higher participation rate widens the tax base by raising labor incomes. To account for this effect, variant 2 assumes that taxes paid by a particular age group depend not only on labor productivity and the number of people in that group but also on the projected labor force participation rate of the age group involved. Table 14.3 compares current age-specific participation rates with projections of these participation rates in 2020 for three alternative scenarios. The

Table 14.4   Assets of Pension Funds, 1991

Country	Assets (% of GDP)
Netherlands[a]	75.9
Germany[a]	15.5
United Kingdom	60.1
France	4.6
Denmark	51.6
Belgium	10.5

Source: Report by the European Commission's Network of Experts on Supplementary Pensions.
[a]1992.

projections for the base case imply that the participation rate of those between 20 and 64 years of age (adjusted for the rise in part-time employment) will rise by about 10 percent (or 6.4 percentage points) between 1995 and 2020. The older age groups are expected to feature the largest boost in labor force participation.

The higher participation rate reduces the generational imbalance substantially. The net tax burden borne by future generations falls from $137,000 in variant 1 to $95,800 in variant 2 (see table 14.1). In the latter variant, the tax burden exceeds that of newborns by only $32,800 (compared to $87,600 in variant 1).

Rising Pension Incomes

A projected increase in private pension incomes is the second factor requiring an adjustment of the age profile. Public pension benefits in the Netherlands are flat (i.e., unrelated to income) so that the public benefit level is relatively low for middle- and high-income earners. For these income groups, collective labor agreements supplement the public benefits with compulsory occupational pension provisions. These provisions are financed by funded pensions funds, which have accumulated financial assets sizable by international standards (see table 14.4). During the coming decades these funds are expected to mature so that an increasing part of the population will have accumulated substantial pension rights when reaching retirement age.

Higher pension incomes strengthen the tax base because retirement benefits are subject to income tax, while indirect taxes are levied on consumption out of these benefits. Variant 3 assumes that average net income of an individual over 65 years of age relative to that of an individual between 35 and 49 years will rise from 78 to 85 percent between 1995 and 2020.[6] The resulting increase in tax payments alleviates the generational imbalance further; future genera-

---

6. These figures are derived from Deelen (1995) and the "European Renaissance" scenario in CPB (1992). This scenario employs projections about future labor force participation similar to the base case in table 14.3.

tions now pay only $16,700 (3.3 percent of lifetime income) more in lifetime taxes than newborns do (table 14.1).

Flatter Age-Earnings Profile

The third phenomenon that calls for an adjustment of the future age profile of taxes is the expected flattening of the age-earnings profile. Wages currently rise rather sharply with age. A number of developments, however, are expected to reduce wages of elderly workers compared to wages of the young. First, market forces increasingly link wages to productivity, thereby reducing the importance of implicit lifetime labor contracts in firms. Second, the aging of the labor force renders younger workers more scarce compared to older workers.

Variant 4 assumes that wages of young workers 20 years old will increase by 9 percent relative to the average wage between 1995 and 2020. A worker 45 years old will experience an average rise in wages. Wages of older workers 60 years old will lag the average by 10 percent.[7] The flattening of the age profile of earnings dampens the rise in tax revenues due to a change in the composition of the labor force toward older workers with higher wages. Hence, it reduces the improvement in the generational imbalance brought about by higher pension incomes and a higher participation rate. Indeed, variant 4 shows a slight rise of the generational imbalance (compared to variant 3) to $24,300, or 4.7 percent of lifetime income (see table 14.1).

The Preferred Case

We believe variant 4 best reflects the impact of future developments on the intergenerational stance of current fiscal policies. Table 14.2 and figure 14.5 provide more detailed information on the differences between the standard variant 1 and our preferred variant 4. Table 14.2 indicates how the additional tax payments in variant 4 are distributed over currently living generations (in present value terms). Figure 14.5 shows the additional current contributions of each age group to the budget in 2020 (in variant 4 compared to variant 1).

14.4.2   Sensitivity Analyses

Interest and Growth Rates

Table 14.5 shows how sensitive the results are with respect to interest and productivity growth rates. A higher interest rate tends to lower the generational imbalance as measured by the difference in the present value of taxes paid by future generations and newborns. The opposite holds for higher productivity growth. However, the dependency on these factors is typically reversed if the generational imbalances are expressed as ratios of the present value of lifetime incomes.

7. These assumptions are based on the "European Renaissance" scenario in CPB (1992) and Deelen (1995).

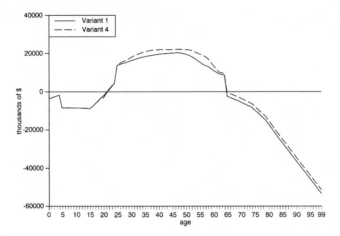

Fig. 14.5   Age profile of total net taxes in 2020: variants 1 and 4

Labor Force Participation

The variants discussed in subsection 14.4.1 employed a base-case assumption for the expected growth of labor force participation. However, in view of the considerable uncertainty surrounding this variable, CPB has constructed two alternative scenarios for the future development of the participation rate (see table 14.3).[8] All three scenarios involve an increase in participation. Whereas the "low" case projects only an accumulated 2 percent growth until 2020, the "high" case involves an accumulated growth of 15 percent. This compares to 10 percent growth in the base case.

Table 14.6 reveals that the generational imbalance is rather sensitive to labor supply. Indeed, in the scenario featuring high labor participation, the additional labor supply offsets the effect of aging so that future generations actually contribute less to the budget than newborns do. This reveals that a high level of labor supply is an important factor in supporting sustainable public finances.

Demographic Developments

Table 14.7 explores the sensitivity of the generational accounts with respect to demographic assumptions. Column (2) of the table contains the accounts if the age structure remains constant. It reveals that without aging, future generations would benefit substantially more from the budget than present generations do. In particular, compared to current generations, they would enjoy an additional lifetime *benefit* of $84,000 (16 percent of lifetime income). This compares with an additional *burden* of $24,000 (4.7 percent of lifetime income) if the prospective change in age structure is taken into account. This contrast reveals that aging puts a heavy burden on public finances. These

---

8. Pomp (1996) describes how these scenarios are constructed.

Table 14.5   Generational Accounts (present value in thousands of U.S. dollars)

	g = 1			g = 1.5			g = 2		
	r = 3	r = 5	r = 7	r = 3	r = 5	r = 7	r = 3	r = 5	r = 7
Variant 1									
Newborns	115	34	4	143	49	3	173	67	12
Future generations	226	117	70	267	137	79	313	161	90
Generational imbalance									
In dollar terms	111	83	66	124	88	76	140	94	78
As a percentage difference	96	239	1,717	87	177	2,355	81	140	664
As a percentage of lifetime income	13.5	18.0	20.7	12.6	17.1	22.8	11.7	15.7	21.1
Variant 4									
Newborns	149	47	2	186	66	10	228	88	20
Future generations	182	70	30	225	90	37	279	114	47
Generational imbalance									
In dollar terms	33	23	28	39	24	27	51	26	27
As a percentage difference	22	48	1,763	21	37	270	22	30	130
As a percentage of lifetime income	4.0	5.0	8.8	4.0	4.7	8.1	4.3	4.4	7.3

Note: g is productivity growth (percent); *r* is discount rate (percent).

Table 14.6   **Sensitivity Analysis: Participation Rate (thousands of U.S. dollars)**

	Low Participation	Average Participation (variant 4)	High Participation
Net taxes of			
Newborns	60.2	65.8	74.3
Future generations	115.4	90.1	67.2
Generational imbalance			
In dollar terms	55.2	24.3	−7.1
As a percentage difference	92	37	−9
As a percentage of lifetime income	10.8	4.7	−1.8
Average GDP growth rate in 1995–2020	1.8	2.1	2.4

Table 14.7   **Sensitivity Analysis: Demographics (thousands of U.S. dollars)**

	Variant 4 (middle birthrate, high life expectancy) (1)	No Change in Age Structure (2)	Low Birthrate, High Life Expectancy (3)	High Birthrate, Low Life Expectancy (4)
Net taxes paid by				
Newborns	66	90	66	67
Future generations	90	6	87	84
Generational imbalance				
In dollar terms	24	−84	21	17
As a percentage difference	37	−93	32	26
As a percentage of lifetime income	4.7	−16.4	4.1	3.3

results underscore the merits of the forward-looking quality of intergenerational accounting.

The assumption of a constant age structure, while useful for analytical purposes, is clearly not realistic. To further pursue the sensitivity analysis with respect to demographic developments, we employ alternative demographic scenarios provided by Statistics Netherlands. In particular, we construct two variants with rather extreme assumptions for the aging of the population. To analyze the impact of substantial aging, the first variant combines the assumption of a low birthrate with that of high life expectancy. The other variant considers the other extreme case by assuming that a high birthrate coincides with low life expectancy. Table 14.8 displays the effects of these alternative assumptions on the elderly dependency ratio. Columns (3) and (4) of table 14.7 show that the consequences of alternative demographic assumptions for the genera-

Table 14.8   **Elderly Dependency Ratios, 1995–2060**

| | | Alternative Assumptions | |
| | Base Case | | |
Year	(middle birthrate, high life expectancy)	Low Birthrate, High Life Expectancy	High Birthrate, Low Life Expectancy
1995	.20	.20	.20
2020	.31	.32	.29
2040	.45	.46	.40
2060	.40	.42	.33

Source: Statistics Netherlands.

Note: Elderly dependency ratio is the number of people aged 65 or older as a percentage of the number of people aged 18 to 64.

Table 14.9   **Sensitivity Analysis: Health Care Costs (thousands of U.S. dollars)**

	Variant 4 (1)	Additional Cost Rise between 1998 and 2020 (2)	Shift of Age Profile (3)
Net taxes paid by			
Newborns	66	57	67
Future generations	90	120	80
Generational imbalance			
In dollar terms	24	62	13
As a percentage difference	37	109	20
As a percentage of lifetime income	4.7	12.1	2.5

tional accounts are relatively minor. The imbalance falls to 4.1 percent of lifetime income in the first case and to 3.3 percent in the second.

The Costs of Health Care

The assumption that (age-specific) costs of health care will grow in line with productivity might not be realistic. In particular, an increase in the relative price of health care services combined with low price elasticity for these services might boost the growth of these expenditures (the so-called Baumol effect). A high income elasticity of health care could further reinforce this cost increase. Table 14.9 explores how sensitive the generational accounts are with respect to the future development of publicly financed health care. We assume no corresponding tax increase and therefore a shift of these additional costs to future generations. Column (2) of the table reveals that an additional increase in the cost of publicly provided health care of 1 percent per year during the period 1998–2020 substantially widens the generational imbalance from 4.7 to 12.1 percent of lifetime income.

Our analysis has assumed that the age profile of health costs is not affected by the increase in life expectancy. An alternative assumption is that as life expectancy rises, an increased portion of the elderly experience good health (see Organization for Economic Cooperation and Development 1996). In that case, the consumption of health services is concentrated more in the period immediately before death. To explore the sensitivity of the generational accounts with respect to alternative assumptions in this respect, we shift the age profile of the cost of health care for the elderly by assuming that these costs are directly related to the number of deaths. In particular, from age 60 on, the age profile of health care is shifted by an increasing margin until it reaches at age 70 a maximum of 1.6 years, being the expected increase in life expectancy. This shift is assumed to occur gradually between 1998 and 2020. Column (3) of table 14.9 shows that a healthier elderly population would reduce the generational imbalance to 2.5 percent of lifetime income.

14.4.3   The Benefits of Government Purchases

The standard practice in generational accounting does not assign the benefits of government purchases to generations. Moreover, it does not distinguish between public consumption and public investment. This section modifies this practice. In particular, we evenly assign over all currently living generations the benefits of both government consumption[9] and the public capital stock. These latter benefits are computed as an imputed rent from the public capital stock.[10]

This alternative treatment of investment improves the generational imbalance significantly (see variant 5 in table 14.10). In fact, the public finances turn out to be almost sustainable: the net contribution of newborns almost equals that of future generations. The main reason for the further improvement in the generational imbalance is that the present level of public investment exceeds the level that is needed to have the public capital stock grow in line with the growth of the economy.

With the assignment of the incidence of government purchases, the net tax burden on future generations measures fiscal "debt" shifted to future generations.[11] Table 14.10 reveals that future generations receive a net benefit from the government of $64,100, or 12.5 percent of lifetime income. Accordingly, current and past generations do not appear to employ fiscal policy to impose a burden on future generations.

9. We assume here that aggregate benefits correspond to the value of spending.

10. In particular, we compute the imputed rent as depreciation plus the product of the interest rate and the public capital stock. The initial stock of government wealth includes the physical capital stock of the government.

11. This is the level measure discussed in the introduction. If we do not assign the benefits from these purchases to generations, the level of the tax burden measures not only this "debt" but also the level of government purchases.

Table 14.10   **Assigning the Incidence of Government Purchases (thousands of U.S. dollars)**

	Variant 4 (not assigning benefits)	Variant 5 (assigning benefits)
Net taxes paid by		
Newborns	65.8	−65.9
Future generations	90.1	−64.1
Generational imbalance		
In dollar terms	24.3	1.8
As a percentage difference	36.9	2.7
As a percentage of lifetime income	4.7	0.4

Table 14.11   **Policies to Achieve Generational Balance: Variant 4**

	Immediate and Permanent Change in Item	
Item	% of Item Itself	% of GDP
Government purchases[a]	−7.9	−1.0
All taxes	2.4	1.0
Income tax	4.3	1.1
Transfer payments net of taxes	−6.1	−1.0
Health	−9.9	−.9
Education	−24.0	−1.1

Note: Real income growth assumed to be 1.5 percent; discount rate, 5 percent.

[a]Government purchases comprise expenditures on defense, general government, and government investment.

14.5   Generational Impact of Alternative Policies

The first part of this section explores a number of policy reforms designed to eliminate the generational imbalance. The second part analyzes the effects of some policy measures that are currently under debate in the Netherlands to contain the burden of aging on the public finances.

14.5.1   Establishing Generational Balance

Table 14.11 indicates the required adjustments for ensuring sustainable public finances by establishing generational balance in our preferred case (variant 4; see subsection 14.4.1). It explores this adjustment for a number of budget items in turn. As could be expected from the small generational imbalance in variant 4, the required policy changes are modest. Indeed, an (immediate and permanent) adjustment in one of these budget items of about 1 percent of GDP would suffice.

Table 14.12   **Effects of Balancing Measures on Tax Burden Borne by Several Generations (present value in thousands of U.S. dollars)**

Item	Future Generations	Newborn	30-Year-Old	60-Year-Old
Government purchases	−24.3	0	0	0
All taxes	−18.6	5.7	8.9	3.2
Income tax	−18.4	5.9	9.2	2.4
Transfer payments net of taxes	−19.4	4.8	7.0	8.1
Health	−19.6	4.7	6.3	8.6
Education	−9.7	14.6	0	0

These required adjustments, when expressed as percentages of GDP, are about the same for all budget items—irrespective of their age profiles. Table 14.12, however, indicates that the measures yield quite different effects on the level of welfare of the various generations. In particular, future generations benefit most from changes in budget items affecting the end of the life cycle, such as health and transfer payments.

14.5.2   Effects of Measures Currently under Debate

In order to reduce the burden of aging on the public finances, Dutch politicians are discussing several policy reforms. This subsection investigates the impact of these reforms on the sustainability of public finances and the net tax burden on future generations.

Taxing the Elderly

Individuals over 65 years of age are currently exempt from contributing to a number of social security schemes, including the public old-age scheme. It has been suggested that the elderly with supplementary occupational pensions should contribute to the public old-age scheme. In this way, not only the young but also the elderly with higher incomes would help to finance the flat public pension benefit. For the elderly, the net effect of the measure is an income tax rise of 40 percent and a reduction in indirect taxes paid of 8 percent. Table 14.13 shows that gradually abolishing the exemption between 1998 and 2020 reduces the generational imbalance by 42 percent. Suddenly eliminating the exemption in 1999 reduces this imbalance by 52 percent by harming those who are currently close to retirement (see the effect on 60-year-olds in table 14.13).

Additional Public Saving

Another policy option currently under debate is to accumulate a social security fund designed to finance some of the additional public pensions for the baby boom generations. We assume that this fund is accumulated by additional public savings rather than a higher deficit in the rest of the public accounts. Hence, this policy package resembles the measures analyzed in subsection 14.5.1. Here we assume that beginning in 1999, indirect taxes are raised by 1.5

Table 14.13   **Taxing the Elderly (thousands of U.S. dollars)**

	Variant 4	Taxing the Elderly Gradually	Taxing the Elderly Immediately
Taxes paid by			
60-year-olds	−40.3	−36.5	−32.0
30-year-olds	245.4	248.7	248.7
Newborns	65.8	67.2	67.2
Future generations	90.1	81.3	78.8
Generational imbalance	24.3	14.1	11.6

Table 14.14   **Raising Public Saving (thousands of U.S. dollars)**

	Variant 4	Higher Indirect Taxes
Net taxes paid by		
60-year-olds	40	40
30-year-olds	245	247
Newborns	66	67
Future generations	90	86
Generational imbalance		
In dollar terms	24	19
As a percentage difference	37	29
As a percentage of lifetime income	4.7	3.7

billion guilders (0.21 percent of GDP). This measure turns out to have only a rather small effect on the generational imbalance of 1.0 percent of lifetime income. (See table 14.14.)

14.6   Conclusion

This paper has provided two main contributions. Its methodological contribution has been to show how generational accounting can accommodate prospective changes in the economic environment in the form of an increasing participation rate, higher pension incomes, and a flatter age-earnings profile. Its second main contribution involves the computation of generational accounts for the Netherlands. The analysis indicates that the main factors affecting the intergenerational stance of present Dutch fiscal policies are the aging of the population, the expected rise in future labor participation rates, rising incomes from private pensions, and high levels of public investment. The first factor threatens the sustainability of public finances and imposes a burden on future generations. The other factors help to reduce this burden. The race between these factors appears to end close to a tie. The additional human capital of women and the additional financial assets of pensioners more or less offset

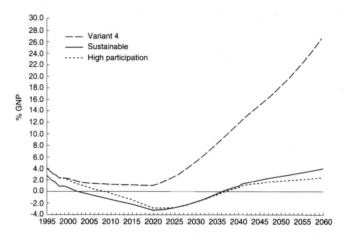

Fig. 14.6   Budget deficits: variant 4, sustainable, and high participation

the aging of the population. This rather optimistic conclusion requires three important caveats.

First, since the rise in participation occurs before the bulk of the aging, the government will have to reduce the deficit in the next two decades to create room for higher age-related spending in later decades. Figure 14.6 indicates how the budget deficit will develop in the period until 2060 in our preferred variant 4. It reveals that present policies produce a soaring deficit, mainly due to an explosion of interest payments. This reflects the unsustainability signaled by the generational accounts. In figure 14.6 we show also how the deficit develops when indirect taxes are raised by an amount that suffices to secure a sustainable policy. In that case, the fiscal balance goes into surplus by 2002. Subsequently, it remains positive for about three decades in order to finance age-related spending.

Second, the results are highly sensitive to projected labor force participation. Figure 14.6 demonstrates this by showing how the deficit develops in the high-participation case, which we referred to in subsection 14.4.2. It indicates that a policy aimed at raising labor force participation seems of great importance in order to ensure the sustainability of the public finances in an aging society. Accordingly, the government may want to stimulate labor supply by further cutting taxes. This would require additional spending cuts.

Third, our analysis does not include intergenerational redistribution occurring outside the government sector, for example, environmental externalities, inheritances within families, and transfers of know-how. Moreover, we do not explore the intergenerational redistribution performed by supplementary, occupational pension schemes. Table 14.4 indicates that these schemes play a major role in the Netherlands. If interest rates turn out to be low compared to the growth rate, these defined-benefit schemes may have to tax the young genera-

tions in the form of higher pension premiums in order to provide pension benefits to the elderly.

References

CBS/CPB. 1997. *Population and labor until 2020: Three scenarios* (in Dutch). The
Hague: Sdu Publishers.

CPB. 1992. *Netherlands in triplo: A scenario study of the Dutch economy* (in Dutch).
The Hague: Sdu Publishers.

————. 1996. *Macroeconomic forecast for 1997* (in Dutch). The Hague: Sdu Publishers.

Deelen, A. P. 1995. The development of the long-term spread in income in the Netherlands (in Dutch). CPB Research Memorandum no. 121. The Hague: CPB.

Hebbink, G. E. 1996. The burden of the public sector on future generations in the Netherlands (in Dutch). Research Memorandum no. 474/9623. Amsterdam: De Neder-
landsche Bank NV.

Kempen, E. J. van. 1996. Will the baby pay for the boom? (in Dutch). *Economisch
Statistiche Berichten* 81 (4 September): 724–28.

Organization for Economic Cooperation and Development. 1996. Ageing population,
pension systems and government budgets: Simulations for 20 OECD countries. Paris:
Organization for Economic Cooperation and Development.

Pomp, M. 1996. A model to project long-term labor supply (in Dutch). Internal CPB
Paper. The Hague: CPB.

15 Generational Accounting in New Zealand

Bruce Baker

15.1 Introduction

This chapter examines the case of generational accounting in New Zealand. In contrast to the experience of most countries in the world, future generations of New Zealanders are likely to face lower net tax burdens than current generations because of the prudent approach to fiscal policy undertaken in the recent past and projected to continue into the future. Under a range of plausible policy outcomes, New Zealand's generational accounts are likely to be close to balance, with a slight bias in favor of future generations.

This result is not accidental. In 1984, New Zealand faced a deep fiscal crisis, which forced fundamental changes in the structure of the economy, and in particular in the structure of the government's finances. A series of reforms, initiated in 1984 by the newly elected Labour government and extended by the National government elected in 1990, reversed years of poor economic performance and bad fiscal management. These reforms culminated in the Fiscal Responsibility Act of 1994, which requires, among other things, that the government balance the budget over the business cycle.

The recent election held on 12 October 1996 will prove to be a historical watershed, not because of the policies of the government brought to power—after all, the policies of the National–New Zealand First coalition are not very different from those of the National-United coalition that preceded it—but

Bruce Baker was formerly senior analyst in the New Zealand Treasury.

This chapter is adapted from the article "Generational Accounting in New Zealand: Is There Generational Balance?" by Alan J. Auerbach, Bruce Baker, Laurence J. Kotlikoff, and Jan Walliser, published in *Journal of International Tax and Public Finance* 4, no. 2 (May 1997): 201–28 and used by permission of Kluwer Academic Publishers.

The views expressed are those of the author and do not necessarily reflect the views of the Treasury.

because it is the first government elected under the new German-style mixed membership proportional (MMP) electoral system.

Under the old English-style system, New Zealand governments were able to deal with crisis efficiently by ramming legislation through the unicameral House of Representatives, often on a strict party vote, and without serious challenge from the opposition. Under MMP, electing a majority party government will be more difficult, raising the likelihood of coalition governments in the future, and the associated problems in passing legislation. Under MMP the reforms initiated in the past 23 years would have been more difficult to implement, but MMP will also make them more difficult to reverse.

In preparing New Zealand's generational accounts, it is assumed that future governments will remain committed to the concept of a balanced budget over the course of the business cycle, as mandated by the Fiscal Responsibility Act. Indeed, even the leftist Alliance Party has promised to fund its social welfare agenda though tax increases, not deficit spending, should it become part of the government.

A more detailed description of the New Zealand economy and current fiscal policy follows in section 15.2. Section 15.3 presents the assumptions behind the generational account calculations, while Section 15.4 presents the findings and discusses their implications and sensitivity to assumptions. Section 15.5 compares these results to a 1995 study of generational accounting in New Zealand (see Auerbach et al. 1997).

15.2   The New Zealand Fiscal Situation

In order to understand New Zealand's current fiscal situation, it is necessary to understand a bit of recent economic history, particularly the reforms that began in 1984 and are continuing today.[1]

From its early days, the government played a dominant role in New Zealand's economy, owning major enterprises in many sectors of the economy, including transport, communications, and finance, and restricting other sectors with stifling regulation. Until the mid-1980s, the domestic economy was sheltered from international competition with extensive import and capital restrictions, and domestic industry was supported with a range of subsidies. The government operated a generous social welfare system and provided universal health care and education. Britain's entry into the European Community in 1973, which ended New Zealand's tariff-free exports to Britain, dealt a severe blow to New Zealand's terms of trade, as did the two oil shocks of the 1970s. The reaction of the government to the second oil shock exacerbated New Zealand's fiscal problems as the government sought to ease the crisis with old-fashioned Keynesian stimulus, financing major infrastructure and energy projects while increasing subsidies to domestic businesses.

This spending, in combination with higher social welfare spending and in-

1. This discussion follows Auerbach et al. (1997).

terest on the burgeoning debt, increased financial net expenditure (which excludes lending activities) from 25.6 percent of GDP in fiscal 1973/74 to 38.3 percent in 1983/84. Part of this spending was financed through higher taxes, as revenue increased from 26.5 percent of GDP to 31.8 percent, but much was financed through borrowing, as the financial balance swung from a surplus of 1.0 percent of GDP to a deficit of 6.5 percent. Net debt grew from just 4.5 percent of GDP in 1973 to 31.5 percent in 1984.

As the fourth Labour government took office in 1984, the New Zealand economy was performing poorly. Real growth had averaged only 2 percent per year from 1973 to 1984. Inflation was enjoying a brief but temporary respite from double-digit rates, and short-term interest rates were about 14 percent. The New Zealand dollar had fallen from U.S.$1.48 in 1973 to below $0.47 by the end of 1984.

The incoming government instituted a series of reforms designed to reduce the deficit, stabilize the economy, and improve efficiency. In its first budget, the government announced cuts in subsidies and reform of the tax system. These measures were designed both to reduce the deficit and to increase economic efficiency.

In terms of macroeconomic stability, the government directed the Reserve Bank to reduce inflation. The Reserve Bank Act of 1989 formalized the requirement that the Reserve Bank's sole focus should be the achievement and maintenance of price stability.

The government set out to improve the performance of the public sector by setting clear goals for public sector managers and giving greater flexibility for their achievement, including the right to set their own salary structures.

The government also introduced major tax reforms aimed at broadening the tax base and reducing marginal rates. A comprehensive goods and services tax was introduced. Personal tax rates were reduced to 24 percent for income up to $30,875 and 33 percent above. Tax rebates to low earners created an additional effective marginal rate of 15 percent up to $9,500. Corporate tax rates were set at 33 percent.

The government also undertook a major deregulation effort, particularly with regard to the financial services sector. The newfound freedoms may have contributed to a speculative bubble on the share market, and when the stock market in New York crashed in 1987, repercussions were deeply felt in New Zealand. While the aftereffects of the crash were relatively minor around the world, in New Zealand the crash coincided with the beginning of a sustained period of difficult times. At the end of September 1992, the level of GDP was about even with that of December 1987.

In October of 1990, a new National Party government took office and embraced the Labour reforms, adding new reforms of its own. The Employment Contracts Act of 1991 substantially removed regulation of the labor markets. The 1991 budget introduced sweeping changes, including reductions in social welfare benefits, introduction of "user pays," and restructuring of the provision of health, education, and housing benefits. The budget also introduced new antievasion and avoidance measures and increases in taxes on alcohol and tobacco.

In 1994, the Fiscal Responsibility Act was passed to enhance fiscal performance over time. The act requires, among other things, that New Zealand's net debt be reduced to "prudent" levels and that the operating balance remain in surplus over time. The act also requires future budgets, beginning with 1994, to use generally accepted accounting principles (GAAP). The new GAAP measures include accrual-based operating statements and balance sheets with cash-based cash-flow and borrowings statements. The new data set allows for a more comprehensive view of the Crown's finances and more sophisticated control.

Through the difficult period of adjustment from 1983/84 to surplus in 1993/94, net financial expenditure initially increased from 38.3 percent of GDP to its high-water mark of 42.1 percent of GDP in 1990/91, before falling off to 35.6 percent in 1993/94. Revenue followed the same path, increasing from 31.8 percent of GDP to a high of 39.9 percent in 1989/90, before falling off to 36.5 percent in 1993/94. The adjusted financial balance rose from a deficit of 6.5 percent of GDP to a surplus of 1.0 percent of GDP in 1993/94. Net debt increased from 31.3 percent in 1983/84 of GDP to a peak of 52.6 percent in 1991/92. With some assistance from asset sales, net debt fell to 43.2 percent of GDP by the end of 1993/94.

Having turned the corner on the deficit, and faced with projections of ever increasing surpluses, the government announced a program of tax reductions, to be implemented in the 1996/97 and 1997/98 fiscal years, provided that net debt was projected to fall within the "prudent" range, that is, under 30 percent of GDP in the first tax cut year. The first tax cut became effective in July 1996 and reduced the lower statutory rate from 24 to 21.5 percent while raising the threshold for the top rate from $30,875 to $34,200. The second tax cut was scheduled to take effect in July 1997.

On 12 October 1996, New Zealand elected its first government under MMP.[2] On election night, National won a plurality of the votes cast with 34 percent, followed by Labour with 28 percent, the populist New Zealand First Party with 13 percent, and the Alliance with 10 percent. The staunchly free market Association of Consumers and Taxpayers won 6 percent of the vote, while the centrist United Party with less than 1 percent of the vote failed to meet the normal 5 percent threshold but gained a single seat in Parliament by winning a constituency seat.[3] The Christian Coalition and other smaller parties failed to meet the threshold and won no seats.

---

2. Proportional representation had been under consideration in New Zealand for many years, driven by the perception that the old first-past-the-post system produced unfair results. E.g., the National Party held power for nine years, from 1975 to 1984, although Labour won more votes in the 1978 and 1981 elections. In the 1993 elections, the last under the old system, the left-wing Alliance Party won 18 percent of the vote but just 2 percent of the seats in Parliament.

3. For a detailed description of MMP election rules, see Electoral Commission of New Zealand (1996).

MMP has been described as a system where the "winner of the bronze determines who gets the gold." After a series of protracted negotiations with both National and Labour, the third-place finisher, New Zealand First, decided to go into coalition with National. While details of the negotiations are still secret, speculation in the press centered on a number of factors that tipped the balance in National's favor. First of all, the combined seats of National and New Zealand First gave the coalition an absolute majority in Parliament. A coalition with Labour would have required the support of the Alliance, who would have expected some kind of payback, an unappealing prospect from the point of view of New Zealand First. Second, New Zealand First was uncomfortable with the amount of new spending proposed by Labour. Finally, National offered the leader of New Zealand First the newly created position of treasurer, carrying substantial power over fiscal and monetary policy.

The coalition agreement between the parties calls for additional spending of about 1.2 percent of GDP in fiscal 1997/98, 1.7 percent in 1998/99, and 2.1 percent in 1999/2000. About 70 percent of the additional spending is earmarked for health and education, two areas that are widely seen as underfunded. Additional revenue in 1997/98 is to be provided by deferring the second round of tax cuts, originally scheduled for 1 July 1997, until one year later. In future years, higher spending is to be paid for out of the currently predicted surpluses.

New Zealand First has also proposed to introduce a compulsory private retirement savings scheme, provided voters approve a referendum on the matter. The scheme would be funded through new withholding taxes, roughly offset by future rounds of tax cuts.

The coalition agreement points to one probable consequence of MMP, which is that future governments will find it harder to control spending. With multiparty coalitions (formal or informal) the most common form of government, it is likely that governments will find it necessary to provide funding for a longer list of budgetary priorities, as "rewards" and "bribes" replace strict party discipline as the glue that holds the government together.

15.3   Assumptions Underlying the Generational Account Calculations

Generational accounts are based on net present values of taxes paid and transfers received by different generations over their remaining lifetimes. Therefore, it is necessary to have long-term projections of taxes, transfers, and other government spending. It is also necessary to have long-term projections of population by age and sex.

To link the aggregate projections of taxes and transfers to the appropriate generations, a series of "profiles" of taxpayers and transfer recipients by age and sex are also required. These projections and profiles are used to form cash flows for each generation. In order to translate the dollar amounts into present values, it is necessary to have a discount rate. Finally, in order to solve the intertemporal budget constraint, it is necessary to have an initial value of government wealth.

Beyond the quantitative assumptions are a number of theoretical assumptions about the incidence of taxes. The general assumption used is that the tax burden is ultimately borne by the payers of each tax type. However, there is one major exception to the rule. For the company income tax, it is assumed that the tax is ultimately borne by workers. Because New Zealand is a small open economy, it is reasonable to assume that taxes on mobile corporate capital are borne by local factors, in this case labor. An alternative simulation was performed assuming that company tax is ultimately borne by the owners of capital.

Population Projections. The population projections used are special very long term extensions of Statistics New Zealand's central population projections (series 6). The projections assume medium fertility (1.90 children per woman), medium mortality (life expectancy rises from 73.6 years in 1994 to 79.5 in 2031 for males, from 79.2 to 84.0 for females), and annual immigration of 5,000 (roughly the average for the past 20 years). Beyond 2031, life expectancy continues to rise, but more slowly than in the first period.

One implication of the medium-fertility assumption, which is below the replacement rate, is that the number of children per person of working age drops from 45.2 percent in 1995 to 35.8 percent in 2100. However, increasing longevity leads the number of elderly per working-age person to more than double, from 19.5 percent in 1995 to 49.7 percent in 2100. Overall, the dependency ratio increases from 64.7 percent in 1995 to 85.4 percent in 2100. See table 15.1.

Fiscal Projections. All fiscal projections were made with Treasury's long-term fiscal model. National fiscal aggregates were supplemented with projections of the relatively small tax and spending activity of local authorities. In New Zealand most governmental activity is funded and provided at the national level. There are no states or provinces.

Taxes are categorized as wage income taxes, nonwage income taxes, corporate income taxes, goods and services tax (GST), excise taxes, local property taxes, and other taxes. Transfer payments are categorized as superannuation benefits, health, unemployment insurance, family and housing benefits, education, and other benefits.

It was necessary to make a number of adjustments to the basic GAAP numbers. New Zealand social welfare benefits are generally taxable, and the GAAP transfer numbers are gross of tax. These taxes were removed from both the income tax and transfers in order to allocate taxes and transfers to generations on a net basis. GST paid by the government to itself was similarly removed. It was also necessary to adjust the GAAP capital spending estimates to a concept compatible with the generational accounting method. In GAAP, capital expen-

Table 15.1   **Population Projections**

	Population (thousands)			Dependency Ratios (%)		
Year	All Ages	Children (0–17)	Working Age (18–64)	Elderly (65+)	Elderly	Child	Total
1995	3,577	981	2,171	424	19.5	45.2	64.7
2000	3,743	1,017	2,273	454	20.0	44.7	64.7
2005	3,887	1,031	2,372	484	20.4	43.5	63.9
2010	4,008	997	2,480	532	21.4	40.2	61.6
2015	4,119	957	2,550	612	24.0	37.5	61.5
2020	4,226	936	2,593	697	26.9	36.1	63.0
2025	4,325	935	2,578	811	31.5	36.3	67.7
2030	4,405	940	2,541	924	36.4	37.0	73.4
2035	4,456	934	2,520	1,002	39.8	37.1	76.9
2040	4,474	914	2,494	1,066	42.7	36.6	79.4
2045	4,468	891	2,504	1,073	42.9	35.6	78.5
2050	4,447	877	2,507	1,063	42.4	35.0	77.4
2055	4,418	871	2,475	1,072	43.3	35.2	78.5
2060	4,387	867	2,423	1,097	45.3	35.8	81.1
2065	4,354	859	2,381	1,113	46.8	36.1	82.8
2070	4,320	846	2,355	1,120	47.6	35.9	83.5
2075	4,285	832	2,338	1,114	47.6	35.6	83.2
2080	4,247	822	2,320	1,105	47.6	35.4	83.1
2085	4,205	813	2,291	1,101	48.1	35.5	83.6
2090	4,162	805	2,256	1,101	48.8	35.7	84.5
2095	4,119	797	2,224	1,098	49.4	35.8	85.2
2100	4,079	787	2,200	1,092	49.7	35.8	85.4

Sources: 1995–2051 from Statistics New Zealand; 2052–2100 from author's calculations.

diture is treated as a financing item, which affects accumulation of debt but is not reflected directly in the operating balance. The operating balance uses depreciation instead. However, in order to correctly attribute spending to the generation that actually paid for it, a timing adjustment was needed. A further adjustment was made to remove administrative expenses from transfers and allocate them to government consumption.

For the current year, 1996/97, the base case was identical to the baseline in the 1996 budget. For the three following years, the coalition agreement was added onto the budget. Beginning in fiscal 2000/01, individual income taxes were reduced to phase out the budget surplus over three years, after which the budget remained in balance year by year. All projections were done in nominal dollars and then converted into constant 1995/96 dollars, the base year for the accounts. The base-case assumption of balanced annual budgets involves a short-run reduction in individual income tax rates relative to current law.

As figure 15.1 shows, the amount of revenue required to balance the budget over the next decade will tend to fall as a percentage of GDP. This is partly due to favorable demographic pressures—the cohort of new retirees, born dur-

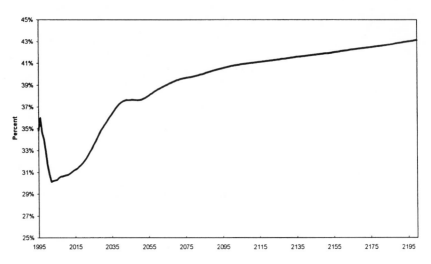

Fig. 15.1   Tax-to-GDP ratio underlying generational account calculations

ing the Depression, is a relatively small cohort, as is the cohort of students now of university age. This effect is also partly due to the legislated increase in the age of qualification for New Zealand superannuation, from 62 to 65 years, being phased in through the year 2000. During this period, the number of superannuitants is projected to fall. However, these favorable circumstances will not last long. Beginning around 2010, the oldest members of the "baby boom" generation will begin to retire and will be joined by their younger brethren in ever larger numbers. Around 2040, the peak of the baby boomers will have passed away, providing a brief fiscal respite, but in the long term, the tension between greater longevity and low fertility will lead to continuing increases in the tax-to-GDP ratios required to balance the budget. Of course, this assumes continuation of retirement at age 65.

The generally sanguine finding of this chapter that future generations of New Zealanders will face a lower *net* tax burden does not deny that future generations will face a higher *gross* tax burden needed to pay the higher health and superannuation costs that come with longer life spans.

Tax and Transfer Profiles. Most of the tax and transfer profiles used in the generational account calculations were developed from Statistics New Zealand's Household Expenditure and Income Survey (HEIS). The HEIS is a survey of about 4,600 New Zealand households.

In New Zealand, health and education are usually provided in kind, and they were thus not included in the survey. For these categories of expenses, profiles were developed from administrative data.

Government Wealth. For government wealth, the measure used is equal to the government's net financial assets, equal to financial assets less gross debt. Although New Zealand has a full balance sheet available, the Crown's tangible assets were excluded from this measure because the flows associated with these assets (both revenues and expenses) are already incorporated in the government's spending and revenue projections. Including the assets would amount to double counting in present value terms. An alternative way of handling productive assets would have been to include the assets and to exclude the revenues and expenditures associated with the assets. In theory, both approaches are equivalent because the present value of the net revenue from the productive assets should equal the asset's value.

Discount Rates. The appropriate discount rate for calculating the present value of future amounts depends on whether these amounts are known with certainty. Future government receipts and expenditures are risky, which suggests that they be discounted by a rate higher than the real rate of interest on government securities. On the other hand, government receipts and expenditures appear to be less volatile than the real return on capital, which suggests that they be discounted by a lower rate than that. The base-case calculations assume a 5 percent real discount rate, which is approximately equal to the government's assumed long-term borrowing rate. Alternative simulations were performed with real discount rates of 3 and 7 percent.

15.4   Findings

This section includes a discussion of the results for the baseline case followed by a sensitivity analysis and a discussion of some alternative scenarios.

15.4.1   Baseline Results

Tables 15.2 and 15.3 present the basic set of generational accounts for males and females for the base year of 1995/96, assuming a 5 percent real discount rate and a 1.5 percent productivity growth rate (table 15.4 reports combined results). For each of several cohorts ranging in age from 0 to 90 the tables list the generational account and the breakdown of this account into the components of household payments and receipts. The row at the bottom of each table labeled "future generations" provides the generational account, adjusted for economic growth, for the representative male or female of each future generation. This account for future generations is calculated as a residual, based on the assumption that current policy will continue to hold for existing generations and the requirement of intertemporal government budget balance.

Looking at the first column of table 15.2, one can observe that the generational account for male newborns is $47,700 (all dollar amounts are expressed in U.S. dollars, converted from New Zealand dollars at a rate of NZ$1.00 =

Table 15.2   Composition of Male Generational Accounts: Base Case (present value of receipts and payments in thousands of U.S. dollars)

		Tax Payments						Transfer Receipts					
Generation's Age in 1995	Net Payment	Wage Income Taxes	Nonwage Income Taxes	Corporate Income Taxes	GST	Excise Taxes	Property Taxes	Super-annuation	Health	UI	Family and Housing	Education	Other Benefits
0	47.7	47.1	14.1	22.7	32.5	8.3	4.6	5.1	21.8	5.4	3.5	39.6	6.3
5	61.2	52.2	16.3	26.7	35.6	9.9	5.6	6.0	18.8	6.4	4.2	42.1	7.5
10	80.3	57.4	18.8	31.4	38.1	11.8	6.8	7.1	19.9	7.7	5.0	35.4	8.8
15	104.6	63.6	21.8	36.6	39.5	13.9	8.1	8.3	20.8	9.0	5.8	24.7	10.4
20	132.3	71.5	25.0	42.4	41.1	15.8	10.0	10.0	22.2	9.8	6.7	12.7	12.1
25	158.9	81.7	30.3	49.5	45.6	18.0	12.1	13.1	25.8	9.1	7.7	8.1	14.5
30	158.5	79.8	32.2	48.8	44.7	17.8	12.8	15.6	27.4	7.3	7.3	6.0	14.1
35	145.0	72.5	33.0	44.3	42.1	16.6	12.9	18.3	28.7	5.8	6.4	4.3	13.0
40	122.4	62.4	33.6	37.9	39.3	15.1	12.6	22.0	30.8	4.8	5.3	3.0	12.5
45	91.0	49.3	33.3	29.5	35.6	13.2	11.9	26.3	32.9	4.1	4.1	1.8	12.6
50	57.9	35.3	32.6	20.8	31.5	11.1	11.1	31.6	33.4	3.4	3.1	0.7	12.1
55	26.3	22.3	31.1	12.8	27.1	9.0	10.1	38.1	34.1	2.3	2.2	0.0	9.5
60	-3.2	12.1	29.0	6.6	22.6	7.0	9.1	46.7	35.7	1.0	1.4	0.0	4.8
65	-35.4	3.8	26.1	1.9	18.2	5.1	8.1	59.4	38.2	0.0	1.0	0.0	0.0
70	-41.1	0.1	22.6	0.0	14.2	3.5	7.0	52.3	35.5	0.0	0.7	0.0	0.0
75	-40.9	0.0	18.4	0.0	10.6	2.3	5.8	43.0	34.4	0.0	0.5	0.0	0.0
80	-36.8	0.0	13.8	0.0	7.6	1.4	4.5	35.0	28.6	0.0	0.4	0.0	0.0
85	-36.1	0.0	9.3	0.0	5.4	0.9	3.1	28.5	25.9	0.0	0.3	0.0	0.0
90	-31.1	0.0	4.7	0.0	3.8	0.6	2.1	22.2	19.7	0.0	0.3	0.0	0.0
Future generations	42.6												
Percentage difference	-10.8												

Note: Productivity growth assumed to be 1.5 percent; real discount rate, 5 percent.

Table 15.3   Composition of Female Generational Accounts: Base Case (present value of receipts and payments in thousands of U.S. dollars)

Generation's Age in 1995	Net Payment	Tax Payments							Transfer Receipts					
		Wage Income Taxes	Nonwage Income Taxes	Corporate Income Taxes	GST	Excise Taxes	Property Taxes	Super-annuation	Health	UI	Family and Housing	Education	Other Benefits
0	-13.3	24.8	10.2	12.2	33.3	5.6	5.3	8.1	28.4	2.7	8.5	39.0	18.1
5	-10.2	27.5	11.8	14.4	36.7	6.7	6.5	9.5	27.8	3.2	10.1	41.6	21.6
10	-2.2	30.5	13.7	17.0	39.4	8.0	7.8	11.3	30.5	3.9	11.9	35.4	25.7
15	9.9	34.4	16.2	20.0	41.2	9.5	9.5	13.3	33.4	4.5	14.0	25.2	30.4
20	25.6	38.9	18.4	22.9	43.7	10.8	11.8	16.3	35.0	4.7	16.3	13.7	35.0
25	34.4	40.6	21.3	24.4	47.6	11.6	14.2	20.8	38.4	3.5	17.3	9.7	35.7
30	36.6	37.3	22.2	22.8	46.0	10.9	14.5	24.2	37.5	2.5	14.5	7.9	30.5
35	36.1	33.8	23.2	20.8	43.7	10.0	14.4	28.6	36.9	2.1	10.8	6.4	24.9
40	31.3	29.8	24.3	18.2	41.1	9.1	14.1	34.6	36.8	1.9	7.5	4.8	19.8
45	20.2	24.3	25.2	14.5	37.7	8.0	13.6	41.7	36.8	1.6	5.0	2.9	15.2
50	1.9	17.4	25.8	10.1	33.9	6.9	13.0	50.5	37.6	1.2	3.6	1.2	11.2
55	-22.0	10.2	25.6	5.8	29.7	5.7	12.3	61.1	38.6	0.7	3.0	0.0	7.9
60	-48.4	4.7	24.6	2.6	25.3	4.5	11.5	74.1	40.3	0.3	2.4	0.0	4.4
65	-66.1	1.3	22.5	0.6	20.9	3.3	10.4	80.6	42.5	0.0	2.0	0.0	0.0
70	-67.3	0.0	19.3	0.0	16.7	2.3	8.9	73.2	39.7	0.0	1.7	0.0	0.0
75	-63.2	0.0	15.3	0.0	13.0	1.5	7.2	61.0	37.9	0.0	1.3	0.0	0.0
80	-54.4	0.0	10.8	0.0	9.8	0.9	5.3	49.3	30.7	0.0	1.1	0.0	0.0
85	-48.2	0.0	6.5	0.0	7.3	0.6	3.5	39.7	25.4	0.0	1.0	0.0	0.0
90	-38.2	0.0	2.9	0.0	5.3	0.4	2.2	29.8	18.6	0.0	0.7	0.0	0.0
Future generations	-11.8												

Note: Productivity growth assumed to be 1.5 percent; real discount rate, 5 percent.

Table 15.4   Composition of Combined Generational Accounts: Base Case (present value of receipts and payments in thousands of U.S. dollars)

Generation's Age in 1995	Tax Payments							Transfer Receipts					
	Net Payment	Wage Income Taxes	Nonwage Income Taxes	Corporate Income Taxes	GST	Excise Taxes	Property Taxes	Super-annuation	Health	UI	Family and Housing	Education	Other Benefits
0	18.0	36.2	12.2	17.6	32.9	7.0	5.0	6.6	25.0	4.1	5.9	39.3	12.1
5	26.4	40.1	14.1	20.7	36.1	8.3	6.0	7.7	23.2	4.9	7.1	41.8	14.4
10	39.0	44.0	16.2	24.2	38.8	9.9	7.3	9.2	25.2	5.8	8.4	35.4	17.3
15	57.9	49.2	19.1	28.4	40.4	11.7	8.8	10.8	27.0	6.8	9.8	25.0	20.3
20	78.7	55.1	21.7	32.6	42.4	13.3	10.9	13.2	28.6	7.2	11.5	13.2	23.6
25	95.3	60.7	25.7	36.7	46.6	14.7	13.2	17.0	32.3	6.2	12.6	8.9	25.3
30	95.9	58.0	27.1	35.4	45.4	14.2	13.7	20.0	32.6	4.8	11.0	7.0	22.5
35	88.7	52.5	27.9	32.1	43.0	13.2	13.6	23.7	32.9	3.9	8.7	5.4	19.1
40	75.1	45.5	28.8	27.6	40.2	12.0	13.4	28.5	33.9	3.3	6.4	3.9	16.3
45	55.6	36.8	29.3	22.0	36.7	10.6	12.8	34.0	34.9	2.9	4.6	2.3	13.9
50	30.3	26.5	29.2	15.5	32.7	9.1	12.0	40.9	35.5	2.3	3.4	1.0	11.7
55	2.4	16.3	28.4	9.3	28.4	7.4	11.2	49.5	36.4	1.5	2.6	0.0	8.7
60	-26.3	8.3	26.8	4.5	24.0	5.7	10.3	60.7	38.1	0.7	1.9	0.0	4.6
65	-50.2	2.6	24.4	1.3	19.5	4.2	9.2	69.6	40.3	0.0	1.5	0.0	0.0
70	-55.8	0.0	20.7	0.0	15.6	2.8	8.1	64.0	37.9	0.0	1.2	0.0	0.0
75	-53.7	0.0	16.6	0.0	12.0	1.8	6.6	53.3	36.4	0.0	1.0	0.0	0.0
80	-47.1	0.0	12.0	0.0	8.9	1.1	4.9	43.4	29.8	0.0	0.8	0.0	0.0
85	-44.5	0.0	7.3	0.0	6.7	0.7	3.4	36.2	25.6	0.0	0.8	0.0	0.0
90	-36.3	0.0	3.4	0.0	4.9	0.5	2.2	27.7	18.9	0.0	0.6	0.0	0.0
Future generations	16.0												
Percentage difference	-10.8												

Note: Productivity growth assumed to be 1.5 percent; real discount rate, 5 percent.

U.S.$0.70). The generational account rises steadily until age 25 and falls thereafter. The initial rise is due to the fact that the heaviest taxpaying years loom closer and closer as one ages from childhood to young adulthood. The fall in the generational account occurs thereafter as more taxpaying years fall into the past and the receipt of old-age pensions and health benefits approaches. The typical 40-year-old has an account of $122,400, while a 65-year-old, entering years of peak transfer receipt, has an account of *minus* $35,400. In interpreting this pattern, it is important to remember that a generation's account equals the present value of its *remaining* lifetime net tax payments to the government. Thus one cannot directly compare the accounts of different current generations to determine their relative *lifetime* burdens.

Perhaps the most salient general observation to make about these accounts is that they indicate that future generations will bear a *lower* lifetime net tax burden than current newborns. That is, under the base-case assumptions, it will be necessary to reduce taxes on or increase transfers to future generations in order to satisfy the government's intertemporal budget constraint. For males and females combined, the reduction in lifetime tax burden is about $2,000, or 10.8 percent of the *net* burden faced by current newborns. While the amount is not great, it stands in marked contrast to those for other countries, which generally indicate that future generations will face a substantially higher burden than current generations.

A second important observation to make about these base-case results is the distinction between males and females. Though males and females have the same general pattern of generational accounts that first rise and then fall with respect to age, the accounts for females at each age are considerably lower than those for males of the same age. While today's newborn males face a lifetime net tax burden of $47,700, females face a burden that is *negative,* −$13,300. That is, they will receive transfers and government educational spending that, in present value, exceed the taxes they will pay during their lifetimes. These results come from a combination of women's lower tax payments and higher transfer receipts. The lower tax payments are due in large part to women's lower projected labor force earnings, which in turn reduce their relative burdens of labor income taxes and corporate income taxes (the latter due to our assumption about the incidence of such taxes being on labor). The higher transfer payments come in part from the fact that social welfare benefits during child-raising years go primarily to women, but even more from women's greater share of superannuation benefits and health benefits in old age, a result due to greater female life expectancy.

Tables 15.2 and 15.3 also permit a number of other interesting observations regarding the New Zealand fiscal system. One is the importance of indirect taxes. For newborn males, over one-third of all lifetime taxes take the form of indirect taxes (GST plus specific excise taxes); for females, this share is nearly one-half. On the transfer side, the largest program for both men and women is education. While, in absolute terms, pension benefits are larger, they occur much later in life and hence have a smaller present value than educational benefits.

15.4.2   Sensitivity Analysis

Generational accounts are sensitive to the assumptions used in their construction. In particular, they are sensitive to the assumed rates of discount and productivity growth. To a lesser extent, they are sensitive to the incidence assumptions.

Table 15.5 presents nine sets of calculations, corresponding to three real, before-tax interest rates (3, 5, and 7 percent) and three rates of multifactor productivity growth (1, 1.5, and 2 percent). The center column corresponds to the base-case assumptions of a 5 percent rate of interest and a 1.5 percent rate of productivity growth. For each combination of discount rate and productivity growth rate, the table shows generational accounts for newborns and future generations, and the difference between the two.

As we move from left to right in the table, we can observe that, for newborns, a rising interest rate lowers the generational account. In fact, with a 7 percent discount rate the generational account of newborns is generally negative, as the present value of the health care currently being received and the benefits of education, soon to be received, slightly outweigh the discounted present value of taxes to be paid later in life. For future generations, the same pattern of falling generational accounts can be observed.

Changes in the assumed rate of productivity growth raise projected levels of both taxes (which depend directly on the level of economic activity) and transfers (through indexing arrangements); thus there is relatively little net impact.

It is clear that the dollar amounts in the generational accounts are quite sensitive to the discount and growth assumptions used. However, the underlying message is that the accounts are in relatively close balance under most combinations of interest rate and growth.

Next is an analysis of alternative incidence assumptions, with the results given in table 15.6. The table provides the results of three simulations, all based on the intermediate discount rate, growth rate assumption ($r = 5.0$, $g = 1.5$), the first of which is simply the base case shown in table 15.4.

As discussed above the basic assumption in the base-case simulations is that the corporate income tax is borne by labor, in proportion to labor income. This assumption is consistent with the view of New Zealand as a small open economy. However, it differs from the assumptions made in the past for other countries, notably the United States, for which corporate taxes have generally been attributed to owners of capital. Thus it is important to know how much the results for New Zealand depend on this difference in assumption, rather than differences in underlying fiscal structure.

The second simulation presented in table 15.6 allocates corporate income taxes according to capital, rather than labor, income. As one would expect, the effect of this change in assumptions is to shift a part of each year's tax burden from the young to the old.

A second difference between the base-case assumptions and those used in

Table 15.5   **Sensitivity Analysis: Discount and Growth Rate Assumptions (thousands of U.S. dollars)**

	r = 3			r = 5			r = 7		
	g = 1	g = 1.5	g = 2	g = 1	g = 1.5	g = 2	g = 1	g = 1.5	g = 2
Generational accounts for									
Newborns	44.2	54.1	64.4	12.3	18.0	24.6	-2.8	-0.1	3.1
Future generations	40.6	50.2	56.4	9.5	16.0	23.5	-4.0	-1.0	2.6
Difference	-3.6	-3.9	-8.0	-2.8	-2.0	-1.1	-1.2	-0.9	-0.5

Note: r is real discount rate (percent); *g* is productivity growth (percent).

Table 15.6   **Alternative Incidence Assumptions (present value of receipts and payments in thousands of U.S. dollars)**

Generation's Age in 1995	Base Case	Corporate Tax Falls on Shareholders	Education in Government Purchases
0	18.0	8.4	57.3
5	26.4	15.2	68.2
10	39.0	26.4	74.4
15	57.9	43.4	82.8
20	78.7	63.4	91.9
25	95.3	81.3	104.2
30	95.9	87.1	102.9
35	88.7	87.1	94.1
40	75.1	82.2	79.0
45	55.6	72.3	57.9
50	30.3	56.9	31.3
55	2.4	37.1	2.5
60	−26.3	13.1	−26.3
65	−50.2	−9.8	−50.2
70	−55.8	−19.5	−55.8
75	−53.7	−24.6	−53.7
80	−47.1	−26.6	−47.1
85	−44.5	−33.5	−44.5
90	−36.3	−32.1	−36.3
Future generations	16.0	6.5	55.3
Difference	−2.0	−1.9	−2.0
Percentage difference	−10.8	−22.0	−3.4

past work by Auerbach, Gokhale, and Kotlikoff (1991) relates to educational expenditures. Here, the benefits of educational expenditures have been allocated to individual generations. Leaving educational expenditures out of the generational account calculations clearly would raise the level of the accounts, as the final column in table 15.6 shows. The accounts rise the most for the young and future generations who will benefit from educational spending. Thus this alternative assumption changes the age profile of generational accounts for existing generations. However, it has relatively little impact on the absolute size of the imbalance between current newborns and future generations. Thus neither changes in discount and growth rates nor alternative incidence assumptions alter the qualitative picture offered by the base-case results.

15.4.3   Generational Balance under Alternative Policies

Generational accounts depend heavily on the fiscal policy projections on which they are based. Obviously, there is considerable uncertainty about the actual course that fiscal policy will take over the next 200 or more years, aside from that indicated in subsection 15.4.2. In this section, a number of scenarios

Table 15.7   **Summary of Alternative Cases (present value of receipts and payments in thousands of U.S. dollars)**

Generation's Age in 1995	Base Case	Alternative Cases		
		Debt Remains at 30% of GDP	Deficit Is 2.2% of GDP	Current Tax Rates
0	18.0	19.7	19.1	11.1
5	26.4	28.2	26.4	22.1
10	39.0	40.9	37.6	38.2
15	57.9	58.9	65.5	60.6
20	78.7	78.6	75.5	84.1
25	95.3	94.3	91.2	103.3
30	95.9	93.9	91.6	105.0
35	88.7	86.1	84.7	97.9
40	75.1	72.0	71.4	83.9
45	55.6	52.4	52.5	63.5
50	30.3	27.4	37.6	37.2
55	2.4	−0.1	0.0	8.5
60	−26.3	−28.6	−28.3	−20.9
65	−50.2	−52.2	−51.9	−45.8
70	−55.8	−57.5	−57.2	−52.2
75	−53.7	−55.3	−54.7	−51.1
80	−47.1	−48.4	−47.6	−45.4
85	−44.5	−45.5	−44.7	−43.5
90	−36.3	−37.0	−36.4	−35.9
Future generations	16.0	18.3	21.9	5.3
Difference	−2.0	−1.4	2.8	−5.8
Percentage difference	−10.8	−7.2	14.6	−51.7

have been constructed to examined the fundamental assumption that individual income taxes will rise and fall in order to balance the budget, year by year. Results are displayed in table 15.7.

The first alternative scenario is a search for generational balance. Under the baseline, the budget remains in balance year by year. A consequence of this assumption is that debt as a share of GDP falls as nominal debt remains constant while nominal GDP rises. In this first alternative scenario, net debt is held constant at 30 percent of GDP instead of falling, as in the baseline.

This scenario is partially successful in balancing the generational accounts, as it reduces the imbalance in favor of future generations relative to newborns from $2,000 to $1,400. However, this result can also be said to reinforce the notion that there is no simple relationship between fiscal balance and generational balance.

The second scenario assumes a return to annual deficits amounting to 2.2 percent of GDP, the average over the past 20 years. Under this scenario, the generational balance swings away from future generations to favor current generations. Under this scenario, future generations face a net burden 14.6 percent higher than current generations. The principal beneficiaries of this policy are young adults, who face a lifetime of lower taxes.

The third scenario assumes that income tax rates remain at 1998/99 rates (after two rounds of tax cuts) instead of falling and then rising as in the baseline scenario. Under this scenario, huge surpluses build up in the current decade, completely retiring the debt by 2005. Aided by interest earnings on a rapidly accumulating stock of financial assets, surpluses eventually build to more than 100 percent of GDP. Under this scenario, future generations would face a net tax burden 51.7 percent less than that on current newborns. There are many reasons to regard this scenario as implausible, not the least of which is the assumption of relatively restrained expenditure growth in the face of huge surpluses.

15.4.4   Achieving Generational Balance

As an alternative to a trial-and-error search for a fiscal policy that balances the generational accounts as in the first alternative simulation, it is possible to solve the accounts backward for the required changes in inputs. Balance in this context means that the ratio of the net payment burden on future generations to that on newborns should be no higher than the rate of multifactor productivity growth. Most of the simulations performed for the sensitivity analysis in table 15.5, and most of the scenarios presented in table 15.7, indicate that future generations will bear a somewhat lower burden than current generations. The implication is that imposing generational balance may require a shift in some of the fiscal burden from current to future generations and is unlikely to require a shift in the other direction.

Of course, many different policies could accomplish generational balance. Starting from the base-case assumptions, we find that each of the following policies would succeed in doing so:

A reduction of 0.8 percent in all income taxes;
A reduction of individual income taxes by 1.1 percent;
An increase in superannuation benefits of 2.7 percent.

15.5   Comparison with Previous New Zealand Study

A 1995 study of generational accounting in New Zealand, prepared for the New Zealand Treasury, was based on fiscal projections from the 1995 budget. The fiscal projections used in this chapter are generally based on the 1996 budget, but with an additional spending package as contained in the new government's coalition agreement. Taxes are also higher in 1997/98 as the second round of tax cuts has been deferred by one year.

Between 1995 and 1996, projections for short-term economic growth were revised downward while projections for spending were revised upward. However, both the 1995 and 1996 budgets projected substantial budget surpluses as far as the eye can see. In practice, these surpluses were overridden by the assumption made in both studies that tax rates would fall and then rise to maintain year-by-year budget balance, although the phase-in of the balanced budget assumption was faster in the 1995 study, balancing in 1998/99 rather than in 2001/02 as in the current study.

Since the 1995 study was completed, there have been a number of important developments that have changed the demographic and fiscal projections underpinning the generational accounts.

New Demographic Projections. Statistics New Zealand has updated its population projections from a 1991 base to a 1994 base. In doing so, it has revisited its assumptions regarding fertility and mortality. It reduced its fertility assumption from 1.95 children per woman to 1.90, while raising life expectancies by nearly two years at 2031 (the ending point for many of its projections), a margin that remains about constant throughout the projections to 2200. The new projections still assume average net immigration of 5,000 but incorporate actual immigration in recent years, which has averaged well above 5,000. Taken together, these changes have adversely affected the dependency ratio throughout the period.

New Fiscal Projections. The earlier study was based largely on the 1995 budget, while the current study is based on the 1996 budget, with adjustments for higher spending. The 1996 budget assumes weaker economic growth than the 1995 budget, with average GDP growth through 2003/04 of 2.5 percent instead of 3.4 percent. The 1996 budget also assumes higher taxes and spending, even without the coalition agreement.

The results from the earlier study were expressed in New Zealand dollars. For ease of comparability, they have been converted to U.S. dollars at the current exchange rate.

Comparison of Results against 1995 Study. Overall, the results are quite similar (as can be seen in table 15.8). The balance between newborns and future generations is substantially the same, with an imbalance of between $2,000 and $3,000 in each case. However, for currently living generations, the results are fairly different, with the current chapter showing net payments about $16,000 higher for 30-year-old persons. This is mainly the effect of higher taxes in the current baseline. With spending accounting for a share of GDP that is about 1.5 percent higher than before, middle-aged persons pay substantially more in taxes.

15.6 Summary and Conclusion

This paper has used generational accounting, a new tool for fiscal analysis and planning, to study New Zealand's long-term fiscal position. Generational

Table 15.8   **Comparison with 1995 Study (present value of receipts and payments in thousands of U.S. dollars)**

Generation's Age in 1995	1996 Base Case	1995 Base Case
0	18.0	18.4
5	26.4	26.4
10	39.0	38.6
15	57.9	54.2
20	78.7	72.6
25	95.3	83.8
30	95.9	79.9
35	88.7	75.6
40	75.1	62.8
45	55.6	44.4
50	30.3	21.0
55	2.4	−5.2
60	−26.3	−31.7
65	−50.2	−55.7
70	−55.8	−58.3
75	−53.7	−55.7
80	−47.1	−49.2
85	−44.5	−44.8
90	−36.3	−36.6
Future generations	16.0	15.7
Difference	−2.0	−2.7
Percentage difference	−10.8	−14.7

accounting emphasizes the importance of implicit as well as explicit government commitments. A key question for New Zealand is whether the country's apparent fiscal health masks large implicit burdens not captured in official debt and deficit measures.

The weight of evidence suggests that behind New Zealand's projected budget surpluses, there is indeed a sound fiscal picture. Even under the base-case scenario of annual budget balance for the foreseeable future, which entails substantial short-run tax reductions, the burden on future generations (relative to income) is projected to fall slightly below that on current newborns. This striking result is not materially changed by the adoption of alternative assumptions about economic or policy parameters. New Zealand appears to have avoided the large fiscal imbalances plaguing the United States and other OECD countries, not by placing large tax burdens on young current generations, but by limiting the size of its commitments. Its fiscal health, therefore, is contingent on the maintenance of such spending discipline.

References

Auerbach, Alan J., Bruce Baker, Laurence J. Kotlikoff, and Jan Walliser. 1997. Generational accounting in New Zealand: Is there generational balance? *Journal of International Tax and Public Finance* 4, no. 2 (May): 201–28.

Auerbach, Alan J., Jagadeesh Gokhale, and Laurence J. Kotlikoff. 1991. Generational accounts: A meaningful alternative to deficit accounting. In *Tax policy and the economy,* vol. 5, ed. D. Bradford, 55–110. Cambridge, Mass.: MIT Press.

Electoral Commission of New Zealand. 1996. *Voting under MMP, New Zealand's electoral system.* Wellington: GP Publications.

16 Generational Accounting and Depletable Natural Resources: The Case of Norway

Erling Steigum, Jr., and Carl Gjersem

16.1 Introduction

Based on a new data set, this paper applies the generational accounting method (Auerbach, Gokhale, and Kotlikoff 1991) to assess the generational impact of current fiscal policies in Norway in terms of net lifetime tax burdens on present and future generations.

Norway has a small population but is endowed with large natural resources. The country has been a producer of oil and natural gas since the 1970s and is now the third largest exporter of oil in the world. More than 80 percent of Norway's petroleum revenues represent government income. Like the other Scandinavian countries, Norway is also a welfare state with a large public sector and a fairly even distribution of income. Most transfers and welfare benefits are financed on a pay-as-you-go basis.

Both GDP and employment growth rates have been relatively high during the past 25 years. Most of the net employment growth can be accounted for by public sector employment, which has increased by 80 percent since 1970.[1] The labor force participation rate is also relatively high, and the rate of unemployment has on average been quite low. Another remarkable fact is that the business cycles in Norway have been larger during the past 15 to 20 years than in the earlier postwar period, despite the automatic stabilizers built into the welfare system. Note, however, that both automatic stabilizers and countercyclical fiscal policy could bias the assessment of the long-run generational impact of

Erling Steigum, Jr., is professor of economics at the Norwegian School of Economics and Business Administration. Carl Gjersem is currently an adviser in the Norwegian Ministry of Finance.

Thanks are due to Laurence J. Kotlikoff for helpful discussions and to the Norwegian Research Council for financial support. Opinions expressed are those of the authors and not those of the Ministry of Finance.

1. At the same time, there has been a remarkable increase in the female participation rate from 44.7 percent in 1972 to 64 percent in 1995 (percentage of those in the age group 16–74).

current fiscal policies because tax revenues, transfers, and other public spending (e.g., on labor market programs) are sensitive to the business cycle and the short-run fiscal policy stance.

The government has long-term fiscal challenges similar to those facing most other OECD countries, such as population aging and increased social security spending when the baby boom generations retire. What makes Norway different is the government's considerable wealth in terms of oil, other energy resources, and net financial assets. The government now runs substantial budget surpluses. The temporary nature of the government's oil revenues represents a special challenge for fiscal planning in addition to the usual problems highlighted in the generational accounting literature.[2] A natural way to deal with this problem is to include an estimate of the government's petroleum resource wealth in the government's intertemporal budget constraint. Indeed, we think that the generational accounting method is a particularly useful tool for long-term fiscal planning and policy analysis in a resource-rich welfare state like Norway.

The method of generational accounting was first applied in Norway for the year 1992 (see Auerbach et al. 1993). This was before the Norwegian economy had recovered from the recession of the late 1980s. Due to the recent recovery, fiscal policy has changed from an expansive policy in 1990–93 to a much more austere policy from 1994 onward. The generational accounting method was discussed and applied in the *National Budget 1995* (released in October 1994), the annual economic policy document of the government. Since then, generational accounting has been used by the government on a regular basis to assess the long-run fiscal balance. The estimated generational imbalance between present and future generations has been reduced remarkably compared with the first results reported by Auerbach et al. (1993). At the present, there is probably generational balance.

The rest of this paper is organized as follows. Section 16.2 looks back on the recent history of the welfare state and fiscal policy in Norway and discusses the ideas behind the State Petroleum Fund, which was established in 1990 to prevent excessive spending of temporary petroleum revenues. In section 16.3, we give a brief description of the data underlying our projections of population, public expenditures and receipts, and government wealth. Section 16.4 reports new results from applying the generational accounting method with 1995 as the base year. Also some sensitivity analysis are reported. Section 16.5 analyzes the impact of alternative policies that hypothetically could equalize the growth-adjusted net tax burdens of present and future generations. Section 16.6 summarizes our results.

---

2. For a recent study of this problem, see Steigum and Thøgersen (1995), who simulate a computable overlapping generations model to illustrate the intergenerational welfare effects of consuming the entire petroleum wealth in the course of the next 40 years.

16.2   Fiscal Policy: Brief History and Present Challenges

16.2.1   The Norwegian Welfare State

The government now spends almost 30 percent of GDP on social protection in the form of various transfers to households, health care, labor market programs, and so forth (see Risa 1996). In addition, the government's expenditures on education total 6.6 percent of GDP. The public sector supplies most educational and health services, including higher education. Consumers pay very little for these services.

The Norwegian welfare state is of recent origin. In 1960, total government spending was 26.4 percent of GDP, which was slightly *lower* than the corresponding number for the United States. The universal and partly earnings-related social security pension scheme was introduced in 1967 and is still maturing. The principle of universalism has been a characteristic of the Scandinavian welfare states. For example, both child support and the old-age pension are universal benefits in Norway. Still, there is a trend away from universalism and toward more targeting in some areas.

The expansion of welfare programs was particularly fast in the 1970s. For example, in 1978 Norway established one of the most generous sickness benefit schemes in the world, involving 100 percent compensation from day one. Government spending on several public assistance programs increased rapidly in the 1980s as well, notably disability pensions, sickness benefits, unemployment benefits, lone parents' allowances, and means-tested municipal economic assistance. This development has caused concern among policymakers. In the 1990s, the government formulated a broad strategy to strengthen the economic foundation and sustainability of the welfare state. An important element of this strategy was the "working approach," aimed at promoting employment and reducing welfare dependency. For example, measures have been taken to curb the growth in spending on unemployment benefits and disability pensions through various labor market programs designed to enhance human capital and increase labor force participation. In recent years, reforms to make the old-age pension system partially funded have also been discussed.[3]

16.2.2   Macroeconomic Planning and Fiscal Policy

In the postwar period, economic policy thinking in Norway has been marked by a strong belief in macroeconomic planning and economic policy activism, beliefs and ideas that can be traced back to the intellectual influence of Nobel laureate Ragnar Frisch (1896–1973) on several generations of Norwegian

---

3. The implications of such reforms for intergenerational distribution of welfare have also been examined, using calibrated overlapping generations models of the Norwegian economy (see Steigum 1993; Raffelhüschen and Risa 1995).

Table 16.1   Net Saving Rates in Norway, Europe, and the United States (percent)

Country/Region and Sector	1970–79	1980–89	1990–94
Norway			
National	11.6	12.3	7.3
Government	7.0	7.6	4.7
Private sector	4.6	4.7	5.5
European countries[a]			
National	13.2	8.3	6.6
Government	1.8	−0.4	−1.6
Private sector	11.4	8.7	8.2
United States			
National	8.5	4.4	2.7
Government	−0.6	−3.0	−3.5
Private sector	9.0	7.4	6.2

Source: Leibfritz et al. (1995, annex 5, table A9).

Note: The definition of public saving captures neither increased social security debt nor changes in the government's petroleum wealth.

[a]Germany, France, Italy, United Kingdom, Austria, Belgium, Denmark, Finland, Norway, and Sweden. Weighted average (1991 GDP weights).

economists.[4] The unique Norwegian system of macroeconomic planning, which was developed in the 1950s and 1960s, may explain why the Norwegian capital market remained particularly underdeveloped for decades, until a long overdue financial deregulation policy was launched in the 1980s. Before the financial deregulation, real rates of interest were kept artificially low—after-tax rates even negative most of the time—private saving was small, and credit rationing and liquidity constraints were widespread. In this institutional setting, fiscal policy was quite potent.

An important fiscal policy goal was to generate enough saving to fulfill the government's ambitious goals with respect to capital accumulation and investment allocation on sectors. The government therefore ran substantial surpluses during most of the postwar period. Table 16.1 highlights the important role of public saving. In the 1980s, government net saving (conventionally measured) was on average 7.6 percent of GDP in Norway, and negative (on average) in Europe.

16.2.3   Oil Revenues: A New Challenge for Fiscal Policy

In the pre-oil period 1950–70, the governments (mostly social democratic ones) were fairly successful in managing the economy, at least in terms of macroeconomic stability.[5] After Norway became a producer of oil and natural

4. Frisch also had very pessimistic views on the social benefits of decentralized resource allocation through the market economy.
5. A likely social cost of the macroeconomic planning system was a low real rate of return from domestic investment.

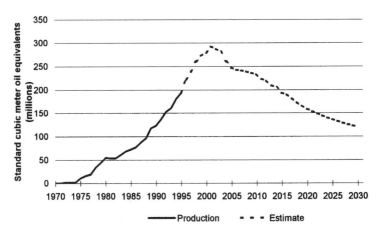

Fig. 16.1   Production of oil and natural gas
Note: See appendix table 16B.1 for data.

gas, however, it turned out to be much harder to manage and stabilize the economy. Norway's macroeconomic problems after OPEC I in 1973–74 were however of a different nature than the stagflationary problems of the oil-importing European countries: in Norway, the main problem after OPEC I was inflationary pressure from very fast growth of domestic aggregate demand. This was due to the positive wealth effect of the oil price shock, a lenient macroeconomic policy to counteract the effects of the international recession, and the aggregate demand effect of a very high rate of investment in the petroleum industry.

Figure 16.1 illustrates the rapid growth of petroleum production since 1975, as well as a projection of petroleum production to 2030. The growth rate of petroleum production has been unexpectedly high during the past 10 years, partly because technological progress has been rapid. The production of oil and natural gas is expected to peak shortly after 2000 and then decline in subsequent decades.

The government's net cash flow from the petroleum sector has been very volatile. It increased dramatically in 1980 due to OPEC II and then fell to almost zero as a result of the oil price plunge in 1985–86. Figure 16.2 shows the government's projection of the net cash flow for the years 2001, 2010, and 2030, as well as for some previous years. In the past 10 years, increased oil production as well as lower operating costs explain most of the remarkable growth of the government's net cash flow from the petroleum sector. Increased production and a lower rate of investment are expected to increase the government's net cash flow to 9 percent of GDP in the year 2001. From then on, the net cash flow is expected to decline. The projection of the net cash flow in figure 16.2 is consistent with the estimates of the government's petroleum wealth used in our calculations of generational accounts.

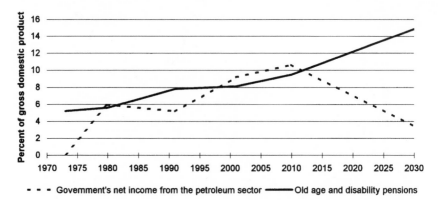

Fig. 16.2   Projected government net income from petroleum sector and old-age and disability pensions

Note: See appendix table 16B.2 for data.

Figure 16.2 also shows a rapid increase in the projected spending on social security pensions as a percentage of GDP in the next century, due to demographics as well as the maturing process of the earnings-related pension scheme. The figure illustrates the expected decline in the importance of the net cash flow from the petroleum sector as a financial resource for the Norwegian welfare state in the future. Since neither changes in petroleum wealth nor social security debt are captured by the conventional budget surplus concept of the government, the latter is a particularly misleading indicator of long-run fiscal balance in the case of Norway.

16.2.4   Business Cycles and Fiscal Policy

Both OPEC I and II had tremendous impacts on Norway's economy. After OPEC I in 1973–74, the fast growth of aggregate demand and huge capital imports led to macroeconomic policy restraint that slowed down the growth in aggregate demand at the end of the decade. The combination of this policy and OPEC II had a very large effect on the external balance, which turned into large surpluses in the current account in the first half of the 1980s. Figure 16.3 indicates that the Norwegian economy has been exposed to larger macroeconomic fluctuations after 1980 than before. This figure shows employment as well as the value added of mainland Norway, that is, GDP net of the petroleum industry and shipping.

The large business cycle in the late 1980s can be traced back to the "credit boom" in the aftermath of the financial deregulation policy in 1984-85.[6] This boom, together with the oil price shock in 1986 and the subsequent deterioration of the current account, triggered a countercyclical fiscal and monetary

---

6. For a discussion of the financial deregulation as well as the fiscal and monetary policy that fueled the credit boom in the 1980s, and the subsequent banking crisis, see Steigum (1992).

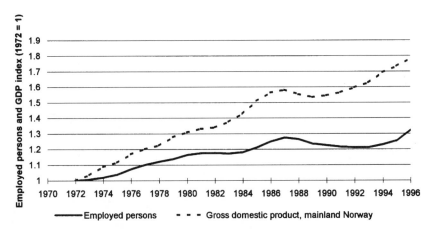

Fig. 16.3   Aggregate employment and GDP for mainland Norway
Note: See appendix table 16B.3 for data.

policy. The credit boom was followed by a quite deep and protracted recession, despite a shift in fiscal policy to boost consumer spending in the beginning of the 1990s. A new business cycle upturn began in 1993, and at present the Norwegian economy is again booming and indeed is running the risk of overheating.

The inflation in the 1970s and 1980s undermined the income tax system and gave rise to large tax wedges in labor and capital markets. In addition to excessive marginal tax rates on labor income, the combination of inflation and unlimited tax deductions of nominal borrowing costs—as well as the government's regulation of nominal interest rates—led to persistently negative after-tax real rates of interest. Marginal tax rates were gradually reduced in the late 1980s, however, and a tax reform was put into effect in 1992. The tax reform broadened the income tax base and reduced the statutory tax rate on nominal capital income to 28 percent, and the maximum marginal tax rate on labor income to 49.5 percent. In addition to its negative effects on economic efficiency and resource allocation, the former tax system also contributed to macroeconomic instability, in particular by excessively stimulating spending financed by credit. Both the volatile petroleum revenues of the government and its countercyclical fiscal policy have contributed to large cycles in the government's budget surplus (see fig. 16.4).

A comparison of figures 16.2 and 16.4 shows quite clearly the influence of the petroleum cash flow on the government's net investment in financial assets. For example, in the period 1981–85 the oil price was very high, leading to a rapid accumulation of government financial assets. When we control for petroleum revenues, however, the government's budget surplus is also very sensitive to the business cycle. During the recessionary period 1988–92, falling tax revenues as well as increased spending on unemployment benefits and labor market

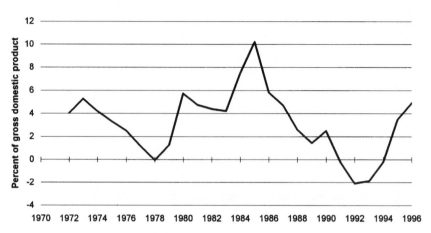

Fig. 16.4   Government net investment in financial assets
Note: See appendix table 16B.4 for data.

programs had a very strong impact on the overall budget balance (see fig. 16.4). Correspondingly, strong employment growth and declining unemployment in recent years have contributed to a remarkable improvement in the budget balance. The surprising cyclical instability of the Norwegian economy during the past 15 to 20 years explains why most of the focus of fiscal policy has been on macroeconomic stability.[7] Still, in recent years there has also been greater awareness of the uncertainties surrounding the government's future petroleum revenues as well as the projected increase in social security pensions and other welfare spending beyond the year 2010, as illustrated in figure 16.2.[8]

16.2.5   The State Petroleum Fund

The large fluctuations in the government's petroleum revenues since the late 1970s have to some extent been absorbed by changes in the government's stock of net financial assets (see figs. 16.2 and 16.4). Still, there has been a growing awareness of the danger that the temporary oil revenues will be spent too quickly. This concern is partly based on previous policy mistakes and partly on the parliamentary situation in Norway, which leads mostly to minority governments. As in most other countries with large public sectors, Norwegian governments are exposed to strong pressure from many influential special interest groups dependent on subsidies, transfers, and other public spending.

As an institutional response to political pressure to spend petroleum revenues quickly, the government established the State Petroleum Fund in 1990.

7. In Norway as in most other small European countries, it is fiscal and not monetary policy that is considered most effective for domestic macroeconomic stabilization. After the financial deregulation, monetary policy in Norway has been geared to stabilization of the exchange rate.

8. This particular illustration first appeared in the government's Long Term Programme in 1993 and has been presented in several national budgets afterward.

Table 16.2   Norway's Demographic Transition

	1995	2015	2050	2100
Population (millions)	4.38	4.78	5.16	5.19
Working age (%)	60.9	61.1	57.4	56.8
Elderly (%)	15.9	17.2	22.2	23.1
Elderly dependency ratio[a] (%)	26	29	40	41

Source: Statistics Norway, *Population Projections 1996–2050: National and Regional Figures,* NOS C H14 (Oslo, 1997), and authors' calculations.

[a]The ratio of those aged 65 or older to those aged 19 to 64.

The goal of the fund is to avoid excessive spending of petroleum revenues and promote a gradual transformation of oil wealth into foreign assets. The fund is likely to make the government's decisions to spend or save petroleum revenues more *visible.* For example, according to the rules of the fund, it is not possible to increase the fund without a budget surplus of the central government. Moreover, future budget deficits will lead to a corresponding decline in the size of the fund. This prevents the creation of an "artificial" fund financed by public borrowing. The year 1995 was the first in which the government ran a budget surplus since the State Petroleum Fund was formally established. Investment in the fund in 1995 was quite small, however; but in 1996 the size of the investment is projected to reach 4.5 percent of GDP. According to the medium-term projection of the government's receipts and expenditures reported in the *National Budget 1997,* the Petroleum Fund will grow rapidly in the rest of the 1990s.

16.3   Data

In this section we revise and update the description of the data sources in Auerbach et al. (1993). More details are given in appendix A. To form generational accounts for current and future generations, we need (1) projections of the population by age and sex, (2) projections of average net taxes for each member of each generation in each year in which as least some of its members will be alive, (3) an estimate of the initial stock of government net wealth, and (4) projections of future government spending on goods and services that are not distributed on age groups.

16.3.1   Population Projection

The projection of population by age and sex from 1995 through 2200 has been provided by Statistics Norway. It builds on recent trends in fertility, mortality, and net immigration. In 1995, Norway's population was 4.38 million, and—as in almost all OECD countries—the population is on average getting older. Table 16.2 shows how this aging process will play out through the next century. The projections assume that the current fertility rate of 1.86 percent

Table 16.3   Public Expenditures and Receipts, 1995 (percent of GDP)

Receipts	
Direct and indirect taxes and social security contributions	42.6
Petroleum taxes	3.0
Indirect taxes, mainland Norway	15.4
Direct taxes and social security contributions, mainland Norway	24.2
Income from capital and wealth	8.6
Total receipts	51.2
Expenditures	
Consumption of goods and services	20.7
Net investment	2.1
Transfers	22.0
Interest payments	2.9
Total expenditures	47.7
Surplus	3.5

Source: National Budget 1997.

will prevail in future years, and that life expectancy at birth will continue to increase, leading to an expected life span of 80 years for males and 84.5 years for females by 2050. The annual net flow of immigrants is assumed to be 7,000 individuals (0.16 percent of total population in 1995). The percentage of Norwegians over age 65 is now 15.9, but by 2050 that figure should hit 22.2. The elderly dependency ratio of 0.26, already quite high, is expected to increase sharply after 2015, reaching 0.40 by the year 2050.

16.3.2   Public Expenditures and Receipts

Our projections of average future taxes and transfers by age and sex begin with the 1995 official totals for all levels of government. Table 16.3 shows the principal components of the Norwegian government's expenditures and receipts in 1995 (both central and local government), based on national accounts definitions. The 1995 budget surplus was positive, 3.5 percent of GDP, after several years of deficits. Looking first at the receipts, we see from table 16.3 that indirect taxes amount to 15.4 percent of GDP. The value-added tax rate is now 23 percent. In addition, there are substantial consumption taxes (excise taxes) on cars, gasoline, alcohol, tobacco, and some other commodities. Excluding petroleum taxes, direct taxes and social security contributions represent 24.2 percent of GDP, most of which are taxes on labor income. Direct taxes on labor income are progressive. Social security contributions are partly a payroll tax and partly a direct tax on labor income. There is full tax deductibility of nominal borrowing costs. Traditionally, households have been heavily indebted. The net tax revenues from capital income have therefore been small and even negative. There is also a progressive wealth tax that may have significant adverse incentive effects on private saving. Property taxes are a minor item. Because the Norwegian government's wealth is huge, income from capital and wealth is large, 8.6 percent of GDP. This number does not include petroleum taxes, however. On the other hand, interest on the government's debt (2.9 percent of GDP) is not deducted; see the last item under "expenditures." The government in Norway is an important financial intermediary, channeling loans through special government financial institutions, called state banks, funded through government bond issues. The gross debt of the government was 42 percent of GDP in 1995. Still the government has positive net financial assets.

Turning to the government expenditures in table 16.3, we see that transfers total 22.0 percent of GDP. Subsidies, primarily agricultural, represent 4.0 percent. In 1995, public expenditures on social security pensions (old-age and disability pensions) amounted to 8 percent of GDP. Social security spending is expected to grow rapidly in the future (see fig. 16.2). Public consumption represented 20.7 percent of GDP in 1995. About 31 percent of total employment is in the public sector, including education and health care organized by local governments. In 1995, public spending on education and health amounted to 6.6 and 6.4 percent of GDP, respectively. To calculate generational accounts, it is assumed that net per capita general government spending (not distributed on age groups as transfers) keeps in line with the productivity growth rate.

16.3.3 Taxes and Transfers

To construct age profiles, taxes are categorized as value-added taxes (VAT), auto excise and gasoline taxes, as well as alcohol, tobacco, and some other excise taxes (EX), social security contributions (SST), and income taxes (YTX), which also include the wealth tax. In table 16.4, the 1995 per capita value of each category, distributed by sex, are presented.[9] Observe that SST and YTX exclude taxes on pension income paid by retirees. Correspondingly, pensions are defined as after-tax pensions. Military service is mandatory for males in Norway. We have not, however, tried to estimate the implicit tax on males (and the corresponding addition to expenditures on defense).

The two far most important tax categories are YTX and SST. On a per capita basis, each Norwegian pays $3,461 in income and other direct taxes (not counting direct income taxes from pensions) and $3,320 in social security contributions (including payroll taxes). The third largest category is VAT ($2,086). Males pay more direct taxes and social security contributions than females, who generally have lower participation rates, more part-time work, and lower hourly compensation. Also, the progressive nature of direct income taxes con-

---

9. Two minor simplifications have been done in the accounts since the first report by Auerbach et al. (1993). In the present version we do not estimate separate time profiles for alcohol and tobacco excise taxes or for the wealth tax.

Table 16.4   Taxes and Transfers and Public Expenditures Related to Age Groups, 1995 (U.S. dollars per capita)

	Males	Females	Sum
Taxes			
Value-added taxes (VAT)	1,035	1,051	2,086
Auto, gasoline, tobacco, and alcohol taxes (EX)	702	713	1,415
Social security contributions (SST)	2,133	1,187	3,320
Income taxes and other direct taxes (YTX)	2,398	1,063	3,461
Sum taxes	6,268	4,014	10,282
Transfers and Expenditures Related to Age Groups			
Transfers			
Old-age pensions, after direct tax (PEN)	908	1,117	2,025
Disability pensions (DIS)	373	348	721
Sickness allowance (SIK)	256	362	618
Family allowance (FAM)	13	406	419
Unemployment (UNM)	343	230	573
Other social security benefits (OTH)	436	600	1,036
Sum transfers	2,329	3,063	5,392
Expenditures			
Old-age support (OLD)	254	439	693
Health benefits (HOS)	374	581	955
Education (EDU)	1,086	1,105	2,191
Sum expenditures	1,714	2,125	3,839
Sum transfers and expenditures	4,043	5,188	9,231
Net Taxes			
Net taxes	2,225	−1,174	1,051
Net taxes excluding EDU	3,311	−69	3,242

Sources: Various data sources, see appendix A.

Note: The numbers in all three columns are aggregates divided by the entire population (4.38 million).

tributes to the large gender difference in tax payments. Existing data do not permit a distribution of VAT and other indirect taxes by sex. Individual tax payments of VAT and EX for each age cohort are therefore assumed to be the same for males and females.

Due to data limitations, there are tax categories that we have not distributed by age and sex, in particular corporate taxes and VAT paid by firms and the public sector itself. Neither are petroleum taxes and taxes paid by hydroelectric power companies included in table 16.4. This is due to the fact that we capitalize the petroleum and hydroelectric power wealth owned by the government and define these as part of total government wealth (see below). In our calculations of generational accounts, the petroleum and energy taxes referred to above are therefore accounted for by the rate of return on government wealth.

In the Norwegian generational accounts, government expenditures on education and some categories of public spending on health and public services to retirees are treated in the same way as transfers to specific age cohorts. Transfer payments distributed by age and sex are categorized as direct old-age-related spending (old-age support, OLD), spending on health benefits that can be traced to age groups (HOS), education (EDU), old-age pensions (PEN; after tax, but including survivors' pensions), disability pensions (DIS), sickness and childbirth benefits (SIK), universal child support (FAM), unemployment benefits and labor market programs (UNM), and other social security benefits (OTH).[10] The per capita values of these categories are also shown in table 16.4. The most important transfer category is PEN, but EDU is very important too. In the generational accounts of some countries, educational spending by the government is not treated as transfers. Since the label of this spending category makes a lot of difference to the accounts, we also present calculations of generational accounts without distributing EDU by age. The other quantitatively important transfer categories are DIS, SIK, FAM, and UNM. The social security system in Norway does not have a general early retirement scheme, and the normal retirement age is 67 years. As a consequence, many individuals above age 60 (particularly males) receive disability pensions and sickness benefits. In addition to unemployment benefits, a substantial part of UNM is spending on labor market programs.

Looking at the distribution of transfers by sex, females have a larger share than males for most categories, the main exception being UNM. Even though the pension scheme is partly earnings related, it gives more transfers to females in the aggregate, due to their longer life expectancy.

Table 16.4 also shows per capita net taxes, which are only $2,225 for males and −$1,174 for females, in sum $1,051. The latter is a very low number compared to the gross per capita taxes in table 16.4, and it illustrates the importance of welfare spending in Norway. The size of the net tax is very sensitive to whether we label public educational spending as transfers or general government spending. In the latter case, the net per capita tax increases to $3,311 for males and −$69 for females, in total $3,242 (see table 16.4).

16.3.4 Government Wealth

Our measure of government net wealth is the sum of four components: (1) petroleum wealth, (2) hydroelectric power wealth, (3) shares and equity capital, and (4) other financial assets (net). Existing data on public wealth are incomplete and generally not based on market values. Our calculations of generational accounts depart from the conventional definition of wealth in the national accounts, primarily because we include natural resource wealth. Since Norway's petroleum wealth is not marked to market, the petroleum wealth estimate is calculated as the present value of expected net future cash flow to the

---

10. Other social security benefits include among other things rehabilitation benefits and lone parents' allowances.

government.[11] In our estimate, future oil prices have been adjusted for risk. The generational accounts presented in tables 16.5 through 16.9 are based on the petroleum wealth estimate in the *National Budget 1997* (released in October 1996), which was 124 percent of GDP (5 percent real rate of interest). In February 1997 the government's estimate of the future time path of oil production was revised upward to a considerable extent, increasing the former petroleum wealth estimate by 29 percent. We shall return to how the revised petroleum wealth affects our results below.

16.4   Basic Findings and Sensitivity Analysis

16.4.1   Basic Findings

Table 16.5 presents the generational accounts for all present and future generations in 1995 under the base-case assumptions (real rate of interest, 5 percent; productivity growth rate, 1.5 percent). The accounts are the present values of the sum of net taxes over the expected remaining lifetime of each generation, assuming that the fiscal policy rules in 1995 apply to all present generations (the 1995 cohort and all older cohorts). Following the generational accounting methodology explained in Auerbach et al. (1991, 1993), the average (growth-adjusted) account for future generations is calculated as a residual from the intertemporal budget constraint of the government.

Comparing the first and last rows of the last column, we see that future generations face a net lifetime tax burden exceeding the account for newborns in 1995 by about $55,900. It is not meaningful to use the percentage difference as a measure of intergenerational tax burden shifting, however, because the average account for newborns in 1995 is close to zero, only $1,400. The low value of the newborns' account is due to the fact that we distribute government educational spending on age groups. For the 5-year-old cohort, the account is even negative. For older generations in 1995 the accounts become larger, reaching a maximum of about $130,000 for 30-year-olds. The average account turns negative for those who are 50 years old in 1995, hitting a minimum for the 70-year-old generation, amounting to about −$180,000.

The gender difference in table 16.5 is significant. The average accounts for newborn boys and girls in 1995 differ by about $170,000. The maximum difference between males and females occurs for 25-year-olds. Then the average account for males is $248,500 and for females only $1,400. For generations older than 60 years, the difference is much smaller. The gender difference can be understood by looking at the more detailed information presented in table 16.6, which splits the base-case results into components of payments and re-

11. Our method does not deal explicitly with the problem of cash-flow risk, which is substantial in the case of petroleum cash flow. Moreover, since the government is not able to diversify away the risk, the precautionary savings motive could be important for Norwegian fiscal policy. This is not captured by the concept of fiscal balance in the present paper.

Table 16.5   **Accounts for All Present and Future Generations: Base Case (thousands of U.S. dollars)**

Generation's Age in 1995	Males	Females	Weighted Sum
0 (newborns)	64.9	−65.8	1.4
5	66.7	−85.5	−7.5
10	104.9	−80.2	14.7
15	163.6	−53.2	58.4
20	225.3	−16.6	106.3
25	248.5	1.4	127.1
30	244.5	8.0	129.6
35	218.0	9.5	116.2
40	172.3	4.9	90.3
45	97.8	−23.1	38.9
50	13.1	−59.1	−22.3
55	−40.5	−106.0	−73.0
60	−124.5	−145.5	−135.3
65	−156.1	−184.1	−170.6
70	−163.2	−194.0	−179.6
75	−150.9	−184.1	−170.0
80	−131.1	−169.7	−155.1
85	−115.8	−150.9	−139.4
90	−101.0	−130.5	−122.6
95	−82.7	−100.4	−96.7
Future generations (account for newborns in 1996)[a]			57.3

Notes: Only the accounts for one-fifth of the present generations are shown. Government spending on education is distributed on age groups. Productivity growth rate assumed to be 1.5 percent; real rate of return, 5 percent; exchange rate, 6.33 kroner per U.S. dollar.

[a] All future newborn generations have the same growth-adjusted account.

ceipts for males and females. Comparing the upper and lower parts of table 16.6, we see that males pay much more in social security taxes (SST) and direct income taxes (YTX) over their lifetimes than females. This is due to lower labor force participation, lower average working hours, and the lower average hourly wage for women than men. In addition, women receive higher lifetime benefits than men, particularly universal child support (FAM),[12] sickness and childbirth benefits (SIK), and health benefits (HOS). Both the higher health benefits and the higher present values of women's pensions (PEN) are mainly due to women's greater longevity.

Looking more closely at the various transfers from the government, the two

12. For simplicity, universal child support has been included in the accounts of the parents (mostly mothers). We could alternatively have distributed these benefits on their children, in which case the gender difference in the accounts of newborns would have been reduced by approximately $20,000, i.e., about 14 percent. On the other hand, the gender difference would probably have been much larger if the implicit military service tax on males had been accounted for.

Table 16.6 Composition of Accounts for All Present Generations: Base Case (present value of receipts and payments in thousands of U.S. dollars)

Generation's Age in 1995	Net Payment	Payment				Receipts								
		VAT	EX	SST	YTX	OLD	HOS	EDU	PEN	DIS	SIK	FAM	UNM	OTH
Males														
0	64.9	54.7	37.1	82.2	87.1	6.7	14.9	102.7	17.1	12.7	9.2	0.5	15.0	18.0
10	104.9	60.1	40.8	116.3	123.4	9.6	18.1	106.0	24.5	17.2	13.1	0.7	21.2	25.4
20	225.3	64.1	43.5	153.5	164.2	12.4	20.8	31.6	33.4	23.0	17.5	1.0	27.6	32.7
30	244.5	57.7	39.1	158.3	179.8	15.2	22.3	6.7	43.3	28.8	20.6	1.2	21.8	30.7
40	172.3	49.8	33.8	133.1	162.9	19.7	25.1	1.8	63.0	36.1	20.5	0.8	16.0	24.4
50	13.1	39.2	26.6	88.1	116.0	25.7	26.3	0.1	112.4	41.5	18.3	0.2	12.6	19.6
60	−124.5	27.3	18.5	38.3	62.4	34.4	27.0	0	148.0	33.3	9.1	0.1	9.6	9.7
70	−163.2	16.2	11.0	6.1	21.6	45.3	20.8	0	148.7	0.1	0.2	0	0.2	2.7
80	−131.1	8.5	5.8	2.6	8.0	62.4	8.0	0	82.6	0	0	0	0	3.0
90	−101.0	4.4	3.0	1.6	3.2	70.1	4.5	0	38.3	0	0	0	0	0.3
Females														
0	−65.8	56.0	38.0	50.2	42.8	9.8	23.4	107.3	23.7	12.0	17.0	19.3	10.8	30.3
10	−80.2	62.2	42.2	71.1	60.7	12.8	30.8	112.2	33.9	17.1	24.1	27.4	15.3	42.7
20	−16.6	66.3	45.0	92.7	79.8	16.6	37.1	37.5	44.4	22.8	31.8	36.3	20.1	53.7
30	8.0	59.8	40.6	88.4	80.5	20.6	32.2	10.2	56.5	28.2	26.6	35.0	15.5	36.4
40	4.9	52.1	35.3	72.2	70.1	27.3	29.5	4.1	73.1	34.0	13.7	13.1	10.3	19.8
50	−59.1	41.9	28.4	46.3	48.2	36.4	30.7	0.4	90.9	35.7	10.3	1.3	7.0	11.1
60	−145.5	30.5	20.7	18.8	21.8	49.9	33.6	0	117.6	24.0	3.7	0	3.2	5.4
70	−194.0	19.1	12.9	2.9	5.2	65.3	30.6	0	135.0	0	0	0	0	3.1
80	−169.7	10.3	7.0	1.4	2.0	82.8	17.2	0	86.6	0	0	0	0	3.8
90	−130.5	5.0	3.4	0.8	0.7	81.2	9.2	0	44.4	0	0	0	0	5.8

Notes: Only the accounts for one-tenth of the present generations are shown. Government spending on education is distributed on age groups. Productivity growth rate assumed to be 1.5 percent; real rate of return, 5 percent; exchange rate, 6.33 kroner per U.S. dollar.

most important are education (EDU) for the youngest cohorts and pensions (PEN) for the oldest. Since the average present value of education is more than $100,000 at birth, it makes an enormous difference to the accounts for newborns whether educational spending is treated as a transfer or not. For the old cohorts, various old-age benefits (OLD) supplied by local governments are also very important for the generational accounts in addition to social security pensions.

16.4.2   Sensitivity to Alternative Assumptions

Table 16.7 shows the results of sensitivity tests with respect to the growth and real interest rates. The accounts of present and future generations (represented by newborn cohorts) have been calculated for nine combinations of growth and interest rate assumptions. In panel A of table 16.7, educational spending has been treated as age-specific transfers just as in tables 16.5 and 16.6. In panel B government spending on education is not treated as a transfer but is included in general government spending. It is hard to judge the interest rate sensitivity of intergenerational tax shifting just from the present values themselves. In panel A, for example, the lifetime net tax burdens of both present and future generations decrease when the interest rate increases, and because the former are either very small or negative, it is not meaningful to compute relative differences. For the same reason, it is also difficult to evaluate how the three different assumptions of growth rates affect our results just by looking at panel A of table 16.7. We therefore turn to panel B.

Panel B of table 16.7 reports the results when government spending on education is not treated as age-specific transfers. This change in labeling alters the definition of "net tax" and increases the size of net taxes for all cohorts who receive subsidized education. To explain how this will change the results, observe that if the age-group distribution of the population is stationary, present and future aggregate government spending will not be altered by the new labeling. Therefore, the difference between the accounts of future and present generations will not change as a result of the new labeling of educational spending. In other words, since fiscal policy does not change, the intergenerational tax shifting must be the same. Note, however, that it is the difference in terms of *present values* that will be invariant under a change in how educational spending is labeled. Clearly, the *relative* difference (percentage change) will decrease, since the new definition of net taxes in panel B involves (much) higher present values of lifetime net tax burdens for newborns than under the former (panel A) definition of net taxes. The relabeling explains almost all of the dramatic fall in relative changes when we go from panel A to panel B in table 16.7. For example, in the base case the relative change in the accounts falls from 4,018 percent in panel A to 60.7 percent in panel B.

The distribution of age groups in the Norwegian population is not stationary over time, however. Due to population aging, the relative size of the young age groups will decrease over time. Since the projection of future general govern-

Table 16.7 Sensitivity to Assumptions about Growth and Interest Rates: Accounts for Newborns in 1995 and Future Generations (thousands of U.S. dollars)

	g = 1			g = 1.5			g = 2		
	r = 3	r = 5	r = 7	r = 3	r = 5	r = 7	r = 3	r = 5	r = 7
	A. Education Distributed on Age Groups								
Present generations	8.6	-2.5	-13.3	5.3	1.4	-11.2	-5.9	5.1	-8.7
Future generations	125.7	22.1	-40.6	169.9	57.3	-15.7	212.0	94.6	10.6
Difference	117.0	24.6	-27.3	164.6	55.9	-4.5	217.9	89.5	19.3
Percentage change[a]	1,344	—	—	3,082	4,018	—	—	1,717	—
	B. No Distribution of Education on Age Groups								
Present generations	138.3	95.2	61.9	145.2	106.3	69.1	145.1	117.8	77.4
Future generations	270.1	128.8	40.4	327.8	173.5	71.7	381.3	220.3	104.9
Difference	131.7	33.6	-21.5	182.6	67.2	2.5	236.3	102.5	27.5
Percentage change[a]	92.9	34.0	-35.0	121.8	60.7	2.6	156.9	82.9	33.4

Note: g is productivity growth rate (percent); r is real rate of interest (percent). Exchange rate assumed to be 6.33 kroner per U.S. dollar.

[a]Growth adjusted.

ment spending (excluding all age-specific transfers) is linked to the development of the *total* population, the sum of future general spending and transfers will be slightly higher when educational spending is relabeled as general government spending. This small change in future fiscal policy explains why the difference between the accounts of future and present generations is larger in panel B than in panel A of table 16.7 for each of the nine combinations of growth and interest rates. For example, in the base case the difference is $55,900 in panel A and $67,200 in panel B. This difference is due to the fact that projected future government spending is somewhat higher in the latter case.

Returning to the question of interest rate and growth rate sensitivity, we can now look at how the relative change between the accounts of present and future generations varies in the nine cases in table 16.7 (panel B). Clearly, we see that in this sense our results are indeed very sensitive to the choice of an interest rate. For example, the 60.7 percent difference in net lifetime tax burdens between present and future generations in the base case increases to 121.8 percent when the rate of interest is 3 percent instead of 5, and it drops to 2.6 percent when the interest rate is 7 percent. Likewise, if the growth rate is 1 percent instead of 1.5 (and the interest rate is 5 percent), the relative difference in generational accounts drops from 60.7 to 34 percent, and if the growth rate is 2 percent, the relative difference increases to 82.9 percent. An important factor behind the interest rate sensitivity is the large wealth of the Norwegian government. A high real rate of interest implies high capital income to the government, counteracting any shifting of tax burdens from present to future generations. In countries where the government is heavily indebted (e.g., Italy), introducing a higher real rate of interest therefore has the opposite intergenerational effect, increasing the tax burdens of future generations relative to the tax burdens of the present.

The large wealth of the government can also explain the positive relation in table 16.7 between the growth rate and the relative difference between the accounts for future and present generations. For a given real rate of interest, a higher growth rate warrants a permanently higher budget surplus to keep the share of capital income in total government income constant. Of course, changes in growth and interest rates have other effects on intergenerational tax shifting besides those stemming from the large income from government wealth, but due to the size of the latter, it is likely that the changes in capital income have a dominant impact on the sensitivity results reported in table 16.7.

Table 16.8 shows the results of some further sensitivity analysis. The first alternative, in column (2), takes into account the medium-term "technical" projection of government expenditures to 2000 reported in the *National Budget 1997*. The medium-term projection assumes a soft landing of the Norwegian economy from the present boom as well as low growth of government spending to keep wages and prices from accelerating. Government spending on unemployment benefits and labor market programs is assumed to decrease due to

Table 16.8   **Sensitivity to Alternative Assumptions: Accounts for Newborns in 1995 and Future Generations (thousands of U.S. dollars)**

	Base Case (1)	Medium-Term Projection[a] (2)	No Demographic Change (3)	Zero Net Financial Assets (4)	50% Reduction in Petroleum Wealth (5)
Present generations	1.4	7.7	14.3	1.4	1.4
Future generations	57.3	35.1	1.2	66.2	112.4
Difference	55.9	27.4	−13.1	64.8	111.0
Change in spending to equalize burdens (% of GDP)	−1.9	−0.95	+0.5	−2.2	−3.8

Notes: Government spending on education is distributed on age groups. Productivity growth rate assumed to be 1.5 percent; real rate of return, 5 percent; exchange rate, 6.33 kroner per U.S. dollar.

[a]A "technical" projection of the government's budget to 2000, reported in the *National Budget 1997.*

expected lower unemployment. The fiscal policy is therefore tighter than in the base-case calculations, decreasing the accounts for future generations. The difference between the accounts for future and present generations decreases from $55,900 in the base case to $27,400, reducing the necessary spending cut to equalize net lifetime tax burdens from 1.9 percent of GDP in the base case to 0.95 percent.

Column (3) in table 16.8 summarizes the results of a counterfactual experiment in which the future demographic structure is identical to the present structure. This leads to slightly lower accounts for future generations than for present newborns. In this sense, population aging "explains" the entire generational imbalance in the base case. Column (4) looks at what happens if the net financial assets of the government in 1995 are removed from the accounts. The increase in intergenerational tax shifting is $8,900 in terms of increased present value of net lifetime taxes on future generations, requiring a spending cut of 2.2 percent of GDP to equalize the net tax burdens.

Column (5) of table 16.8 summarizes the results when the petroleum wealth of the government is reduced by 50 percent. This is not a very unlikely shock. For example, the oil price shock in the winter of 1985–86 more than halved the petroleum wealth between 1985 and 1986. Table 16.8 shows that the intergenerational impact is huge, increasing the necessary spending cut to equalize burdens from 1.9 percent of GDP in the base case to 3.8 percent of GDP.

In section 16.3 we reported the recent increase in the petroleum wealth estimate due to higher expected oil production in the future. Adopting the new petroleum wealth, the necessary spending cut to equalize the net tax burdens of present and future newborns is reduced from 1.9 to 0.8 percent of GDP.

16.5   The Generational Impact of Alternative Policies

In section 16.4, we showed that a permanent spending cut amounting to 1.9 percent of GDP would restore the generational accounts of newborns and future Norwegians to fiscal balance in the sense that the growth-adjusted present value of net lifetime taxes of future newborns is brought in line with the account of the 1995 newborns in the base case (see table 16.8).[13] In this section, we discuss the effects on present generations of increasing taxes or reducing pensions to restore long-run fiscal balance. The following three alternatives will be considered: (1) an increase in VAT revenues by 1.8 percent of GDP, (2) an increase in direct income tax revenues (YTX) by 1.8 percent of GDP, and (3) a cut in social security pensions (PEN) by 1.3 percent of GDP. Alternative 1 involves an increase in the VAT rate from 23 to 27.6 percent, and alternative 2 corresponds to an increase in direct taxes from 24.1 to 27.9 percent of total wage income. Finally, the reduction in PEN amounts to a cut in after-tax pensions by 24.3 percent. Table 16.9 shows the effects of the three alternative policies.

In the case of increased VAT, we see that an increase of the growth-adjusted account for newborns in 1995 to $18,500 is sufficient to obtain full long-run fiscal balance. Increasing YTX to achieve fiscal balance, involves a slightly lower account for both present and future newborns ($13,700), and reducing PEN leads to an even lower account for present and future newborns ($6,800). Considering how different generations living in 1995 are affected, the cut in pensions has a much larger effect on those over 50 years old than the corresponding increases in VAT and YTX in table 16.9. For a 70-year-old individual in 1995, for example, the present value of net taxes will be $38,000 higher than in the base case, and more than $30,000 higher than under the two alternative policies in table 16.9. This of course benefits the younger generations in 1995 as well as all future generations, if the alternatives are increases in VAT or YTX. Such cuts in current pensions are, however, politically very unlikely. For example, in 1992 the rules of the earnings-related pension system were changed, affecting only pensions far in the future. Taken in isolation, this policy change probably *increased* the imbalance between the net tax burdens of present and future generations. A more likely future reform, however, is to remove some exclusive tax benefits for retired individuals, benefits that were introduced before the social security reform in 1967.

There are also some minor differences between increasing VAT and YTX to achieve fiscal balance. The increase in direct taxes will affect those 15 to 60 years old somewhat more than it will the youngest and oldest age cohorts. In the past it appears to have been easier for Norwegian politicians to increase

---

13. In the autumn of 1998, the oil price fell to half of its average 1997 level. This new information has not been taken into consideration in tables 16.5 through 16.9.

Table 16.9   Eliminating the Generational Imbalance: Accounts for All Present and Future Generations (thousands of U.S. dollars)

Generation's Age in 1995	Base Case	Increasing VAT by 1.8% of GDP	Increasing YTX by 1.8% of GDP	Reducing PEN by 1.3% of GDP
0	1.4	18.5	13.7	6.8
5	−7.5	10.1	6.9	−1.1
10	14.7	33.6	32.2	22.6
15	58.4	78.4	79.0	67.6
20	106.3	126.5	129.4	116.8
25	127.1	146.6	151.6	139.1
30	129.6	147.8	154.4	143.0
35	116.2	133.2	140.2	132.3
40	90.3	106.0	112.4	108.6
45	38.9	53.2	58.3	62.3
50	−22.3	−9.7	−6.7	5.3
55	−73.0	−62.3	−61.3	−43.9
60	−135.3	−126.3	−127.5	−99.5
65	−170.6	−163.6	−166.1	−130.8
70	−179.6	−174.3	−177.4	−141.6
75	−170.0	−165.9	−168.7	−138.8
80	−155.1	−152.1	−154.4	−132.1
85	−139.4	−137.2	−139.0	−123.0
90	−122.6	−121.2	−122.4	−111.1
95	−96.7	−95.7	−96.7	−88.7
Future generations	57.3			

Notes: Government spending on education is distributed on age groups. Productivity growth rate assumed to be 1.5 percent; real rate of return, 5 percent; exchange rate, 6.33 kroner per U.S. dollar.

the VAT rate and other indirect taxes than direct taxes on labor and capital. The VAT rate was increased from 20 to 23 percent in the early 1990s. Norway also has the future option of broadening the VAT base to include services in the same manner as Sweden did some years ago.

It is worth emphasizing that the estimated size of the generational imbalance is much smaller in the present paper than in Auerbach et al. (1993). As we saw in section 16.4 above, it is also very sensitive to the projected real interest rate and the rate of productivity growth.

16.6   Conclusions

As a consequence of the government's large petroleum revenues, as well as of the expected increase in pensions and other welfare spending due to population aging, the government's budget surplus is quite misleading as an indicator of long-run fiscal balance. In a country like Norway, therefore, generational accounting appears to be a particularly useful method to assess the generational impact of current fiscal policy.

Adopting the base-case assumptions, the estimated imbalance in net tax burdens between future generations and present newborns in 1995 is relatively small. For example, a permanent spending cut of 1.9 percent of GDP would be sufficient to restore long-run fiscal balance in the sense that the growth-adjusted present value of net lifetime taxes of future newborns is reduced and brought in line with the account for the 1995 newborns. If we adopt the medium-term projections of public spending and taxes in the *National Budget 1997*, the corresponding spending cut to achieve long-run fiscal balance is reduced to 1 percent of GDP. Also the recent increase in the petroleum wealth estimate reduces the generational imbalance significantly. We considered three different policies that would also restore long-run fiscal balance in the sense explained above. These were an increase in VAT revenues, an increase in direct income taxes, and a cut in pensions. The generational imbalance in 1995 is much smaller than in a previous study based on 1992 data. This is due both to the strong recent business cycle upturn and to a shift to a more austere fiscal policy. Using the most recent information on the government's wealth and its fiscal policy for 1997, there is probably generational balance in 1997.

In addition to the sensitivity to the present business cycle, our results are sensitive to the choice of assumptions about future rates of interest and productivity growth. If the real interest rate is lower than the base-case assumption of 5 percent, the generational imbalance increases. The interest rate sensitivity is mainly a consequence of the large public petroleum wealth, because a higher real rate of interest will increase permanent income. We also looked at the effects of a reduction in petroleum wealth by 50 percent. Adopting the base-case assumptions, such a reduction would increase the necessary spending cut to achieve long-run fiscal balance from 1.9 to 3.8 percent of GDP. The government's considerable exposure to oil price risk therefore represents an additional element of uncertainty in our assessment of the generational impact of current fiscal policy in Norway.

Appendix A
Data Sources

Age Profiles

We distribute the 1995 totals of each tax and transfer by age and sex based on corresponding distributions in cross-sectional survey data. Age and sex profiles for SST, YTX, WTX, PEN, DIS, SIK, FAM, UNM, and OTH are all constructed on the basis of the 1994 Income and Wealth Survey, which contains cross-sectional information on 41,112 individuals (1 percent of the population). Individual tax returns are linked to the data collected by the survey. The estimated age profiles were smoothed, using a seven-period moving average, with weights reflecting the number of observations in each age group.

Due to the future maturing of the old-age pension scheme, the estimated age profiles from cross-sectional data will drift upward over time. To account for the expected average growth in future per capita old-age pensions, we use estimates provided by the microsimulation model MOSART developed by Statistics Norway.

Our age-sex profile for VAT is estimated from the 1990 Survey of Consumer Expenditures. This is a survey of 1,201 households containing 3,216 individuals. In distributing household consumption, we assumed that each child under age 17 consumed 70 percent of what adults consume. Various excise taxes on gasoline and cars, as well as excises on tobacco, beer, and other alcoholic drinks are aggregated into one single age profile based on the 1990 Survey of Consumer Expenditures, corresponding to EX in table 16.4.

For education (EDU), we adopted coverage rates and costs per student of various educational institutions based on public education statistics. While the age and sex profiles for primary and secondary education are quite accurate, we had to resort to a subjective estimate of profiles for college education.

Due to incomplete and missing data, most public health expenditures are not distributed by age and sex. The OLD category in table 16.4 represents public spending on old-age homes, wards, and dwellings; home nursing and assistance; and other public support to retirees living in their own homes. This profile is based on the MAKKO model.[14] The age profile of public hospital services (HOS) has been constructed using coverage rates and average nursing time data from public hospital statistics.

Government Wealth

The petroleum wealth estimate is calculated as the present value of expected net future cash flow to the government, assuming a given time path of oil prices and field-specific natural gas prices, investment outlays, and production costs, as well as a projection of the future speed of reserve depletion (source: Ministry of Finance). The revenues are both petroleum taxes paid by the oil companies and capital income from the government's ownership of oil and gas fields in the North Sea. Since future oil prices, production costs, reserves, and other factors are highly uncertain, estimates of petroleum wealth are very sensitive to assumptions. When performing sensitivity analyses, the wealth estimate as well as the permanent petroleum income will depend on the chosen real rate of interest.

Hydroelectric power wealth has also been estimated as a present value of a projection of future public revenues from this sector. Due to incomplete data, the estimate is very crude. The estimated value of shares and equity capital owned by the government has been provided by the Ministry of Finance. Another important asset is the public telephone company. Its value is estimated simply on the basis of a crude net cash-flow estimate. We have not attempted to estimate the values of other public enterprises.

---

14. MAKKO has also been developed by Statistics Norway.

Appendix B

Table 16B.1   Production of Oil and Natural Gas

Year	Production Estimate (million standard m³ oil equivalents)	Year	Production Estimate (million standard m³ oil equivalents)	Year	Production Estimate (million standard m³ oil equivalents)
1972	1.9	1992	153.2	2012	219.9
1973	1.9	1993	160.8	2013	209.4
1974	2.0	1994	180.3	2014	205.2
1975	11.0	1995	193.4	2015	193.9
1976	16.2	1996	222.4	2016	190.7
1977	19.3	1997	238.7	2017	182.2
1978	34.9	1998	260.6	2018	173.9
1979	43.9	1999	272.0	2019	165.9
1980	55.0	2000	279.5	2020	159.1
1981	53.9	2001	292.3	2021	154.0
1982	54.1	2002	287.3	2022	149.2
1983	61.1	2003	281.4	2023	144.7
1984	68.8	2004	260.6	2024	140.5
1985	72.9	2005	247.4	2025	136.5
1986	77.5	2006	242.7	2026	132.9
1987	87.9	2007	241.4	2027	129.4
1988	96.4	2008	239.3	2028	126.2
1989	118.0	2009	236.2	2029	123.2
1990	123.4	2010	233.7	2030	120.4
1991	136.8	2011	223.3		

Note: Numbers after 1995 are projections.

Table 16B.2   Projected Government Net Income from Petroleum Sector and Old-Age and Disability Pensions (percent of GDP)

Year	Government Net Income from Petroleum Sector	Old-age and Disability Pensions
1973	0.1	5.2
1980	5.95	5.57
1991	5.17	7.8
2001	9	8.11
2010	11	9.47
2030	3	14.86

Table 16B.3   Aggregate Employment and GDP for Mainland Norway (1972 = 1)

Year	GDP, Mainland Norway	Employed Persons	Year	GDP, Mainland Norway	Employed Persons
1972	1.00	1.00	1984	1.43	1.18
1973	1.04	1.01	1985	1.51	1.21
1974	1.09	1.02	1986	1.56	1.25
1975	1.12	1.04	1987	1.58	1.27
1976	1.17	1.07	1988	1.55	1.27
1977	1.20	1.10	1989	1.54	1.24
1978	1.23	1.12	1990	1.55	1.23
1979	1.28	1.14	1991	1.57	1.22
1980	1.31	1.16	1992	1.60	1.21
1981	1.33	1.18	1993	1.63	1.21
1982	1.34	1.18	1994	1.69	1.23
1983	1.38	1.17	1995	1.73	1.25

Table 16B.4   Government Net Investment in Financial Assets

Year	Net Investment (% of GDP)	Year	Net Investment (% of GDP)	Year	Net Investment (% of GDP)
1972	4	1981	5	1990	2
1973	5	1982	4	1991	0
1974	4	1983	4	1992	2
1975	3	1984	7	1993	2
1976	3	1985	10	1994	0
1977	1	1986	6	1995	3
1978	0	1987	5	1996	5
1979	1	1988	3		
1980	6	1989	1		

References

Auerbach, Alan J., Jagadeesh Gokhale, and Laurence J. Kotlikoff. 1991. Generational accounts: A meaningful alternative to deficit accounting. In *Tax policy and the economy,* vol. 5, ed. D. Bradford, 55–110. Cambridge, Mass.: MIT Press.

Auerbach, Alan J., Jagadeesh Gokhale, Laurence J. Kotlikoff, and Erling Steigum, Jr. 1993. Generational accounting in Norway: Is Norway overconsuming its petroleum wealth? SNF Report no. 75/1993. Bergen: Foundation for Research in Economics and Business Administration. Also Ruth Pollak Working Paper Series on Economics, no. 24. Boston: Boston University, Department of Economics, October 1993.

Leibfritz, Willi, Deborah Roseveare, Douglas Fore, and Eckhard Wurzel. 1995. Ageing populations, pension systems and government budgets: How do they affect saving? Economics Department Working Paper no. 156. Paris: Organization for Economic Cooperation and Development.

Raffelhüschen, Bernd, and Alf Erling Risa. 1995. Reforming social security in a small open economy. *European Journal of Political Economy* 11:469–86.

Risa, Alf Erling. 1996. Objectives and strategies in the development of the Norwegian welfare state. Working Paper no. 0396. Bergen: University of Bergen, Department of Economics, February.

Steigum, Erling, Jr. 1992. Financial deregulation, credit boom, and banking crisis: The case of Norway. Discussion Paper no. 15/92. Bergen: Norwegian School of Economics and Business Administration, Department of Economics. Also *PTT Katsaus* (Finland) 4 (1992): 10–31.

———. 1993. Accounting for long-run effects of fiscal policy by means of computable overlapping generations models. In *Macroeconomic modelling and policy implications,* ed. S. Honkapohja and M. Ingberg, 45–67. Amsterdam: Elsevier.

Steigum, Erling, Jr., and Øystein Thøgersen. 1995. Petroleum wealth, debt policy and intergenerational welfare: The case of Norway. *Journal of Policy Modeling* 17: 427–42.

17 Generational Accounts in Sweden

Robert P. Hagemann and Christoph John

17.1 Introduction and Overview

The calculation of generational accounts is especially appropriate and timely for Sweden, for several reasons. First, reflecting the progressive expansion of the welfare state during the past 30 years, Sweden's tax-transfer system is one of the most complex among developed countries. To the extent that the incidence of taxes and transfer payments varies across age groups in the population, estimated generational accounts will reflect the lifetime impacts of the taxes and transfers. Second, the first half of the 1990s has witnessed very wide swings in public finances in Sweden. As successive governments have introduced discretionary measures to consolidate public finances, it is important to have a sense of the net impact of such measures on the lifetime disposable incomes of living and, notably, future generations. Third, a blueprint for a significant reform of the pension system was endorsed by the major parties in 1994 that aims at reducing pension outlays over the long term. This reform would clearly have a substantial impact on the net taxes of different generations, and generational accounting is a framework especially well suited to assess the impact of the reform.

This chapter presents estimates of generational accounts for Sweden based on projections as of September 1996. The estimates also take into account the

Robert P. Hagemann is senior economist in the Office in Europe of the International Monetary Fund. Christoph John is with the economics department of the Chamber of Commerce, Hamburg, Germany. At the time this paper was written, he was at the Faculty of Economics, University of Konstanz, Germany.

The authors thank Anette Granberg and Lars Erik Lindholm of the Swedish Ministry of Finance, Leif Johansson of the National Institute of Statistics, and Laura Shrestha and Eduard Bos of the World Bank for providing extensive data. The authors are also grateful to Johan Fritzell of the University of Stockholm for data on age- and sex-specific patterns of consumption of education. The views expressed are those of the authors and not necessarily those of their respective institutions.

prospective pension reform and the consolidation program as of June 1995. In addition, we present estimates that incorporate the impacts of a package of additional measures that was proposed by the government in April 1996 but that had not yet been approved by the Parliament.

The estimated generational accounts vary substantially across generations. Males and females over age 56 benefit from the current tax-transfer system in Sweden, as reflected in the negative values of future net taxes.[1] On the other hand, the accounts of newborns are substantially positive; newborn males could be expected to pay $213,600 in lifetime net taxes on the basis of policies in place in September 1996, while their female counterparts could expect to face a lower but still large net lifetime net tax of $153,600. The net tax liabilities rise steadily across living generations, reaching a maximum of $357,200 for males and $230,300 for females at around age 25. In general, accounts for females are lower than those of males largely because, although high by international standards, the labor force participation rates of women are lower than those of men (so that lifetime gross taxes are correspondingly lower) while their pensions are roughly comparable to those of men.

The estimates suggest that the present fiscal system in Sweden results in substantial intergenerational transfers: unborn generations face very high net tax burdens. As a result of the combined effects of consolidation measures taken in recent years and the pension reform, however, the net tax burden of unborn generations is 22 percent *lower* than those of today's newborns. This reflects the substantial future impact on transfers and taxes of recent measures, if implemented on a sustained basis.

17.2 Recent Fiscal Developments

17.2.1 The First Half of the 1990s

The late 1980s and early 1990s witnessed a substantial deterioration of public finances in Sweden. In 1989, the budget balance of the general government—central government, local governments, and the social security system—recorded a sizable surplus of about 5.5 percent of GDP. On a deterioration of the aggregate revenue ratio from 65.7 percent to 60.1 percent and a surge in spending from 60.3 percent of GDP to 70.5 percent, the general government budget balance moved into substantial deficit, settling at 10.4 percent of GDP in 1994 after peaking at 13.4 percent the previous year. Neither

---

1. Results presented in this chapter are based on a treatment of public educational outlays as government consumption. Estimates based on their treatment as transfer payments are reported in chap. 1 of this volume. In both cases, estimates of generational accounts for Sweden are based on all *future* taxes and transfers. Estimates of *lifetime* net taxes could differ from those reported here to the extent that generations alive today have paid higher or lower net taxes in the past than the estimated net taxes projected during the remainder of their lives.

trend is explained entirely by the weakening of economic activity.[2] Most of the increase in the share of public spending was due to increases in transfer payments, which account for a sizable portion of household income. Transfer payments increased by 5 percent of GDP during the period 1990–94, reaching 25.5 percent in 1994. Approximately half of this increase was attributable to higher unemployment benefits and spending on labor market programs, with higher pension outlays accounting for an equivalent share of the increase in the spending ratio.

The deterioration of Sweden's public finances, together with the prospective further weakening of the fiscal situation, had substantial adverse macroeconomic effects that, in turn, placed additional pressures on the authorities to redress the situation. Successive policy packages were, however, inadequate, and the outlook for public finances over the medium term remained tenuous at best. It was estimated that a swing of about 10 percent of GDP in the public sector's primary balance was still required to stabilize the debt ratio (see Lachman et al. 1995).

The poor budgetary outlook was also well reflected in estimates of generational accounts at that time. On the basis of the policies in place as of early autumn 1994, it appeared that future generations would be facing very substantial net tax burdens. Unborn males and females faced prospective net tax payments of $209,700 and $124,700, respectively.[3] These estimated net tax bills were 37 percent *higher* than those facing the youngest living generations at that time.

Following the elections in September 1994, the newly elected Social-Democrat government proposed a number of further measures aimed at putting Sweden's public finances back on a sustainable track. These measures (table 17.1), totaling some SKr 56.4 billion, together with SKr 19.4 billion of additional measures to be included in the subsequent budget and the major pension reform that had been separately approved by the Parliament, had a very substantial impact on the fiscal outlook.[4] Reflecting the effects of these prospective measures, in particular of the reductions in future pension benefits, the

---

2. A large portion of the decline in the revenue ratio resulted from an unanticipated loss of revenue due to the 1990–91 tax reform. Some of the decline was also attributable to a lowering of the payroll tax rate by 4 percentage points, which nonetheless remained high at 33 percent in 1994. Estimates of the share of the cyclical component of the deterioration of the general government budget balance range from 50 percent to over 60 percent. In either case, a substantial portion is attributable to the structural imbalance in Swedish public finances at that time.

3. These estimates are based on assumed productivity growth of 1.5 percent and a discount rate of 4.65 percent. Moreover, these estimates are based on an age-consumption profile observed in the United States, which differs significantly from that observed in Nordic countries.

4. The principal features of the pension reform were (1) replacement of the two-pension system (basic pension and earnings-related pension) by a single, multitiered pension consisting of a defined-benefit component and a defined-contribution component and (2) tightening the linkage between real wage developments and indexation of the defined-benefit pension. See Ministry of Health and Social Affairs (1994) and Hagemann and John (1995, 1997).

Table 17.1   Consolidation Measures, 1994–96

Measure	Amount (billion SKr)
Measures taken prior to November 1994	18.3
November 1994 package	56.4
Revenue increases	36.6
Taxation of dividends and capital gains on stocks	6.5
Higher tax rate on private pension income	2.0
Retained tax on wealth	2.0
Higher tax on property	2.5
Limited indexation of income tax allowances	4.5
Contribution to sickness insurance	14.1
State income tax raised from 20% to 25%	4.3
Other revenue increases, net	0.7
Spending reductions	24.5
Abolition of special child allowance	3.2
Reforms of family support	3.7
Early retirement pensions	4.3
Military spending	4.0
Reduced state consumption	2.0
Limited indexation of pensions, etc.	8.4
Slower phasing down of interest rate support	−2.0
Other spending reductions	0.9
Induced reduction in revenues due to spending cuts	−4.7
1995/96 Budget proposal, January 1995	19.3
Spending reductions	24.6
Lower child allowances and compensation in family allowances	3.6
Pensions	3.8
Sickness insurance	1.5
Reduced investment in roads and railways	2.7
Reduced spending on tertiary education	1.0
Reduced training subsidy in ALMP	1.0
Reduced support for enterprise-based training	1.4
Labor Market Fund	3.9
Other	5.7
Induced reduction in revenues due to spending cuts	−2.1
Other	−3.2
1995/96 Budget proposal, April 1995	3.6
Spending reductions	8.7
Reduced unemployment, sickness, and parental insurance benefits	3.8
Reduced housing benefits	1.2
Changed rules concerning compensation in ALMP	2.5
Other	2.5
Revenue measures	−5.1
Lower VAT on food	−7.7
Other	2.5
April 1996 measures	8.0
Spending reductions	6.0
Revenue measures	2.0
Total consolidation measures	125.6

Sources: OECD (1997) and Swedish authorities.

Table 17.2   **Profile of Savings of Consolidation Program (percent of GDP)**

Year	Annual Impact	Cumulative Impact
1995	3.5	3.5
1996	2.0	5.5
1997	1.5	7.0
1998	1.0	8.0

Source: OECD (1997).

net tax burdens of unborn males and females were reduced to $141,500 and $89,200, respectively. Moreover, the net tax burdens of the unborn were estimated to fall *below* those of newborns at that time, a result attributable mostly to the impact of the pension reform.

Despite the improved fiscal outlook, the government saw the need for additional measures, motivated in part by the goal of achieving the fiscal targets of the Maastricht Treaty. In June 1995, the government presented the "convergence program," aimed at meeting the Maastricht budgetary criteria for entry into the Economic and Monetary Union by 1998. Measures to improve permanently public finances (the "consolidation program") played a major role. In April 1996, additional measures totaling a net amount of SKr 8 billion were proposed, three-quarters of which consisted of expenditure cuts. The net effect of all these measures was estimated to reach SKr 125 billion by 1998, or 8 percent of GDP (see table 17.2).

17.2.2   The Outlook to 2000

Reflecting in part the expected effects of the measures adopted to date, the fiscal outlook has improved considerably (table 17.3). Discretionary measures do not alone account for the improved prospects for public finances, however. A significant portion of the strengthened fiscal outlook is attributable to an improved economic forecast. With wage growth projected at twice the rate of GDP growth during the initial years of the period 1996–2000, the growth of wage tax receipts is projected to outpace GDP growth. Additional revenue measures, including higher real estate taxes and a change in value-added tax (VAT) collection—which should have only a temporary positive impact on revenues—will raise the share of revenue in GDP by close to 1 percent on a sustained basis by the year 2000.

Further measures are expected on the expenditure side as well. Public consumption will increase initially during the period 1996–2000, reflecting mostly delayed procurement of defense-related hardware. It also reflects the shift into 1996 of the increase for public sector wages, which had been approved in 1995. By holding the growth in outlays below the growth in nominal GDP, public consumption is projected to fall from 27 percent of GDP in 1996 to 24.4 percent in 2000, while overall public spending should fall from 68 percent of GDP to 60.2 percent. In turn, the overall fiscal balance is expected to continue to

Table 17.3   **Public Sector Finances, 1995–2000**

	1995	1996	1997	1998	1999	2000
	In Billions of Kronor					
Revenue	983	1,059	1,101	1,153	1,200	1,256
Taxes and charges	824	897	942	990	1,037	1,088
Capital income	94	89	86	88	86	90
Other income	65	73	73	75	77	78
Expenditures	1,115	1,144	1,158	1,168	1,188	1,219
Transfers to households	397	393	396	401	409	420
Subsidies	130	125	126	122	121	121
Interest	116	127	128	126	126	129
Consumption	423	448	458	468	479	494
Investment	49	52	50	51	53	55
Financial balance	−132	−85	−57	−14	12	37
Central government	−144	−102	−62	−19	3	28
National pension fund	18	16	15	14	−14	12
Local government	−6	0	−11	−10	−5	−3
Central government borrowing requirement (net)	139	76	59	16	−5	−25
Primary balance	−109	−48	−15	23	51	76
	In Percent of GDP					
Revenue	60.1	62.8	62.5	62.3	61.8	62.0
Taxes and charges	50.4	53.2	53.5	53.5	53.4	53.7
Capital income	5.7	5.3	4.9	4.8	4.4	4.4
Other income	4.0	4.3	4.1	4.1	4.0	3.9
Expenditures	68.2	67.9	65.7	63.1	61.2	60.2
Transfers to households	24.3	23.3	22.5	21.7	21.1	20.7
Subsidies	7.9	7.4	7.2	6.6	6.2	6.0
Interest	7.1	7.5	7.3	6.8	6.5	6.4
Consumption	25.9	26.6	26.0	25.3	24.7	24.4
Investment	3.0	3.1	2.8	2.8	2.7	2.7
Financial balance	−8.1	−5.1	−3.2	−0.8	−0.6	1.8
Central government	−8.8	−6.0	−3.5	−1.0	−0.2	1.4
National pension fund	1.1	0.9	0.9	0.8	−0.7	0.6
Local government	−0.4	0.0	−0.6	−0.5	−0.3	−0.1
Central government borrowing requirement (net)	8.5	4.5	3.3	0.9	−0.3	−1.2
Primary balance	−6.7	−2.8	−0.9	1.2	2.6	3.8
	Memorandum Items					
GDP (billion SKr)	1,636	1,686	1,762	1,851	1,942	2,026
Net debt (billion SKr)	454	540	584	603	598	572
Net debt (% of GDP)	27.8	32.0	33.2	32.6	30.8	28.2
Gross debt (billion SKr)	1,303	1,375	1,432	1,456	1,456	1,437
Gross debt (% of GDP)	79.7	81.5	81.3	78.7	75.0	70.9

Source: Ministry of Finance, *Sweden's Economy* (Stockholm, April 1996), 59.

improve during the remainder of the decade. The general government primary balance is projected to move into surplus in 1998, followed by a surplus in the overall balance in 1999. Correspondingly, the ratio of gross debt to GDP would peak in 1997 and begin to decline in 1999. The ratio of net debt to GDP would begin to decline sooner, however, reflecting improvements in the financial balance of the pension system.

The paper now turns to a presentation of estimated generational accounts, preceded by a brief description of the data and key assumptions used in the estimates.

17.3 Data Sources

The construction of generational accounts requires estimation of three components: (1) the present value of net tax payments of living generations, (2) government net wealth in the base year, and (3) the present value of future government consumption. The intertemporal government budget constraint then allows the derivation of net tax payments imposed on future generations as a residual.

17.3.1 Taxes and Transfers

The main ingredients in the calculation of generational accounts of living generations are simulations of their net lifetime tax payments (taxes paid minus transfers received). These are obtained by projecting the per capita taxes and transfers by age and sex group derived from the most recent (1994) Income Distribution Survey (IDS). In each year from 1995 to 2000, per capita taxes and transfers derived from the IDS were calibrated to yield projected aggregate spending and receipts, which take into account the anticipated effects of the ongoing consolidation program (see above and table 17.3). Thereafter, per capita amounts are assumed to increase at the same rate as labor productivity growth.

Several taxes and transfers have been distinguished in estimating generational accounts in Sweden. Of the eight taxes used in this study, age- and sex-specific per capita estimates for seven were obtained from the IDS: (1) taxes on personal income paid to the central government, (2) taxes on personal income paid to local governments, (3) property taxes, (4) wealth taxes, (5) taxes on capital income, (6) taxes on income from self-employment, and (7) social security contributions. Finally, as no age- or sex-specific information was available on VAT and excise taxes, aggregate amounts were distributed across age groups using consumption patterns observed in Norway.[5]

Per capita estimates of transfer payments are available from the IDS for nine transfer items: (1) pensions, (2) sick pay, (3) labor market assistance,

---

5. The authors are grateful to Carl Gjersem (Ministry of Finance, Norway) for providing these data.

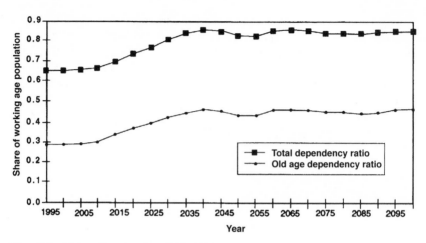

Fig. 17.1   Dependency ratios, 1995–2100

(4) parental allowances, (5) educational grants, (6) housing allowances, (7) child allowances, (8) social assistance, and (9) allowances to single parents and other allowances. As in the case of taxes, transfers are assumed to increase at the rate of productivity growth after the year 2000. The IDS does not provide information on the age- and sex-specific distribution for benefits-in-kind (education, child care, etc.). Therefore, these expenditures were included in government consumption.[6]

Demographic projections obtained from the World Bank (as of July 1996) were used. These projections assume a net reproduction rate growing from 0.969 in 1995 to 1.000 in 2030, leading to a stable population over the long run. During the same period, the total dependency ratio is expected to rise from 65.2 to 80.4 percent, reflecting entirely the increase in the old-age dependency ratio from 28.7 to 42.6 percent (see fig. 17.1).[7]

17.3.2   Government Net Wealth and Government Consumption

Government net wealth consists of the difference between government financial assets and gross debt. At the beginning of 1995, public sector net financial liabilities equaled 23.5 percent of GDP (see Organization for Economic Cooperation and Development [OECD] 1995, table A35). This figure comprises consolidated net liabilities of central and local governments and the social security sector. The present value of government consumption—including consumption, investment, and nonhousehold subsidies—was obtained us-

---

6. But see chap. 1 in this volume for estimates based on a treatment of educational outlays as transfer payments.

7. The total dependency ratio is the sum of the number of children under age 18 and the number of persons aged 65 or older as a percentage of the population aged 18 to 64. The old-age dependency ratio is the number of persons aged 65 or older as a percentage of the population aged 18 to 64.

ing the estimates and projections of the Ministry of Finance for 1995–2000. After 2000, it is assumed that expenditures on these items grow with the assumed rate of labor productivity growth.

17.3.3 Labor Productivity Growth and the Discount Rate

The rate of labor productivity growth and the discount rate are critical parameters in generational accounting. Higher labor productivity growth is assumed to result in higher taxes, transfers, and government consumption, leading in turn to higher net tax payments of living as well as of future generations. The higher the discount rate, on the other hand, the lower the present value of taxes, transfers, and government consumption. The base-case scenario assumes labor productivity growth of 1.5 percent per annum and a constant 5 percent discount rate.[8] In order to demonstrate the sensitivity of the results to differences in both labor productivity growth and discount rates, generational accounts have also been calculated using labor productivity growth rates of 1 and 2 percent and discount rates of 3 and 7 percent.

17.4 Results

17.4.1 Base-Case Scenario

Base-case results are presented in table 17.4. Column (1) shows age-specific generational accounts for combined male and female generations, both living and future; estimates for males and females separately are shown in columns (2) and (3). In order to facilitate comparisons with the results of other countries, the estimates are shown in U.S. dollars.[9] The accounts display a familiar pattern. Older generations are net beneficiaries of the existing system; generations under age 60 can expect to face a *positive* net tax burden, while the tax burdens of older generations are *negative*. The accounts reach their maximum at age 25. Tax burdens for the very young generations are lower, reflecting the substantial transfers paid to them (child allowances, educational grants, etc.). Generations older than age 25, on the other hand, face less heavy tax burdens since the present value of the transfers they receive (pensions, health insurance) increases slowly. Reflecting their old-age pensions, generations aged 60 or older can expect to receive net transfers over their remaining lifetimes. Table 17.5 decomposes the base-case results into different tax and transfer items. Results indicate that the present value of social security payments for newborns is almost as high as direct tax payments. Older people face high pension payments, but they also pay considerable amounts of taxes.

The consecutive consolidation programs adopted in recent years in Sweden

8. This is close to the average rates that prevailed in Sweden over the past decades. See Hagemann and John (1995, 1997).
9. The exchange rate applied was 7.133 Swedish kronor per U.S. dollar, which is the average exchange rate for 1995. See International Monetary Fund (1996).

Table 17.4   Generational Accounts: Base Case (U.S. dollars)

	Present Value of Net Tax Payments		
Generation's Age in 1995	Joint (1)	Male (2)	Female (3)
0	184,347	213,631	153,599
5	203,429	238,046	167,003
10	226,351	267,260	182,938
15	253,510	310,979	202,010
20	281,194	338,327	221,982
25	295,229	357,188	230,272
30	283,714	341,329	222,320
35	261,900	310,973	209,443
40	228,488	267,844	186,320
45	177,195	206,811	146,190
50	105,251	127,801	81,224
55	16,514	22,667	10,232
60	−66,304	−72,493	−60,262
65	−110,848	−127,728	−95,202
70	−97,797	−112,413	−85,130
75	−79,722	−86,939	−74,003
80	−58,074	−59,159	−57,344
85	−33,182	−30,020	−34,954
90	−6,481	−5,758	−6,747
Future generations	143,474		
Generational imbalance[a]	−22.2		

Source: Authors' calculations.

Note: Labor productivity growth assumed to be 1.5 percent; discount rate, 5 percent.

[a]Difference between present values of net tax payments of future generations and newborns as a percentage of present value of net tax payments of newborns.

have had a substantial impact on public finances. To the extent that these deficit reductions have been effected by measures that—if sustained—will have lasting effects on Swedish households, these are also reflected in the generational accounts. In 1994, at a time when the fiscal deficit reached 11.7 percent of GDP, future generations faced tax burdens estimated to be roughly 37 percent higher than those of newborns at the time. Taking into account the long-term impacts of subsequent and future deficit reduction measures, the estimated net tax burden of future generations—though still positive—is *lower* than that of newborns in 1995.[10]

10. In addition to the effects of discounting, this result also reflects the assumption used in this study that per capita transfers and taxes grow at the rate of productivity growth beyond the year 2000. Given the targeted budgetary surplus in 2000 (1.8 percent of GDP), this implies that budgetary surpluses are sustained thereafter. The importance to generational accounting of taking into full account the long-term implications of budgetary measures adopted today is illustrated by a comparison of the results presented here and those obtained by the Swedish Ministry of Finance, as reported in OECD (1997). There, future generations are estimated to face a substantially *higher*

Table 17.5   **Composition of Joint Generational Accounts: Base Case (U.S. dollars)**

	Present Value of Tax and Transfer Payments						
Generation's Age in 1995	Total	Direct Taxes	Social Security	Indirect Taxes	Pensions	Labor Market Programs	Other
0	184,347	87,835	83,733	105,965	40,484	23,595	29,107
5	203,429	104,041	99,201	110,557	47,947	27,957	34,475
10	226,351	123,250	117,601	116,122	56,694	33,144	40,785
15	253,510	145,585	139,237	123,069	66,560	39,300	48,521
20	281,194	169,929	161,497	127,711	77,622	46,737	53,586
25	295,229	182,721	166,292	127,953	91,496	40,560	49,702
30	283,714	186,716	159,890	122,200	107,481	34,988	42,622
35	261,900	186,576	147,762	115,872	125,640	29,948	32,722
40	228,488	181,743	131,155	109,336	146,183	25,460	22,104
45	177,195	171,504	108,962	101,119	168,542	21,744	14,105
50	105,251	155,998	81,962	91,176	194,532	17,739	11,614
55	16,514	129,700	50,108	80,148	219,986	12,280	11,177
60	−66,304	105,349	19,212	69,237	242,477	5,871	11,753
65	−110,848	81,533	0	57,263	236,977	202	12,464
70	−97,797	58,885	0	46,270	189,994	21	12,937
75	−79,722	41,336	0	35,203	143,557	1	12,703
80	−58,074	24,461	0	24,770	95,741	1	11,563
85	−33,182	11,017	0	14,219	50,272	0	8,147
90	−6,481	1,612	0	2,284	8,613	0	1,764

Source: Authors' calculations.

Note: Labor productivity growth assumed to be 1.5 percent; discount rate, 5 percent.

It is useful to emphasize, however, that the improvement in the generational accounts of future generations reflects in large part the very high tax payments facing living Swedes. This is illustrated by comparing the estimated lifetime tax burdens of newborns in Denmark and Norway, who face much lower net tax burdens—$84,000 and $106,300, respectively—than their Swedish counterparts (see chaps. 10 and 16 in this volume). When account is taken of lower average incomes in Sweden than in Denmark and Norway, the effective tax burdens faced by Swedish newborns would also appear to be high.[11]

17.4.2   Sensitivity Analysis

Generational accounts are very sensitive to two assumptions: labor productivity growth and the discount rate. Table 17.6 reports the estimated accounts

---

tax burden (150 to 200 percent higher) than newborns. These estimates are based, however, on the assumption that the policies that yielded the deficit of 8.1 percent of GDP in 1995 would remain in place in the future, no account having been taken of the expected effects of the consolidation program.

11. World Bank data report per capita GDP (1994, adjusted for purchasing power parity) of $17,850 in Sweden, $20,800 in Denmark, and $21,120 in Norway.

Table 17.6   Generational Accounts under Different Assumptions (U.S. dollars)

	g = 1			g = 1.5			g = 2		
	r = 3	r = 5	r = 7	r = 3	r = 5	r = 7	r = 3	r = 5	r = 7
Present generation[a]	292,419	163,206	97,469	333,009	184,347	108,258	378,757	208,756	120,741
Future generations	268,292	119,236	40,780	309,630	143,474	53,164	351,439	171,249	67,534
Generational imbalance[b]	−8.3	−26.9	−58.2	−7.0	−22.2	−50.9	−7.2	−18.0	−44.1

Note: g is labor productivity growth (percent); r is discount rate (percent).

[a] Account of newborns in the base year, 1995.

[b] Difference between present values of net taxes of future generations and newborns as a percentage of present value of net taxes of newborns in 1995.

for newborns and future generations under different assumptions. Although the sensitivity of the estimates is evident, the principal conclusion emerging from the base-case scenario is robust to different assumptions: a sustained implementation of the consolidation program approved to date will reduce substantially the net tax burden of future generations, to a level that is below the lifetime tax burdens of many living generations.

In general, the higher the discount rate, the lower the generational accounts of future generations. This reflects the fact that a higher discount rate assigns a lower weight to future flows. With higher labor productivity, the absolute burden on future generations rises, whereas the relative burden falls. Over their life cycles, individuals first receive net transfers, then make net tax payments, and subsequently again receive net transfers when old. In this framework, a rise in productivity boosts taxes and transfers equally after 2000. However, since taxes tend to be higher than transfers during the early years of the projection, this leads to higher generational accounts for current newborns. By contrast, future generations initially face a lower level of debt inherited from living generations. Subsequently, their accounts rise more quickly.[12] This results in a lower generational account for future generations and, correspondingly, a larger difference between living and future generations.

17.4.3   Generational Accounts under Different Policy Scenarios

An important virtue of generational accounting is that it enables assessments of the intergenerational impact of policy *changes* (see Kotlikoff 1992). This section reports the results of various policies on generational accounts in Sweden. The section first describes potential policy changes that could restore generational equity and then presents the quantitative impact of these policies on generational accounts on the assumption that these policies would have been implemented on a sustained basis beginning in the base year (1995). In a subsequent simulation, the impact of policies envisaged in April 1996 are estimated.

Policies to Restore Generational Equity

The base-case calculations suggest that future generations will be better off than newborns. From an intergenerational equity perspective, a more balanced sharing of the burden could be considered. This could be achieved by (1) raising government spending permanently, from which living generations will benefit; (2) reducing permanently gross taxes (i.e., gross of transfers); or (3) increasing permanently gross transfers.

Table 17.7 reports the results of several such simulations. Each simulation assumes a permanent change in one or another policy lever (e.g., tax revenues sufficient to yield an equal net tax burden for newborns and future generations). Each row of table 17.7 reports the level of the targeted variable as a

---

12. It should be recalled that net tax payments of any future generation equal the net tax payments of the preceding future generation augmented by the rate of productivity growth.

Table 17.7   Policy Options to Achieve Generational Equity

Policy Option	1995	1996	1997	1998	1999	2000
Increase government consumption by 7.6%	27.8	28.6	28.0	27.2	26.6	26.2
Lower all taxes by 3.4%	48.8	51.5	51.7	51.7	51.6	51.9
Reduce income tax rates by 9.3%	17.1	17.5	17.4	17.3	17.1	17.3
Increase household transfers by 7.7%	26.2	25.1	24.2	23.3	22.7	22.4

Source: Authors' calculations.
Note: Table reports level of targeted variable as share of GDP.

share of GDP in each year from 1995 to 2000 needed to achieve intergenerational equity. Thus, for instance, a permanent reduction of 3.4 percent of GDP in all taxes, including social security contributions, would, in achieving intergenerational equity, result in a revenue ratio of 51.9 percent of GDP, versus 53.7 percent under the base-case scenario.

Supplementary Budget Bill of April 1996

The consolidation program of June 1995 targeted a reduction of the general government deficit to 5.2 percent in 1996, 3 percent in 1997, and a balanced budget by 1998.[13] By April 1996, although the projected budget deficit for 1996 had been lowered to 4.0 percent of GDP, the fiscal targets for 1997 and 1998—needed to meet the Maastricht budgetary criteria—could not be met. The government therefore announced a number of additional permanent measures in the supplementary budget bill in April 1996. First, a number of already specified measures totaling SKr 8 billion would be introduced in 1997 and 1998, with heavy front-loading. Three-fourths of the measures consist of expenditure cuts. Revenue increases are to come in particular from higher central government income taxes and an increase in deposit insurance premiums.[14] Second, the government announced that it will implement measures in 1998 to achieve additional savings of SKr 6 billion, although these have not yet been specified. Taking these measures into account, the deficit would fall to 2.6 percent of GDP in 1997 and would be eliminated in the following year. The impact of these measures on the estimated generational accounts is vividly evident in table 17.8. Reflecting the substantial impact of these additional measures on living generations, the net tax burdens of future generations would fall yet further.

13. For a recent assessment of the convergence and the included consolidation program, see Ministry of Finance (1996).
14. These measures were specified by the government, but most of them have not yet been adopted by the Parliament. This is in contrast to the consolidation program: the Swedish Parliament has adopted decisions on the entire program.

Table 17.8   **Generational Accounts under the Policy Scenario**

Generation's Age in 1995	Present Value of Net Tax Payments		
	Joint	Male	Female
0	188,751	218,536	157,476
5	208,428	243,656	171,377
10	232,062	273,670	187,906
15	259,987	309,283	207,610
20	288,058	346,135	227,869
25	302,077	365,025	236,083
30	290,334	348,932	227,893
35	268,158	318,185	214,679
40	234,217	274,485	191,072
45	182,198	212,695	150,271
50	109,329	132,630	84,500
55	19,614	26,421	12,665
60	−64,063	−69,715	−58,544
65	−109,181	−125,639	−93,928
70	−96,565	−110,861	−84,176
75	−78,892	−85,889	−73,347
80	−57,606	−58,560	−56,964
85	−33,040	−29,847	−34,830
90	−6,481	−5,758	−6,747
Future generations	132,244	152,979	110,236
Generational imbalance[a]	−29.9		

Source: Authors' calculations.

Note: Labor productivity growth assumed to be 1.5 percent; discount rate, 5 percent.

[a]Difference between present values of net tax payments of future generations and newborns as a percentage of present value of net tax payments of newborns.

17.5   Conclusion

Motivated in part by concerns about the potentially substantial adverse macroeconomic consequences of an unsustainable budgetary position and in part by the goal of meeting the fiscal criteria of the Maastricht Treaty, Swedish authorities have introduced substantial budget consolidation measures in recent years. The consequences for public finances as traditionally measured in terms of the cash-flow budget balance and projected public debt levels are evident. The potency of the measures is also evident from an intergenerational accounting perspective, wherein the net tax burdens of future generations—though still positive and large—are estimated to fall below those of living generations. Whether this shift in the relative tax burdens of living and future generations is desirable rests on normative considerations.

References

Hagemann, Robert P., and Christoph John. 1995. Fiscal policy in Sweden: A generational accounting perspective. IMF Working Paper no. 95/105. Washington, D.C.: International Monetary Fund, September.

———. 1997. Fiscal reform in Sweden: What generational accounting tells us. *Contemporary Economic Policy* 15 (3): 1–12.

International Monetary Fund. 1996. *International financial statistics.* Washington, D.C.: International Monetary Fund, August.

Kotlikoff, Laurence. 1992. *Generational accounting: Knowing who pays, and when, for what we spend.* New York: Free Press.

Lachman, Desmond, et al. 1995. Challenges to the Swedish welfare state. IMF Occasional Paper no. 130. Washington, D.C.: International Monetary Fund, July.

Ministry of Finance. 1996. Review of the Swedish convergence program. Stockholm: Ministry of Finance, September.

Ministry of Health and Social Affairs. 1994. *Pension reform in Sweden: A short summary.* Stockholm: Ministry of Health and Social Affairs.

Organization for Economic Cooperation and Development (OECD). 1995. *Economic outlook,* vol. 58. Paris: Organization for Economic Cooperation and Development, December.

———. 1997. *Economic surveys—Sweden 1996–97.* Paris: Organization for Economic Cooperation and Development.

18 Thailand's Generational Accounts

Nanak Kakwani and Medhi Krongkaew

18.1 Introduction

Like many other countries in East Asia, Thailand has a long history of extended family relationships in which family members across generations provide help to one another throughout their lifetimes. The state or government in this case plays a relatively minor role (vis-à-vis families) in assisting individuals in their lives and livelihood. Until 1993 Thailand did not have a well-defined social security system, and although some systems of public assistance were always in existence, the size and extent of this public assistance was not large. Therefore, whether the government would create an intergenerational fiscal burden on future generations as a result of present tax and transfer policies has yet to become a hot issue. Things may change with the full operation of the social security system in 1998, when Thailand will add an old-age pension to the existing four areas of coverage, namely, sickness not related to work, maternity leave, invalidity, and death.

The involvement of the state in the lives of its citizens is manifest in the traditional instrument of the public sector—fiscal policy. The government taxes the people to transfer resources from private hands to public hands. By so doing the government effects change in both the level and the distribution of welfare of people in the posttax situation. The level and distribution of public welfare change again with the spending of the public money raised from

Nanak Kakwani is professor of econometrics at the University of New South Wales, Sydney, Australia. Medhi Krongkaew is director of the Institute of East Asian Studies and the APEC Study Centre, Thammasat University, Bangkok. He also teaches economics at the Faculty of Economics of the same university, specializing in public economics, economic development, and the Thai economy.

This paper draws heavily on a previous study by Nanak Kakwani, Laurence J. Kotlikoff, Medhi Krongkaew, Sudhir Shetty, and Jan Walliser. See Kakwani et al. (1996).

taxes and other revenue sources. The net effect of these tax-transfer policies, or the net fiscal incidence, can be linked with the concern about intergenerational fiscal burden to answer the question of whether the government through its fiscal policy helps or hurts future generations.

This paper uses a recently developed technique called generational accounting to assess the sustainability of Thailand's fiscal policy. Generational accounting determines whether the spending policies currently in place can be maintained without raising the net lifetime tax payments (tax paid net of transfers received) of future generations. Several studies in OECD countries have suggested the existence of serious generational imbalances (see Auerbach, Gokhale, and Kotlikoff 1991; Franco et al. 1993; Auerbach et al. 1993; Gokhale, Raffelhüschen, and Walliser 1995; Hagemann and John 1995). An application of generational accounting to Thailand is therefore of particular interest because it can shed light on the intergenerational stance of fiscal policy in a developing country. It has been observed that many developing countries' economic and demographic structures contrast sharply with those of developed countries. Specifically, populations tend to be very young, with the fraction below age 25 often exceeding 50 percent of the total population. Productivity growth rates are generally either much higher or much lower than in industrialized countries.[1] In addition, the tax systems in developing countries are often characterized by limited personal income taxation and transfer payments.

Countries with limited transfer payments are likely to have more favorable generational policies because transfer programs typically benefit the elderly at the expense of current young and future generations. However, the structure of the tax-transfer system in many developing countries is subject to change—change that may produce imbalances in generational policies. What can we say about the situation in Thailand? Have Thai fiscal policies a tendency to favor present or future generations? Will the pay-as-you-go social security system that Thailand launched in 1993 create an unfair intergenerational burden on future Thai generations? What kind of fiscal planning is needed for a more balanced generational account? And so on. These are some of the questions we will be dealing with in this paper.

In what follows, section 18.2 describes the demographic and fiscal structures of Thailand. It will emphasize the changes in tax and expenditure structures of the Thai government in the past two and half decades to see their prospective impacts the population as a whole. Section 18.3 discusses the construction of generational accounts and the data used. Section 18.4 presents the results, along with some policy simulations. Section 18.5 summarizes the findings and concludes.

---

1. See Kotlikoff and Walliser (1995) for more detailed description of how these characteristics may affect generational accounts.

Table 18.1   **Population by Age Group (percent of total population)**

Year	Age 0–24	Age 25–64	Age 65+
1993	52.2	43.8	3.9
1995	50.3	45.5	4.2
2000	46.6	48.6	4.8
2010	41.4	52.9	5.7
2020	38.8	53.7	7.6
2030	36.2	52.9	10.9
2040	34.3	51.0	14.7
2050	33.3	49.5	17.1
2060	32.4	49.7	17.9
2070	31.7	49.2	19.0
2080	31.2	48.5	20.3
2090	30.8	48.2	21.0
2100	30.5	47.9	21.6

Source: Data provided by Eduard Bos of the World Bank.

18.2   Demographic and Fiscal Structures of Thailand

Thailand had a population of about 60 million in 1995. Due to very high fertility rates in the 1960s and 1970s, the population is very young. As table 18.1 shows, 52 percent of the population was under age 25 in 1993, whereas only 4 percent was over age 65. However, the rapid reduction in the fertility rate, from 5.4 to 2.8, experienced over the past 20 years combined with an increase in life expectancy will cause a significant change in the Thai population structure. As shown in table 18.1, by the year 2030 the population under age 25 is predicted to fall to 36 percent, and the percentage of elderly over age 65 will rise to 11 percent. In 2080, the corresponding numbers will be 31 and 20 percent, respectively.

The reduction of population growth rates in the 1980s was accompanied by an acceleration of economic growth. Between 1980 and 1990, Thailand's GDP expanded at a rate of 8 percent per annum and continued to grow at this rate during the first half of the 1990s. GNP per capita reached a level of 69,000 baht, or about U.S.$2,760, in 1995, characterizing Thailand as a middle-income country at the level achieved by Korea in mid-1980s. What is more, economic growth occurred with moderate levels of inflation.

During the 1980s, annual inflation measured by the percentage change in the GDP deflator averaged less than 4 percent per year. As a consequence of economic transformation, the Thai economy has a declining agricultural sector, which in 1995 accounted for just 10.9 percent of GDP. In that year, industrial production accounted for 46.8 percent of GDP, of which 28.9 percent originated from manufacturing activities.

Like many other Southeast Asian and East Asian countries before it, Thailand is an export-oriented country. Exports of manufactured products such as garments, electronic components, electrical appliances, processed food, gems and jewelry, and traditional primary commodities such as rice, rubber, cassava, and sugar have combined to enable Thailand to achieve its present high economic growth rate. Thailand, however, is also a trade deficit country, with revenue from export trade that always falls below its purchase of imported goods. In 1995, for example, the trade deficit of Thailand amounted to some U.S.$14.9 billion. And although the service account shows some surplus, it was not large enough to compensate for this huge trade deficit. Therefore, the current account deficit for that year was about U.S.$13.5 billion, or about 8 percent of GDP. This high level of current account deficit has worried Thai economic leaders, but some have argued that since Thailand's gross national savings rate of 33.6 percent in 1995 is very high, the Thai current account deficit was not being driven by overconsumption but rather by spending on investment goods and by a desire among foreign investors to invest in Thailand.

This picture of a fundamentally sound Thai economy is reinforced by an analysis of its fiscal policy. As a unitary state with a long history of independence and noncolonization by any Western powers, the government in Thailand is very centralized and has strong political power. And yet the size of the government is not large by the standards of developed, industrialized countries as measured by the share of government revenue or expenditure in GDP. In 1961 when Thailand launched its first national economic development plan, the share of central government revenue in GDP was only about 10 percent. The share of government expenditure in the country's GDP was slightly higher, at 12 percent. Of course the role of the Thai government expanded with overall economic development as these shares increased in later years and peaked at around 16 percent for revenue and 20 percent for expenditure in the mid-1980s. The change in the absolute size of the government as seen through its revenue and expenditure shares of GDP could give a misleading or confusing picture of the role of the Thai government if not seen within the context of other changes that had taken place in the structure and composition of government revenue and expenditure. This is what we turn to next.

18.2.1   Government Revenue

Strictly speaking, "government" here means only central government. So government revenue here does not include the revenues of the other two bodies of the public sector, namely, state-owned enterprises and local governments. If we assume, however, that state enterprises operate in a manner similar to private, commercial enterprises, their exclusion should not affect the traditional role of the state too much. As for local governments, their economic importance in the context of the role of the public sector is small because the size of revenue of local governments has always been around 5 or 6 percent of the central government's. Therefore, it is not inappropriate to analyze the role of the Thai state by looking only at the revenue (and expenditure) of the central government.[2]

Tables 18.2A and 18.2B give the structure and distribution of revenue of the central government of Thailand between 1970 and 1995. It may be seen from this table that the major source of government revenue was taxation, ranging between 90.31 and 92.73 percent of total revenue. While it was true that as in many other developing economies, the majority of tax revenues in Thailand came from indirect taxes, there has been a drastic change in the composition and proportion of direct taxes vis-à-vis indirect taxes during the past decade or so. For example, the share of income taxes in 1970 was only 11.89 percent, whereas the share of indirect taxes was 76.37 percent. There was little change in the share of indirect taxes during the 1970s, but the beginning of the 1980s saw a downward shift of this share to around 68 percent. This downward shift continued in the first half of the 1990s, when the share of indirect taxes was less than 60 percent. In step with the gradual loss of dominance of indirect taxes in the Thai revenue structure is the rising share of direct tax revenue in total revenue. Indeed, this share doubled to 20.90 percent during 1981–85 and more than tripled to 32.01 percent in 1995. Looking inside the composition of direct taxes, the contribution from corporate income tax is a major factor explaining the rapid increase of the direct tax share. In 1995, for example, the corporate income tax contributed a full 20.25 percent of the total revenue of the central government. Personal income tax also increased its share of total revenue (from 7.02 percent in 1970 to 11.34 percent in 1995), but not as fast as the corporate income tax. The direction makes clear, however, that the government will attempt to improve its collection of personal income tax from richer income earners.

Within the indirect tax structure, three taxes have dominated. These are import duties, business taxes (and later the value-added tax), and excise or selective sales taxes. During the past decade, however, one can see a drastic decline in the share of import taxes, from 29.21 percent in 1970 to 16.39 percent in 1995. This has been the result of gradual reduction in Thai import tariffs as the government tries to reduce the rate of protection of domestic industries and to liberalize its foreign trade under the agreements of greater regional and global cooperation in the form of the ASEAN Free Trade Area, the Asia Pacific Economic Cooperation, and the GATT Uruguay Round trade negotiations and the subsequent World Trade Organization.

Beginning in 1995, the Thai authorities adopted a simplified tariff schedule whereby the number of tariff rates was reduced from about sixty to just five. These five rates were zero percent for raw materials in short supply within the country, 5 percent for other raw materials, 10 percent for intermediate

---

2. Of course, if and when necessary, we can make some adjustments to central government figures by adding the revenue contributions of local governments and state-owned enterprises.

Table 18.2A   Structure of Central Government Revenue, 1970–95 (millions of baht)

	1970	1971–75	1976–80	1981–85	1986–90	1991–95	1995
Taxation	16,776	26,320	62,203	123,247	253,887	547,305	711,357
Income taxes	2,200	3,899	11,613	28,437	58,749	176,673	248,827
Personal	1,298	1,918	5,146	14,551	26,688	62,356	88,170
Corporation	902	1,981	6,467	13,886	31,587	111,154	157,430
Petroleum	0	0	0	0	474	3,162	3,227
Indirect taxes	14,130	21,892	49,714	92,818	187,954	356,639	445,917
Import duties	5,404	6,939	14,678	26,105	58,833	104,560	127,389
Export duties	848	1,659	2,278	2,033	692	12	12
Business taxes	3,408	5,761	13,603	25,882	54,415	23,413	699
Value-added tax	0	0	0	0	0	88,199	142,955
Selective sales taxes	3,049	5,263	13,728	31,344	61,914	125,365	161,170
Fiscal monopoly	647	1,240	2,269	2,369	4,250	7,087	7,890
Royalties	399	578	2,580	2,925	2,553	3,860	4,233
Licenses and fees	375	451	580	2,159	5,298	4,142	1,569
Other taxes	446	530	875	1,992	7,185	13,993	16,613
Nontaxation	1,727	2,823	5,220	12,783	19,893	54,037	66,147
Sales and charges	483	780	1,242	2,081	3,987	8,198	7,773
Contribution from government enterprises and dividends	623	1,088	1,814	4,017	8,014	29,875	36,766
Miscellaneous revenue and income	621	955	2,165	6,685	7,893	15,964	21,609
Total revenue	18,503	29,143	67,421	136,030	273,784	601,296	777,286

Source: Bank of Thailand, *Monthly Bulletin* (various years).

Table 18.2B Distribution of Central Government Revenue, 1970–95 (percent)

	1970	1971–75	1976–80	1981–85	1986–90	1991–95	1995
Taxation	90.67	90.31	92.26	90.60	92.73	91.02	91.52
Income taxes	11.89	13.38	17.22	20.90	21.46	29.38	32.01
Personal	7.02	6.58	7.63	10.70	9.75	10.37	11.34
Corporation	4.87	6.80	9.59	10.21	11.54	18.49	20.25
Petroleum	0.00	0.00	0.00	0.00	0.17	0.53	0.42
Indirect taxes	76.37	75.12	73.74	68.23	68.65	59.31	57.37
Import duties	29.21	23.81	21.77	19.19	21.49	17.39	16.39
Export duties	4.58	5.69	3.38	1.49	0.25	0.00	0.00
Business taxes	18.42	19.77	20.18	19.03	19.88	3.89	0.09
Value-added tax	0.00	0.00	0.00	0.00	0.00	14.67	18.39
Selective sales taxes	16.48	18.06	20.36	23.04	22.61	20.85	20.73
Fiscal monopoly	3.50	4.26	3.37	1.74	1.55	1.18	1.02
Royalties	2.16	1.98	3.83	2.15	0.93	0.64	0.54
Licenses and fees	2.03	1.55	0.86	1.59	1.94	0.69	0.20
Other taxes	2.41	1.82	1.30	1.46	2.62	2.33	2.14
Nontaxation	9.33	9.69	7.74	9.40	7.27	8.99	8.51
Sales and charges	2.61	2.68	1.84	1.53	1.46	1.36	1.00
Contribution from government enterprises and dividends	3.37	3.73	2.69	2.95	2.93	4.97	4.73
Miscellaneous revenue and income	3.36	3.28	3.21	4.91	2.88	2.65	2.78
Total revenue	100.00	100.00	100.00	100.00	100.00	100.00	100.00

Source: Bank of Thailand, *Monthly Bulletin* (various years).

products, 20 percent for finished manufactured products, and over 20 percent for products whose domestic protection was still needed. Specifically it is expected that by the year 2003, the tariff rates for all products traded among ASEAN countries will be reduced to no more than 5 percent.

In the 1950s taxes on rice exports were the largest revenue item for the government. As the burden of these taxes was believed to fall on domestic producers the majority of whom were poor, there was a concerted effort to abolish these taxes to reduce the tax burden as well as to increase the return to these farmers. The government succeeded in removing rice export taxes and most other export taxes in the late 1980s.

Another important indirect tax in Thailand is the business tax. This is a kind of sales tax levied on producers and importers of goods and services based on their gross sale receipts or import values. As each point of sale is subject to this tax it was in fact a turnover tax whose cascading effects were large and created distortions in resource allocation and posed an unfair burden on consumers. In the early 1980s, the Thai tax authorities had proposed to replace this indirect consumption tax with a value-added tax and spent more than 10 years preparing for the eventual adoption of the new tax, which became a reality in 1992 with a consumption-type value-added tax with a beginning tax rate of 7 percent. The changeover caused a slight fall in tax collection in initial periods, but as the tax office gained experience the public became more familiar with the tax, value-added tax collection has begun to increase markedly in the past few years.

Excise taxes in Thailand are levied on a few sumptuary items such as tobacco and liquor and on petroleum products. The contributions of these taxes to overall revenue have always been large. In the future these excise taxes may even be used to supplement the single-rate value-added tax if more curbing of consumption is required. The contributions from fiscal monopolies and royalties have declined in share in recent years because the government has adopted greater liberalization and privatization policies, allowing price and other production and management adjustments in government agencies and state-owned enterprises. This privatization has shown some success recently as the contributions of these state-owned enterprises to the government have increased in the past few years.

In all, it may be concluded that the Thai government has started to rely more on direct income taxes as a source of revenue. Indirect taxes, which were often regarded as regressive, have continued to lose their share. The use of a value-added tax has increased the efficiency of the tax system and also is expected to increase tax collection due to the built-in tax control. In the future, greater taxing power will be given to local governments, who will concentrate on property and wealth taxes, which are currently very weak. The size of the government in the future may grow if the present rapid economic growth continues as the government finds it necessary to spend more on public infrastructure as well as public welfare. This point will become clear as we look at government expenditure in the next subsection.

In closing, we would like to make one comment about the state of personal income taxation in Thailand. As seen from table 18.2B, the personal income tax contributes only 11.34 percent to total revenue. As has been noted by many studies, including that of Kakwani (1997), income inequality in Thailand is extremely high. The Gini index of per capita income in 1992 was as high as 0.53. It is possible that many people with high income are not paying their due share of income tax. Rich people tend to consume more imported goods. Thus these people also benefit from a continuous lowering of tariffs. The government should be looking at reforming personal income taxation so that rich people pay their due share of taxation. This will also have an impact on the current account deficit because it will lower the propensity of rich people to consume imported goods.

18.2.2   Government Expenditure

As a rule, the Thai government decides how much it will spend each year on the strength of its revenue projection. If it expects healthy revenue collection, the tendency to spend more is likely to be greater than when prospective public income is small. The practice of changing taxes or tax rates or raising other revenues as a precondition for a package of future spending is simply not followed in Thailand. This does not mean, however, that the budget in Thailand must always be in balance. The government can, and often does, borrow internally and externally to compensate for budget deficits and to finance public projects that it believes to be worthwhile or important. However, past records have shown the Thai government to be a cautious spender and borrower. This is due partly to budget laws that set effective controls on government borrowing and partly to the slow manner in which the government deliberates on the benefits and costs of public projects. As a result, Thailand has avoided foreign debt traps that have crushed many developing countries, especially during the mid-1980s.

Tables 18.3A and 18.3B show the structure and distribution of expenditure of the Thai government classified into budget type and function. First, the annual budget is classified into current and capital expenditure. Current expenditure includes the part of the budget that goes into wages and salaries of public officials and the maintenance of existing official services, whereas capital expenditure includes the purchase of land and other immovable properties, necessary equipment and materials, and the construction of public buildings and other infrastructure projects. It may be observed that during the 1970s and 1980s, a large proportion of the government budget was spent on current expenditure with little left for capital spending. This was necessary because of the relatively large size of public servants. Since the early 1980s, however, the government has frozen the expansion of the size of public servants to no more

Table 18.3A   Government Expenditure Classified by Type and Function (millions of baht)

	1970	1971–75	1976–80	1981–85	1986–90	1991–95	1995
Total expenditures	25,135	33,801	82,341	167,961	241,525	509,355	642,321
Economic classification							
Current	17,204	25,711	62,884	137,987	204,632	362,407	442,456
Capital	7,931	8,091	19,457	29,974	36,894	146,948	199,865
Major functional classification							
Economic services	7,324	7,827	17,460	28,239	37,133	133,386	169,964
Social services	6,622	9,671	25,142	50,084	72,816	185,244	242,417
Defense	4,403	6,493	16,115	33,634	46,402	78,692	96,331
General administration and services	3,554	4,919	10,970	22,437	31,824	58,509	72,974
Unallocated items	3,232	4,891	12,656	33,568	53,349	53,523	60,635

Source: Bank of Thailand, *Monthly Bulletin* (various issues).

Table 18.3B   Distribution of Government Expenditure Classified by Type and Function (percent)

	1970	1971–75	1976–80	1981–85	1986–90	1991–95	1995
Total expenditures	100.00	100.00	100.00	100.00	100.00	100.00	100.00
Economic classification							
Current	68.45	76.06	76.37	82.15	84.72	71.15	68.88
Capital	31.55	23.94	23.63	17.85	15.28	28.85	31.12
Major functional classification							
Economic services	29.14	23.16	21.20	16.81	15.37	26.19	26.46
Social services	26.35	28.61	30.53	29.82	30.15	36.37	37.74
Defense	17.52	19.21	19.57	20.02	19.21	15.45	15.00
General administration and services	14.14	14.55	13.32	13.36	13.18	11.49	11.36
Unallocated items	12.86	14.47	15.37	19.99	22.09	10.51	9.44

Source: Bank of Thailand, *Monthly Bulletin* (various issues).

than 2 percent a year, which slowed down the share of current expenditure some years later.

The slowdown in public expenditure during the mid-1980s was also appropriate considering the fiscal difficulties that the government experienced with revenue shortfalls and huge budget deficits. However, the economy rebounded in the latter half of the 1980s with extraordinary export growth, a large influx of foreign investment, especially from Japan, and successful promotion of foreign tourism in Thailand. This has led to unexpected increases in government revenue from all kinds of taxes, especially income and sales taxes. The economic boom in Thailand that started in 1987 continued until 1991 when the country suffered a slight setback due to internal political problems. During this period problems with infrastructure shortages became very apparent, prompting the government to decide to spend more on infrastructure such as roads and rails, telecommunications, power and utilities, and traffic management systems. By the early 1990s, the central government had already accumulated a large sum of treasury surplus, something experienced only once in the postwar history of Thailand. The government then started to spend on capital projects. From table 18.3B, it may be seen that the average share of capital expenditure in total government expenditure during 1991–95 was 28.85 percent, compared to only 15.28 percent in the previous five years. This part of government spending is still growing. In 1995, its share was 31.12 percent.

More could be said about this pattern of government spending during the past few years. During the start of the economic boom period during the last half of the 1980s, the nonspending of the government while taking in large fiscal surpluses acted in a beneficent countercyclical manner in the economy, effectively forestalling inflationary pressure. When the private-sector-led economic boom was coming to an end in the early 1990s, the government decided to use its large public savings on numerous public projects, thus easing the crash landing of the economy. This appropriate policy by the Thai government has won accolades from many international organizations such as the International Monetary Fund and the World Bank, although we must contend that the Thai government was just lucky.

But how much luck will continue to befall the Thai government? Treasury reserves at the end of 1996 stood at more than U.S.$12 billion, the highest in recorded history. And indeed, it could be said that this huge budget surplus enabled the Thai authorities to agree to participate equally in the tripartite system of social security contributions. (They were not inclined to make any contributions earlier.) The economic slowdown in 1996 due to dismal performance in the export sector, high inflation, and the tight monetary situation gave a clear warning that the good times may have come to an end. The government may be required to return to its cautious mode of spending again.

The bottom half of table 18.3B shows the distribution of government expenditures classified by function. Of the four major functions, namely, economic services, social services, defense, and general administration, social services now rank first in terms of share of total expenditure. Looking back to the situation in the 1970s and 1980s, one can see an interesting change in the function of the Thai budget. The defense allocation, which was as high as 20 percent of total expenditure, gradually declined in the latter half of the 1980s, falling as low as 15.01 percent in 1995. Social services, which have traditionally assumed a major share of the Thai budget (because they include educational spending, which in the past was the largest budget item, and health spending, which has enjoyed a phenomenal rate of growth in the past decade and a half), have increased their share even more during this decade. And so have expenditures on economic services, which include spending on agricultural development and industrial infrastructure. The comparison between productive economic and social services and nonproductive defense spending alone should make most public finance specialists happy.

It has been alluded to earlier that countries with limited transfer payments are likely to have more favorable generational policies. Will the recent changes in the budget composition of the Thai government make Thai generational accounts less favorable? No one could give a clear answer until empirical generational accounting studies like this one could be undertaken frequently enough. It suffices to say at this juncture that it is unlikely that the Thai government will get carried away with spending on anything when the revenue situation does not warrant it. If the government were able to mobilize domestic resources in an efficient way, it should be in a position to spend more on neglected sectors such as poverty and rural areas. Present Thai economic development has come about partly as a result of sacrifice of the agricultural sector and the farmers. It can only be proper to return more of the fruits of development to this sector and these people.

Before concluding this section, a word should be said about fiscal incidence, or the impact of fiscal policy on the income distribution of the country. We have maintained that despite the correct development policy of the Thai government—giving investment initiatives to the private sector during the past three decades of economic development while the government concentrated on infrastructure and other economic institution building—the government has not done much in terms of poverty alleviation and the improvement of income inequality until recently. On poverty alleviation, the incidence of poverty based on the traditional poverty line stayed very high at around 20 percent throughout the 1970s and much of the 1980s. Only when the economy entered the private-sector-led economic boom in the latter part of the 1980s and early 1990s did the incidence of poverty show some marked reduction, mainly through the rise in personal or household income. On income inequality, a study by one of the present authors on the incidence of the Thai fiscal system during the 1960s and the early 1970s has shown that the equalizing effects of government expenditure were not large enough to overwhelm the disequalizing effects of government taxation, leading to, at best, a neutral overall effect of fiscal policy on the Thai income distribution (Medhi 1980). Generational accounting can indeed be looked upon as a fiscal incidence study, but the impact is measured on people of different ages and sexes rather than on people with different incomes.

18.3   Construction of Generational Accounts

Generational accounting is based on the government's intertemporal budget constraint. This constraint requires that the future net tax payments of current and future generations be sufficient, in present value, to cover the present value of future government consumption as well as to service the government's initial net indebtedness.[3] In order to solve this budget constraint, we require (1) a population projection, (2) projections of average net taxes by age and sex, (3) an estimate of government net wealth, (4) a discount rate, and (5) a projection of government purchases.

18.3.1   Population Projections

Our demographic projection as shown in table 18.1 comes from the World Bank and incorporates its long-term forecasts for fertility and life expectancy.[4] Specifically, total fertility is assumed to reach a level of 2.1 by the year 2000, which guarantees that the population slowly settles into a stationary distribution. Life expectancy at birth is expected to increase from 65 years in 1990 to 72 years in 2010, 77 years in 2030, and 80 years in 2050.

18.3.2   Projection of Taxes and Transfers

Average tax and benefit payments by age and sex were obtained from the 1992 Socioeconomic Survey (SES) conducted by the National Statistical Office, which is described in appendix B. In this survey, 13,458 households selected by a two-stage cluster sampling were asked about their household income and expenditure and other household socioeconomic characteristics. In order to account for the different sizes of clusters, observations are weighted according to their sampling probabilities. Since the survey provides data for total households as well as individuals, a calculation of age- and sex-specific average payments is possible. In particular, data from the 1992 SES have been used to distribute by age and sex revenues from personal and corporate income taxes, monopoly profits, petroleum taxes, motor vehicle taxes, duties, state lottery revenues, and local taxes. Incidence assumptions are given in appendix C.

In some cases, specific incidence assumptions were necessary. Personal income taxes, for example, are only available at the household level. They have been distributed to individual household members according to their share of

---

3. Appendix A of this paper gives a brief discussion of the methodology of generational accounting. Readers who are not familiar with the technique of generational accounting can find some technical information there.

4. We thank Eduard Bos of the World Bank for providing us with special demographic tabulations for Thailand.

total household taxable income. We proceed similarly with property taxes. Corporate taxes are allocated to individuals according to their wage and salary income since in a small open economy the capital tax incidence is on labor.[5] Value-added taxes are distributed in proportion to household consumption and then divided within the family according to an equivalence scale that gives lower weight to children. Finally, excise taxes are divided equally among adult household members with the exception of petroleum and motor vehicle taxes, which are allocated only to the household head.

As far as benefits are concerned, we distribute education and health expenditures by age and sex. Educational spending is allocated evenly among all individuals attending schools and universities. Payments of old-age pensions to former government workers are included with government spending on goods and services since these payments may be viewed as part of the compensation package that the Thai government needed to offer these workers to solicit their employment. Unfortunately, there are no data available to allocate health care expenditure by age and sex. For this profile, we used the corresponding German profile of relative health expenditures by age and sex described in Gokhale, Raffelhüschen, and Walliser (1994). The German data entail higher per capita health care expenditures by age, with per capita expenditures on 80-year-olds equal to roughly twice that on 40-year-olds. All raw profiles obtained in the described manner have then been smoothed with an eighth-order polynomial. Finally, we rescale all average tax and benefit payments to accord with 1993 fiscal aggregates.[6]

18.3.3   Government Net Wealth

We take government financial wealth as our estimate for 1993 government net worth. As previously mentioned, this number is 224.6 billion baht, or 6.4 percent of GDP in 1993.

18.3.4   Growth and Discount Rates

For productivity growth we assume a rate of 2 percent per year, in line with other recent studies of the Thai economy (see Hagemann, Amieva-Huerta, and Ross 1992). Future government receipts are risky, which suggests that they be discounted with a higher rate than the real interest on government securities. However, government receipts and expenditures appear less volatile than the return on capital, which suggests that they be discounted with a lower rate than

---

5. See Fehr and Kotlikoff (chap. 3 in this volume) for an analysis of the capital tax incidence in a small open economy.

6. We have used the fiscal aggregates of 1993 as a proper consequence of the availability of household income and expenditure statistics for 1992 (the 1992 SES). At the end of 1996, the latest socioeconomic survey data—the 1994 SES—also became available, which should enable us to construct generational accounts for 1995. But the time and resources needed to analyze the new data set were not available, so we have to contend with the fiscal situation of 1993 for the time being.

that.[7] Our discount rate of 6 percent therefore reflects a long-term risk-free interest rate augmented by a risk premium but is smaller that the rate of return on capital.

18.3.5 Government Consumption

Finally, we assume that government spending after 1993 grows with the overall economy. For 1993, government spending is calculated as the sum of all non-age-specific government expenditures net of revenues not distributed by age and sex. In this calculation, profits from state enterprises and other nontax revenues are treated as negative government spending.

18.4   Results

18.4.1   Major Findings

Tables 18.4A and 18.4B present generational accounts for the Thai male and female populations, respectively. The accounts exhibit a life cycle pattern with the maximum expected future net payment peaking at age 30 for males and age 25 for females. Male newborns, whose generational accounts reflect their entire lifetime net tax payments, can anticipate a net tax burden of $7,700 in present value. For females, the lifetime net tax burden is $4,000. The highest expected tax burden facing these newborns comes from corporate income tax, followed by value-added taxes and other excise taxes. This is not surprising; developing countries rely heavily on indirect taxes and corporate taxes since the collection of personal income taxes requires a fairly sophisticated tax system.

The age pattern of the present value of future taxes differs for each tax. Whereas the present values of remaining lifetime personal income taxes and, due to our incidence assumption, corporate taxes peak between ages 25 and 30, the present value of remaining lifetime property taxes peaks at age 45. Clearly, corporate and personal income taxes reflect the present value of expected future wages and salaries whereas property taxes depend on wealth, which is accumulated more slowly over the life cycle. Additionally, some taxes, specifically value-added taxes and other consumption taxes, are more evenly spread over the life cycle than are, say, personal income taxes. Note that generational accounts at all ages are positive. This is in contrast to most developed countries, which show generational accounts eventually becoming negative due to welfare programs targeted at the elderly.

Tables 18.4A and 18.4B also indicate that the residual fiscal burden facing future generations is negative. If current Thais make the remaining lifetime net tax payments indicated in these tables, the Thai government will have sufficient resources to provide a very large subsidy to future Thais. Is this result

---

7. For a more detailed discussion of the choice of a discount rate, see Auerbach et al. (1991, 1994).

Table 18.4A   **Composition of Male Generational Accounts: Present Value of Receipts and Payments (thousands of baht)**

Generation's Age in 1993	Net Payment	Tax Payments								Transfer Receipts		
		Personal Income	Corporate Income	Property and Local	VAT	Alcohol and Tobacco	Petroleum and Vehicle	Duties	State Lottery	University Education	Education	Health
0	163.5	24.0	52.6	21.5	43.8	16.6	41.8	41.6	1.3	6.9	55.1	17.6
5	196.5	29.2	64.1	26.0	48.2	20.2	50.8	45.9	1.6	8.4	62.0	19.1
10	262.3	35.3	77.7	31.2	52.1	24.5	61.3	49.5	1.9	10.2	40.2	20.6
15	337.4	42.8	93.3	37.4	54.2	29.7	74.0	51.6	2.3	12.4	13.1	22.3
20	400.3	51.8	106.8	44.8	54.5	34.7	88.3	51.8	2.7	9.7	1.6	23.8
25	441.6	59.4	114.2	53.4	53.1	35.5	100.3	50.5	2.9	2.8	0	25.0
30	452.1	62.8	112.8	62.5	50.3	33.9	105.5	47.9	2.8	0.7	0	25.6
35	436.4	61.2	102.9	71.3	46.7	30.4	103.1	44.4	2.5	0.2	0	26.0
40	396.0	54.4	85.7	77.6	42.4	25.8	93.9	40.3	2.1	0	0	26.2
45	338.4	43.8	64.7	79.7	37.6	21.0	80.5	35.8	1.7	0	0	26.2
50	273.7	31.6	43.4	76.9	32.7	16.6	66.1	31.1	1.4	0	0	26.0
55	209.4	19.8	25.0	68.9	27.8	13.0	52.8	26.4	1.1	0	0	25.4
60	154.0	10.4	11.4	56.7	23.2	10.3	41.9	22.0	0.8	0	0	22.9
65	109.3	4.4	3.4	41.9	19.0	8.3	32.9	18.0	0.7	0	0	19.3
70	75.8	1.8	0.2	27.5	15.3	6.6	25.2	14.6	0.5	0	0	15.9
75	48.7	0.8	0	14.6	11.5	4.9	17.7	10.9	0.3	0	0	12.1
80	29.7	0.5	0	6.1	8.6	3.4	11.8	8.2	0.2	0	0	9.2
85	17.2	0.3	0	1.6	6.4	2.2	7.4	6.1	0.1	0	0	7.0
90	9.0	0.2	0	0.2	4.2	1.1	4.0	4.0	0.1	0	0	4.7
Future generations	−189.3											
Percentage difference	−215.8											

Note: Productivity growth assumed to be 2 percent; discount rate, 6 percent.

Table 18.4B Composition of Female Generational Accounts: Present Value of Receipts and Payments (thousands of baht)

Generation's Age in 1993	Net Payment	Tax Payments								Transfer Receipts		
		Personal Income	Corporate Income	Property and Local	VAT	Alcohol and Tobacco	Petroleum and Vehicle	Duties	State Lottery	University Education	Education	Health
0	84.2	13.8	28.2	11.5	45.4	14.0	7.2	43.2	1.3	8.7	51.7	20.1
5	96.4	16.8	34.4	13.9	50.0	17.0	8.7	47.6	1.6	10.7	60.8	22.0
10	139.9	20.3	41.7	16.6	54.2	20.5	10.4	51.5	1.9	13.0	40.1	24.1
15	192.2	24.7	50.3	19.8	56.7	24.8	12.4	53.9	2.3	15.8	10.5	26.3
20	224.2	28.4	55.3	23.9	57.2	28.4	14.3	54.4	2.6	11.1	1.1	28.0
25	239.1	30.6	55.8	28.9	55.7	28.9	15.9	53.0	2.7	2.4	0.2	29.0
30	236.1	30.5	51.3	33.7	52.6	27.6	17.3	50.0	2.6	0.4	0	29.1
35	218.1	28.1	43.0	35.4	48.6	25.1	18.1	46.2	2.4	0	0	28.9
40	191.2	23.9	32.5	34.3	44.2	22.0	18.6	42.1	2.0	0	0	28.4
45	160.2	18.6	21.7	31.3	39.6	18.8	18.5	37.7	1.7	0	0	27.7
50	131.2	13.3	12.5	28.1	31.3	15.9	18.0	33.5	1.3	0	0	26.7
55	107.4	8.6	5.9	26.0	27.1	13.6	17.1	29.5	1.0	0	0	25.4
60	90.3	5.0	2.1	25.6	23.1	11.6	15.7	25.8	0.8	0	0	23.5
65	77.8	2.8	0.5	26.2	19.1	10.0	13.8	22.0	0.6	0	0	21.1
70	67.8	1.6	0.1	26.4	15.3	8.3	11.3	18.2	0.5	0	0	17.6
75	57.5	1.1	0	25.0	12.1	6.7	8.6	14.5	0.3	0	0	14.1
80	46.2	0.9	0	21.5	9.2	5.2	6.1	11.5	0.2	0	0	11.2
85	32.4	0.6	0	15.0	5.8	3.7	3.8	8.7	0.2	0	0	8.7
90	15.0	0.2	0	5.6	4.2	2.1	1.6	5.5	0.1	0	0	5.9
Future generations	−97.4											

Note: Productivity growth assumed to be 2 percent; discount rate, 6 percent.

Table 18.5   **Sensitivity Analysis: Percentage Difference between Generational Accounts of Newborns and Future Generations for Alternative Growth and Interest Rates**

Interest Rate (%)	Growth Rate (%)		
	1	2	3
5	−218.6	−155.2	−111.5
6	−307.0	−215.8	−153.8
7	−435.9	−301.9	−213.0

Source: See text.

surprising? Not if one reconsiders the demographic and fiscal scenario. Remember, 52.2 percent of the 1993 population was less than 25 years old. Under baseline policy, all these people can be expected to contribute net payments of between $6,128 and $16,852 in present value. Given that the Thai government already runs a surplus, this implies a very large accumulation of government wealth over the next 40 years, when the currently young are at their peak earning years, which can be used to subsidize the next generation. Additionally, the aging of the Thai population will not, under baseline policy, put a substantial strain on government expenditures because there is, under baseline policy, no national social security system that would potentially leave elderly Thais with negative annual net taxes.

Table 18.5 demonstrates that our finding that baseline Thai policy is, generationally speaking, highly favorable holds for a range of interest and growth rates. Though the percentage difference in lifetime net tax payments between current and future newborns varies somewhat, in all cases future generations are much better off than are current newborns. In fact, if we were to balance the burden between currently living generations in the base case we could permanently lower personal and corporate income taxes, value-added taxes, and property tax by about 70 percent. Alternatively, a reduction of all taxes by 36 percent would suffice. Would we recommend such a policy? No, particularly given the introduction of pay-as-you-go social security by the Thai government.

18.4.2   The Generational Implications of Introducing Pay-As-You-Go Social Security

We now consider how our generational accounts change with the Thai government's introduction of a pay-as-you-go system in 1993. In particular we follow the current plan by choosing a level of aggregate social security benefits equal to 9 percent of wages and assuming that a third of these benefits will be financed by the Thai budgetary surplus without raising taxes and the rest financed through a payroll tax.[8] All revenues are divided equally among the pop-

8. We assume a GDP labor share of 50 percent, consistent with the estimate in Pranee and Chalongphob (1994).

ulation over the age 65. Tables 18.6A and 18.6B present the results for males and females, respectively. Since payroll taxes are allocated according to wage income, they are included in the corporate tax column. Social security benefits are shown in a separate column. All other payments remain unchanged. Compared to the baseline results, net payments of male newborns are reduced since they can now expect social security benefits over 48,000 baht in present value exceeding the present value of payroll taxes by 11,000 baht. Furthermore, accounts of males over age 55 turn negative, indicating that future benefits exceed future tax payments in present value. Similar results hold for females. Net payments of female newborns are reduced by more than those of males due to a lower payroll tax burden facing females.

Despite the reduction of net payments by living generations, future generations are still better off than current newborns assuming a 2 percent growth rate and a 6 percent discount rate. Note though that their net tax payments are now positive; under pay-as-you-go social security, future generations can no longer expect a net transfer from the government. Table 18.7 recognizes the introduction of pay-as-you-go social security in 1993 and shows the percentage difference between lifetime net tax payments of current and future newborns under alternative discount and growth rates. As table 18.7 indicates, in a high-growth environment future generations may face considerably higher lifetime net tax burdens than current newborns as a result of introducing pay-as-you-go social security. Furthermore, as mentioned earlier, because the expenditures of the existing welfare system are more likely to grow until 2030 than in our base-case social security simulation, we find that future generations must pay net taxes that are 40.7 percent higher than those of 1993 newborns.

18.5   Summary and Conclusion

This paper has applied generational accounting—a new method of assessing the sustainability of fiscal policy—to Thailand. We find that Thailand's current fiscal policy is, generationally speaking, very favorable. Indeed, it is favorable enough that future Thais are likely to bear substantially smaller fiscal burdens and might even be, on net, subsidized by the fiscal system. This finding could, however, be reversed by the planned introduction in Thailand of a pay-as-you-go social security system. Depending on the scale and other features of the system, this policy could leave future Thais with a significantly higher growth-adjusted lifetime net tax burden than that faced by current Thais. Consequently, this paper's message for Thailand is that it should consider introducing a funded, rather than an unfunded, social security system if it wants to preserve its well-deserved reputation for fiscal prudence and generational responsibility.

Lest our readers feel too uncomfortable about our analysis of pay-as-you-go social security in Thailand and its impact on the balance of intergenerational burden, we would offer a caveat that the Thai government has been very careful about the present and future operations of its social security fund. Although it is not a fully funded system, the present Thai social security system has started

Table 18.6A   **Composition of Male Generational Accounts with Social Security: Present Value of Receipts and Payments (thousands of baht)**

Generation's Age in 1993	Net Payment	Tax Payments								Transfer Receipts			
		Personal Income	Corporate Income	Property and Local	VAT	Alcohol and Tobacco	Petroleum and Vehicle	Duties	State Lottery	University Education	Education	Social Security	Health
0	152.5	24.0	89.6	21.5	43.8	16.6	41.8	41.6	1.3	6.9	51.7	61.0	20.1
5	185.2	29.2	109.2	26.0	48.2	20.2	50.8	45.9	1.6	8.4	60.8	71.6	22.0
10	251.7	35.3	132.4	31.2	52.1	24.5	61.3	49.5	1.9	10.2	40.1	82.6	24.1
15	327.5	42.8	158.9	37.4	54.2	29.7	74.0	51.6	2.3	12.4	10.5	95.5	26.3
20	387.4	51.8	181.9	44.8	54.5	34.7	88.3	51.8	2.7	9.7	1.1	111.0	28.0
25	418.9	59.4	194.7	53.4	53.1	35.5	100.3	50.5	2.9	2.8	0.2	129.6	29.0
30	410.7	62.8	192.2	62.5	50.3	33.9	105.5	47.9	2.8	0.7	0	151.8	29.1
35	366.0	61.2	175.3	71.3	46.7	30.4	103.1	44.4	2.5	0.2	0	178.6	28.9
40	286.6	54.4	146.1	77.6	42.4	25.8	93.9	40.3	2.1	0	0	211.9	28.4
45	179.8	43.8	110.2	79.7	37.6	21.0	80.5	35.8	1.7	0	0	253.3	27.7
50	52.6	31.6	74.0	76.9	32.7	16.6	66.1	31.1	1.4	0	0	308.3	26.7
55	−92.8	19.8	42.6	68.9	27.8	13.0	52.8	26.4	1.1	0	0	384.9	25.4
60	−260.9	10.4	19.5	56.7	23.2	10.3	41.9	22.0	0.8	0	0	496.2	23.5
65	−473.3	4.4	5.8	41.9	19.0	8.3	32.9	18.0	0.7	0	0	656.9	21.1
70	−405.0	1.8	0.4	27.5	15.3	6.6	25.2	14.6	0.5	0	0	539.4	17.6
75	−318.4	0.8	0	14.6	11.5	4.9	17.7	10.9	0.3	0	0	429.6	14.1
80	−248.1	0.5	0	6.1	8.6	3.2	11.8	8.2	0.2	0	0	340.6	11.2
85	−193.5	0.3	0	1.6	6.4	2.2	7.4	6.1	0.1	0	0	265.6	8.7
90	−133.4	0.2	0	0.2	4.2	1.1	4.0	4.0	0.1	0	0	178.6	5.9
Future generations	108.6												
Percentage difference	−28.8												

Note: Productivity growth assumed to be 2 percent; discount rate, 6 percent.

Table 18.6B   Composition of Female Generational Accounts with Social Security: Present Value of Receipts and Payments (thousands of baht)

Generation's Age in 1993	Net Payment	Tax Payments								Transfer Receipts			
		Personal Income	Corporate Income	Property and Local	VAT	Alcohol and Tobacco	Petroleum and Vehicle	Duties	State Lottery	University Education	Edu-cation	Social Security	Health
0	43.0	13.8	48.1	11.5	45.4	14.0	7.2	43.2	1.3	8.7	51.7	61.0	20.1
5	49.1	16.8	58.6	13.9	50.0	17.0	8.7	47.6	1.6	10.7	60.8	71.6	22.0
10	86.6	20.3	71.0	16.6	54.2	20.5	10.4	51.5	1.9	13.0	40.1	82.6	24.1
15	132.1	24.7	85.7	19.8	56.7	24.8	12.4	53.9	2.3	15.8	10.5	95.9	26.3
20	152.2	28.4	94.3	23.9	57.2	28.4	14.3	54.4	2.6	11.1	1.1	111.0	28.0
25	149.5	30.6	95.1	28.9	55.7	28.9	15.9	53.0	2.7	2.4	0.2	129.6	29.0
30	120.5	30.5	87.5	33.7	52.6	27.6	17.3	50.0	2.6	0.4	0	151.8	29.1
35	69.7	28.1	73.3	35.4	48.6	25.1	18.1	46.2	2.4	0	0	178.6	28.9
40	2.2	23.9	55.4	34.3	44.2	22.0	18.6	42.1	2.0	0	0	211.9	28.4
45	−77.8	18.6	37.0	31.3	39.6	18.8	18.5	37.7	1.7	0	0	253.3	27.7
50	−168.3	13.3	21.4	28.1	35.2	15.9	18.0	33.5	1.3	0	0	308.3	26.7
55	−273.4	8.6	10.1	26.0	31.1	13.6	17.1	29.5	1.0	0	0	384.9	25.4
60	−404.4	5.0	3.5	25.6	27.1	11.6	15.7	25.8	0.8	0	0	496.2	23.5
65	−578.7	2.8	0.8	26.2	23.1	10.0	13.8	22.0	0.6	0	0	656.9	21.1
70	−471.6	1.6	0.1	26.4	19.1	8.3	11.3	18.2	0.5	0	0	539.4	17.6
75	−372.1	1.1	0	25.0	15.3	6.7	8.6	14.5	0.3	0	0	429.6	14.1
80	−294.4	0.9	0	21.5	12.1	5.2	6.1	11.5	0.2	0	0	340.6	11.2
85	−233.3	0.6	0	15.0	9.2	3.7	3.8	8.7	0.2	0	0	265.6	8.7
90	−163.5	0.2	0	5.6	5.8	2.1	1.6	5.5	0.1	0	0	178.6	5.9
Future generations	30.6												

Note: Productivity growth assumed to be 2 percent; discount rate, 6 percent.

Table 18.7   **Sensitivity Analysis: Percentage Difference between Generational Accounts of Newborns and Future Generations for Alternative Growth and Interest Rates with Social Security**

	Growth Rate (%)		
Interest Rate (%)	1	2	3
5	−30.4	−11.1	−65.7
6	−73.4	−28.8	−12.3
7	−127.4	−71.1	−27.3

Source: See text.

with a large reserve fund as a result of very few claims during the first few years of operations and generous financial support from the government. Its current financial condition should go a long way toward cushioning future contingencies. Moreover, the government has aggressively sought ways to profitably invest this fund at this early stage of social security operations so as to expand its financial capability. It has also expressed deep interest in adopting a microsimulation study of how Thais will work and spend in the future so that it can even be more prepared to face future financial emergency. These facts should allay some fear that the present social security system is generationally unsound.

Appendix A
Methodology of Generational Accounting

Generational accounting is based on the government's intertemporal budget constraint.[9] This constraint, written as equation (A1), requires that the future net tax payments of current and future generations be sufficient, in present value, to cover the present value of future government consumption as well as to service the government's initial net indebtedness:[10]

$$\text{(A1)} \qquad \sum_{s=0}^{D} N_{t,t-s} + \sum_{s=1}^{\infty} N_{t,t+s} = \sum_{s=t}^{\infty} G_s (1 + r)^{-(s-t)} - W_t^g.$$

The first summation on the left-hand side of equation (A1) adds together the generational accounts (the present value of the remaining lifetime net payments) of existing generations. The term $N_{t,k}$ stands for the account of the gen-

9. This section only briefly describes the method of generational accounting. For an in-depth explanation of the methodology, see Auerbach et al. (1991).
10. It is not necessary to repay the debt in order to satisfy the intertemporal budget constraint. It is enough that the growth rate of debt not exceed the discount rate.

eration born in year k. The index s in this summation runs from age 0 to age D, the maximum length of life.[11]

The second summation on the left-hand side of equation (A1) adds together the present values of remaining net payments of future generations. The first term on the right-hand side of equation (A1) expresses the present value of government consumption. In this summation the value of government consumption in year s, given by G_s, is discounted by the pretax real interest rate, r. The remaining term on the right-hand side, W_t^g, denotes the government's net wealth in year t, its assets minus its debt.

Equation (A1) indicates the zero-sum nature of intergenerational fiscal policy. Holding the present value of government consumption fixed, a reduction in the present value of net taxes extracted from current generations (a decline in the first summation on the left-hand side of eq. [A1]) necessitates an increase in the present value of net tax payments of future generations.

The term $N_{t,k}$ is defined by

$$\text{(A2)} \qquad N_{t,k} = \sum_{s=\max(t+k)}^{k+D} T_{s,k} P_{s,k} (1 + r)^{-(s-t)}.$$

In expression (A2) $T_{s,k}$ stands for the projected average net tax payment to the government made in year s by a member of the generation born in year k. The term $P_{s,k}$ stands for the number of surviving members of the cohort in year s who were born in year k. For generations who are born in year k, where $k > t$, the summation begins in year k. Regardless of the generation's year of birth, the discounting is always back to year t.

A set of generational accounts is simply a set of values of $N_{t,k}$, one for each existing and future generation, with the property that the combined present values add up to the right-hand side of equation (A1). Though we distinguish between male and female cohorts in our results, we suppress sex subscripts in equations (A1) and (A2) to ease notation.

Note that generational accounts reflect only taxes paid less transfers received. With the exception of government expenditures on education, which are treated as transfer payments, the accounts do not impute to particular generations the value of the government's purchases of goods and services because it is difficult to attribute the benefits of such purchases. Therefore, the accounts do not show the full net benefit or burden that any generation receives from government policy as a whole, although they can show a generation's net benefit or burden from a particular policy change that affects only taxes and transfers. Thus generational accounting tells us which generations will pay for government spending, rather than which generations will benefit from the spending.

---

11. Hence, the first element of this summation is $N_{t,t}$, which is the present value of net payments of the generation born in year t; the last term is $N_{t,t-D}$, the present value of remaining net payments of the oldest generation alive in year t, namely, those born in year $t - D$.

Assessing the Fiscal Burden Facing Future Generations. Given the right-hand side of equation (A1) and the first term on the left-hand side of equation (A1), we determine, as a residual the value of the second term on the right-hand side of equation (A1), which is the collective payment, measured as a time *t* present value, required of future generations. Based on this amount, we determine the average present value lifetime net tax payment of each member of each future generation under the assumption that the average lifetime tax payment of successive generations rises at the economy's rate of productivity growth. (This makes the lifetime payment a constant share of lifetime income.) Leaving out this growth adjustment, the lifetime net tax payments of future generations are directly comparable with those of current newborns, since the generational accounts of both newborns and future generations take into account net tax payments over these generations' entire lifetimes. Note that our assumption that the generational accounts of all future generations are equal, except for a growth adjustment, is just one of many assumptions we could make about the distribution across future generations of their collective net payment to the government. We could, for example, assume a phase-in of the additional fiscal burden (positive or negative) to be imposed on future generations, allocating a greater share of the burden to later future generations and a smaller share to earlier ones. Clearly, such a phase-in would mean that generations born after the phase-in period has elapsed would face larger values of lifetime burdens (the $N_{t,s}$) than we are calculating here.

Appendix B
Thailand's Socioeconomic Survey 1992

The present study uses data obtained from the SES 1992. Although the National Statistical Office (NSO) of Thailand conducted its first household expenditure survey in 1957, it did not begin to conduct these surveys on regular basis until 1968–69. The surveys were repeated every five years. In 1986, the NSO started conducting the surveys every two years. The SES 1992 is the eleventh survey of this kind. The survey covered all private, noninstitutional households residing permanently in municipal areas, sanitary districts (a form of administrative unit), and villages. However, it excluded that part of the population living in transient hotels or rooming houses, boarding schools, military barracks, temples, hospitals, prisons, and other such institutions (NSO 1994).

Sampling Design
The simplest household survey would be one in which each household has an equal probability of being selected. This is called simple random sampling. It is impractical to conduct large surveys in which each household in the popu-

Table 18B.1   Number of Blocks/Villages Sampled

Region	Municipal Areas	Sanitary Districts	Nonmunicipal Areas	Total
North	54	83	222	359
Northeast	41	84	264	389
Centre	54	84	197	335
South	54	71	154	279
Bangkok Metropolis	249	0	0	249
Remainder	12	18	33	63
Total	464	340	870	1,674

lation has an equal chance of inclusion. It is more economical and efficient to use stratified sampling procedures. The SES surveys were conducted using a stratified two-stage cluster sampling.

The entire country was divided into six regions: (1) North, (2) Northeast, (3) Centre (excluding regions 5 and 6), (4) South, (5) Bangkok Metropolis, (6) Remainder (Nonthaburi, Pathum Thani, and Samut Prakan). Each region was further divided into three parts according to the type of local administration, namely, municipal areas, sanitary districts, and nonmunicipal areas outside sanitary districts. Thus the sampling design consisted of 18 strata, 3 strata in each region. The primary sampling units were blocks for municipal areas and sanitary districts, villages for nonmunicipal areas outside sanitary districts. At the first stage of sampling, blocks/villages were randomly selected from each stratum by using probability proportional to size (the total number of households). The total number of blocks/villages was 1,674, from 77,981 blocks/villages.

Table 18B.1 presents the number of blocks/villages sampled from each stratum. The secondary sampling units were the private households that were sampled from each selected block/village. A systematic sample of 15 households was selected from each of sample blocks, while 9 and 7 households were selected from each of sample villages in sanitary districts and nonmunicipal areas outside sanitary districts, respectively. Table 18B.2 presents the total number of sample private households selected for enumeration.

It is often the case that not all households selected in the sample respond. Some households are unwilling to respond, and others provide incorrect information. Also errors are made in recording and coding data. The sample of households finally selected in the survey is smaller than the number of initially selected households. The difference between the two causes nonsampling errors in the survey. If the nonresponding households are distributed uniformly across various groups, the impact of nonsampling error is small. Since it is difficult to know the distribution of nonresponding households, it is not possible to estimate the overall degree of accuracy in the survey results.

Table 18B.3 presents the actual number of households in the final sample.

Table 18B.2   **Number of Sample Households Selected for Enumeration**

Region	Municipal Areas	Sanitary Districts	Nonmunicipal Areas	Total
North	810	747	1,554	3,111
Northeast	615	756	1,848	3,219
Centre	810	756	1,379	2,945
South	810	639	1,078	2,527
Bangkok Metropolis	3,735	0	0	3,735
Remainder	180	162	231	573
Total	6,960	3,060	6,090	16,110

Table 18B.3   **Actual Numbers of Private Households Selected in Survey**

Region	Municipal Areas	Sanitary Districts	Nonmunicipal Areas	Total
North	614	665	1,441	2,720
Northeast	507	667	1,737	2,911
Centre	628	633	1,274	2,535
South	632	546	964	2,142
Bangkok Metropolis	2,698	0	0	2,698
Remainder	129	130	193	452
Total	5,208	2,641	5,609	13,458

Table 18B.4   **Nonsampling Error by Region and Community**

Region	Municipal Areas	Sanitary Districts	Nonmunicipal Areas	Total
North	24.20	10.98	7.27	12.57
Northeast	17.56	11.77	6.01	9.57
Centre	22.47	6.33	12.74	25.35
South	21.98	14.55	10.58	21.42
Bangkok Metropolis	27.76	0	0	27.76
Remainder	28.33	19.75	16.45	21.12
Total	25.17	13.69	7.90	16.46

The percentage differences between tables 18B.2 and 18B.3 provide the magnitude of nonresponding households (expressed in percentage). These results are presented in table 18B.4.

Of 16,110 households initially selected, 13,458 households were eligible for inclusion in the survey, giving a response rate of 83.54 percent. The response rate of 83.54 percent can be considered satisfactory considering the nature of the survey. It is interesting to note from table 18B.4 that the nonresponse rate is much higher in urban areas than in rural areas. In Bangkok Metropolis, the

nonresponse rate is very high, 27.76 percent compared to the average nonresponse rate of 16.46 percent for the whole country. Since the sample size is so
large in Bangkok, however, a higher level of nonresponse will not bias the
results too much.

Weighting Sampling Observations

Expansion factors ("weights") need to be inserted in respondent household
records to enable the data provided by these households to be expanded to
obtain estimates for the defined population. For instance, if N is the total number of households in the population and n is the number of households selected
in the survey, the weight attached to the ith household will be given by

(B1) $w_i = \dfrac{N}{n}$ such that $\sum_{i=1}^{n} w_i = N$ (the total household population).

The weight in equation (B1) is derived on the assumption that every household
in the population has exactly the same probability of being selected in the
survey. Generally, the design of the survey will not imply that each household
in the population has exactly the same probability of being selected. Hence the
weight given to each respondent household must be determined by its probability of selection within a stratum adjusted to take account of nonresponding
households. This is what we do below.

Let k be the serial number of a household and j the serial number of a block/
village. Index areas by i, where i is 1 for municipal areas, 2 for sanitary districts, and 3 for nonmunicipal areas outside sanitary districts. Index regions by
h, where h is 1 for North, 2 for Northeast, 3 for Centre, 4 for South, 5 for
Bangkok Metropolis, and 6 for Remainder. Now suppose N_{hij} and P_{hij} are the
total number of households selected for enumeration and the probability of
selection in the jth sample block/village, ith area, and hth region, respectively, then

$$H'_{hi} = \frac{N_{hij}}{P_{hij}}$$

will be the estimated number of population households in the ith area and hth
region. H'_{hi} will be the same in each selected block/village because the probability of selecting a block/village is proportional to the number of households
in each population block/village. If m_{hi} is the number of sample blocks/villages
selected in the ith area and hth region, then H_{hi}/m_{hi} will be the estimated number of population households allocated to each of the selected block/villages.
If n_{hij} is the number of interviewed households in the ith area, hth region, and
jth block/village, then the estimated number of population households allocated to the kth interviewed household in the ith area, hth region, and jth block
will be given by

Table 18B.5   **Number of Households as of July 1992**

Region	Municipal Areas	Sanitary Districts	Nonmunicipal Areas	Total
North	278,376	352,525	2,405,145	3,036,046
Northeast	247,841	374,332	4,063,994	4,686,167
Centre	3,242,666	455,988	2,052,994	2,851,648
South	303,126	144,158	1,484,637	1,931,921
Bangkok Metropolis	1,653,115	–	–	1,653,115
Remainder	374,691	156,506	306,392	837,589
Total	31,996,486	1,483,509	10,313,162	14,996,486

(B2)
$$H'_{hi} = \frac{1}{m_{hi}n_{hij}} \cdot \frac{N_{hij}}{P_{hij}},$$

where H'_{hi} will be the same number for all interviewed households in the ith area, hth region, and jth block. Note that

$$H'_{hi} = \frac{1}{m_{hi}} \sum_{j=1}^{m_{hi}} \frac{N_{hij}}{P_{hij}} \cdot \frac{1}{n_{hij}}.$$

H'_{hi} is the estimated number of population households in the ith area and hth region. Suppose H_{hi} is the actual number of population households, based on the household projections as obtained from NSO (1994; see table 18B.5), then the household weight attached to each interviewed household will be given by

(B3)
$$W_{hijk} = \frac{H_{hi}}{H'_{hi}} \cdot \frac{N_{hij}}{P_{hij}} \cdot \frac{1}{m_{hi}n_{hij}},$$

where $W_{hijk} = W_{hij}$ for all k.

Note from equation (B3) that

$$H_{hi} = \sum_{j=1}^{m_{hi}} W_{hij},$$

and if H is the total number of households in the entire population, then

$$H = \sum_{h=1}^{6} \sum_{i=1}^{3} H_{hi}.$$

From table 18B.5, it can be seen that the total number of households in Thailand is 14,996,486. If we multiply the household size by its household weight, we get the population weight for each household. If we add all the population weights, we get unbiased estimates of the population in Thailand. The population estimates are presented in table 18B.6.

Table 18B.6   Population as of July 1992 (millions)

Region	Municipal Areas	Sanitary Districts	Nonmunicipal Areas	Total
North	0.95	1.21	8.97	11.13
Northeast	0.90	1.47	17.58	19.96
Centre	1.15	1.60	7.93	10.68
South	1.05	0.53	6.20	7.78
Bangkok Metropolis	5.54	–	–	5.54
Remainder	1.41	0.56	1.09	3.06
Total	11.0	5.37	41.77	58.15
Percentage of total	18.92	9.23	71.83	100.00

The total population of Thailand is estimated to be 58.15 million. The population of Bangkok Metropolis is 5.54 million. Of the total population in Thailand 71.83 percent lives in nonmunicipal areas outside sanitary districts. Thus a large majority of population in Thailand lives in rural areas.

Appendix C
Incidence Assumptions

Definition of Taxable Income. The following income sources can be allocated to individuals who earn them (whose age and sex are given): (1) wage and salary; (2) profit, nonfarm; (3) profit from farm; (4) transfer payments; (5) property income; and (6) other money receipts. Taxable income is defined as total money income minus all taxes paid. We obtained the individual age and sex profiles for taxable income and property income.

Income Tax (method 1). Income tax was available at the household level. From the taxable incomes of individuals we calculated the taxable income for each household. Given taxable income and income tax for each household, we computed the tax rate for each household. Given this information, we allocated the household income tax to each individual within the household in proportion to the taxable income of the individual (using the household tax rate). This allowed us to calculate the age and sex profile for each individual. This procedure does not assume that the income tax is proportional to the taxable income in the country. The assumption of proportionality is rather strong because the income tax is generally progressive. In the above allocation, we assumed that income tax is proportional within each household. This is not entirely satisfactory, but it is better that assuming that taxes are proportional in the entire economy. Many households had positive taxable income but did not pay any income tax. The assumption of proportionality would allocate taxes to households and then to individuals even if these households did not actually pay any income tax.

Income Tax (method 2). This method allocates income tax to individuals in proportion to their taxable income. This method assumes that income tax is proportional in the economy. This method is less accurate than method 1.

Property Tax (method 1). This method is exactly the same as income tax method 1. The property tax is available at the household level and property income at the individual level. So we calculated the tax rates for each household and allocated property tax to individuals within the households in proportion to each individual's share of property income.

Property Tax (method 2). The property tax is allocated to individuals within the economy in proportion to the individual's property income. This method assumes proportionality in the economy.

Corporate Tax. We assumed that corporate income taxes are borne by labor because of international capital mobility. So we allocated corporate taxes in proportion to wage and salary income, which is available at the individual level, giving immediately the age and sex profile of corporate taxes.

Value-Added Tax (VAT). The value-added tax was allocated to households in proportion to each household's total expenditure. The allocation of VAT within households was done in proportion to the following equivalence scale:

Age 0–5 years	0.5
Age 6–11 years	0.6
Age 12–15 years	0.7
Age 16–18 years	0.8
Age 18+ years	1.0

We used this equivalence scale in order to take account of the differing needs of household members of different ages.

Import Duty. The allocation of import duty follows exactly the same procedure as for VAT.

Tobacco, Alcohol, and State Lottery. Taxes on alcohol, tobacco, and gambling were allocated to households in proportion to household expenditures on these items. Within households, these taxes are allocated only to adults (giving zero weight to children aged 18 or younger). This is referred to as method 1. Since in Asian countries, alcohol and tobacco are generally consumed by males only, in method 2 none of these taxes are allocated to females within households.

Petroleum Products and Motor Vehicles. The excise on petroleum products and motor vehicles is allocated to the household head according to the household consumption of these items.

Expenditures on Education. Current and capital expenditures on education were allocated in proportion to the number of persons attending school or university. In Thailand about 22 percent of the population is attending school of some kind. University expenditures were allocated to individuals attending a university and other educational expenditures were allocated to individuals attending institutions and schools other than a university.

Social Security. Expenditure on social security is allocated to the household head according to pensions and disability payments received by the household. It should be noted that the Thai government gives pensions only to government employees.

Local Government Revenue. In 1993–94, local government revenue was 47.3 billion baht, which on dividing by population gives a per person tax (per month) paid equal to 813.5 baht. This amount can be allocated to individuals in proportion to the property tax.

References

Auerbach, Alan J., Jagadeesh Gokhale, and Laurence J. Kotlikoff. 1991. Generational accounts: A meaningful alternative to deficit accounting. In *Tax policy and the economy,* vol. 5, ed. D. Bradford, 55–110. Cambridge, Mass.: MIT Press.

———. 1994. Generational accounting: A meaningful way to assess fiscal policy. *Journal of Economic Perspectives* 8 (1): 73–94.

Auerbach, Alan J., Jagadeesh Gokhale, Laurence J. Kotlikoff, and Erling Steigum, Jr. 1993. Generational accounting in Norway: Is Norway overconsuming its petroleum wealth? Ruth Pollak Working Paper Series on Economics, no. 24. Boston: Boston University, Department of Economics, October.

Franco, Danielle, Jagadeesh Gokhale, Luis Guiso, Laurence J. Kotlikoff, and Nicola Sartor. 1993. Generational accounting—The case of Italy. In *Saving and the accumulation of wealth,* ed. A. Ando, L. Guiso, and I. Visco, 128–62. Cambridge: Cambridge University Press.

Gokhale, Jagadeesh, Bernd Raffelhüschen, and Jan Walliser. 1995. The burden of German unification: A generational accounting approach. *Finanzarchiv* 52:141–65.

Hagemann, Robert P., Juan Amieva-Huerta, and Stanford Ross. 1992. Thailand: Developing the social security system. Washington, D.C.: International Monetary Fund. Mimeograph.

Hagemann, Robert P., and Christoph John. 1995. The fiscal stance in Sweden: A generational accounting perspective. IMF Working Paper no. 95/105. Washington, D.C.: International Monetary Fund.

Kakwani, Nanak. 1997. Economic growth and income inequality in Thailand. In *Specific issues*. Bangkok: National Economic and Social Development Board, Develop Evaluation Division.

Kakwani, Nanak, Laurence J. Kotlikoff, Medhi Krongkaew, Sudhir Shetty, and Jan Walliser. 1996. Generational accounting in Thailand. Economic Growth, Poverty and Income Inequality in the Asia Pacific Region Working Paper Series, no. WP 2/96. Sydney: University of New South Wales, School of Economics.

Kotlikoff, Laurence J. 1992. *Generational accounting*. New York: Free Press.

Kotlikoff, Laurence J., and Jan Walliser. 1995. Applying generational accounting to developing countries. Boston: Boston University. Mimeograph.

Medhi Krongkaew. 1980. *The government and the income gap of the people* (in Thai). Bangkok: Thammasat University Press.

National Statistical Office (NSO). 1994. *Report of the 1992 Household Socioeconomic Survey*. Bangkok: National Statistical Office.

Pranee Tinakorn and Chalongphob Sussangkam. 1994. Productivity growth in Thailand. Bangkok: Thailand Development Research Institute. Mimeograph.

19   Generational Accounting in Japan

Noriyuki Takayama, Yukinobu Kitamura, and Hiroshi Yoshida

19.1   Introduction

Although the importance of the concept of generational accounting has been well recognized in Japan as the aging of the population proceeds, there has been no definitive study on the subject. This work intends to rectify this omission by providing the most comprehensive analysis of generational accounts in Japan to date.

Given certain conditions such as the prospect of low economic growth and the rapid aging of society, which cannot easily be changed, the government has to implement dramatic reform on both the revenue and expenditure sides of public finances. Although future prospects with respect to public finances are uncertain and policy objectives to avoid any worsening of the fiscal position are unclear, there is no doubt that the government must reduce the public debt. In this context, one fiscal measure that is attracting attention among policy-makers is the gross public burden ratio (i.e., all taxes and the social security contributions divided by national income). For 1996, the ratio is expected to be 37.2 percent, compared with 25.7 percent in 1975. As a rule of thumb, the government is expected to maintain this ratio at around 45 percent at the beginning of the twenty-first century and below 50 percent even when the elderly population reaches its peak, say, in 2020.

We should identify some basic principles for future fiscal reform. First, all agents (individuals, firms, and the government) should take full responsibility for their decisions. A simple cost-benefit analysis, such as the generational accounting presented here, can be a very useful tool in making individual fiscal positions more transparent. Second, competitive market mechanisms must be

Noriyuki Takayama is professor of economics at Hitotsubashi University. Yukinobu Kitamura is an associate professor at Keio University and economist at the Bank of Japan. Hiroshi Yoshida is an associate professor at Tohoku University.

used to ensure the efficient allocation of government funds, which means institutional and political compromises should be avoided if they do not satisfy competitive market mechanisms. Third, as future generations do not yet have a political voice, if the government does not think of them, they will have to bear a huge debt burden to pay for the benefits accruing to current generations. In principle, it is the government that adjusts the burdens and benefits of public transfers and objectively decides the fairness of intergenerational burden sharing.

A summary of our main conclusions is as follows: The base-case calculation of the generational imbalance between present and future generations is 169 percent for case A (educational expenditures are treated as consumption) and 338 percent for case B (educational expenditures are treated as transfers) if the current fiscal policy stance is to be maintained (where real income growth is 1.5 percent and the discount rate is 5 percent). This implies that future generations will have to bear 2.7 to 4.4 times the fiscal burden that present generations do, a huge imbalance by international standards.

For the base case, four basic scenarios and two additional scenarios to resolve this generational imbalance are considered. In the four basic scenarios, government purchases must be cut 26 to 30 percent, or all taxes need to be raised about 16 percent, or income tax has to be increased 54 percent, or transfer payments must be cut by some 25 to 29 percent. In the additional scenarios, both government purchases and transfers are to be cut 14 percent, and if all taxes are reduced by 50 percent, then both purchases and transfers need to be cut by 57 percent, which makes the size of government expenditures one-quarter of the current level.

Another simulation indicates that the generational imbalance is due not to the fiscal debt outstanding per se but to changes in demographic structure. Indeed, if the demographic structure were to remain unchanged, the generational imbalance would fall substantially. This is probably the main implication of generational accounting, not only in Japan but also in other countries.

We also consider the concept of *fixed lifetime relative position* suggested in Musgrave (1981). This concept differs from *generational imbalance* in generational accounting. That is, the fixed lifetime relative position sets contributions and benefits so as to keep constant the ratio of per capita earnings of those in working generations to the per capita benefits of retirees. This concept evaluates the benefits of retirees in terms not of their own net burden but of the earnings of current working generations. In other words, this concept per se includes generational interaction. The result shows that a balanced budget will be achieved and the fixed lifetime relative position kept constant, if taxes are increased 10 to 15 percent and transfer benefits are reduced 10 to 13 percent. In this case, the generational imbalance remains less than 13 percent for case A and 73 percent for case B.

19.2   Brief History of Fiscal Policy and Current Fiscal Debates

19.2.1   Brief History of Fiscal Policy in Japan[1]

In 1947, after the Second World War, the government decided to seek a balanced budget, a principle that was applied not only to the general budget but also to the special budget and other governmental organizations. Then, in 1950, fundamental tax reform, the so-called Shoup mission tax reform, was implemented, which laid the foundation of Japan's tax system on direct taxation with a special emphasis on fairness. A deep economic recession in 1949 suddenly ended when special procurement by the U.S. military due to the Korean War commenced.

During 1951–55, active fiscal policy was implemented from time to time. However, under capital market and foreign exchange controls, the economic boom was suppressed when the balance of payments worsened. For example, fiscal policy was tightened in 1954–55 along with tight monetary policy. This type of stop-and-go policy continued until the mid-1960s.

A period of high economic growth started in 1955. The government budget had been increased steadily to finance public investment, social security expenditures among others. Because of the natural increase in tax revenues reflecting high economic growth, the principle of having a balanced general budget was strictly adhered to. Furthermore, a tax reduction was effected almost annually so as to keep the average ratio of tax revenue to GNP at around 19 percent. In addition, the government paved the way for the introduction of a comprehensive social security system, namely, the public pension and medical insurance system, which was intended to cover all citizens in Japan. The fiscal authority in these halcyon days of 1955–64 actually ran fiscal surpluses that fluctuated from year to year and functioned as something of a built-in stabilizer. Looking at the long term, the government invested heavily in fixed public capital formation, and tax incentives to encourage personal savings and corporate investment worked well.

In 1965, the economy entered a recession after policy tightening in 1963. Although the budget was balanced in the original plan, tax revenues fell short and the government thus decided to issue government bonds for the first time since the Second World War. In 1966, the government intended only to issue bonds for the purpose of construction investment, but in so doing it obtained a very useful but potentially dangerous free hand in terms of demand management. This was its historic departure from the principle of a balanced budget.

After that first issue of government bonds, the debt dependency ratio increased (see table 19.1). In 1968, fiscal discipline was the goal, and easy reliance on bond finance halted; as a result, the debt dependency ratio dropped dramatically in 1970.

1. This section draws heavily from Tamura (1996, sec. 4).

Table 19.1   Basic Fiscal Statistics

	General Account (100 million yen)			Debt Dependency Ratio[a] (%)	Tax Burden Ratio[b] (%)
Year	Expenditure	Tax Revenue	Bond Issue		
1960	17,431	16,183			18.9
1965	37,230	30,496	1,972		18.0
1970	81,877	72,958	3,472	4.2	18.9
1975	208,609	137,527	52,805	25.3	18.3
1980	434,050	268,687	141,702	32.6	22.2
1985	530,045	381,988	123,080	23.2	24.0
1990	692,687	601,059	73,120	10.6	27.8
1991	705,472	598,204	67,300	9.5	27.1
1992	704,974	544,453	95,360	13.5	24.9
1993	751,025	541,262	161,740	21.5	24.4
1994	736,136	508,160	164,900	22.4	23.2
1995	780,340	537,310	125,980	28.2	23.3

Source: Ministry of Finance.
[a]Debt dependency ratio is bond issue/expenditure.
[b]Tax burden ratio is all tax revenues/national income.

In 1971, the Nixon administration suspended gold convertibility and imposed a 50 percent import tax as part of a new economic policy—the so-called Nixon shock—which had a serious impact on the Japanese economy. In response, the Japanese government adopted expansionary fiscal policies to increase public investment and to reduce taxes during 1971–72, along with an easy monetary policy. The first oil shock in October 1973 pushed inflation above 20 percent in 1974. Although dramatic reform of the social security system was implemented in 1973, by which 100 percent of the medical expenditures of the elderly and 70 percent of those of nonworking spouses and children were covered, the government otherwise maintained a very tight fiscal policy stance and a lot of public investment was suspended or postponed; 1974 saw zero growth in public investment expenditures.

The economy fell into recession in 1974 and experienced negative growth for the first time since the Second World War. The government could not help but implement aggressive fiscal policy to stimulate the economy. As a consequence of the recession, tax revenues fell short and the government thus again turned to bond financing, but this time, it was permitted to issue bonds that were not for the purpose of public investment. The debt dependency ratio jumped from 11.3 percent in 1974 to 25.3 percent in 1975 and remained high until the late 1980s, with a peak of 34.7 percent in 1979. We consider 1975 a second turning point for fiscal policy.

During 1980–84, after the second oil shock in 1979, the government tried to implement substantial fiscal reform to escape its heavy reliance on debt financing. After 1983, the following reforms were adopted: some fiscal expenditures were cut, the public pension and medical insurance system was reformed, local government finances were revamped, subsidies were reduced, food management expenditures were revised, and public corporations were privatized. As a result, the debt dependency ratio fell to 23.2 percent in 1985.

From 1985 to 1990, the government continued to pursue various fiscal reform measures. In September 1985, the major Organization for Economic Cooperation and Development (OECD) economies agreed to adjust exchange rates against the U.S. dollar by international policy coordination (the Plaza Agreement). In order to avoid repercussions on the Japanese economy from the rapid appreciation of the yen, the government pursued aggressive fiscal policy through an easy monetary policy (i.e., the official discount rate was kept at 2.5 percent for over two years). These policies stimulated the economy, which, in turn, enjoyed a long boom in the latter half of the 1980s. From 1983 to 1987, general government expenditures were cut annually. Thanks to increased tax revenue due to the boom, in 1990 the government succeeded in reducing debt financing by a substantial margin for the first time in 15 years.

In 1991, the economy started contracting as a result of the bursting of the bubble economy, and a deep recession ensued. The government implemented extraordinary fiscal policy packages during 1992–95, and the official discount rate was reduced to a record low 0.5 percent in September 1995. As a consequence, the debt dependency ratio has increased since 1991 (see table 19.1). Debt outstanding reached 200 trillion yen at the end of 1994 (the ratio of gross debt to GDP in 1994 was 73.2 percent) and is expected to reach some 240 trillion yen at the end of 1996; if local government debt (i.e., municipal bonds) were included, the figure would be 442 trillion yen (and the ratio of gross debt to GDP in 1996 would be 87.4 percent). In this respect, the fiscal stance of the Japanese government has been going from bad to worse in recent years.

19.2.2 Current Fiscal Debates[2]

In reaction to the recent rapid deterioration in its fiscal position and the rapid aging of society toward the twenty-first century, the Japanese government as well as the private sector, including academic economists, has started asserting openly the urgent need to improve the current fiscal position and for more fundamental structural reform of public finance in general.

To clarify the situation, let us first look at the general budget plan for 1996. Of 75.1 trillion yen in expenditures, social-security-related items account for 14.3 trillion yen (19 percent); public investment for infrastructure (i.e., roads, bridges, housing, etc.), 9.7 trillion yen (13 percent); educational and science-research-related expenditures, 6.2 trillion yen (8 percent); transfers to municipal governments, 13.6 trillion yen (18 percent); and other small expenditures for defense, official development assistance, energy-related items, and the promotion of small and medium-sized enterprises, 6.8 trillion yen (9.1 percent).

---

2. This section mainly relies on Ishi (1996, chap. 1).

In addition to these expenditures, government-bond-related items (i.e., interest payments and the repayment of principal) require 16.4 trillion yen (22 percent), which is the biggest expenditure item. On the revenue side, income tax provides 19.3 trillion yen; corporate tax, 13.5 trillion yen; inheritance tax, 2.6 trillion yen; and consumption tax, 5.9 trillion yen. Together with other tax revenues and stamp duties, tax revenues total 51.3 trillion yen. The gap between expenditures and revenues is mainly filled by public debt, 21 trillion yen (28 percent of total revenues).

On both the expenditure and revenue sides, public-debt-related items account for the biggest shares, an alarming picture of the fiscal position in Japan. To put it into perspective, compare the statistics with those for the other major OECD economies (OECD 1996): while the ratio of gross public debt to GDP in Japan increased from 65.1 percent in 1990 to 80.7 percent in 1995, in the United States it rose from 55.6 to 64.3 percent, in the United Kingdom from 39.3 to 60.0 percent, in Germany from 45.5 to 61.6 percent, and in France from 40.2 to 60.0 percent. As these statistics show, Japan is in the worst position among major OECD countries.

There are some causes and reasons for the worsening of the fiscal position. First, tax revenue growth remains very low as the economy itself has grown very slowly in recent years. Second, the population is aging at an accelerated pace (see table 19.2). Third, expenditures on institutional arrangements, such as the social security system, have been increasing. Fourth, because of the extraordinary fiscal policy packages in 1992–95 to stimulate the economy amid a deep recession, public debt has increased by 68 trillion yen in the past five years.

Prospects with respect to the future fiscal position and policy objectives to avoid a worsening of the fiscal position are still unknown. Without doubt, however, the government must avoid issuing bonds that are not used to provide public capital because such bonds merely transfer the burden without providing any benefits to future generations. A simulation suggests that the government will have to issue bonds simply for repayment purposes until 2003 even if there is no growth in general expenditures from 1997 onward (which means general expenditures 20 percent lower than the natural growth path in 2001). In other words, without any substantial reduction in real terms, government expenditures cannot be maintained, and even if maintained, the government has to issue bonds until 2003.

One fiscal concept that is attracting attention among policymakers is the gross public burden ratio (i.e., all taxes and the social security burden divided by national income, which is a larger concept than the tax burden rate in table 19.1). The ratio in 1996 is expected to be 37.2 percent, compared with 25.3 percent in 1975. As a rule of thumb, the government is expected to maintain this ratio at around 45 percent at the beginning of the twenty-first century and below 50 percent even at the peak of the elderly population, say, in 2020. Note that this measure itself does not take into account public debt and the genera-

Table 19.2   **Demographic Projection**

	Population			Dependency Ratio[a]		
Year	Total	Children Ages 0–17	Working Ages 18–64	Old Ages 65+	Elderly	Child	Total
1995	125,570,246	24,989,428	82,303,927	18,276,891	22.21	30.36	52.57
2000	126,892,162	23,043,161	81,978,714	21,870,288	26.68	28.11	54.79
2005	127,683,764	22,050,991	80,627,184	25,005,587	31.01	27.35	58.36
2010	127,622,805	21,875,387	77,621,677	28,125,744	36.23	28.18	64.42
2015	126,443,541	21,583,315	72,977,324	31,882,900	43.69	29.58	73.26
2020	124,133,164	20,709,028	70,088,953	33,335,184	47.56	29.55	77.11
2025	120,913,146	19,424,577	68,372,447	33,116,115	48.43	28.41	76.84
2030	117,149,082	18,239,653	66,141,892	32,767,534	49.54	27.58	77.12
2035	113,114,063	17,436,911	62,890,562	32,786,592	52.13	27.73	79.86
2040	108,964,036	16,965,244	58,272,787	33,726,002	57.88	29.11	86.99
2045	104,758,334	16,552,487	54,708,560	33,497,281	61.23	30.26	91.48
2050	100,496,300	15,954,267	52,087,946	32,454,089	62.31	30.63	92.94
2055	96,188,065	15,202,042	50,288,102	30,697,922	61.04	30.23	91.27
2060	91,848,186	14,486,333	48,858,470	28,503,387	58.34	29.65	87.99
2065	87,636,413	13,964,828	47,121,932	26,549,657	56.34	29.64	85.98
2070	83,773,434	13,652,110	45,023,103	25,098,219	55.75	30.32	86.07
2075	80,367,936	13,404,853	42,899,729	24,063,357	56.09	31.25	87.34
2080	77,375,135	13,106,607	41,068,281	23,200,243	56.49	31.91	88.41
2085	74,639,896	12,736,928	39,624,936	22,278,029	56.22	32.14	88.37
2090	72,067,533	12,364,880	38,445,282	21,257,378	55.29	32.16	87.45
2095	69,634,513	12,073,791	37,293,925	20,266,797	54.34	32.37	86.72
2100	67,365,808	11,887,962	36,068,378	19,409,469	53.81	32.96	86.77

Source: Medium variant projection of future population conducted in 1997 by the Institute of Population Problems, Ministry of Health and Welfare.

Note: The medium variant projection is based on the following assumptions: (1) The base population distribution was estimated on 1 October 1995. (2) The total fertility rate was 1.42 in 1995, dropped to 1.38 in 2000, and then gradually rose to 1.61 in 2030. (3) Life expectancies at birth were 76.36 years for men and 82.84 for women in 1995, rising to 77.40 and 84.12 in 2000 and 79.43 and 86.47 in 2050. (4) The net international migration rate remains very small for Japan (a maximum of 1.5 per million for male immigrants aged 25). Data on net migration is based on the five-year average from 1 October 1990 to 30 September 1995 and is assumed constant from 1 October 1995 onward.

We assume that the population after 2100 will reach a steady state so that the demographic structure remains the same as in 2100.

[a]Elderly dependency ratio is the old population as a percentage of the working population. Child dependency ratio is the child population as a percentage of the working population. Total dependency ratio is old plus child populations as a percentage of the working population. In Japan, it is conventional to assume that children are aged 0 to 14, the working population, aged 15 to 64, and the old, aged 65 or older. Therefore, officially announced dependency ratios differ from those reported in the table.

tional distribution of the burden. Government expenditures can be increased without raising the gross public burden ratio as long as the gap between expenditures and revenues is financed by public debt. Thus the usefulness of this concept seems rather limited.

All in all, given certain conditions such as prospects of low economic growth and the rapid aging of society, which cannot be easily changed, the government has to implement dramatic reform on both the revenue and expenditure sides. Several principles for such reform can be put forward. First, all agents (individuals, firms, and the government) must take full responsibility for their decisions; self-help is a rather old but still valid idea. With respect to the burden and benefits of the old social security system, a reasonable balance must be found; that is, benefits cannot go beyond the means of society. Second, competitive market mechanisms must be used in implementing the efficient allocation of government expenditures. Institutional and political compromises should be avoided if they do not satisfy the market mechanism. Third, the stabilization role of public finance has been weakened, if not abandoned completely, in all major OECD countries but Japan. Indeed, stabilization policy has come to be viewed more as one aspect of government intervention to alleviate market failure, and the effectiveness of fiscal stimuli has been very limited, as the recent Japanese experience shows. Finally, as future generations do not have a political voice at the moment, if the government does not consider them, they will have to bear a huge burden of debt that only benefits current generations. In principle, it is the government that adjusts the burden and benefit of public transfers and objectively judges the fairness of intergenerational burden sharing.

19.3   The Data

Government revenues and expenditures are based on the 1995 *Annual Report on National Accounts* (Economic Planning Agency). Tax revenue estimates are from the third 1995 supplementary budget shown in the April 1996 issue of the *Ministry of Finance Statistics Monthly* (vol. 528), municipal government revenues and expenditures are from the *Municipal Government Finance Plan* for 1995, and income from interest and stock sales is from the 1994 *National Tax Bureau Annual Report* (no. 120). Government fixed capital formation is obtained from the general account and not the special account.

Consumption and income for each generation are distributed according to age distribution information from the 1994 National Survey of Family Income and Expenditure (Statistics Bureau, Management and Coordination Agency) by expenditure, savings, and loans for households with two or more members (issued 27 December 1995) and assets (issued 25 May 1996). As age distribution is reported at five-year intervals from ages 20 to 65, and those aged 70 or older are treated equally, we allocate the same value for those aged 70 to 95.

Social security transfers in kind (mainly medical transfers) are calculated according to age distribution information from the 1993 Survey of Income Redistribution (Ministry of Health and Welfare).

Population projections are taken from the medium variant projection of future population conducted in 1997 by the Institute of Population Problems, Ministry of Health and Welfare. The base population is the 1995 population census of Japan.

Table 19.3 **Generational Accounts: Base Case (thousands of U.S. dollars)**

Generation's Age in 1995	Case A: Education as Consumption	Case B: Education as Transfer
0	143.4	73.0
5	169.3	90.9
10	200.1	135.4
15	235.9	187.4
20	278.1	257.4
25	295.2	295.2
30	297.8	297.8
35	287.4	287.4
40	263.8	263.8
45	227.7	227.7
50	173.1	173.1
55	99.0	99.0
60	11.9	11.9
65	−47.7	−47.7
70	−44.8	−44.8
75	−36.0	−36.0
80	−26.7	−26.7
85	−18.2	−18.2
90	−9.7	−9.7
Future generations	386.2	319.4
Generational imbalance (%)	169.3	337.8

Note: Case A: Educational expenditures treated as consumption. Case B: Educational expenditures treated as transfers. Exchange rate assumed to be 93.37 yen per U.S dollar (1995 average); real income growth, 1.5 percent; discount rate, 5 percent.

Per capita educational expenditure for each age is allocated from 1993 school expenditure data (excluding donations) in the 1996 *Ministry of Education Statistics Handbook.*

19.4 Main Findings and Sensitivity Analysis

Table 19.3 presents the basic results of generational accounting in Japan (1995 base year). They are divided into two cases: case A, in which educational expenditures are treated as consumption, and case B, in which they are treated as transfers. This distinction makes for some differences for generations between ages 0 and 24. The percentage imbalance between newborn and future generations is 169 percent for case A and 338 percent for case B, implying that future generations must pay about 2.7 times for case A and about 4.4 times for case B as much tax (net basis) as newborn generations, a huge difference.

Note, however, that such a large generational imbalance does not immediately imply a heavy burden or pain for future generations. That is to say, if the net present value of payments as a proportion of lifetime income for future generations is reasonably small, this large imbalance might not induce a burden for future generations that is 2.7 to 4.4 times as much as that on newborn generations. In other words, an absolute value comparison of net payments makes sense as far as the generational imbalance is concerned. The net present value of net payments as a proportion of lifetime income for future generations (i.e., the relative burden of future generations), however, cannot be identified solely by the absolute value of net payments because lifetime incomes differ substantially.

In the following, we calculate the net present value of payments as a percentage of lifetime income. Taking the working generations as those aged 0 to 64, the present value of average lifetime income for employees (evaluated at age 0) is approximately $487,800 (in the case of 1.5 percent growth with a 5.0 percent discount rate). According to table 19.3, case A, the net present value of payments for the present generation is $143,400, implying that the lifetime net tax rate is 29 percent. It is 79 percent for future generations. Even if we take into consideration pension benefits, net tax payments of nearly 80 percent of lifetime income would be a heavy burden.

However, it is worth noting that because future generations will benefit from government consumption, the 80 percent of lifetime income is not meant to be collected for nothing. In fact, the net tax payments of each generation will be used as government consumption, mostly for one's own generation and the rest for future generations. Government consumption used for future generations can be interpreted as a net burden on the current generation because it is a form of intergenerational transfer via the government. In case B (in which educational expenditures are treated as transfers), the lifetime net tax rate is 15 percent for present generations and 65 percent for future generations.

In addition to the base-case assumptions of 1.5 percent real income growth and 5.0 percent discount rate, table 19.4 assesses various growth and discount rate combinations (see also fig. 19.1). In particular, we include the case of a 2.0 percent discount rate because the standard discount rates in this volume seem rather high (i.e., 3, 5, and 7 percent) by Japanese standards, while the real growth rates are low (i.e., 1, 1.5, 2, and 3 percent).

Given the same fiscal policy, the generational imbalance is very sensitive to real income growth and discount rate assumptions. According to demographic projections, the aging process will reach a peak in 2050, after which society will get younger. The fiscal position is also expected to ease after 2050. The higher real income growth rate reduces the burden of future generations because of a bigger improvement in fiscal position after 2050. On the other hand, the higher discount rate increases the burden of future generations because the fiscal position is heavily discounted.

Because the demographic projection includes a lot of uncertainty, nothing can be said for sure. But if the demographic structure remains stationary after the aging process reaches its peak, the effects of real income growth and the

Table 19.4   Sensitivity Analysis of Generational Imbalance (thousands of U.S. dollars)

	$g = 1$				$g = 1.5$				$g = 2$				$g = 3$			
	$r = 2$	$r = 3$	$r = 5$	$r = 7$	$r = 2$	$r = 3$	$r = 5$	$r = 7$	$r = 2$	$r = 3$	$r = 5$	$r = 7$	$r = 2$	$r = 3$	$r = 5$	$r = 7$
Case A: Education as Consumption																
Present generations	348.6	242.1	120.1	62.4	419.5	291.0	143.4	73.8	n.a.	349.8	171.4	87.4	n.a.	n.a.	245.6	123.3
Future generations	595.2	510.6	356.5	283.3	730.7	571.5	386.2	297.6	n.a.	644.3	421.6	314.9	n.a.	n.a.	514.7	360.6
Generational imbalance (%)	70.7	110.9	196.9	354.3	74.2	96.4	169.3	303.5	n.a.	84.2	146.0	260.3	n.a.	n.a.	109.6	192.5
Case B: Education as Transfer																
Present generations	256.3	159.7	53.3	7.4	321.7	203.8	73.0	16.0	n.a.	257.5	97.1	26.7	n.a.	n.a.	162.7	56.0
Future generations	553.3	431.3	293.6	232.5	635.3	487.2	319.4	243.9	n.a.	554.7	350.9	258.1	n.a.	n.a.	435.0	297.1
Generational imbalance (%)	115.9	170.1	450.7	3,038.4	97.5	139.0	337.8	1,424.3	n.a.	115.4	261.4	868.5	n.a.	n.a.	167.3	430.6

Note: Exchange rate assumed to be 93.37 yen per U.S. dollar (1995 average); g is real income growth (percent); r is discount rate (percent). Situations where real growth and discount rates are identical are not available.

Case A

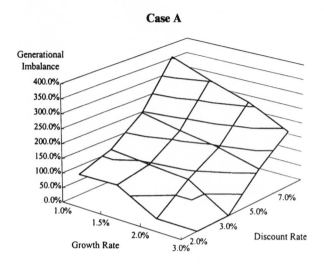

Case B

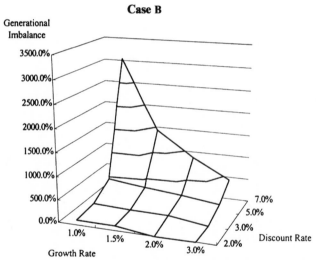

Fig. 19.1   Sensitivity of generational imbalance to growth and discount rate assumptions

Note: Case A, Educational expenditures treated as consumption. Case B, Educational expenditures treated as transfer.

discount rate work in opposite directions. A reasonable scenario would be a real income growth rate of 1.5 percent and a discount rate of 3.0 percent. In this case, the generational imbalance is 96.4 percent for case A and 139 percent for case B. These are much smaller than the imbalances in the base case (i.e., a real income growth rate of 1.5 percent and a discount rate of 5 percent).

Table 19.5   **Decomposition of Generational Imbalance (percent)**

Case	Base Case	No Demographic Change	Zero Debt
A	169.3	42.19	154.40
B	337.8	77.21	308.64

Note: Case A: Educational expenditures treated as consumption. Case B: Educational expenditures treated as transfers. Real income growth assumed to be 1.5 percent; discount rate, 5 percent.

If we are concerned only with the net present values of payments after 1995, table 19.3 indicates that they are positive for generations aged 64 or younger and negative for generations aged 65 or older. This is partly due to the fact that tax payments and social security contributions that old generations made when they were young are ignored in this calculation and also partly due to large intergenerational transfers from young to old generations via fiscal policy. If redistribution policy is biased toward old generations, the fiscal burden of future generations will increase as the aging process advances. Table 19.5 eloquently indicates this.

Table 19.5 decomposes the generational imbalance into two factors: demographic change and fiscal debt position. Even if we assume no debt outstanding (zero debt) in 1995, there will remain generational imbalances of 155 percent for case A and 309 percent for case B. Hence, current debt outstanding per se is not the main reason for the generational imbalance. On the other hand, if we assume no demographic change after 1995, the generational imbalance shrinks substantially to 42 percent for case A and 77 percent for case B. This implies that in Japan the generational imbalance is largely due to the aging of the demographic structure and intergenerational transfers via fiscal policy.

An important aspect of generational accounting in Japan is the role of the government's fixed capital formation. So far, future generations seem to be forced to bear an unjustifiably huge fiscal burden to finance current and future old generations. However, at the same time, future generations will enjoy without explicit repayment the benefits of public capital accumulated by the previous (old) generations. In order to make a fair judgment of intergenerational income redistribution, it is necessary to evaluate imputed benefits from public capital inherited from previous (old) generations (on this, see the appendix). As for the private sector, young generations either buy private capital or borrow it (paying rent) from old generations. As for the household sector, bequest and gift transfers from old to young generations are made with no repayment except taxes.

Table 19.6 shows the percentage share of public capital formation in total gross domestic fixed capital formation. As is evident, the Japanese government has been investing heavily in public capital formation, probably most heavily among OECD countries. In fact, we can say that the government transfers its gross fixed capital formation to future generations via public capital investment financed by current taxes. We think it is fair to discount the burden of future

Table 19.6   Gross Domestic Fixed Capital Formation in Major OECD Countries, 1995

	A Gross Domestic Fixed Capital Formation	B Private Sector Investment	C Public Sector Investment (A − B)	D Share of Public Sector Investment (%) C/A	Unit
Japan	136,695	95,054	41,641	30.5	Yen (billion)
United Kingdom	104,024	87,283	16,741	16.1	Pounds (million)
Germany	7,534	6,674	860	11.4	Marks (million)
France	13,807	11,403	2,404	17.4	Francs (100 million)
Italy	301,039	261,083	39,956	13.3	Lira (billion)

Source: Bank of Japan, *Comparative Economic and Financial Statistics: Japan and Other Major Countries* (Tokyo, 1996).
Note: Because of the National Income and Product Accounts basis, U.S. data are not shown.

generations because they enjoy benefits from public capital. Unfortunately, the framework we use here makes no distinction between government consumption and investment for public capital formation that will benefit future generations. In the following section, we will discuss the impact of alternative policies and the fairness of intergenerational transfers.

19.5   Generational Impact of Alternative Policies

19.5.1   Six Different Policy Simulations

This section conducts six different policy simulations and an "alternative fairness" exercise for intergenerational transfers. The six different policy simulations are based on the following assumptions to achieve generational balance: (a) an immediate and permanent cut in government purchases, (b) an immediate and permanent increase in all tax revenues, (c) an immediate increase in income tax revenues, (d) an immediate and permanent cut in transfer payments, (e) an immediate and permanent cut in both purchases and transfers, and (f) an immediate and permanent 50 percent cut in all taxes and reduction in both purchases and transfers. The results are reported in table 19.7 under both case A and case B. Let us first look at the base case, with real growth of 1.5 percent and a discount rate of 5.0 percent.

First, policy (a) implies that government purchases and fixed capital investment must be cut by about 26 to 30 percent to achieve generational balance. As the ratio between private and public demand with respect to gross domestic expenditures is about 4:1, an immediate cut in government purchases of 26 to 30 percent implies a reduction in gross domestic expenditure of 5 to 6 percent, which would have a big macroeconomic impact.

Second, policy (b) means an approximate 16 percent increase in tax pay-

Table 19.7   **Generational Impact of Alternative Policies**

Base Case (real income growth of 1.5%; discount rate of 5.0%)

Policy	Change (%)	Result (%)
Case A: Education as Consumption		
Cut in government purchases	26.0 cut	74.0
Increase in all taxes[a]	15.5 up	115.5
Increase in income tax	53.6 up	153.6
Cut in transfer payments	28.6 cut	71.4
Cut in both purchases and transfers	13.6 cut	86.4
All taxes cut by half and both purchases and transfers reduced[a]	57.4 cut	42.6
Case B: Education as Transfer		
Cut in government purchases	29.5 cut	70.5
Increase in all taxes[a]	15.5 up	115.5
Increase in income tax	53.6 up	153.6
Cut in transfer payments	25.3 cut	74.7
Cut in both purchases and transfers	13.6 cut	86.4
All taxes cut by half and both purchases and transfers reduced[a]	57.4 cut	42.6

Alternative Case (real income growth of 1.5%; discount rate of 3.0%)

Policy	Change (%)	Result (%)
Case A: Education as Consumption		
Cut in government purchases	29.7 cut	70.3
Increase in all taxes[a]	17.8 up	117.8
Increase in income tax	60.8 up	160.8
Cut in transfer payments	31.3 cut	68.7
Cut in both purchases and transfers	15.2 cut	84.8
All taxes cut by half and both purchases and transfers reduced[a]	57.9 cut	42.1
Case B: Education as Transfer		
Cut in government purchases	33.5 cut	66.5
Increase in all taxes[a]	17.8 up	117.8
increase in income tax	60.8 up	160.8
Cut in transfer payments	28.0 cut	72.0
Cut in both purchases and transfers	15.2 cut	84.8
All taxes cut by half and both purchases and transfers reduced[a]	57.9 cut	42.1

[a]Local tax and social insurance contribution (the Japanese counterpart of the social security tax) are included in taxes.

ments. Tax payments and social security contributions as a percentage of national income (the so-called gross public burden ratio) in 1995 were 36.8 percent. If scenario (b) is selected, the gross public burden ratio will jump to 41 percent. If this scenario is not selected, the net tax payment of future generations will be 2.7 to 4.4 times that of present generations, as seen in table 19.3. In such a case, the gross public burden ratio would certainly exceed 50 percent. Therefore, this scenario, with a gross public burden ratio of around 40 percent, could be accepted by the public, as long as it is sustainable.

Third, policy (c) implies a 54 percent increase in income tax. Compared with policy (b), it is rather high. Given the percentage share of income tax in total government tax revenue (35.5 percent in 1995), simple arithmetic implies that (c) requires three times as much of an increase as (b). Policy (c) affects mostly current working generations. As the income tax rate is already rather high, it would be very difficult to raise income tax further.

Fourth, policy (d) requires a 29 percent cut in transfer payments for case A and a 25 percent cut for case B. The ratio of social security transfers to national income was 17.5 percent in 1995. A slightly less than 30 percent cut in transfer payments implies a 5 percent decrease in the national income ratio.

We consider two additional scenarios, which seek "small government." Fifth, policy (e) is concerned with an immediate cut in both purchases and transfers to achieve generational balance. Here, a 13.6 percent cut in gross government expenditures is needed. This scenario seems to be reasonable and acceptable.

Sixth, policy (f) is an immediate 50 percent cut in all taxes and a reduction in both purchases and transfers. Gross government expenditures must be cut by 57.4 percent. This implies that the size of government in terms of expenditure shrinks to one-quarter of the current level.

Now look at an alternative case, real income growth of 1.5 percent and a discount rate of 3.0 percent. This case is considered because, as shown in table 19.4, it cuts the generational imbalance to half of that in the base case. In general, with a lower discount rate, the generational impact of alternative policies becomes larger (i.e., larger cuts in purchases and transfers and larger increases in taxes). But the difference between the base case and the alternative case is not as large as we expect. In other words, the generational impact of alternative policies remains robust.

Table 19.8 presents results for the same policy simulations as in table 19.7 with the additional assumption that current policy will be kept for 10 years (i.e., until 2005) and then the listed policy action will be implemented afterward. The underlying assumption is that the government may not be able to implement immediately the policy action needed to achieve generational balance. It is worthwhile examining how the generational impact of alternative policies would change if the government failed to conduct prompt policy action. As expected, the generational impact is larger for all scenarios. This implies that the sooner a policy action is implemented, the more easily generational balance is obtained. In contrast with the results in table 19.7, this exercise shows that policies in the alternative case with a lower discount rate have generational impacts slightly smaller than in the base case.

19.5.2 Alternative Measure of Intergenerational Transfers: The Musgrave Criterion

So far we have examined generational accounting in terms of absolute generational imbalance between present and future generations. In this section, we

Table 19.8   **Generational Impact of Alternative Policies after Maintaining Current Policy for 10 Years**

Base Case (real income growth of 1.5%; discount rate of 5.0%)

Policy	Change (%)	Result (%)
Case A: Education as Consumption		
Cut in government purchases	37.8 cut	62.2
Increase in all taxes[a]	22.5 up	122.5
Increase in income tax	76.6 up	176.6
Cut in transfer payments	39.3 cut	60.7
Cut in both purchases and transfers	19.3 cut	80.7
All taxes cut by half and both purchases and transfers reduced[a]	62.0 cut	38.0
Case B: Education as Transfer		
Cut in government purchases	42.5 cut	57.5
Increase in all taxes[a]	22.5 up	122.5
Increase in income tax	76.6 up	176.6
Cut in transfer payments	35.2 cut	64.8
Cut in both purchases and transfers	19.3 cut	80.7
All taxes cut by half and both purchases and transfers reduced[a]	62.3 cut	38.0

Alternative Case (real income growth of 1.5%; discount rate of 3.0%)

Policy	Change (%)	Result (%)
Case A: Education as Consumption		
Cut in government purchases	35.6 cut	64.4
Increase in all taxes[a]	21.4 up	121.4
Increase in income tax	72.4 up	172.4
Cut in transfer payments	36.5 cut	63.5
Cut in both purchases and transfers	18.0 cut	82.0
All taxes cut by half and both purchases and transfers reduced[a]	60.0 cut	40.0
Case B: Education as Transfer		
Cut in government purchases	40.0 cut	60.0
Increase in all taxes[a]	21.4 up	121.4
Increase in income tax	72.4 up	172.4
Cut in transfer payments	32.7 cut	67.3
Cut in both purchases and transfers	18.0 cut	82.0
All taxes cut by half and both purchases and transfers reduced[a]	60.0 cut	40.0

[a]Local tax and social insurance contribution (the Japanese counterpart of the social security tax) are included in taxes.

propose an alternative criterion to measure the fairness of intergenerational transfers, that is, a concept of intergenerational social contract upon which a social security system may be designed. Richard Musgrave (1981, 97) considers six alternative contracts:

1. *Intergenerational neutrality:* Each generation finances its own retirement, without claims on following generations or obligations to preceding generations.

2. *Ad hoc provision:* The agreement may be a very loose one, allowing the voters of each period to decide the level of support.

3. *Fixed replacement rate:* Retirees are entitled to receive a given fraction of their gross earnings in the form of benefits. With the replacement rate fixed, the working generation must adjust its contribution rate accordingly. Thus the tax rate changes.

4. *Fixed replacement rate, adjusted:* The replacement rate is fixed, as under the fixed replacement rate contract, but the earning base of retirees to which this rate is applied is adjusted upward to allow for the productivity gains and higher wage rates enjoyed by subsequent working generations.

5. *Fixed contribution rate:* The working population is required to contribute a given fraction of its gross earnings for the support of retirees. With the contribution rate thus fixed over generations, the replacement rate has to be changed. However, it seems impossible to maintain a fixed contribution rate throughout the aging process, and the contribution rate has been changed frequently (in an intergenerationally redistributive way) and it would be very costly to maintain.

6. *Fixed relative position:* Contributions and benefits are set so as to hold constant the ratio of per capita earnings of those in working generations (net of contribution) to the per capita benefits of retirees.

In the following, we will consider the concept of fixed relative position in detail. This means that government transfers to the "old" generation as a percentage of disposable income of the "young" generation is *fixed*. This resembles the concept of "net income indexation" in the case of public pension transfers.[3]

Denoting transfer benefits to the old generation by B_o, gross wage income of the working (young) generation by W_y, and social security tax, pension contributions, and all other taxes of the working generation by T_y, the fixed relative position k can be expressed as

$$(1) \qquad\qquad k = B_o / (W_y - T_y).$$

As long as k remains constant, transfer benefits to the old generation will not increase even if the aging process advances. This is because the disposable income of the working generation binds transfers as equation (1) shows.

Now, let us denote the number of people in the old generation by N_o and that in the working generation by N_y. Under the fully pay-as-you-go social security system,

$$(2) \qquad\qquad B_o N_o = N_y T_y \quad \text{or} \quad T_y = B_o (N_o / N_y)$$

Substituting equation (2) into equation (1) yields

---

3. Net income indexation is a concept in which pension benefits for pensioners are a given fraction of the disposable income of pension contributors, the working generation. This concept has been adopted in Germany and Japan.

(3) $\qquad k = B_o / [W_y - B_o(N_o/N_y)] = B_o/(W_y - B_o \cdot a),$

where $a = N_o/N_y$, the ratio of the old generation to the working generation. Solving for B_o, we obtain

(4) $\qquad\qquad\qquad B_o = kW_y/(1 + ak).$

Given that k is constant, transfer benefits to the old generation increase as gross wage income increases and decrease as the ratio of the old generation to the working generation increases.

The main characteristics of this fixed relative position can be summarized as follows. First, it includes interaction with other generations within society, while the concept of net present value of payments for each generation as discussed in sections 19.4 and 19.5.1 is an individualistic one, meaning that it is a closed accounting system within a generation. Fixed relative position is suitable for the current social security system, which is virtually a pay-as-you-go system. Furthermore, at the end of section 19.4, we pointed out that intergenerational transfers of fixed public capital to future generations are prevalent and, therefore, it is important to take account of a productivity increase due to public capital that, in turn, is reflected in the income of the working generation. The fixed relative position takes income changes of the working generation into full account.

Second, the concept of fixed relative position allows for policy changes such as reductions in transfer payments and tax cuts, as long as k remains constant. On the other hand, generational accounting of the net present value of payments assumes once-for-all policy changes and a balanced budget in the infinite future. In practice, political pressure increasingly imposes heavy restrictions on annual budget deficits and allows frequent changes in policy stance. The concept of fixed relative position can be used as an alternative (or a complement) to generational accounting of the net present value of payments. Note also that fixed relative position is not a discretionary policy but a rule with some intrinsic flexibility.

Third, the policy authority can manage this policy rule of fixed relative position easily because it only needs to pay attention to the relative relationship between old and working generations on an annual basis. In addition, this rule may be politically acceptable because it avoids direct generational conflict as to who bears the fiscal burden of the aging process.

In order to calculate fixed relative position in Japan, we extend this concept over life. The working period is defined as ages 0 to 64 and the old period as age 65 and older. We then calculate disposable income (gross earnings minus net tax burden) of the working period and transfer benefits for the old period. Our fixed lifetime relative position is defined as

(5) $\qquad\qquad k(1995) = \sum_{t=65}^{99} B_{ot} / \sum_{t=0}^{64} (W_{yt} - T_{yt}).$

Table 19.9   **Fixed Lifetime Relative Position: Simulation**

Year	a	b	g	$h(1)$	$h(2)$	$i(n)$
Case A: Education as Consumption						
1995	17.0	Start	0.699	Start	Start	Start
2020	36.7	16.3 up	0.816	9.6 cut	10.9 up	5.4
2045	47.7	23.4 up	0.880	13.3 cut	15.1 up	13.0
2070	42.8	21.3 up	0.860	12.2 cut	13.9 up	10.8
Case B: Education as Transfer						
1995	17.0	Start	0.699	Start	Start	Start
2020	36.7	16.3 up	0.816	9.2 cut	10.5 up	52.3
2045	47.7	23.4 up	0.880	12.8 cut	14.6 up	72.8
2070	42.8	21.3 up	0.860	11.8 cut	13.4 up	66.9

Note: Real income growth assumed to be 1.5 percent; discount rate, 5 percent. "Up" and "cut" imply percentage changes from the base year, 1995.

Definitions of simulation:

a = Ratio of old generation to working generation (percent).
b = Increase in taxes from 1995 level to achieve a balanced budget.
g = Value of fixed relative position k under tax increase b.
$h(1)$ = Cut in transfer benefits to maintain k ($= 0.699$).
$h(2)$ = Increase in taxes from 1995 level under transfer cut $h(1)$ and constant k ($= 0.699$).
$i(n)$ = Generational imbalance to maintain k ($= 0.699$), where it is defined as lifetime net taxes
        of the future generation born in year n divided by that of the 1995 generation (percent).

As table 19.9 shows, the fixed lifetime relative position in 1995 is 0.699. Suppose the policy stance in 1995 is kept for the future, then the fixed lifetime relative position will be high, at 0.88, when the aging process approaches its peak in 2045. Note that T_y includes taxes other than income tax (e.g., corporate tax) so that the high value of fixed lifetime relative position, k, does not necessarily imply a very small lifetime disposable income.

We have conducted two additional policy simulations: (g) an increase in taxes and reduction in transfer benefits to achieve a balanced budget every year from now on and (h) a reduction in transfer benefits ($h(1)$) and an increase in taxes ($h(2)$) in order to maintain the level of the fixed lifetime relative position in 1995 ($= 0.699$). Table 19.9 shows that a balanced budget will be achieved and that the fixed lifetime relative position will be maintained constant if transfer benefits are reduced 9 to 13 percent and taxes are increased by some 10 to 15 percent. These policy simulation results appear politically acceptable as they satisfy the political trade-off between some transfer benefit reductions (i.e., a cut in the size of the government) and some tax increases (i.e., to sustain decent economic policy in an aging society). To put it differently, if the fixed lifetime relative position is kept constant at $k = 0.699$, the generational imbalance would be less than 13 percent for case A and 73 percent for case B, even at the peak of the aging process.[4]

---

4. In this exercise, the generational imbalance is defined as lifetime net tax of the generation born in year n divided by that of the generation born in 1995.

Nevertheless, some problems remain. First, it is difficult to determine the base-year value of k, the fixed lifetime relative position. Second, it may not be politically easy to change policies such as reductions in transfer payments, given an arbitrary value of k.

19.6 Brief Summary and Conclusion

This study has presented the most comprehensive picture of generational accounting in Japan to date. The main results are summarized as follows: The base-case calculation of the generational imbalance between present and future generations is 69 percent for case A and 338 percent for case B, assuming the current fiscal policy stance is to be maintained and real income growth of 1.5 percent and a discount rate of 5 percent. This implies that future generations have to bear 2.7 to 4.4 times the fiscal burden facing present generations over their lifetimes. This imbalance is very large by international standards.

For the base case, four basic scenarios and two additional scenarios to resolve such a generational imbalance are considered. In the four basic scenarios, government purchases have to be cut 26 to 30 percent, or all taxes have to be raised about 16 percent, or the income tax has to be increased 54 percent, or transfer payments must be reduced 25 to 29 percent. In the additional scenarios, both government purchases and transfers have to be reduced 14 percent; if all taxes are cut by 50 percent, then both purchases and transfers have to be cut by 57 percent, shrinking government expenditures to one-quarter of the current level.

Another simulation indicates that the generational imbalance is due not to fiscal debt outstanding per se but to change in the demographic structure. Indeed, if the demographic structure were to remain stationary, the generational imbalance would fall substantially. This is probably the main implication from the study of generational accounts, not only in Japan but in other countries as well.

Because of the relatively low stock of public capital, the Japanese government has been investing heavily. In flow statistics, the share of government investment in total gross domestic fixed capital formation has been much higher than in other OECD economies. And a portion of present government expenditure is used to accumulate public capital that will benefit future generations without repayment. In this respect, present generations transfer benefits, via the government, to future generations.

To take into account this aspect of public capital accruing to future generations, we consider the concept of fixed lifetime relative position. The result shows that balanced budgets will be achieved annually and that the fixed lifetime relative position will remain constant if taxes are increased by 10 to 15 percent and transfer benefits are reduced by 10 to 13 percent. In this case, the generational imbalance remains less than 13 percent for case A and 73 percent for case B.

Some problems and topics for future research remain. First, generational accounting in general and the generational imbalance in particular are very sensitive to real interest rate and income growth assumptions. It is very difficult to set reasonable assumptions for these parameters over a long period. It may be interesting to estimate alternatively the real income growth rate needed to minimize the generational imbalance for a given discount rate.

Second, and somehow related to the first point, generational accounting is based on a comparative static framework. It would be much more realistic to formulate a dynamic general equilibrium framework in which economic growth and interest rates are determined endogenously, as discussed in Auerbach and Kotlikoff (1987).

Third, the standard framework of generational accounting ignores benefits from government consumption. Suppose a cut in government purchases is made to achieve generational balance; future generations may not enjoy this situation because of reduced benefits from government consumption. The same argument can be applied to government investment and public capital, as has been discussed elsewhere in this study.

Fourth, the demographic projections we use in this study assume a gradual increase in the fertility rate in the mid-twenty-first century. But, in fact, there is no guarantee of this happening. If the demographic structure in 2050 remains as it is, the intergenerational imbalance will be larger.

Appendix
Evaluation of Imputed Benefits from Public Capital

There are at least three approaches to evaluating the imputed benefits stemming from public capital inherited from previous (old) generations.

Simple Distribution of Public Capital among Current Generations. The simplest approach is to estimate the monetary value of public capital. According to our calculations, per capita public capital in 1954 was $99,800 (1993 value), and in 1993 it was $610,400 (1993 value). This significant increase may indicate that intergenerational transfers in the form of public capital are rather huge. This approach, however, has two drawbacks. First, a large portion of public capital inherited from previous generations, such as roads, public buildings, and sewage systems, cannot be disposed of by individuals or a generation but is simply handed over to future generations. Second, the value of public capital stock may not necessarily correspond to the benefit to current generations.

Evaluation of Imputed Benefits from Public Capital. The second drawback we raised above can be avoided by estimating imputed benefits, which can be obtained by multiplying public capital stock by its annual return. However, this approach does not solve the problem of how imputed benefits are distributed among generations (e.g., through consumption, income, or assets).

Evaluation of Public Capital in Terms of Wage Rate. This approach evaluates benefits stemming from public capital in terms of labor productivity; that is, young generations enjoy marginally higher production levels because of inherited public capital from previous (old) generations. This fact must be reflected in the wage rate. Assume a production function such that

(A1) $$Y = F(G, K, L),$$

where G is public capital, K is private capital, and L is labor input. Differentiate Y with respect to L; it must be equal to the wage rate W:

(A2) $$W = \frac{\partial Y}{\partial L} = \frac{\partial F(G, K, L)}{\partial L} = H(G).$$

Now the wage rate becomes a function of public capital G. The sign condition of G on W is positive. With this approach, we can evaluate the net present value of payments for each generation in comparison with the lifetime income of each generation, which includes benefits stemming from public capital.

References

Auerbach, A. J., and L. J. Kotlikoff. 1987. *Dynamic fiscal policy.* Cambridge: Cambridge University Press.

Ishi, H., ed. 1996. White paper on structural reform of public finance (in Japanese). Tokyo: Toyokeizai.

Musgrave, R. 1981. A reappraisal of social security financing. In *Social security financing,* ed. F. Skidmore. Cambridge, Mass.: MIT Press.

Organization for Economic Cooperation and Development (OECD). 1996. *Economic outlook,* no. 60. Paris: Organization for Economic Cooperation and Development, December.

Tamura, Y., ed. 1996. *Public finance in Japan* (in Japanese). Tokyo: Toyokeizai.

20   Generational Accounting
in Portugal

Alan J. Auerbach, Jorge Braga de Macedo, José Braz,
Laurence J. Kotlikoff, and Jan Walliser

20.1 Introduction

This study uses generational accounting, a new method of long-term fiscal planning, to derive the future net taxes that will balance Portugal's government budget accounts. Specifically, it computes a set of generational accounts and uses them to reach an important conclusion: Portuguese fiscal policy is unsustainable.

Current budgetary policy includes ceilings on the budget and the debt until the year 2000, which fulfill the convergence criteria set out in the Treaty on European Union for accession to the euro. Yet, under current fiscal rules, future Portuguese generations face a net tax (taxes paid net of transfer payments received) burden, relative to income, that is well in excess of that faced by current generations. Significant increases in taxes or reductions in expenditures are required to satisfy the government's long-term (intertemporal) budget constraint and avoid unfairly burdening future generations.

Generational accounting offers an intuitive measure of the sustainability of fiscal policy, namely, *generational balance*—the condition that future genera-

Alan J. Auerbach is the Robert D. Burch Professor of Economics and Law at the University of California, Berkeley, and a research associate of the National Bureau of Economic Research. Jorge Braga de Macedo is professor of economics at Nova University, Lisbon; a research fellow of the Centre for Economic Policy Research, London; and a research associate of the National Bureau of Economic Research. He served as minister of finance of Portugal between 1991 and 1993. José Braz is managing partner of TEcFinance, Lda, Lisbon; former secretary of state for the Treasury of Portugal; and former president of the Portuguese supervisory authority for insurance and pension fund activity. Laurence J. Kotlikoff is professor of economics at Boston University and a research associate of the National Bureau of Economic Research. Jan Walliser is an economist in the Macroeconomic Analysis Division of the Congressional Budget Office.

A longer version, with the title "Future Net Taxes in Portugal," is available as Nova Economics Working Paper no. 293, April 1997. The views expressed do not necessarily reflect the positions of the Congressional Budget Office or of any current or past affiliation of the authors. Auerbach and Kotlikoff thank the Instituto de Seguros de Portugal for research support.

tions pay the same share of their lifetime labor income in net taxes (taxes paid net of transfer payments received) as is paid by current generations. In addition to showing the substantial current imbalance in Portuguese generational policy, alternative means of achieving generational balance are suggested in this study.

Because it is forward looking and deals explicitly with implicit as well as explicit liabilities, generational accounting can provide more insight into a nation's fiscal affairs than can the simple consideration of its official budget deficit. Generational accounting is particularly helpful in understanding the prospects for national economies, such as the Portuguese, undergoing profound change in their fiscal and monetary regimes. Section 20.2 describes recent Portuguese economic reforms, traces out their implications, and suggests additional measures needed for Portugal to attract foreign investment and to converge to European levels of income. The size of the net tax burden facing future generations is documented by section 20.3's generational accounting and the alternative means of facing it are contrasted. As stated in the conclusion, section 20.4, Portugal's generational accounts provide a way for international investors to judge whether fiscal stability is actually being achieved by the Portuguese government.

20.2   Regime Change and Fiscal Evolution

European economic integration influenced Portugal for decades, even when restricted civil rights and the absence of political parties hindered mutual political responsiveness with the member states of the Common Market. Export-led growth of the 1960s, associated with membership in the European Free Trade Association, changed much of Portuguese industry. Agriculture and finance, however, remained traditional. Large-scale industrial projects were directed toward fostering economic integration with the African colonies, whereas trade and emigration were overwhelmingly directed toward Europe. Following decades of conservative social and economic policies, a bloodless military coup (the "carnation revolution") in April 1974 paved the way for a radical swing to the left, with widespread nationalizations and the adoption of many philosophical and institutional tenets of central planning.

Under pressure from military leaders, the two newly created major political parties, the left-of-center Partido Socialista (PS) and right-of-center Partido Social Democrata (PSD), approved a constitution in 1976 that included an explicit prohibition of privatization. With traditional agriculture in the hands of cooperatives and a state-owned financial system (which incorporated most large-scale industrial projects), the only sizable firms remaining in private hands were in export-oriented manufacturing.

The main constraint on inflationary policies came from the balance of payments and led to attempts to restore external balance via exchange rate depreciation and credit restrictions, which introduced a marked "stop and go" pattern

Table 20.1   **Convergence Indicators**

Year	Growth Rate of Labor Productivity[a]	Nominal Real Wage Growth Rate[a]	Long-Term Nominal Interest Rate[a]	Real Exchange Rate	Deficit (% of GDP)
1989	1.8	8.9	7.0	−3.2	2.5
1990	1.7	12.4	5.9	−8.7	5.6
1991	−1.8	12.5	8.1	−15.1	6.7
1992	0.5	2.6	5.6	−6.0	3.6
1993	−0.7	4.9	4.5	1.0	6.9
1994	−2.3	4.9	2.0	−2.2	5.8
1995	1.0	1.9	3.0	−3.1	5.1
1996	0.5	2.4	1.4	−1.8	4.0
1997	0.5	1.8	0.8	−2.0	2.9
1998	0.4	0.9	0.6	−0.6	2.9

[a]Portugal vs. EU average as presented in Braga de Macedo (1997).

in private economic activity. Market-oriented policies for internal balance did not begin to regain prominence until EU accession in 1986.

Under the leadership of Cavaco Silva the PSD obtained a majority in two successive general elections in July 1987 and in October 1991. Between 1985 and 1995, the PSD rule achieved a stable democratic government and rapid convergence toward European levels of most economic and social indicators. Indeed, Portugal now appears to be a serious contender for inclusion in the initial group of countries to join the Economic and Monetary Union (EMU) and adopt the euro as a single currency.

20.2.1   The Change in Economic Regime

In order to reduce the public sector of the Portuguese economy, a constitutional amendment allowing privatization was necessary. This amendment required a two-thirds majority and, thus, had to be supported by both the PS and PSD parties. This bipartisan support was achieved in the summer of 1989. Table 20.1 reports indicators of real and nominal convergence between Portugal and the average of its EU partners. The indicators are the rate of labor productivity growth, the rate of nominal wage growth, and long-term nominal interest rates according to the European Commission forecasts of winter 1996. The real effective exchange rate relative to the Organization for Economic Cooperation and Development (OECD) average (up is depreciation) and the general government deficit as a percentage of GDP are also reported in table 20.1.

The decade from 1974 to 1985 had been a period of severe economic disequilibrium, with the International Monetary Fund (IMF) twice being called to intervene with standby arrangements. The fiscal deficit averaged close to 10 percent of GDP during this period, and inflation rates reached nearly 30 percent. Politically, the situation was equally unstable, with governments of average duration around one year, which is one-fourth of the normal parliamentary term.

Recognizing that convergence toward the price stability and living standards of the European Community required a multiyear program, the government prepared the Program to Correct External Imbalances and Unemployment (PCEDED), or P1, which was approved in March 1987. Thanks to the international boom, and the terms-of-trade improvement, real convergence was accompanied by the elimination of the payments deficits and by sustained job creation.

The inflation differential relative to the Community average initially fell but later rose again and the debt-to-GDP ratio peaked at approximately 75 percent in 1988. In July 1989, following the acceptance of the EMU at the European Council in Madrid, the government approved a revised version of the PCEDED called P2. Under this revised program, fiscal adjustment was based on the newly reformed tax system, which introduced comprehensive income taxation for the first time. The concomitant revenue increases led the official government deficit to fall below 3 percent of GDP in 1989 (table 20.1).

The multiyear fiscal adjustment strategy contained in P2 was gradual, and before the change of the constitution, the size of the public sector remained essentially constant until 1990. Moreover, the rekindling of inflation led to an equally gradual abandonment of the policy of expected depreciation (crawling peg), which had been in place since 1977. While this mechanism was replaced in the spring of 1990 with shadowing the European Community's Exchange Rate Mechanism (ERM), the change was never announced publicly. Moreover, controls on capital inflows were introduced on top of the traditional restrictions on outflows. Because it was not based on clear rules, this shadow exchange arrangement managed by the central bank turned out to be more opaque and rigid than ERM membership. Because it preceded inflation convergence, it also brought greater volatility to the real exchange rate, as shown in table 20.1.

In 1990 and 1991, the Portuguese economy grew at approximately 1 percentage point above the Community average, while the inflation differential fell from 8 to 7 points. However, the official budget deficit deteriorated to almost 7 percent of GDP, and a reform of public sector pay led to wage increases that were 12 percentage points greater than the EU average. Exchange controls, in turn, increased rates on public bonds to 8 percentage points above the EU average. This was inconsistent with the exchange rate regime change implicit in the National Adjustment Framework for the Transition to Economic and Monetary Union, known as QUANTUM (or Q1), approved in June 1990.

The second PSD government, elected at the end of 1991, made the strategy of full participation in EMU a central part of its economic program.[1] In the convergence program for 1992–95 approved by the European Council (Ecofin)

1. The relevant national and European Community documents are summarized and interpreted in Braz (1992) and Braga de Macedo (1997) and literature cited therein.

in December, and dubbed Q2, fiscal, structural, and income policies were set in a macroeconomic framework consistent with a single European currency to which the escudo would be credibly pegged. Central features of the program were the inflation objective and the principle of nonaccommodation of nominal budgetary expenditures to any slippage in the inflation outcome. The budget process started with an overall expenditure ceiling in nominal terms, which was mandatory for the central government and recommended for the general government. To avoid higher other spending after the expected fall in interest rates, these ceilings were expressed net of interest payments on government debt. The next stage was the determination of the corresponding sources of revenue and financing. Finally, decisions were made regarding the allocation of the general government budget and, more specifically, of the central government budget.

Moderation in public sector wage increases was fundamental to compliance with the expenditure ceiling. As a participant in the process determining income policy, the government proposed target ranges for inflation consistent with convergence to the EU best performers. The average inflation range envisaged in Q2 was 7 to 9 percent in 1992 and 4 to 6 percent in the period 1993–95. At the same time, strict restraint on increases in other general government expenditures was essential to permit a significant increase in public investment in real terms, which was desirable to ease the catching-up process.

Monetary policy was kept compatible with the shadow exchange rate regime until the entry of the escudo in the ERM in April 1992, opening the way for the removal of the controls on capital inflows that had been introduced in 1991 and full liberalization of capital movements in December 1992.

Budgetary and structural policies were also important features of Q2. One goal was the reduction of the public sector deficit. In line with the projected macroeconomic framework, the general government deficit was to decline to 3 percent of GDP and the debt-to-GDP ratio to 53 percent on average for the three-year period 1993–95. With the anticipated reduction in interest rates, the interest burden was expected to fall from 9 percent of GDP in 1991–92 to 5 percent on average in 1993–95. The 1992 budget placed an overall ceiling on total noninterest expenditures, requiring stable noninvestment spending but allowing increasing public capital expenditures. A major revision of indirect taxation—mainly changes in the value-added tax (VAT) base and rates—was responsible for increasing revenue, while the speeding up of privatization allowed the repayment of public debt.

The outcome for 1992 was in line with the program, and the general government deficit declined to 3.6 percent, from 6.7 percent in 1991. Public debt fell from 69.3 to 61.4 percent of GDP, while inflation declined from 11.4 to 8.9 percent. Output growth, however, continued to slow, and GDP growth fell to 1.7 percent in 1992, from 2.3 percent in 1991. Monetary policy continued to be very cautious and real interest rates remained very high (by the end of 1992, real lending rates exceeded 10 percent on average).

The economic downturn continued in 1993, with serious consequences for the fiscal position. The nominal expenditure ceiling for the central government was adhered to, despite higher unemployment benefits, but revenues fell sharply, reflecting a weakening of tax collection in a more difficult economic climate and as a consequence of the abolition of customs within the European Union. The general government deficit doubled to about 7 percent of GDP and public debt rose to 66.6 percent, instead of declining as anticipated. The only economic variable that improved as planned was inflation, declining to 6.5 percent. Real GDP fell by 1.2 percent. A revised convergence program was presented with the 1994 budget and approved by the Monetary Committee on 30 November 1993, when the budget itself was approved in Parliament. The revised program extended the expenditure ceilings into 1997 when it was replaced by the Convergence Stability and Growth Program (CSGP), which brought the fiscal adjustment path forward until the year 2000.

Economic policy in 1994 and 1995 was geared toward gradually recovering the growth and convergence path. The overall deficit was reduced to 5.8 percent in 1994 and 5.1 percent in 1995, with the bulk of the improvement coming from reduced interest payments. The public debt service declined from 6.6 percent of GDP in 1993 to 5.6 percent in 1995, despite a continued increase in the stock of public debt (71.5 percent of GDP in 1995, up from 66.6 percent in 1993). The implicit interest rate on public debt fell from 10.6 percent in 1993 to 8.1 percent in 1995, to an estimated 7.6 percent in 1996. Inflation continued to decline, to 4 percent in 1995, and output growth recovered modestly, to 1 percent in 1994 and 2.8 percent in 1995. Economic recovery continued with ever greater vigor in 1996 and in 1997, helping considerably the attainment of the debt-to-GDP and deficit-to-GDP targets required for participation in the EMU.

The data on relative productivity reported in table 20.1 suggest a double-dip recession, in 1991 and 1994, when productivity growth in Portugal was 2 percent below the EU average. In 1991 this was mostly due to high employment growth, whereas in 1994 it was a consequence of a delayed recovery from the 1993 trough. This pattern may explain why the perception of the change in regime was delayed until the end of the recession. It is also consistent with the observed slowdown of structural reforms.

20.2.2   Structural Reforms

Since the mid-1980s, the evolution of the public finances has been determined by several major structural reforms. In 1986, a VAT was introduced and subsequently has been harmonized with EU levels. Comprehensive income taxation was introduced in 1989. In 1993, tax exemptions were rationalized and a reform of tax administration initiated; the reform was further consolidated in 1994 and 1995. This involved successive tax amnesty plans, especially for firms and for the self-employed. The method has continued to be used by the new government, under the so-called Mateus plan. It is difficult, however, to sort out the effects of amnesty and improved tax collection from the general improvement in profitability and consumer confidence stemming from the recovery in economic activity.

The privatization law opened the way for a large-scale privatization program, with the bulk of the proceeds allocated to the reduction of public debt. Until 1993, a mandatory 80 percent of privatization receipts was used for debt reduction; thereafter, at least 40 percent had to be used for that purpose, with the remainder used to provide capital for the restructuring of public enterprises. Between 1989 and 1995, Portugal's privatization program raised an amount equivalent to about 10 percent of GDP, which made Portugal the OECD's third largest privatizer after the United Kingdom and New Zealand. The state's presence in the economy (particularly the financial sector) was reduced from about 20 percent of value added in 1989 to 10 percent in 1994, and from 6.5 percent of employment to 3 percent. Major privatizations in 1994 included banking and cement enterprises, and in 1995 the privatization of the telecommunications sector was initiated. The process continued with the PS government and has benefited from the recovery in economic activity.

Debt management policy led to a shift from central bank borrowing to market-based domestic and foreign borrowing and the introduction of long-term fixed rate instruments. In the late 1980s, central bank policy came to depend increasingly on issuing short-term domestic debt to compensate for the growing capital inflows attracted not only by the favorable investment climate but also, increasingly, by the highly remunerative real interest rates to be earned on pure arbitrage operations. In spite of strict controls on capital inflows, the central bank's foreign reserves more than doubled, from $10 billion in 1989 to $20.6 billion in 1991, with disastrous consequences for the bank's operating results. The bank was effectively accumulating huge dollar deposits earning a 5 percent rate of return, while paying 20 percent on the escudo debt being issued to mop up the resultant "excess" liquidity. The cost of this policy, during the period 1990–92, is estimated to have exceeded the structural funds received from the European Community in the same period.

Following entry in the ERM, the currency became fully convertible for the first time since leaving the gold standard in 1891 (except for a short-lived attempt in 1931). As real interest rates declined, maturities were lengthened, with the issue of three-year, five-year, and eight-year government bonds (previously, practically all borrowing was at three- and six-month maturities). Further downward pressure on domestic interest rates was achieved by shifting some of the government's borrowing needs abroad. Benchmark issues in yen and deutsche mark in the first half of 1993 were followed by an upgrade of Portugal's rating to AA− grade and the successful placement of a U.S. dollar global issue in September and a global ECU issue in early 1994. These operations opened the way for Portuguese enterprises to borrow directly abroad, ending the long-lasting protectionism enjoyed by the financial sector. In mid-1996, the Azores Regional Government became the first Portuguese quasi-sovereign entity to borrow abroad without state guarantees. One year later, the approval of the CSGP by Ecofin was widely seen as the culmination of the medium-term-oriented macroeconomic policy initiated six years earlier.

Despite the achievements of the past decade, several areas require further attention. There is general consensus that the justice, education, and health delivery systems benefited from significant investment in expanding facilities during the past 10 years but that the quantitative increase now needs to be complemented by improvements in quality and efficiency. However, public sector reform and social security reform are more germane to the fiscal discussion.

The government elected at the end of 1991 made some progress in restructuring the major spending ministries, but the double-dip recession, subsequent slow recovery, and rising unemployment have effectively removed public sector reform from the political agenda.

Within public sector reform, the most important item, in terms of financial magnitude and fiscal pressures, is social security.[2] Portugal's growth in per capita expenditure on social protection benefits during 1985–95 was the highest in the European Union, albeit from relatively low initial levels. The social security system provides pensions and a wide range of welfare benefits, mostly on a universal basis. Funding is from payroll contributions and residually by the state. The contribution rate (almost 40 percent, including compulsory accident insurance) is one of the highest in the European Union and amounts to a very significant tax on labor utilization, contributing to unemployment.

With an aging population and real increases in benefits reflecting real wage increases of the past decade, the financial imbalance will continue to grow. The dependency ratio is projected to peak at 44 percent in 2045, from 37 percent in 1995 (table 20.2). The residual financing from the state budget will continue to increase unless the system is reformed. Additionally, civil servant pensions cost 3 percent of GDP in 1995 and are projected to increase further. Unless significant reform is undertaken soon, the social security financial imbalance promises to be the major economic problem facing future generations.

20.3   Portuguese Generational Accounts

The generational accounts technique requires a choice of base year, in this case 1995, and future population projections and an accounting of fiscal aggregates for the base year. Using incidence profiles, all taxes and transfers in the base year are distributed across existing generations, obtaining per capita measures of taxes and transfers for each cohort, broken down by age (from 0 to 90 years) and sex. Generational accounts for existing generations are then calculated by projecting these tax and transfer profiles forward based on an assumed

---

2. See Kotlikoff (1996). Braga de Macedo's introduction to United Nations (1997) has a discussion of convergence and divergence in social security policies.

Table 20.2   **Dependency Ratios, 1995–2070**

Year	Elderly	Children	Total
1995	0.15	0.22	0.37
2000	0.16	0.21	0.36
2005	0.16	0.20	0.36
2010	0.16	0.20	0.37
2015	0.17	0.20	0.37
2020	0.18	0.20	0.38
2025	0.19	0.20	0.39
2030	0.20	0.20	0.40
2035	0.21	0.20	0.41
2040	0.23	0.21	0.43
2045	0.24	0.21	0.44
2050	0.23	0.21	0.44
2055	0.22	0.21	0.43
2060	0.20	0.22	0.42
2065	0.20	0.22	0.41
2070	0.19	0.22	0.41

Source: Authors' calculation based on population data of the World Bank.

rate of productivity growth and discounting back to the present with an assumed discount rate. Generational accounts for future generations are obtained as a residual, equal to the sum of existing government net debt and the present value of future government purchases, less the generational accounts of all existing generations.

20.3.1   Data and Basic Assumptions

Our population data come from the World Bank.[3] Table 20.2 shows the projections of the dependency ratios, expressed as the ratio of children (younger than age 18) and the elderly (those older than age 64) to the working-age population (18 to 64 years). As is true in most other developed countries, the elderly dependency ratio is projected to grow during the coming decades, increasing by more than half over the next 50 years.

Fiscal data come primarily from the OECD general government accounts. In 1995, direct taxes amounted to 1,469.0 billion escudos. They were distributed across workers according to wages earned, based on a profile of wage earnings estimated from the household survey Inquérito ao Patrimônio e Endividamento das Famílias de 1994. (This survey was also used to estimate profiles for consumption, self-employment plus property income, and receipt of transfer payments.)[4]

This assignment of all income taxes, including corporate income taxes, to

3. We thank Eduard Bos for making his projections available.
4. We are grateful to Pedro Neves of Banco de Portugal for providing his data. Carlos Andrade of the Catholic University of Portugal also did some of the initial data work.

labor reflects our assumption that as a small open economy, Portugal cannot impose a burden on internationally mobile capital. Because they are imposed as employment taxes, social security contributions of 1,783.4 billion escudos were also distributed according to the wage profile. Indirect taxes of 2,207.6 billion escudos, generally taxes on consumption, were distributed according to a consumption profile. Property and entrepreneurial taxes of 354.5 billion escudos were distributed according to a combined self-employment plus property profile.

On the transfer side, the only breakdown is between social security and other transfers. These two categories, a total of 2,516.8 billion escudos, are lumped together and distributed according to a profile of general transfer receipts.

Government spending is the sum of government consumption (2,730.9 billion escudos), subsidies (136.6 billion escudos), and government net investment (437.2 billion escudos) minus transfers received, primarily from the European Union (121.9 billion escudos). The resulting total of government purchases is 3,182.8 billion escudos. By our measures, the resulting government primary surplus (taxes less transfers and government purchases) in 1995 was 114.9 billion escudos. The government net financial debt (obtained from Portugal's own fiscal accounts) is 10,724.9 billion escudos.

As an alternative to treating government expenditures on education as a government purchase, as done in the base case, we treat these expenditures as transfer payments, allocated across cohorts.[5]

To maintain comparability with the estimates for the other countries in this project, all generational accounts are converted into U.S. dollars, using the exchange rate of 0.006104 dollars per escudo.

For future years, the profiles for taxes, transfers, and educational expenditures remain fixed, except for productivity growth. This means that shifts in the composition of the population will exert an impact on the GDP shares of each of these items, as cohorts vary in their intensity of tax payments and receipt of transfers and educational expenditures. We assume that government purchases other than education grow with productivity and contrast the case in which education is a government purchase with the one in which the benefits are directed toward the younger generations, thus lowering their net lifetime taxes relative to what they would otherwise be.

20.3.2   Generational Accounts

Table 20.3A presents the base-case generational accounts for males and females combined, using a discount rate of 5 percent and a productivity growth rate of 1.5 percent and treating government educational expenditures as government purchases (i.e., not allocated to individual generations). For cohorts at

5. The data, based on unpublished Portuguese government data on expenditures by educational level, were provided by Jose Manuel Bracinha Vieira, former education secretary, to whom we wish to express our gratitude.

Table 20.3A   **Generational Accounts for Males and Females Combined: Base Case (thousands of U.S. dollars)**

Generation's Age in 1995	Net Payment	Income Taxes	Property and Proprietors	Social Insurance Contribution	Indirect Taxes	Trans- fers	Edu- cation
0	61.8	17.8	3.9	21.6	36.4	17.9	0.0
5	67.1	21.0	4.5	25.6	37.1	21.1	0.0
10	73.0	24.8	5.3	30.1	37.6	24.7	0.0
15	79.6	29.1	6.3	35.4	37.9	29.0	0.0
20	86.0	33.7	7.3	41.0	37.9	33.9	0.0
25	85.1	35.5	8.3	43.1	37.6	39.3	0.0
30	75.0	33.9	8.6	41.2	36.2	45.0	0.0
35	60.0	30.9	8.5	37.5	33.8	50.7	0.0
40	39.7	26.3	7.8	32.0	30.5	56.8	0.0
45	15.9	20.9	6.8	25.4	26.7	63.9	0.0
50	−10.6	14.6	5.4	17.7	22.2	70.6	0.0
55	−33.9	8.9	4.1	10.9	17.7	75.4	0.0
60	−47.1	5.0	2.8	6.1	13.7	74.6	0.0
65	−49.4	2.7	1.8	3.2	10.5	67.6	0.0
70	−42.7	1.4	1.1	1.7	8.0	54.9	0.0
75	−33.3	0.6	0.6	0.8	5.9	41.2	0.0
80	−24.8	0.0	0.4	0.0	4.0	29.3	0.0
85	−15.4	0.0	0.2	0.0	2.5	18.1	0.0
90	−4.1	0.0	0.1	0.0	0.6	4.8	0.0
Future generations	91.8						
Percentage difference	48.7						

five-year intervals between ages 0 and 90, the table shows the total generational account (the net present value fiscal burden over that generation's remaining lifetime) as well as the tax and transfer components of that generational account. According to the table, a representative newborn in 1995 faces a generational account of $61,800, the difference between taxes of $79,700 and transfers of $17,900. Following the typical pattern, the accounts increase initially with age, as generations move closer to the primary taxpaying years, and then decline, as the retirement years of lower taxes and higher receipt of transfer payments approach. The highest value of the account, $86,000, occurs at age 20, with the accounts turning negative after age 45.

Under current policy, a representative member of future generations will have to pay $91,800 adjusted for productivity growth, or 48.7 percent more than current newborns, who are assumed to pay taxes and receive transfer payments according to current fiscal rules.

Table 20.3B presents the generational accounts for current and future generations allocating educational spending to individuals. Because educational spending is heavily concentrated among the young, the net payment of Portu-

Table 20.3B   **Generational Accounts for Males and Females Combined: Base Case, Education Treated as Transfer Payments (thousands of U.S. dollars)**

Generation's Age in 1995	Net Payment	Income Taxes	Property and Proprietors	Social Insurance Contribution	Indirect Taxes	Trans- fers	Edu- cation
0	43.5	17.8	3.9	21.6	36.4	17.9	18.2
5	45.5	21.0	4.5	25.6	37.1	21.1	21.6
10	50.9	24.8	5.3	30.1	37.6	24.7	22.0
15	65.3	29.1	6.3	35.4	37.9	29.0	14.3
20	82.7	33.7	7.3	41.0	37.9	33.9	3.3
25	84.5	35.5	8.3	43.1	37.6	39.3	0.6
30	75.0	33.9	8.6	41.2	36.2	45.0	0.0
35	60.0	30.9	8.5	37.5	33.8	50.7	0.0
40	39.7	26.3	7.8	32.0	30.5	56.8	0.0
45	15.9	20.9	6.8	25.4	26.7	63.9	0.0
50	−10.6	14.6	5.4	17.7	22.2	70.6	0.0
55	−33.9	8.9	4.1	10.9	17.7	75.4	0.0
60	−47.1	5.0	2.8	6.1	13.7	74.6	0.0
65	−49.4	2.7	1.8	3.2	10.5	67.6	0.0
70	−42.7	1.4	1.1	1.7	8.0	54.9	0.0
75	−33.3	0.6	0.6	0.8	5.9	41.2	0.0
80	−24.8	0.0	0.4	0.0	4.0	29.3	0.0
85	−15.4	0.0	0.2	0.0	2.5	18.1	0.0
90	−4.1	0.0	0.1	0.0	0.6	4.8	0.0
Future generations	73.2						
Percentage difference	68.3						

guese aged 25 or younger is smaller once educational spending is accounted for. The net payment of Portuguese newborns is thus $18,200 smaller in table 20.3B than in table 20.3A. Allocating education to individuals also changes the percentage difference between the payments of current and future generations. As table 20.3B shows, future generations face a 68.3 percent higher burden than current generations under that calculation.

Tables 20.4 (males) and 20.5 (females) break down the generational account in table 20.3A by sex, based on the assumption of equal percentage imbalances by sex between current and future newborns. A comparison of these tables shows that males face higher generational accounts because of their higher tax payments, due to higher labor market earnings, and their lower receipt of transfer payments, attributable primarily to their lower life expectancy.

Table 20.6A presents alternative estimates, for males and females combined, for three different discount rates (3, 5, and 7 percent) and three different rates of productivity growth (1, 1.5, and 2 percent), a total of nine combinations that span a broad range of possible values. Our base-case results from table 20.3A, for an interest rate, r, of 5 percent and a productivity growth rate, g, of 1.5 percent, are presented in boldface, in the center column of the table.

Table 20.4A   **Generational Accounts for Males: Base Case (thousands of U.S. dollars)**

Generation's Age in 1995	Net Payment	Income Taxes	Property and Proprietors	Social Insurance Contribution	Indirect Taxes	Trans-fers	Edu-cation
0	71.1	21.5	5.5	26.1	36.6	18.6	0.0
5	78.7	25.5	6.5	31.0	37.7	22.0	0.0
10	86.9	30.0	7.6	36.4	38.6	25.8	0.0
15	96.3	35.3	9.0	42.8	39.4	30.2	0.0
20	105.9	41.2	10.5	50.0	39.9	35.6	0.0
25	107.2	43.8	12.0	53.2	40.0	41.9	0.0
30	98.5	42.9	12.9	52.1	39.1	48.6	0.0
35	83.1	39.9	13.0	48.4	37.2	55.4	0.0
40	60.6	34.9	12.2	42.4	34.2	63.0	0.0
45	32.4	28.4	10.7	34.5	30.3	71.5	0.0
50	0.4	20.7	8.8	25.2	25.5	79.9	0.0
55	−29.9	13.0	6.7	15.8	20.3	85.8	0.0
60	−49.1	7.4	4.7	9.0	15.7	85.9	0.0
65	−55.3	3.7	3.0	4.5	12.0	78.5	0.0
70	−48.2	1.9	1.8	2.4	9.0	63.4	0.0
75	−37.9	0.8	1.1	1.0	6.5	47.3	0.0
80	−29.1	0.0	0.8	0.0	4.4	34.3	0.0
85	−18.8	0.0	0.5	0.0	2.6	21.9	0.0
90	−5.5	0.0	0.2	0.0	0.7	6.3	0.0
Future generations	105.7						

Table 20.4B   **Generational Accounts for Males: Base Case, Education Treated as Transfer Payments (thousands of U.S. dollars)**

Generation's Age in 1995	Net Payment	Income Taxes	Property and Proprietors	Social Insurance Contribution	Indirect Taxes	Trans-fers	Edu-cation
0	52.9	21.5	5.5	26.1	36.6	18.6	18.2
5	57.1	25.5	6.5	31.0	37.7	22.0	21.6
10	64.8	30.0	7.6	36.4	38.6	25.8	22.0
15	81.9	35.3	9.0	42.8	39.4	30.2	14.3
20	102.6	41.2	10.5	50.0	39.9	35.6	3.3
25	106.6	43.8	12.0	53.2	40.0	41.9	0.6
30	98.5	42.9	12.9	52.1	39.1	48.6	0.0
35	83.1	39.9	13.0	48.4	37.2	55.4	0.0
40	60.6	34.9	12.2	42.4	34.2	63.0	0.0
45	32.4	28.4	10.7	34.5	30.3	71.5	0.0
50	0.4	20.7	8.8	25.2	25.5	79.9	0.0
55	−29.9	13.0	6.7	15.8	20.3	85.8	0.0
60	−49.1	7.4	4.7	9.0	15.7	85.9	0.0
65	−53.3	3.7	3.0	4.5	12.0	78.5	0.0
70	−48.2	1.9	1.8	2.4	9.0	63.4	0.0
75	−37.9	0.8	1.1	1.0	6.5	47.3	0.0
80	−29.1	0.0	0.8	0.0	4.4	34.3	0.0
85	−18.8	0.0	0.5	0.0	2.6	21.9	0.0
90	−5.5	0.0	0.2	0.0	0.7	6.3	0.0
Future generations	88.9						

Table 20.5A   **Generational Accounts for Females: Base Case (thousands of U.S. dollars)**

Generation's Age in 1995	Net Payment	Income Taxes	Property and Proprietors	Social Insurance Contribution	Indirect Taxes	Trans- fers	Edu- cation
0	51.8	13.9	2.1	16.8	36.1	17.1	0.0
5	55.1	16.4	2.5	20.0	36.4	20.2	0.0
10	58.5	19.3	2.9	23.5	36.5	23.6	0.0
15	62.3	22.7	3.4	27.6	36.3	27.7	0.0
20	65.5	26.1	4.0	31.7	35.9	32.2	0.0
25	62.5	26.9	4.4	32.7	35.1	36.7	0.0
30	51.7	25.0	4.4	30.4	33.3	41.4	0.0
35	37.4	22.2	4.1	26.9	30.4	46.1	0.0
40	20.0	18.2	3.7	22.1	27.0	51.0	0.0
45	0.0	13.7	3.1	16.6	23.3	56.7	0.0
50	−20.6	9.1	2.4	11.0	19.2	62.3	0.0
55	−37.5	5.3	1.7	6.4	15.3	66.1	0.0
60	−45.4	2.9	1.1	3.5	12.0	64.9	0.0
65	−44.5	1.8	0.8	2.1	9.3	58.5	0.0
70	−38.5	1.0	0.5	1.2	7.2	48.4	0.0
75	−30.0	0.5	0.3	0.6	5.4	36.9	0.0
80	−22.2	0.0	0.2	0.0	3.8	26.2	0.0
85	−13.8	0.0	0.1	0.0	2.4	16.3	0.0
90	−3.6	0.0	0.0	0.0	0.6	4.2	0.0
Future generations	77.0						

Table 20.5B   **Generational Accounts for Females: Base Case, Education Treated as Transfer Payments (thousands of U.S. dollars)**

Generation's Age in 1995	Net Payment	Income Taxes	Property and Proprietors	Social Insurance Contribution	Indirect Taxes	Trans- fers	Edu- cation
0	33.5	13.9	2.1	16.8	36.1	17.1	18.3
5	33.5	16.4	2.5	20.0	36.4	20.2	21.6
10	36.4	19.3	2.9	23.5	36.5	23.6	22.1
15	48.0	22.7	3.4	27.6	36.3	27.7	14.3
20	62.2	26.1	4.0	31.7	35.9	32.2	3.3
25	61.9	26.9	4.4	32.7	35.1	36.7	0.6
30	51.7	25.0	4.4	30.4	33.3	41.4	0.0
35	37.4	22.2	4.1	26.9	30.4	46.1	0.0
40	20.0	18.2	3.7	22.1	27.0	51.0	0.0
45	0.0	13.7	3.1	16.6	23.3	56.7	0.0
50	−20.6	9.1	2.4	11.0	19.2	62.3	0.0
55	−37.5	5.3	1.7	6.4	15.3	66.1	0.0
60	−45.4	2.9	1.1	3.5	12.0	64.9	0.0
65	−44.5	1.8	0.8	2.1	9.3	58.5	0.0
70	−38.5	1.0	0.5	1.2	7.2	48.4	0.0
75	−30.0	0.5	0.3	0.6	5.4	36.9	0.0
80	−22.2	0.0	0.2	0.0	3.8	26.2	0.0
85	−13.8	0.0	0.1	0.0	2.4	16.3	0.0
90	−3.6	0.0	0.0	0.0	0.6	4.2	0.0
Future generations	56.4						

Table 20.6A   Sensitivity Analysis (thousands of U.S. dollars)

	g = 1			g = 1.5			g = 2		
	r = 3	r = 5	r = 7	r = 3	r = 5	r = 7	r = 3	r = 5	r = 7
Net payment of newborns	86.9	54.8	35.5	97.2	61.8	39.6	107.9	69.6	44.3
Net payment of future generations	116.9	85.4	69.9	127.6	91.8	72.7	138.5	99.4	69.5
Difference in net payments									
Absolute	30.0	30.5	34.5	30.3	30.1	33.1	30.6	29.8	25.2
Percentage	34.5	55.7	97.2	31.2	48.7	83.7	28.4	42.8	56.9

Note: g is productivity growth rate (percent); *r* is discount rate (percent).

Table 20.6B   Sensitivity Analysis: Education Treated as Transfer Payments (thousands of U.S. dollars)

	g = 1			g = 1.5			g = 2		
	r = 3	r = 5	r = 7	r = 3	r = 5	r = 7	r = 3	r = 5	r = 7
Net payment of newborns	64.5	37.9	22.4	73.1	43.5	25.6	82.0	50.0	29.4
Net payment of future generations	93.9	68.0	56.7	102.7	73.2	58.5	111.8	79.4	61.0
Difference in net payments									
Absolute	29.4	30.2	34.2	29.7	29.7	32.8	29.8	29.4	31.6
Percentage	45.6	79.7	152.7	40.6	68.2	128.0	36.4	58.8	107.7

Note: g is productivity growth rate (percent); *r* is discount rate (percent).

For both current and future generations, the generational accounts fall with an increase in the interest rate and rise with an increase in the growth rate. Each of these phenomena is easily understood. For a newborn generation, a generational account equals the present value of future taxes less future transfers. Discounting these future flows more heavily (with a higher value of r) acts to decrease the present value of both taxes and transfers and hence their difference, the generational account, as well. In principle, there is an offsetting impact, in that transfers, which typically occur later in life, should be discounted even more heavily. However, because transfers are relatively small compared to taxes in the Portuguese case, this effect is not strong enough to offset the former effect.

For a given discount rate, a higher rate of productivity growth means higher taxes and transfers in the future and, following the same logic as above, has two effects. The first is to raise the value of both taxes and transfers. The second is to raise the present value of transfers, which occur later in life, more. Again, because transfers are relatively small, the first effect dominates, and higher growth leads to a higher net tax payment in present value (generational account). In terms of the generational imbalance, the percentage gap between current and future generations rises with the interest rate and falls with the growth rate.

While the accounts may appear sensitive to these changes in r and g, note that the important calculation—the imbalance between current and future generations—is quite robust. The absolute difference between current and future newborns ranges only between $25,200 and $34,500, both values quite close to our base-case estimate of $30,100; and while the percentage differences vary more, all estimates indicate a substantial percentage difference between current and future generations.

As seen in tables 20.4B, 20.5B, and 20.6B, which correspond to tables 20.4A, 20.5A, and 20.6A for the base-case assumption for educational spending, allocating educational spending to individuals lowers the generational accounts of young and newborn current generations, who are the beneficiaries of educational spending. As shown in table 20.6B this alternative assumption has essentially no impact on the difference between the generational accounts of current newborns and future generations, which, implicitly in the calculation, also are being credited with the benefits of educational spending.

20.3.3   Understanding Portugal's Generational Imbalance

Given the small reported primary surplus in the base year, it may seem surprising that future generations face such steep tax increases. However, there are two straightforward explanations for this finding, one relating to the past, the other to the future.

The first explanation is that, as discussed above, past fiscal policy has accumulated a large financial debt, the burden of which remains. Were the current stock of financial debt zero, this would eliminate about two-thirds of the ex-

isting imbalance between current and future generations—from 48.7 percent
to 16.2 percent.

Even zero debt and a current primary surplus leaves some imbalance because the changing demographic composition of the country is leading to an
older population that will receive more transfers and pay less taxes. As discussed above, the dependency ratio is expected to increase sharply over the
coming decades. Were the population age structure to remain constant, instead
of undergoing this shift, current policy would be much closer to balance, even
with the existing stock of debt—just 17.5 percent, just over a third of its current estimated level.

Given the existing stock of debt and the changing structure of the population, though, the imbalance is large, requiring net taxes to increase nearly by
half if no policy changes are enacted that affect current generations. However,
policy changes enacted immediately would require less draconian measures,
for they would be spread over a larger population that includes those presently alive.

20.3.4   Achieving Generational Balance

We estimate that policy could be made sustainable—the difference between
the generational accounts of current and future newborns eliminated—through
any of the following immediate and permanent policy changes (or some combination of them):

7.6 percent reduction in government purchases (including education),

9.8 percent reduction in government purchases (excluding education),

9.6 percent reduction in all transfer payments,

4.2 percent increase in all taxes, or

13.3 percent increase in direct income taxes.

Although each change would eliminate the generational imbalance, the policies vary in the extent to which the burden would be borne by different generations. For example, a reduction in transfer payments would place a larger burden on the current elderly, while an increase in income taxes would have a
much smaller impact on them and burden the young more.

20.4   Conclusions

Portugal has made significant changes in its monetary and fiscal policies
over the past decade. Its current macroeconomic policies, directed toward inclusion in the new European Economic and Monetary Union, are now supported by the two major political parties. These facts notwithstanding, our
findings suggest that Portugal remains far from achieving a truly sustainable
fiscal policy, specifically, one that entails generational balance. Under our baseline assumptions future generations face a roughly 50 percent higher fiscal
burden than do current newborns. This imbalance reflects Portugal's past debt

accumulation and the aging of its population. A variety of alternative tax increase and expenditure reduction policies can be used to achieve generational balance. Which of those policies spreads the burden most appropriately among old and young current generations is a matter for political debate.

Achieving generational balance in Portuguese fiscal policy would not only improve economic prospects for future Portuguese citizens. It would also indicate to foreign investors that Portugal is not likely to expropriate their investments in the future through extraordinary fiscal levies. While actually producing generational balance in Portuguese fiscal policy may prove difficult, the longer the delay, the more painful will be the requisite fiscal adjustments. The generational accounts constructed here can help the Portuguese public to understand the true cost of adjusting the tax and transfer system.

References

Braga de Macedo, Jorge. 1997. Crises? What crises? The escudo from ECU to EMU. Nova Economics Working Paper no. 313. Lisbon: Nova University, December. (Available at http://www.fe.unl.pt/~jbmacedo/papers/wider.htm)
Braz, José. 1992. Portugal from P1 to Q2: A strategy of sustained regime change. In *A single currency for Europe,* ed. Clive Crook. London: Centre for Economic Policy Research.
Kotlikoff, Laurence. 1996. Privatizing social security at home and abroad. *American Economic Review* 86 (2): 368–72.
United Nations. 1997. *Sustaining social security.* New York: United Nations.

21 Generational Accounts for the United States: An Update

Jagadeesh Gokhale, Benjamin R. Page,
and John R. Sturrock

To pay for all the goods and services that a government ever buys, someone of some generation must pay at some time. If one generation pays less, another must pay more. If the government does not pay for what it purchases with current taxes, it must raise them later—either to retire the ensuing debt or to pay interest forever. Sooner or later, someone pays.

This idea underlies the intertemporal government budget constraint, which states that the present value of prospective government purchases must be financed from the sum of three sources: the current net wealth of government, the present value of the prospective net taxes of current generations (people now alive), and the present value of the prospective net taxes of future generations (people not yet born).[1] Thus the constraint reveals the way in which government purchases involve a fiscal burden that someone must bear.

For the prospective purchases implied by a given fiscal policy, generational accounting estimates how much of that total burden will fall on current versus future generations.[2] The analysis begins by calculating the present value of prospective purchases for a given policy. The first source of financing (the government's current net wealth) is given. The second source (the present value of current generations' net taxes) is obtained by estimating the per capita net taxes that each living generation will pay during its remaining lifetime, actuarially discounting the payments back to the present, and summing over the dis-

Jagadeesh Gokhale is an economic advisor at the Federal Reserve Bank of Cleveland. Benjamin R. Page and John R. Sturrock are economic analysts at the Congressional Budget Office.

The authors thank Robert Kilpatrick and Laurence Kotlikoff for helpful discussions. The views reflected herein are those of the authors and not necessarily those of the Federal Reserve Bank of Cleveland, the Federal Reserve System, or the Congressional Budget Office.

1. Net taxes are taxes minus transfers.
2. The technique of generational accounting was developed in Auerbach, Gokhale, and Kotlikoff (1991). See also Auerbach, Gokhale, and Kotlikoff (1994).

counted values to obtain a generational account for each generation.[3] Those respective generational accounts are then added over everyone currently alive to find their combined contribution to prospective purchases. Having calculated the present value of prospective purchases and the first two sources of financing, the third source (the present value of unborn generations' net taxes) can be computed as a residual. This residual expresses the fiscal burden that must be placed on unborn generations for the government to remain solvent forever.

Finally, generational accounting compares all living generations on a lifetime basis by estimating the effective rate at which each pays net taxes over its *entire* life—its lifetime net tax rate. The method estimates past and prospective net taxes and labor income that each living generation earns over its life. The lifetime net tax rate is then stated as a percentage, namely, the present value, at birth, of a generation's lifetime net taxes as a share of the present value, at birth, of its lifetime labor income.

As an illustrative device, generational accounting further supposes that future generations share the residual burden equally (with an adjustment for economic growth). This implies that males and females born in each future year will face the same lifetime net tax rate. Thus the method compares all generations on the same basis—the effective rate at which they pay net taxes over their entire lives.

Generational accounts help us judge whether fiscal policy is generationally balanced, that is, whether future generations will pay, on average, the same lifetime net tax rate as current newborns (people born in the base year). A generationally balanced policy is *sustainable,* meaning that it can be followed forever without changing its scheduled effective rates for taxes, transfers, and spending. Conversely, a policy is imbalanced (or unsustainable) if it implies that future generations must pay a different net tax rate than current newborns.

An imbalance implies that to pay for prospective purchases, the scheduled rates of effective net taxes must change—if not for current generations, then for future ones. If an imbalance implies that the future rate will be higher than the current rate, the rate must eventually rise. If the imbalance is large, then the rate for some living or future generations will have to increase substantially and may harm their incentives to work, save, and invest. Hence, the finding of a large generational imbalance points to the potential for weaker future economic performance. Conversely, if an imbalance implies that the future rate will be lower than the current one, someone must pay less to keep the government's net wealth from growing so big that government owns all of the nation's assets. Generational accounting can estimate the sizes of policy changes that would restore sustainability and generational balance.

3. An actuarial calculation allows for the fact that the current number of people in a generation will later be decreased by death or increased by immigration.

Section 21.1 reports generational accounts and the associated lifetime net tax rates for the United States. The results suggest that U.S. fiscal policy is generationally imbalanced. If living generations pay net taxes as scheduled, future generations will have to pay a lifetime net tax rate far exceeding that of current newborns—49.2 versus 28.6 percent, an arithmetic difference of 20.6 percentage points.

Ordinarily, generational accounting does not estimate by age who benefits from prospective purchases, only who pays for them with their net taxes. In this study, however, we also calculate an alternative set of accounts that assign to each living generation the benefit from its share of government spending on education. The recalculated accounts show a similar arithmetic difference in lifetime net tax rates.

These results depend on a "reference" scenario for fiscal policy, the economy, and the population. The reference policy used here cuts the deficit, splitting the reduction evenly between Medicare and discretionary spending and balancing the budget in the years from 2002 through 2007. After that, however, it allows the deficit to widen, reflecting an aging population, slowing labor force growth, and rising per capita medical costs. Through 2070, the reference scenario depends on three factors: the federal tax and spending schedule, the "no-feedback" economic projection of the Congressional Budget Office (CBO), and the Social Security Administration's (SSA's) intermediate population projection (SSA 1997; CBO 1997b; 1997c, chap. 1). Beyond 2070, the reference scenario extends those fiscal, economic, and demographic projections by the methods described below.

The reference scenario does not include the recent budget reconciliation package (the Balanced Budget Act of 1997 and the Taxpayer Relief Act of 1997) because long-term projections under that package are not yet available. Other things equal, the results under the reference scenario should roughly correspond to those under the reconciliation package because both policies cut base spending on health care and other (non–social security) programs in about the same proportions. However, the most recent budget projections yield more than just midterm budget balance; they show a small surplus in 2002, which rises to about 0.7 percent of GDP in 2007 (CBO 1997a). Therefore, the current fiscal stance is likely to produce a smaller generational imbalance than the one we report based on the reference policy. Even so, in contrast to the accounts reported earlier, the reference scenario implies a sharp decline in the degree of generational imbalance.[4]

Section 21.2 details the reasons for that decline, which occurred largely because per capita costs for medical programs have recently grown more slowly than expected. Section 21.3 reports the amounts by which generational accounts change when we alter the assumptions for population growth, govern-

---

4. The results here update those in Auerbach, Gokhale, and Kotlikoff (1995).

ment spending, and economic growth or discount rates. Generational accounts move into or near balance under some of these assumptions but remain imbalanced under most.

Section 21.4 considers *hypothetical* policy actions that achieve generational balance by changing the reference policy's schedule for purchases or for the net taxes that living generations will pay. The required size of such a change depends on whether it cuts prospective purchases or raises prospective net taxes for current generations. For instance, under the reference assumptions, balance could now be restored by proportional cuts of 15.4 percent in purchases or 18.5 percent in transfers, or by an increase of 8.9 percent in taxes. (The changes differ because the programs involve different initial dollar amounts, and the effects of the changes depend on both how fast the programs expand and which generations are most affected.) Although we examine these policies only as examples of the magnitude of the imbalance, it is clear that the longer the status quo persists, the more difficult it will be to restore generational balance. Section 21.5 concludes the paper.

21.1   The Generational Stance of U.S. Fiscal Policy

21.1.1   Intertemporal Government Budget Constraint

The intertemporal government budget constraint is expressed as

$$(1) \qquad \qquad PVG_t = NWG_t - PVL_t + PVF_t,$$

where PVG_t is the present value of government purchases, NWG_t is the current value of government financial net wealth, PVL_t is the total present value of net taxes that living generations will pay over the rest of their lives, and PVF_t is the residual fiscal burden that future generations must bear.[5]

To calculate those values for a base case, we assume the following: (1) The real discount rate is 6 percent. (2) Labor productivity growth through 2070 is given by the reference scenario; beyond 2070, it is assumed to be 1.2 percent per year (its average annual growth rate for most of the reference scenario). (3) Aggregate taxes, transfers, and purchases through 2070 are given by the reference projection; beyond 2070, they are assumed to grow at a rate consistent with per capita growth at the same rate as labor productivity. (4) The population through 2070 is the SSA's intermediate projection; from 2070 through

---

5. The constraint includes all debt, taxes, transfers, and purchases at every level of government. Unlike the National Income and Product Accounts, generational accounting treats spending on medical, disability, and retirement benefits for veterans and government workers as purchases (payment for past services), rather than as transfers. For an explanation of how generational accounts treat taxes, transfers, and purchases, see Auerbach, Gokhale, and Kotlikoff (1991).

NWG_t excludes the value of tangible government assets, and PVG_t excludes the service flows of those assets. If NWG_t included the assets, PVG_t would have to include the service flows. Because (in equilibrium) the assets and their service flows are equal in present value, they would cancel each other if they were both included in eq. (1).

2200, we extend that projection by assuming that fertility, mortality, and net immigration rates remain at their 2070 values; beyond 2200, we assume that the size and the age composition of the population remain fixed.

Under the reference policy and the assumptions mentioned earlier, PVG_t equals $29.4 trillion, and NWG_t (calculated as the algebraic sum of past real government surpluses) amounts to $-$2.1 trillion. Loosely, NWG_t is the negative of net public debt, NDG_t. PVL_t equals $22.1 trillion, and PVF_t is $9.4 trillion.[6]

It is PVF_t, rather than NDG_t, that more meaningfully reflects the fiscal burden that the reference policy imposes on future generations. NDG_t includes only the explicit legal obligations of U.S. governments, not their implicit obligations. For example, the current debt ignores the unfunded liabilities of Medicare, social security, and government retirement programs. Outlays for these programs will accelerate in the future as the baby boom generations retire and as the costs of health care programs mount. In contrast to the debt, PVF_t includes all prospective government liabilities, implicit as well as explicit. We calculate that PVF_t is more than four times as large as NDG_t: $9.4 trillion versus $2.1 trillion.

21.1.2   Generational Accounts

A generational account is the present value of the per capita net taxes that a generation will pay for the rest of its life under the assumed fiscal policy. (Generational accounting defines a generation by sex and year of birth.) To obtain each generation's prospective per capita values through 2070, generational accounting first distributes among the generations the reference projections for aggregate taxes and transfers. The distribution assumes that the current ratios of per capita taxes and transfers by age and sex remain fixed. For instance, in a given year, 50-year-old women always pay 38 percent as much in per capita payroll taxes as do 40-year-old men.[7] Beyond 2070, generational accounting assumes that the per capita amount of each type of tax or transfer by age or sex grows at the same rate as labor productivity. The resulting streams of per capita net taxes are actuarially discounted to the base year in order to calculate the generational account for each living generation. (The base year in this case is 1995, the latest year for which we have the ratios of per capita taxes and transfers by age and sex.)

As tables 21.1 and 21.2 show, generational accounts follow a life cycle pattern. Young generations at or near working age will pay a significant amount

---

6. All dollar figures are reported in constant 1995 dollars.

7. The ratios are estimated from official survey data. For details of the procedure, see Auerbach et al. (1991); for a description of the respective ratios of per capita net payments by age and sex, see CBO (1995, 7–8).

For social security and government retirement programs, the generational accounts shown here reflect the way in which productivity growth feeds gradually into benefits under current schedules. Thus the ratios of per capita benefits by age and sex for these programs need not remain fixed. See CBO (1997b).

Table 21.1 Composition of Male Generational Accounts under Reference Assumptions (present value in thousands of 1995 dollars)

Generation's Age in 1995	Net Tax Payment	Tax Payments				Transfer Receipts		
		Labor Income	Capital Income	Payroll	Other[a]	OASDI	Health	Other
0	77.4	33.5	9.0	34.3	31.5	7.2	19.6	4.2
5	95.7	41.6	11.2	42.8	36.6	8.8	22.5	5.2
10	119.5	52.1	14.3	53.9	42.5	10.6	26.3	6.5
15	149.1	65.1	18.1	67.8	48.6	12.1	30.4	8.1
20	182.2	79.5	23.5	83.6	53.4	13.7	34.4	9.7
25	196.2	86.0	27.9	90.6	53.5	16.4	35.4	10.1
30	196.8	86.3	33.7	90.2	52.7	19.9	36.4	9.8
35	189.0	82.9	40.7	86.0	51.4	24.6	38.2	9.2
40	171.2	76.0	46.6	78.6	50.4	30.8	40.9	8.7
45	139.2	65.1	50.2	67.4	47.7	38.8	44.3	8.1
50	93.7	50.8	51.3	52.9	43.7	49.3	48.0	7.6
55	37.5	34.6	49.7	36.3	38.7	62.8	52.0	7.0
60	−25.5	18.6	46.3	19.5	32.9	80.1	56.5	6.3
65	−77.7	7.4	41.2	7.5	27.5	91.8	63.8	5.7
70	−89.2	3.2	33.0	3.3	22.2	85.0	60.9	5.1
75	−87.9	1.6	22.4	1.7	16.9	71.7	54.5	4.2
80	−77.2	0.9	11.2	1.0	11.9	54.8	44.4	3.1
85	−68.3	0.7	0.0	0.7	8.0	42.6	32.9	2.1
90	−53.8	0.5	0.0	0.5	6.3	33.7	25.9	1.7
Future generations	134.6							
Percentage difference	71.9							

Source: Authors' calculations.

Note: Future generations are those born in 1996 and thereafter. The net tax payment represents a present value as of 1996. The percentage difference between the net tax payments of future generations and current newborns is calculated after adjustment for growth (see text).

[a] Includes excise and other indirect taxes, property taxes, and other taxes.

Table 21.2 Composition of Female Generational Accounts under Reference Assumptions (present value in thousands of 1995 dollars)

Generation's Age in 1995	Net Tax Payment	Tax Payments				Transfer Receipts		
		Labor Income	Capital Income	Payroll	Other[a]	OASDI	Health	Other
0	51.9	19.4	9.5	20.9	30.4	6.8	14.8	6.8
5	63.4	24.1	11.9	26.1	35.2	8.3	16.9	8.5
10	78.1	30.2	15.1	32.9	40.5	10.0	19.9	10.6
15	95.7	37.7	19.3	41.3	45.6	11.3	23.4	13.5
20	115.0	45.7	24.8	50.7	49.8	12.7	26.6	16.8
25	122.6	48.1	30.3	53.7	50.4	15.3	28.9	15.7
30	120.7	46.2	36.2	51.6	50.1	18.6	31.7	13.2
35	113.8	42.8	42.3	47.9	49.8	23.0	35.2	10.8
40	99.0	38.2	46.3	43.0	48.6	28.8	39.6	8.7
45	72.8	31.6	47.7	35.7	46.2	36.5	45.0	7.0
50	37.4	23.6	46.8	26.9	42.3	46.9	49.5	5.6
55	−5.2	15.0	44.8	17.2	37.6	60.6	54.5	4.8
60	−52.0	7.6	41.6	8.7	32.4	78.6	59.5	4.2
65	−91.2	2.7	35.6	3.1	27.1	89.3	66.5	3.8
70	−101.0	1.0	25.3	1.2	22.2	83.4	63.9	3.4
75	−101.0	0.5	14.1	0.6	16.9	71.6	58.5	2.9
80	−90.2	0.3	5.3	0.3	12.4	57.2	48.8	2.4
85	−73.5	0.1	0.0	0.1	9.4	43.5	37.8	1.9
90	−55.8	0.1	0.0	0.1	7.2	33.2	28.5	1.5
Future generations	90.2							

Source: Authors' calculations.

Note: Future generations are those born in 1996 and thereafter. The net tax payment represents a present value as of 1996.

[a]Includes excise and other indirect taxes, property taxes, and other taxes.

of taxes for several years before they retire and collect social security and Medicare benefits. Hence, their generational accounts are positive and high. By contrast, older generations in or near retirement will pay low taxes and receive high transfers for most of their remaining years. Thus their generational accounts are negative.

The generational accounts for women of any age are lower (or more negative) than those for men of the same age. On average, women pay lower taxes because they are less likely to work in the marketplace and earn less when they do. Moreover, they live longer and often receive payments as widows on their husbands' accounts. Therefore, relative to their earnings, they receive more in transfers, especially for medical care and social security.

Generational accounts compare on the same lifetime basis the net payments of current newborns (those born in 1995) and future generations (those born later). That is, the accounts show the present value of per capita net taxes that each group will pay over its entire life. How do their accounts compare? Under the reference policy, the generational account for a 1995 newborn is $77,400 for a male and $51,900 for a female. As mentioned earlier, the residual burden on future generations is $9.4 trillion, but there is no way to know how they would share that burden. To get around this problem, generational accounting assumes that future generations split the burden equally on a growth-adjusted basis. As noted, this assumption amounts to specifying that males and females born in each future year will pay combined lifetime net taxes at a uniform rate.[8] Given this assumption, the reference policy implies that males born in 1996 will pay an average of $134,600 (in present value as of 1996), while females will pay an average of $90,200. These payments are larger than the corresponding payments of current newborns, indicating that the reference policy is out of generational balance.

21.1.3   Lifetime Net Tax Rates

So far, it has been legitimate to compare directly only the generational accounts of current newborns and future generations. These accounts give each group's net payment over its *entire* life. Other generations, however, are at varying stages of their life cycles. Thus their accounts are not directly comparable because their net payments are stated only over their *remaining* lives. For instance, the generational account of a 40-year-old man is higher than that of a

8. The calculation assumes that labor productivity (and hence, eventually, per capita income) grows each year at rate g. In that case, an equal growth-adjusted share of the burden means that the per capita net payment of each future generation is $1 + g$ times that of its immediate predecessor. If males born in 1996 pay Y dollars each, then males born in 1997 pay $Y(1 + g)$ dollars each, males born in 1998 pay $Y(1 + g)^2$ dollars each, and so forth. (Generational accounting gives those per capita net payments in present value as of year of the generation's birth.) Similarly, if females born in 1996 pay X dollars each, then females born in 1997 pay $X(1 + g)$ dollars each, and so on. This procedure amounts to assuming that all future males pay lifetime net taxes at a uniform rate— their lifetime net taxes grow generation by generation at the same rate as their lifetime incomes. Future females also pay lifetime net taxes at a uniform rate, but it is lower than the rate for males.

Table 21.3   **Lifetime Net Tax Rates for Living and Future Generations under Reference Assumptions**

Generation's Year of Birth	Net Tax Rate	Components of Net Tax Rate	
		Gross Tax Rate	Gross Transfer Rate
1900	23.9	28.0	4.0
1910	27.5	33.4	6.0
1920	29.6	36.4	6.7
1930	31.3	38.4	7.1
1940	32.5	40.3	7.8
1950	33.4	43.0	9.5
1960	33.3	44.1	10.8
1970	32.4	44.3	11.9
1980	30.8	43.0	12.2
1990	29.3	42.1	12.8
1995	28.6	41.7	13.1
Future generations	49.2		

Source: Authors' calculations

Note: Future generations are those born in 1996 and thereafter. Numbers may not add up because of rounding.

50-year-old man because the 40-year-old has 10 more years of taxes to pay and is 10 years farther from receiving social security and Medicare benefits. But the accounts cannot say whether the 40-year-old paid net taxes in the past at the same effective rate as the 50-year-old when he was 40. Nor do the accounts state how a 60-year-old woman's current negative account compares with her past net taxes.

To compare everyone on the same basis, generational accounting calculates the effective rate at which each generation pays net taxes over its entire life— its lifetime net tax rate. The method first estimates each generation's past net taxes (in addition to its prospective net taxes) to find its per capita lifetime net taxes. Those per capita net taxes are then discounted to the year in which the generation was born in order to find its generational account at birth. Similarly, the procedure estimates each generation's per capita lifetime labor income and finds its present value at birth. The generational account at birth is then divided by the present value at birth of per capita lifetime labor income to yield the generation's lifetime net tax rate. A lifetime net tax rate compares all generations on the same basis—the effective share of labor income that its members will pay in net taxes over their entire lives.

As table 21.3 shows, the lifetime net tax rate for successive generations has both risen and fallen over the century. It started at 23.9 percent for people born in 1900, climbed to 33.4 percent for those born in 1950, then fell to 28.6 percent for those born in 1995.[9] The rise in the rate for successive generations

9. The rates are ratios of population-weighted net taxes to population-weighted labor incomes.

through 1950 coincided with a similar increase in the share of output devoted to government purchases. The decline in the rate for successive generations since 1950 stems mostly from three factors: longer life expectancies, a decline in the effective rate of excise taxes, and—most important—the rapid growth in per capita health care and social security transfers that began in the 1960s.[10]

The results shown in table 21.3 indicate that the reference policy is unsustainable. Either prospective purchases must fall or the effective schedule at which people pay net taxes must rise—if not for current generations, then for future ones. If current generations pay net taxes as scheduled by the reference policy, current newborns will pay lifetime net taxes of 28.6 percent, and future generations will pay 49.2 percent.[11]

We can use these lifetime net tax rates to quantify the notion of generational imbalance. The degree of such imbalance is given as a percentage, namely, the arithmetic difference between the lifetime net tax rates of future generations and current newborns as a fraction of the lifetime net tax rate of current newborns. Thus the degree of imbalance under the reference scenario is 72 percent (the difference between 49.2 and 28.6 as a percentage of 28.6). A degree of zero indicates generational balance while a negative degree indicates an imbalance in favor of the future.

21.1.4 Benefits of Government Spending on Education by Age and Sex

How would this outcome differ if the accounts assigned, by age, the benefits that living generations receive from government purchases? It is impossible to assign the benefits from many purchases, such as those for defense or administration, because they generate public services that apply equally to everyone.[12] Arguably, however, we can estimate by age the per capita benefits from one category of purchases—educational spending (now about one-fifth of total government purchases). Below, we recalculate the generational accounts by treating all prospective government spending for education as a transfer rather than a purchase, then distributing that spending by age.[13]

The recalculation substantially lowers the lifetime net taxes of those under age 25 (see tables 21.4 and 21.5), since they receive most of the benefits from

10. Excise taxes affect a generational account at birth more than do other taxes. Generational accounting prorates excise taxes among all family members, including children. Therefore, a decline in the excise tax lowers the estimated taxes that a child pays early in life. An earlier payment has a higher present value at birth than does the same payment at a later time. Hence, a cut in the excise tax lowers lifetime net tax rates by more than does a cut in another tax that reduces current revenue by the same amount.

11. These figures do not predict what *will* happen, only what *would* happen if the reference policy applied to current generations for the rest of their lives.

12. Beyond 2070 (the end of the reference projection), generational accounting prorates each year's per capita cost of such purchases to everyone alive in that year. However, the method is used only to estimate total prospective purchases, not to try to assign the benefits of those purchases by age.

13. Data used in the calculation are from the Department of Education (1997).

Table 21.4 **Composition of Male Generational Accounts under Reference Assumptions: Benefits of Educational Expenditure Distributed by Age and Sex (present value in thousands of 1995 dollars)**

Generation's Age in 1995	Net Tax Payment	Tax Payments				Transfer Receipts			
		Labor Income	Capital Income	Payroll	Other[a]	OASDI	Health	Other	Education
0	25.7	33.5	9.0	34.3	31.5	7.2	19.6	4.2	51.7
5	33.1	41.6	11.2	42.8	36.6	8.8	22.5	5.2	62.6
10	71.4	52.1	14.3	53.9	42.5	10.6	26.3	6.5	48.1
15	120.1	65.1	18.1	67.8	48.6	12.1	30.4	8.1	28.9
20	172.7	79.5	23.5	83.6	53.4	13.7	34.4	9.7	9.5
25	193.3	86.0	27.9	90.6	53.5	16.4	35.4	10.1	2.9
30	195.1	86.3	33.7	90.2	52.7	19.9	36.4	9.8	1.7
35	187.8	82.9	40.7	86.0	51.4	24.6	38.2	9.2	1.2
40	170.4	76.0	46.6	78.6	50.4	30.8	40.9	8.7	.7
45	138.7	65.1	50.2	67.4	47.7	38.8	44.3	8.1	.5
50	93.6	50.8	51.3	52.9	43.7	49.3	48.0	7.6	.2
55	37.3	34.6	49.7	36.3	38.7	62.8	52.0	7.0	.1
60	−25.6	18.6	46.3	19.5	32.9	80.1	56.5	6.3	.1
65	−77.7	7.4	41.2	7.5	27.5	91.8	63.8	5.7	.0
70	−89.2	3.2	33.0	3.3	22.2	85.0	60.9	5.1	.0
75	−87.9	1.6	22.4	1.7	16.9	71.7	54.5	4.2	.0
80	−77.3	.9	11.2	1.0	11.9	54.8	44.4	3.1	.0
85	−68.3	.7	.0	.7	8.0	42.6	32.9	2.1	.0
90	−53.8	.5	.0	.5	6.3	33.7	25.9	1.7	.0
Future generations	114.3								
Percentage difference	340.3								

Source: Authors' calculations.

Note: Future generations are those born in 1996 and thereafter. The net tax payment represents a present value as of 1996. The percentage difference between the net tax payments of future generations and current newborns is calculated after adjustment for growth (see text).

[a]Includes excise and other indirect taxes, property taxes, and other taxes.

Table 21.5   Composition of Female Generational Accounts under Reference Assumptions: Benefits of Educational Expenditure Distributed by Age and Sex (present value in thousands of 1995 dollars)

Generation's Age in 1995	Net Tax Payment	Tax Payments				Transfer Receipts			
		Labor Income	Capital Income	Payroll	Other[a]	OASDI	Health	Other	Education
0	.1	19.4	9.5	20.9	30.4	6.8	14.8	6.8	51.8
5	.8	24.1	11.9	26.1	35.2	8.3	16.9	8.5	62.6
10	29.9	30.2	15.1	32.9	40.5	10.0	19.9	10.6	48.2
15	66.8	37.7	19.3	41.3	45.6	11.3	23.4	13.5	28.9
20	105.5	45.7	24.8	50.7	49.8	12.7	26.6	16.8	9.5
25	119.7	48.1	30.3	53.7	50.4	15.3	28.9	15.7	3.0
30	119.0	46.2	36.2	51.6	50.1	18.6	31.7	13.2	1.7
35	112.6	42.8	42.3	47.9	49.8	23.0	35.2	10.8	1.2
40	98.3	38.2	46.3	43.0	48.6	28.8	39.6	8.7	.8
45	72.2	31.6	47.7	35.7	46.2	36.5	45.0	7.0	.6
50	37.3	23.6	46.8	26.9	42.3	46.9	49.5	5.6	.2
55	-5.3	15.0	44.8	17.2	37.6	60.6	54.5	4.8	.2
60	-52.1	7.6	41.6	8.7	32.4	78.6	59.5	4.2	.1
65	-91.2	2.7	35.6	3.1	27.1	89.3	66.5	3.8	.0
70	-101.1	1.0	25.3	1.2	22.2	83.4	63.9	3.4	.0
75	-101.0	.5	14.1	.6	16.9	71.6	58.5	2.9	.0
80	-90.2	.3	5.3	.3	12.4	57.2	48.8	2.4	.0
85	-73.6	.1	.0	.1	9.4	43.5	37.8	1.9	.0
90	-55.8	.1	.0	.1	7.2	33.2	28.5	1.5	.0
Future generations	0.3								

Source: Authors' calculations.

Note: Future generations are those born in 1996 and thereafter. The net tax payment represents a present value as of 1996. The percentage difference between the net tax payments of future generations and current newborns is calculated after adjustment for growth (see text).

[a]Includes excise and other indirect taxes, property taxes, and other taxes.

such spending. The recalculated generational account for males born in 1995 is only $25,700, and for females, only $100. Thus educational spending cancels much of the net taxes that the rest of the reference policy imposes on the youngest generations.

At the same time, the recalculation also lowers projected purchases (by classifying educational outlays as transfers) and thereby reduces the residual burden on future generations. Thus, at 19.8 percentage points, the arithmetic difference in the recalculated lifetime net tax rates of future generations and current newborns is nearly as large as when educational outlays are counted as purchases.

21.2   Recent Improvement in the Generational Stance of U.S. Fiscal Policy

In the past two years, the generational stance of U.S. fiscal policy has improved markedly from that reported in the accounts using 1993 as the base year (GA1993).[14] Given the economic outlook and policy schedule of two years ago, GA1993 estimated that future generations would pay a lifetime net tax rate of 84.4 percent. That rate falls to 49.2 percent under the reference scenario for the base year 1995 (GA1995).

What explains this improvement? Most of it stems from lower projected federal spending for medical care, which is now about 10 percent less than what was expected two or three years ago. As a result, projected transfer spending for health care is growing from a lower base and remains a smaller share of output (see fig. 21.1). The output shares of other projected taxes, transfers, and government purchases are also below levels seen two years ago. The reason for lower purchases growth is that projections for state and local government purchases are below GA1993 levels.

We examine the effects of moving from GA1993 to GA1995 by cumulatively updating their underlying assumptions. The change from base year 1993 to 1995 means that the accounts treat people born in 1994 and 1995 as current rather than as future generations. In GA1995, these two generations no longer assume a share of the accumulating residual burden that falls on future generations. Thus time and compound interest alone raise the lifetime net tax rate on future generations to 87.4 percent (see table 21.6). The updated projections for population, however, reduce that rate to 85.3 percent. As noted, the newer projections for transfers (especially for health care) decrease the rate much farther—more than 40 percentage points. The smaller transfers projected for

---

14. See Auerbach et al. (1995). The base calculation in 1993 used the Office of Management and Budget's economic and budget projections through 2030. Those projections were extended by assuming that per capita taxes, transfers, and purchases by age and sex grew at the same rate as labor productivity.

These calculations, and those that follow, treat government outlays for education as purchases.

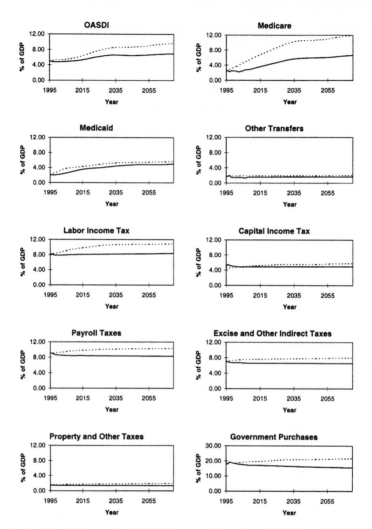

Fig. 21.1   Comparison of projected budget aggregates: GA1993 and GA1995
Source: Office of Management and Budget; Congressional Budget Office; authors' calculations.
Note: Dashed line is GA1993; solid line is GA1995. "Excise and other indirect taxes" excludes property taxes.

GA1995 entail higher net taxes on living generations and thus a lower residual burden on future ones. The more recent estimates of current government net wealth and projected purchases by state and local governments lighten that burden still more. By contrast, the lower revenue projections of GA1995 reduce the lifetime net tax rate on current newborns and raise that on future generations.

Table 21.6   **Generational Accounts, 1993 versus 1995: Cumulative Impact of Updating Demographic and Fiscal Projections**

	Lifetime Net Tax Rates		
	Newborns	Future Generations	Percentage Difference
1993 Accounts	34.2	84.4	147.1
Freeze 1993 policy for two years	34.1	87.4	156.0
Update demographic projections	33.6	85.3	154.1
Fiscal projections			
Transfers			
1. Social security	34.6	76.4	121.2
2. Medicare and Medicaid	36.9	46.9	27.1
3. Other	37.7	44.5	18.1
Government purchases			
1. Federal	37.7	46.0	22.0
2. State and local	37.7	21.5	−42.9
Government wealth	37.7	20.8	−44.8
Taxes			
1. Income (labor and capital)	33.6	32.5	−3.2
2. Payroll	31.1	40.5	30.5
3. Excise and other indirect	29.1	46.7	60.4
4. Property and other	28.7	49.3	71.9
Projected labor income	28.6	49.2	71.9
1995 Accounts	28.6	49.2	71.9

Source: Authors' calculations.

21.3 Sensitivity to Alternative Assumptions

21.3.1 Alternative Projections for Government Purchases and Health Care

The reported calculations depend on many uncertain or arguable economic and budgetary assumptions. For instance, the reference scenario assumes that real federal discretionary spending falls through 2007 at an average rate of 1.3 percent per year; after that, it grows at the same rate as output. By contrast, the Balanced Budget Act of 1997 limits discretionary spending only through 2002, although subsequent legislation may extend such limits even more.[15]

In the near term, both the budget act and the reference policy would intensify the post–Korean War period's secular decline in discretionary spending as a share of output. In the long run, however, it may be difficult to keep such a tight rein on discretionary spending (mostly purchases). For instance, federal nondefense purchases since the 1950s have varied little as a share of output. Moreover, the current replacement schedule for aging defense systems may strain prospective budgets.

15. The act itself extended the limits on discretionary spending set by the Omnibus Budget and Reconciliation Act of 1993.

Similar uncertainty besets projections of federal mandatory spending (mostly transfers), especially for health care. Through 2007, the reference scenario assumes that real per capita Medicare outlays by age outpace labor productivity by an average of 3.4 percentage points per year. That difference tapers to zero by 2020, after which Medicare spending is assumed to grow at the same rate as labor productivity. On average through 2020, per capita Medicare spending by age grows 2.4 percentage points per year faster than labor productivity.[16]

Projections for health care outlays are notoriously uncertain. For many years, analysts underpredicted per capita spending for these rapidly expanding programs. In the past several years, however, such outlays have increased much more slowly than expected. No one is entirely sure of the reasons behind this slowdown, and it is possible that rapid growth may resume. On the other hand, growth may continue at its slower pace or slacken even more, and budgetary pressures may require limits on the expansion of medical programs.

How much do the accounts change if we look at alternative budgetary assumptions in order to allow for uncertainty or ambiguity? To find out, we examine the effects of two optimistic policies that specify lower spending for purchases and health care.[17] The first holds real federal purchases constant after 2000; the second slows the growth rate of per capita Medicare outlays by age. Under the latter policy, per capita medical spending through 2003 grows at an average rate that is 2 percentage points per year slower than under the reference policy. After 2003, per capita outlays expand at the same rate as labor productivity.

These policies depart significantly from current conditions and from the reference policy. For example, federal purchases now represent 6.0 percent of output. In 2070, that share is 4.2 percent under the reference policy, but only 1.5 percent if real federal purchases stay constant after 2000. Total spending for Medicare is now equal to 2.7 percent of output. In 2070, it reaches 7.1 percent under the reference policy, but only 4.3 percent if that spending grows more slowly.

Given the other reference assumptions, these alternative policies reduce the generational imbalance but do not eliminate it. If real federal purchases remain constant after 2000, the lifetime net taxes of living generations remain unchanged. However, the policy lowers projected spending for purchases. That decrease leaves a smaller residual burden on future generations, reducing their lifetime net tax rate from 49.2 to 44.6 percent (see table 21.7). Unlike constant purchases, slow Medicare growth boosts the per capita net taxes of every living generation (because it lowers their projected transfers). Like constant purchases, however, slow Medicare growth lessens the burden that current genera-

---

16. The Health Care Financing Administration (1997) makes similar assumptions.

17. Projected federal purchases under this assumption serve as a proxy for federal discretionary outlays. Purchases now make up about 90 percent of federal discretionary spending, which in turn accounts for around 37 percent of noninterest federal outlays.

Table 21.7   **Lifetime Net Tax Rates under Alternative Health Care and Federal Purchases Assumptions**

Generation's Year of Birth	Reference	Slower Purchases Growth[a]	Slower Health Care Growth[b]	Slower Health Care and Purchases Growth
1900	23.9	23.9	23.9	23.9
1910	27.5	27.5	27.5	27.5
1920	29.6	29.6	29.7	29.7
1930	31.3	31.3	31.4	31.4
1940	32.5	32.5	32.9	32.9
1950	33.4	33.4	34.0	34.0
1960	33.3	33.3	34.1	34.1
1970	32.4	32.4	33.6	33.6
1980	30.8	30.8	32.4	32.4
1990	29.3	29.3	31.4	31.4
1995	28.6	28.6	30.9	30.9
Future generations	49.2	44.6	38.1	33.5

Source: Authors' calculations.

[a]Federal purchases are held constant in real terms after the year 2000.

[b]Per capita spending by age for health care grows 2 percentage points slower than under reference policy through 2003 and grows at the same rate as labor productivity thereafter.

tions leave for future generations, and their lifetime net tax rate falls to 38.1 percent. A policy of both constant real federal purchases and slow Medicare growth yields lifetime net tax rates of 33.5 percent for future generations and 30.9 percent for current newborns. Therefore, a small generational imbalance remains despite optimistic assumptions for federal purchases and Medicare outlays.

The response of lifetime net tax rates to slower Medicare growth may seem paradoxical. Slow growth raises the lifetime net tax rate for the oldest generation the least, although that generation receives the lower transfers now. By contrast, slow growth increases that rate for the youngest generation the most, although these individuals collect the lower benefits later. This pattern occurs in part because people over age 65 will receive the smaller benefits for fewer years until death, a fact that reduces its cumulative lifetime impact.

More fundamentally, the pattern occurs because slower growth makes a greater difference over a long time horizon. For instance, if per capita benefits rise 1 percentage point per year less, benefits at age 65 will be 1 percent lower for this year's 64-year-old, 2 percent lower for this year's 63-year-old, and so forth. Moreover, the decline in benefits at age 65 is discounted not to the base year but to the generation's year of birth. Thus slow Medicare growth cuts the present value of the newborn's benefit at age 65 by proportionately more than that of the one-year-old. Slower growth thus raises the lifetime net taxes (reduces the lifetime net transfers) of the current newborn by more than those of the one-year-old, boosts the net taxes of a one-year-old by more than those of a two-year-old, and so on.

21.3.2   Alternative Discount and Productivity Growth Rates

The accounts also depend on uncertain assumptions about the rates of discount and productivity growth. As noted, the reference case uses a real discount rate of 6 percent ($r = 0.06$) and assumes that labor productivity eventually increases 1.2 percent per year ($g = 0.012$).

A 6 percent discount rate is roughly equal to the historical real rate of return on equity, but there are arguments for using a lower or higher rate. For example, it may be reasonable to use a discount rate closer to the real rate of return on long-term government debt (2 or 3 percent), or to the real pretax rate of return on private capital (10 or 12 percent). That range reflects ambiguity about how to deal with such issues as risk, opportunity cost, and the equity-premium puzzle (see CBO 1995, 41–43).

In the same vein, the trend of labor productivity has varied significantly in the past, growing at an average annual rate of 1.3 percent from 1902 to 1929, 1.2 percent from 1929 to 1948, 2.8 percent from 1948 to 1966, and 0.9 percent from 1966 to 1996.[18] Moreover, productivity growth swung wildly during the 1929–48 period in response to the Depression, World War II, and demobilization. To examine how sensitive the results are to these assumptions, we next calculate generational accounts using alternative discount and productivity growth rates. The alternative assumptions are 3 and 9 percent for the discount rate and 0.7 and 1.7 percent for the productivity growth rate.

Given the reference policy, generational accounts remain imbalanced under all combinations of these growth rates, with the degree of imbalance ranging from 53 to 334 percent (see table 21.8). Given the alternative spending policies, some combinations of discount and productivity growth rates tip the generational scales in favor of the future. Most do not, however, and the degree of imbalance ranges from −4 to 155 percent (see table 21.9). Lifetime net tax rates on future generations fall below those on current newborns only at a low discount rate and a moderate or high growth rate.

The degree of imbalance responds more to the differences considered for the discount rate than to those for the productivity growth rate. A higher discount rate typically makes the residual burden accumulate faster and thereby raises the degree of imbalance.[19] On the other hand, higher productivity growth tends to boost income and output, and they in turn feed into higher values for

---

18. For consistent comparison, labor productivity is defined in this example as GDP per worker. The periods seem to define growth epochs, with the first three spanning nonsuccessive peaks in the annual business cycle. There was no peak in 1966, but economists generally agree that the trend in labor productivity growth changed about then. Neither was 1996 a peak year, but it is the most recent full year for which we have data and comes after a long (six-year) expansion.

19. This statement is true as long as the sum of the current value of the net debt of government, NWG_t, plus the present value of prospective government purchases, PVG_t, exceeds the present value of prospective net taxes of living generations, PVL_t. The condition is easily satisfied for any reasonable values.

Table 21.8   **Percentage Difference in Lifetime Net Tax Rates of Future Generations and Current Newborns under Alternative Discount and Growth Rate Assumptions**

Discount Rate	Growth Rate		
	0.007	0.012	0.017
0.03	84	53	83
0.06	160	72	127
0.09	334	130	253

Source: Authors' calculations.

Table 21.9   **Percentage Difference in Lifetime Net Tax Rates of Future Generations and Current Newborns under Alternative Discount and Growth Rate Assumptions with Slower Health Care Growth and Constant Real Federal Purchases**

Discount Rate	Growth Rate		
	0.007	0.012	0.017
0.03	24	−4	10
0.06	85	8	53
0.09	126	45	155

Source: Authors' calculations.

purchases and the net taxes of living generations (see CBO 1997b). That phased-in response dilutes the impact of higher productivity growth on the lifetime net tax rates of all generations.[20]

21.3.3   Alternative Demographic Projections

Uncertainty about population growth also afflicts generational accounts (or any other long-run projection). As noted, the accounts use the SSA's intermediate projection for a base case (and extend it as described earlier). However, the SSA also projects high- and low-growth paths to try to describe a reasonable range of uncertainty about its estimates for the probable actuarial balance of

20. Seemingly paradoxical reversals sometimes occur. For example, suppose that the discount and productivity growth rates shown in table 21.8 move, respectively, from 3 to 6 percent and from 0.7 to 1.2 percent. The degree of imbalance then falls from 84 to 72 percent. However, it subsequently rises to 253 percent as the discount and productivity growth rates move higher, to 9 percent and 1.7 percent, respectively. Such reversals occur both because the degree of imbalance is a percentage ratio and because the discounting process can lead to the same kind of "reswitching" issues that arise in capital theory. A higher discount rate reduces the absolute present value in any year a tax is paid or a wage transfer is received. A higher productivity growth rate raises those absolute present values. Therefore, a lifetime net tax rate may go up or down if both the discount and productivity growth rates are higher. Moreover, people generally pay taxes in youth and middle age and receive transfers in old age. Other things equal, a higher discount rate reduces the present value of both taxes and transfers, so that the present value of net taxes (taxes less transfers) may rise or fall. A higher discount rate is more likely to raise the present value of net taxes in the

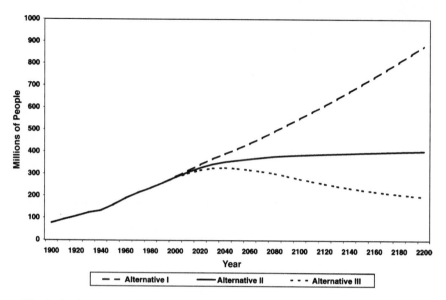

Fig. 21.2   Population 1900–1990 and projections 2000–2200

the social security trust fund. The three population projections represent low-cost (alternative I), mid-cost (alternative II), and high-cost (alternative III) outcomes.

The differences in populations depend on differences in their fertility, mortality, and net immigration rates. Alternative I assumes the highest rates for all of those demographic factors, and alternative III assumes the lowest. Higher rates imply more workers paying taxes and fewer retirees receiving transfers; lower rates imply the opposite. The population of alternative I grows to about twice that of alternative II, while the population of alternative III falls to about half the size (see fig. 21.2).[21]

All of the alternatives show a rise in the old-age dependency ratio—the population aged 65 or older as a share of the population aged 20 to 64. As the baby boom generations retire, that ratio increases during the years from about 2010 to 2035 (see fig. 21.3). The ratio for alternative II then levels off, with fertility and immigration rates largely offsetting its mortality rates to roughly stabilize the size and the age composition of the population. The ratio for alter-

following cases: the initial discount or productivity growth rate is higher, the recipient receives a given transfer at a later age, or the recipient gets a larger transfer at a given age (as in the earlier case of slow Medicare growth, when the newborn's benefit at age 65 was cut by proportionately more than that of the one-year-old).

21. Another way to compare these alternatives is to look at their populations in 2200 as ratios of the population in 1995. Under alternative I, the population increases by the year 2200 to more than 300 percent of its 1995 level; under alternative II, it rises to about 150 percent of its 1995 level; and under alternative III, it declines to about 70 percent of its 1995 level.

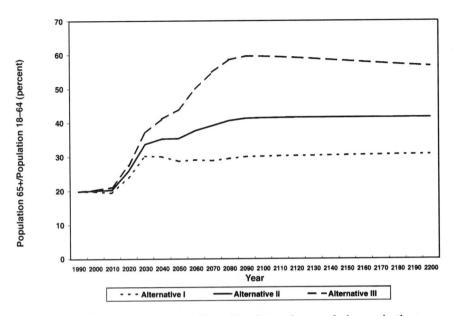

Fig. 21.3   Old-age dependency ratios under alternative population projections

native I falls, since higher mortality rates reduce the relative number of old people, and higher fertility and immigration rates expand the relative number of working-age people. The opposite occurs under alternative III.

For living generations, higher mortality and immigration rates usually imply higher generational accounts for the old and lower ones for the young (see table 21.10). For instance, the accounts of old generations are higher (less negative) under alternative I than under alternative II, while the accounts of very young generations are lower. The higher mortality rates associated with alternative I imply that fewer people of any age live to any given year in the future. People now old will receive less in transfers, and people now young will pay less in taxes (whose present value is greater than that of the later transfers that they would otherwise receive).

The pattern is not strictly consistent because net immigration boosts the later size of some young generations. For instance, the generational account for 20-year-old males is highest under alternative I. That apparent anomaly reflects the prospective U.S. net taxes of the current foreign 20-year-old males who will immigrate later. That is, the population count in the base year excludes their present numbers, but the generational account includes their prospective taxes and transfers. In effect, the accounts assign those prospective net taxes to the current population of 20-year-old U.S. males. That assignment raises the (per capita) generational account; a higher immigration rate increases it still more.

The accounts of living generations typically vary by less than 2 percent in

Table 21.10   **Generational Accounts under Alternative Demographic Assumptions (present value in thousands of 1995 dollars)**

Generation's Age in 1995	Net Tax Payments under Alternatives					
	I		II		III	
	Male	Female	Male	Female	Male	Female
0	75.4	50.3	77.4	51.9	79.8	53.6
5	94.1	62.1	95.7	63.4	97.7	65.0
10	118.8	77.1	119.5	78.1	121.0	79.4
15	149.3	95.1	149.1	95.7	149.8	96.7
20	183.3	114.8	182.2	115.0	181.9	115.6
25	195.8	121.7	196.2	122.6	196.5	123.6
30	195.7	119.4	196.8	120.7	197.2	121.8
35	187.7	112.5	189.0	113.8	189.2	114.8
40	170.0	98.1	171.2	99.0	171.7	99.7
45	138.3	72.2	139.2	72.8	139.8	73.2
50	93.3	37.3	93.7	37.4	94.0	37.4
55	37.6	−4.8	37.5	−5.2	37.3	−5.7
60	−24.8	−51.0	−25.5	−52.0	−26.3	−53.0
65	−76.3	−89.4	−77.7	−91.2	−79.0	−92.8
70	−87.5	−98.8	−89.2	−101.0	−90.9	−103.1
75	−86.1	−98.6	−89.9	−101.0	−89.7	−103.2
80	−75.6	−88.1	−77.2	−90.2	−78.9	−92.2
85	−66.9	−72.0	−68.3	−73.5	−69.6	−75.1
90	−52.8	−54.8	−53.8	−55.8	−54.8	−56.8
Future generations	116.6	77.8	134.6	90.2	153.7	103.3
Percentage difference	52.1	52.1	71.9	71.9	89.5	89.5
Lifetime net tax rates[a] (%)						
Current newborns	26.8		28.6		30.3	
Future generations	40.9		49.2		57.6	

Source: Authors' calculations.

[a]Lifetime net tax rates are population-weighted averages across males and females.

response to population differences. The percentage differences tend to be greatest at the ages with the highest mortality rates—newborns and seniors. The alternative populations assume greater *differences* in their mortality rates and thus imply greater proportional differences in their generational accounts. Fertility rates affect only the population of future generations, not the accounts of current generations.

For future generations, fertility, mortality, and net immigration rates all play a role. The higher fertility rates of alternative I imply larger future generations to share the residual burden, thereby reducing their lifetime net tax rates. Higher mortality rates play a smaller and partly offsetting role. Fewer young people live to pay taxes in middle age, fewer middle-aged people live to collect benefits in old age, and fewer old people live to collect them for as long a period. Given the age pattern of net immigration, a higher immigration rate implies relatively more workers.

The lifetime net tax rates of future generations respond more to alternative populations than do those of current newborns. Even if differences in mortality produce a relatively small change in the account of any one current generation, their combined effect produces a relatively large change in the residual burden on future generations. Under the various population assumptions, the lifetime net tax rate for future generations ranges from about 41 percent under alternative I to about 58 percent under alternative III. The degree of generational imbalance ranges from 52 percent under alternative I to 90 percent under alternative III. Thus, even under optimistic assumptions about the population, the reference policy remains unsustainable.

21.4   Policies for Eliminating Generational Imbalance

21.4.1   Alternative Ways to Indicate the Extent of Generational Imbalance

So far, we have assumed that living generations pay net taxes as scheduled for the rest of their lives. The spending side of the fiscal schedules examined here have followed the reference policy or an alternative policy (either constant real federal purchases or slow growth in Medicare outlays, or both). We have further assumed that all future generations share the resulting residual burden proportionately by paying the same lifetime net tax rate. Given the other reference assumptions, each policy we have considered has been generationally imbalanced (i.e., future generations must pay a higher lifetime net tax rate than current newborns) and is thus unsustainable.

Some observers have criticized this way of analyzing the generational stance of fiscal policy, arguing that if a fiscal schedule is unsustainable, lawmakers will change it so that some or all living generations will pay higher net taxes, and future generations will pay less than they otherwise would have (see, e.g., Eisner 1994; Haveman 1994).[22] To address this concern, we now calculate policy changes that would equalize the lifetime net tax rates of current newborns and future generations. The policies we examine involve permanently raising particular taxes or cutting particular outlays by a policy-specific percentage starting in 1998, 2003, or 2016. The different policies result in different equalized lifetime net tax rates on current newborn and future generations and require different dollar amounts of tax increases or outlay cuts in the first year of their implementation.

---

22. Another criticism stems from the Ricardian equivalence proposition, which states that current generations, perceiving that higher current deficits entail higher net taxes on future generations, will respond by increasing their saving and bequests. However, formal tests fail to detect the altruistic behavior required for Ricardian equivalence to hold. See Altonji, Hayashi, and Kotlikoff (1992, 1997).

21.4.2   Percentage Changes Needed in Various Programs to Reach Balance

The first two rows of table 21.11 repeat the lifetime net tax rates on current newborns and future generations under the alternative assumptions. The remaining rows list alternative tax, transfer, or purchase policies that may be used to restore generational balance, while the columns indicate the assumptions (reference, constant real purchases, slow health care growth, and so on) underlying the calculations. Columns (1)–(4) show the required percentage change, and columns (5)–(8) indicate the equalized value of the lifetime net tax rate under each row-specific policy and column-specific assumption.[23]

Given the other reference assumptions, balance can be achieved in 1998 by permanently raising the schedules for all income taxes on current generations by 20.4 percent (panel A, row 1, col. [1]). That equalizes lifetime tax rates at 31.9 percent, raising the rate on current newborns from 28.6 percent and lowering the rate on future newborns from 49.2 percent (panel A, row 1, col. [5]). If real federal purchases remain constant after 2000, the required hike in income taxes is 15.8 percent, implying an equalized lifetime net tax rate of 31.1 percent (panel A, row 1, cols. [2] and [6]). If Medicare spending grows slowly, the income tax hike is even smaller (7.1 percent), but the equalized lifetime net tax rate rises (32.1 percent). With constant real federal purchases and a deceleration in Medicare outlays, the required tax increase is smaller yet (2.6 percent), and the equalized lifetime net tax rate is 31.3 percent.

Similarly, if we fix the other reference assumptions and change the various fiscal programs, balance can be reached via several alternative policies, including a hike in taxes of 8.9 percent, a cut in social security transfers of 47.5 percent, a cut in health care outlays of 36.8 percent, or a reduction in all purchases of 15.4 percent (col. [1]). These policies equalize the lifetime net tax rates of current newborns and future generations at values that differ by policy, namely, 32.3 percent for raising all taxes, 30.1 percent for cutting social security benefits, 31.3 percent for cutting all health care benefits, 31.0 percent for cutting all transfers, and 28.6 percent for cutting all purchases. (The reasons for these differences are explained below.)

21.4.3   Variation in Percentage Changes and
          Equalized Lifetime Net Tax Rates

Why do the percentage changes and the equalized lifetime net tax rates differ across each row and down each column of table 21.11? Moving across each row, the respective percentage changes are lower because the underlying assumptions involve progressively smaller degrees of initial imbalance. Hence, restoring balance requires progressively smaller percentage changes in a row-specific policy.

---

23. A table indicating the initial dollar amounts of revenue increases and transfer or purchase reductions for each of the policies considered in table 21.11 is available upon request from the authors.

Table 21.11   Policies for Equalizing the Lifetime Net Tax Rates of Newborn and Future Generations

	Percentage Change				Equalized Lifetime Net Tax Rate			
	Reference (1)	Slower Purchases Growth[a] (2)	Slower Health Care Growth[b] (3)	Slower Health Care and Purchases Growth (4)	Reference (5)	Slower Purchases Growth[a] (6)	Slower Health Care Growth[b] (7)	Slower Health Care and Purchases Growth (8)
No Change Lifetime Net Tax Rates								
Newborns					28.6	28.6	30.9	30.9
Future generations					49.2	44.6	38.1	33.5
A. Policy Change in 1998								
Percentage tax increases								
Income tax[c]	20.4	15.8	7.1	2.6	31.9	31.1	32.1	31.3
Income tax (federal only)	24.9	19.4	8.7	3.1	31.9	31.1	32.1	31.3
Payroll tax	31.0	24.1	10.8	3.9	32.4	31.6	32.3	31.4
Other taxes[d]	39.7	30.8	13.9	5.0	33.3	32.2	32.6	31.5
All taxes	8.9	6.9	3.1	1.1	32.3	31.5	32.2	31.4
Percentage transfer cuts								
Social security	47.5	36.9	16.5	5.9	30.1	29.8	31.4	31.1
Health	36.8	28.6	16.8	6.0	31.3	30.7	31.8	31.2
All transfers	18.5	14.3	7.3	2.6	31.0	30.5	31.7	31.2
Percentage purchases cuts								
Entire government	15.4	12.3	5.3	2.0	28.6	28.6	30.9	30.9
Federal	38.7	31.1	13.5	5.0	28.6	28.6	30.9	30.9
B. Policy Change in 2003								
Percentage tax increases								
Income tax[c]	25.3	19.7	8.8	3.2	32.6	31.7	32.3	31.4
Income tax (federal only)	31.0	24.1	10.8	3.9	32.6	31.7	32.3	31.4
Payroll tax	38.7	30.1	13.5	4.8	33.4	32.3	32.6	31.5
Other taxes[d]	50.8	39.5	17.7	6.4	34.0	32.8	32.8	31.6
All taxes	11.2	8.7	3.9	1.4	33.1	32.1	32.5	31.5

(continued)

Table 21.11   (continued)

	Percentage Change				Equalized Lifetime Net Tax Rate			
	Reference (1)	Slower Purchases Growth[a] (2)	Slower Health Care Growth[b] (3)	Slower Health Care and Purchases Growth (4)	Reference (5)	Slower Purchases Growth[a] (6)	Slower Health Care Growth[b] (7)	Slower Health Care and Purchases Growth (8)
Percentage transfer cuts								
Social security	57.4	44.6	20.0	7.2	30.3	29.9	31.5	31.1
Health	42.2	32.8	20.2	7.3	31.6	31.0	31.9	31.3
All transfers	21.8	16.9	8.8	3.2	31.3	30.7	31.8	31.3
Percentage purchases cuts								
Entire government	19.5	15.8	6.8	2.5	28.6	28.6	30.9	30.9
Federal	50.1	40.6	17.4	6.5	28.6	28.6	30.9	30.9
			C. Policy Change in 2016					
Percentage tax increases								
Income tax[c]	45.4	35.2	15.8	5.7	35.5	34.0	33.3	31.8
Income tax (federal only)	55.3	43.0	19.2	6.9	35.6	34.0	33.3	31.8
Payroll tax	70.3	54.6	24.5	8.8	36.9	35.0	33.8	32.0
Other taxes[d]	102.0	79.2	35.5	12.8	35.9	34.3	33.5	31.9
All taxes	20.6	16.0	7.2	2.6	35.9	34.3	33.5	31.8
Percentage transfer cuts								
Social security	94.9	73.8	33.0	11.9	30.8	30.3	31.7	31.2
Health	63.7	49.5	32.7	11.7	32.7	31.8	32.3	31.4
All transfers	34.6	26.9	14.6	5.2	32.4	31.5	32.2	31.4
Percentage purchases cuts								
Entire government	35.4	30.0	12.3	4.8	28.6	28.6	30.9	30.9
Federal	92.5	78.4	32.2	12.6	28.6	28.6	30.9	30.9

Source: Authors' calculations.

Note: Calculations incorporate projections by the Congressional Budget Office (CBO). "Newborn" refers to generations born in 1995; future generations are as of 1995.

[a]Federal purchases are held constant in real terms after the year 2000.

[b]Per capita spending by age on health care grows 2 percentage points slower than under reference policy through 2003 then grows at the same rate as labor productivity growth.

[c]Refers to federal, state, and local income taxes.

[d]Includes excise and other indirect taxes, property taxes, and other taxes.

Across each row, there is no general pattern for the *level* of the equalized lifetime net tax rate, but there is a pattern for the *change* in the lifetime net tax rate of current newborns. For a change in a given tax or transfer, the change in that lifetime rate is smaller as we move across each row. For example, an increase in the income tax that restores balance raises the lifetime net tax rate of current newborns by 3.3 percentage points under the reference policy (31.9 percent vs. 28.6 percent). But that lifetime rate rises by 2.5 percentage points when real purchases remain constant, by 1.2 percentage points when Medicare spending grows slowly, and by 0.4 percentage point when real purchases remain constant and Medicare spending grows slowly.

For a cut in purchases, the net taxes of all living generations remain unchanged, so the lifetime net tax rate of current newborns stays at its initial value as we move across each row. However, cutting purchases lowers the residual burden on future generations, and achieving balance requires that the cut be large enough to reduce the rate on future generations until it equals that on current newborns.

For a column-specific initial policy, the variation in the outcome depends largely on which generations are most affected by the row-specific change in policy. On average, older individuals pay more in taxes on capital income and receive more in transfers from social security, Medicare, and Medicaid. Thus, a change in the schedule for such a tax or transfer will make every living generation contribute more—the old now, the young later. By contrast, a change in the schedule for a program that primarily affects young individuals effectively reduces the number of generations that make additional contributions. Therefore, between two programs of the same initial size, an equalizing policy that affects the old more than the young will require both a smaller percentage change and a smaller increase in the lifetime net tax rate on current newborns. The aging of the population and the rapid rise in medical costs greatly magnifies these effects.

21.4.4   Costs of Waiting

Waiting for five years, until 2003, before undertaking such policies requires larger changes than acting sooner (compare columns [1]–[4] in panel B with those in panel A). Under the reference scenario, the delay in trimming purchases again leaves the equalized lifetime net tax rate at the same level as that for current newborns. However, the required percentage cut is larger than when action is taken sooner (19.5 vs. 15.4 percent). Acting later to raise taxes or to cut transfers results in a higher equalized lifetime net tax rate than does acting sooner. The delay implies that some living generations escape the higher taxes or lower transfers, meaning that living and future generations must each bear higher lifetime net tax rates.

Waiting until the year 2016—about the time the largest baby boom generations will retire—requires even greater changes (see panel C). Again, except for purchase cuts, the lifetime net tax rates in panel C are higher than their counterparts in panel B. Such a long delay in restoring balance will involve unrealistically high tax increases, benefit cuts, or purchase reductions. For example, it would involve defaulting on 95 percent of social security's implicit obligations to living generations.

21.5   Conclusion

Reasonable economic and demographic assumptions imply that the generational stance of U.S. fiscal policy remains seriously imbalanced. Although the degree of this imbalance has declined from two years ago, the reference scenario implies lifetime net tax rates of 49.2 percent for future generations and 28.6 percent for current newborns. The schedule of such a policy cannot persist. At some point, projected government purchases must fall or scheduled net tax rates must rise—if not for living generations, then for future ones. We have described the sizes of hypothetical policy changes that would restore generational balance. They appear large, but failure to act soon will require even bigger changes in the future.

References

Altonji, J., F. Hayashi, and L. J. Kotlikoff. 1992. Is the extended family altruistically linked? *American Economic Review* 82, no. 5 (December): 1177–98.
———. 1997. Parental altruism and inter-vivos transfers: Theory and evidence. *Journal of Political Economy* 105, no. 6 (December): 1121–66.
Auerbach, A. J., J. Gokhale, and L. J. Kotlikoff. 1991. Generational accounts: A meaningful alternative to deficit accounting. In *Tax policy and the economy,* vol. 5, ed. D. Bradford, 55–110. Cambridge, Mass.: MIT Press.
———. 1994. Generational accounting: A meaningful way to evaluate fiscal policy. *Journal of Economic Perspectives* 8, no. 1 (winter): 73–94.
———. 1995. Restoring generational balance in U.S. fiscal policy: What will it take? *Federal Reserve Bank of Cleveland Economic Review* 31, no. 1 (quarter 1): 2–12.
Congressional Budget Office (CBO). 1995. *Who pays and when: An assessment of generational accounting.* Washington, D.C.: Government Printing Office, November.
———. 1997a. *The economic and budget outlook: An update.* Washington, D.C.: Government Printing Office, September.
———. 1997b. *An economic model for long-run budget simulations.* Washington, D.C.: Government Printing Office.
———. 1997c. *Long-term budgetary pressures and policy options.* Washington, D.C.: Government Printing Office, March.
Department of Education. Office of Educational Research and Improvement. National Center for Education Statistics. 1997. *Digest of education statistics, 1995.* Washington, D.C.: Government Printing Office.
Eisner, R. 1994. The grandkids can relax. *Wall Street Journal,* 9 November.
Haveman, R. 1994. Should generational accounts replace public budgets and deficits? *Journal of Economic Perspectives* 8, no. 1 (winter): 95–111.

Health Care Financing Administration. 1997. *The annual report of the Board of Trustees of the Federal Hospital Insurance Trust Fund.* Washington, D.C.: Health Care Financing Administration.

Social Security Administration (SSA). 1997. *Annual report of the Board of Trustees of the Federal Old-Age and Survivors Insurance and Disability Trust Funds.* Washington, D.C.: Social Security Administration.

Contributors

John Ablett
Department of Economics and Finance
Faculty of Business and Technology
University of Western Sydney, Macarthur
P.O. Box 555
Campbelltown, NSW 2560
Australia

Marcelo F. Altamiranda
Philip Morris International Inc.
800 Westchester Avenue, 4N-041
Rye Brook, NY 10573

Alan J. Auerbach
Department of Economics
University of California
549 Evans Hall
Berkeley, CA 94720

Bruce Baker
6907 Chestnut Avenue
Falls Church, VA 22042

A. Lans Bovenberg
CentER
Tilburg University
P.O. Box 90153
5000 LE Tilburg
The Netherlands

Jorge Braga de Macedo
Faculdade de Economia
Universidade Nova de Lisboa
Travessa Estevao Pinto
Campolide, 1070 Lisboa
Portugal

José Braz
TEcFinance, Lda.
Rua Pascoal de Melo, 120, 2 Esq.
1000 Lisboa
Portugal

Ousmane Doré
European I Department
International Monetary Fund
700 19th Street NW
Washington, DC 20431

Hans Fehr
University of Tübingen
Department of Economics
Mohlstrasse 36
D-72074 Tübingen
Germany

Carl Gjersem
Ministry of Finance
P.O. Box 8008 Dep
N-0030 Oslo
Norway

Jagadeesh Gokhale
Research Department
Federal Reserve Bank of Cleveland
East Sixth and Superior
Cleveland, OH 44116

Robert P. Hagemann
66, avenue d'Iéna
75017 Paris
France

Svend E. Hougaard Jensen
Economic Policy Research Unit
University of Copenhagen
Studiestraede 6
DK-1455 Copenhagen K
Denmark

Christoph John
Handelskammer Hamburg
Stabsbereich Volkswirtschaft
Adolphsplatz 1
20457 Hamburg
Germany

Nanak Kakwani
School of Economics
University of New South Wales
Sydney, NSW 2052
Australia

Yukinobu Kitamura
Faculty of Business and Commerce
Keio University
Mita 2-15-45, Minato-ku
Tokyo 108-8345
Japan

Laurence J. Kotlikoff
Department of Economics
Boston University
270 Bay State Road
Boston, MA 02215

Willi Leibfritz
Department for Macroeconomics Analy-
    sis and Fiscal Studies
ifo Institute for Economic Research
Poschingerstrasse 5
Postfach 860460
D-81679 München
Germany

Joaquim Levy
European I Department
International Monetary Fund
700 19th Street NW
Washington, DC 20431

Regina Villela Malvar
2302 233d Avenue NE
Redmond, WA 98053

Medhi Krongkaew
Institute of East Asian Studies
Thammasat University, Rangsit Campus
Pathum Thani 12121
Thailand

Philip Oreopoulos
Department of Economics
University of California
549 Evans Hall
Berkeley, CA 94720

Benjamin R. Page
Congressional Budget Office
Room 456
2d and D Streets SW
Washington, DC 20515

Bernd Raffelhüschen
Institut für Finanzwissenschaft I
Albert-Ludwigs-Universitaet Freiburg
Platz der alten Synagoge 1
D-79085 Freiburg
Germany

Harry ter Rele
CPB Netherlands Bureau for Economic
    Policy Analysis
P.O. Box 80510
2508 GM The Hague
The Netherlands

Nicola Sartor
Istituto di Diritto Pubblico
Via dell'Artigliere, 19
37129 Verona
Italy

Erling Steigum, Jr.
Department of Economics
Norwegian School of Economics and
    Business Administration
N-5035 Bergen-Sandviken
Norway

Jean-Philippe Stijns
Department of Economics
University of California
549 Evans Hall
Berkeley, CA 94720

John R. Sturrock
Congressional Budget Office
Room 456
2d and D Streets SW
Washington, DC 20515

Noriyuki Takayama
Department of Economics
Hitotsubashi University
47-3 Yuhigaoka
Hiratsuka 254-0806
Japan

Jan Walliser
1201 S. Eads Street, #307
Arlington, VA 22202

Hiroshi Yoshida
Faculty of Economics
Tohoku University
Kawauchi, Sendai 980
Japan

Author Index

Abel, B. A., 301n5
Ablett, J., 141, 153, 164t, 166, 173
Alesina, A., 301n3
Almeida, S. C., 181
Altamiranda, Marcelo F., 103n1
Altonji, J. G., 21, 511n22
Ambrosini, G. C., 311n21
Amieva-Huerta, Juan, 427
ANSeS (Administración Nacional de la Segur-
idad Social), Argentina, 107n13
Artoni, R., 317n30
Atkinson, A. B., 219n1
Auerbach, Alan, 1, 2, 10, 25, 31, 37, 43n1, 44,
50, 59n11, 62, 115n42, 118n48, 161, 166,
172, 200n3, 224, 247, 261, 277, 284,
348, 362, 369, 370, 377, 379n9, 382,
414, 428n7, 435n9, 468, 489n2, 491n4,
492n5, 493n7, 501n14
Australian Bureau of Statistics, 144

BACEN (Banco Central do Brasil), 180, 184t,
185
Banca d'Italia, 300f, 302f
Bayet, Alain, 271
Blau, F., 154n7
Boll, Stephan, 44n2, 281, 294n10
Bordt, Michael, 205n6
Borjas, G. J., 153n5
Bos, Eduard, 113n33, 240t, 241t
Boskin, Michael, 10
Bouillot, M., 171n11
Braga de Macedo, Jorge, 473t, 474n1, 478n2
Braz, José, 474n1

Briet, Raoul, 246, 269
Bröcker, J., 280, 285
Brosio, G., 305
Buiter, W. H., 2, 232n6, 255, 301, 321n34
Bund-Länder-Kommission, Germany, 283
Burda, M., 285

Cairns, Alan, 199n1
Caisse Générale d'Epargne et des Retraite, Bel-
gium, 164
Callataÿ, E. de, 171n11
Callensen, P., 223
Cameron, Grant J., 205
Campagne, Nathalie, 271
Canadian Institute of Actuaries, 207
Canceill, G., 271
Canziani, P., 317n30
Castelar Pinheiro, Armando, 111n31, 185n11
Castellino, O., 307n14
Caussat, Laurent, 272
Cavalcanti, C. E. G., 181
Centre for International Economics, Australia,
154n7
Chalongphob Sussangkam, 431n8
Chamley, C., 10
Cigno, A., 311n22
Clokeur, R., 166
Colin, Christel, 271
Commission pour l'Inventaire, Belgium, 167
Congressional Budget Office (CBO), United
States, 491, 493nn7, 8, 507
Contenci, Didier, 271
Corsetti, G., 321n34

CPB, Netherlands, 329, 330n5, 334n6, 335n7
Cristini, Marcela, 132n71
Cutler, David, 2, 45, 74–75n1

Danmarks Statistik, 224
Deelen, A. P., 329, 334n6, 335n7
Demekas, D. G., 317n30
Deutsche Bundesbank, 280t, 283
Diamond, Peter, 2, 38n4
Dinh Quang Chi, 255
Direction de l'Animation de la Recherchée,
    des Etudes et des Statistiques (DARES),
    France, 255, 266, 271
Doré, Ousmane, 257n10, 260n12
Drèze, J., 219

Eisner, Robert, 10, 511
Electoral Commission of New Zealand, 350n3

Fasquelle, N., 164
Fehr, Hans, 232n6, 427n5
Feldstein, Martin, 10, 28
Fernandes, Fernando, 183n8
FIEL–Consejo Empresario Argentino,
    132nn71, 73, 133n78
Flood, M. Cristina V. de, 115n40
Förster, M., 221
Franco, Daniele, 44n2, 271, 305, 312, 313,
    317n30, 320n32, 414
Frasca, F., 317n30
Frisch, Ragnar, 371–72
Funke, M., 285

Ganugi, P., 301nn2, 4, 303n7, 304n8
Gasparini, Leonardo, 115n40
Giambiagi, F., 185n11
Giavazzi, F., 308n16
Gillespie, Irwin W., 202n4
Glaude, Michel, 272
Gokhale, Jagadeesh, 1, 2, 31, 37, 43n1, 44n2,
    115n42, 118n48, 161, 166, 172, 200n3,
    224, 247, 261, 277, 287, 290n9, 362,
    369, 414, 427, 489n2, 491n4, 492n5
Grilli, V., 303

Habakkuk, H. J., 74–75n1
Hagemann, Robert P., 272, 399n4, 405n8,
    414, 427
Hagen, K., 219–20n1
Haveman, Robert, 2, 511
Hayashi, F., 19–21, 58, 511n22
Health Canada, 205

Health Care Financing Administration
    (HCFA), United States, 504n16
Hebbink, G. E., 325n1
Huber, A. M., 10

INDEC (Instituto Nacional de Estadística y
    Censos), Argentina, 110n27, 113n33,
    114, 115n43, 118n50
Ingerslev, O., 223
INSEE (Institut National de la Statistique et
    des Etudes Economiques), France, 249,
    252–54t, 271, 272
Institut National de Statistique, Belgium, 164
Instituto Brasileiro de Geografia e Estatística
    (IBGE), Brazil, 182, 184t
Instituto de Pesquisa Econômica Aplicada,
    Brazil, 183
International Monetary Fund (IMF), 265n16,
    405n9
Ishi H., 451n2
Istituto Centrale di Statistica (ISTAT), Italy,
    310f, 311
Istituto di Recherche sulla Popolazione, Italy,
    311n24
Isuani, Ernesto A., 107n12

Jensen, L., 154n7
Jensen, S. H., 223, 227, 230
John, Cristoph, 272, 399n4, 405n8, 414

Kakwani, Nanak, 413n, 421
Kempen, E. J. van, 325n1
Kneebone, Ronald D., 203n5
Koch, C., 222
Kotlikoff, Laurence, 1, 2, 10, 25, 31, 37,
    43n1, 44, 50, 62, 115n42, 118n48, 133,
    134, 161, 166, 171n12, 172, 200n3, 224,
    242, 247, 261, 277, 362, 369, 409, 414,
    427n5, 468, 478n2, 489n2, 491n4,
    492n5, 511n22
Kuné, J., 244n2

Lachman, Desmond, 399
Laitner, J., 25
Lambrecht, M., 164
Latin American Demographic Center, Brazil,
    183n7
Leibfritz, Willi, 1
Lenseigne, F., 246
Leonard, H. B., 10
Levy, Joaquim, 257n10, 260n12
Lindbeck, A., 219

Lollivier, S., 271
Lundvik, Petter, 86n2, 98n3, 100n5
Lüth, Erik, 86n2, 98n3, 100n5
Lykketoft, M., 234

Malinvaud, E., 219
Masciandaro, D., 303
Medhi Krongkaew, 425
Melconian, Carlos A., 130n67, 131t
MEyOySP (Ministerio de Economía y Obras
    y Servicios Públicos), Argentina, 112t,
    113t, 115nn40, 41, 42, 116t, 131t
Ministère de l'Education Nationale, France, 272
Ministério da Educaçao e do Desporto, Brazil,
    184t
Ministério da Previdência e Assistência So-
    cial, Brazil, 181
Ministero del Tesoro, Italy, 300f, 302f, 311n23
Ministry of Finance, Denmark, 221, 232
Ministry of Finance, Sweden, 402t
Ministry of Health and Social Affairs, Swe-
    den, 399n4
Mizhari, A., 272, 273
Morcaldo, G., 302f
Musgrave, Richard, 448, 463

National Bank of Belgium, 163t, 164
National Fiscal Outlook, Australia, 142, 151
National Statistical Office (NSO), Thailand,
    437
Nielsen, S. B., 223
Northcott, Herbert C., 204

Office of the Superintendent of Financial Insti-
    tutions, Canada, 204
Onofri, R., 307n13
Oreopoulos, Philip, 200, 204, 205–6, 213n10,
    215n11
Organization for Economic Cooperation and
    Development (OECD), 162n1, 171, 221,
    240t, 305, 308, 400t, 401t, 404, 406n10,
    452

Palomba, R., 310–11n20
Perelman, S., 166, 171n11
Perotin, Virginie, 271
Persson, T., 303
Petit, W., 244n2
Pieper, P. J., 10
Pinheiro, A. C., 111n31, 185n11
Pinxt, A., 244n2
Ploug, N., 223

Pomp, M., 336n8
Porta, P., 317n30
Pranee Tinakorn, 431n8

Raffelhüschen, Bernd, 1, 44n2, 86n2, 98n3,
    100n5, 227, 232n6, 279n2, 280, 281,
    285, 287, 371n3, 414, 427
Ricordeau, P., 246
Risa, Alf Erling, 232n6, 371
Robinson, M. S., 10
Roineau, Christelle, 271
Rosati, F. C., 311n22
Ross, Stanford, 427
Rossi Sciumè, G., 311n21
Roubini, N., 321n34
Rubenstein, Jean-Christophe, 246, 269

Sachverständigenrat, 278n1, 280t
San Martino, Jorge A., 107n12
Santángelo, Rodolfo A., 130n67, 131t
Saraceno, P., 317n30
Sartor, Nicola, 98n3, 304, 313, 317n30, 320,
    321n33
Schneider, Ross, 111n27
Siebert, H., 279n2
Simon, Julian L., 74n1, 154n7
Sinn, G., 279n2
Sinn, H.-W., 279n2
Siow, A., 21
Social Security Administration, United States,
    491
Sommer, B., 281, 282
Sorensen, P. B., 221
Spaventa, L., 308n16
Statistics Canada, 204, 205
Statistisches Bundesamt, Germany, 282t
Steigum, Erling, Jr., 370n2, 371n3, 374n6
Sturrock, John, 1, 271, 272
Summers, Lawrence H., 10
Superintendencia de Administradoras, Argen-
    tina, 133, 134

Tabellini, G., 303
Tamura, Y., 449n1
Thorgersen, Oystein, 370n2
Toniolo, G., 301nn2, 4, 303n7, 304n8
Turtelboom, B., 171n11

United Nations, 311n24
U.S. Department of Education, 498n13
U.S. Office of Management and Budget
    (OMB), 44n2

Valliancourt, François, 200, 205–6, 215n11
Verger, D., 271

Walker, J. R., 312n26
Walliser, Jan, 44n2, 281, 287, 414, 427
Wattenberg, B. J., 74–75n1
Weemaes, S., 164
Whiteford, P., 154

Wolfson, Michael C., 205
Wroberl, Marion G., 203n5

Yotsuzuka, T., 19

Zaidman, Catherine, 246, 269
Zamagni, V., 300n1, 301n2
Zanardi, A., 317n30

Subject Index

Accelerated Cost Recovery System (1981), United States, 28

Argentina
convertibility plan (1991), 104–7, 135
demographic projections (1991–2200), 114
generational balance, 127–37
Integrated Pension System (IPS), 107–10
privatization program, 103–4, 110–13, 129–31

Australia
compulsory saving for retirement, 144
current account deficit, 144
current fiscal debate, 142–44
deregulation, 142–43
effect of immigration on generational accounting, 153–59
history and current debates in fiscal policy, 142–44

Balanced Budget Act (1997), United States, 491, 503

Balanced budget rule, 11, 26

Belgium
economic policy, 171–73
generational balance, 164–71
public debt, 162–64

Bonds, indexed, 37

Brazil
Constitution of 1988, 177–79, 190
fiscal debates, 178–83
generational accounts, 185–97
informal economy, 181

Budget constraint, intertemporal
generational accounting based on government's, 43
of government, 31, 74
of government in two-period model, 39

Budget deficit
as economic concept, 10
Brazil, 180
Canada, 199–200, 202–4
France, 243
Germany, West and East, 278–79
Italy, 299–304, 320
Netherlands, 327–29
Sweden, 398–99

Budget surplus, Norway, 370, 375–76

Canada
generational balance, 207–16
welfare state, 199–204

Constitution
Brazil, 181, 182
Portugal, 472

Data sources
Argentina, 111, 113–14
Australia, 144–46
Belgium, 164
Brazil, 183
Canada, 204–7
France, 248–49, 270–72
Italy, 312–13
Japan, 454–55

Data sources (*cont.*)
  Netherlands, 329
  Norway, 377, 391–92
  Portugal, 479
  Sweden, 403–5
  Thailand, 426, 437
Deficit accounting
  compared to generational accounting,
    87–88
  to measure fiscal policy, 10–21
  problem with, 4
  Belgium: fiscal policy, 161–64
  Canada, 204–5
  Netherlands, 327
Demographic projections
  trends in countries studied, 75–77
  Argentina, 114
  Australia, 144–45
  Brazil, 183–84
  Canada, 205
  Denmark, 224
  France, 246
  Germany, 282
  Italy, 310–13
  Japan, 452–54
  Netherlands, 336–39
  New Zealand, 352, 365
  Norway, 377
  Sweden, 404
  Thailand, 415t, 426
  United States: alternative, 507–11; effect on
    updated generational accounts, 501–3
Demographics
  producing generational imbalances, 73
  related to generational imbalances, 96–97
  trends in countries studied, 75–77
Denmark
  fiscal policy debates, 221–24
  generational balance, 225–36
  income distribution, 221
  welfare state, 219–21
Discount rates
  in estimating generational accounts, 40–41
  in generational accounts, 37
  risk-adjusted, 37–40
  sensitivity of generational accounts to,
    88–95
  Argentina, 119–27
  Belgium, 166
  Canada, 207
  New Zealand, 355, 360–62
  Thailand, 427–28

Economic and Monetary Union (EMU)
  Denmark's nonparticipation in, 222
  France's consolidation of accounts under,
    240, 242, 244
  Italy's criteria for joining, 321
  Netherlands' fiscal policy under, 329
  Portugal's plans to join, 472
Economic performance
  Argentina, 103–6
  Australia, 142
  Brazil, 177, 179–80
  Canada, 199–201
  France, 244–46
  Germany, West and East, 278–79
  Japan, 447
  New Zealand, 348–51
  Thailand, 415–16
Educational spending
  in generational accounts, 32
  Belgium, 173–74
  Canada, 207–10
  Denmark, 225–31
  New Zealand: present value of benefits,
    359; sensitivity of generational accounts
    to benefits of, 362
  Portugal, 481–84, 486
  Thailand, 427
Electoral system, New Zealand, 348, 350–51
Employment Contracts Act (1991), New
  Zealand, 349
EMU. *See* Economic and Monetary Union
  (EMU)

Fiscal balance rule
  basis for, 11
  defined, 9–10
  function of, 27–28
  implementation of, 28–29
  use of, 23–26, 29
  See also Balanced budget rule
Fiscal burden
  of future generations, 33, 490
  incidence as distribution of generational, 4
  with intertemporal government budget con-
    straint, 489
  relation to generational balance, 74
  Belgium, 168–73
  Japan, 448
  Thailand, 428–32
Fiscal incidence
  assumptions in generational accounting, 44
  as distribution of tax burden, 4

Thailand, 425, 442–44
See also Tax incidence
Fiscal policy
arbitrary nature of labels, 14–15, 17
effect of changes on factor returns, 45–49,
51–70
information in generational accounting related to, 32–33, 43–44
intergenerational, 32
labeling and relabeling, 15, 38–39
loose, 17
in neoclassical macroeconomic indicators
models, 10
nondistortionary and distortionary, 17–19,
22–23, 27
reform changes in generations' utilities,
48–49, 51–70
sources of imbalances in, 96–97
sustainability of current, 2
uncertain, 15–17
using fiscal balance rule, 25–26
Argentina: generational impact of alternative, 127–36; privatization, 103–6,
110–13; social security system, 107–10
Australia: generational impact of alternative, 147–59; history and current debates,
142–44; impact on generational accounts
of alternative, 147–59
Belgium: meeting Maastricht Treaty criteria,
162; structural corrective measures, 162
Brazil: alteration in (1988), 177–78; burden
on future generations, 178; effect of policy changes, 193–96
Canada: historical (1960 to present),
200–204
Denmark: generational imbalance related
to, 235; tax reform, 221–22
France: adjustments to achieve generational
balance, 264–65; effect on income distribution, 242
Germany: convergence with unification,
284–85; effect of unification on, 277–78;
tax burden of unification, 289–95
Japan: future reform, 447–48; history
(1947–95), 449–54; impact on generational accounts of alternative, 460–67; reform proposals, 454
Netherlands: historical, 327–29; reform proposals, 342–43; standard method in generational accounting, 330
New Zealand: generational accounts dependent on, 362–64

Norway: impact of alternative, 389–91;
related to oil and gas wealth, 372–77;
revised (1994), 370
Portugal: to achieve generational balance,
471; current, 471
Thailand, 425, 442–44
United States: to eliminate generational im-
balance, 511–16; generational accounts
updates (1993, 1995), 501–3
Fiscal policy, loose
in two-period life cycle model, 12–15,
25–26
United States (1990s), 28–29
Fiscal projections
France, 273–74
New Zealand, 352–55, 364–65
Norway, 378–79
Fiscal Responsibility Act (1994), New
Zealand, 347–50
Fiscal system, Brazil, 181
France
baby boomers' generational accounts,
261–63
generational balance, 247–61, 263–70
welfare state, 239–46

Generally accepted accounting principles
(GAAP), New Zealand, 350, 352–53
Generational accounting
advantages and limitations, 44
analogy to tax incidence, 46–49
assumptions, 33–34, 44, 74
Auerbach-Kotlikoff dynamic life cycle
model to study, 44–45
basis for, 2, 31
in closed economy, 52–64
compared to deficit accounting, 87–88
estimate of change in welfare of those born
in the long run, 56
estimates of effective rate of taxation, 490
estimates related to fiscal burden, 489
explanations of, 4
functions of, 2–3
information related to generational distribution, 32–33, 43–44
measure yielded by, 325–26
in small open economy, 64–71
software package, 75
tracking generations' utility using, 51–69
uses for, 44, 73
Brazil: methodology, 187; used to assess
policy changes, 193–96

Generational accounting (*cont.*)
  Canada, 204–5
  Italy, 312
  Japan, 455
  Thailand, 435–44
Generational accounts
  based on government's intertemporal budget
    constraints, 74
  changes in under deficit-financed tax cut,
    57
  with changes in fiscal policy, 51–70
  defined, 31–32, 74, 248, 493
  life cycle pattern of, 493–96
  measurement by, 43
  of newborns and future generations, 33, 74
  present value in countries studied, 77–81
  production of, 33–34
  relation to government spending, 247–48
  scaling of countries studied, 81–85
  sensitivity to discount rates and labor pro-
    ductivity, 88–95
  in two-period life cycle model, 47–49
  using range of discount rates to estimate, 41
  Argentina: central assumptions and baseline
    cases (1994), 119–23; imbalance in, 103;
    projections, 111, 113–14; sensitivity anal-
    ysis, 119, 123–27, 136
  Australia, 153–59
  Belgium, 164–71
  Brazil, 185–96; with alternative fiscal pol-
    icy changes, 193–97; base case, 186–90;
    with social insurance changes, 190–92
  Canada: under alternative fiscal policies,
    210–15; base case, 207–10
  Denmark, 232–35
  France: of baby boomers, 261–63; construc-
    tion, 248–58; with slower growth in
    health care spending, 265–66
  Germany, 292–96
  Italy, 315–16
  Japan, 460–67
  New Zealand: assumptions underlying cal-
    culation of, 351–55; dependence on alter-
    native fiscal policies, 362–64; for males
    and females (1995–96), 355–59; new-
    borns and future generations, 360–62;
    sensitivity of, 360–62
  Norway, 382–85
  Portugal, 480–86
  Sweden: under alternative policies, 409–11;
    base case, 405–7; under different assump-
    tions, 407–9
  Thailand, 431–32

  See also Generational balance; Sensitivity
    analysis
Generational balance
  achieving, 74, 97–100
  comparison among countries of imbalances,
    85–95
  defined, 100
  imbalance implication, 490
  imbalances in countries studied, 78–80t,
    85–87, 97–101
  measuring imbalance, 326
  restoring, 97–98
  Argentina, 127–36
  Australia, 141
  Belgium: imbalance, 166; policies to
    achieve, 171–73
  Canada: under alternative policies, 210–15;
    imbalance, 207–10
  Denmark: existence of imbalance, 230; poli-
    cies to achieve, 230–35
  France: imbalance, 242, 261–64; policies to
    achieve, 264–69
  Germany: factors influencing imbalance,
    287–89; policies to achieve, 289, 292–95
  Italy: imbalance, 299, 317–20; with pension
    reform, 299; potential policies to achieve,
    317–20
  Japan, 455–60, 467
  Netherlands: imbalance, 326, 330; policies
    to achieve, 340–43
  New Zealand: under alternative fiscal poli-
    cies, 363–64; policies to achieve, 364
  Norway, 370, 391
  Portugal, 471–72, 486–87
  United States, 511–16
Generations
  in Auerbach-Kotlikoff model, 50
  defined for generational accounting, 493
  fiscal burden of future, 33
  generational accounts of living, 77–85
Germany
  aging-related policies, 292, 294–96
  convergence of East and West, 284–92
  fiscal policy with unification, 277–78, 289–91
  increased elderly dependence ratio, 277–78,
    281
  macroeconomic performance, 278–81
Government
  forecasts of taxes and transfer payments, 34
  reporting under loose fiscal policy, 17
  use of distortionary fiscal policy, 17–19
Government budget constraint, intertemporal,
  489

expression of, 492–93
fiscal balance rule based on, 9, 11
generational accounting based on, 2
Government purchases. *See* Spending, government
Government wealth
   in generational accounting, 32, 34
   as source of financing purchases, 489
   Argentina, 103–4, 115–16
   France, 249–50
   Germany, 283–84
   Japan, 468–69
   Norway's petroleum, natural gas, and hydroelectric, 372–77, 392–93
   Sweden, 404–5
   Thailand, 427–28

Health care spending
   in generational accounts, 32
   Australia, 143
   Brazil, 178–79
   France, 239–40, 245–46, 265–66
   Netherlands, 339–40

Immigration, Australia, 153–59
Income tax
   capital marginal and inframarginal, 34–37
   corporate, 34
   to restore generational balance, 99
   Argentina: on labor and capital income, 118
   Denmark, 221–22
   Germany, 292–95
   Thailand, 421
Institutions, international, 6–7
Interest rates, 37–41
   See also Discount rates
Intergenerational redistribution
   consequences of, 197
   life cycle model of, 11–15
   occurrence of, 10–11
   through Social Security in the United States (1960s and 1970s), 28
   Brazil: imbalance, 189–90, 196
   Canada, 207–10
   Germany, 290–96
   Japan, 462–67
Italy
   demographic changes, 310–14
   generational balance, 315–21
   government spending role, 304–9
   public debt, 299–304
   use of generational accounting, 44

Japan
   current and historical fiscal policy, 449
   fixed lifetime relative position, 448
   generational balance, 455–68
   public debt, 447
   use of generational accounting, 44

Labor force participation
   Denmark, 220, 222–23, 232
   France: benefits, 246; effect of raising rate of, 266–70
   Netherlands: proposed policy to increase, 344; rising, 332–34; in sensitivity analysis, 336
   Norway, 369, 374–75
Labor productivity
   sensitivity of generational accounts to, 88–95
   Argentina, 119–27
   Canada, 207–10
   Denmark, 222–23
   New Zealand, 360–62
   Thailand, 427–28
Life cycle model
   Auerbach-Kotlikoff dynamic, 44–45, 50
   with distortionary fiscal policy, 18
   government redistribution in two-period, 11–15
   government transfer from young to old, 15–16
   tax incidence in two-period, 47–49
Lifetime net payment (LNP), 22–24, 26, 31
Living standards, 81, 85

Maastricht Treaty
   Belgium: meeting criteria of, 162
   Denmark: adherence to convergence criteria, 222
   France: consolidation of accounts under, 240, 242, 244
   Italy: fiscal policy to fulfill criteria of, 321
   Netherlands: meeting convergence criteria, 329
   Sweden: meeting fiscal targets of, 401
   See also Economic and Monetary Union (EMU)
Macroeconomic policy, Norway, 371–74
Migration, Australia, 141

Netherlands
   generational balance, 329–44
   historical and current fiscal policy, 327–35
Net lifetime payment (NLP). *See* Lifetime net payment (LNP)

New Zealand
    current fiscal situation, 348–51
    fiscal policy reform, 347–48
    generational accounting study (1995),
        364–66
    generational balance, 347, 351–64
    use of generational accounting, 44
Norway
    application of generational accounting, 370
    generational balance, 382–91
    government investment of wealth, 394
    government petroleum revenues, 369, 371–
        77, 392–94
    use of generational accounting, 44
    welfare state, 371–77

Pension system
    Argentina, 107–10
    France, 239–40, 245, 265–70
    Netherlands, 334–35
    New Zealand, 359
    Norway, 371, 378–79
    Thailand, 427
Population aging
    effect on fiscal accounting, 2
    Australia, 144
    Brazil, 178, 183
    Canada, 204
    Denmark, 220, 223
    France, 239–41, 245
    Germany, 277–78, 281
    Italy, 311–12
    Japan, 447, 452
    Netherlands, 329
    Norway, 370, 377–78, 385, 388
Population projections. *See* Demographic pro-
    jections
Portugal
    European influences on fiscal policy,
        472–78
    generational balance, 471, 478–88
    International Monetary Fund intervention
        in, 473
Privatization program
    Argentina: fiscal role of, 103–6, 110–11;
        generational account effects of, 129–31,
        136
    Australia, 142–43
Public sector
    Argentina, 103–7
    Brazil, 178
    Denmark, 219–20

France, 244–45
Norway, 369–70
Sweden, 401–3
Thailand, 416

Reserve Bank Act (1989), New Zealand, 349
Retirement, Australia, 144
Revenues
    discount rate to calculate, 37
    government forecasts of, 34
    Argentina, 115–16
    Australia, 142
    Brazil, 184–85
    Denmark, 221, 224–25
    Norway, 369–70, 372–79
    Thailand: projection, 426–27; structure and
        distribution of, 416–21
Risk adjustment
    discounting, 37–39
    of fiscal flows, 40
    generation-specific, 39
    intergenerational sharing, 40

Saving, Norway, 371–72
Sensitivity analysis
    of generational accounts in countries stud-
        ied, 88–95
    Argentina, 119, 123–27, 136
    Australia, 146–47
    Brazil, 193
    Canada, 207–10
    Denmark, 227–30
    France, 258–61
    Germany, 292–93
    Japan, 455–60
    Netherlands, 329, 335–41
    New Zealand, 360–62
    Norway, 382–88
    Sweden, 407–9
Social insurance
    Argentina: components and reform of, 103,
        107–10; generational account effects of
        reform, 131–37
    Australia, 143
    Brazil, 179; impact of changes in, 190–92,
        196–97; new rules and proposals for
        (1991–92), 181–83; reform (1988),
        177–79
    Canada, 199–202
    France, 239–40, 245
    Germany, 280, 282–83
    Thailand, 413, 428, 431–32, 435

Spending, government
  in generational accounting, 34
  sources of financing for, 489–90
  tax-financed, 52–55
  Argentina, 115–16
  Australia: historical, 142; social security
    and Medicare, 143
  Belgium, 173–74
  Brazil, 177–78
  Canada: deficit, 199; indexing of some,
    200
  Denmark, 224–25
  France: current, 251–55; growth, 243–45;
    increases in (1970s–1990s), 244–45
  Germany: in generational accounting,
    284–89; related to unification, 277–82
  Italy: on health and pensions, 299; histori-
    cal, 300–309
  Netherlands, 340–41
  New Zealand, 348–51
  Norway: current revenues and, 379–81; on
    education, 385; projections of receipts
    and, 378–79; related to petroleum reve-
    nues, 376–77; for social protection, edu-
    cation, and health care, 371, 378–79; for
    social security, 378–79
  Sweden, 398–99
  Thailand, 421–26
Stabilization plans, Brazil, 179–80
State Petroleum Fund, Norway, 370, 376–77
Subsidies, Norway, 379
Superannuation Guarantee Charge (SGC),
    Australia, 144
Sweden
  generational balance, 405–11
  recent fiscal policy, 398–403
  welfare state, 397–98

Taxation
  of current generation, 2
  deficit-financed tax cut, 57–58
  in generational accounting, 34
  Canada, 205–7
  Denmark, 220–21
  France: computation of weights, 272–73;
    increased (1990s), 243–44; projected for
    future generations, 250–51; revenues,
    239–40
  Germany: related to unification spending,
    277–78; with unification, 280–84,
    289–91
  Italy, 313–14

New Zealand, 352, 356–59
  See also Income tax
Tax burden
  of newborns and future generations, 2, 326
  yielded by generational accounting, 325–26
  Canada, 200
  France, 242
  Netherlands, 327–29
  New Zealand, 347, 359
  Sweden, 398, 411
  Thailand, 428–31
Tax incidence
  in generational accounting, 4, 34
  generational accounting analogy to, 46–49
  life cycle model, 47–49
  Brazil, 181
  France, 249–50
Tax Reform Act (1986), United States, 28
Tax system
  Argentina's federal and provincial, 106
  Australia's proposed reform, 143
  Brazil: decentralization of, 178–79; overlap-
    ping and temporary, 181–82
  Denmark: green tax reform (1993), 221–22;
    structure, 221
  New Zealand, 349–50
  Norway: categories, 379; reform (1992),
    375
  Sweden, 397
  Thailand, 417–21
Thailand
  fiscal and demographic structures in,
    415–26
  generational balance, 426–35
  government role in, 413
Transfer payments
  in generational accounting, 34
  health care and education in generational
    accounts, 32
  Belgium, 171
  Brazil, 184–85
  Canada, 205–7
  Denmark: educational, 224–27; increases
    in, 222–23
  France: increases (1980–95), 244–45; pro-
    jected future, 250–51
  Germany: with unification, 280–81, 283
  New Zealand, 352, 356–59
  Norway, 378–81
  Portugal, 481–84, 486
  Sweden, 397–98
  Thailand, 426–27

Uncertainty, 37
United States
  Balanced Budget Act (1997), 491
  generational balance, 493–516
  intertemporal government budget con-
    straint, 492–93
  use of generational accounting, 44

Universalism principle, Norway, 371

Welfare system
  France, 239
  Norway, 369–71